D1255641

FROM BUILDINGS AND LOANS TO BAIL-OUTS

For most Americans, the savings and loan industry is defined by the fraud, ineptitude, and failures of the 1980s. These events, however, overshadow a long history in which thrifts played a key role in helping thousands of households buy homes. First appearing in the 1830s, savings and loans, then known as building and loans, encouraged their working-class members to adhere to the principles of thrift and mutual cooperation as a way to achieve the "American Dream" of home ownership. This book traces the development of this industry, from its origins as a "movement" of a loosely affiliated collection of institutions into a major element of America's financial markets. It also analyzes how diverse groups of Americans, including women, ethnic Americans, and African Americans, used thrifts to improve their lives and elevate their positions in society. Finally, the overall historical perspective sheds new light on the events of the 1980s and analyzes the efforts to rehabilitate the industry in the 1990s.

David L. Mason is Assistant Professor of History at Young Harris College. Prior to earning his Ph.D. in Business History from The Ohio State University, he served as a corporate banker for nearly a decade, holding positions at the Bank of America and the Resolution Trust Corporation. He is also the author of articles for *Essays in Economic and Business History* and *Proceedings of the Ohio Academy of History*.

FROM BUILDINGS AND LOANS TO BAIL-OUTS

A History of the American Savings and Loan Industry, 1831–1995

DAVID L. MASON

Young Harris College

 CAMBRIDGE
UNIVERSITY PRESS

PUBLISHED BY THE PRESS SYNDICATE OF THE UNIVERSITY OF CAMBRIDGE
The Pitt Building, Trumpington Street, Cambridge, United Kingdom

CAMBRIDGE UNIVERSITY PRESS
The Edinburgh Building, Cambridge CB2 2RU, UK
40 West 20th Street, New York, NY 10011-4211, USA
477 Williamstown Road, Port Melbourne, VIC 3207, Australia
Ruiz de Alarcón 13, 28014 Madrid, Spain
Dock House, The Waterfront, Cape Town 8001, South Africa

http://www.cambridge.org

First published 2004

Printed in the United States of America

Typeface Sabon 10/12 pt.   *System* LATEX 2$_\varepsilon$ [TB]

A catalog record for this book is available from the British Library.

Library of Congress Cataloging in Publication data
Mason David Lawrence.
From buildings and loans to bail-outs : a history of the American savings
and loan industry, 1831–1995 / David L. Mason.
p. cm.
ISBN 0-521-82754-X (hbk)
1. Savings and loan associations – United States – History.   2. Savings and loan association
failures – United States – History.   I. Title.
HG2151.M37   2004
332.3′2′0973 – dc22   2003069691

ISBN 0 521 82754 X hardback

For Dad

CONTENTS

Contents

LIST OF TABLES

ACKNOWLEDGMENTS

Completing this project would not have been possible without the aid and support of many individuals. While I was fortunate to have access to nearly one hundred years of trade journals and conference proceedings with regard to thrifts from dozens of libraries across the country, making sense of this material was a daunting task. It was made immeasurably easier by my advisor Mansel G. Blackford, who kept my work focused and helped me develop my ideas on the effects S&Ls had on American society. William R. Childs provided me with valuable insights into the history of government/business relations, and led me to think seriously about just when S&Ls became a true financial industry. Likewise, the seminars I took under the guidance of K. Austin Kerr helped me formulate my basic approach to writing this history.

My research could not have been completed without the assistance of several talented and friendly archivists. Allen Fisher at the Lyndon B. Johnson Presidential Library provided invaluable assistance researching the collections of that impressive repository. Pat Wildenberg and Dale Mayer at the Herbert Hoover Presidential Library helped me to better understand Herbert Hoover's devotion to the needs of families and better housing. Don Shewe at the Jimmy Carter Presidential Library provided both invaluable assistance and stories about the OSU History Department faculty while he was a graduate student in the 1960s. I also deeply appreciate the financial assistance used to complete my work from the Herbert Hoover Presidential Library and the Franklin and Eleanor Roosevelt Research Institute. Special thanks go to Robert Surabian, who provided me with unrestricted access to the records of Medford Cooperative Bank, and Lorraine Silva, who regaled me with stories of her life as a community banker.

Preparing any manuscript for publication is a daunting task, but for me the process was made infinitely less stressful by the fact that I worked with some very patient people. Frank Smith at Cambridge University Press was very understanding when the inevitable delays occurred, and his enthusiasm for the project was always appreciated. I especially want to thank my readers Paul Miranti and Ed Perkins for their insightful and constructive comments and suggestions; every author should be fortunate enough to have such supportive peers. Eric Crahan and Catherine Felgar at Cambridge University Press and Shubhendu Bhattacharya at TechBooks also provided invaluable assistance in the editing process. Mistakes, however, are inevitable, and I take full responsibility for them. Finally, I would like to thank my mother for always asking me how the book was coming, and thanks to Jeff and Sandy for never bringing up the subject.

INTRODUCTION

In his movie *It's a Wonderful Life* the director Frank Capra tells the story of George Bailey, the manager of the Bailey Bros. Building and Loan. This thrift association is in Bedford Falls, a small community where people know each other, families are stable, and personal morals are strong. Although the town also has a bank, most of the working-class residents belong to the local building and loan. A turning point in George's life comes on Christmas Eve when an audit reveals that $5,000 is missing from the thrift. George is unable to account for the funds, and after the banker Henry Potter accuses him of stealing the money, George panics and considers suicide. To prevent this, George's guardian angel Clarence lets him see what life in Bedford Falls would be like if he were never born, and by extension if his thrift did not exist. In a world without George and his building and loan, Potter controls the town and dominates the lives of its residents. Called Pottersville, the town is no longer peaceful and happy but a place where drinking, vice, and debauchery reign supreme. Most of the people rent apartments from Potter, have dysfunctional families, and generally regard each other warily. The experience makes George realize how important he and his work are to the community, which causes him to keep on living and face arrest for malfeasance. In the end, the people of Bedford Falls rally to support George with donations that not only cover the missing funds but also lead the authorities to drop the criminal charges against him.[1]

---

[1] One journalist described this as the nation's "first S&L bail out." Kathleen Day, *S & L Hell: The People and the Politics Behind the $1 Trillion Savings & Loan Scandal* (New York: W. W. Norton & Co., 1993), 38; *It's A Wonderful Life* (Metro-Goldwyn-Mayer, 1948); Vito Zagarrio, "It Is (Not) a Wonderful Life: For a Counter-reading of Frank Capra," in Robert Sklar and Vito Zagarrio, editors, *Frank Capra: Authorship and the Studio System* (Philadelphia: Temple University Press, 1998), 64–94; James Agee, *Agee on Film* (New York: Grosset & Dunlap, 1969), 233–4; Ray Carney, *American Vision: The Films of Frank Capra* (New York: Cambridge University Press, 1986), 379, 381–2; "*It's a Wonderful Life*," *Savings and Loan News* 67 (February 1947), 17.

In this cinematic masterpiece, Capra's main objective was to "encourage audiences to recognize the heroism involved in merely living a helpful but ordinary life." However, Capra also provided an accurate sketch of America's thrift industry during its heyday of the late 1940s and early 1950s. An examination of the movie from the perspective of the Bailey Bros. Building and Loan reveals that the primary goal of a thrift was to help working-class men and women become homeowners. By following the basic principles of systematic savings and mutual cooperation, thrift members could borrow money to buy their homes. The movie also revealed the widespread assumption of Americans that private homes provided the best environment for raising a family, and that pride of owning a home generated higher personal self-esteem and good citizenship. Finally, because the building and loan was such an integral part of Bedford Falls, when events threatened to close this thrift, the town fought to save it.[2]

Although Capra apparently never intended *It's a Wonderful Life* to be an homage to the savings and loan industry, he nonetheless provided a useful snapshot of a business that, to date, has not received much scholarly examination. This is not to say that historians have ignored the study of finance in America, as evidenced by many valuable histories of investment and commercial banking.[3] One reason for the growing number of works on these industries is that each was critical in financing big business and making America an economic superpower. Similarly, historians have closely examined the relationship between business and government, especially those actions that helped the federal government assume greater economic and social responsibilities in the twentieth century.[4] Finally, while scholars have explored the role financial intermediaries played in the growth of American cities and suburbs, the majority of works in this area focus on federal government activities and not on those of savings and loans.[5] Because my project

---

[2] Wes D. Gehring, *Populism and the Capra Legacy* (Westport, CT: Greenwood Press, 1995), quote 112.

[3] For representative histories, see Vincent P. Carosso, *Investment Banking in America, a History* (Cambridge, MA: Harvard University Press, 1970); Benjamin J. Klebaner, *American Commercial Banking: A History* (Boston: Twayne Publishers, 1990); Ron Chernow, *The House of Morgan: An American Banking Dynasty and the Rise of Modern Finance* (New York: Atlantic Monthly Press, 1990); William F. Hixson, *Triumph of the Bankers: Money and Banking in the Eighteenth and Nineteenth Centuries* (Westport, CN: Praeger, 1993); Edwin J. Perkins, *Wall Street to Main Street: Charles Merrill and Middle-Class Investors* (New York: Cambridge University Press, 1999).

[4] Seminal works include Thomas K. McCraw, *Prophets of Regulation: Charles Francis Adams, Louis D. Brandeis, James M. Landis, Alfred E. Kahn* (Cambridge, MA: Belknap Press of Harvard University Press, 1984); Thomas K. McCraw, editor, *Regulation in Perspective: Historical Essays* (Cambridge, MA: Harvard University Press, 1981); Richard H. K. Vietor, *Contrived Competition: Regulation and Deregulation in America* (Cambridge, MA: Belknap Press of Harvard University Press, 1994).

[5] See Sam Bass Warner, *Streetcar Suburbs: The Process of Growth in Boston, 1870–1900* (Cambridge, MA: Harvard University Press, 1978); Kenneth T. Jackson, *Crabgrass Frontier:*

combines elements from all three areas into one study, it fills the scholarly gap in the literature on S&Ls, and helps define their overall role in American business history.

At the end of the twentieth century, America's 1,103 thrift institutions controlled more than $863 billion (in US billion) in assets, equivalent to about 8 percent of the nation's gross domestic product in 1999. Thrifts continue to serve as a significant source of residential home mortgages and are the second-largest repositories for consumer savings in the country.[6] Despite their critical importance to the financial structure of the United States, thrifts have been grossly neglected by scholars. Only five extensive histories of this industry are available. All were written by industry insiders, and none cover the events of the S&L crisis.[7] Conversely, books and articles on the financial debacle of the 1980s abound. Unfortunately, many are journalistic accounts that focus on the criminal misconduct associated with individual thrift failures. Furthermore, only a handful of these works place the events of the decade in any historic perspective.[8]

This study attempts to correct these deficiencies in three ways. First, by examining the entire history of the American savings and loan industry, I

The Suburbanization of the United States (New York: Oxford University Press, 1985); Robert Fishman, *Bourgeois Utopias* (New York: Basic Books, 1987).

[6] Office of Thrift Supervision. *2002 Fact Book: A Statistical Profile on the United States Thrift Industry* (Washington, DC: Office of Thrift Supervision, April 2003), 1, 4.

[7] H. Morton Bodfish, *History of Building and Loan in the United States* (Chicago: United States Building and Loan League, 1931); Horace Russell, *Savings and Loan Associations* (Albany: M. Bender, 1960); Josephine Hedges Ewalt, *A Business Reborn: The Savings and Loan Story, 1930–1960* (Chicago: American Savings and Loan Institute Press, 1962); Leon T. Kendall, *The Savings and Loan Business: Its Purposes, Functions, and Economic Justification* (Englewood Cliffs, NJ: Prentice-Hall, 1962); A. D. Theobald, *Forty-Five Years on the Up Escalator* (privately published, 1979). Bodfish wrote his history to celebrate the centennial of the industry, and it was distributed at the annual convention of the thrift trade association. Russell's work is primarily a memoir of the author's career at the Federal Home Loan Bank Board, while Ewalt wrote her book while serving as the chief publicist of the thrift trade association. Kendall was the chief economist for the United States Savings and Loan League and wrote his monograph for the Commission on Money and Credit. Theobald's book is the only detailed history of the thrift industry between 1930 and 1979.

[8] Representative books include Paul Zane Pilzer, *Other People's Money: The Inside Story of the S&L Mess* (New York: Simon and Schuster, 1989); Stephen Puzzo, Mary Fricker, and Paul Muolo, *Inside Job: The Looting of America's Savings and Loans* (New York: McGraw-Hill, 1989); James O'Shea, *The Daisy Chain: How Borrowed Billions Sank a Texas S&L* (New York: Pocket Books, 1991). Among the few books that include a basic history of the thrift industry are James Ring Adams, *The Big Fix: Inside the S&L Scandal* (New York: John Wiley & Sons, 1989); Kathleen Day, *S&L Hell: The People and Politics Behind the $1 Trillion Savings and Loan Scandal* (New York: W. W. Norton, 1993); Ned Eichler, *The Thrift Debacle* (Berkeley: University of California Press, 1989); James Barth, *The Great Savings and Loan Debacle* (Washington, DC: AEI Press, 1991); Mark Carl Rom, *Public Spirit in the Thrift Tragedy* (Pittsburgh: University of Pittsburgh Press, 1996); Kitty Calavita, Henry N. Pontell, and Robert H. Tillman, *Big Money Crime: Fraud and Politics in the Savings and Loan Crisis* (Berkeley: University of California Press, 1997).

not only place the recent past in a broad context, but also offer new insights into the development of consumer finance. Second, my extensive use of industry sources provides a different perspective about how and why S&Ls responded to the array of different economic conditions and crises that they faced over the years. Finally, by accessing previously untapped government archival documents I enhance our understanding of the relationship between the industry and federal regulators.

Given this multifaceted approach, my work should interest scholars in a variety of fields. For economic and business historians, this study strengthens our understanding of how American finance developed over time; in particular the role small enterprises play in meeting the financial needs of consumers. It also contributes to the literature on government-business relations and thus will be of interest to scholars of political science. Similarly, scholars focusing on "household" finance will find this work a valuable resource on the development of various types of lending, such as installment and mortgage loans. Meanwhile, business professionals will learn more about how financial firms evolve over time. Finally, academics focused on African American, ethnic American, and women's studies will find new information that expands and breaks new ground in understanding the relationship between these groups and American business.

Although a chronological history, this study is organized around four broad themes. The first focuses on the evolution of saving and loans business practices. Thrifts began as a way for working-class men and women to obtain affordable long-term home mortgages and simultaneously have access to a safe repository for savings. They were typically nonprofit cooperatives, which were owned by their members and often relied on word-of-mouth advertising to attract business. As neighborhood businesses, civic leaders usually served in top leadership positions, and the close ties these managers maintained with the local community allowed thrift members to better monitor the association's lending activities. Finally, thrifts employed a variety of legal structures and lending procedures that were tailor-made to meet member needs. While such eclectic practices often served members well and met local financial needs, they also made thrifts appear to be less prestigious than commercial banks.[9]

The thrift industry remained a small but important source of consumer finance for the first one hundred years of its existence, and although S&Ls used more uniform practices, they remained member-owned institutions. This changed after World War II when the postwar housing boom produced

---

[9] For a discussion of the role of agency in business and finance see Jonathan Barron Baskin and Paul J. Miranti, Jr., *A History of Corporate Finance* (New York: Cambridge University Press, 1999), 20–24 and Jonathan Barron Baskin, "The Development of Corporate Financial Markets in Britain and the United States, 1600–1914: Overcoming Asymmetric Information," *Business History Review* 62 (Summer 1988), 199–237.

an unprecedented demand for mortgages. To meet this demand, the industry developed innovative business procedures, and some thrifts even began to raise funds by selling stock on the open market. The growth that resulted from this period significantly enhanced the image of thrifts as financial institutions, and gave the industry greater political and business clout. It also, however, caused the industry to become divided into a handful of large institutions capable of competing directly with commercial banks and thousands of smaller, more traditional, associations. Although competition between thrifts and banks for funds was especially high during the 1960s, in terms of lending S&Ls continued to be undiversified, with mortgages accounting for more than 80 percent of industry assets. Because most S&Ls used relatively short-term variable-rate deposits to make these long-term fixed-rate loans, the industry was in a very vulnerable position when the economy deteriorated and interest rates rose sharply in the late 1970s.

Despite efforts by the industry to create loan structures that minimized the effects of high rates on consumers, S&Ls lost millions during this period. These problems became so severe that the industry was allowed to enter new lending fields and diversify their loan portfolios. Unfortunately, many of these new business areas were riskier than traditional mortgage finance, and managers had to acquire new skills to participate in them profitably. The fact that hundreds of S&Ls became insolvent during the 1980s showed that not all associations successfully made the transition. While fraud played a role in some S&L failures, the vast majority of these insolvencies resulted from ill-advised lending decisions and the inability of managers to respond to the problems associated with rapid growth. Significantly, a common trait among the thrifts that survived the 1980s was that they approached deregulation more cautiously and remained focused on meeting the consumer finance needs of their local service territories.

The process of how thrifts refined their operating and management procedures reveals that both external forces and internal initiative drove change. For the first one hundred years of the industry's existence, thrifts faced few competitive challenges, in part because they were relatively small and narrowly specialized financial institutions. After World War II, however, competitive pressures from commercial banks and the federal government forced thrifts to adopt more formal business procedures, and in the extreme to rethink their mission as financial institutions. Some responded by offering services that made them virtually identical to banks, while others remained focused on providing home mortgages and consumer loans. Other innovations occurred because managers were proactive. S&Ls were among the first financial institutions to offer fully amortizing mortgages, a very consumer-friendly form of finance, and pay compound interest on deposits. Similarly, their emphasis on service led thrifts to pioneer the use of drive-up windows, branch offices, and consumer technology such as automated teller machines.

The second theme examines the role of the national thrift trade association in the development of the industry.[10] While thrifts organized local, state and regional trade groups to promote their business interests, it was the United States Savings and Loan League, the industry's national trade group that proved to be the most influential. Like trade associations in other industries, the League began as an informal organization whose chief function was to act as a forum for thrift leaders to meet. This role changed significantly in the 1920s and 1930s, as the League assumed new responsibilities that included the development of uniform business practices in accounting, real estate appraising. It also played a larger role in publicizing both the industry and the ideals of thrift and home ownership. A key figure in this transformation was Morton Bodfish, who led the League from the late 1920s to after World War II. His organizational improvements gave the trade group the capacity to take a leading role in the industry's growth after the war.

The League was at its height of power in the 1950s and early 1960s when thrifts were emerging as an important source of consumer finance. Under the leadership of Norman Strunk, the national trade association continued to portray thrifts as modern, innovative, and local financial institutions. Such efforts helped the industry attain its present status as a dominant source for long-term home finance and a major repository for savings. As the industry grew, however, the League's work was hindered by the competing interests of large and small thrifts, which limited its ability to present unified positions on political and business issues. One consequence of this industry disharmony was that the League played only a nominal role in the process of deregulation. Although the League regained its political influence in the 1980s, the severity of the S&L crisis discredited the trade group and in 1991 it was disbanded.

Despite the broad successes achieved by the League during its nearly one hundred years of existence, this study clearly shows that industry support for its national trade association was very inconsistent. During the early twentieth century, the League often encountered stiff resistance from members in its efforts to change industry practices. Similarly, the creation of the system of federal regulation required the League to not only lobby Congress, but also wage an extensive promotional campaign to convince thrifts how various governmental programs would benefit them. Another important characteristic of the League's history was that even though a majority of all thrifts belonged to the trade association, its policies usually favored the interests of its largest members. This growing inability to represent the needs of smaller

---

[10] Seminal studies on trade associations include Louis Galambos, *Competition & Cooperation; The Emergence of a National Trade Association* (Baltimore: Johns Hopkins Press, 1966); William R. Childs, *Trucking and the Public Interest: the Emergence of Federal Regulation, 1914–1940* (Knoxville: University of Tennessee Press, 1985); Robert F. Himmelberg, *The Origins of the National Recovery Administration: Business, Government, and the Trade Association Issue, 1921–1933* (New York: Fordham University Press, 1993).

thrifts was critical in the formation of competing trade associations that challenged the League's authority.

The third theme focuses on the evolution of relations between the thrift industry and government. Thrift leaders, like those in other financial industries, generally regarded government regulation as both a blessing and a curse. While they approved of measures designed to protect and promote their business, they also wanted the government to give them free reign to grow and broaden operations. Thrift regulation first began in the late nineteenth century at the state level. Initially it was well received because state oversight helped limit competition and produced more uniform business practices that, in turn, increased public confidence. The economic turmoil of the Great Depression led to federal regulation of thrifts, and by 1934 S&Ls had the support of a central reserve credit bank, a program of deposit insurance, and a system of federal chartering. Significantly, League leaders took an active role in designing these laws, which they saw as important in protecting thrifts from competition and promoting their growth. Furthermore, because the League used the close ties it developed with regulators over the years to influence the formation of thrift regulations, some observers claimed that the industry had captured these agencies.

The most recent period of major change in government-business relations happened in the 1980s, when Congress deregulated the thrift industry. Following the financial losses associated with the unprecedented changes in interest rates in the late 1970s, regulators realized that a more flexible system of regulation and oversight was needed if the thrift industry was to remain strong. Significantly, commercial banks, investment banks, and financial services firms faced many of the same challenges as S&Ls, and all these industries underwent dramatic change during the decade. The goal of deregulation was to make thrifts more competitive by allowing them to diversify their loan portfolios into areas beyond consumer finance. These included the right to make commercial loans, hold junk bonds, and make direct equity investments in real estate.

Financial deregulation was not, however, a straightforward process. Because the federal government insured the deposits of both thrifts and banks, legislators had to ensure that allowing these firms to enter new business areas would not result in greater risks to the insurance funds. Consequently, when regulators relaxed the restrictions on thrifts, they should also have increased the level of oversight and enforced greater lender discipline. Unfortunately, regulatory supervision of S&Ls declined in the early 1980s for a variety of reasons, and despite efforts to impose stricter controls beginning in 1984, industry oversight at both the state and federal levels remained inadequate. Consequently, lenders who made well-intentioned but ill-advised loans were not held strictly accountable for their actions, and managers intent on fraud found it easier to commit their illegal acts. The result was one of the worst financial disasters in American history that has directly cost taxpayers more than $160 billion to resolve. Given the magnitude of the thrift crisis, in 1989 Congress imposed greater restrictions on thrifts, and while not complete re-regulation the new rules were intent on refocusing S&Ls on their core mission of providing home finance.

The analysis of thrift oversight reveals two consistent characteristics. First, changes in the level of government regulation were rarely proactive but rather came in response to economic downturns and industry crises. State oversight of thrifts began after the Depression of 1893, federal regulation occurred during the Great Depression, and deregulation was driven by rising interest rates in the late 1970s. The second trend was that when change did occur, larger S&Ls tended to be among the first to utilize the benefits of regulation and deregulation, while smaller associations took a more deliberate "wait and see" attitude. For example, it took nearly twenty years for a majority of thrifts to become members of the federal deposit insurance system. While internal disagreements over the level of regulation were not unique to the thrift industry, they also often reflected broader divisions within the industry.

The final theme in this study focuses on the role savings and loans played in promoting home ownership and popularizing the home as one element of the "American Dream" of individual home ownership. When industrialization in the nineteenth century allowed for the separation of commercial and domestic activities, the image of the home underwent a radical transformation. Rather than being a place where family and work chores occurred simultaneously, the home came to be regarded as a distinct environment where parents could focus on raising children. Interestingly, the "new" family-oriented home also became the place where people learned the moral values that made them good citizens. Thrifts readily identified with the changed image of the home, and by the 1890s were publicizing to working-class men and women how owning a home offered not only financial security and a healthy place to raise a family, but also led to greater personal self-esteem and ultimately a stronger country. This image was best captured in the slogan for the national thrift trade association – "The American Home. The Safeguard of American Liberties."

Aside from popularizing the idea that thrifts produced "good Americans," the industry played a major role in changing where Americans wanted to live. One trend in the demographic history of the United States has been the steady movement of people from rural to urban and suburban areas. While the growth of cities and suburbs required a variety of changes, ranging from improvements in transportation to how homes were built, the availability of affordable financing was also critical. The "democratization" of the home loan by the thrift industry, which involved making it easier to qualify for and repay a mortgage, helped transform suburbia from a nineteenth-century retreat for the rich to the predominant residence for the twentieth-century middle class. It also helped give the United States one of the highest percentage of private home ownership in the world and helped make home equity a major source of household wealth.

It clearly would be an exaggeration to claim that S&Ls were responsible for changing how Americans viewed the home, or determining where people wanted to live, but it is fair to say that the romantic ideals held by many thrift leaders allowed the industry to play a crucial role in shaping these processes. For the first one hundred years of the industry's existence, S&L publications emphasized thrifts as being part of a social uplift movement that was more concerned with improving people's lives than making a profit. While this belief was greatly eroded by the 1950s, S&L managers continued to stress their commitment to the local community as the key difference between their institutions and other financiers. Even at the end of the twentieth century, these ideals still resonate with consumers and remain a defining characteristic of the industry.

I have divided this work so that each chapter focuses on a major period of change or innovation. Chapter 1 traces the development of thrifts during the nineteenth century and focuses on four major topics: how and why the thrift industry began, why savings and loan leaders cultivated an image of their business as a self-help movement, the role of women in encouraging industry growth, and the rise and fall of "national" thrifts and their impact on the industry. Chapter 2 covers the years 1900 to 1929, a period when the national trade association emerged as the true leader in the thrift industry. The major topics include how the trade association encouraged thrifts to adopt more uniform business practices, its efforts to promote thrift development and home ownership, the rise of ethnic savings and loans, and how the prosperity of the 1920s affected the thrift industry.

Chapter 3 analyzes how and why state and federal regulation began, and the effects these laws had on the industry. Because thrift leaders played an active role in securing regulation, the programs created often protected and promoted industry interests. Still, not all managers agreed on the need for regulation, and the League worked hard to gather industry support for the federal programs to ensure their success. Chapter 4 focuses on business and organizational changes from 1930 to 1945 and includes an analysis of how the industry dealt with the financial hardships of the Great Depression, as well as the competitive challenges associated with increased federal involvement in home finance. Chapter 5 covers the first decade after World War II, which is generally considered the thrift industry's "glory years." This section details how the industry took advantage of the natural postwar demand for housing to become the dominant institutional source of residential finance in the country. While the growth of suburbia was important to this expansion, League promotional activities, favorable regulations, and innovations by individual thrift managers also contributed to this process.

Chapters 6 and 7 analyze the events of the twenty-five years that preceded deregulation of S&Ls in the 1980s. While the industry continued to post steady growth, an overarching theme is the widening gap between large and small associations. Among the sources of disagreement were, first, how to respond to the competitive threats posed by commercial banks and federal housing programs, and second, how best to utilize an ever-increasingly growing array of technological innovations. At the same time, the industry had to contend with the problems associated with greater regulatory scrutiny and congressional actions that included the loss of their tax-exempt status and the imposition of interest rate controls. This section ends with a review of how the unprecedented economic problems of the 1970s affected the industry and contributed to thrift deregulation.

Chapter 8 focuses on thrift deregulation and an overview of the S&L crisis of the 1980s. A review of key legislation passed during this decade and the events surrounding the failure of hundreds of thrifts provides evidence that this financial debacle resulted from a combination of forces, and that there is no one dominant cause. While fraud was a factor in the failure of dozens of thrifts, bad lending decisions and lax supervision were clearly the leading causes of insolvency. Chapter 9 discusses thrift re-regulation and examines the efforts to liquidate the billions in assets held by insolvent thrifts. It includes a critical assessment of the major reasons why thrifts failed, and examines the state of the thrift industry toward the end of the twentieth century. Chapter 10 concludes the study by evaluating the overall roles that regulators, trade groups, outside competitive pressures, and internal forces played in shaping the development of the thrift industry during its long history.

An appendix includes case studies of two savings and loan associations, which are intended to illustrate elements of success and failure in the industry. The first is of Empire Saving and Loan Association, a thrift located near Dallas, Texas, which failed in 1983 as a result of criminal activity. An analysis of this insolvency reveals that, although management fraud was critical to the collapse, an equally important factor was the inability of regulators to intervene in a timely manner. The second case study is of Medford Cooperative Bank, near Boston, which was formed in 1887 and continues to profitably meet the financial needs in its local community. This analysis reveals that a key reason for success was that it was committed to serving the financial needs of the local community it served, a trait that traditionally has been associated with the thrift industry.

My examination of the American savings and loan industry indicates that thrifts have served, and continue to serve, a vital function in this country's financial system. Thrifts are responsible for perfecting the system of home finance that has become the standard used by the federal government and all other home lenders. Also, by making mortgages affordable to ordinary Americans, thrifts made owning a home a reality for millions of families and in turn helped make home ownership the chief source of household wealth. At the same time, because thrifts are the only financial institutions that trace their roots to a broad cooperative movement, these businesses promoted self-help ideals and helped create an image of the home that have since become integral elements of American popular culture. Finally, the fact that most thrifts continue to operate as community-based businesses committed to specialized areas of consumer finance shows it is possible to operate successfully in an increasingly competitive financial marketplace dominated by large, diversified institutions.

I

A MOVEMENT TAKES SHAPE, 1831–1899

The creation and early development of a savings and loan industry in America reflected many of the broad social and economic changes that occurred during the nineteenth century. Building and loan associations (B&Ls) first appeared in 1831 as a way to help working-class men and women have the opportunity to become homeowners. B&Ls patterned themselves after the British building societies that pioneered a system of home finance based on systematic savings and mutual cooperation between society members. While the American thrift business grew slowly during the first forty years of its existence, growth accelerated in the 1880s, and soon thrifts were in operation across the country. While a steady stream of innovations designed to make thrifts more efficient accounts for part of this growth, the businesses also benefited from increased publicity by thrift leaders directed at both the working class and Progressive era social reformers. These people portrayed B&Ls as being part of a self-help movement capable of improving the lives of working-class men and women and alleviating many of the social ills affecting industrial cities. Although these changes led to strong business expansion, their success also spawned the creation of "national" B&Ls whose primary objective was to enrich their organizers at the expense of their members. The failure of these fraudulent thrifts during the 1890s significantly tarnished the image of the thrift business, but the "nationals" crisis also led to the formation of state and national trade associations, called Leagues, intent on promoting and protecting B&L business interests. Eventually, a national League would become the central force in preparing the thrift movement for the challenges of the twentieth century.

BRITISH TRADITIONS OF HOME FINANCE

Although private financing of homes first began in China more than five thousand years ago, institutional lending for residential purposes originated in eighteenth-century England. The building society movement was the first effort to help people not in the upper classes become homeowners, and its creation resulted from a variety of forces. The first of these was the effort by yeoman farmers to become private landowners. Traditionally, British elites had controlled most of the arable land in the country, which they rented to farmers, but in the 1640s small groups of merchants with excess capital challenged this arrangement by forming land buyers' societies. First appearing in the English Midlands, these businesses bought large tracts of land, which they subdivided and sold outright to farmers. The upper classes, however, realized that making farmers direct landowners and not tenants reduced their power base, and they tried to suppress these groups. Despite such opposition, land buyer societies flourished well into the eighteenth century.[1]

The second development that contributed to the appearance of British building societies was the friendly society movement, which also began in the British Midlands in the late 1600s. Friendly societies were self-help cooperatives whose mostly working-class members made regular contributions into a common fund and in times of need received benefits in the form of interest-free loans. Members could make a claim for hardships caused by unemployment, illness, or losses associated with fire and robbery. In the eighteenth century, the number of societies grew rapidly, in part because of the religious revival known as the "Great Awakening." This evangelical movement emphasized the need for social holiness in which men should work to help the poor, sick, and underprivileged. This focus on "helping your fellow man" in a spirit of self-help and self-reliance, combined with broader social changes associated with industrialization, led to the formation of more than 7,000 societies by 1800. Also, the popularity of the movement led to the first government involvement in the activities of a cooperative movement when the passage of The Friendly Societies Act of 1793 required these groups to register with Parliament.[2]

The third force that aided the rise of British building societies was the growth of cities during the First Industrial Revolution. The rise of factories caused a tremendous demand for unskilled labor, and, as people responded to this demand nearly every major British city experienced unprecedented growth. Between 1800 and 1850, the populations of London and Edinburgh rose by 240 percent. Glasgow experienced a 460 percent increase, while Birmingham and Manchester more than tripled in size. One consequence of urban expansion was that housing conditions began to deteriorate, since the low wages earned by most workers forced them to live in crowded tenements. For skilled workers with higher incomes, an alternative to the tenement was home ownership, but rising real estate prices in the city made it hard for these

[1] Seymour J. Price, *Building Societies: Their Origin and History* (London: Franey, 1958), 1, 5–7.

[2] E. J. Cleary, *The Building Society Movement* (London: Elek Books, 1965), 9–11, quote 9; Price, *Building Societies*, 10–12, quote 11; Peter Gray, "A Brief History of Friendly Societies," *http://www.afs.org.uk/research/researchpgrayhistorypage.htm*, accessed 31 August 2003.

people to save enough to buy a house outright. If they wanted to borrow from traditional mortgage lenders, they had to make substantial down payments, and they often had to repay the full loan in just a few years.[3]

In 1781, the experience of the land buyers and friendly societies, which showed how mutual cooperation and systematic savings could achieve goals difficult for individuals alone, combined with the need for urban housing led to the creation of the first building society in Birmingham. As in the case of other cooperatives, people joined by subscribing to shares in the society, which made them all part owners. Because few of these middle-class members could buy these shares at their face value, they paid for them over time in regular monthly installments. When enough money accumulated, the society held a lottery to see who would receive a loan to buy a home, but because the loan was equal to the face value of the subscribed shares, it was actually an advance on the unpaid shares. To repay these loans, members continued to make their regular monthly share payments to which was added interest for the loan. This interest, along with any fines and initiation fees, was profit for the building society that the officers distributed to the members as dividends. When all members had taken out and repaid their home loans, the building society terminated operations.[4]

Because building societies succeeded only if all members adhered to the ideals of mutual cooperation and systematic savings, once people joined they could not transfer or withdraw their money. Also, failure to make timely share or loan payments resulted in fines and penalties. Furthermore, anyone who joined after a society began business had to make a first payment large enough so that the value invested in the new shares was the same as the total amount paid by the original shareholders. This was necessary to ensure that all members shared equally in any dividends. Given such stringent requirements, most societies had fewer than twenty-five members, but it was also common for building societies to admit both men and women as members and treat them as equals. Another characteristic of these societies was that the officers, who were often society members or community leaders, usually served without pay, and meetings were held at local taverns – all in an effort to minimize operating expenses. This last trait often resulted from behests of pub owners, who sold food and drink to the members during the meetings. As a result, many building societies named themselves after their meeting places.[5]

---

[3] B. R. Mitchell, *European Historical Statistics 1750–1970* (New York: Columbia University Press, 1978), 12–14; J. B. Leaver, *Building Societies, Past, Present and Future* (London: J. M. Dent and Sons Ltd., 1942), 6–8; Price, *Building Societies*, 14.

[4] Leaver, *Building Societies*, 8–9; Cleary, *Building Societies*, 16; Price, *Building Societies*, 5–16. Price dates the first society to 1775 in Birmingham.

[5] Sir Harold Bellman, *The Thrift Three Millions* (London: Abbey Road Building Society, 1935), 24–5, 30.

The growth of industrial cities gave rise to another important financial institution, the mutual savings bank. These were the first financial institutions specifically designed to help those of limited means save for the future, and their organizers were motivated to help the needy based on the moral argument that they were "deserving poor." The first mutual savings bank, called the Tottenham Benefit Bank, was organized by the prominent social reformer Priscilla Wakefield in 1804. Believing that "the only true secret of assisting the poor is to make them agents in bettering their own condition," Wakefield wanted her bank to teach its members how to save and not squander their earnings. To do this, she adopted the share purchase plan used by building societies, in which members had to make regular savings contributions or face penalties. The bank placed these funds in very secure investments, and the interest earned was credited to the member accounts. Similarly, when the shares matured, the member could either withdraw the money or keep it on account. Because mutual savings banks were simple to operate and served socially acceptable purposes, they were so popular that by the end of the nineteenth century they held more than £57 million for their 1.6 million depositors.[6]

By 1825, sixty-nine building societies operated in Great Britain, primarily in the industrial regions of the Midlands and the North. As more of these informal groups were organized, it became necessary for the government to provide them with some type of legal definition and recognition. Initially, Parliament placed them within the jurisdiction of the Friendly Societies Act, but their more specialized operations led to the creation of the Building Society Act, passed in 1836. At the same time, societies developed standardized operating procedures, which made forming a new association easier. The number of new societies multiplied to 2,050 by 1851 and to more than 3,642 by 1895. The assets of these groups also grew rapidly, increasing from approximately £17 million to £54.8 million over the same period. The fact that asset growth exceeded the number of new societies is particularly interesting since the period from 1876 to 1896 was a deflationary period in Great Britain; this underlines how important these nascent financial institutions were to their members. A final consequence of this growth was that as people emigrated from England, they often took the building society ideals with them to their new homes.[7]

---

[6] H. Oliver Horne, *A History of Savings Banks* (London: Oxford University Press, 1947), 23–6; Mary B. Murrell, "Women's Place in the Building Association Movement," *Financial Review and American Building Association News* [hereafter *FRABAN*] 12 (November 1893), 279; Minnie F. Phillips, "Woman's Relation to Building and Loan Associations," *American Building Association News* [hereafter *ABAN*] 18 (January 1899), 22.

[7] Donald McKillop and Charles Ferguson, *Building Societies: Structure, Performance and Change* (London: Graham & Trotman, 1993), 5–25; Leaver, *Building Societies*, 7, 12–15; Bellman, *Thrift Three Millions*, 15, 329.

THE STATE OF HOME FINANCE IN AMERICA

In eighteenth-century America, institutional home finance was virtually nonexistent, primarily because few people needed to borrow to buy a house. Land was relatively cheap, if not free, and raw materials to build homes was abundant. These conditions began to change during the First Industrial Revolution, when urban centers like Philadelphia and New York experienced rapid growth. Between 1790 and 1830, the populations of these cities rose 380 percent and 595 percent, respectively, and one consequence of this was that city housing became more expensive, often requiring some form of outside financing. Initially, private individuals with excess capital provided most of this credit; but because these were loans based on personal connections this system of finance was not widely available, and there were many inconsistencies between lenders regarding loan terms and conditions.[8]

While private mortgage lending was the leading source of home finance in America well into the twentieth century, there were other institutional alternatives. One was the commercial bank, which offered the advantages of greater availability of money for lending and more standardized loan terms than private individuals. There were, however, several drawbacks to borrowing from a bank for a mortgage. Because bank deposits could be withdrawn on demand, bank loans had to be fairly liquid, and to compensate for the low liquidity of real estate, home buyers had to make substantial down payments (up to 60 percent of appraised value) in order to receive a loan. The structure of bank loans was also problematic, since mortgagees usually made interest-only payments during the life of the loan with the full principal due at maturity, a period of no more than five years. A final limitation of commercial bank finance was that only state banks could make mortgages, since national banks by law could not make real estate loans except to buy farm land for agricultural purposes.[9]

Another institutional lender involved in residential finance was the mutual savings bank, which also came to America from England in 1819. Similar to the associations inspired by Priscilla Wakefield, mutual savings banks were neighborhood institutions designed to help the poor and working class save

---

[8] Kenneth A. Snowden, "Mortgage Lending and American Urbanization, 1880-1890," *Journal of Economic History* 48 (June, 1988), 274–7; Kenneth T. Jackson, *Crabgrass Frontier: The Suburbanization of the United States* (New York: Oxford University Press, 1985), 115–27; James Johnson, *Showing America a New Way Home* (San Francisco: Jossey-Bass Publishers, 1989), 32–7; Naomi R. Lamoreaux, "Information Problems and Banks' Specialization in Short-Term Commercial Lending: New England in the Nineteenth Century," in Peter Temin, editor, *Inside the Business Enterprise: Historical Perspectives on the Use of Information* (Chicago: University of Chicago Press, 1991), 161–204.

[9] Morton Bodfish and A. D. Theobald, *Savings and Loan Principles* (New York: Prentice-Hall, 1936), 18–23; Benjamin J. Klebaner, *American Commercial Banking: A History* (Boston: Twayne Publishers, 1990), 72–4; Nelson L. North and DeWitt Van Buren, *Real Estate Finance* (New York: Prentice-Hall, 1928), 36–7.

for the future. Despite the use of the term "mutual," savings banks were not owned by their customers but rather were managed by a group of trustees who made loans on behalf of the depositors. To fulfill their mission as safe repositories, savings banks usually invested in low-risk and highly liquid state and municipal bonds, but since these deposits were also long term the banks also made home loans. While these mortgages had longer terms than commercial banks, the need to ensure safety meant that savings banks also required large down payments from borrowers. Furthermore, mutual savings banks were not national and could only be found in the Northeast.[10]

A third institutional source for real estate finance was the insurance company. The first modern insurance company was Lloyd's of London, a mutually owned British firm founded around 1688. The basic operating plan of this and other mutual insurance companies was that the members pooled their funds and agreed to provide protection to their clients against the risk of loss resulting from a variety of hazards. By the nineteenth century, insurance companies had expanded their lines of business to provide benefits if the policyholder died. While the main reason people had life insurance policies was to provide financial security for their beneficiaries, they also used them as savings accounts since most companies paid dividends on the policies and allowed policyholders to borrow from or withdraw these funds after a certain period of time. To cover policy claims and earn a return for investors, insurance companies invested their money in bonds as well as long-term commercial and residential mortgages. Similar to other institutional lenders, insurance companies required a large down payment from the borrower.[11]

CREATING AN AMERICAN THRIFT BUSINESS

Although home buyers could obtain residential mortgages from a variety of financial institutions, the lending restrictions often limited their availability to people with substantial savings. This situation created an opportunity to create an American version of the British building society, which occurred in January 1831 when forty-five men in the suburban Philadelphia town

[10] Alan Teck, *Mutual Savings Banks and Savings and Loan Associations: Aspect of Growth* (New York: Columbia University Press, 1968), 9–17; James Henry Hamilton, *Savings and Savings Institutions* (New York: Macmillian Company, 1902), 30–45; "Building Associations and Savings Banks," *Gunton's Magazine* 10 (April 1896), 246–7; Edwin J. Perkins, *American Public Finance and Financial Services, 1700–1815,* (Columbus: Ohio State University Press), 1994, 151.

[11] Robert F. Bingham and Elmore L. Andrews, *Financing Real Estate* (Cleveland: Stanley McMichael Publishing, 1924), 95–100; Bodfish and Theobald, *Savings and Loan Principles,* 32–5; Perkins, *American Public Finance and Financial Services,* 299; Kenneth A. Snowden, "The Evolution of Interregional Mortgage Lending Changes 1870–1940: The Life Insurance–Mortgage Company Connection," in Naomi Lamoreaux and Daniel M. G. Raff, editors, *Coordination and Information: Historical Perspectives on the Organization of Enterprise* (Chicago: University of Chicago Press, 1995), 242–4.

of Frankford formed the Oxford Provident Building Association, the first savings and loan association in the United States. Because many of these organizers came from the English Midlands and were familiar with building societies, the operating plan of their new financial institution closely resembled that of its British counterparts. Members subscribed to shares in the association and paid for them in monthly installments. They received loan advances on these shares to buy homes through an auction by submitting bids indicating the loan fee and interest rate they would pay. The member/borrower then continued to make the monthly payments on the shares, as well as the loan interest and a portion of the loan fee, and the officers distributed these profits to the members as dividends. Finally, when the members repaid all their loans or paid for their shares in full, Oxford Provident ended business.[12]

While the main purpose of this first thrift was to provide home loans, an equally important objective was to instill habits of systematic savings and mutual cooperation in members. Not only did late payments incur fines, but anyone withdrawing funds prior to maturity had to pay a substantial penalty. Similarly, the highest bidder for a loan did not automatically receive an advance. Rather, an officers' committee had to declare a person eligible to receive a loan by checking the property, which the member pledged along with the subscribed shares as security, as well as the member's "character" and ability to pay the debt. Similarly, members did not receive dividends in cash; rather, the B&L officers credited these funds to the account of each member. Not only did this requirement preserve the money available for lending, but because the amount owed on the shares fell, members realized compound interest on their investments.[13]

"AMERICANIZING" THE THRIFT BUSINESS

Although building and loans were an effective way for people of modest means to become homeowners, there were a number of operational problems that limited their ability to serve large groups of people. First, it was hard for anyone to join a thrift after it began business. Because all members shared equally in thrift dividends, new members had to make back payments to put them on a par with existing shareholders. Another problem appeared when thrift shares neared maturity and the money received from loan repayments increased. Because this potentially meant the association would have

---

[12] H. Morton Bodfish, "$9,000,000,000 in Small Homes," *The Ladies Home Journal* 47 (January 1931), 21; Horace Clark and Frank Chase, *Elements of the Modern Building and Loan Association* (New York: Macmillan, 1930), 15–17; Henry Rosenthal, *Cyclopedia of Building, Loan and Savings Associations,* Fifth Edition (Cincinnati: American Building Association News Publishing, 1928), 101–3.

[13] Seymour Dexter, *A Treatise on Cooperative Savings and Loan Associations* (New York: D. Appleton, 1889), 66–74.

idle funds, thrift officers would often force nonborrowing members to take advances, or require them to liquidate their shares prior to maturity. Finally, the biggest limitation to this original "terminating plan" of operations was that the association was not a permanent entity and had to end business after the members repaid their loans or paid for their shares in full.[14]

To correct these structural weaknesses, B&Ls began to issue shares periodically on set dates. This minor innovation, which appeared in the 1850s and became known as the "serial plan" of organization, accomplished several goals. First, the steady issuance of shares made the thrift a perpetual entity since members could join over time. Also, by treating each issue of shares as a separate transaction, members could share equally in dividends without having to make back payments. Similarly, the steady addition of new members helped ensure a high demand for loans, which in turn allowed people to join a thrift simply to save long term. While the serial plan quickly replaced the terminating plan, this new structure also had problems. Since each series had individual dividend and payment requirements, officers needed more complex record-keeping systems to track account balances and had to employ more precise cash management skills to ensure that enough funds were available to pay off each series as it came due. Also, if members wanted to keep their money in the thrift after shares matured, they had to subscribe to new shares and resume making monthly payments. Finally, in areas with rapid growth issuing shares only on set dates could unduly limit business activity.[15]

By the late 1870s, these shortcomings led to a new form of thrift structure, the "permanent plan," in which the B&L issued shares whenever the need arose. The permanent plan introduced a number of innovations, including passbooks in which to record deposits and dividends, and the matured share given to members who did not want to withdraw their savings after the original shares came due. The permanent plan also led to the widespread use of reserve funds to account for loan losses. Under the terminating and serial plans, each shareholder had the same amount of money invested in the thrift, which meant it was possible for the thrift to directly charge loan losses as they occurred against profits while still treating all members equally when calculating dividends. When thrifts issued shares individually, however,

---

[14] Edmund Wrigley, *How to Manage Building Associations,* Fourth Edition (Philadelphia: J. P. Lippencott, 1894), 81–7; Herbert Francis DeBower, "Building and Loan Associations Make Both Men and Women," in Robert Marion LaFollette, *The Making of America,* v. 10, *Public Welfare* (Chicago: The Making of America Company, 1908), 229.

[15] Because the first thrift to issue multiple series of shares was the Third Oxford Provident Building Association, the serial plan also was known as the "Philadelphia plan;" Rosenthal, *Cyclopedia of Building, Loan and Savings Associations,* 108–11; C. Floyd Byers, "Building and Loan Associations" (unpublished M.A. thesis, The Ohio State University, 1927), 47; H. Morton Bodfish, "The Serial Era," in H. Morton Bodfish, editor, *History of Building and Loan* (Chicago: United States Building and Loan League, 1931), 91–2.

the share balance of each shareholder was different, and so if the thrift continued to subtract actual losses from profits newer members suffered more. To correct this inequality, thrifts set aside up to 5 percent of earnings into reserve funds for potential defaults and calculated dividends out of the remainder. When actual losses occurred, they were charged against the reserves and not profits.[16]

A fourth form of thrift operating structure was the "Dayton plan," which was introduced in the mid-1880s by the Mutual Home and Savings Association of Dayton, Ohio. Thrifts using the Dayton plan, which was based on procedures developed by the English building societies, also issued shares individually, but members were allowed to apply for loan amounts that exceeded the value of their subscribed shares. In addition, these associations often accepted deposits and made loans to nonmembers, although the interest rates on these accounts were inferior to share holders. Other innovations under the Dayton plan included allowing members to make share payments at any time and in any amount, as well as the ability to withdraw money prior to maturity without penalties. Finally, these thrifts eliminated the use of loan auctions and made mortgages at set rates determined by the officers.[17]

The most significant innovation of the Dayton plan, however, lay in how it calculated loan repayments. A typical B&L loan was repaid through the "sinking fund" method in which the loan matured when the member paid for the subscribed shares in full. One problem with this repayment scheme was that the interest portion of the loan remained constant even as the principal balance fell. Also, it was hard to set a precise loan maturity date when repayment was affected by the level of dividends paid by the association. Dayton plan thrifts improved on this by tying loan payments to the interest rate rather than the dividend rate, which meant using the outstanding principal balance to calculate the interest portion of the loan payment. While this change allowed borrowers to know exactly when their loans would mature, the primary benefit was that the loan accrued lower interest charges than the sinking fund calculation method. These innovations marked the birth of the modern amortizing mortgage, a consumer-friendly home loan that was available only from thrifts for nearly forty years.[18]

---

[16] Henry Rosenthal, *Building, Loan and Savings Associations* (Cincinnati: American Building Association News, 1911), 56–8; Rosenthal, *Cyclopedia of Building Loan and Savings Associations*, 117–18.

[17] Reuben M. Goldstein, *Building and Loan Associations of Ohio* (unpublished B.A. thesis, University of Cincinnati, 1923), 18–22; Byers, "Building and Loan Associations," 15–16; Bodfish and Theobald, *Savings and Loan Principles*, 47–50.

[18] H. E. Buker, "Building and Loan Association Fundamentals and Methods: The Ohio Plan," *Proceedings of the Thirty-Second Annual Meeting of the United States League of Local Building and Loan Associations* (Chicago: American Building Association News Publishing Co., 1924),

A fifth major operating plan appeared in the late 1890s and was used primarily in Oregon, Kansas, and California. This structure, which became known as the "guarantee stock plan," required thrift directors to purchase nonwithdrawable stock as a form of reserve and guarantee that members would earn a specific dividend rate on deposits. If profits exceeded the required dividend payments, the officer/stockholders received the excess, but if profits were insufficient to meet the required payments, the balance came from the stock fund, which stockholders had to replenish. One benefit of this plan was that the reserve fund gave members greater confidence in the overall safety of the association. Also, since the thrift officers held this stock, management had an incentive to operate as efficiently as possible. Finally, thrifts that used this plan could advertise dividend rates with certainty, which was a strong marketing tool to attract funds.[19]

An overarching characteristic of all these different operating procedures was that their success required the close cooperation of thrift members and management. Similar to the British building societies, most American thrift officers were community leaders elected by the membership. One advantage of such close relationships was that many of the risks associated with borrowing and lending money could be better controlled. Because borrowers naturally know more about their own creditworthiness than lenders do, lenders must be cautious in selecting between safe and risky loan applicants as well as ensure that borrowers do not engage in risky activities with loan proceeds. B&Ls managed these risks in a number of ways. First, borrowers typically had to be shareholders, which gave them a financial stake in the success of the thrift. Second, many thrift managers used a borrower's character as part of the loan approval process. Third, rules enforcing systematic savings and mutual cooperation provided an additional safeguard on member defaults or loan losses. Finally, the visibility of thrift management and their willingness to offer products tailor-made to meet member needs gave shareholders confidence that their savings were being invested prudently.

143; Josephine Hedges Ewalt, *A Business Reborn* (Chicago: American Savings and Loan Institute Press, 1962), 39; A. D. Theobald, *Forty-Five Years on the Up Escalator* (Chicago: privately published, 1979), 245.

[19] The guarantee stock plan appeared in Oregon, Kansas, and California because of the problems these states experienced during the nationals crisis; R. Holtby Meyers, *Building and Loans Explained* (Cincinnati: American Building Association News, 1924), 27–31; R. Holtby Meyers, "The California Guarantee Stock Plan," *ABAN* 41 (December 1921), 552; Wilfred George Donley, "An Analysis of Building and Loan Associations in California, 1920–1935," (unpublished doctoral dissertation, University of California, Berkeley, 1937), 20–7; R. Holtby Meyers, "The Guarantee Sock Plan," *Proceedings of the Thirty-Second Annual Meeting of the United States League of Local Building and Loan Associations*, 149–52; Joseph H. Sundheim, *Law of Building and Loan Associations*, Third Edition (Chicago: Callaghan and Company, 1933), 16.

DEFINING THE THRIFT MOVEMENT

By the late 1870s, B&Ls began to appear across the Northeast and Midwest, and as business grew thrift leaders saw the need to create a more uniform public image of their business. Significantly, they described the thrift business as a "movement" not an industry; and this deliberate word choice reflected the fact that many of these leaders identified with the broader effort in America during the late nineteenth century to encourage greater political, social, and economic cooperation. The most prominent of these cooperative efforts included the Knights of Labor, the Farmer's Alliances, Populism, and organized social reform campaigns – all of which were formed as ways to help their members cope with the changes created by industrialization. Like the thrift movement these movements relied on grassroots organization and mutual assistance to achieve growth. Moreover, while material benefits were important, each group tried to achieve far-reaching and often idealistic social goals that would improve the nation as a whole. This combination of practical benefit and social uplift was a common trait in all these popular movements.[20]

The Knights of Labor was one of the first movements to gain national attention in the nineteenth century. Founded in 1869, the Knights objected to the control that monopolies and bankers exercised over the economy and sought to emancipate workers from wage "slavery." The Knights wanted to organize all workers regardless of skill in a "great brotherhood." These wage earners would in turn pool their resources into producers' cooperatives and use these groups to gain greater power and help them enter the capitalist class. The Knights had other goals for bettering the conditions of the working class, including an end to contract and child labor and the creation of the eight-hour day, which they argued were needed to give workers leisure time for improving their social lives. The Knights were an inclusive organization accepting workers of all skill levels and both sexes; blacks were included after 1883 (though in segregated locals). By 1886 the Knights had more than 700,000 members, but membership fell rapidly after the movement became associated with the deadly Haymarket Square Riot that year; by the end of the century it had vanished into obscurity.[21]

Another area where cooperative efforts were strong was among the farming communities of the Great Plains. Often isolated from their neighbors,

[20] Ellen Furlough and Carl Strikwerda, "Economics, Consumer Culture, and Gender: An Introduction to the Politics of Consumer Cooperation," in Ellen Furlough and Carl Strikwerda, editors, *Consumers Against Capitalism? Consumer Cooperation in Europe, North America, and Japan, 1840–1990* (Lanham, MD: Rowman & Littlefield, 1999), 6–27.

[21] Steven Leiken, "The Citizen Producer: The Rise and Fall of Working-Class Cooperatives in the United States," in Furlough and Strikwerda, *Consumers Against Capitalism?* 101–3; Leon Fink, *Workingmen's Democracy: The Knights of Labor and American Politics* (Urbana: University of Illinois Press, 1983), xii–xiv, 13–35.

farmers were at the mercy of railroads to send their crops to market and to big businesses for everyday goods. To increase their economic power, farmers formed cooperatives under the auspices of the Grange and Farmers' Alliance, which pooled the resources of growers into one entity and gave farmers greater leverage to negotiate prices with shippers. They also formed local cooperative stores to buy machines and other goods in large quantities and at lower costs. By 1890, the Farmers' Alliance claimed more than three million members, and in 1892 it expanded its activities into politics with the People's Party. Also known as the Populists, this grassroots political group advocated state ownership of railroads, a graduated income tax, lower tariffs, and easier access to money through the free coinage of silver and a "subtreasury" plan. Populism was successful at the state and local levels, and its ideas on government activism ultimately had important effects on both the Democratic and Republican parties.[22]

A third movement of the late nineteenth century was the rise of organized social reform groups led by religious leaders and women. Organizations such as the Young Women's Christian Association, the Woman's Christian Temperance Union, and Hull House focused on alleviating the economic and social problems experienced by the urban poor. Reformers preached a "social gospel," which maintained that in order for people to lead pure lives they had to have decent homes and opportunities to develop their talents. To create these opportunities, reformers organized vocational instruction programs, ran shelters and hospitals, and promoted physical fitness and temperance. They also advocated civil service reform, an end to child labor, and greater government regulation of big business. Much of this work was coordinated locally with women taking a leading role, and while the participants in these programs realized practical benefits the organizers also emphasized the moral effects of self-improvement.[23]

The Knights of Labor, the Farmers' Alliances, and to a lesser extent Populism and the social gospelers shared several important characteristics with thrifts that helped define them as movements. First, these were nonprofit groups that relied on mutual cooperation for their success. Second, they were primarily grassroots organizations that were easy to form. Third, they were often based on democratic principles, with the leaders usually coming from the membership. Fourth, these movements focused primarily on the least

[22] Norman Pollock, *The Populist Mind* (Indianapolis: Bobbs-Merrill, 1967), xli; Lawrence Goodwyn, *Democratic Promise: The Populist Movement in America* (New York: Oxford University Press, 1976), xi–xxiii; Michael Kazin, *The Populist Persuasion: An American History* (Ithaca, NY: Cornell University Press, 1998), 1–7; Robert C. McMath, Jr., *American Populism: A Social History, 1877–1898* (New York: Hill and Wang, 1993), 83–107.

[23] Samuel P. Hays, *The Response to Industrialism, 1885–1914* (Chicago: University of Chicago Press, 1995), 92–110; Kathleen Donohue, "From Cooperative Commonwealth to Cooperative Democracy: The American Cooperative Ideal, 1880–1940," in Furlough and Strikwerda, *Consumers Against Capitalism?* 115–30.

advantaged members of American society and promoted self-improvement as the best way for advancement. Finally, these groups wanted to achieve broad economic and social goals for their members and the nation as a whole. It is this sense of idealism bordering on evangelism that distinguishes a movement from other forms of organization, and this helped make thrifts unique among America's financial institutions.[24]

The formation of popular movements by groups of Americans seeking to protect their self-interest was not unique, and in the late nineteenth century business leaders and various professions also began to organize to promote their interests. One reason for doing this was to help rationalize industries racked by increased competition resulting from changes caused by the Second Industrial Revolution. Forming trade associations gave businesses forums to discuss issues affecting their industries; and, while this helped leaders share information, it also raised problems of collusion. Professionals, such as doctors and bankers, also formed organizations for many of the same reasons as businessmen, but they also wanted to use these groups to set standards for members and instill greater public confidence in their work. Thrifts ultimately followed this same course, and like other businesses, the trade association B&L leaders formed became a dominant force in shaping future growth.[25]

REACHING THE WORKING CLASS

In order to publicize the benefits of belonging to the thrift movement, its leaders wrote books and circulated pamphlets targeted at working-class men and women. While these works emphasized the practical and economic benefits of owning a home, they also gave equal treatment to the beneficial effects home ownership had on morals and character. One of the earliest of these works appeared in 1852. Its authors described in detail how B&Ls operated as well as how they were good places to invest financially. They noted how private homes were superior to tenements for families, and they stressed that thrifts developed in their members the positive habits of self-restraint, respect for property, and interest in the community. They concluded that from "both a moral and political point of view, these associations assume a position of vital importance."[26]

---

[24] Furlough and Strikwerda, "Economics, Consumer Culture, and Gender," in Furlough and Strikwerda, *Consumers Against Capitalism?* 30–42.

[25] Louis Galambos, "The Emerging Organizational Synthesis in Modern American History," *Business History Review* 44 (Autumn 1970), 279–90; Louis Galambos, "Technology, Political Economy, and Professionalization: Central Themes in the Organizational Synthesis," *Business History Review* 57 (Winter 1983), 472–93; Brian Balogh, "Reorganizing the Organizational Synthesis: Federal Professional Relations in Modern America," *Studies in American Political Development* 5 (Spring 1991), 119–72.

[26] *Mutual Benefit Building and Loan Associations: Their History, Principles and Plans of Operation* (Charleston, SC: Walker and James, 1852), 1–4, 21.

The first thrift publication to gain national prominence was *The Working-Man's Way to Wealth* by Edmund Wrigley, published in 1869. Wrigley developed two basic themes that became the basis of most early books on B&Ls. The first focused on the principles of thrift and mutual cooperation as the foundations of successful B&Ls. Wrigley provided a "how to" guide for organizing a B&L and explained in detail how shares accrued compound interest and the ways in which loans were made and repaid. Because such procedures were easy to understand and financially sound, Wrigley concluded that "the building association is the only plan by which the working man can become his own capitalist." The second major theme of the book emphasized how developing the habits of systematic savings and mutual cooperation by joining a thrift could improve personal morals and increase self-esteem and self-sufficiency. The book was so popular that it went through six editions; in 1873 Wrigley wrote the first practical thrift operating manual.[27]

Thrift leaders also relied on public addresses to reach potential members, and like B&L books and articles, these speeches cited the practical and moral benefits of joining a thrift. One speaker stressed the importance of mutual cooperation in determining the success of a thrift, noting that "it is very easy to help another man. It is very hard to help yourself. The chance here offered by these associations may be the cornerstone of your prosperous life. The spirit must be, first to encourage thrift; then to aid one after another to own his own home; and in and through it all a spirit of cordial cooperation." Other speeches about the movement described B&Ls as the essence of democratic institutions, claiming that they "possess the only plan by which the working man can become his own capitalist . . . [and] create a community in which communism, socialism and anarchy will not be tolerated." Thrifts, however, were not the only financial institutions to use such moral arguments to attract members, since life insurance companies had used similar methods for years.[28]

Daily newspaper advertising, however, was the most prominent form of B&L publicity. Given the space constraints of newspapers, associations focused more on the concrete financial rewards of joining a thrift, such as good dividend earnings or safety of operations. Some advertisements also stressed how joining a B&L would help a person end the financial waste

---

[27] Edmund Wrigley, *The Working-Man's Way to Wealth*, Third Edition (Philadelphia: J. K. Simon, 1874), 1–2; Edmund Wrigley, *How to Manage Building Associations*, Third Edition (Philadelphia: J. K. Simon, 1880), vii–viii; Henry S. Rosenthal, "Building and Loan Literature," in Bodfish, editor, *History of Building and Loan*, 236–8; Henry Rosenthal, *Manual for Building and Loan Associations* (Cincinnati: S. Rosenthal & Co, 1891), iii.

[28] Robert Treat Paine, Jr., *Cooperative Savings Banks or Building Associations* (Boston: Tolman and White, 1880), quote 12; F. W. Bell, *Building Associations, How Operated, Advantages, Etc. Read before the Office Men's Club, June 10, 1886*, Pamphlets in American History, Cooperative Societies (s.l.:s.n., 1886), quote. On life insurance companies, see Viviana A. Rotman Zelizer, *Morals and Markets: The Development of Life Insurance in the United States* (New York: Columbia University Press, 1979), 94–117.

of paying rent. The copy of a typical advertisement included the following: "Young man and Woman, stop and reflect! The money you fritter away uselessly will make you independent. Today sign the magna charter of your independence and like our forefathers, in about eight years you will, in a great degree, be independent by saving only thirty-three cents each day. In that time you will realize $2,000 or have a home and be independent of the landlord." In cities like Philadelphia, Cincinnati, and Chicago associations also published cooperative weekly or monthly papers to give working-class people more complete information about the movement. While designed to promote thrifts, some of these publications also served as trade journals, and over time they became important business organs.[29]

REACHING THE SOCIAL REFORMERS

In addition to publicizing the thrift movement to potential members, thrift leaders worked to gain support for the movement from social reformers and urban elites. This effort reflected the fact that many thrift directors were drawn from such community leaders. One of the first groups to monitor thrift activities was the American Social Science Association (ASSA), an organization founded in 1869 to "promote personal interaction between individuals interested in promoting educational, financial, sanitary, charitable and other social reforms and progress." ASSA members included leading academics, scientists, and reformers who corresponded with affiliate organizations mostly in the Northeast, Midwest, and Europe. In 1884, the ASSA Social Economy Department had completed its first report on these "cooperative building associations," which marveled at the success thrifts had in helping working-class people become homeowners. For the next twenty years the department provided annual reports on the progress of the movement, and over time several ASSA members, including Robert Treat Paine, Jr., of Boston and Judge Seymour Dexter of New York, became active in the movement and prominent thrift leaders.[30]

In addition to the work of organizations like the ASSA, thrift leaders wrote articles for mass-circulation publications like *Scribner's Magazine* and

[29] "A Hundred Thousand Homes and How They are Financed," *Scribner's Magazine* 3 (February 1876), quote 481; Henry Rosenthal, "Building Association Literature," *FRABAN* 15 (August 1896), 23–4.

[30] "American Social Science Association: Constitution, List of Officers Committees and Members," *Journal of Social Science* 12 (December 1880), 165–7. Anna Hallowell, "The Care and Saving of Neglected Children," *Journal of Social Science* 12 (December 1880), 117–24; Edmund Wrigley, "The Advantages of the Cooperative Feature of the Building Association as Compared to Other Plans of Savings," *Philadelphia Social Science Association, Papers on Building Associations*. Reprinted from *Penn Monthly* for July and August 1876 (Philadelphia: Philadelphia Social Science Association, 1876), 1–16; F. B. Sanborn, "Co-operative Building Associations," *Journal of Social Science* 25 (December 1888), 112–13; H. Morton Bodfish, "Seymour Dexter," in Bodfish, editor, *History of Building and Loan*, 177–85.

North American Review, which were read by middle-class and upper-class men and women. Many of these works argued that because the thrift movement worked to increase home ownership among the working class it was an effective way to alleviate the problems of congested urban centers. One author argued that thrifts would "remedy the difficulties and disabilities under which New York labors in the housing of her skilled workmen and great laboring class," and that the lack of B&Ls would hurt the city's future as a commercial and manufacturing center. Others appealed to the ideals associated with home ownership and saw the movement as a way to "remove the youth of the nation from the terrible ever present temptations of the crowded tenement dens." Finally, B&Ls "encourage the development of thrift and providence among wage-earners... and has a social and moral value in counteracting the tendency... to a wider divergence between rich and poor, and the development of a proletariat class."[31]

Another theme used to gain the support of social reformers focused on how thrift membership improved personal morals and strengthened community spirit. Often these writers emphasized the fact that the movement was not a charity, but was "essentially advancement of self-help.... There is nothing philanthropic about it. The man or woman who joins a building association and builds a house sacrifices nothing of self-respect and nothing of dignity. Indeed self-respect and dignity are increased." Philadelphia newspaper publisher Addison Burke noted that because the movement encourages self-sufficiency, a B&L "does more good for the community than the philanthropist who, in helping workmen to acquire homes through gifts of money... leads them to look forward with a beggar's wistful eye to a means of getting money without working for it." Furthermore, when thrifts helped people acquire their own homes, "steadiness, morality and thrift are encouraged, and lawlessness is held in check."[32]

To convince upper-class Americans that the movement could improve citizenship and reduce social unrest, which was "the dream of the reformer," thrift leaders argued that "you cannot make a rioter out of a [homeowner].

[31] Erastus Wiman, "The Hope of a Home," *The North American Review* 156 (February 1893), 228–35, quote 233; Willis Paine, *The Laws of the State of New York Relating to Building Associations* (New York: L. K. Strousse, 1889), quote iii; Robert Treat Paine, Jr., "Homes for the People," *Journal of Social Science* 15 (February 1882), 104–20, quote 110; Talcott Williams, "Philadelphia – A City of Homes," *St. Nicholas: An Illustrated Magazine for Young Folks* 20 part 1 (March 1893), 331–2; Seymour Dexter, "Building and Loan Associations as Related to the Future Political and Social Welfare of the United States," *The American Journal of Politics* 1 (December 1892), 624; W. A. Linn, "Building and Loan Associations," *Scribner's Magazine* 5 (June 1889): 709; Francis B. Thurber, "Industrial and Financial Cooperation," *The North American Review* 153 (July 1891), 85–6.

[32] D. A. Tompkins, "Working People's Homes," *Cassier's Magazine* 23 (March 1903), 612–15, quote 613; Joseph Lee, "Preventive Work," *The Charities Review* 10 (November 1900), 383–4, quote 383; Addison Burke, "The City of Homes and Its Building Societies," *Journal of Social Science* 15 (February 1882), 120–3, quote 121.

TABLE I.I. *Number of Thrifts and Assets – 1888 to 1900*

Year	No. of B&L	Change/Year	Assets (000)	Change/Year
1888	3,500	–	$300,000	–
1893	5,598	9.8%	$473,137	9.5%
1898	5,576	0.0%	$600,135	4.9%
1900	5,356	(0.2%)	$571,367	(2.4%)

Source: Carroll D. Wright, *Ninth Annual Report of the Commissioner of Labor, Building and Loan Associations* (Washington, DC: USGPO, 1894), 214; Ewalt, *A Business Reborn*, 391; F. B. Sanborn, "Address of the Chairman," *Journal of Social Science* 25 (December 1888), 98.
All monetary figures in this study are in current dollars.
B&L: Building and Loan associations.

He is a 'capitalist;' he will never be a turbulent striker." Similarly, because the movement encouraged mutual cooperation, thrifts helped produce "a community of patient, diligent, frugal and contented workers . . . [who instead] of wasting their hours and strength to useless opposition [and] listening to the idle talk of the demagogue, they unite, not for the purpose of overthrowing capital, but with the design of becoming in good time capitalists themselves." Given these benefits, they argued that "this movement . . . deserves the support and encouragement of all employers of labor as well as those devoting their energies to moral, patriotic, or philanthropic purposes."[33]

GILDED AGE GROWTH

The combination of increased promotion among both potential working-class members and reformers, improved organizational structures, and refinements in lending procedures contributed to the impressive growth of the thrift movement in the late nineteenth century as seen in Table 1.1.

One important aspect of the early history of the thrift movement is that the vast majority of all B&Ls were small. The average thrift held less than $90,000 in assets, and nearly 60 percent of all associations had fewer than 200 members; 28 percent had fewer than 100. These trends reflect the fact that most B&Ls were local institutions that served well-defined groups of aspiring homeowners. For example, Philadelphia had more than 900 thrifts by 1890, which caused it to be known as the "City of Homes"; similar concentrations of B&Ls were found in Baltimore, Chicago, and Cincinnati. Furthermore, when the federal government conducted its first survey of all B&Ls in 1893, it found that these associations were helping people of limited

[33] Wrigley, "The Advantages of the Cooperative Feature of the Building Association as Compared to Other Plans of Savings," 1–16, quote 3; J. W. Jenks, "Report on Savings Banks and Building Associations of Illinois," *Journal of Social Science* 15 (February 1882), quote 134; Paine, *Laws of New York*, quote iii; Dexter, "Building and Loan Associations as Related to the Future Political and Social Welfare of the United States," 622–7, quote 624.

financial means. It reported that 26.9 percent of all members were laborers and factory workers, 17.7 percent were housewives and housekeepers, 14.5 percent were artisans and mechanics, 12.3 percent were merchants and dealers, and just 2.9 percent were defined as "capitalists."[34]

A second trend is the rapid growth and relative stability of these institutions. The 1893 survey showed that more than 85 percent of all thrifts were organized under the serial or permanent plans of operation, and the age of the average thrift was just over six years. It also found that the financial condition of most B&Ls was very sound. The liabilities of the average thrift consisted of more than 15 percent retained profits, which can be seen as the capital base of the institution. Similarly, the assets of the average thrift consisted of about 90 percent real estate mortgages, with the balance roughly evenly divided between loans on B&L shares, cash, and other assets. Furthermore, the overwhelming majority of all thrift loans were paid as scheduled, since the movement posted a foreclosure rate of just 2.4 percent; ironically, however, the first loan ever made by an American thrift ended in foreclosure.[35]

A final trend not revealed by these figures was that the expansion of the thrift movement across the country was very uneven. Initially, thrifts were concentrated in Pennsylvania, New Jersey, Massachusetts, New York, and Maryland, but by 1866 migration westward had led to the formation of B&Ls in California, Texas, and Illinois. Surprisingly, thrifts did not appear in states like Ohio, Tennessee, and Rhode Island until much later; one reason for this spotty expansion pattern is that settlers in the West learned about thrifts while living in the East and took the idea with them. Also, the rapid growth of cities like Chicago and San Francisco made forming thrifts a logical solution. By 1880, all but five states had at least one thrift, and just ten years later B&Ls operated in every state or territory, including Hawaii.[36]

THE ROLE OF WOMEN IN B&LS

The 1893 federal survey of the thrift movement revealed the importance of women in helping B&Ls grow. The first thrift to admit female members was the Second Oxford Provident in 1841, and the first B&L organized and

---

[34] The number of B&Ls reporting member occupations was 909, and those reporting gender were 4,260. Wright, *Ninth Annual Report*, 24–31, 292; Bodfish and Theobald, *Savings and Loan Principles*, 50; Dexter, *Cooperative Saving and Loan Associations*, 44; D. Eldredge, *Massachusetts Cooperative Banks or Building Associations* (Boston: G. H. Ellis, 1893), 1; H. F. Cellarius, "The Financial Growth of Building and Loan," in Bodfish, editor, *History of Building and Loan*, 133–40; Kenneth A. Snowden, "Building and Loan Associations in the United States, 1880–1893: The Origins of Localization in the Residential Mortgage Market," *Research in Economics* 51 (1997), 227–50.

[35] Wright, *Ninth Annual Report*, 280, 316–19, 336.

[36] H. Morton Bodfish, "The Spread of the Building and Loan Movement in the United States," in Bodfish, editor, *History of Building and Loan*, 79–84; Sanborn, "Address of the Chairman," 98–9.

managed by women opened its doors in 1880. The government also reported that more than 25 percent of all thrift members were women; indeed, of the 4,260 associations surveyed, only twenty-seven had no female members. Furthermore, female members held shares and borrowed money in their names and had rights equal to those of male members. Women even served as elected delegates at League conventions. One reason women were so involved in the movement was because most early thrifts relied on word-of-mouth publicity and personal referrals to attract new members. These characteristics meshed with the strong networking skills and community support groups of women, especially among the urban working class. One female thrift manager noted that because B&Ls were well suited to women's "rare facility of utilizing with power the small forces of life that are often regarded by men as unworthy of their attention," they were "in conception and practical workings essentially feminine."[37]

Another important reason women joined thrifts arose from the close ties between home ownership and the traditional role of women as family leaders. In the late nineteenth century, most men and women recognized that the primary female responsibility was to raise the family, and as such it was logical that women should also be involved in social and economic pursuits that furthered this goal. One key area of this "woman's sphere" of influence lay in providing a proper home environment, and since B&Ls helped in this respect thrift leaders often considered it a duty of women to become thrift members. According to one female thrift leader, the relationship between B&Ls and women was "as close and binding as home and church." Another asked "where else do we find two great spheres into which we may class all women – the business on the one hand and the domestic on the other – coming together as closely and intimately as in the building and loan?" Male thrift leaders similarly advised associations to "encourage the securing of women as investors and borrowers, as she generally succeeds in her undertakings" to improve the home. They further noted that women tended to be thriftier than men and that they were also good credit risks.[38]

---

[37] Wright, *Ninth Annual Report*, 291, 323; H. Morton Bodfish, "The Spread of the Building and Loan Movement in the United States," in Bodfish, editor, *History of Building and Loan*, 75; "Activity of Women in Building and Loan Circles," *ABAN* 19 (September 1900), 258; Genevieve N. Gildersleeve, *Women in Banking* (Washington, DC: Public Affairs Press, 1959), 17, 26–7; "The Field Now Being Open to Women," *ABAN* 20 (September 1900), 258; Nancy A. Hewitt, "Beyond the Search for Sisterhood: American Woman's History in the 1980s," in Vicki L. Ruiz and Ellen Carol DuBois, editors, *Unequal Sisters*, Second Edition (New York: Routledge, 1994), 6; Anna E. Cardell, "A Woman's Building and Loan Association," *Proceedings of the Seventh Annual Meeting of the United States League of Local Building and Loan Associations* (Chicago: The Press of the American Building Association News Press, 1899), 25; Murrell, "Women's Place in the Building Association Movement," quote 279.

[38] Phillips, "Woman's Relation to Building and Loan Associations," quote 22; M. S. Jones, "Woman's Influence in Building and Loan Associations," *ABAN* 20 (January 1900), quote 6; F. D. Gay, "How Can We Better Our Associations?" *ABAN* 18 (January 1899), quote 4;

A second aspect of the woman's sphere that corresponded to the work of B&Ls was the strengthening of personal morals and character. While securing a home was the main goal of most members, thrift leaders considered developing the habit of systematic savings equally important, since thrift taught men and women "industry, frugality and patriotism." Similarly, homeowners learned values associated with pride of ownership and pride in their communities. Since women were "the teachers of thrift and helpful principles," men wanted them to help instill these ideas in others. They noted how female members often made their husbands join in order to become thrifty and work toward the goal of owning a home. One of their greatest contributions as thrift members, however, was teaching these values to children. Women saw thrift as a virtue that children needed to have, and associations assisted in building this virtue by allowing minors to have accounts in their names. They also developed school savings programs, and some even maintained separate juvenile annexes.[39]

Women also closely identified with the self-help elements of thrift work that some connected to the broader goals of Progressivism. As one female B&L executive suggested, promoting thrift and home ownership among the working class would "bring about a condition of affairs...as fruitful of perfect happiness as is pictured by Mr. Bellamy in his 'Looking Backward.'" Related to this image of thrifts as social reformers was the idea that thrift-inspired home ownership could protect traditional values such as patriotism and personal freedom, which some women included as part of the women's sphere of influence. As one female thrift leader asked rhetorically, "what is the [thrift] ideal? Surely a home. What does it signify? Safeguard of American liberty. Here Woman's Day has always been."[40]

"Women Are Good Payers," *FRABAN* 14 (January 1895), 23. Women were also active in savings banks, since these institutions, like B&Ls, offered a way to provide for the welfare of families through long-term savings. See George Alter, Claudia Goldin, and Elyce Rotella, "The Savings of Ordinary Americans: The Philadelphia Saving Fund Society in the Mid-Nineteenth Century," *The Journal of Economic History* 54 (December 1994), 735–67.

[39] A. B. Sbarboro, "The Beneficial Effect of Women in Building and Loan Associations," *FRABAN* 13 (January 1893), quote 4; Jones, "Woman's Influence in Building and Loan Associations," *ABAN* 20 (January 1900), 6; "Little Savings Banks for Public Schools," *ABAN* 22 (May 1903), 22; "Juvenile Saver Annex," *ABAN* 23 (June 1904), 23; William Corbin, "Building and Loan Associations in Relation to Our Public Schools," *ABAN* 31 (July 1911), 316–17; James Clarency, "The Laboring Man in Building Associations," *Proceedings of the Fourth Annual Meeting of the United States League of Local Building and Loan Associations* (Chicago: The Press of the Financial Review and American Building Association News Press, 1896), 76; L. J. Wolcott, "Woman's Work in Building and Loan Associations," *Proceedings of the Sixth Annual Meeting of the United States League of Local Building and Loan Associations* (Chicago: The Press of the Financial Review and American Building Association News Press, 1898), 95–102.

[40] William Pieplow, *Century Lessons of Building and Loan Associations* (Appleton, WI: C. C. Nelson Publishing, 1931), 11–13, 31–2, 56–7; George McKinnis, "Building and Loan as a Moral Force," *Proceedings of the Twenty-Ninth Annual Convention of the United States League*

Finally, women became thrift members as a way to achieve long-term financial security. Because monthly share payments were small, women of all ages, marital status, and employment status could use these associations to save for the future. In Massachusetts, where thrift share payments averaged just $1.25 per month, more than 12,000 women owned shares valued at $11.5 million. Most single female workers used their memberships to save for their well-being, while married women joined to have a financial cushion should their husbands lose their jobs, become disabled, or die. Similarly, some women became members after their husbands borrowed from B&Ls in order to provide for new households. Several states recognized these motives and allowed married women to hold accounts as individuals with ownership rights separate from their husbands. Similarly, managers often commented on how women tried to calculate dividend payments on their own and were eager to learn more about their accounts.[41]

THE "NATIONALS" CRISIS

By the late 1880s, the growth of the thrift movement contributed to the creation of a new type of B&L that applied the ideals of systematic savings and mutual cooperation on a national level. These new associations, which became known as "national" B&Ls, had the potential to enhance greatly the stature of the thrift business by extending the movement beyond urban centers into rural areas. Typically headquartered in a city like Minneapolis or Chicago, nationals were often formed by bankers or industrialists and had on their Boards prominent people like state governors and congressmen. The organizers also owned the $5 million in capital stock that most of these thrifts held as equity. The majority of nationals operated on the serial plan and employed promoters to sell shares by forming local branches primarily in the Midwest and South. Significantly, because the number of votes for the typical national member was based on the number of shares held, these institutions were more open to control by wealthy individuals than traditional B&Ls, which tended to limit each shareholder to one vote.[42]

of Local Building and Loan Associations (Chicago: American Building Association News Publishing, 1921), 74–8; "Building and Loan Program Aims to Get More for Homeowners," *Business Week*, 30 July 1930, quote 22; B. S. Twichell, "Ideas, Facts and Figures," *ABAN* 20 (March 1901), quote 83.

[41] Phillips, "Woman's Relation to Building and Loan Associations," 22; Jones, "Woman's Influence in Building and Loan Associations," 6; Elene D. Loeb, "Bitter Bread," *ABAN* 49 (June 1929), 336–7; Wright, *Ninth Annual Report*, 615, 626, 671; "Women Shareholders Increasing," *ABAN* 24 (December 1905), 235; Jones, "Woman's Influence in Building and Loan Associations," *ABAN* 19 (January 1900), 6; "Mrs. B. S. Twitchell," *ABAN* 19 (November 1900), 325.

[42] A. A. Winters, "A Review of the Growth, Methods, Failures and Manners of the So-Called National Building and Loan Associations," *FRABAN* 12 (September 1893), 228–9; "National Installment Loan Companies," *ABAN* 43 (April 1923), 167–71; "National

The members of the nationals made their share payments at their local branch, and the money was then sent to the home office, where it was pooled with other funds and made available for home loans. This plan of collecting money from across the country and concentrating it into a larger loan pool was in principle an ideal way of bringing the benefits of B&Ls to areas too sparsely populated to have their own associations. There were, however, several problems with how the nationals operated that limited their effectiveness. First, national B&Ls were for-profit businesses whose organizers expected to make a return on their investment. Furthermore, the organizers, officers, and promoters all earned hefty salaries, and most nationals spent from 6 percent to 11 percent of revenues on operating expenses. By contrast, the rate for traditional B&Ls was just 1 percent to 2 percent of revenues.[43]

While these abnormally high expenses naturally reduced the amount of money the nationals could use for home loans, the problem was exacerbated by the practice of segregating member payments into different funds and setting this money aside to cover actual and contingent expenses. For example, most nationals had insurance funds to pay the par value of the shares to the heirs of a deceased member. Unfortunately, after making these deductions only about 80 percent of the total members' payments was available for loans. In contrast, virtually all member dues at a traditional B&L was lent as mortgages. Such a difference may account for why, in 1893, just 13.8 percent of all nationals members were borrowers, compared to 29.8 percent for the "locals."[44]

Despite such drawbacks, the nationals were extremely successful and spread quickly across the country. By 1893, more than 290 such associations were in business, a figure that rose to 361 three years later. Some nationals were among the largest financial institutions in the country, with assets in the millions and membership in the tens of thousands. In contrast, the typical local was a fraction as big. At their height, the nationals controlled more than $139 million in assets, and branches of these associations could be found in every state. Although most people became national members to obtain a home loan, another equally important reason to join was that nationals seemed to offer a way to get rich quick, since their advertised dividend rates were three to four times as high as those available from any other financial institution.[45]

Installment Loan Companies," *ABAN* 43 (May 1923), 210–12; Wright, *Ninth Annual Report*, 360–1.

43 The National Building and Loan Association, Milwaukee, WI, *Plain Answers to Sensible Questions* (Milwaukee: n. p. 1894?), 15; James P. Fritze, *Investment Building and Loan: Reasons Why* (Peoria, IL: n. p., 1892), 8–9; Wright, *Ninth Annual Report*, 297–8.

44 "The National Associations," *FRABAN* 12 (January 1893), 3; "The 'American' of Minneapolis," *FRABAN* 15 (March 1896), 9; Wright, *Ninth Annual Report*, 299.

45 The People's Building and Loan Association of Bloomington Illinois, *The People's Building and Loan Association of Bloomington, Illinois* (Bloomington, IL: J. E. Burke & Co., 1893),

Although the nationals did not actually guarantee that investors would earn high returns on savings, these rates were implied because these associations did guarantee that their shares would mature after a set number of monthly payments. The nationals maintained this was possible because they were high-volume lenders that would generate large amounts of interest income. An examination of the nationals income statements, however, revealed that these thrifts also relied on up to fourteen different types of fees and fines (many of which were quite exorbitant) for revenue. Furthermore, the mortgage agreements the nationals used had strict payment requirements that increased the potential of foreclosure by the lender. Finally, members faced severe restrictions on premature withdrawals, and nationals commonly required that deposits be held with the thrift for a minimum number of years to avoid penalties. Some also operated under a "tontine" arrangement in which withdrawals or any late payments resulted in the complete forfeiture of member savings.[46]

By the mid-1890s, the leaders of traditional thrifts, who began to refer to their B&Ls as the "locals," began to publicize how procedures used by the nationals could lead to financial problems. One such practice was the requirement that all branch loan applications be approved by the home office. Because many of these officers were unfamiliar with the real estate conditions where the branch was located, many loan approvals were based on overvalued appraisals or inadequate security. Also, since branch agents were paid according to the number of new members they attracted, and not the quality of the loans, borrower credit risks were potentially quite high. The locals contended that such procedures virtually guaranteed a loan portfolio of such low quality that the safety of the entire institution would be at risk. The locals, however, rarely faced such risks since the officers and directors who approved their loans came from the local community.[47]

1, 11, 17; National Building and Loan, *Plain Answers to Sensible Questions*, 3–8; G. Gunby Jordan, *The ABC Primer of a Building and Loan Association* (New York: Uncle Ben Publishing, 1889), 2–7; H. Morton Bodfish, "The Rise and Fall of the 'Nationals,'" in Bodfish, editor, *History of Building and Loan*, 102; "A New Plea for the Nationals," *FRABAN* 14 (September 1895), 11.

[46] People's B&L, *The People's Building and Loan Association*, 3–5, 13; National Building, Loan and Provident Association, *By-Laws of the National Building, Loan and Provident Association* (Wilmington, DE: National Building, Loan and Provident Association, n. d.), 1–15; Bodfish and Theobald, *Savings and Loan Principles*, 51; Bodfish, "The Rise and Fall of the 'Nationals'" in Bodfish, editor, *History of Building and Loan*, 101; "Nebraska: Review of the Progress of Loan and Building Associations," *FRABAN* 12 (January 1893), 31–2; "Locals vs. Nationals," *FRABAN* 12 (February 1893), 27; Fritze, *Investment Building and Loan*, 7.

[47] "How It Works," *FRABAN* 14 (March 1895), 3; J. H. Westover, "The Difference Between National and Local Building Associations," *FRABAN* 16 (May 1897), 5; "National Installment Loan Companies," *ABAN* 43 (June 1923), 254–7; "National Installment Loan Companies," *ABAN* 43 (July 1923), 311–13; D. A. Emery, "The National Building Associations

Another line of attack on the nationals exposed the contradiction in the promises made by these thrifts to offer low interest rates on mortgages and pay high returns on savings. According to the critics, "these magic workers think nothing of promising that the borrower shall pay only six percent for his money, six to eight percent shall be deducted for expenses, and yet the depositor will realize from seventeen to fifty percent on his investment." By showing how these B&Ls imposed many restrictions on member savings, the locals graphically demonstrated that a person would have to hold money in a national for up to four years to avoid losing money, while earning a paltry 1.5 percent return. As the nationals began to post unfavorable financial results, the problems predicted by the locals gained credibility, and one critic wondered how a national with annual management expenses of nearly 10 percent of total income "can keep going and pay even a small percentage of interest. Yet this particular St. Paul company offers 24 percent interest. Comment is hardly needed here. It is plain to see that somebody is going to be greatly disappointed."[48]

The nationals defended their work, contending they were not in competition with the locals but rather complemented these thrifts by distributing funds more equitably between areas of high and low loan demand. Because most nationals were wholesale lenders, they needed far more full-time employees to "expand the usefulness." In fact the average national had twice as many agents, bankers, and brokers as members as the average local. Furthermore, the leaders of the nationals contended that their thrifts were safer than traditional B&Ls, since they limited their mortgages to just 50 percent of appraised value, unlike the locals, which lent up to two-thirds of the value. Contrary evidence on the safety issue was found in the 1893 federal government survey of B&Ls, which found that the nationals experienced the same rate of foreclosures as the locals. Overall, the report concluded that the nationals were "conducting business with the same integrity as the locals."[49]

of Twenty Years Ago," *Proceedings of the Thirty-Second Annual Meeting of the United States League of Local Building and Loan Associations* (Cincinnati: American Building Association News Publishing, 1924), 112, 115.

[48] "The Nationals of Illinois," *FRABAN* 12 (January 1893), 1–2; "Stopped! the use of the word 'National' by the so-called National Building and Loan Associations," *FRABAN* 12 (November 1893), 283; "Building and Loan Finance," *FRABAN* 15 (September 1896), 25; A. A. Winters, "National Building Associations," *Cooperative News*, 1 February 1890, quote in Bodfish, "The Rise and Fall of the 'Nationals,'" in Bodfish, editor, *History of Building and Loan*, 103; F. B. Sanborn, "Annual Report on Co-operative Building and Loan Associations," *Journal of Social Science* 27 (October 1890), quote lvi.

[49] "Editorial," *The National Building and Loan Herald*, 15 November 1889, quote in Bodfish, "The Rise and Fall of the 'Nationals,'" in Bodfish, editor, *History of Building and Loan*, 103; Bird Robinson, *A Paper on Building and Loan Associations* (s.l.:s.n.), 6–7, 17–18, 21–2; Fritze, *Investment Building and Loan*, 8–9, 12; "National Installment Loan Companies," *ABAN* 43 (September 1923), 416–17; Wright, *Ninth Annual Report*, quote 16.

As leaders of both nationals and locals fought each other, they began for the first time to actively press state legislators to enact laws governing all B&Ls. Although national leaders scored some modest victories, the locals were more effective and secured a number of anti-national restrictions. These included prohibiting "foreign" associations from opening branches in a state, capping officers' salaries as well as fines and fees, and even banning the use of the word "national" in the name of an association. These efforts occurred throughout the country, and in states such as Illinois, Indiana, West Virginia, and Missouri, local thrift leaders essentially drafted the laws passed by their legislatures. Most laws were not simply designed to limit the nationals, but were an attempt to promote the local movement by producing better business standards. In Ohio, the thrift trade group secured the adoption of a "model building association code," and by 1900 nearly every state passed some form of thrift law.[50]

While legislation did hinder the nationals business, what ultimately caused these thrifts to disappear was the Depression of 1893. Even before the economic downturn, most nationals were only marginally profitable, averaging just less than $87 in profits per shareholder; by contrast the average local had nearly $303 in profits per shareholder. Furthermore, since the nationals relied heavily on membership and loan fees, which in some cases accounted for more than 25 percent of total income, profitability plummeted when these B&Ls could no longer attract new members and borrowers. Consequently, by the mid-1890s, many nationals had trouble covering both their hefty expenses and large dividend payments.[51]

In addition to declining membership, another important factor that crippled the nationals was the collapse in real estate prices. During the late 1880s, real estate prices rose to such an extent that even if borrowers defaulted on their loans, the lenders who acquired these properties could still resell them and make a profit. During the deflationary period of the depression, real estate prices fell to such an extent that when a thrift acquired properties through foreclosure they were worth a fraction of their original value. Because the average national had less equity and held just one-tenth as much

[50] "Notes on Legislation," *FRABAN* 14 (February 1895), 4–6; "Must Have Legislation," *FRABAN* 14 (January 1895), 23; "Building and Loan Legislation in Iowa," *FRABAN* 15 (March 1896), 33; F. D. Kilborn, "Supervision of Building and Loan Associations," *FRABAN* 18 (21 September 1899), 231; "The Leagues," *FRABAN* 13 (February 1894), 36; "Kansas Building Associations," *FRABAN* 13 (November 1894), 266; F. B. Sanborn, "Report on Co-operative Building and Loan Associations," *Journal of Social Science* 26 (February 1890), 123; "Once More the Nationals," *FRABAN* 13 (November 1894), 270; "Building Association Press," *FRABAN* 14 (September 1895), 17; James W. Carr, *A History of Savings and Loan Associations in the State of Ohio* (unpublished B.S. thesis, University of Cincinnati, 1949), 30–1; Ewalt, *A Business Reborn*, 381–2, 385–6.

[51] Bird, *A Paper on Building Associations*, 26; Otto Fowler, "Review of the Character and Extent of Business Done by Nationals in Michigan," *FRABAN* 15 (October 1896), 5; "The Breaking Storm," *FRABAN* 16 (March 1897), 15; Wright, *Ninth Annual Report*, 15, 299.

cash as its local counterpart, few nationals were able to absorb the losses on these loans or maintain their liquidity.[52]

By the end of the decade, the number of prominent nationals that went out of business began to skyrocket, and in their wake thousands of working-class members were left penniless. The most shocking aspect of these failures, however, was that they revealed the magnitude of these thrifts' self-dealing practices. One Minneapolis association, with branches throughout the Midwest and assets of more than $2.1 million, had spent $1.2 million on expenses during its seven years of operation. Another national with only $170,000 in assets spent nearly $40,000 annually on operating expenses. Between 1893 and 1897, more than half of all nationals were out of business, and local thrift leaders estimated that these failures cost their members a quarter of a billion dollars. The death knell for the nationals came when the largest, the Southern Building and Loan Association of Knoxville, Tennessee, with $5 million in assets collapsed in 1897. This thrift had a broad network of branches across the South, and its failure sparked a number of banking scares that fueled a general loss of confidence in all nationals. By the end of the century only a handful of nationals remained, and all were gone by 1910. Such a rapid rise and fall of thrifts that generated profits for their owners at the expense of the members would, unfortunately, occur again during the 1980s.[53]

THE LEGACY OF THE NATIONALS

The rise and fall of the national B&Ls had important consequences for the thrift movement. One negative effect was that the wholesale failure of the nationals sparked a general loss of public confidence in all B&Ls. This situation was especially true in the South, and in states like Tennessee, where in 1893 sixty-one local and seventeen national B&Ls existed, a total of just fifteen thrifts were in business by 1910. In Georgia, which had thirty-one locals and twelve nationals in the 1890s, only one thrift was still in business by 1900. The crisis also tarnished the reputation of the thrift movement and did much to undermine the image of B&Ls as friends of the working class.

---

[52] Wright, *Ninth Annual Report*, 316–19; "Report of the Southern Building and Loan Association of Knoxville, Tennessee," *FRABAN* 16 (January 1897), 3; "National Installment Loan Companies," *ABAN* 43 (October 1923), 460–3.

[53] "Proceedings of the United States League of Local Building and Loan Associations," *FRABAN* 14 (January 1895), 1; "Turning on the X Rays," *FRABAN* 15 (May 1896), 23; "The Granite State Provident Association" *FRABAN* 15 (February 1896), 3; "Reached the End" *FRABAN* 15 (February 1896), 1; "The 'American' of Illinois," *FRABAN* 15 (March 1896), 9; "The Illinois National," *FRABAN* 13 (November 1894), 255; "Another National Follows the Long Line of Those that Have Gone Before," *FRABAN* 14 (August 1895), 5; "The Southern of Knoxville, Tennessee," *FRABAN* (March 1897), 25; Thomas J. Fitzmorris, "Some Fruits of National Methods," *FRABAN* 16 (November 1897), 28–30; Ewalt, *A Business Reborn*, 387.

Because the nationals were so similar to the locals in terms of operation and nomenclature, it was hard to convince people that any building and loan was still safe. As one thrift leader commented, "it will be years before it will be possible to establish a genuine building and loan association in a community after the name of building associations has been besmirched and prostituted, and brought into grave disrepute through the action of schemers who have run these bogus concerns."[54]

Among the positive consequences of the nationals crisis was that thrift leaders became aware of the economic benefits offered by government regulation. While movement officials used state laws to drive the nationals out of business, they also sought regulation as a way to limit competition and promote the movement by restoring public confidence in legitimate B&Ls. The movement also took responsibility for seeing that legislators updated these laws periodically and often took the lead in drafting desired legislation. A second important positive consequence was that B&L managers realized the importance of maintaining loan loss reserves as a way of reducing the possibility of failure when real estate values fell, and by the early twentieth century most thrifts began voluntarily to create such funds. Finally, the nationals experience directly led to the creation of the guarantee stock plan, which required thrift directors to create and maintain a permanent capital fund and guarantee their dividend rates.[55]

The most significant consequence of the nationals crisis was that it showed thrift leaders the importance of greater internal organization through trade associations. As early as the 1870s, B&Ls began to form state trade associations called "leagues," and by 1890 twelve were in operation. As the nationals crisis grew, these leaders formed the United States League of Local Building and Loan Associations in 1892 to provide a forum for state leagues. Although some thrift leaders saw the national League as a temporary body limited to defeating the nationals, its founders had long-range plans for this organization. As outlined by its first president, Seymour Dexter, the League would "magnify the movement we represent not for our own welfare, save as citizens, but for the welfare of the Republic." The primary way to do this was to popularize the positive benefits of thrift and home ownership, the importance of which was evident in the League motto: "The American Home. The Safe-Guard of American Liberties." During the next thirty years,

---

[54] Horace Russell, *Savings and Loan Associations* (New York: Matthew Bender & Co., 1960), 27–8; "Downfall of the 'Nationals,'" *FRABAN* 15 (March 1896), quote 8; Mark Carl Rom, *Public Spirit in the Thrift Tragedy* (Pittsburgh: University of Pittsburgh Press, 1996), 21–2.

[55] Charles S. Elliott, "Kansas," in Bodfish, editor, *History of Building and Loan*, 396–9; H. Morton Bodfish, "State Supervision of Building and Loan Associations," in Bodfish, editor, *History of Building and Loan*, 121–2; Clark and Chase, *Elements of the Modern Building and Loan*, 50–1; C. W. Nagle, "The Reserve Fund," *FRABAN* 16 (June 1897), 29; Bodfish, "The Rise and Fall of the 'Nationals,'" in Bodfish, editor, *History of Building and Loan*, 114; Ewalt, *A Business Reborn*, 388–9.

the League became an important force that promoted the thrift movement, created uniform business practices, and encouraged the passage of favorable legislation.[56]

CONCLUSIONS

From the appearance of the first thrift in Philadelphia in the 1830s, American B&Ls had, by the end of the nineteenth century, spread from coast to coast. These institutions, which helped people of modest means save for the future and acquire homes were popular for several reasons. First, they were local, mutually owned, and easy to organize and operate, traits that gave thrift members high degrees of confidence and agency in their management. Second, thrift leaders aggressively promoted their businesses and the benefits of thrift and home ownership not only to the working class but also to socially conscious reformers. These factors helped build a successful thrift movement, which in turn spawned a host of competitors including the national B&Ls. These B&Ls, which grew rapidly during the prosperous 1880s, seemed like traditional thrifts but explicitly promised high returns for investors, which proved a fatal flaw when the nation sank into a prolonged depression during the 1890s. The collapse of the nationals cost thousands of members their life savings, and in the process tarnished the image of traditional B&Ls.

The nationals crisis represented the first major challenge the thrift movement faced in its brief history, and the experience had a number of important consequences. One of the most long-lasting was the realization by thrift leaders of the need for greater internal organization. In 1892, these leaders formed the United States League of Local Building and Loan Associations as a national trade association to promote the principles of thrift and home ownership as well as the political and economic interests of the thrift movement. As the League entered the twentieth century, its dual role of encouraging the basic tenets of the thrift movement and shaping the direction of the thrift business would help repair the image of B&Ls and help them assume a greater role in residential and consumer finance.

[56] "Constitution," *FRABAN* 12 (August 1893), 198; "President's Address," *FRABAN* 12 (July 1893), 167–8; H. F. Cellarius, "The United States League of Local Building and Loan Associations – Its Work and Relation to State League," *FRABAN* 16 (June 1897), 28; H. F. Cellarius, "The United States League: Its Organization and Other Historical Data," in Bodfish, editor, *History of Building and Loan*, 141–7; Clark and Chase, *Elements of Building and Loan*, 50–1.

2

THE RISE OF THE LEAGUE,
1900–1929

By the turn of the twentieth century, the "nationals" crisis was over and the thrift movement faced the challenge of restoring its image and returning to prosperity. At the forefront of these efforts was the movement's trade association, the United States League of Local Building and Loan Associations. The League focused on three major objectives. The first and most important was to repair the damage caused by the nationals crisis and to reestablish the role of B&Ls in promoting the ideals of thrift and home ownership. Elements of Progressive era reform movements partially aided this effort, since improving urban housing conditions was also a goal of these social reformers. A second objective focused on generating greater advertising and publicity for the movement. The League advised associations on useful advertising methods, encouraged their participation in national promotions of thrift and home ownership, and took steps to build better relations with housing-related industries. The final objective of the League was launching programs to help create a more professional public image for the movement. These initiatives, which met with varying degrees of success, included formal education classes for thrift managers, creation of more uniform business practices and lending systems, and efforts to encourage the modernization of the physical appearance of B&Ls.

These efforts, combined with economic prosperity and increased consumerism in the 1920s, helped the B&L movement recover fully and emerge as an important source of consumer finance. The success of the movement did not go unnoticed by others, however, and the result was greater competition from banks as well as increased public scrutiny into how thrifts conducted their work. Despite these developments, the experience of the first two decades of the twentieth century helped the League mature as a trade association and gave it the capacity to aid the movement once the nation sank into the Great Depression of the 1930s.

PROGRESSIVISM AND THE THRIFT MOVEMENT

The major focus of the League at the turn of the century was to restore and strengthen the tarnished public image of the B&L movement following the nationals debacle. While the actual damage in terms of failed associations during the 1890s was nominal, thrift leaders were still concerned that legitimate B&Ls had been smeared by the episode. To rebuild public trust and confidence in these institutions, the League resumed its efforts to promote knowledge of how B&Ls helped their members acquire the habit of thrift and the benefits of home ownership. These themes had been critical in helping the movement grow in the 1880s, and in the early twentieth century the League hoped they would attract the favorable attention of the Progressives who were also trying to improve housing conditions for the working class. Despite similar goals, these reformers did not always consider the creation of B&Ls as a way to solve the nation's problems.[1]

The rise of Progressive reform movements in the early 1900s resulted in part as a way to address the social changes caused by the Second Industrial Revolution. One aspect of the work of reformers lay in improving the substandard and overcrowded living conditions of the urban lower classes. Although reformers began addressing this problem as early as the 1860s, it was only after muck-raking journalists brought greater attention to the evils of the infamous "dumbbell" tenements that substantive changes were made. In 1900, New York Governor Theodore Roosevelt formed the nation's first state housing commission to address these problems. Its success in creating substantive tenement reform laws led to the formation of similar commissions in other industrial cities. Eventually, the mission of improving tenements became a national movement when urban reformers founded the National Housing Association (NHA) in 1911. The NHA, like other Progressive organizations, approached the housing problem scientifically and collected all forms of data on urban tenements, educated the public on the need for change, and secured corrective legislation that could be enforced.[2]

While the NHA believed that teaching the public how to live better was an important part of housing reform, it did not try to encourage these people

[1] H. Morton Bodfish, "The Future of Building and Loan in the United States," in H. Morton Bodfish, editor, *History of Building and Loan in the United States* (Chicago: United States Building and Loan League, 1931), 288–300.

[2] Erastus Wiman, "Hope of a Home," *North American Review* 156 (February 1893), 229–30; Jacob Riis, "How the Other Half Lives," *Scribner's Magazine* 6 (December 1889), 647–8; "Tenements of Greater New York," *American Building Association News* [hereafter *ABAN*] 32 (December 1912), 534–5; Kenneth T. Jackson, *Crabgrass Frontiers* (New York: Oxford University Press, 1985), 191–2; "Dumb-Bell Tenements in New York," *ABAN* 31 (May 1911), 199; Robert DeForest, "President's Address," and Lawrence Veillor, "A Program for Housing Reform," *Proceedings of the Academy of Political Science* (New York: The Academy of Political Science, Columbia University, 1912), 239, 10H.

to join thrifts and become homeowners. One reason for not doing so was a matter of priorities. As NHA leader Lawrence Veillor noted, "any effort toward considering more interesting and attractive forms of housing had to wait" until tenement conditions were improved. He saw the immediate conditions as the more "serious social menace which threatens to overwhelm American institutions." Nor was Veillor entirely convinced that home ownership would produce lasting reforms. He claimed that "in cities where the workingman owns his own home ... sanitary authorities have the greatest difficulty meeting health needs, securing adequate appropriations, and enforcing higher standards." The final reason why the NHA may not have considered B&Ls as a viable solution was that these reformers were focused on helping the poorest elements of society who did not have the financial capacity to join thrifts. As Robert Treat Paine, Jr., a thrift leader and president of Boston's Associated Charities noted, tenement reformers aimed to help "the class who have sunk to the very bottom and propose to stay there." Thrifts, however, wanted as members "the classes above the lowest" because these people had more stable incomes. This requirement that members have steady incomes was important because systematic savings were critical to the success of any B&L.[3]

Although few Progressives advocated organizing B&Ls as an immediate solution to urban housing problems, they did agree that teaching the habit of thrift would help solve another tenement problem, that of loan sharks and pawnbrokers who preyed on immigrants. Urban reformers supported the creation of remedial banks and employee cooperative savings banks to provide personal finance at reasonable terms and conditions. These mutual banks were not charities, but rather self-help organizations that operated much like B&Ls by issuing shares to members who paid for them over time. The only real difference was that remedial bank loans were small and used for household needs. Given such similarities, it is likely that when lower working class borrowers advanced into higher wage positions, they would already have the financial habits needed to join a B&L and make a final exit from life in the tenements. Consequently, it may be best to view such NHA reforms as a stepping stone to the ultimate goal of home ownership through a building and loan association.[4]

<hr />

[3] Veillor, "A Program for Housing Reform," quotes 10G; "Housing and Health," *ABAN* 38 (November 1918), 481–3; "The Relation of Building and Loan Associations to the Housing Problem," *American City* 9 (September 1913), 250–1; Robert Treat Paine Jr., "Homes for the People," *Journal of Social Science* 25 (February 1882), 117–8, quote 118; Lendol Calder, *Financing the American Dream: A Cultural History of Consumer Credit* (Princeton: Princeton University Press, 1999), 111–56.

[4] Edward Ewing Pratt, "Cooperative Savings and Loan Associations," *Proceedings of the Academy of Political Science* (1912), 139–48; Elizabeth Moran, "Public Loan Association Proposed for Relief of Milwaukee Poor People," *ABAN* 21 (January 1902), 8; "Loan Association for Store Workers," *ABAN* 31 (September 1911), 391.

Another goal of Progressive reformers was to bring immigrants into the American mainstream. Achieving this objective took a variety of forms, including "social hygiene," settlement house, health education, and temperance movements. Because this work involved making immigrants "better" citizens, thrift leaders felt this was an area they could play a role in. Since the 1870s, B&L movement leaders had maintained that increasing home ownership would reduce the threats of socialism and labor unrest, since owning a home "adds dignity and earnestness to life." Also, homeowners, they claimed, took a greater interest in government and would "demand as a matter of right purer water, better sanitation, better schools and better moral surroundings." Finally, developing the habit of thrift in immigrants would reduce "wasteful" spending on socially harmful goods such as cigarettes, gum, and alcohol. Initially, however, most Progressives continued not to see the creation of thrifts as part of their work.[5]

By the mid-1910s, the rise of "good citizenship" and "Americanization" movements finally caused reformers to recognize the potential of thrifts to improve personal morals and character. Because the majority of the estimated 9.3 million immigrants who came to America between 1873 and 1910 were from southern and eastern Europe, some "traditional" Americans saw these people as a threat to the American way of life and value system. One business leader even contended that "the greatest danger ... upon our country's future prosperity is the emigration to our shores of thousands upon thousands of the ignorant lower classes of the old world." To address this perceived problem reformers tried to "Americanize" immigrants by forming national organizations like the YMCA, and local bodies like settlement houses. The League recognized the potential benefits of participating in these movements, and encouraged thrift managers to make "special efforts ... to secure the foreign element as members," because "every time you make a home you make a citizen."[6]

As this work to encourage immigrants to join thrifts grew, people associated with the Americanization effort began to give greater recognition to

[5] R. M. Gillan, "Building and Loan Association – Its Influence on Private Citizenship," *ABAN* 22 (December 1903), 257; Rev. Denis O'Donaghue, "The Building Association: Its Influence on the Community," *ABAN* 20 (March, 1901), 71-2, quote 72; W. E. N. Hemperly, "The Position of the Savings and Loan Association in the Community," *ABAN* 21 (October 1902), quote 343; F. A. Chase, "Citizenship and Thrift," *Proceedings of the Twenty-Ninth Annual Convention of the United States League of Local Building and Loan Associations* (Chicago: American Building and Loan News Publishing Co., 1921), 74-8.

[6] Edward Hartmann, *The Movement to Americanize the Immigrant* (New York: AMS Press, 1967), 8-11; Gerd Korman, *Industrialization, Immigrants, and Americanizers; the View from Milwaukee, 1866-1921* (Madison: State Historical Society of Wisconsin, 1967), 117-20; "Competition to House Immigrants," *ABAN* 36 (May 1916), 207; F. P. Cleveland, "Homes," *FRABAN* 15 (July 1896), quote 5; "Benefits of Building and Loan Associations," *ABAN* 35 (November 1915), 500; "Americanization," *ABAN* 37 (March 1917), quote 103; *ABAN* 35 (December 1915), 519.

the B&L movement. The president of the Kalamazoo Michigan Chamber of Commerce said that the best way to Americanize aliens was to form B&Ls for them so that they could learn how to manage their own finances and possess their own homes. Governor Woodrow Wilson of New Jersey noted that the real significance of B&Ls was its "moral influence on members. It is a movement for the conservation of the character of citizenship." New Jersey Chamber of Commerce President George Viehmann spoke for many when he said there was "no greater force for the Americanization of the immigrant than is being exerted by the building and loan association." He also noted that immigrant homeowners "take a taxpayer's interest in good government and politics." One reason why 'good citizenship' groups used thrifts to promote Americanization while housing reformers were generally averse to the idea was that "Americanizers" often had more diverse social backgrounds and were not drawn simply from urban elites.[7]

A third aspect of Progressivism that shared a similar goal with the B&L movement was the effort to promote thrift by reducing personal and national wastefulness. To do this, however, efficiency advocates had to convince people that thrift was not a negative trait associated with parsimony and miserliness. This task became much easier during World War I when all Americans were urged to make financial sacrifices in order to achieve victory. One example of this was the need to raise money to finance the war effort, since 77 percent of all war expenditures were covered by issuing federal debt. Significantly, much of this debt was sold to individual Americans in the form of small denomination Liberty Loans and War Savings Stamps. The idea to involve the general public in financing the war came from Treasury Secretary William MacAdoo who created campaigns that portrayed buying government bonds as a patriotic duty of all citizens. The result was overwhelming national participation, and by the end of the war 22 million people held more than $17.8 billion in government debt, up from the $1 billion held by 200,000 people in 1914.[8]

---

[7] "Good Accomplished by Leagues," *ABAN* 31 (July 1911), 291; "Benefits of Building and Loan Association," *ABAN* 35 (November 1915), 500; *ABAN* 36 (May 1916), quote 195; "Thrift and Building and Loan Associations," *ABAN* 37 (January 1917), 16–17, quote 16; "Makes Good Citizens," *ABAN* 38 (February 1918), quotes 53; Taylor O. B. Eaton, "The Building and Loan: An Institution for the People," *Proceedings of the Eighteenth Annual Meeting of The United States League of Local Building and Loan Associations* (Chicago: The Press of the American Building Association News Press, 1910), 116–23.

[8] Samuel P. Hays, *The Response to Industrialism, 1885–1914* (Chicago: University of Chicago Press, 1995), 197–8; Samuel Haber, *Efficiency and Uplift: Scientific Management in the Progressive era, 1890–1920* (Chicago, University of Chicago Press, 1964), 13–15; Guy Alchon, *The Invisible Hand of Planning* (Princeton: Princeton University Press, 1985), 15–17; Henry Raymond Massey, editor, "Influence of Saving on Character," *Proceedings of the Academy of Political Science*, 12–14; "'Acquired' Rather than 'Natural' Resources Should Claim Conservationists," *ABAN* 32 (August 1912), 344–5; E. L. Kellogg, "To Increase Efficiency in Home Building," *The Survey* 33 (October 11, 1914), 67; Charles Gilbert, *American Financing of World War I* (Westport, CT: Greenwood Publishing, 1970), 65–70, 117–20, 164–5.

Such broad popular support for Liberty Loans encouraged reformers to continue their work of encouraging thrift after the war and to change what the *Cleveland Plain Dealer* described as a national motto of "easy come; easy go." One reason that reformers felt it was possible to sustain these efforts was that the war experience had created a new concept of thrift in which people "realized for the first time it was a matter of life and death whether they wasted or whether they consumed." Consequently, while the government ended most wartime conservation programs in 1918, the Treasury Department continued to sell savings stamps to help perpetuate the habit of thrift. Similarly, academic and civic leaders tried to promote the idea of a "New American Thrift" by designing standardized budgets that would achieve the "proper use" of resources, and creating classes to teach children the benefits of thrift.[9]

The high point of this renewal of thrift came in 1919 when the Treasury Department urged the YMCA and other national civic organizations to create a nationwide celebration of financial awareness called National Thrift Week. Designed to increase public education about the benefits of sound financial planning, each day of National Thrift Week had a specific theme, such as "National Thrift Day," "Share with Others Day," and "Pay Your Bills Promptly Day." To give this celebration added importance, it was held around the January 17 birthday of Benjamin Franklin, whose *Poor Richard's Almanac* contained many well-known stories on the benefits of thrift. Because the goals of the National Thrift Week and the B&L movement dovetailed, the League strongly endorsed the event and urged associations to sponsor speakers, produce literature, and create advertisements highlighting the messages of each day. Although the initial Thrift Week celebrations were successful, interest in the movement waned during the consumer-oriented 1920s, and the League eventually assumed responsibility for the annual event. The League established an affiliate organization, the nonprofit National Thrift Week Committee, to coordinate these activities.[10]

Another related national celebration the B&L movement took an active role in was the Better Homes Week. Commerce Secretary Herbert Hoover developed the idea of Better Homes Week in 1922 to encourage home ownership among people of lesser incomes, as well as to promote better housing design and more efficient construction methods. To further these goals, he directed the Commerce Department to encourage the systematization of

[9] "The Army of Thrift," *ABAN* 39 (January 1919), quote 13; "Thrift," *ABAN* 40 (January, 1920), 5. Roy G. Blakey, "America's New Conception of Thrift," *The Annals of The American Academy of Political and Social Science* 87 (Philadelphia: The American Academy of Political and Social Science, 1920), 1–4; B. R. Andrews, "Thrift as a Family and Individual Problem," *Ibid*, 13–18; Alvin Johnson, "The Promotion of Thrift in America," *Ibid*, 233–9.

[10] James B. Morman, "Cooperative Credit Institutions in the United States," *Ibid*, 87, 173–6; "Keep Up the Savings Habit, Says the Government," *ABAN* 39 (March 1919), 103; "National Thrift Week," *ABAN* 39 (December 1919), 546–51.

building standards across the country. Although Better Homes Week was not a government program, Hoover was the honorary president of the volunteer organization called Better Homes of America, whose more than 30,000 mostly female members coordinated the activities. Each year the League encouraged associations to get involved in these promotions not by publicizing their own business, but by focusing on the benefits of home ownership to the public. While this work brought greater attention to the thrift movement, Better Homes Week also created the opportunity for greater interaction with other housing industries.[11]

THE RISE OF THRIFT MOVEMENT ADVERTISING AND PROMOTION

A second major focus of the League in the early twentieth century involved getting more B&Ls to advertise and promote their associations broadly to the general public. In the late-nineteenth century, most thrift managers relied primarily on word-of-mouth advertising and member referrals to promote their associations. Some tried to build ties with the community by allowing civic groups to meet in thrift offices and by sponsoring public lectures. By the 1910s, the use of window displays by associations with ground-floor windows was also popular. These advertisements usually were dioramas based on the themes of thrift and home ownership. This form of publicity became so commonplace and effective that the League began an annual contest for the best-designed window advertising. Finally, newspaper advertising was an important way of reaching the public, and while some managers used this medium to promote the self-help virtues of thrift membership, by World War I the majority of print advertising emphasized interest rates for deposits and loans.[12]

11 Herbert C. Hoover, *The Memoirs of Herbert Hoover: The Cabinet and the Presidency, 1920–1933* (New York: The Macmillan Co., 1952), 92–6; Letter from Herbert Hoover to Miss J. Alison Hunter, December 28, 1922; Collected Speeches of Herbert Hoover [hereafter "The Bible"] No. 274; Herbert Hoover Presidential Library (HHPL); Letter from Herbert Hoover to Irving B. Heitt, September 13, 1922; Building and Housing, Better Homes in America Previous to Incorporation, 1921–1923; Commerce Papers; HHPL; Herbert Hoover, "Better Homes Drive Due to Women," *The Washington Times*, 11 May 1923, 12; Letter from James Ford to Herbert Hoover, 13 July 1925; Building and Housing, Better Homes in America, 1925; Commerce Papers; HHPL; Letter from Herbert Hoover to Mrs. William Brown Meloney, 26 January 1926, 1–5; Building and Housing, Better Homes in America, 1926; Commerce Papers; HHPL; "Better Homes Week, October 9–14," *ABAN* 42 (November 1922), 394–5. *Better Homes in America: Guidebook for Demonstration Week, May 11 to 18 1924* (Washington, D.C.: USGPO, 1924), 4–8.
12 W. G. McClain, "Profitable Advertising," *ABAN* 21 (January 1902), 11; O. H. Roetken, "Advertising the Building Association," *ABAN* 32 (May 1912), 210–1; "Advertising by Word-of-Mouth," and "The Need for More Publicity," *ABAN* 34 (April 1914), 200–1, 210–1; K. V. Haymaker, "Distinction Between a Publicity Program and an Advertising Program," *ABAN* 47 (August 1927), 413–5; R. W. Pearson, "We Need Publicity. How Can We Get It?" *ABAN* 47 (November 1927), 520–2; A. W. Anderson, "The Need for Building and Loan

While the League approved of the increase in advertising, it also wanted B&Ls to produce more polished publicity efforts. In 1899, the League's trade journal began to run a regular column on effective thrift advertising, and by the 1920s its editors invited advertising experts to write articles on how to design more effective types of promotions. Significantly, the League did not want managers to lose sight of the spirit of self-improvement that was central to the thrift movement. J. R. Moorehead, a leader of both the thrift and lumber trade associations, compared the mission of B&L officers to that of religious crusaders, and he exhorted them to "spread the gospel of savings and home ownership." He insisted that managers had an obligation to "sell the building and loan association to all people for their own good," and urged "the apostles of thrift and home ownership [to] send out men to preach the gospel you profess to believe."[13]

Another way of increasing thrift publicity was to build cooperative alliances with other housing-related industries to promote home ownership. In 1927, thrift leaders launched the Better Relations campaign to increase interactions between the lumber and real estate trade associations and coordinate joint promotions. In 1929, local chapters of these various trade groups sponsored advertising campaigns that often stressed the importance of using experts in real estate, construction and finance when buying a home. Finally, thrifts also benefited from the number of "how-to" articles that appeared in popular press magazines during the 1920s, many of which were targeted at female readers. Like the how-to books of the nineteenth century, these works advised home buyers on the strengths and weaknesses of different types of home financing, and highlighted how B&L mortgages offered the most consumer-friendly terms.[14]

Publicity," *ABAN* 48 (January 1928); 21; "Persistent Advertising a Necessity," *ABAN* 40 (June 1920), 386; Burl D. Knight, "Getting New Members," *ABAN* 47 (September 1927), 421; Robert Riegel and J. Russell Doubman, *The Building-and-Loan Association* (New York: J. Wiley and Sons, 1927), 44.

[13] "How to Advertise," *ABAN* 18 (January 1899), 47; "Publicity for Savings and Loan Associations," *ABAN* 33 (May 1913), 201–4; M. George. DeLucas, "Some Suggestions on Advertising," *ABAN* 47 (March 1927), 124–5; "Why We Don't Know More About Building and Loan Association," *ABAN* 44 (December 1924), 532–3; "The Purpose of Advertising," *ABAN* 47 (August 1927), 363; J. R. Moorehead, "Are You Selling the Building and Loan Association to the Public?" *Proceedings of the Twenty-Eighth Annual Convention of the United States League of Local Building and Loan Associations* (Chicago: American Building Association News Publishing Co., 1920), 103–5, quotes, 112; "Spreading the Gospel," *ABAN* 45 (August 1925), 349; Walter F. McDowell, "The Social Value of Savings and Loan Association," *Proceedings of the Thirtieth Annual Convention of the United States League of Local Building and Loan Associations* (Chicago: American Building Association News Publishing Co., 1922), 89–90; George E. McKinnis, "Building and Loan Associations as a Moral Force," *Proceedings of the Twenty-Ninth Annual Convention of the United States League of Local Building and Loan Associations*, 80–1.

[14] R. Holtby Myers, "Education for Building and Loan Service," *ABAN* 41 (December 1921), 514; K. V. Haymaker, "The Importance and Value of Building and Loan Associations,"

MAKING THE THRIFT MOVEMENT MORE PROFESSIONAL

A third major objective of the League in the early twentieth century was to enhance the status of the movement as a profession and to better standardize business operations. The Progressive era drive to professionalize the image of everything from industrial occupations to the sciences was done in part to increase public respect for the specialized nature of different lines of work. For the League, the key reason to make B&Ls appear more professional was to give the movement the same status people gave to other financial institutions. To do this, the League wanted managers to become knowledgeable with the latest developments in finance, an area in which bankers had a decided edge. An important reason for this advantage was that the American Bankers Association, which began the professionalization of banking in the mid-nineteenth century, had formed the American Bankers Institute in 1900 to design formal financial education classes. As consumer finance increased in complexity during the 1920s, the lack of a similar program for B&L executives led one League leader to conclude that "the next generation of building and loan executives will surely need an education in keeping with the times."[15]

In 1922, representatives from the thrift, lumber, and real estate trade associations organized the American Savings, Building and Loan Institute (ASBLI) to improve manager education. The ASBLI created courses in savings and loan business principles, salesmanship and advertising, and accounting and property appraisals – all of which were made available through local ASBLI chapters or home study. Each course took about sixteen weeks to complete, and students received a diploma certifying their accreditation as B&L professionals. The ASBLI curriculum used a college-level text, which was also the first modern standardized manual for thrift operations, and the ASBLI even helped colleges design their own courses in building and loan

National Real Estate Journal 23 (17 July 1922), 22–5; "Better Relations Program Under Way," *ABAN* 47 (October 1927), 454–5; "Tie Up with a Realtor in November," *ABAN* 47 (November 1927), 506–7; "Better Relations Proves Effective for Local Association," *ABAN* 48 (April 1928), 171–2; "Better Relations Commission Announces the New Co-operative Advertising Service," *ABAN* 48 (July 1928), 290–3; 35–43; C. M. Keys, "How to Finance the Building of a Little Home," *The Ladies Home Journal* 30 (October 1913), 36; Henry T. Theis, "If You are Thinking of Building a House," *The American Magazine* 86 (August 1918), 106.

[15] Robert H. Wiebe, *The Search for Order, 1877–1920* (New York: Hill and Wang, 1967), 120–4, "American Bankers Association," *ABAN* 19 (December 1900), 1; Naomi R. Lamoreaux, *Insider Lending: Banks, Personal Connections, and Economic Development in Industrial New England*, (Cambridge: Cambridge University Press, 1994), 107–19; R. Holtby Meyers, "Education for Building and Loan Service," *ABAN* 41 (December 1921), 514–5, quote 514; Frank A. Chase, "Educational Development, Part I: Organization of the American Savings, Building and Loan Institute," in Bodfish, editor, *History of Building and Loan*, 253–7; "Get Behind the American Savings, Building and Loan Institute," *ABAN* 43 (May 1923), 196–8.

methods. In 1924, the Institute graduated its first class of twenty men and seven women, and by the end of the decade it had a national network of chapters educating hundreds of B&L managers. Initially, the ASBLI was an independent organization run by the Kansas City Building and Loan League and the Southern Lumbermen's Association, but in 1930 it became an official affiliate of the League.[16]

While creating a formal thrift-manager education program was a major success in the campaign to professionalize the movement's image, other initiatives were less successful. One of these was the effort to encourage managers to improve the physical appearance of their offices. Although few B&Ls held meetings in taverns as in the old days, it was equally true that most did not own their own offices. Most thrifts, in fact, rented upper-floor space in bank buildings. Furthermore, few associations were open on every business day, because most transactions, like share payments and making loans, occurred only on certain days of the month. The League wanted managers who could afford the expense to acquire separate office buildings or at the least rent ground-floor space. It also wanted thrift offices to look like banks by using classical architecture styles, marble and brass fixtures, and the ubiquitous "teller's cage" as a way to convey financial strength. Despite these urgings, few managers wanted to spend money in this manner as reflected in the fact that in 1930 less than half of all thrifts owned their own offices.[17]

Another partial failure in this campaign to professionalize the B&L movement was the effort to institute standardized business procedures. The 1893 federal survey of B&Ls showed that thrifts calculated dividends, loan premiums, and fees by dozens of different methods. Most associations also used

---

[16] The first college course on B&L practices appeared at The Ohio State University. See "The American Savings, Building and Loan Institute," *ABAN* 42 (December 1922), 533–6; Franklin Stevens, "Building and Loan Education," *Proceedings of the Thirty-Second Annual Meeting of the United States League of Local Building and Loan Associations* (Chicago: American Building Association News Publishing Co., 1924), 108; H. F. Clark, "Modern Building and Loan Education," *ABAN* 44 (December 1924), 549–52; "Popularity of Home-Study Course," *ABAN* 45 (April 1925), 172; Horace F. Clark and Frank A. Chase, *Elements of the Modern Building and Loan Associations* (New York: Macmillian and Co., 1925), vi; Horace F. Clark, "Educational Development, Part II: The Institute at Work," in Bodfish, editor, *History of Building and Loan*, 262–6; Philip Lieber, "Educational Development, Part III: Recent Institute History," in Bodfish, editor, *History of Building and Loan*, 267.

[17] George Walker, "Some Defects in the Building and Loan Association System," *Financial Review and American Building Association News* [hereafter *FRABAN*] 15 (August 1896), 27; J. J. Stoddart, "The Status of Building and Loan Associations as Financial Institutions," *ABAN* 23 (February 1904), p. 28; "Homes for Building Associations," *ABAN* 39 (July 1919), 308; Frank A. Chase, "What are the Facts About Building and Loan Associations?" *The Magazine of Wall Street* 40 (11 April 1925), 998–1000; Horace F. Clark, "The Extension of State Regulation to the Building and Loan Association," *The Journal of Political Economy* 32 (December 1924), 632–3; Angel Kwolek-Folland, *Engendering Business: Men and Women in the Corporate Office, 1870–1930* (Baltimore: Johns Hopkins University Press, 1994), 171–2.

rudimentary accounting systems that primarily tracked just the receipt and disbursement of cash, and which were inadequate for complex tasks such as calculating multiple-share dividends and amortization schedules. Furthermore, financial statements used terms such as "installments" and "dues," or "gains" and "profits" interchangeably, which the League saw as needlessly confusing to outsiders. The survey's author noted the overall "lack of uniformity in bookkeeping methods" as a significant flaw within the movement. One League leader later charged that such inconsistency in thrift practices "places obstacles in the way of a [B&L's] effectiveness," and was the main reason why "we do not have the definite strong standing before the public." In the 1920s, state League-sponsored legislation requiring greater uniformity did reduce some of these problems, but resistance to change was so strong that substantive alterations came only during the economic crisis of the Great Depression.[18]

Another standardization effort that failed was having the movement use a common name to describe their business. From the beginning of the thrift movement, B&Ls deliberately chose very descriptive names for their businesses, names that often described the ethnic or occupational background of the members. Also, thrifts used the words "building," "loan," "savings," and "investment" seemingly at random. These practices were so pervasive that by 1925 thrifts used more than 140 forms of corporate titles. Adding to this confusion was the fact that B&Ls went by different names depending on where they were located. Thrifts in Massachusetts were called "cooperative banks," while in Louisiana thrifts were known as "homestead associations." In New York the most common title for a B&L was "savings and loan association." A related problem lay in how the movement should describe its occupation. Thrift employees were not in the strict sense bankers, given their different functions, and most managers were loathe to use the term.[19]

---

[18] F. D. Gay, "How Can We Better Our Associations?" *FRABAN* 18 (January 1899), 4; Addison B. Burke, "Uniformity in Nomenclature and Reports," *Proceedings of the Fourteenth Annual Meeting of The United States League of Local Building and Loan Associations* (Chicago: The Press of the American Building Association News Press, 1906), 75–7; "Complete Reports Essential," *ABAN* 21 (October 1902), 291; H. G. Comstock, "A Practical Accounting System for Building and Loan Associations," *ABAN* 35 (November 1915), 511; Wright, *Ninth Annual Report*, quote 316; "Proceedings of the United States League of Local Building and Loan Associations," *FRABAN* 14 (August 1895), quotes 2; P. M. Endsley, "Necessity of Reformation of Local Building and Loan Association," *FRABAN* 15 (July 1896), 17; "The Twenty-Fifth Annual Meeting of the United States League of Local Building and Loan Associations," *ABAN* 37 (August 1917), 347; William J. Byrne, "Uniform Methods," *ABAN* 48 (February 1928), 53; James W. Carr, *A History of Savings and Loan Associations in Ohio* (unpublished B. S. thesis, University of Cincinnati, 1949), 30–1, 39; Clark and Chase, *Elements of Building and Loan*, 60–1.

[19] Joseph Sundheim, *Law of Building and Loan Associations*, Third Edition (Philadelphia: Smith-Edwards Co., 1922), 24–7; Clark and Chase, *Elements of Building and Loan*, 13.

League members failed to agree on how to solve these problems. Despite pleas to adopt "some sort of standardization, so a man dealing with an association in California will, upon moving to Texas, feel a sense of security with an association in Houston," thrifts refused to give up what they considered to be their own unique identities. The effort to describe the B&L occupation also produced a wide range of terms. In 1922, the League sponsored a contest and encouraged "anyone who can put 'building-loan-savings-investment-association-company-homestead-cooperative-bank' into a melting pot and produce a simple term that will be readily understood everywhere" to enter. The most popular suggestions included "Co-operative Banker," "Savings-Loaner," "B-Lator" (a take-off on "Realtor"), "Thriftor" and "Frugalator." The League eventually decided not to pick a single term, leaving the issue of what to call the thrift professional to local preference. While these were relatively minor defeats for the League, the inability to unify the thrift business at such a basic level was symptomatic of how managers still placed local concerns above those that affected the movement as a whole.[20]

NEW LEAGUE STRATEGY, NEW LEAGUE STRUCTURE

Another reason why the League had mixed success at standardizing and professionalizing the B&L movement was that the League itself was not a very professional organization. In fact, during its first thirty years of existence the main functions of the League were to publish a monthly newsletter and hold a gala annual convention where state trade association leaders could meet. These tasks were easily accomplished with a staff of part-time employees who worked in two small offices in Cincinnati and Chicago. Even elected officials worked for the League part time, primarily because they were also still managers of their local institutions. All these factors made it difficult initially for the League to expand its scope of activities and services in an effective manner.[21]

One way by which the League tried to expand its presence within the movement was by improving the quality and quantity of communication with its members. In 1899, the League combined the two major thrift publications into one monthly journal, which became the official trade association organ. It also refined its content to make it more informative and useful to managers. In the past, thrift journals had consisted of speeches by movement leaders and stories on thrift and home ownership that gave them distinctly home-spun qualities. The new League journal carried more articles

[20] Burke, "Uniformity in Nomenclature and Reports," 71–4; A. S. Keister, "What's Wrong with Building and Loan," *ABAN* 49 (October 1929), 587, 623; "Committee on State Legislation," *Building and Loan Annals, 1930* (Chicago: United States Building and Loan League, 1930), 654–5; "Let's Name Ourselves," *ABAN* 42 (August 1922), 340–2; "Can You Think of a Better Name?" *ABAN* 44 (January 1924), 11.
[21] "Retrospective," *FRABAN* 12 (December 1893), 310; Ewalt, *A Business Reborn*, 25.

written specifically on business issues affecting thrifts, and by 1909 it switched from a newspaper format to that of a professionally edited magazine. The League also began to include inserts with articles important to a particular area written by local thrift leaders to help customize the journal for state Leagues. Finally, the League published more general thrift texts and manuals written by experts, and made sure these works were updated often.[22]

Two other changes greatly enhanced the organizational capabilities of the League. The first was the 1924 decision to let individual thrifts become members. Although some executives objected to this change because of fears that the trade group would become dominated by large B&Ls, it was necessary to improve the ailing financial condition of the League. This situation was so severe that during most of the 1910s the League was virtually bankrupt. The second, and more important change, came in 1929 when the League created the position of full-time executive manager. This move, along with the decision to consolidate operations into one modern Chicago high-rise office, not only gave the trade group a permanent leader but also for the first time allowed it to hire a large professional staff dedicated to League activities.[23]

PROGRESSIVE ERA RECOVERY

As the nationals crisis of the 1890s faded from memory and the League worked to revitalize the movement, the thrift business experienced an extended period of steady growth as is shown in Table 2.1.

This expansion reveals a number of trends in the development of the movement during the early twentieth century. First, as total asset growth exceeded the increase in the number of associations, individual B&Ls were larger than ever before. The assets of the average thrift rose from just $106,000 in 1900

---

[22] "American Building Association News" *ABAN*, (January 1899), 1; "Announcement" *ABAN* 29 (January 1909), 1; H. H. C. "Our Official Organ: Its Function," *ABAN* 37 (May 1917), 202–3; E. W. Stillwell, "Better Relations Report Reviewed by an Expert," *ABAN* 47 (September 1927), 416; "Your Magazine and Your Movement," *ABAN* 48 (February 1928), 65; Henry Rosenthal, *Cyclopedia of Building, Loan and Savings Associations* (Cincinnati: American Building Association News Publishing Co., 1923), 10–12; "President's Address," *Proceedings of the Thirty-First Annual Meeting of the United States League of Local Building and Loan Associations* (Chicago: American Building Association News Publishing Co., 1923), 24–25.

[23] The League also removed the word "Local" from its name in 1927 to make the movement appear modern and progressive. "Busy Days of a U.S. League President," *ABAN* 43 (November 1923), 489–90; K. V. Haymaker, "The U.S. League – Its Membership and Finance," *ABAN* 41 (September 1921), 247–8; "The Thirty-First Annual Convention of the United States League," *ABAN* 43 (August 1923), 354; Ewalt, *A Business Reborn*, 26. See Louis Galambos, *Competition & Cooperation: The Emergence of a National Trade Association* (Baltimore: Johns Hopkins Press, 1966), for how trade associations in other industries widen their membership roles during this period.

TABLE 2.1. *Number of Thrifts and Assets – 1900 to 1920*

Year	No. of B&L	Change/Year	Assets (000)	Change/Year
1900	5,356	–	$571,367	–
1907	5,424	0.2%	$731,508	3.6%
1914	6,616	2.9%	$1,357,708	9.2%
1920	8,633	4.5%	$2,519,915	10.8%

Source: Josephine Hedges Ewalt, *A Business Reborn: The Savings and Loan Story, 1930–1960* (Chicago: American Savings and Loan Institute Publishing Co., 1962), 391.

to nearly $292,000 twenty years later. Second, the B&L movement proved to be fairly resilient to short-term economic crises such as the Panic of 1907, which caused dozens of banks to fail, but which barely affected thrifts. While one reason for this was that many B&Ls were literally not open when the crisis swept through their areas, the key factor was that B&Ls had a different legal relationship with their members than that between banks and their customers. Commercial bank depositors were legally considered creditors, which gave them the right to demand immediate withdrawal of deposits. B&L members, however, owned their thrift and could not legally demand immediate payouts. They instead had to submit withdrawal requests, which the thrift had to honor within thirty days. This delay helped diffuse potential problems associated with deposit runs and permitted more effective cash management.[24]

During World War I, the main concern for the thrift movement was finding ways to invest the surge in new deposits they received from members working in the defense industries. This was a problem because mortgage lending, which was the heart of the thrift business, fell sharply when the government diverted materials used for home construction and repair to the war effort. To prevent the accumulation of idle funds, thrift managers invested in government debt, such as Liberty Loans. While these securities earned lower interest rates than what could be earned from making home loans, associations saw this work as a way of showing their patriotism and support of the war effort. When the war ended, the major increase in the demand for homes helped boost the share of all residential mortgages provided

---

[24] "Effect of Panic on Associations," *ABAN* 27 (November 1908), 202; L. L. Rankin, *Financial Panic of 1907 and Its Lessons to Building and Loan Associations* (Columbus: Champlain Printing Company, 1908), 307; Charles O'Conner Hennessey, "Building and Loan Associations and Financial Panics," *Proceedings of the Sixteenth Annual Meeting of The United States League of Local Building and Loan Associations* (Chicago: The Press of the American Building Association News Press, 1908), 75–9; Clark and Chase, *Elements of Building and Loan Associations*, 470–1; Sundheim, *Law of Building and Loan*, 27–9.

by thrifts from 15 percent in 1915 to 20 percent by 1922. Furthermore, this market share remained steady during the 1920s.[25]

THE RISE OF ETHNIC THRIFTS

One reason why the thrift business grew so quickly during this period was that ethnic groups became very active in the movement. Beginning in the late-nineteenth century millions of immigrants began to settle in America's industrial cities, and to acquire better homes they often created B&Ls to serve specific ethnic communities. By 1894, more than 550 ethnic thrifts were in business serving German, Irish, Scottish, Polish, Hungarian, Serbian, Croatian, Yugoslavian, Italian, Lithuanian, Estonian, Latvian, and Russian communities. Some thrifts even served people of specific religions. The League approved of these developments, and encouraged greater involvement by ethnic groups, noting that thrifts are "being rapidly carried forward among the foreign element which is truly for the good of the local community."[26]

There are several reasons why thrifts appealed to these ethnic groups, one of which was that thrifts were traditionally small neighborhood organizations. The average thrift had just 300 members, and it was common for a single city to have more than 200 associations. Similarly, word-of-mouth advertising used to attract B&L members was a trait ideally suited to the tight-knit nature of ethnic communities. Finally, because states often allowed thrifts to conduct business from almost any location, some ethnic associations operated out of local taverns that were often the center of neighborhood social activity. Such characteristics, however, did not mean ethnic thrifts were small financially. In Chicago, one Bohemian association that used no formal advertising and drew all its members from a neighborhood four miles long and one mile wide held more than $5 million in assets. Furthermore, these B&Ls were not "clannish," but often attracted members from a variety of ethnic groups.[27]

---

[25] Morton Bodfish and A. D. Theobald, *Savings and Loan Principles* (New York: Prentice-Hall, 1938), 57–9; J. R. Moorehead, "Wartime Activities Affecting Building and Loan Associations," *American Lumberman*, 27 July 1918, 47; "What To Do With Surplus Funds," *ABAN* 38 (March 1918), 151; "Building Associations and the Liberty Loan," *ABAN* 38 (May 1918), 200.

[26] Carroll Wright, *Ninth Annual Report of the Commissioner of Labor, Building and Loan Associations* (Washington, D.C.: USGPO, 1894), 291, 323; "Organization of Associations Among Foreigners," *ABAN* 29 (January 1910), quote 187.

[27] Wright, *Ninth Annual Report*, 291; "Monthly Dues," *ABAN* 22 (November 1903), 244; "Loan Associations for Store Workers," *ABAN* 31 (September 1911), 391; Sundheim, *Law of Building and* Loan, 33–9; "Irish-American of Buffalo," *ABAN* 29 (March 1909), 127; "Tavern Societies," *ABAN* 29 (April 1909), 149; John Novak, "The Bohemian People and Their Building and Loan Associations in the United States," *Proceedings of the Thirty-Sixth*

The most important trait that endeared thrifts to ethnic Americans was the high degree of agency these people had in the management of their associations. As was true with most thrifts, members of ethnic B&Ls often knew each other and usually had open access to the officers, both critical factors in establishing this confidence. Also, because these thrifts conducted meetings and printed documents in their members' native languages, immigrants felt less like "strangers in a strange land." According to one Polish thrift executive, "the work of the [thrift] is more on the line of a social organization. Perhaps it is the fact that the members know personally their own officers which they have chosen . . . that gives them so much confidence in the [association]." This need for trust was important, since unscrupulous businessmen often preyed upon financially ignorant immigrants to fleece them of their savings. In contrast, officers in ethnic associations worked to make sure their members understood how the association worked, and even tried to avoid foreclosing on a home if immigrant borrowers fell on hard times.[28]

Another reason that there were close connections between immigrants and thrifts was that similar savings associations operated throughout Europe in the early 1900s. In Poland, the "People's Banks" were a very popular form of mutual-aid cooperative, and in the Province of Posen more than 141,000 working-class Poles entrusted $87.7 million in assets with these banks. Germany also had a very strong history of cooperative finance that included the Housewives Societies (*hausfrauen vereins*) and Friendly Societies for Building (*Baughenossenschaften*). The friendly societies were so popular with the German working class that by 1914 over 1,400 were in operation throughout the country. Similar examples of cooperative home financing existed in other countries such as France, Denmark, and Sweden. Furthermore, because the operating procedures used by many foreign associations were also derived from the British system of home credit, immigrants tended to be more familiar with the business practices of American thrifts.[29]

A third reason why ethnic Americans joined B&Ls was that they saw membership as a way to help them assimilate into society and become better citizens. This factor became especially important by the 1910s when Americanization movements swept the nation. One German thrift leader noted that the ethnic B&Ls in Cincinnati encourage "not only the assimilation of the immigrant population, but inculcate anew the spirit which prompted the

Annual Meeting of the Building Association League of Illinois (Chicago: American Building Association News Publishing, 1916), quote 103.

[28] Albert Wachowski, "Polish United Building and Loan Associations," *ABAN* 31 (December 1911), 492–3; H. S. Rosenthal, "Possibilities of Building and Loan Movement," *Proceedings of the Thirty-Sixth Annual Meeting of the Building Association League of Illinois*, 105–8; Upton Sinclair, *The Jungle* (New York: The Jungle Publishing, 1906), 44–53.

[29] Mary Hinman Abel, "Housekeepers' Clubs in Germany," *FRABAN* 12 (June 1893), 90; "The Housing Question in Germany," *ABAN* 24 (December 1905), 235; "The International Aspect of Home Financing Institutions," *ABAN* 52 (August 1933), 359, 385–6.

early pioneers of America in the pride of the home." Ethnic thrift leaders
also stressed that ethnic thrifts instilled in their members proper "American" values and morals. A Polish thrift officer noted that "our organizations
help to make better citizens, and greatly add to the wealth and prosperity of
our nation," while another called attention to the homes financed by ethnic
B&Ls and "erected by the foreign-speaking element who became citizens
by adoption." During World War I, these thrift members reinforced their
standing as "good Americans" by participating in Liberty Bond drives as a
way to prove that "we do our bit."[30]

Although nearly every major industrial city had ethnic thrifts, Chicago had
the most diverse mix of associations. The city had over 120 thrifts that served
Bohemian residents, fifty-two with primarily Polish members, and overall
four different trade groups based on nationality. Bohemians were particularly
active in forming thrifts, and their ethnic leaders attributed this not only to
their "natural thriftiness," but also to the fact that "we Bohemians believe
home owning is the highest test of citizenship." A leader of Chicago's Polish
B&L trade association also noted that "Poles see in the building and loan
the foundation of everything that is democratic and free." The commonality
of these attitudes led one state League official to claim that thrifts have
"contributed in no small measure to Americanize the thousands of aliens
who have come from different parts of the world to make Chicago their
home." Another city with a diverse collection of ethnic thrifts, including one
restricted to Catholics, was Minneapolis. A student of these B&Ls noted
that "their social and moral value is in counteracting the tendency to wider
divergence between rich and poor, and to the development of a proletariat
class."[31]

---

[30] Gustav Wexner, "Future of Building and Loan Associations," *ABAN* 19 (February 1900),
38; *Ohio Savings and Loan League: A Century of Service* (s.l.: s.n., 1988), 5; Wade Ellis, "The
American Home," *Proceedings of the Fifteenth Annual Meeting of the Ohio Building Association
League* (Cincinnati: American Building Association News Publishing, 1903), 22–4 quote 23;
George Thomas, "The Building and Loan Association and the Foreigner," *Proceedings of the
Twenty-Fifth Annual Meeting of the Ohio Building Association League* (Cincinnati: American
Building Association News Publishing Co., 1913), 27–30; "Monthly Dues," quote 244;
Albert Wachowski, "Progress of the United Polish-American Building and Loan Association
of Chicago," *ABAN* 36 (February 1917), quote 70; John Novak, "Report of the Bohemian
Building and Loan Association of Chicago, Ill," *Proceedings of the Thirty-Seventh Annual
Meeting of the Building Association League of Illinois* (Chicago: American Building Association
News Publishing Co., 1916), 93; Konrad Ricker, "The Opinion of a Foreign-Born Citizen on
the American Building and Loan Association," *Proceedings of the Eighteenth Annual Meeting
of The United States League of Local Building and Loan Associations*, quote 123; "Building and
Loan Associations Doing Their Bit," *ABAN* 36 (September 1917), quote 391.

[31] Albert Wachowski, "The Polish Nationality and Their Building and Loan Associations,"
ABAN 29 (January 1909), 24–5, quote 24; Albert Wachowski, "The Democratic Spirit
of the Polish People and Its Fondness for Democratic Institutions as Our Building and
Loan Associations," *Proceedings of the Thirty-Eighth Annual Meeting the United States League
of Local Building and Loan Associations* (Cincinnati: American Building Association News

THRIFTS IN THE DECADE OF CONSUMERISM

The 1920s was an economically prosperous time for most Americans, and one characteristic of this decade was the increased consumption of goods intended to last more than two or three years, items commonly called "consumer durables." An important factor in the rise of consumer-durable purchases was the development of installment credit, which allowed people to buy goods immediately and not wait until they had saved the full purchase price. Under this arrangement, a seller allowed a buyer to purchase a product by paying only a portion of the price in cash at the time of sale, with the balance paid in installments over time. Initially, many Americans were uneasy about buying anything other than a house with credit because of the social stigma of being in debt. This attitude, however, changed as advertisers urged people to consume and take on more personal debt. Not only would such consumption improve the material lives of people, but the need to repay these loans meant that debt was good because it helped to instill a stronger work ethic. The resulting increase in consumer credit was so great that by the mid-1920s some people described the nation as "installment mad."[32]

While increased durable goods sales were one sign of the prosperity in the decade of consumerism, another economic sector to benefit was housing. Because wartime restrictions on building produced a severe housing shortage, new home construction soared after the war and remained high throughout the decade. This was especially true in urban areas where nearly 80 percent of all houses were built between 1923 and 1928. Significantly, new home prices did not also rise steadily, and after initial increases, they began to level off. While one reason for this was the eventual saturation of the housing market, the increased use of standardized materials, such as floor plans, lumber, and plumbing and ventilation systems, also reduced overall costs.

Publishing Co., 1917), quote 117; John Novak, "The Bohemian League of Building and Loan Associations of Chicago," *Proceedings of the Twenty-Third Annual Meeting the United States League of Local Building and Loan Associations* (Cincinnati: American Building Association News Publishing Co., 1914), 278–9 quote 279; C. C. Burford, "Illinois," in H. Morton Bodfish, editor, *History of Building and Loan in the United States* (Chicago: United States Building and Loan League, 1931), quote, 377; Albert Shaw, *Cooperation in a Western City* 1 no. 4 (Baltimore: American Economic Association, 1886), 278–90; Albert Shaw, *History of Cooperation in the United States* (Baltimore: Johns Hopkins University, 1888), quote, 296.

[32] Ellis W. Hawley, *The Great War and the Search for a Modern Order*, Second Edition (New York: St. Martin's Press, 1992), 66–71; "American Income," *ABAN* 47 (August 1927), 357; James J. Flink, *The Car Culture* (Cambridge: The MIT Press, 1975), 56; Martha N. Olney, *Buy Now Pay Later: Advertising, Credit, and Consumer Durables in the 1920s* (Chapel Hill: University of North Carolina Press, 1991), 95, 102–7; Calder, *Financing the American Dream*, 156–209; "Building and Loan a Great Savings Institution," *World's Work* 50 (August 1925), 444; "The Fly in the Ointment," *ABAN* 46 (March 1926), 168–70; "Elwood Lloyd, "Buy Today – Pay Tomorrow," *ABAN* 46 (June 1926), 251; "Extension of Credit," *ABAN* 46 (February 1926), 71–2.

The result was that the average price of a house actually fell by 8 percent between 1925 and 1929. For consumers with significant installment debt, however, these changes did not mean that it was easier to buy a home in the 1920s. One reason for this was that most lenders still required a down payment of between 33 percent and 60 percent of the purchase price in order to obtain a mortgage.[33]

To obtain this equity, home buyers often took out second mortgages, which, like installment credit, grew in popularity during the 1920s. There were drawbacks, however, with this type of financing. Because these mortgages were secured by a second lien on the property, if borrowers defaulted the lender did not get repaid until the first mortgage was paid off. Also, because of the higher level of debt on the property, if property values fell there was a risk that the second mortgage would no longer be covered by the underlying security. To compensate for these risks, second mortgage lenders collected from their borrowers up-front fees of up to 20 percent of the loan amount and charged interest rates that were on average twice as high as rates on first mortgages. Finally, second mortgages usually matured within three years, and often incurred additional fees to renew.[34]

While most states prohibited B&Ls from making second mortgages, associations in Philadelphia found a way of providing this service that was both profitable and relatively low risk. This arrangement required a home buyer to take out a short-term, non-amortizing first mortgage from any lender, and a long-term amortizing second mortgage from a B&L. The borrower then paid off the second in installments while paying interest only on the first mortgage, and renewing the first each time it came due. This plan saved borrowers money because the loan renewal fees for a first mortgage were far less than for a second. Also, the borrowers built up equity on their homes as the B&L second mortgage was repaid. Like all second mortgage lenders, thrifts charged higher rates for this service, but because these managers also used better loan approval and appraisal processes they were better able to measure risks, which resulted in very favorable rates of loan loss.[35]

---

[33] Edith Elmer Wood, *Recent Trends in American Housing* (New York: Macmillian, 1931), 2–3; National Housing Administration, *Housing After World War I: Will History Repeat Itself?"* National Housing Bulletin No. 4 (Washington, D.C.: USGPO, December 1945), 37–9.

[34] Nelson North and Dewitt Van Buren, *Real Estate Financing* (New York: Prentice Hall, 1928), 59–61, 64–5; Joseph A. Uhl, *Financing the Purchase of Real Estate* (unpublished B.A. thesis, University of Cincinnati, 1928), 35–43. Keys, "How to Finance the Building of a Little Home," 36.

[35] Samuel N. Reep, "Second Mortgages by Building and Loan Associations," *ABAN* 49 (March 1930, 194–5, 234; Samuel N. Reep, "Second Mortgages by Building and Loan Associations," *ABAN* 49 (April 1930), 256–7, 286; William Loucks, *The Philadelphia Plan of Home Financing: a Study of the Second Mortgage Lending of Philadelphia Building and Loan Associations* (Chicago: Institute for Research in Land Utility and Public Economics, 1929), 1–8, 42–5; David Thomas Rowlands, *Two Decades of Building and Loan Associations in Pennsylvania* (Ph.D. Dissertation, University of Pennsylvania, 1940), 126–7.

Thrifts also helped home buyers by making it easier for them to qualify for mortgages. One way to accomplish this goal was by reducing the monthly payment amount by extending the maturity of the loan. Between 1900 and 1930, the average thrift mortgage term rose from eight to twelve years, a term length that was both more than twice as long as commercial bank mortgages, and very close to the fifteen-year maturity most homeowners preferred. B&Ls also replaced the loan auction method of determining interest rates and began making loans with interest rates set by the thrift's directors. To this was added a premium that was negotiated by the lender and the borrower. Furthermore, more thrifts used escrow accounts to pay property taxes and insurance, and sold credit life insurance as a way of protecting both the borrower and lender. Finally, more thrifts began using commercially prepared credit reports and credit-scoring systems that incorporated ratio analysis, which made lending decisions more precise and "scientific." These changes also allowed managers to correlate loan risks and returns better.[36]

Another way thrifts tried to make it easier to buy a new house was by consolidating the different forms of construction finance into simpler loan packages. Prior to the 1920s, new homes were usually built to order, and financing was a multistep process. The home buyer first had to acquire the land outright, then use a short-term bank loan to pay for the construction. This interim loan was then refinanced with a permanent mortgage. Such an awkward system of finance was used because few lenders were willing to assume all the risks associated with transactions between so many different parties. This situation changed, however, when developers begin building multihome projects to meet the postwar demand for housing. Because the developer controlled everything, from raw land acquisition to final home sales, lenders were better able to measure the financial risks. Some B&Ls gained an edge in this type of financing by also providing home buyers with design and construction supervision services.[37]

---

[36] H. Morton Bodfish, *Lending Practices of Building and Loan Associations in Ohio*, Bureau of Business Research, Monograph No. 8 (Columbus: The Ohio State University Press, 1927), 14–5, 20–2, 57–63; Bodfish and Theobald, *Savings and Loan Principles*, 202–6; R. J. Richardson, "Building and Loan or Straight Mortgage?" *ABAN* 47 (August 1927), 382–3; George L. Bliss, "Monthly Reduction Mortgage Aids Business," *ABAN* 49 (April 1929), 214; "What is the Real Cost of Borrowing from Building & Loan Associations?" *The Magazine of Wall Street* 40 (21 November 1925), 116–7; Alex Carr, "Future Loan Plans and Rates for Building and Loan Money," *ABAN* 45 (April 1925), 170–2.

[37] John M. Wyman, "Financing Small Homes Through Local Building Loan Associations," *Building Age and National Builder* 48 (April 1926), 232–3; Philip Lieber, "Some Services to Help Beat the Competition" *ABAN*, (January 1929), 8–9, 50; "Planning the Home," *ABAN* 48 (February 1928), 70; John M. Gries, "The Building and Loan Association as Advisor to the Home Seeker," *Proceedings of the Thirty-First Annual Meeting of the United States League of Local Building and Loan Associations* (Cincinnati: American Building Association News Publishing Co., 1923), 108–18.

TABLE 2.2. *Number of Thrifts and Assets – 1920 to 1930*

Year	No. B&L	Change/Year	Assets (000)	Change/Year
1920	8,633	–	$2,519,915	–
1924	11,844	7.4%	$4,765,937	17.2%
1927	12,804	2.6%	$7,178,562	14.7%
1930	11,777	(2.7%)	$8,828,612	7.1%

Source: Ewalt, *A Business Reborn*, 391.

Although most of the prominent B&L innovations in the 1920s improved lending services, thrifts also broadened their savings options for members. One of these was increased use of juvenile annexes to attract more children as members and teach them the value of thrift. While accounts for minors had long been a part of most B&L activities, giving children separate services like their own passbooks to record deposits and withdrawals made them feel more responsible for their accounts. While the League noted this work was typical of "uplifting organizations" such as thrifts, encouraging child members also built relations with B&Ls that lasted into adulthood. Another popular savings option was the fully paid share issued to members who wanted to make one initial lump-sum deposit to pay for the share completely. Most managers liked using these shares because they earned lower dividends than regular shares, and thus were cheaper sources of funds. In addition, despite concerns that these shareholders would withdraw their money whenever rates changed, these accounts attracted stable and long-term investors.[38]

POSTWAR PROSPERITY

Although the thrift movement recovered fully from the nationals crisis by the end of World War I, during the 1920s it truly blossomed, as shown in Table 2.2.

An analysis of this expansion reveals several important trends. First, individual B&Ls continued to grow in resources with the average thrift in 1929 controlling $704,000 in assets, up from $205,000 in 1914. Furthermore, one hundred thrifts had over $10 million in assets each, with the largest association exceeding $52 million. Second, this expansion was not uniform, but rather more pronounced in the West which experienced higher population growth. While thrifts in states such as Pennsylvania and Ohio

---

[38] "Little Savings Banks for Public Schools," *ABAN* 22 (May 1903); 22; "Juvenile Saver Annex," *ABAN* 23 (June 1904), 23; Edwin M. Einstein, "School Savings," *ABAN* 47 (October 1927), 54–5; H. Morton Bodfish, *Historical Balance Sheet Analysis of Ohio Building*, Bureau of Business Research, College of Commerce and Administration (Columbus, The Ohio State University Press, 1928); 28–30; Charles Elliott, "Full Paid Stock," *ABAN* 26 (November 1907); 212; "Fitting the Investment to the Investor" *The Magazine of Wall Street* 45 (29 November 1930); 171; Bodfish and Theobald, *Savings and Loan Principles*, 140–6.

experienced average annual asset growth of 35 percent between 1914 and 1929, in California thrifts saw their assets double annually. This growth was so fast that by the end of the decade California accounted for 6 percent of all B&Ls and assets, up from less than 1 percent in 1914. A third trend was that the percentage of people who belonged to B&Ls rose steadily. By 1929, one in ten of all Americans were thrift members, up from 4 percent in 1919, and just 2.5 percent in 1900. These changes helped make thrifts one of the leading institutional home lenders in the country, providing 22 percent of all mortgages and an estimated one thousand loans a day by 1930.[39]

Another important change for the movement during the 1920s lay in the type of people who were joining these associations. For nearly one hundred years, thrift members had come almost exclusively from the working class, with many associations serving specific occupations or ethnic groups. By the 1920s, the increased use of fully paid shares and services such as deposit by mail attracted upper-class and upper-middle-class men and women with more disposable income. While many of these new members used B&Ls to acquire homes, others joined to invest money safely and earn good returns. By 1925, *The Magazine of Wall Street*, a leading personal finance and investment weekly, was carrying regular stories on thrifts in its "Building Your Future Income" column. It recommended thrift shares to young professionals as an ideal way to balance their stock and bond investment portfolio risks. Such favorable exposure to people, who would not otherwise have come in contact with the B&L movement, was critical in broadening the appeal of thrifts and generating growth.[40]

While the natural increase in demand for housing may account for the success of the movement in the early twentieth century, the work of thrift leaders who took advantage of opportunities in areas under-served by other

39 Individuals and noninstitutional sources provided 39 percent of all mortgages, while mutual savings banks accounted for 17 percent, and banks and insurance companies make 11 percent each. Ewalt, *A Business Reborn*, 391; Milton M. Schayer, "Where is the Money Coming From?" *The Magazine of Wall Street* 44 (18 May 1929): 140–1; Floyd F. Burtchett, "What's Behind the Growth of California Associations?" *ABAN* 49 (May 1929), 282–3; Arthur Millard, "Tracing the Growth of Building and Loan Ass'ns," *The Magazine of Wall Street* 42 (19 November 1927): 132–3; "Secretary's Address," *Proceedings of the Thirty-Seventh Annual Meeting of the United States League of Local Building and Loan Associations* (Chicago: American Building Association News Publishing Co., 1929), 57–9; Bureau of the Census, *Historical Statistics of the United States, Colonial Times to 1957* (Washington, D.C.: USGPO, 1961), 396.

40 "Small Investors Money for Home Building," *World's Work* 26 (May 1913), 31–3; Theis, "If You are Thinking of Building A Home," 108; J. Lloyd McMaster, "The B&L Plan as First Aid for the Home-Maker," *The Magazine of Wall Street* 43 (7 April 1928), 1049; Stephen Valiant "Weighed in the Balance!" *The Magazine of Wall Street* 44 (23 March 1929), 959; Milton M. Schayer, "'Paid-Up' Building and Loan Certificates Attractive for Investment" *The Magazine of Wall Street* 44 (24 August 1929): 770–1; "Rating Building & Loan Investments by States," *The Magazine of Wall Street* 41 (9 October 1926), 1128, 1179; "Investing in Building and Loan Associations," *World's Work* 48 (October 1924), 675–6.

institutions cannot be ignored. B&Ls captured a disproportionately large share of the 1920s home finance market in large part because the first and second mortgages they offered were more affordable than bank loans. Similarly, innovations in savings options, which were needed in part to fund the rising demand for loans, also reflected the fact that managers wanted to broaden the appeal of B&Ls beyond the traditional working class and directly challenge the supremacy of banks and trust companies in the long-term savings market.[41]

WOMEN MOVE TO THE FORE

Another factor in the success of the B&L movement during the early twentieth century was the increased role of women in local and national affairs. The League boasted that thrifts had more female managers and directors than other financial industries and encouraged their involvement noting, "if they can induce more of their sisters to emulate their example, the movement will be better for it." One sign of this change was the effort by thrifts in the 1920s to broaden their appeal to working women with services such as "women's departments" to provide specialized financial planning and advice for female customers. Another example of greater female involvement in the movement was the appearance of thrifts organized and managed by women. One of the most successful of these associations was the Women's Building and Loan of Cleveland, formed in 1922. The only difference between the Women's B&L and that managed by men, according to one observer, was the absence of cigar smoke in the boardroom. This B&L was so successful that in its first nine years of business it reportedly had to foreclose on only one loan.[42]

Women also became more active in thrift trade organizations, and in the 1920s several states formed women's auxiliaries to address issues affecting female thrift officers. While several women achieved prominence as the leaders of state trade associations, few had the same degree of success as Ann Rae. Rae began her thrift career in the late 1900s at the Niagara Permanent Savings and Loan Association in Niagara, New York. In 1917, she became thrift president, and when she retired in 1930 her association was one of the largest in the nation with over $16 million in assets. Rae was also involved in both state and national trade association work. In 1921, she became president of

41 Ewalt, *A Business Reborn*, 30–5.
42 "Then and Now," *ABAN* 41 (June 1921), quote, 296; "Women in Building Associations," *ABAN* 46 (June 1926), 257; Bessie Q. Mott, "Why Building and Loan Shares Appeal to Women," *ABAN* 49 (May 1929), 268–8; McMaster, "The B&L Plan as First Aid for the Home-Maker," 1049; Susan Bozung, "Are Building and Loan Associations Keeping in Step with the Times?" *ABAN* 49 (December 1929), 714–5; Anna Caldwell, "A Woman's Building and Loan Association," *ABAN* 20 (January 1900), 6; Nina Donberg, "Are Women Good Financiers?" *ABAN* 51 (June 1931), 273, 292–4.

the New York League, and two years later she was elected unanimously as the first female president of the national League, a selection that was "not a function of gallantry or even courtesy, but was the logical choice." As president, Rae spoke across the country to thrift and housing industry groups, and urged ways to improve movement. She remained involved in the League even after her term, and in 1931 was the American delegate to the International Thrift Convention. When Rae died in 1932, the movement recognized her passing with a full-page tribute in its trade journal.[43]

THE CONSEQUENCES OF GROWTH

The rapid expansion of the thrift movement in the 1910s and 1920s did not go unnoticed by other financial groups. This was especially true with the commercial banking industry, which for the first time saw B&Ls as a real competitive threat. Traditionally, banks had not regarded thrifts as competitors, in part because each offered different financial products. Banks made primarily short-term loans funded by demand deposits, while thrifts made long-term mortgages using longer-term savings. The main interaction between the two was that banks provided thrifts with liquidity loans and depository services. Both financial institutions benefited from this symbiotic relationship, in that thrifts could use the loans to meet unanticipated mortgage demands, while banks gained low-risk loans and fees from ancillary business such as title and trust work. Given this dependency and the prominence of commercial banks in the American financial system, it was generally acknowledged that "in relation to banks building and loans have always occupied a subordinate position."[44]

Throughout the 1920s, however, thrifts and banks began to compete more directly for funds, with the result that the percentage of consumer savings

[43] Lydia Cellarius, "Women and the Home," *Proceedings of the Thirty-Sixth Annual Meeting of the Ohio Building Association League* (Cincinnati: American Building Association News Publishing, 1925), 153–4; "Women's Auxiliary in Ohio," *ABAN* (September 1921), 391; "A Woman Elected President," *ABAN* 37 (March 1917), 104; *ABAN* 50 (January 1930), 114; "Then and Now," 296; "First Woman President of the U.S. League," *ABAN* 43 (August 1923), quote 341; "Tireless Work of the League President," *ABAN* 43 (November 1923), n.p.; "Woman's Auxiliary of the U.S. League to be Organized at the Cleveland Meeting," *ABAN* 44 (February 1924), 59; "Death of Miss Ann E. Rae," *ABAN* 52 (November 1932), 486.

[44] Thomas B. Fulmer, "Trust Companies and Building and Loan Associations," *ABAN* 24 (December 1905), 246; I. H. C. Royse, "The Legitimate Sphere of the Building and Loan Associations Considered in Its Relation to Banks and Trust Companies," *ABAN* 23 (October 1904), 209–11; "Associations Have a Field of Their Own," *ABAN* 29 (November 1909), 502–3; James M. McKay "The Building and Loan Movement in the United States," *Proceedings of the Annual Convention of the American Bankers Association* (New York: American Banker's Association, 1910), 539–40; Samuel McK. Perry, "The Financial Relationship Between Banks and Building and Loan Associations in Pennsylvania," *The Bankers Magazine* 115 (August 1927), 147–9.

held by thrifts rose from 10 percent to 16 percent over the course of the decade. While bankers knew a key reason for this increase was that thrifts paid dividend rates that were up to three times higher than those paid by banks, they also alleged that B&Ls used unfair methods to obtain these funds. Bankers claimed that thrifts used house-to-house solicitors to lure people into opening new accounts. They also objected to B&Ls making unsecured share loans and issuing fully paid shares, activities that made thrifts less like mutual organizations and more like ordinary for-profit stock corporations. Their greatest complaint, however, was that B&Ls advertised that share account funds were available on demand like bank accounts when in fact most thrifts technically required members to give advance notice for withdrawals. The banking community insisted that if this common practice continued B&Ls should be placed under the same rules as banks.[45]

To counter thrift competition, commercial bankers followed several strategies. They filed complaints with state regulators to stop improper B&L advertising, and launched consumer education campaigns that detailed what services banks and thrifts could legally offer. Bankers also lobbied for laws to require thrifts to hold additional reserves if they made unsecured share loans and paid deposits on demand since these activities involved greater risks. Forcing thrifts to set aside more earnings as reserves had the added benefit of reducing the amount of dividends they could pay. Finally, national banks wanted the right to make residential mortgage loans, something they were prohibited by law from doing. Eventually, these efforts to "level the playing field" led to the inclusion of language in the McFadden Act in 1927, to allow national banks to lend up to one-half of their savings deposits on real estate mortgages. Despite the increased hostility toward B&Ls, bankers were never intent on destroying these businesses and readily admitted that thrifts served a useful role in American finance.[46]

While thrift leaders grudgingly admitted some criticism was warranted, they insisted that the practices bankers objected to represented only isolated cases of abuse. While the League publically opposed any efforts to require B&Ls to establish large reserves, citing the historically low rate of loan losses

[45] C. F. Schwenker, "Building and Loan Competition with Banks," *American Banking Association Journal* 21 (August 1928), 129–31; H. L. Standeven, "To Stop Unfair Competition" *American Bankers Association Journal* 22 (May 1929), 1110, 1156–7; Reuben A. Lewis, Jr., "A Growing Competitor for Savings," *American Banking Association Journal* 20 (February 1927), 561–2; W. S. Webb "An Invasion of Savings Banking" *American Banking Association Journal* 20 (July 1927), 7–8; Bodfish and Theobald, *Savings and Loan Principles*, 59.

[46] Standeven, "To Stop Unfair Competition," 1156; James E. Clark, "A Way to Meet Unfair Building and Loan Competition," *American Banking Association Journal* 23 (June 1930), 1108–1109, 1095; "Banks Up in Arms," *Kansas League Section of the American Building Association News* 46 (November 1926), iii; "National Banks May Enter Real Estate Loan Field." *American Banking Association Journal* 20 (February 1927), 617; Peter G. Cameron, "Regulating the Building and Loan Associations," *American Bankers Association Journal* 18 (February 1926), 82–3, 111–2.

for the movement as a whole, it privately encouraged thrifts to build reserves voluntarily to blunt further attacks. Interestingly, some bankers agreed with the League that the criticism was extreme, and instead felt the real reason for the competition was that conservative bank practices allowed thrifts to steal customers. They also accused bankers of hypocrisy by "condemning all building and loans to [their] official family at the very moment [they] send salesmen down-state to see if they can't knock off a few more of 'those good building and loan accounts.'" The debate over the financial roles of thrifts and banks would continue for the next fifty years. Over time, the leaders in each group insisted on gaining powers that were the other group's strengths: banks wanted greater ability to make mortgages, while thrifts sought the right to make consumer and personal loans. The debate would finally end when deregulation in the 1980s removed most barriers separating thrifts and banks.[47]

Aside from increased criticism from bankers, thrifts faced other competitive challenges in the 1920s. One of these was from mortgage brokers which were firms that specialized in connecting home lenders from different areas with borrowers for a fee. The more significant threat, however, came from mortgage companies, which were an insignificant source of finance prior to 1910 but grew to account for 5 percent of all residential mortgages by 1929. Mortgage companies made direct loans using funds from the sale of stock or mortgage-backed securities, and although these were quasi-financial institutions they were generally unregulated. Also, since these firms focused on providing high-rate second mortgages they were also very profitable. Unfortunately, few mortgage companies held substantial reserves and equity capital so that when the Great Depression began, losses from foreclosed properties forced hundreds of the companies into bankruptcy. One important consequence of this collapse was that the second mortgage market virtually disappeared.[48]

---

[47] Jay W. Sutton, "Unfair Treatment of Building and Loan Associations From Within and From Without," *Proceedings of the Thirteenth Annual Meeting of The United States League of Local Building and Loan Associations* (Chicago: The Press of the American Building Association News Press, 1905), 153–61; K. V. Haymaker, "One Vital Difference Between Banks and Building Associations," *ABAN* 47 (December 1927), 561; Ralph Beaton, "Building and Loan Associations and Banks," *ABAN* 45 (May 1925), 196–7; "Illegal and Unethical Advertising," *ABAN* 44 (December 1924), 537; "Criticism Due," *Kansas League Section of the American Building Association News* 47 (December 1927), iii; W. L. Bowersox, "Is There Any Reason Why?" *ABAN* 48 (February 1928), 62–4; H. Morton Bodfish, "Unfair Building and Loan Competition – An Answer," *ABAN* 50 (August 1930), 458–485; T. N. T. "Banks and Building and Loan Associations," *The Bankers Magazine* 114 (February 1927), 167–70; H. B. Lewis, "Can Banks Meet Present Building and Loan Competition?" *The Bankers Magazine* 116 (May 1928), 652–5.

[48] *Historical Statistics of the United States*, 396; North and Van Buren, *Real Estate Financing*, 59–63; John M. Gries and Thomas M. Curran, *Present Home Financing Methods*, (Washington, D.C.: USGPO, 1928), 5–6, 9; Milton M. Schayer, "New Factors in Building and Loan Field,"

Another new source of mortgage competition came from the federal government, which in the 1910s entered the farm mortgage field in order to ease a severe credit crunch. The main reason for the lack of credit from private sources was that in the early 1900s the demand for farm land had caused land prices to more than double, which ultimately absorbed almost all available funds from traditional lenders. In 1916, Congress passed the Federal Farm Loan Act, which created a system of federal land banks to increase liquidity for agricultural lenders. Patterned after the Federal Reserve banks, the land banks made loans to commercial banks, pledging existing farm mortgages as collateral. One provision of this law was that farm loans had to be long term and be amortized in monthly installments. While the League was pleased the land banks were using the repayment system pioneered by the movement, its members also feared this was the first step toward government involvement in residential finance. As one thrift leader stated, "it will be but a short time before the city housing problem will be included in its operations... [T]his chain of land banks is designed to, and is capable of, taking over our place in the financial world." As a result, thrift leaders worked to ensure this program remained narrowly defined.[49]

Aside from legitimate forms of competition, thrifts had to contend with fraudulent home finance businesses throughout this period. One of the most serious came after World War I when "Three Percent" Loan Companies spread rapidly in the South and Midwest. Members signed a contract that required them to pay $10 per month to the lender, and at maturity they could withdraw the accumulated savings, which earned no interest, plus an amount equal to $1,000; the borrower then paid 3 percent interest on the additional funds. Several states outlawed these companies because they were essentially lotteries that relied on steady membership growth to make them work. Members received loans based on when they signed their contracts, which matured based on how quickly money accumulated. This meant that the only way for people who joined late to receive a loan was after they made close to $1,000 in payments to the lender. While such shady lending operations were not unique to the 1920s, the fact that dishonest financiers

Magazine of Wall Street, 43 (17 November 1928), 134–5; Letter from Charles W. Carlson to James S. Taylor, 23 November 1931; Finance Committee; White House Conference on Home Building and Home Ownership; Herbert Hoover Presidential Library.

49 Sally H. Clarke, *Regulation and the Revolution in United States Farm Productivity* (New York: Cambridge University Press, 1994), 113–4, 140–2; E. N. Breitang, "Money for Farms," *ABAN* 33 (June 1913), 246–8; James McKay, "The Building and Loan Association and Loans to Farms," *ABAN* 33 (July 1913), 300–1; Wilber Hedrick, "Building and Loan Associations the Solution of the Rural Credit Problem," *The Scientific Monthly* 2 (May 1914), 453–6; Edwin F. Howell, "Land Banks and the Housing Question," *Proceedings of the Twenty-Second Annual Meeting of the United States League of Local Building and Loan Associations* (Cincinnati: American Building Association News Publishing Co., 1914), 42–4; K. V. Haymaker, "Farm Loans and Building Associations," *ABAN* 37 (July 1917), 318–9.

could still attract business was a sign that the nation needed a more systematic and available system of home finance, an issue that would be addressed by the thrift movement and the federal government in the 1930s.[50]

While the majority of all thrifts were honest operations, when signs of fraud did occur they often drew close public scrutiny. The largest and most publicized instance occurred in 1925 when Pennsylvania regulators closed seventeen Philadelphia thrifts for unethical banking practices. Each B&L was controlled by interlocking directorates, which allowed a small group of investors to manipulate the lending processes for their own personal gain. Among the illegal activities they engaged in were approving loans for more than what a property was worth and accepting kickbacks from developers. While most of the accused officers contended they were acting out of ignorance and not criminal intent, several were convicted of defalcation. One consequence of this incident was that the League, like many businesses of the 1920s, adopted a code of ethics for all officers to follow. Still, despite such problems, the overall record of thrift failures during the 1920s was superior to the record for banks. During the decade, just 2.3 percent of all thrifts failed, while 21.3 percent of all banks, most of which were small and rural, went out of business. In 1924 alone over 700 bank failures cost depositors $182 million, while the eighteen B&Ls that failed during the year resulted in losses of less than $398,500. This record of financial strength, however, would change once the nation entered the Great Depression.[51]

[50] T. J. Fitzmorris, "Cooperative Home Finance Companies," *Proceedings of the Tenth Annual Meeting of The United States League of Local Building and Loan Associations* (Chicago: The Press of the American Building Association News Press, 1902), 108–12; Morris Mechanic, *The Development of the Building and Loan Associations* (unpublished M. A. thesis, Johns Hopkins University, 1921), 21–3; "Promoters in the Insurance and Building and Loan Fields," *Worlds Work* 44 (July 1922), 247–8; L. E. Roush, "The Impossible Three Per Cent Loan Contract," *Proceedings of the Thirtieth Annual Meeting of the United States League of Local Building and Loan Associations*, 128–40; Maco Stewart, "Contract Loan Companies – Frauds and Lotteries," *Proceedings of the Thirty-First Annual Meeting of the United States League of Local Building and Loan Associations*, 179–90; "Three Percent Concerns Under Fire," *ABAN* 42 (September 1922), 393; W. G. Akers, "Inside View of 3 Per Cent Contract Loan Companies," *ABAN* 43 (January 1923), 14–16.

[51] J. G. Medlenka, "Some of the Causes Which Lead to the Failure of Building and Loan Associations," *Proceedings of the Seventeenth Annual Meeting of The United States League of Local Building and Loan Associations* (Chicago: The Press of the American Building Association News Press, 1909), 126–9; "State Closes 17 B and L Associations," *The Philadelphia Inquirer*, 15 July 1925, 1; "Criminal Charges Hinted in Probe of Loan Associations," *The Philadelphia Inquirer*, 16 July 1925, 1, 6; William D. Gordon, "Irregular Practices in Building and Loan Associations," in Clyde L. King, editor, *Modern Crime: Its Prevention and Punishment* (Philadelphia: The American Academy of Political and Social Science, 1926), 49–54; "The Philadelphia Case," *ABAN* 46 (July 1926), 296–7; "Building and Loan a Great Savings Institution," *World's Work* 50 (August 1925), 444–65; "Code of Ethics," *ABAN* 46 (September 1926), 408–9; Horace Russell, *Savings and Loan Principles*, Second Edition (Albany, NY: Matthew Bender & Co., 1960), 654.

CONCLUSIONS

By the end of the 1920s, the thrift movement had not only recovered fully from the nationals crisis of the 1890s, but had also become a leading force in consumer finance. One reason for this growth was the role of ethnic Americans in forming new associations as a way to both improve the material condition of their lives and show their desire to become good citizens in their new country. Women also helped bolster the movement in the early twentieth century, as evidenced by their increased participation in various trade association activities as well as in the organization of female-managed associations. Like other financial institutions, B&Ls benefited from the booming consumer-oriented economy in the 1920s, and by designing more affordable mortgage products and savings options thrifts attracted members from broader segments of society. Such innovations reflected how B&Ls responded to competitive challenges and took advantage of new business opportunities. Another critical factor in the growth of the movement was the work of the national trade association, the United States League of Building and Loan Associations. During the first three decades of the twentieth century, the League worked to reinforce the relationship between B&Ls and ideals of thrift and home ownership, a campaign that seemed to be well suited to the rising spirit of Progressivism sweeping the nation. It also launched initiatives to improve the professionalism of the thrift managers through greater education and the use of more standardized business practices. Through this work, the League matured as a trade association and by the end of the decade had implemented organizational changes that allowed it to improve its level of service and leadership, attributes that would be tested during the Great Depression.

3

FROM STATE TO FEDERAL OVERSIGHT

By the end of the 1920s, the thrift movement was larger and stronger than at any time in its history, but despite the best efforts of the United States League of Building and Loan Associations it still was not completely unified. One way to change this situation was to promote government oversight, since comprehensive regulation might result in greater public respect and recognition for B&Ls, protection from competition, and increased standardization within the movement. Government oversight of thrifts had begun at the state level in the 1860s, and by 1900 nearly every state had passed some form of thrift regulation, much of which was done at the behest of thrift leaders with relatively little public input. The fact that these laws were not uniform and often lacked detail led the League to consider federal regulation as a way to correct these inconsistencies. The movement, however, was not fully supportive of federal oversight, and resisted efforts to create a national mortgage credit bank after World War I. This attitude changed when the Great Depression caused massive economic turmoil, and between 1930 and 1934 Congress created a comprehensive set of thrift regulations, including a reserve banking system, federally chartered institutions, and deposit insurance. The process of securing these laws was difficult, however, since thrift leaders had to overcome considerable opposition from legislators, other financial institutions, and dissent within their own movement. Despite such obstacles, intense lobbying by League leaders helped ensure the passage of new legislation favorable to the thrift business. Securing these laws represented a milestone that proved to be instrumental in finally creating a group identity for thrifts, as well as providing a base for their continued growth in the decades that followed.

THE STRUGGLE OVER STATE REGULATION

When the thrift movement first appeared in the 1830s, there was little need to have government supervision for these associations, since most B&Ls were temporary organizations. By the 1860s, the movement had expanded to such an extent that some thrift leaders began seeking greater state oversight. Their arguments focused on three basic objectives. First, regulation would promote safe operations that would check poor business practices, as well as prevent dishonest people from using their positions of trust for personal gain. Second, regulation would lead to greater standardization that would help increase public confidence in all associations. Finally, state supervision could be used to protect thrifts from competition by giving B&Ls favorable treatment and preferences. Given these potential benefits, movement leaders felt that government oversight would both improve the integrity of the thrift business and represent a state "seal of approval" for well-managed associations.[1]

One of the earliest thrift leaders to elucidate these reasons for state oversight was League founder Judge Seymour Dexter. Dexter, who was a thrift president and author of many New York B&L laws, advocated that all states should pass laws that were not only consistent with those for other financial institutions, but would also promote the mission of thrifts in advancing the condition of the wage-earning working classes. One way of preserving the local nature of thrift business and encouraging the formation of hundreds of new B&Ls was to have the state limit the territory in which thrifts could operate and prohibit the creation of branches. The goal, according to Dexter, was that a thrift would be located in "every business center of the state having a population of 500, all operating under one law requiring uniformity in the essential methods and elements of safety."[2]

Despite the potential benefits of state supervision, the process of securing legislation was initially limited to states where B&Ls were numerous and active. Ohio, Pennsylvania, and Illinois were the first states to enact comprehensive codes to regulate thrift formation and operation, all of which aided B&L growth in those states. In 1875, New York became the first state to require that thrifts file annual reports with the banking commissioner, and twelve years later it was the first to require state examinations. The progress in securing state regulation increased dramatically during the nationals crisis

---

[1] H. Morton Bodfish, "State Supervision," in H. Morton Bodfish, editor, *History of Building and Loan in the United States* (Chicago: United States Building and Loan League, 1931), 123–7, quote 123; Stacy W. Wade, "The Attitude of the Supervising Official Toward the Individual Association as a Whole," *Proceedings of the United States League of Building and Loan Associations* (Chicago: American Building Association News Publishing, 1927), 296; J. C. Shumway, "The Effects and Results of State Inspection," *Financial Review and American Building Association News* [hereafter *FRABAN*] 13 (July 1894), 166–7; "California Associations," *FRABAN* 13 (December 1894), 292; "Proceedings of the United States League of Local Building and Loan Associations, *FRABAN* 14 (August 1895), 2; P. M. Endsley, "Necessity of Reformation of Local Building and Loan Association," *FRABAN* 15 (July 1896), 17.

[2] Seymour Dexter, "State Supervision," *FRABAN* 14 (October 1895), 22; Seymour Dexter, "Cooperative Building and Loan Associations in New York," *Journal of Social Science* 25 (December 1888), 146–8, quote 148; Seymour Dexter, "Cooperative Building and Loan Associations," *Quarterly Journal of Economics* 3 (April 1889), 335.

of the 1890s. The scandals associated with these for-profit businesses led to dozens of new thrift laws, many of which state League leaders drafted for the legislators. By 1900, nearly every state had some form of thrift code, and state Leagues continued to work with legislators to ensure that these laws were enforced and updated. Such work led one League leader to later claim "it would be difficult to find any other business which is so anxious to restrict itself in the interests of the public welfare."[3]

Although this initial wave of thrift regulation was an important accomplishment for the movement, the process was not a complete success since many of these laws were confusing, incomplete, and not uniform. By the 1920s, thirty-six of the forty-eight states directly supervised thrifts, while ten states included these associations in their "blue-sky" laws that required certain financial disclosures; only Maryland and South Carolina had no B&L-specific rules. Four states maintained separate building and loan commissions, with the majority of the other states giving their banking or insurance commissions responsibility for B&L oversight. While nearly every state mandated that thrifts should file annual reports, in twelve states the laws did not indicate how to meet this requirement. Furthermore, while thrift supervisors in some states could prohibit "unnecessary or unsatisfactory associations" from entering business, other states granted charters to anyone who applied. Finally, having a law did not guarantee adequate supervision since some states refused to fund their regulatory agencies.[4]

The haphazard development of state laws was frustrating for thrift leaders as well as potential members. Although thrifts were receiving greater and more favorable publicity from the financial press by the 1920s, publications such as the *Magazine of Wall Street* counseled investors to use caution before opening accounts, in part because of the vagaries of state laws. In 1926, this magazine rated the quality of state laws governing thrifts and found that only twenty-seven states provided high or reasonable degrees of safety, while fourteen had only minimal depositor safeguards. For seven states with particularly weak thrift laws it recommended that only in-state residents should open B&L accounts. The amazement and disbelief at the inconsistencies of the state laws governing thrifts was best summarized by two Wharton School of Business professors who stated that "not only do

---

3 "Notes on Legislation," *FRABAN* 14 (February 1895), 4–6; "Must Have Legislation," *FRABAN* 14 (January 1895), 23; "Building and Loan Legislation in Iowa," *FRABAN* 15 (March 1896), 33; F. D. Kilborn, "Supervision of Building and Loan Associations," *FRABAN* 18 (21 September 1899), 231; "The Leagues," *FRABAN* 13 (February 1894), 36; "Kansas Building Associations," *FRABAN* 13 (November 1894), 266; "Notes on Legislation," *FRABAN* 14 (February 1895), 4; Bodfish, "State Supervision," quote 127.

4 Horace F. Clark and Frank A. Chase, *Elements of the Modern Building and Loan Associations* (New York: The Macmillian Co., 1927), 378–83, quote 380; William Stephen Marlowe, "Rating Building and Loan Investments by State," *The Magazine of Wall Street* 41 (9 October 1926), 1129–30.

important subjects frequently go without legislation, but where regulations exist they are so dispersed as to make mental grasp thereof difficult, and oversight easy."[5]

Another factor complicating the passage of uniform codes was that not everyone in the movement agreed on the need for state supervision. Many smaller associations objected to the expense of examinations and increased paperwork associated with these regulations. These managers also considered state supervision as an infringement on individual rights and an unwarranted extension of government power into business. When government increased its oversight of railroads, banks, and insurance companies during the Progressive era, some B&L leaders still contended that they should not be regulated because those industries performed "public functions" that thrifts did not. Finally, opponents to regulation insisted that the individual member and not the state was best suited to judge a thrift's condition, and any effort to change this smacked of socialism. Such differences in opinion invariably affected the level of individual state oversight during the early twentieth century.[6]

As more associations operated under state oversight, thrift leaders realized that active supervision often resulted in official efforts to promote the movement. As North Carolina Commissioner Stacy Wade stated, "the supervising official's attitude should be one of never-failing interest and enthusiasm. . . . If there is need of a building and loan association anywhere, and I can help to get it going, I let nothing short of a serious illness stand between me and active participation in the movement." The League encouraged associations to advertise that they were under state supervision as a sign of their safety, since such supervision represented to the layman "a sort of Pure Food Law of Building and Loan Associations." Over time, the relationship between the movement and thrift regulators grew so close that when state supervisors formed a national organization in 1920, they held their annual meetings in conjunction with the League "to share information and cooperate with building and loan leaders for the furtherance of the best interests of the movement."[7]

---

[5] Horace F. Clark, "The Extension of State Regulation to the Building and Loan Association," *The Journal of Political Economy* 32 (December 1924), 622–4, 632–5; Robert Reigel and J. Russell Doubman, *The Building-and-Loan Association* (New York: J. Wiley and Sons, 1927), 230–42, quote 242.

[6] J. H. Westover, "Expert Examination or State Inspection, Which?" *FRABAN* 19 (June 1900), 164; "Dexter on State Supervision," *FRABAN* 18 (20 October 1899), 273–4; William Brace, "State Interference with the Business of Building Associations; Its Tendencies and Results," *FRABAN* 18 (21 September 1899), 237–41.

[7] John S. Fisher, "How Building and Loan Associations Help Solve the Housing Problem," *National Real Estate Journal* 22 (21 November 1921), 36–7; Wade, "The Attitude of the State Supervising Official," quote, 297; Ben H. Hazen, "How Supervisory Departments Can Best Promote Growth and Development of Building and Loan Associations," *Proceedings of the United States League of Local Building and Loan Associations* (Cincinnati: American Building

The evolution of state thrift laws reveals important trends that would reappear during the effort to secure federal regulation in the 1930s. First, movement leaders were usually responsible for initiating thrift supervision, and they often cited public interest concerns in support of regulation. Little public input, however, went into the design of these laws; rather, state trade associations often dictated their wording and their passage. Second, these regulations were specific to the businesses, and there was little uniformity among the states, characteristics that were typical of early Progressive era efforts to reform business. Finally, the level of internal support for oversight varied widely, with states that had active thrift leaders passing the most complete laws and states with smaller and more rural associations having the least comprehensive codes.[8]

Another important observation is that the creation of close and supportive relationships between regulators and thrifts was not unique, but was also found in capital-intensive industries such as railroads. In the late nineteenth century, officials in several states enacted laws designed to rationalize the increasingly competitive railroad industry, and the leaders of these firms realized that such supervision had many benefits for their business. First, uniform standards for rates, timetables, and operations not only improved public confidence and safety, but helped reduce cutthroat competition. The result was that these businesses were able to grow profitably, while at the same time providing more efficient service. The development of closer government-business relations spread from the state to the federal level in 1888 with the creation of the Interstate Commerce Commission. Like state railroad commissions, this federal agency encouraged more uniform business practices, often with the cooperation of the firms they regulated.[9]

Finally, the basic reasons given to justify thrift oversight were similar to those used to regulate other industries. While the need for government regulation is driven by a variety of factors, they can be grouped into two broad

---

Association News Publishing, 1927), 313–15, quote 314; "American Society of Building and Loan Association Supervisors," *American Building Association News* [hereafter *ABAN*] 40 (September 1920), quote 387; Bodfish, "State Supervision," 132.

[8] For details on other Progressive era efforts by business to secure regulation see Gabriel Kolko, *The Triumph of Conservatism: A Re-interpretation of American History, 1900–1916* (Chicago: Quadrangle Books, 1967); Robert Wiebe, *Businessmen and Reform: A Study of the Progressive Movement* (Chicago: Quadrangle Books, 1968), and Morton Keller, "Social and Economic Regulation in the Progressive Era," in Sidney M. Milkis and Jerome M. Mileur, editors, *Progressivism and the New Democracy* (Amherst: University of Massachusetts Press, 1999), 126–44.

[9] For more on how regulation developed at both the state and federal levels, see Thomas K. McCraw, *Prophets of Regulation: Charles Francis Adams, Louis D. Brandeis, James M. Landis, Alfred E. Kahn* (Cambridge, MA: Belknap Press of Harvard University Press, 1984), Thomas K. McCraw, editor, *Regulation in Perspective: Historical Essays* (Cambridge, MA: Distributed by Harvard University Press, 1981) and K. Austin Kerr, *American Railroad Politics, 1914–1920; Rates, Wages, and Efficiency* (Pittsburgh: University of Pittsburgh Press, 1968).

areas. The first is to protect the public interest, which can be accomplished with rules requiring disclosure and publicity of information, or standards to ensure consumer safety. The second goal of regulation is to protect and promote private interests. This area includes restricting business competition by erecting barriers to entry or promoting fair competition by controlling monopolies. Other beneficial regulations include those that help legitimize their functions to the public. While protecting public and private interests may seem like contradictory objectives, instances abound in which regulators accomplished both goals. In the case of thrifts, establishing minimum net worth standards helped consumers by making associations safer, while B&Ls benefited because those unable to meet the rules were forced out of business, which helped reduce competition. Furthermore, the arguments used to justify federal regulation of thrifts will be similar to those used to create state oversight.[10]

THE LEAGUE AND THE FEDERAL GOVERNMENT

While the League generally supported the creation of state regulation, such was not the case for federal involvement in the movement. The first evidence of recalcitrance appeared in 1894 when Congress tried to include thrifts in a proposed national tax on corporations. To prevent this, the League used a variety of arguments. First, it contended that B&Ls should not pay federal taxes because B&Ls were not for-profit businesses, but cooperatives that distributed earnings back to their members. Second, because thrifts helped members of the working class improve their lives through home ownership, the League contended they should be treated like other tax-exempt charitable organizations. Finally, they saw the proposed federal tax as an "injustice to the workingman," since a national levy would represent double taxation for those who paid state real estate taxes. By positioning thrifts as semicharitable organizations that constituted a movement, and not as for-profit businesses that were part of an industry, the League secured exemptions from Congress for all federal tariffs, revenue acts, and income taxes, for the next fifty-eight years.[11]

---

[10] McCraw, *Prophets of Regulation*, 299–309; Richard H. K. Vietor, *Contrived Competition: Regulation and Deregulation in America*, (Cambridge, MA: Harvard University Press, 1994), 311–13.

[11] "The Proposed Income Tax," *FRABAN* 13 (January 1894), 13; "The Taxation Question in Illinois," *FRABAN* 13 (January 1894), 1; "The Tax Question in New York," *FRABAN* 15 (December 1896), 1; Joseph H. Sundheim, *Law of Building and Loan Associations* (Chicago: Callaghan & Co., 1933), 7, 216–20; Julius Stern, "The Necessity for, and Justification of, the Exemption From Taxation of Local Building and Loan Associations," *FRABAN* 13 (September 1894), 219; "Victory in Sight!" *FRABAN* 13 (June 1894), 1; Thomas F. Larkin, "Taxation and its Effect on Individual Homeowning," *FRABAN* 18 (20 October 1899), 295; Josephine

Thrifts were not alone in their wariness of federal regulation, as commercial banks were also deeply divided on the issue. Following the Panic of 1907, however, federal involvement in commercial banking expanded significantly with the creation of the Federal Reserve in 1913 and the Federal Land Banks in 1916. One responsibility of these credit reserve systems was to improve the liquidity of banks by making low-cost loans to their members, who in turn pledged a portion of their existing loan assets as collateral (a process known as "rediscounting"). A second equally important function was to establish uniform rules for its members, including minimum standards for reserves, lending guidelines, and depository services. While all banks with national charters had to join the Federal Reserve, membership for state-chartered banks was optional. While few state banks saw the need for a backup source of liquidity during the prosperous 1920s, the value of Fed membership quickly became apparent during the banking crises of the 1930s. Of the 12,576 bank failures between 1929 and 1939, more than 80 percent had state charters.[12]

Although few League leaders saw the need for a similar credit reserve system for thrifts, their attitudes changed by the end of the 1910s as the nation grappled with the severe post–World War I housing shortage. Because new home construction had virtually ground to a halt during the war, once the conflict ended government officials estimated that the nation needed two million units to satisfy existing demand. Significantly, more than half of these homes were needed in urban areas. Unfortunately, remedying this situation was hindered by a number of factors including labor unrest and material shortages. At the same time, the rebuilding effort was hampered by the fact that demand for loans by manufacturers converting back to peacetime production had caused a scarcity of mortgage funds.[13]

Hedges Ewalt, *A Business Reborn: the Savings and Loan Story, 1930–1960* (Chicago: American Savings and Loan Institute Press, 1962), 390.

[12] New York was the first to organize a reserve bank specifically for B&Ls in 1915. See "New York Land Bank Ready for Business," *ABAN* 24 (January 1915), 10–11; Frank Bailey, "Waste in Borrowing on Real Estate," *The American Review of Reviews* 45 (January 1916), 39; F. R. Howe, "Federal Aid to Home Building," *The Architectural Forum* 30 (May 1919), 137–40; "Success of Federal Land Bank," *ABAN* 28 (January 1919), 20; Benjamin J. Klebaner, *American Commercial Banking: A History* (Boston: Twayne Publishers, 1990), 34; Glenn G. Munn, *Encyclopedia of Banking and Finance* (Boston: Bankers Publishing Co., 1983), 365; Horace Russell, *Savings and Loan Associations* (Albany, NY: Matthew Bender& Company, 1960), 654.

[13] Hume McPherson, "Aid for Home Builders," *The Survey* 42 (16 August 1919), 723–4; J. R. Moorehead, "Wartime Activities Affecting Building and Loan Associations," *American Lumberman* 12 (27 July 1918), 47; "Building and Loans and the Building Revival," *American Architect* 114 (7 August 1918), 167; "Labor Unrest Must Be Settled Before Advancing Building Material Prices Can Be Stabilized," *American Architect* 116 (20 August 1919), 249; "Financing Home Building is the Problem Today," *American Architect* 116 (7 September 1919), 387–8; "Manufacturers Unable to Supply Demand for Building Materials," *American Architect* 116

Given the severity of this crisis, in January 1919 the White House called housing industry leaders to Washington for a housing and home finance conference. Because one objective of this meeting was to find ways to extend federal aid to B&Ls, League leaders came prepared with a proposal to organize a credit reserve system for thrifts similar to that available to banks. Under the League's plan, the thrift credit bank, like the Federal Reserve, would consist of a national network of up to twelve banks whose members could obtain short-term loans by pledging a portion of their mortgage assets as collateral. Unlike the Federal Reserve, the thrift members would own these banks, and their operations would be funded through the sale of tax-exempt bonds to the public. This last requirement was in keeping with the tax-exempt status of B&Ls. The White House endorsed the League plan, and worked with its leaders to draft a bill for Congress. In July, long-time B&L supporter Sen. William Calder (R-NY) and Rep. John Nolan (R-CA) co-sponsored the Federal Building Loan Bank Act, more commonly called the Calder-Nolan Bill. Both the House and Senate held hearings on the bill in October 1919.[14]

Although the League helped create the Federal Building Loan Bank Act, the movement was not united in support of the measure. A Department of Labor poll conducted after the bill was introduced showed that only 45 percent of thrift executives favored creating a central bank, while 9 percent were opposed and 46 percent were undecided. One reason for the indecision was that more than 60 percent of all B&Ls, most of which were smaller associations, felt they had ample funds in hand to meet existing loan demand. Similarly, an increase in funds might lead some managers to take greater lending risks that might harm their association's safety. Also, the traditional wariness of thrifts regarding political involvement in their affairs led to fears that such a system would lead to socialism in housing. To counter this internal opposition, the League emphasized that a reserve bank would increase the

(7 September 1919), 388; "Demands for and Obstacles to Building," *ABAN* 39 (April 1919), 169; "The Situation Regarding Building Loan Money," *Architectural Forum* 32 (April, 1920), 163; Henry R. Brigham, "How to Meet the Housing Situation," *The Atlantic Monthly* 127 (March 1921), 405, 411.

[14] "The Washington Conference," *ABAN* 39 (February 1919), 49–56; Charles O'Conner Hennessy, "A Proposed Federal Building-Loan Bank System," *Housing Problems in America, Proceedings of the Eighth National Conference on Housing* (New York: National Housing Association, 1920), 31–2; "Conference at Washington," *ABAN* 39 (January 1919), 22–3; J. R. Moorehead, "The Financing of Home Building," *American Lumberman* 13 (19 April 1919), 48–9; Abram I. Elkus, "How to Finance the New Home," *The Delineator* 95 (December 1918), 60; "The Proposed Federal Home Loan Bank," *ABAN* 39 (March 1919), 99–101; "Senator Calder Urges 2 Billion 'Home Loan Bank' Measure," *American Architect* 116 (20 August 1919), 248–9; "Senator Calder on the Home Loan Bank Bill," *ABAN* 39 (July 1919), 310–1; David A. Bridewell, *The Federal Home Loan Bank and Its Agencies* (Washington, DC: Federal Home Loan Bank Board, 14 May 1938), 10, 14–25.

prestige of the movement, which could be irreparably damaged if B&Ls did not meet the overwhelming demand for new homes.[15]

For legislators concerns over the bill focused on two issues. Some Congressmen questioned the need to create a new federal agency, which they saw as duplicating existing government functions, while others disliked using tax-exempt debt to fund the bank. Few lawmakers, however, opposed the basic intent of the federal building and loan bank, and, in fact, favored a thrift reserve system in principle. Unfortunately, because the proposal came at a time when the government was trying to dismantle wartime agencies and reduce spending, backers could not muster enough support, and the Calder-Nolan Bill died in committee. This failure did not deter the League, and throughout the 1920s it lobbied Congress to reintroduce a mortgage credit bank measure. These efforts consistently failed largely because most B&Ls remained apathetic on the issue. As the housing shortage began to disappear after 1922, enthusiasm for the idea declined further, and finally in 1928 the League formally withdrew its support of a home loan bank.[16]

Interest in forming a home loan bank reappeared two years later to help thrifts and other home lenders contend with the financial crises of the Great Depression. One of the biggest problems these institutions faced was meeting the growing demand for withdrawal of consumer savings. Initially, B&Ls followed their common practice of honoring these requests immediately, but as withdrawals mounted some associations invoked the rules requiring members to wait up to thirty days to receive their funds. They were able to do this because B&L members were the legal owners of the thrift, and unlike bank customers they could not demand immediate withdrawal of deposits. This helped insulate B&Ls from "runs" that had forced many commercial banks to close, with the result that in the year following the October 1929 stock market crash more than 6 percent of all banks failed, as compared

---

[15] "Attitude of Building Associations to Proposed Federal Home Loan Bank Plan," *ABAN* 39 (April 1919), 202–3; "Views Pro and Con on the Proposed Federal Home Loan Bank Plan," *ABAN* 39 (June 1919), 267–75; "President Keesler on the Building Loan Bill," *ABAN* 39 (July 1919), 309; "Building-Loan Bank Urgently Needed," *ABAN* 40 (March 1920), 1.

[16] "Federal Building-Loan Banks Opposed," *ABAN* 39 (October, 1919), 1; A. C. Comey "A Proposed Federal Building-Loan Bank System,"*Housing Problems in America*, 234–7; "Report of the Federal Legislative Committee," *Twenty-Eighth Annual Convention of the United States League of Local Building and Loan Associations*, (Chicago: American Building and Loan News Press, 1920), 160–3; G. P. Woodruff, "Financing Building Operations," *Building Age* 42 (February 1920), 35–7; "The Calder Bill to Aid Housing," *Domestic Engineering* 94 (22 January 1921), 227; "Proposed Federal Loans to Stimulate Construction," *Engineering and Contracting* 55 (27 April 1921), 427; W. V. M. Robertson, "Building and Loan Associations Should Have a Federal Reserve System," *ABAN* 49 (December 1929), 738; George L. Bliss, "Building and Loan Associations as Home Financing Agencies" *Housing Problems in America, Proceedings of the Tenth National Conference on Housing*, (New York: American Housing Association, 1929), 63, 67; C. Clinton James," History of the Home Loan Bank Bill," *ABAN* 50 (February 1930), 94.

to just 1 percent of all thrifts. In fact, thrift assets in some states grew as investors saw B&Ls as a safer place to hold money.[17]

Beginning in 1931, however, the financial situation for thrifts worsened considerably. Not only did withdrawal requests continue to rise, but deposits also fell off as rising unemployment affected the ability of thrift members to make loan and share payments. While these conditions were serious, even worse problems began when more of the correspondent commercial banks used by B&Ls went under. Traditionally, thrifts relied on commercial banks to provide them with a variety of depository services and checking accounts. As a result, when these institutions closed their doors, the B&Ls, like other customers, usually lost all their money. Moreover, because most B&Ls had credit lines with these banks that were typically payable on demand, when these lenders called in their thrift loans most associations lacked the funds to make immediate repayment and were forced into bankruptcy. Despite such problems, B&Ls faired remarkably well compared to commercial banks. Between 1931 and 1932 almost 20 percent of all banks went out of business while just over 2 percent of all thrifts met a similar fate.[18]

HERBERT HOOVER AND THE HOME LOAN BANK

While the deepening financial crisis of the early 1930s was important in generating support for a home loan bank, another key reason plans moved forward was that Herbert Hoover occupied the White House. An engineer by training, Hoover gained national prominence after World War I when he led famine relief efforts in Belgium. Hoover embraced many of the ideals first developed by the Progressives, and among these was a belief that a proper living environment had a salutary effect on individual morals and improved personal character. In the 1920s, Hoover was the secretary of commerce in both the Harding and Coolidge Administrations, and he directly expanded the role of government in promoting home ownership in two major respects. First, he organized the Better Homes campaign as a way

---

[17] "The Home-Owner Gets Pinched," *Business Week* 9 (November 1929), 35; "Building and Loan and the Stock Market," *ABAN* 49 (December 1929), 709–10; "Building and Loan Put Up Stout Resistance," *Business Week*, 21 (September 1932), 43; "Billions of Dollars for Residential Building," *American Builder and Building Age* 50 (October 1930), 100–1; K. V. Haymaker, "The Rule for Paying Withdrawals," *ABAN* 43 (January 1933), 58, 96; Sundheim, *Law of Building and Loan*, 216–24; Russell, *Savings and Loan Associations*, 654.

[18] A discussion of how B&Ls coped with the financial hardships of the Great Depression is contained in Chapter 4. "Loans for Small Homes Tend Towards Increase," *Business Week*, 17 (December 1930) 20; C. A. Sterling, "The Successful Handling of Repossessed Property," *ABAN* 51 (September 1931), 512–3; "Building and Loans Advertise to Combat Withdrawals," *Printer's Ink* 159 (14 July 1932), 52; Ewalt, *A Business Reborn*, 14–8; Oscar Kreutz, *The Way It Happened* (St. Petersburg, FL: St. Petersburg Printing Co., 1972), 9; *The Federal Home Loan Bank System* (Washington, D.C.: Federal Home Loan Bank Board, 1952), 6; Russell, *Savings and Loan Associations*, 654.

of standardizing housing conditions, and second he formed the Division of Building and Housing in the Bureau of Standards to improve construction efficiency, and the availability of housing and home finance.[19]

As Commerce Secretary Hoover also indirectly promoted the growth of home ownership through his policy of "associationalism," in which government encouraged businesses to cooperate in the public interest. He organized a series of conferences that brought together representatives from the housing and financial sectors to share information on ways to improve the state of housing in America. These conferences not only received a positive reception from the media and trade groups, but also brought Hoover into contact with the thrift movement and its leaders. Although he did not maintain close ties with the League, Hoover did voice his support of the movement, noting "the Department of Commerce has been in thorough sympathy with the work you have been carrying on, and is at least an agency of government that believes the results which you attain are of the most fundamental to our American people."[20]

As early as 1921 Hoover expressed an interest in creating a home loan bank as a way to extend home ownership and end the problems associated with using second mortgages to buy houses. While the commerce secretary believed that "the government has no notion whatever of going into the housing business either directly or indirectly," he did feel it had a responsibility to improve the flow of housing credit. Consequently, Hoover closely followed the postwar efforts to form a rediscount bank, and over the years corresponded with League and housing industry leaders on this subject. Although

---

[19] Joan Hoff Wilson, *Herbert Hoover: Forgotten Progressive* (New York: Little Brown & Co., 1975), 110–11; Robert K. Murray, "Herbert Hoover and the Harding Cabinet," in Ellis Hawley, editor, *Herbert Hoover as Secretary of Commerce: Studies in New era Thought and Practice* (Ames, IA: University of Iowa Press, 1981), 25–6; Herbert Hoover, "Home Building and Home Ownership: Their National Significance," *Child Welfare Magazine* 21 (April 1927), 357–8; "Ohio Building Association League – Speech Before 'Billion Dollar Convention,' Columbus," 21 (October 1926), 4; Collected Speeches of Herbert Hoover [hereafter The Bible] #654; Herbert Hoover Presidential Library (HHPL); Herbert Hoover, "Home Ownership," *Liberty Magazine* 3 (11 May 1926), 5; "America a Nation of Homes is the Goal of Many Forces, Declares Secretary Hoover," *Christian Science Monitor*, 25 March 1925, 12; "The United States League Convention," *ABAN* 43 (August 1923), 339.

[20] Graham Taylor, "Better Housing for the Wage Earner," *The Chicago Daily News*, 17 April 1926, 14; William J. Barber, *From New Era to New Deal* (New York: Cambridge University Press, 1985), 96–7; Ellis Hawley, "Herbert Hoover and Economic Stabilization, 1921–22," in Hawley, *Herbert Hoover as Secretary of Commerce*, 54–5; Wilson, *Herbert Hoover*, 157–9; "Hoover Again Endorses Building Association," *ABAN* 43 (July 1923), 292; "Hoover Endorses Fight to Stabilize Business," *New York Evening Post*, 18 March 1922, 12; Press Release of the Department of Commerce, 11 March 1921, 1, 3; The Bible No 134; HHPL; Press Release, "Trade Association Activities – Correspondence Between Departments of Commerce and Justice," 16 February 1922; The Bible No 206; HHPL; "U.S. League of Local Building and Loan Associations – Remarks Before the Thirty-Fourth Annual Meeting, Minneapolis," 20 July 1926, quote 2; The Bible No 609; HHPL.

Hoover pledged to the League he would sponsor congressional legislation to create a home loan bank if he became president, it was only when the crisis facing homeowners and lenders became truly serious that he appeared ready to use a home loan bank as one way of alleviating problems faced by homeowners and revive residential construction.[21]

In early 1931, Hoover announced plans for a White House Conference on Home Building and Home Ownership to study all aspects of the national housing problem and provide recommendations for ways to increase home building and home ownership. To provide the conferees with the necessary information to create these plans, the conference consisted of several committees made up of government and business leaders to gather facts and study the housing question from a variety of perspectives, including housing design and construction, residential planning, urban renewal, and the availability of homes in rural areas and for minorities. One of the central issues the conference would address was finding ways to improve the availability of home mortgages, which was an area Hoover felt was "not as soundly organized as other branches of credit." To assist in this effort, in November Hoover met privately with banking, insurance, real estate, and thrift leaders to discuss preliminary ideas on these and other related issues.[22]

One of the participants at the White House meetings with the League was the trade group's new executive manager, H. Morton Bodfish. Although just twenty-seven years old, Bodfish was already a recognized authority on the movement. He had attended The Ohio State University where he wrote extensively on B&L operations, and after graduation he had become an instructor in real estate at Northwestern University and a consultant for the national real estate trade association. Once he joined the League, Bodfish established himself as a strong and effective leader; and, while some associates described him as arrogant and opinionated, he was above all else passionate

---

[21] "Address before the National Association of Real Estate Boards, Chicago, Ill.," 15 July 1921, 6–9, quote 6; The Bible No 164; HHPL; Memorandum from F. T. Miller to Secretary Hoover, 20 June 1921; F. T. Miller, June–August, 1921 and undated; Building and Housing, Home Finance 1921–1929; Commerce Papers; HHPL; Letter from Herbert Hoover to Wilber Walling, 5 March 1925; Kingsley, William H.; Home Financing; Building and Housing, Home Finance 1921–1929; Commerce Papers; HHPL; The Herbert Hoover Presidential Library has dozens of letters from homeowners to the president requesting something be done to help them renew their mortgages or pay their taxes to avoid foreclosure. See handwritten memorandum from Arthur Mertzke to Dr. Gries and Mr. Ellington with attachments, 21 April 1932; Circular Letter, Finance Committee, Reduction of Foreclosure Plans; White House Conference on Home Building and Home Ownership (WHCHBHO); HHPL.

[22] "The Chance for Civilized Housing," *The New Republic*, 17 September 1930, 115–7; *Housing Objectives and Programs*, President's Conference on Home Building and Home Ownership, (Washington, D.C.: USGPO, 1933), 1–20; "Money for Homes," *American Builder* 52 (December 1931), 30; *Confidential Bulletin of the United States Building and Loan League* [hereafter *Confidential Bulletin*] 1 (26 October 1931), 5; Charles O'Conner Hennesy, "Savings and Loan Statesmanship," *Building and Loan Annals, 1931* (Chicago: United States Building and Loan League, 1931), quote 59.

about the B&L business. This commitment, combined with an innate ability to influence people, proved very useful when Bodfish began to represent the League on Capitol Hill. To keep thrifts informed of his work he began a League members-only *Confidential Bulletin,* which proved to be an important tool in rallying support for federal thrift laws.[23]

During its meeting with Hoover, the League leadership presented its plan to ease the problems facing home lenders. Like Hoover, they agreed that providing a stable source of liquidity was an important part of the solution, and they wanted to let thrifts become members in the Federal Reserve and use its funds to make home loans. They reasoned that because the crisis demanded quick action including B&Ls in an existing rediscounting system was more expedient than creating a new reserve bank; it would also enhance the prestige of the movement. Hoover, however, suspected that Congress would strongly resist tampering with the Federal Reserve and quickly rejected the idea. He instead commented on a proposal outlined at the annual meeting of the National Association of Real Estate Boards in May 1931 to create a central mortgage reserve bank. Hoover then pulled from his desk a detailed plan for such a mortgage reserve bank that he intended to give to Congress and wanted the League to review.[24]

Shocked by this revelation, the League tried to rally support for their ideas with legislators, but they soon learned that Hoover's concerns were accurate. Consequently, League leaders fell in line with Hoover, and worked to ensure that any mortgage bank would serve the interests of the movement, since, as Bodfish noted, "we must do something, or something may be done to us." Unfortunately, when the housing conference began, League representatives on the conference's Finance Committee quickly learned that the main concern was not creating a mortgage bank, but rather finding ways to reduce the need for high-risk second mortgages. One reason for this was that the committee was chaired by an insurance company executive and was dominated by banking and insurance interests who likely had little interest

---

[23] Bodfish remained on the Northwestern faculty until 1940 when he retired a full professor. See M. E. Irwin, "Meet the New Executive Manager," *ABAN* 50 (June 1930), 333, 365; Henry Morton Bodfish, *Money Lending Practices of Building and Loan Associations in Ohio* (unpublished masters thesis, The Ohio State University, 1927); H. Morton Bodfish, *Historical Balance Sheet Analysis of Ohio Building and Loan Associations* (Columbus, OH: Bureau of Business Research, College of Commerce and Administration, The Ohio State University, 1928); "The Road to Success," *The Chicago Daily Tribune,* 22 August 1953, 7; Kreutz, *The Way It Happened,* 88; A. D. Theobald, *Forty-Five Years on the Up Escalator* (Chicago: n.p. 1979), 4–7, 32.

[24] *Confidential Bulletin* 1 (26 October 1931), 2, 8–11; *Confidential Bulletin* 2 (10 November 1931), 2–4; *Confidential Bulletin* 4 (23 December 1931), 7; Mortgage Bankers Association, "Central Residential Mortgage Bank," *Letter to Members* 40 (30 June 1931), 1–2; Letter from Herbert Hoover to Roy A. Young, 30 March 1930, 1–2, Letter from Roy Young to Herbert Hoover, 28 March 1930, and Memorandum from E. A. Goldwater to Roy Young, 11 April 1930, 1–6; Federal Home Loan Bank Board Correspondence, 1930; Presidential Papers – Subject File; HHPL.

in bolstering the status of the thrift movement. Furthermore, many of these people not only questioned the basic premise of a funding shortage but also did not want federal government directly involved in the mortgage business and insisted that any program created to help lenders be temporary in order to "meet the present emergency."[25]

While the Finance Committee was compiling housing data and evaluating various alternatives, on November 13 Hoover announced his proposal to create a federal home loan bank capable of advancing up to $2 billion to home lenders. Patterned on the organization and operational structure of the Federal Reserve, this new reserve banking system would consist of twelve banks owned by B&Ls and other institutions that joined by subscribing to bank stock. These members could receive liquidity loans from the banks by pledging a portion of their mortgage assets as collateral. The reserve bank would issue bonds to investors to fund these loans, but initial funding would come directly from the government. Furthermore, Hoover insisted that this home loan bank should become a permanent addition to the nation's financial system to "further the promotion of home ownership, particularly through the financial strength thus made available to building and loan associations."[26]

The announcement of the new home loan bank plan received a very cool reception from the conference attendees. The main objections came from banking and insurance interests who disliked creating a permanent organization, and one that was so narrowly defined. Furthermore, they considered the large size of the bank as an extreme response to a temporary emergency,

[25] The committee received dozens of suggestions from businessmen and homeowners for solving the home finance problem, including the creation of a limited number of large, urban federally chartered savings and loans that would loans directly to individuals. Memorandum from James Taylor to Mr. Baker with attachment, 19 September 1930, Finance Committee, 1930, WHCHBHO, HHPL; Notes on First Meeting of the Committee of Finance of the President's Conference on Home Building and Home Ownership, 23 April 1931, 1–4, and Addendum to Notes on Second Meeting of the Committee of Finance of the President's Conference on Home Building and Home Ownership, 29 May 1931, 1–2; Home Financing, 1931, April–May; WHCHBHO; HHPL; Notes on First Meeting of Division on Mortgage Structure of the Committee of Finance of the President's Conference, etc., June 29, 1931, 1–4, quote 4 and handwritten notes of Division on Mortgage Structure Meeting, 29 June 1931, 1–6; Home Financing, 1931, June–July; WHCHBHO; HHPL; handwritten notes of Division on Mortgage Structure Meeting, 22 September 1931, 1–5; Home Financing, 1931, August–September; WHCHBHO; HHPL; *Confidential Bulletin* 2 (10 November 1931), 1–6.

[26] Letter from Herbert Hoover to Secretary of Commerce with attachment, 23 December 1931; Federal Home Loan Bank Board Correspondence, December 1931; Presidential Papers – Subject File; HHPL; Paul M. Mazur, "Huge Home Building Credit Viewed as a Business Lever," *The New York Times*, 25 October 1931, sec. 9, 3; "Propose to Hoover Home Credits Plan," *The New York Times*, 3 November 1931, 4; "Sound Basis Urged for New Credit Plan," *The New York Times*, 9 November 1931, 36; William Best, "Building and Loan Looks at the President's Plan," *ABAN* 51 (December 1931), 545; "President's Statement on Home Loan Plan," *The New York Times*, 14 November 1931, quote 2.

especially because B&Ls could gain access to funds through existing federal agencies such as the Reconstruction Finance Corporation (RFC). Supporters countered that because the maximum term for RFC loans was only one year, it was ill-suited for long-term mortgage lenders; and, in fact, of the $2 billion lent by the RFC through 1933 only $125 million went to thrifts. Despite this overall negative reaction, the conference wanted to be supportive of the president and in its final report gave his plan a mild endorsement. Hoover was undeterred by this tepid response, and in his opening message to the new session of Congress on December 8, 1931 he called for legislators to establish a permanent home loan bank.[27]

In January 1932, representatives from the Commerce Department, the Federal Reserve, and the League met to draft the Federal Home Loan Bank Act, which Rep. Robert Luce (R-MA) and Sen. James Watson (R-IN) co-sponsored in Congress. While the basic outline of the final draft matched the Hoover plan, it also contained elements of the original Calder-Nolan bill, including a restriction on bank membership to only B&Ls and a provision allowing the government to use tax-exempt bonds to fund the bank. The bill had the backing of the League, the National Association of Real Estate Boards, home building trades, and consumer groups; and in their testimony to legislators representatives of these groups argued that increased home financing through the home loan banks would create new jobs and ease the national economic crisis. The home loan bank would also complement the federal credit reserve systems for banks and agricultural lenders, and thus place B&Ls on par with these financial institutions.[28]

[27] James Ford, "The Practical Significance of the President's Conference," *ABAN* 52 (January 1932), 10, 13; *Home Finance and Taxation*, President's Conference on Home Building and Home Ownership (Washington: USGPO, 1933), 8–9, 47–9; "Hoover Moves to Form Twelve Home Loan Banks as Spur to Construction," *The New York Times*, 14 November 1931, p. 1; Bridewell, *The Federal Home Loan Bank*, 31–35; *Confidential Bulletin* 5 (30 January 1932), 2–8; *Confidential Bulletin* 6 (25 March 1932), 6; "Building Loan Groups Get Help from RFC," *Business Week*, 4 May 1932, 26; Letter from Edward Bertram to James Taylor, 21 June 1932 and Letter from James Taylor to Edward Bertram, 6 July 1932; Personal Experiences and Finance Plans, 1931; Finance Committee; WHCHBHO; HHPL James S. Olson, *Herbert Hoover and the Reconstruction Finance Corporation, 1931–1933* (Ames, IA: Iowa State University Press, 1977), 14, 60–61; Article by Joseph Day, "More and Better Mortgages," n.p., n.d.; References to Finance Committee Reports; Finance Committee; WHCHBHO; HHPL; handwritten comments by James S. Taylor, References to Finance Committee Reports; Finance Committee; WHCHBHO; HHPL; Memorandum from James S. Taylor to Secretary Lamont, 24 November 1931; Correspondence and Memoranda. Home Finance Report and Recommendations of the Committee on Home Finance; WHCHBHO; HHPL; Kreutz, *The Way It Happened*, 10–15.

[28] Bridewell, *The Federal Home Loan Bank*, 46–7; "Hoover Asks Speed on Relief Bills; Congress Chiefs Pledge Quick Action; Democrats Offer Their Tariff Plan," *The New York Times*, 5 January 1932, 1; "Witnesses Boost Home Loan Bank Bill," *ABAN* 52 (March 1932), 106–112; Horace Russell, "The Public Needs the Home Loan Bank System." *ABAN* 52 (April 1932), 188; "House Committee Hears B and L Men Support Home Loan System," *ABAN*

Bankers and insurance companies were the main opponents to the bill, and they raised the same objections used to defeat the Calder-Nolan bill in 1920. They opposed limiting bank membership to just thrifts, and alleged that using government bonds to fund the bank would lead to inflation. They also feared that increasing the availability of home loans would lead to "another wild spree in real estate" with overbuilding resulting in lower home values. Given these criticisms, the House Banking and Commerce Committee dropped the Luce-Watson measure and substituted a broader bill drafted by Rep. Michael Reilly (D-WI) that was supported House Speaker Jake Garner (D-TX) who wanted to "make short work of getting a home loan bill passed...." The Reilly bill allowed virtually any mortgage lender to join the home loan bank, which made the new bank appear to be less a special interest for thrifts but also resulted in strong criticism from both the League and White House officials.[29]

The Reilly Bill was reported to the full House on June 10, and during five days of lackluster hearings representatives raised only two substantive objections, the first of which involved a general disapproval of creating "another army of federal officers, agents and employees" to handle what some saw as a short-term problem. The other, more contentious, issue was using tax-exempt bonds to fund the banks, since legislators feared this would increase the national debt. Despite these concerns, the majority of representatives voted in favor of the bill, and sent the measure to the Senate on June 16. When the Senate Committee on Banking and Currency reported it to the full body after only four days of hearings, the White House was so confident it would pass that officials began making plans for putting the home loan bank into operation. Their optimism quickly ended, however, as debate in the Senate dragged on for almost a month. As Congress neared the end of its session, officials feared the bill would not pass and would have to be reintroduced in the next session in December.[30]

---

52 (April 1932), 172; Letter from L. C. Irvine to Lawrence Ritchie, n.d.; Federal Home Loan Bank Board Correspondence, January, 1932; Presidential Papers – Subject File; HHPL; Letter from Conrad Mann to Herbert Hoover, 27 February 1932, 1–2; Federal Home Loan Bank Board Correspondence, February, 1932; Presidential Papers – Subject File; HHPL; Letter from G. E. De Nike to Herbert Hoover, March, 1932; Federal Home Loan Bank Board Correspondence, March–May, 1932; Presidential Papers – Subject File; HHPL.

29 I. Friedlander, "The Home Loan Bank Bill vs. Special Privilege Monopolies," *ABAN* 52 (April 1932), 152–3; "Says Federal Plan Fails Homeowner" *The New York Times*, 24 January 1932, sec. 9, 8; "Hoover May Drop Home Loan Banks," *The New York Times*, 8 February 1932, 30; Bridewell, *The Federal Home Loan Bank*, 53–6; "Same Horse – With a New Name," *ABAN* 52 (May 1932), 196; *Confidential Bulletin 6* (25 March 1932), 1–2; "Throws Down Gauntley to Insurance Companies," *ABAN* 52 (March 1932), 130; handwritten memorandum, author unknown, quote; Federal Home Loan Bank Legislation, 1931–1932; Presidential Papers – Subject File; HHPL; Memorandum from John M. Gries to Secretary Lamont, 16 April 1932, 1–2; Federal Home Loan Bank Legislation, 1931–1932; Presidential Papers – Subject File; HHPL.

30 Bridewell, *The Federal Home Loan Bank*, 73–89, quote 78; *Confidential Bulletin* M9 (12 July 1932), 1; "New Laws and Legislative Matters," *Building and Loan Annals*, 1932, 666–70;

The main reason for the delay was that several influential senators, including Carter Glass (D-VA), William Borah (R-ID), and James Couzens (R-MI), strongly opposed the measure. While Glass and Borah expressed concerns similar to those raised in the House debate, Couzens felt the purpose of the bill was misdirected. Instead of making loans to mortgage lenders, Couzens wanted the home loan bank to make loans directly to individual homeowners. He argued that if government were to become involved in home finance, any system it created had to provide direct relief to those who needed it the most. Given this formidable opposition, the Senate approved the bill only after Couzens amended it to permit the bank to make direct loans to homeowners who could not get money from a B&L or bank. On July 12, just nine days before Congress was scheduled to adjourn, House and Senate members met in a joint conference committee to iron out their differences over the much-amended bill.[31]

By July 16, the House had accepted the Couzens Amendment, and had agreed on all other issues except for an amendment inserted by Glass, designed in part to defeat the bill, to expand the currency. For the next five days, final approval of the home loan bank bill hinged on this one provision, until finally on the last day of the session the House agreed to accept the amendment to ensure its passage. Opponents to the bill, however, could still nullify it by not authorizing money to fund bank operations. Because Senate rules required an appropriation bill to lie over for one day before it

Memorandum from John M. Gries to Secretary Lamont, 15(?) January 1932; Federal Home Loan Bank Legislation, 1931–1932; Presidential Papers – Subject File; HHPL; Telegram from Ohio Bankers Association to Herbert Hoover, 29 January 1932; Federal Home Loan Bank Board Correspondence, January, 1932; Presidential Papers – Subject File; HHPL; Letter from Herbert Nelson to Walter Newton, 1 February 1932; Federal Home Loan Bank Board Correspondence, February, 1932; Presidential Papers – Subject File; HHPL; Memorandum from the United States Building and Loan League to Herbert Hoover, n.d.; Federal Home Loan Bank Board Correspondence, March–May, 1932; Presidential Papers – Subject File; HHPL; Letter from Clarence Seaman to Herbert Hoover, 17 May 1932; Federal Home Loan Bank Board Correspondence, March–May, 1932; Presidential Papers – Subject File; HHPL.

31 Bridewell, *The Federal Home Loan Bank*, 93–111; Robert Luce, "The Federal Program and Building and Loan." *Building and Loan Annals, 1932* (Chicago: United States Building and Loan League, 1932), 21–3; "Couzens Gets Shift in Home Loan Bill," *The New York Times*, 7 July 1932, 12; Phone Message from Secretary Lamont to Herbert Hoover, 5 February 1932; Federal Home Loan Bank Board Correspondence, February, 1932; Presidential Papers – Subject File; HHPL; Letter from Secretary Lamont to Secretary Newton with attachment, 24 June 1932; Federal Home Loan Bank Board Correspondence, June 1932; Presidential Papers – Subject File; HHPL; Memorandum from Lawrence Ritchie to Herbert Hoover with attached letter from Wilson W. Mills to Lawrence Ritchie, 6 January 1932; Federal Home Loan Bank Correspondence, January 1932; Presidential Papers – Subject File; HHPL; "Senate Approves Home Loan Bill," *The New York Times*, 13 July 1932, 2; Thomas B. Marvell, *The Federal Home Loan Bank Board*, (New York: Praeger & Co., 1969), 22–3; Robert Luce, "The Federal Program and Building and Loan, *Building and Loan Annals, 1934* (Chicago: United States Building and Loan League, 1934), 23–5; The Legislative History of the Bill H. R. 12280; Federal Home Loan Bank Board; Federal Home Loan Bank Legislation, 1931–1932; Presidential Papers – Subject File; HHPL.

could be considered, it appeared as if the home loan bank would in fact be a dead letter law. Then, just minutes before adjournment, Sen. Wesley Jones (R-WA), using an obscure parliamentary maneuver, attached the appropriation to another pending bill, which allowed the Senate to vote on the funding immediately. Caught off guard, Couzens protested this legislative "sleight of hand" to no avail, and by voice vote the appropriation passed, followed by a motion to adjourn. On July 22, 1932, President Hoover signed the Federal Home Loan Bank Act into law.[32]

The creation of a federal home loan bank culminated a twelve-year effort to give thrifts a liquidity reserve system, and passage of the law reflected the differences between the 1930s and the 1920s. First, the crisis of the 1930s was clearly more severe than that of a decade earlier, and the need to give homeowners some form of relief was an important concern for legislators. Also, opponents to the home loan bank did not wage a coordinated attack to defeat the bill, as both the Mortgage Bankers Association and the American Bankers Association put up only nominal resistance. In the final analysis, the passage benefited from much stronger support from within the thrift movement which overwhelmingly believed the bank would improve their financial condition. This factor, combined with intense lobbying by League leaders, caused Reilly to later compliment the League saying, "the reason why you have a Federal Home Loan Bank Bill . . . is because of the efforts put forth by this organization."[33]

FORMING THE BANK AND FAILED EXPECTATIONS

In August 1932, Hoover appointed the first Federal Home Loan Bank Board (FHLBB) to put the home loan bank into operation. Its members were Commerce Department housing advisor John Greis, banker Nathan Adams,

---

[32] "Conferees Blocked on Home Loan Bill," *The New York Times*, 15 July 1932, 2; "Deadlock Over the Relief Bill Broken; Congress Expected to Adjourn Today; Hoover Cuts Pay $15,000, Cabinet, 15%," *The New York Times*, 16 July 1932, 1; "Home-Loan Measure in All-Day Snarl," *The New York Times*, 17 July 1932, 1; "72d Congress Adjourns Near Midnight; Relief and Home Loan Bank Bills Pass Senate in Flurry Over Dry Law Repeal," *The New York Times*, 17 July 1932, 1; "Hoover Approves Home Loans Bill, Predicts Jobs Rise," *The New York Times*, 23 July 1932, 1; Bridewell, *The Federal Home Loan Bank*, 136–55.

[33] *Confidential Bulletin* 7 (21 May 1932), 2; *Confidential Bulletin* M9 (12 July 1932), 1; "Lamont Will Urge Home Loan Banks," *The New York Times*, 6 February 1932, 2; "Get Behind the Home Loan Bank Bill," *ABAN* 52 (March, 1932), 100; Railroad Cooperative Building and Loan Association, *Financing Home Ownership*, 3–4; Martin, George A.; Finance Committee, Correspondence; White House Conference on Housing and Home Building; HHPL; "United We Stand," *ABAN* 52 (June 1932), 244; "Building and Loan Men Cautious About New Plan," *American Builder* 51 (September 1931), 77, 98; "Mortgage Bankers Hit Home Loan Bill," *The New York Times*, 15 February 1932, 33; I. Friedlander, "Membership," *Building and Loan Annals 1933*, 69–70; Rep. Michael K. Reilly, "Passing the Bill," *Building and Loan Annals, 1932*, 51–4, quote, 51.

League president William Best, League manager Morton Bodfish, and banker Franklin Fort as chairman. The first task of the Board was to divide the country into districts for each Federal Home Loan Bank; and, although it could have used the existing Federal Reserve districts, the members deliberately chose different boundaries so as to combine states that had adequate mortgage financing with those that had severe shortages. Next, the Board got states to pass laws that would allow thrifts to pledge their mortgages as collateral for bank loans, something most prohibited because during the nationals era thrifts had used these assets for speculative purposes.[34]

In October 1932, the Board announced the federal home loan bank system was fully operational and ready to make loans to its members. The bank had total capital of $134 million, consisting of $122 million from the government and $12 million from the bank members. Although the bank was open to all types of residential lenders, all of the first members were thrifts, a trend that continued throughout the life of the home loan bank. Within a few months, the Board approved $98.8 million in loans to members and had an additional $53.4 million in pending applications. By March 1933, lending volume exceeded $5 million per day, and, while the additional liquidity did not dramatically improve conditions, it did help. Thrift managers reported to the League that they experienced a decline in withdrawal requests following their joining the home loan bank, and in some instances people opened new accounts reflecting greater public confidence that B&Ls had money to lend.[35]

Despite such overall progress, the Board did have major trouble in meeting the objective of making direct loans to homeowners as required by the Couzens Amendment. Because the home loan bank was, like the Federal Reserve, a wholesale lender to other financial institutions, it did not have the manpower to effectively operate a retail lending system as envisioned by Couzens. The lack of personnel was so acute that the Board had difficulty just

---

34 The Board also chose to locate these banks in small cities such as Winston-Salem, NC and Little Rock, AR because it was more in keeping with the "local" nature of thrift business. "Hoover Appoints Home Loan Board; Headed by Fort," *The New York Times*, 7 August 1932, 1; *Confidential Bulletin* M11 (10 August 1932), 1–2; "Convention Highlights," *ABAN* 52 (September 1932), 399–400; "The Home Loan Bank System," *ABAN* 52 (August 1932), 340–1; Franklin W. Fort, "Federal Home Loan Bank System," *Building and Loan Annals 1933*, 1–4; Bridewell, *The Federal Home Loan Bank*, 157–61.

35 Press Release, Federal Home Loan Bank Board, 14 October 1932, 1–3; Federal Home Loan Bank Board; Federal Home Loan Bank Legislation, 1931–1932; Presidential Papers – Subject File; HHPL; H. Morton Bodfish, "The Home Loan Bank System," *ABAN* 52 (October, 1932), 454–5; *Confidential Bulletin* M11 (18 November 1932), 3–4; *Confidential Bulletin* M18 (22 December 1932), 1–3; "Members of the Home Loan Bank," *ABAN* 53 (May 1933), 75; Address of Horace Russell, General Counsel, Federal Home Loan Bank Board before the Carolina Lumber and Building Material Dealers' Association, 8 February 1933, 1–4; Federal Home Loan Bank Board; Federal Home Loan Bank Legislation, 1931–1932; Presidential Papers, Subject File; HHPL.

responding to the avalanche of requests it received from mortgagees seeking relief. Another problem was that Congress did not specify what lending criteria the Board should use to evaluate individual loan requests. Because of this omission, the Board was forced to treat applications from homeowners by the same standards it used to approve loan requests from private lenders. This meant that small loans had to have a minimum loan-to-value ratio of between 60 percent and 70 percent, which, given the steady erosion of property values, was virtually impossible to meet. The result was that of the more than 41,000 homeowner requests for direct loans received by the Board through March 1933, only three were approved.[36]

These problems in meeting the direct loan provision ultimately led to public criticism of the Board. Since several newspapers followed the progress of organizing the regional banks on an almost daily basis, the public had heightened expectations that the home loan bank would provide immediate assistance. This attitude was reinforced by the constant attention given to the Couzens Amendment. The Board, however, stressed that its primary role was as a source of liquidity for home lenders. Consequently, it would take time for these institutions to use this money to make mortgages, and the Board urged the public to be patient and have faith that things would improve. Despite such pleas, the rising tide of foreclosures combined with the virtual absence of direct loans caused a steady rise in criticism. Attitudes were so negative, that the "failure" of the home loan bank to help suffering homeowners became a Democratic party campaign issue in the 1932 presidential election.[37]

Nor did Congress like this lack of direct lending to homeowners, and some congressmen thought the Board was purposely avoiding the mandate legislators had given it. Among them was Sen. Borah who accused the Board of operating the home loan bank as a self-serving institution to help only B&Ls. He introduced bills to abolish the bank in December 1932 and

---

[36] *Confidential Bulletin* M17 (18 November 1932), 1–2; Bridewell, *The Federal Home Loan Bank*, 162–5; Marvell, *The Federal Home Loan Bank Board*, 24; "Government Pushes Big Recovery Plans," *The New York Times*, 24 July 1932, 2; Address of Nathan Adams Before the Autumn Meeting of the Board of the Associated General Contractors of America, 10 October 1932, 1–3; Federal Home Loan Bank Board; Federal Home Loan Bank Legislation, 1931–1932; Presidential Papers – Subject File; HHPL; Address of Horace Russell, 8 February 1933, 5–6; "LaGuardia Warns of Home Loan Evils, *The New York Times*, 19 August 1932 32; Ewalt, *A Business Reborn*, 52.

[37] Seventy-seven articles appeared in *The New York Times* between 7 August 1932 and 7 December 1932, detailing the progress of the home loan bank. For representative stories see "Fort Reports Every Good Mortgage in the U.S. Will Become Liquid When 12 District Banks Open for Business," *The New York Times*, 14 October 1932, 3 and "No Loans Made as Yet,"*The New York Times*, 16 November 1932, 28; Address of Horace Russell, 8 February 1933, 3; Address of Nathan Adams, 10 October 1932, 1; Letter from Rolfe Cobleigh to Theodore Joslin, 20 October 1932; Federal Home Loan Bank Board; Federal Home Loan Bank Legislation, 1931–1932; Presidential Papers, Subject File; HHPL; Marvell, *The Federal Home Loan Bank Board*, 21–4; Ewalt, *A Business Reborn*, 66–9.

March 1933. The Board defended its record by citing the problems it had in interpreting and implementing the law. It also noted how the bank was steadily increasing its membership, as well as its success in meeting member loan demand. Although neither of Borah's bills was reported to the full Senate, the debate over the value of a home loan bank highlighted the need to find a more effective way to provide homeowners with direct relief from their delinquent mortgage debts. This issue, along with rescuing the nation's rapidly faltering banking system, would be one of the top priorities of the new president, Franklin D. Roosevelt.[38]

ROOSEVELT TAKES COMMAND

By the time Franklin D. Roosevelt took the oath of office on March 4, 1933, the problems facing homeowners were reaching epidemic proportions. According to federal statistics, roughly 45 percent of the more than 10.6 million homes in the country had either first, second, or third mortgages. The government estimated that 43 percent of all first mortgages were in default with an average arrearage of fifteen months. Furthermore, more than half of all homes with second and third mortgages were in default and in arrears an average of eighteen months. Officials concluded that nearly 25 percent of all homeowners with mortgages were in danger of losing their property. In fact, lenders were initiating an average of 24,000 foreclosures per month by 1933, a rate that was nearly five times more than that of just six years earlier. Significantly, the number of foreclosures would have been much higher, except that many lenders refused to take possession of a property, because doing so would have forced them to recognize a financial loss given the steep decline in real estate values.[39]

---

[38] Ward Whitlock, Statement on Behalf of the United States Building and Loan League to the Banking and Currency Committee of the United States Senate, and the Banking and Currency Committee of the House of Representatives, 20 December 1932, 1–3; Federal Home Loan Bank Board; Federal Home Loan Bank Legislation, 1931–1932; Presidential Papers, Subject File; HHPL; "Plans Fight to Revise Home Loan Bank Law," *The New York Times*, 19 November 1932, 28; I. Friedlander, "Permanency of the Federal Home Loan Bank System," *ABAN* 52 (December 1932), 535, 573; "Credit – Not Magic," *ABAN* 52 (September 1932), 388–9; "Borah Asks Repeal of Home Loan Act," *The New York Times*, 8 December 1932, 2; "Opposes Changes in Home Loan Act," *The New York Times*, 21 December 1932, 2; "Bill Offered to Amend Home Loan Bank Act, Granting Borrowers 80% of Assessed Valuation," *The New York Times*, 13 December 1932), 1; "Home Loan Bank Act's Sponsor Rises to its Defense in Congress," *ABAN* 53 (April 1933), 150, 185.

[39] Bureau of the Census, *Historical Statistics of the United States, Colonial Times to 1970* (Washington, D.C.: USGPO, 1976), 651; Ewalt, *A Business Reborn*, 60–6; Bridewell, *The Federal Home Loan Bank*, 170–5; Marvel, *The Federal Home Loan Bank Board*, 23; Russell, *Savings and Loan Associations*, 35, 53–5; "Plight of the Homeowner Burdened with a Mortgage," *The New York Times*, 26 March 1933, sec. 8, 4.

A more immediate problem, however, was the increase in commercial bank failures over the previous six months. Between October 1932 and February 1933, waves of panic and deposit runs forced nearly 6 percent of all commercial banks to cease operations, and significantly these failures were nationwide, affecting both rural and urban areas. In order to preserve the integrity of the banking system, by January 1933 some states began to order shutdowns of all banks by declaring "bank holidays." State officials used any convenient reason to justify their actions, such as the Louisiana bank holiday called to celebrate the sixteenth anniversary of America's breaking of diplomatic relations with Germany during World War I. By March 1, ten states had declared bank holidays, and while these actions may have prevented local deposit runs, in states where banks remained open people feared that their institutions would be the next to initiate other deposit runs. This created a domino effect that ultimately forced dozens of states to enact banking moratoriums, so that on the eve of Roosevelt's inaugural, so many states had declared bank holidays that the nation's banking system was essentially inoperative.[40]

Roosevelt devoted a large portion of his inaugural speech to his plan to deal with the banking crisis. He declared a national bank holiday and called legislators back into session, which began the famous "Hundred Days" Congress. While thrifts and the home loan bank were included in the Roosevelt bank holiday, by March 13 the home loan bank was allowed to reopen and it began immediately making loans to members. This quick response by the Board helped dozens of thrifts meet withdrawal requests, and this action went a long way toward improving the agency's tarnished public image. While this assistance was important, another reason why B&Ls stayed solvent was the support individual members gave their associations. Thrift managers appealed to the cooperative spirit that had helped create the thrift movement and asked members to limit their withdrawals to meeting essential needs such as buying food. As a result, no B&Ls failed during the national bank holiday.[41]

Even though the home loan bank had proven its worth during the national bank holiday, thrift leaders still feared that the White House was intent on terminating what some Roosevelt insiders referred to as the "Hoover banks." Because the term of the FHLBB members expired on March 4, rumors abounded that the expirations would be used as an excuse to abolish the

[40] Sue C. Patrick, *Reform of the Federal Reserve System in the Early 1930s: The Politics of Money and Banking* (New York: Garland Publishing, 1993), 132–4; *Confidential Bulletin* M22 (29 March 1933), quote 2; *Confidential Bulletin* M36 (12 December 1933), 3; Susan Estabrook Kennedy, *The Banking Crisis of 1933* (Lexington: University of Kentucky Press, 1973), 74–7, 214–7.

[41] "*Confidential Bulletin* M20 (4 March 1933), 1–2; *Confidential Bulletin* M21 (7 March 1933), 1–4; *Confidential Bulletin* M22 (29 March 1933), 1–3; "The Crisis and the Strong Measures that are Being Used," *ABAN* 53 (March 1933), 100–1; Henry S. Rosenthal, "We are Facing the Keenest Competition in the History of the Movement," *ABAN* 53 (March 1933), 196–7.

system, and these fears appeared to be confirmed when Roosevelt failed to reappoint any of the original Board members. The new Board consisted of South Carolina Congressman William Stevensen, newspaper publisher John Fahey, and three bankers, none of whom had ties with the thrift movement. Stevensen was chairman, and thrift leaders assumed he was the "hatchet man" who would disassemble the bank. To the surprise of many, instead of ending its existence the White House was ready to make the home loan bank a key element of its plans to provide direct relief to homeowners.[42]

CREATING FEDERAL SAVINGS AND LOAN INSTITUTIONS

One of the first tasks Roosevelt gave the new Board was to design an effective way to give immediate relief to homeowners. Although one flaw in the home loan bank was the requirement of homeowners to apply directly to the home loan bank for a loan, two other problems also needed attention if any direct assistance program were to be feasible. The first involved reducing the risks associated with lending money on properties that were highly leveraged, a situation that resulted from the extensive use of second and third mortgages in the 1920s. The Board had to find a way to not only refinance all the liens, but also reduce the monthly payment of the new mortgage over a longer term. The second problem involved increasing the availability of home loans nationally, since the hundreds of bank and thrift failures left one-third of all counties in the nation without any local source for mortgages.[43]

Administration officials met with the FHLBB on April 2, 1933 to discuss different proposals to implement a direct lending program. This meeting produced a number of ideas, and the task of crafting them into legislation fell to the Board's general counsel Horace Russell, a former president of Atlanta's largest B&L. On April 4, Russell presented his draft of a bill he titled the "Emergency Mortgage Act of 1933." The bill repealed the Couzens direct loan provision, and created a temporary agency operated by the home loan bank to help home lenders refinance individual mortgages. These loans would be made for up to 80 percent of the appraised property value and would be amortized in equal monthly installments for a period not exceeding eighteen years. Homeowners who possessed unencumbered property could also apply for an HOLC cash loan for up to 40 percent of the appraised value. Finally, the bill created a national charter for thrifts to be called "federal savings and loan associations." These privately run thrifts were intended

---

[42] *Confidential Bulletin* M22 (29 March 1933), 3–4; *Confidential Bulletin* M23 (15 April 1933), 2; Russell, *Savings and Loan Associations*, 46–7; "United We Stand – Divided We Fall," *ABAN* 53 (March 1933), 99; Ewalt, *A Business Reborn*, 66–8; Kreutz, *The Way It Happened*, 19–23.

[43] Bridewell, *The Federal Home Loan Bank*, 175–7; Russell, *Savings and Loan Associations*, 54; Ewalt, *A Business Reborn*, 75–6; William Stevenson, "The Homeowners Loan Corporation and the Home Loan Bank System," *Building and Loan Annals, 1933* (Chicago: United States Building and Loan League, 1933), 225.

not to compete with existing B&Ls, but would serve areas that lacked any mortgage institutions. The bill also gave the Board funds to promote their creation, and allowed the government to provide "seed money" of up to $100,000 per association to help this system get started.[44]

When Roosevelt read the Russell draft, he immediately approved it but changed its name to the "Homeowners' Loan Act." He also renamed the mortgage refinance agency to the Homeowners' Loan Corporation (HOLC). On April 13, he sent the bill to Congress, and two weeks later the House overwhelmingly approved it after only 90 minutes of debate. The Senate took longer to consider the bill because of the large volume of pending legislation; but on June 6, after two days of hearings, it also passed the act, which Roosevelt then signed into law a week later. Although congressional action on the Homeowners' Loan Act was unusually fast, it was not because of a lack of controversy. In fact, several legislators objected to the federal savings and loan provision, and they questioned how these associations could give relief to those in immediate danger of losing their homes in a timely manner. They also opposed using public funds to promote federal thrifts, which they viewed as just propaganda for the thrift movement. League leaders, however, urged legislators to view federal thrifts not only as replacements for the thousands of bankrupt lenders, but also as a long-term solution to improve the availability of mortgage finance, noting they will "give more relief to homeowners over the next few years than any other legislation that could be enacted."[45]

As was true with the home loan bank, this new government role in the thrift business was not completely embraced by those in the thrift movement. Some managers feared that federally chartered thrifts would be formed in areas already adequately served by B&Ls and thus increase competition. Other officials, including state regulators, disliked this plan because it was

---

[44] The plan to form a system of national-charter thrifts was the brainchild of Horace Russell, who felt it would be less expensive than the initial White House proposal to create a network of federally operated mortgage associations. It would also would keep the government from entering the direct mortgage market. Bridewell, *The Federal Home Loan Bank*, 179–85; *Confidential Bulletin* M22 (29 March 1933), 2–4; Russell, *Savings and Loan Associations*, 55–6; "Federal Savings and Loans: A Provision of the Homeowners Loan Act," *ABAN*, 53 (October 1933), 502–3; Horace Russell, "Federal Savings and Loan Associations," *Building and Loan Annals 1933*, 21–8.

[45] Government investment in these thrifts was not unique, since the Emergency Banking Act of 1933 allowed the government to invest in the preferred stock of national banks. Bridewell, *The Federal Home Loan Bank*, 182–290; "Aid to Homeowners Sped by Roosevelt," *The New York Times*, 4 April 1933, 1; "Home Mortgages," *The New York Times*, 17 April 1933, 12; "Homeowners Act Reaches Final Stages in Congress," *ABAN* 53 (May 1933), 201; "Home Loan Bank Retained in Bill," *The New York Times*, 30 April 1933, sec 11 and 12, 1. Patrick, *Reform of the Federal Reserve System*, 145–65; Russell, *Savings and Loan Associations*, 56–7; Horace Russell, "Federal Savings and Loan Associations," *Building and Loan Annals 1933*, 21–8; *Confidential Bulletin* M24 (10 May 1933), 2; *Confidential Bulletin* M25 (3 June 1933), 2, 6; *Confidential Bulletin* M26 (1 July 1933), 6–9, quote 8.

an intrusion by the federal government into their affairs. To assuage these concerns, the League received assurances from the Board that it would not grant federal charters lavishly or in an unwise manner. Rather, because these new associations would complement existing thrifts serving areas not covered by other home lenders, the League portrayed them as a way to bring the gospel of thrift to new communities. It also contended that the new "federal" identity would significantly enhance the image and reputation of the thrift business. Finally, League leaders looked to these more standardized institutions as a way to increase the overall uniformity of thrift operations across the country.[46]

SECURING DEPOSIT INSURANCE

Although the Homeowner's Loan Act was the piece of legislation which had the greatest impact on thrifts during the First New Deal, the Banking Act of 1933 was another key measure that had an indirect effect on the movement. While this law gave thrifts a competitive advantage by restricting the ability of banks to pay interest on savings, its creation of the Federal Deposit Insurance Corporation (FDIC) to insure commercial bank deposits also placed thrifts at a disadvantage. The FDIC, however, was highly controversial, and at first the banking community vehemently opposed it. The Roosevelt Administration also considered it unworkable, but supported it because of pressure from the public and the bill's cosponsor, Rep. Henry Steagall (D-AL). Since the law required all Federal Reserve members to join the FDIC, within a year nearly all commercial banks had coverage, and the psychological effect of this on the nation was profound. By giving depositors assurances that they would not lose their money if an insured institution failed, the FDIC helped restore public confidence in the national banking system. Evidence of this is seen in the fact that while 1,275 Federal Reserve member banks failed in 1933 alone, just 21 member banks became insolvent over the next six years.[47]

Like most bankers, Bodfish initially thought the FDIC was "essentially an unwise and unsound program" and took a wait-and-see attitude on whether to seek deposit insurance for thrifts. By the end of 1933, the effect of the FDIC

---

[46] Russell, *Savings and Loan Associations*, 62–3; *Confidential Bulletin* M23 (15 April 1933), 3; *Confidential Bulletin* M28 (21 July 1933), 9; Philip Lieber, "In Double Harness," *ABAN* 53 (December 1933), 549; Philip Lieber, "Emphasize the Federal Savings and Loan Idea," *ABAN* 53 (May 1933), 213, 239; M. E. Bristow, "Federalization of Building and Loan Associations," *Building and Loan Annals 1934*, 329–32.

[47] Patrick, *Reform of the Federal Reserve System*, 168–71; Burns, *The American Banking Community and New Deal Banking Reforms, 1933–1935* (Westport, CT: Greenwood Press, 1974), 66–8, 85–93; Morton Bodfish, "Glass Bill Raises Important Issues," *ABAN* (May 1932), 212, 234; Milton Friedman and Anna Schwartz, *A Monetary History of the United States, 1867–1960* (Princeton: Princeton University Press, 1963), chapter 7.

on the public caused the League executive manager to change his mind, noting if "commercial bank savings are insured, then should not thrifts . . . enjoy the same privileges?" This desire to stay competitive with banks led the League to meet with the FHLBB in November 1933 to discuss a system of deposit insurance for B&Ls. While gaining parity with commercial banks was one goal for thrift leaders, they also saw deposit insurance as a way of increasing membership in the home loan bank, spur the creation of federal associations, and reduce the flight of deposits from thrifts to insured commercial banks. From these meetings, Board counsel Russell outlined a plan for a Federal Savings and Loan Insurance Corporation (FSLIC), which the League reviewed in February 1934.[48]

Although both the FSLIC and FDIC insured consumer deposits, there were several important differences between the two programs. First, the FSLIC was under the control of the Board, whereas the FDIC was an autonomous agency. Second, since thrifts were not required to pay deposits on demand, the FSLIC would also pay off depositors within three years; in contrast, the FDIC made immediate payments since it insured demand accounts. Third, the only associations required to join the FSLIC were those with federal charters, which reflected the fear that state regulators would put troubled state-chartered thrifts into involuntary liquidation and let the FSLIC pay off depositors. The one significant similarity between the two programs was that all FSLIC members would have to build their reserves to equal 5 percent of their assets. While the League generally supported this plan, it strongly objected to the reserve requirement; but Russell insisted it should not be changed since it would force managers to take greater responsibility for their lending decisions and also improve public confidence in insured thrifts. Consequently, this one section caused the League to give the FSLIC a weak endorsement saying, "if we must have an insurance corporation, this is the right approach."[49]

While the White House favored thrift insurance, its greater concern was the continued doldrums in the housing industries. In 1933, new mortgages and home improvement loans were just 25 percent and 12.5 percent, respectively, of pre-depression levels. Furthermore, an estimated two million housing industry workers were still without jobs. In light of these facts, the Roosevelt Administration sidetracked consideration of thrift deposit insurance and focused instead on creating a program federal mortgage insurance to increase home lending. The rationale behind this decision was that if the risk of loss due to foreclosure could be minimized, lenders would make more loans, and in turn generate more jobs. The initial administration

---

[48] *Confidential Bulletin* M22 (29 March 1933), quotes 2; *Confidential Bulletin* M36 (12 December 1933), 3; Bridewell, *The Federal Home Loan Bank*, 364–77; Russell, *Savings and Loan Associations*, 97–8.

[49] Ewalt, *A Business Reborn*, 97–9, Quote 98; I. Friedlander, "Business Stimulating Possibilities of Building and Loan Insurance Plan," *ABAN* 54 (May 1934), 205–6.

plan involved backing mortgages with a federal guarantee that entitled lenders who foreclosed on an insured loan to receive a bond equal to the unpaid principal. This bond would then be paid off over the original mortgage term. Because this represented a radical extension of government involvement in home finance, Russell roundly condemned it, fearing also that it would lead to speculative building and unnecessary foreclosures as a way to receive guaranteed government funds.[50]

Nonetheless, the administration wanted some form of mortgage insurance, and the Board directed Russell to prepare the desired legislation. The result was the National Housing Act of 1934, which consisted of four major sections. Title I created a mortgage insurance program that guaranteed payment of a home loan in an amount of up to the appraised value of the underlying security. Title II authorized the government to charter tax-exempt national mortgage associations to make loans directly to home buyers as well as invest in mortgages. Title III established a voluntary deposit insurance program that any B&L could join, while Title IV authorized the Board to make loans for home improvements and repair projects. This last section was part of a broader administration plan for a government-sponsored home modernization drive that would hopefully increase employment.[51]

The bill also created a new government agency, the Federal Housing Administration (FHA), to administer all the programs, with the exception of the FSLIC which the Board would control. The White House insisted on this separate housing agency primarily because it would diffuse the power of the FHLBB, which was already coming under the influence of the League. While the administration was wary of this close relationship, thrift leaders such as Bodfish thought that because thrifts owned the individual home loan banks, they should also control how they were managed. In fact, when Bodfish was a Board member, he personally selected several regional bank officers and developed a list of criteria for choosing future officials as a way of preventing "liberalizing" forces from taking over. Consequently, given the dislike of the National Housing Act by the League, it was not surprising that the administration feared the Board would not administer these programs in a wholehearted manner.[52]

---

[50] Bridewell, *The Federal Home Loan Bank*, 389–96, *Confidential Bulletin* M38 (22 February 1934), 1–2; Edward Baltz, "Building and Loan and the Distressed Condition of the Construction Industry," *ABAN* 54 (February 1934), 76–8; "Building Survey Shows Home Building Ready to Go if Federal Loans are Offered," *American Builder* (February 1934), 62–5; Russell, *Savings and Loan Associations*, 84–7.

[51] Memorandum from the National Emergency Council, 4 May 1934, cited in Bridewell, *The Federal Home Loan Bank*, 411–7; "Congress Pushes Home Renovation," *Washington Star*, 15 May 1934), 3; Russell, *Savings and Loan Associations*, 103–6; Ewalt, *A Business Reborn*, 97, 99–100.

[52] *Confidential Bulletin* S19 (29 July 1933), Quotes 1; Charles W. Thompson, "Relations with the Federal Home Loan Bank Board," *Building and Loan Annals, 1933*, 241; Marvell, *The Federal Home Loan Bank Board*, 27–28; Theobald, *Forty-Five Years*, 33–5, 64–6.

Roosevelt sent the National Housing Act to Congress on May 14, 1934, and the House Banking and Currency Committee held hearings shortly thereafter. While the League disliked the idea of mortgage insurance, it considered the national mortgage associations the greatest threat to their business. The main reason for this fear was that these associations would be tax exempt, which was one of the few advantages B&Ls had over other mortgage lenders. Bodfish lobbied so hard to prevent the creation of these potential competitors that when the Committee sent the bill to the full House on June 12, the national mortgage association section had been removed and replaced with a provision to increase the HOLC investment in federal savings and loans from $100 million to $500 million. Because the current session was almost over, the revised bill was made a special order of business which limited debate to four hours. Despite this restriction, the debate was lively, acrimonious, and focused on League-inspired changes, which some referred to as the "Bodfish Amendment."[53]

Unlike earlier congressional debates on thrift bills, in which legislators generally praised Bodfish and the movement, the mood in the House was decidedly hostile toward the League. Representatives accused the Committee of abandoning the administration by submitting a bill that was the product of a self-serving thrift lobby. As a result, the full House rejected the Committee's revisions to Title II and restored the original White House proposal. One sign of anti-League sentiment was that Rep. Reilly, who supported the movement and was instrumental in passing the Home Loan Bank Act, was among those voting to drop the Bodfish Amendment. In the Senate, support for the national mortgage association idea was strong, and some senators asserted that it would help thrifts. According to Sen. Robert Bulkley (D-OH), "building-and-loan associations at first feared that active competition would be started by the proposed mortgage associations . . . [But now] at least a large part of the building-and-loan associations feel that the competition will not be dangerous." Roosevelt finally signed the National Housing Act into law on June 27, 1934.[54]

While the League did manage to modify the final bill in their favor by preventing the national mortgage associations from making direct loans and

[53] *Confidential Bulletin* M40 (19 March 1934), 4–5; *Confidential Bulletin* M41 (24 April 1934), 4; *Confidential Bulletin* M42 (15 May 1934), 1–3; *Confidential Bulletin* M44 (20 June 1934), Addenda 1, "Report Favors Housing Bill Widely Altered," *Washington Star*, 9 June 1934, 4.

[54] Bridewell, *The Federal Home Loan Bank*, 440–531, quote 523; *Confidential Bulletin* S25 (5 June 1934), 1–2; *Confidential Bulletin* M43 (26 May 1934), 1–2; *Confidential Bulletin*, M44, (20 June 1934), 3; "Roosevelt Ban Put on Altered Housing Bill," *New York Herald-Tribune*, 10 June 1934, 2; "Roosevelt Wins First Test Vote on Housing Bill," *New York Herald-Tribune*, 13 June 1934, 3; "Senate and House Approve Bill in Roosevelt Form," *The New York Times*, 19 June 1934, 35; "Report of the Federal Legislative Committee, National Housing Act," *Building and Loan Annals*, 1934, 522–3; "The NHA Becomes Law," *Architectural Forum* 61 (July 1934), 66.

making them taxable businesses, the overall reaction to the Act from the movement was one of fear and foreboding. Thrift leaders considered mortgage insurance an expensive program that would lead to fraud and unsound financial practices. Bodfish in particular believed that the law was the first step toward socialism in housing in which the government ultimately would control all aspects of home finance. The League's greatest concern, however, lay in how successful the national mortgage associations would be. Aside from problems of competition, the League feared that the access these associations would have to low-cost government funds would drive down all mortgage rates and hurt thrift profitability. Despite such fundamental concerns, the League pledged to support the law and hoped for the best regarding its implementation.[55]

One consequence of the struggle to pass the National Housing Act was that Bodfish gained greater national recognition and even notoriety, given his ability to alter the bill during the House hearings. The Roosevelt Administration was incensed at what Bodfish did, and late in 1934 it called for an investigation of what it called a powerful and influential thrift lobby. Much to its chagrin, the White House did not find instances of unethical influence peddling, but rather legitimate lobbying designed to protect the interests of B&Ls. In fact, both friends and enemies of Bodfish on Capitol Hill praised him as a talented and effective lobbyist. The most appreciative group, however, was the League, and following passage of each law its leaders heaped praise on their executive manager. They not only recognized his ability to influence the creation of thrift laws, but lauded his work to promote the work of B&Ls among legislators. This work also assisted Bodfish's rise to power within the League, and helped in his other efforts to transform and modernize the character and nature of the thrift movement.[56]

CONCLUSIONS

By the end of 1934, the thrift movement was governed by a comprehensive system of federal regulations, complementing existing state regulations.

---

[55] Russell, *Savings and Loan Associations*, 98–9; Ewalt, *A Business Reborn*, 98–9; "Insurance and Building and Loan Shares and Mortgage Insurance," *ABAN*, 54 (June 1934), 248; *Confidential Bulletin*, M44 (20 June 1934), 1–2, 4; "Housing Bills Socialism Hit by Loan Chief," *Washington Post*, 23 May 1934, 2; "Private Handling of Housing Fought," *Philadelphia Record*, 12 June 1934, 5; I. Friedlander, "Building and Loan and National Housing Act,"*ABAN*, 54 (July 1934), 293–4; "How Building and Loan Leaders View the National Housing Act," *ABAN*, 54 (August 1934), 377; *Confidential Bulletin* M44 (20 June 1934), 4; J. Howard Aubrey, "Mutual Mortgage Insurance and National Mortgage Associations" *Building and Loan Annals 1934*, 36–9.

[56] Friedlander, "Building and Loan and National Housing Act," 293; *Confidential Bulletin* M44 (20 June 1934), 4; Philip Lieber, "Presidential Address," *Building and Loan Annals, 1934*, 397–8, 406–8; Theobald, *Forty-Five Years*, 26–9.

In principle, League leaders approved of government oversight, since they viewed it as a way of accomplishing certain goals that would improve their movement as a whole. Laws governing how a B&L should be organized and operated led to greater uniformity among associations and helped generate greater public confidence in the institutions. While the thrift movement generally supported state oversight, initially the pursuit of federal oversight was half-hearted at best. Prior to 1930, the only major federal issue with which B&Ls concerned themselves was taxation, and the League was vigilant in making sure all thrifts were exempt from federal taxes. The major reason for this lack of interest in federal oversight was that thrifts were local institutions that they felt should be regulated by the states.

This attitude of indifference changed, however, during the Great Depression when economic upheaval ravaged all financial businesses. As unemployed homeowners faced the risk of foreclosure, President Hoover, who was himself a supporter of the thrift movement, decided in 1931 to create a federal home loan bank as a way of alleviating these hardships. The League, while initially hesitant, eventually jumped on Board and worked hard for passage of the Federal Home Loan Bank Act. While deteriorating financial conditions for thrifts were important in shifting opinions, another critical factor was that the League's new executive director, Morton Bodfish, was able to work with legislators to make sure the new bank would serve the interests of the movement. In fact, his role was so significant that Hoover appointed Bodfish to serve on the first Board. Unfortunately, the new home loan bank met with operational problems, and its inability to meet the pressing demands of homeowners to refinance mortgages almost led to its demise.

The other two major elements of federal involvement in the thrift business came during the Roosevelt Administration. The first of these was the creation of a system of federally chartered thrifts to serve areas without sources for mortgages. The federal identity of these thrifts also enhanced the status of the movement and had the potential to introduce more uniform business practices. The idea of federal charters for thrifts was part of the Homeowner's Loan Act of 1933, a law that also improved the home loan bank by creating the Homeowner's Loan Corporation to assume responsibility for making loans to individuals. The last aspect of federal oversight of the movement was the creation of a deposit insurance under the National Housing Act in 1934. While thrift leaders were skeptical of deposit insurance prior to 1933, the success of the FDIC convinced them of the desirability of a similar system for B&Ls.

Although the majority of B&Ls were either ambivalent to or resisted federal oversight of their business, the creation of a reserve bank, federal charters and deposit insurance were very important milestones. In just two years, the thrift movement acquired a regulatory system that had taken banks more than sixty years to obtain. Many of these accomplishments resulted from the work of the League and in particular Bodfish. Bodfish's attention to lobbying key Congressmen helped ensure that federal oversight would be favorable to the interests of B&Ls and be one that would help the movement grow and prosper. Moreover, this work was just one aspect of the League's broader efforts to institute change during the 1930s. Under the leadership of Bodfish, the League would finally achieve success in its long-sought goal of unifying the movement, and in turn transforming it into an industry.

4

THE MOVEMENT BECOMES AN INDUSTRY, 1930–1945

The Great Depression and World War II were pivotal in the development of a modern thrift business. The broad changes that occurred during this period came in three major areas. The first of these involved improvements in the structure of the thrift trade association. Under the leadership of its executive manager Morton Bodfish, the League became better organized and more useful to its members through the development of new programs designed to improve thrift business practices. At the same time, Bodfish and the League helped transform the mindset of thrift leaders to think of their business less as a movement and more as an industry, in part by urging associations to adopt the common term "savings and loan" to replace the older "building and loan" nomenclature. A second body of changes affecting the thrift business centered on the consequences of the Great Depression. While the financial turmoil associated with deposit runs and loan foreclosures led to a number of thrift failures, most associations survived the period, and this experience strengthened the industry by improving the financial acumen of most managers. The final major changes affecting thrifts involved the work of the newly created federal regulatory system, including the Federal Home Loan Bank Board, the Federal Savings and Loan Insurance Corporation, and the system of federal charters for savings and loans. Each program steadily attracted members, and by the end of World War II they were firmly established as part of the American financial system. This success resulted in part from the leadership of the Board and its chairman John Fahey, who petitioned Congress to modify these programs to improve their effectiveness. Combined, these three areas of change helped enable the thrift business to experience virtually uninterrupted prosperity for nearly two decades following the end of the war.

BODFISH AND THE LEAGUE

The 1930s saw a number of major changes for thrifts, not the least of which was the development of a trade association better equipped to meet the needs of its members. The League became a well-regarded and multifaceted organization by the end of the decade, with much of this improvement due to its executive manager, Morton Bodfish. Bodfish was twenty-seven years old when he joined the League in 1929, but he already had a broad understanding of real estate finance. His mission as manager was to unleash the potential of the thrift business, which he likened to a sleeping giant. However, to achieve this goal, he first had to transform the League into an efficient organization capable of handling a variety of tasks. For years, the League was a loosely run entity with mostly part-time employees. The new executive manager created the first organization chart for the trade group, which included several new positions that were to be staffed by experienced executives. To improve the League's long-term strategic planning capacity, Bodfish expanded the number of standing committees and encouraged more leaders from individual B&Ls to serve as members.[1]

In addition to formalizing its structure, the League improved the level of its communications with members. It expanded the content of its monthly trade journal, and began to publish its annual convention proceedings as a professionally edited volume instead of a verbatim transcript. Bodfish formed a full-time publicity department to coordinate releases to newspapers and national wire services, and began two monthly newsletters: the *Confidential Bulletin*, which focused on federal legislative and regulatory developments, and the *Legal Bulletin*, which concentrated on state and federal litigation affecting thrifts. Most of these publications were directed to member thrifts, but the League also distributed them to schools, libraries, legislators, and chambers of commerce to heighten the visibility of thrift work and make people more aware of thrift business activities.[2]

Finally, Bodfish worked hard to increase the number of associations which belonged to the League. Although thrift trade associations often flourished at the state, regional, and even local levels, the national association had trouble attracting members, since many managers did not feel that the benefits of membership justified the costs. Just 12 percent of all thrifts were League members by 1931, and this low participation hurt the credibility of

[1] Harold Donaldson, "Our National Organization," *American Building Association News* [hereafter *ABAN*] 55 (May 1935), 217–8; R. Holtby Myers, "Presidential Address," *Building and Loan Annals, 1931* (Chicago: United States Building and Loan League, 1931), 908–9; Fred G. Sticker, "Practical Program for Future League Work," *ABAN* 55 (August 1935), 237–9; Ernest Hale, "Reviewing the Past Ten Years," *American Savings and Loan News* [hereafter *ASLN*] (June 1940), 249–52; Morton Bodfish and A. D. Theobald, *Savings and Loan Principles* (New York: Prentice-Hall, 1938), 595–8; A. D. Theobald, *Forty-Five Years on the Up Escalator* (Chicago: privately published, 1979), 86–8.

[2] Philip Lieber, "President' Annual Address," *Building and Loan Annals, 1934* (Chicago: United States Building and Loan League, 1934), 389–91; I. Friedlander, "President's Annual Address," *Building and Loan Annals, 1935* (Chicago: United States League of Building and Loan Associations, 1935), 419; Harold Donaldson, "What the National Organization Has to Offer," *ABAN* 56 (July 1936), 309–11; "Anniversary Reflections," *ASLN* 60 (January 1940), 2.

its leaders who testified for the passage of federal regulation. To change this, Bodfish and League officials literally hounded managers to join the trade association, and as the legislative influence of the League led to the passage of favorable laws, thrifts began to join in large numbers. By 1935, 42 percent of all associations were part of the League, and these members accounted for more than 75 percent of total thrift assets. This growth also made the League financially secure, giving it the ability to fund its new programs.[3]

While Bodfish helped make the League a more powerful organization, his work also increased his own standing within the thrift business. The executive manager influenced the selection of state League leaders, and he showed them how to use grassroots lobbying techniques such as letter writing campaigns to secure favorable legislation. These activities proved so successful and gained such an awesome reputation that the mere threat of their use was enough to sway wavering legislators. Bodfish also tried to affect the direction of federal oversight, and during his brief tenure on the Federal Home Loan Bank Board (FHLBB) he made sure that the twelve reserve banks were controlled by people who were "loyal organization men." Even after leaving the Board, federal officials continued to consult with Bodfish before making appointments or issuing new regulations. The net effect of this work at the local, state, and national levels was the creation of a virtual "Bodfish machine" of thrift leaders who supported the vision of the executive manager.[4]

MOVING TOWARD OPERATIONAL UNIFORMITY

The second major goal of the League was to improve the level of uniformity and standardization of business practices within the thrift business. To do this, it focused primarily on improving management education, thrift accounting practices, and real estate appraisal techniques. A key element

---

3 Thomas Fitzmorris, "Advantages of National and State Leagues," *Financial Review and American Building Association News* 18 (May 1899), 165; J. G. Elder, "The Benefits to be Derived from Membership in the State and United States Building and Loan League," *ABAN* 26 (October 1907), 195; Joseph McNamee, "The Necessity and Value of Organization in Building and Loan Work," *ABAN*, 35 (November 1915), 503–5; "Why Not Join a League?" *ABAN* 41 (September 1921), 390; William Best, "Growing Unity of the Building and Loan Business," *ABAN* 52 (May 1932), 216–17; John R. B. Byers, "How to Change the Rope of Sand into a Rope of Steel," *ABAN* 53 (April 1933), 153, 181; "No More Free Rides," *ABAN* 53 (August 1933), 344; "United States Building and Loan League Launches Membership Campaign," *ABAN* 54 (August 1933), 345; J. J. O'Malley, "The Reasons Why Your Association Should be a National Member," *ABAN* 53 (February 1934), 71–2; "Membership Campaign Shows Results," *ABAN* 55 (October 1935), 453.

4 Oscar Kreutz, *The Way It Happened* (St. Petersburg, FL: St. Petersburg Printing Co., 1972), 68; I. Friedlander, "Membership," *Building and Loan Annals 1933* (Chicago: United States Building and Loan League, 1933), 73–4; "Leaders in Convention Plans for 1932: A Biographical Sketch," *ABAN* 52 (July 1932), 325; "The NHA Becomes Law," *Architectural Review* 77 (July 1934), 36; A. D. Theobald, *Forty-Five Years*, 130.

in achieving this standardization was the American Savings and Loan Institute (ASLI), formed in the mid-1920s and made a League affiliate in 1930. The need for increased financial education became apparent during the Great Depression, which had "revealed that [thrifts], like all cooperatives and quasi-public enterprises, suffer from a lack of skilled management and staff services." The ASLI met this challenge in 1939 with the creation of the Graduate School of Savings and Loan. Held at Northwestern University during the summer, this three-year program offered a complete curriculum of courses ranging from accounting and business forecasting to personnel management and thrift law. It soon had a positive reputation for its education program, and eventually became a training center for academicians and others wanting to know more about thrift business practices.[5]

Another major project of the ASLI was creating a standardized thrift accounting system. Because state laws rarely addressed accounting issues, associations had over time developed a myriad of financial procedures. While this was not necessarily a major business problem, the trade association did see this lack of uniformity as detrimental to their business image. In 1934, the League created the Accounting Division, which designed a series of standardized reporting forms that the FHLBB and thirty states later adopted for their own use. In 1936, the ASLI expanded on this work by organizing the first standard accounting system that created uniform classifications for all types of thrift assets, liabilities, and equity. Hailed by the League as "the most significant nonlegislative work accomplished by the organized savings and loan business in many years," this plan soon became the standard for all associations. This system consisted of a balance sheet, a profit and loss report, and a reconciliation of net worth, which were laid out in such precise detail that the level of financial reporting accuracy rose markedly. This system was also a boon to the League and regulators since it produced a wealth of new industry data.[6]

---

[5] Ernest Hale, "Presidential Address," *Building and Loan Annals, 1930* (Chicago: United States Building and Loan League, 1930), 533–4; Clarence T. Rice, "The Institute Widens Its Service," *ABAN* 53 (February 1933), 67; Josephine Hedges Ewalt, *A Business Reborn: The Savings and Loan Industry, 1930–1960* (Chicago: American Savings and Loan Institute Press, 1962), 126, 152; "Savings Bodies Need Trained Officials," *The New York Times,* 16 October 1938, sec. 10, 4; Lawrence Marston, "Another Step Towards Qualifying Executives," *ABAN* 56 (April 1936), 173–4; John Sierocinsky, "Progress in Educating Future Leaders," *ABAN* 57 (August 1937), 445; Justin Langille, "Savings and Loan Management as a Professional Career," *Building and Loan Annals, 1937* (Chicago: United States Building and Loan League, 1937), 184–7; Morton Bodfish, *Depression Experience of Savings and Loan Associations in the United States* (n.p., September 1935), quote 10; Ewalt, *A Business Reborn,* 283; "Savings and Loan Graduate Schools," *Federal Home Loan Bank Review* [hereafter *FHLB Review*] 7 (October 1940), 11–12.

[6] L. R. Richards, "The Place of the Accountant and Accountancy in Our Business," *ABAN* 52 (December 1932), 537, 559; "Standard Report Forms for Savings and Loan Associations," *FHLB Review* 2 (December 1935), 69–73; John R. B. Byers, "What Should a Model Savings, Building and Loan Accounting System Do," *ABAN* 54 (April 1934), 69–70; "A Forward Step

A final project of the Institute focused on designing a uniform real estate appraisal system that all associations could use. Although obtaining an accurate property value was critical to any mortgage lending decision, making a valuation was traditionally regarded as more of an art than a science. Most B&L appraisals were completed by directors with real estate or construction backgrounds; but because they often lacked formal training in appraising, their reports were usually cursory reviews of the property and neighborhood. This lack of detail reflected the fact that lenders generally considered the moral risk of a borrower to be as important, if not more so, than the value of the underlying collateral. As a result, loan reports frequently contained interviews with friends, creditors, or employers of the applicant. Even some League leaders felt that "the value of a property should [only] be a safeguard . . . in case the judgement of the borrower as a credit risk should prove wrong."[7]

In 1926, real estate appraising became a more distinct and recognized profession when the National Association of Real Estate Boards formed the American Institute of Real Estate Appraisers (AIREA) to design the first accreditation system for appraisers. Unfortunately, because most of its members were with banks or insurance companies, the AIREA gave little attention to improving residential appraisal practices. In 1931, the League addressed this problem by forming the Appraisal Division, which created uniform guidelines for appraising residential real estate, as well as a standard appraisal form used by federal regulators. In 1934, the League sponsored the formation of the Society of Real Estate Appraisers to design specialized education programs in residential appraising, as well as a separate accreditation system and code of ethics.[8]

towards Standardized Accounting," *ABAN* 55 (December 1935), 559–60; James T. Wilkes, "Background of the New Model Accounting System," and R. F. DuBois, "Installing the New Accounting System," *Building and Loan Annals, 1935*, 137–46, 147–53; "Standard Report Forms for Savings and Loan Associations," *FHLB Review* 2 (December 1935), 69–73; Walter J. Sherry, "Financial Statements for Management," *ABAN* 57 (December 1937), 673–8; "Standard Reports and Accounting Systems for Savings and Loan Associations," *FHLB Review* 2 (August 1936), 374–6; "Report of the Accounting Division," *Building and Loan Annals, 1937*, 425–33, quote 425.

7 Letter from A. D. Theobald, to Arthur Mertzke, May 24, 1932, and Richard B. Thift, "Appraisal Machinery of Building and Loan Associations in Washington, D.C.," 1–4; Finance Committee, Appraising; White House Conference on Home Building and Home Ownership; Herbert Hoover Presidential Library; Bodfish and Theobald, *Savings and Loan Principles*, 197–202, 215; Marc A. Weiss, *The Rise of the Community Builders: The American Real Estate Industry and Urban Land Planning* (New York: Columbia University Press, 1987), 31–6; "Calls Character Security Value," *The New York Times*, 6 June 1937, sec. 9, quote 6.

8 Edwin Einstein, "The Society for Real Estate Appraisers," *ABAN* 55 (November 1935), 523–4; Fred T. Greene, "Significant Post-Depression Changes in Savings and Loan Practices," *Journal of Land and Public Utility Economics* 16 (February 1940), 31–4; Ewalt, *A Business Reborn*, 125; Bodfish and Theobald, *Savings and Loan Principles*, 197–202, 215; Edwin Einstein, "The Society for Real Estate Appraisers," *ABAN* 54 (December 1934), 549–50; H. O. Walther,

THE LEAGUE AND THRIFT ADVERTISING

The third major objective of the League in the 1930s was to improve the overall public impression of thrifts, primarily by encouraging greater advertising and publicity. A 1934 survey found that, given a choice of different forms of investment, consumers ranked building and loan shares next to last in terms of desirability. Furthermore, only 10 percent of respondents would recommend a thrift investment to others. Even more troublesome to League leaders was that just 29 percent would obtain a home loan from a thrift, while nearly half would use a commercial bank. To change this perception the League emphasized to managers the importance of well-designed advertising, and in 1935 it organized the Advertising Division to assist in this effort. One project of the division involved creating generic advertising packages that thrifts could have customized for their association. It also helped managers produce advertising for special events like office openings, dividend declarations, or anniversaries.[9]

In addition to these forms of local advertising, the League wanted thrifts to participate in regional and national publicity campaigns. Greater use of radio advertising was an important way to achieve this, and by 1940 nearly 20 percent of all money in thrift publicity budgets was spent on this medium. State thrift trade associations also cooperated to produce regional campaigns in traditional print media. Unfortunately, the League had little success in producing a national campaign because of the high costs involved. This changed, however, in 1937, when the League launched its first national advertising program that targeted residential professionals including Realtors, architects, and builders. The advertising division placed advertisements in building trade publications that detailed the benefits of thrift financing, and urged these housing "middlemen" to support "your *local* savings or building and loan association."[10]

"Residential Appraisers' Society Appeals to New Group," *ABAN* 56 (March 1936), 116; *Confidential Bulletin of the United States Building and Loan League* [hereafter *Confidential Bulletin*] M77 (30 May 1937), 7–8.

9 Fred T. Greene, "What Twenty Four Hundred People Said about Building and Loan," *ABAN* 54 (December 1934), 545–6; Ross H. Ryder, "Your Best Friends Won't Tell You," *ABAN* 56 (December 1936), 525–6; "Building and Loans are Mirrored," *Architectural Forum* 61, suppl. 36 (October 1934), 36; "Advertising and Publicity for Federal Savings and Loan Associations," *FHLB Review* 1 (January 1935), 202; "Window Displays and Outdoor Advertising for Savings and Loan Associations," *FHLB Review* 4 (July 1938), 362–5; "Publicity Department Utilizes 100th Anniversary in Getting Editorial Comment," *Ohio League Section of ABAN* 51 (January 1931), i–iii; "Announcement of Dividends Occasion for Effective Advertising," *FHLB Review* 4 (December 1937), 82–4.

10 "Building and Loan Airs Its Advertising Problems," *ABAN* 55 (December 1935), 553–4; Gustav Flexner, "Business Development by Radio," *Building and Loan Annals, 1935*, 168–9; "Radio Advertising by Savings and Loan Associations," *FHLB Review* 7 (October 1940), 3–5; "Cooperative Advertising," *FHLB Review* 4 (June 1938), 322–4; "B-L Takes First Step Towards National Advertising Campaign," *ABAN* 54 (January 1934), 29–30; *Confidential*

The focus and content of thrift advertising also changed in the 1930s. The hard times of the depression required managers to stress the financial soundness of their organizations, and their willingness to lend money in the community. Another important message in thrift advertising was that members often knew and had access to the officers, which gave them a strong degree of agency and confidence in their associations. The League urged associations to "tell about your reserves, tell about your management, the standing of your directors [and] do it all in a positive, aggressive, confident and 'we are doing business as usual' manner." It also wanted managers to tout their participation in the federal home loan bank and deposit insurance systems as a way to further highlight their commitment to a safe and sound management. While such recommendations made practical business sense, the League also hoped that an emphasis on financial integrity and managerial expertise would professionalize the image of thrifts.[11]

THE "B&L" BECOMES THE "S&L"

The fourth major objective of Bodfish and the League was to modernize the way in which thrift executives viewed themselves and their business. Since the nineteenth century, thrift leaders had consistently referred to their business as a social and financial self-help movement. The League consciously linked its mission of encouraging thrift and home ownership to patriotism, personal liberty, and community values – an attitude neatly summarized in its slogan, "The American Home. The Safeguard of American Liberties." Furthermore, people often served as thrift managers out of a sense of service to the members and their community. Given these beliefs, it is not surprising that the League traditionally glorified its work as an altruistic mission that improved personal morals and the general welfare of the nation. In many ways, thrift leaders wanted the public to think of these associations more like religious institutions than as financial ones.[12]

Bulletin M45 (12 July 1934), 14; *Confidential Bulletin* M90 (21 December 1938), 3–4; Ewalt, *A Business Reborn*, 110–11, 126–8, 161–2.

[11] Louis V. Sams Jr., "Balance Sheet Advertising," *ABAN* 55 (February 1935), 79; Philip Lieber, "Combating the Insidious Propaganda Directed at Building and Loan," *ABAN* 54 (February 1934), 59–62; I. Friedlander, "President's Annual Address," *Building and Loan Annals 1935*, 352; "Truth in Savings and Loan Advertising," *FHLB Review* 1 (September 1935), 441–2; "Keeping to the Facts in Savings and Loan Advertising," *FHLB Review* 2 (December 1935), 85–6; *Confidential Bulletin* M24 (10 May 1933), quote 6; Ewalt, *A Business Reborn*, 179.

[12] William Pieplow, *Century Lessons of Building and Loan Associations* (Appleton, WI: C. C. Nelson Publishing, 1931), 11–13, 31–2, 56–7; George McKinnis, "Building and Loan as a Moral Force," *Proceedings of the Twenty-Ninth Annual Convention of the United States League of Local Building and Loan Associations* (Chicago: American Building Association New Press, 1921), 74–8; T. L. Mathews, "The Spirit of the Building and Loan Association," *Proceedings of the Thirty-Third Annual Convention of the United States League of Local Building and Loan Associations* (Chicago: American Building Association News Press, 1925), 143–5.

The rapid expansion of the thrift business during the 1920s led some observers to question the effectiveness of maintaining this type of image. *Business Week* noted wryly that "the 'movement' – they still call it that – is imbued with a tinge of evangelism," implying that thrifts were not on a par with other financial institutions like banks. Another critic chided the League for "relying too much on sentiment and moralizing for support." At the same time, the inclusion of thrifts under federal regulation had brought greater attention to B&Ls as distinct financial businesses. As a result, some thrift leaders began to tone down their references to "the movement," and Bodfish was among them. He noted in 1935 that "while the thrift and home financing institutions may be appropriately referred to in their social significance as a 'movement' there seems to be a definite need... to develop the concept of these institutions as a business. While the business remains essentially cooperative and quasi-public, it must be continued as a business procedure with the same demands for skill and managerial ability which characterize any business enterprise." Such an attitude was reflected in his efforts to have the League take the lead in professionalizing and standardizing the thrift business.[13]

Another sign of how thrift leaders were trying to change their identity away from a movement toward a financial industry, lay in their efforts to get all associations to adopt uniform nomenclature. For decades, thrifts had used a wide variety of descriptive association names, but by 1933 the creation of the federal savings and loan system led to a concerted campaign to persuade all thrifts to adopt the term "savings and loan" in their names. According to Bodfish, "the opinion is gradually developing that the term 'savings and loan'... is the more appropriate since it emphasizes the investment and systematic savings phase as well as the provision for home ownership." To encourage these efforts, the League changed its name to the United States Savings and Loan League in 1939. While Massachusetts thrifts continued to be called "cooperative banks," associations in nearly every other state dropped the older term "building and loan" in favor of "savings and loan." By the end of World War II the transition was virtually complete, marking another major step toward greater industry unity.[14]

---

[13] In 1933 the League drafted a Uniform Savings and Loan Act as a way to encourage standardized state regulations. Henry S. Rosenthal, "A Plan for Better Public Relations," *ABAN* 56 (July 1936), 291–2; "Building and Loan Program Aims to Get More for Homeowners," *Business Week*, 30 July 1930, quote 22; A. S. Keister, "What's Wrong with Building and Loan?" *ABAN* 49 (October 1929), quote 634; "Building and Loan Still – Of the People; By the People and For the People," *ABAN* 54 (March 1934), 38; "Bankers and Building and Loan Men," *American Bankers Association Journal* 26 (June 1934), 75; Bodfish, *Depression Experience*, quote 1; Bodfish and Theobald, *Savings and Loan Principles*, 637–43; "Ask Uniform Laws for Loan Bodies," *The New York Times*, 21 March 1937, sec. 9, 1.

[14] The League changed its name to the United States Building and Loan League in 1929. Isabella F. Henderson, "What's In a Name? There Should Be a Lot," *ABAN* 51 (February 1931), 82;

EXERCISING THE REGULATORY MACHINE

While the League worked to modernize and unify the S&L industry during the 1930s, the government focused on establishing its new role in home finance through the Federal Home Loan Bank, the Federal Savings and Loan Insurance Corporation (FSLIC), and the federal savings and loan system. Even though the League strongly supported the home loan bank, initially few thrifts became members, primarily because managers were not convinced they needed a reserve bank. As a result, after four years of operation just 33 percent of all S&Ls representing 49 percent of total industry assets were home loan bank members. Over the next five years, however, membership increased steadily, and by 1941 associations representing more than 90 percent of S&L assets were part of the home loan bank. Still, many smaller associations and those in strong financial condition resisted joining, in part because of the cost of membership as well as a basic dislike of government involvement in their affairs. This resistance persisted for years, and only in 1960 did this credit reserve bank system acquire a numerical majority of all thrifts as members.[15]

One reason for the growth in membership in the late 1930s was that the FHLBB worked hard to make itself more useful to bank members. The Board published a monthly magazine with articles on business and regulatory issues. It also began the systematic collection of financial statistics so that managers could compare their associations with other institutions. In 1936, the Board launched the Federal Home Building Service Plan (FHBSP) as a way to help thrifts satisfy the public demand for low-cost homes. The FHBSP was a comprehensive package of design, construction and financing services that S&Ls used to advise home buyers, and even included a certificate of recognition from the government given to the new homeowner. In addition to stimulating construction of affordable housing, the FHLBB hoped that combining multiple services into one package would improve the public perception of thrifts as experts in residential finance. While the FHBSP was

Bodfish, *Depression Experience*, quote 1; "110 Years of Thrift," *Business Week*, 18 January 1941, 60; "Committee on Names," *Savings and Loan Annals, 1949* (Chicago: United States Savings and Loan League, 1949), 252–5.

[15] Henry Kissell, "Home Loan Banks Can Help B&L Get in Step with New Conditions," *ABAN* 53 (August 1933), 352, 370; "Third Annual Federal Home Loan Bank Report," *ABAN* 56 (April 1936), 135–7; J. E. McDonough, "The Federal Home Loan Bank System," *The American Economic Review* 24 (December 1934), 673–4; Edward Baltz, "President's Annual Address," *Building and Loan Annals, 1938* (Chicago: United States Building and Loan League, 1938), 352; John M. Gries, "Our New System of Home Loan Banks," *Review of Reviews and World's Work* 61 (October 1932), 22–4; John H. Fahey, "Federal Aid in Home Finance," *Building and Loan Annals, 1935*, 41; "Federal Home Loan Banks," *FHLB Review* 3 (October 1936), 22–6; Morton Bodfish, "Toward an Understanding of the Federal Home Loan Bank System," *The Journal of Land & Public Utility Economics* 15 (November 1939), 416–9; Ewalt, *A Business Reborn*, 57, 68–9; *Savings and Loan Fact Book, 1960* (Chicago: United States Savings and Loan League, 1960), 53–5, 83.

advertised extensively, with the American Institute of Architects supplying more than 500 different home designs, it got off to a slow start and after one year was available in only three Midwestern cities.[16]

Thrifts were initially reluctant to use the FHBSP, fearing it would lead to speculative building and lower real estate values. Others did not feel that home buyers would use such a broad array of services. Both the Board and the League worked with association managers to allay their fears, and by 1938 the program had spread to more than twenty cities. Local newspapers also began to feature these projects, which led to greater business for the participants. An additional benefit of the FHBSP was that thrifts began to cooperate more with other home-building trades, which further enhanced the reputation and visibility of the industry. By 1941 the plan was so firmly established that the Board transferred its administration to the individual home loan banks.[17]

While the home loan bank generally received strong support, the FSLIC was much slower to gain acceptance, but the reasons for this had little to do with the idea of deposit insurance. Most thrift managers approved of insuring accounts, especially given the positive experience banks received with the FDIC. Their main objection was that the FSLIC charged thrifts an insurance premium that was twice the rate for bank insurance. Not only did this action reduce the amount of profits available for dividends, but it also gave the perception that thrifts were not as safe as banks. They also disliked the asset reserve requirement since it restricted their ability to allocate resources. Finally, the League objected to the broad regulatory powers the FSLIC had

[16] "Introducing the *Review*," *FHLB Review* 1 (October 1934), 8; *Confidential Bulletin* M17 (18 November 1932), 3; "Proposal for a Home-Building Service Plan," *FHLB Review* 2 (January 1936), 116–20; "Steps in the Operation of the Home-Building Service Plan," *FHLB Review* 2 (April 1936), 248–50; "Federal Home Building Service Plan," *FHLB Review* 3 (January 1937), 121–4; "A Complete Home Building Service," n.d.; Records on Advertising the Home Service Program; Records of the Federal Home Loan Bank Board, Record Group 195 (RG 195); National Archives, College Park (NACP); "A Home Building Service for Members of the Federal Home Loan Bank System," 1 April 1935, 1–5, and Minority Report on the Home Building Service Plan, 3 May 1939, 1–3; Records Regarding the Role of Private Trade Associations in the Home Service Program; RG 195; NACP.

[17] "Home Building Service Being Provided for Small Income Owners in Many Cities," *The New York Times*, 16 October 1938, 24; "The Experience of Several Associations in a Home Building Service," *FHLB Review* 2 (February 1936), 164–6; "A Discussion of the Home Building Service Plan," *ABAN* 57 (August 1937), 443–4; "Preliminary Suggestions to Field Representatives for Organizing Industry Cooperation Under the Federal Home Building Service Plan," n.d., 1–4; Programs for Intensive Development of Areas 1–6, 1939; RG 195; NACP; Memorandum from Fred T. Greene, B. H. Wooton, Walter D. Schultz, W. H. Neaves, William F. Penneman, D. H. McNeal, and William H. Husband to the Members of the Federal Home Loan Bank Board, 3 May 1939, 1–3; Records Regarding the Role of Private Trade Associations in the Home Service Program; RG 195; NACP; "First Home Built Here Under Federal Service Plan," *St. Paul Pioneer Press*, 14 May 1939, 24; "Recent Changes in the Operation of the Registered Home Service," *FHLB Review* 7 (June 1941), 298–301.

assumed, especially because these rules were made by "inexperienced persons and brain trusters" who appeared to focus more on political infighting than thrift matters.[18]

Because of these concerns, Congress passed legislation to make the FSLIC more attractive to the thrift industry. The Banking Act of 1935 lowered the insurance premium to that of the FDIC, extended the reserve creation period to twenty years, and gave the FSLIC authority to infuse cash into a "sick" thrift in order to restore solvency as opposed to simply closing it. These improvements led the League to change its official position on deposit insurance from "use it only if you need it" to recommending that all thrifts join the agency. In 1938, the League reaffirmed its support of the FSLIC when it noted that "its earlier 'reform-em and regulate-em' spirit [had] pass[ed]." Between 1935 and 1940, the number of thrifts with deposit insurance rose from 11 percent to 30 percent of all associations. Significantly, most of the new members were among the largest S&Ls, since 51 percent of total industry assets had insurance, a trend that mirrored the experience for the home loan bank.[19]

The least successful of the major federal thrift programs in the 1930s was the federal savings and loan association system. Despite strong promotional efforts, three years after federal charters became available in 1933, only 10 percent of all thrifts were federal associations. The main reason for the resistance was that the federal associations had fewer powers than thrifts with state charters. There was also strong resistance to coming under federal scrutiny, especially given the uncertainty as to how similar federal regulations would be to state rules. Feelings among local thrift leaders were so negative that federal thrift organizers felt like pariahs when attending trade meetings. At one such gathering in Florida, a speaker announced that "if there was a federal man in the audience [he] was going to throw him out." The League was also apprehensive about how the public would accept federally chartered thrifts, and as Bodfish said, "frankly, I can't seem

---

[18] I. Friedlander, "Stimulating Possibilities for Share Insurance," *ABAN* 54 (May 1934), 205–6; Brent Spence, "Reduce the Premium for Insured Institutions," *ABAN* 57 (November 1937), 622–5; Ewalt, *A Business Reborn*, 68–70, 104–5; L. W. Pellett, "Prospects for Share Insurance," *ABAN* 55 (January 1935), 11–12; William E. Best, "Shall We Insure Our Shares?" *ABAN* 55 (February 1935), 67–70, 91, quote 70; *Confidential Bulletin* M47 (17 September 1934), 5–8; "Federal Savings and Loan Insurance Corporation," *FHLB Review* 2 (October 1935), 23–4; Kreutz, *The Way It Happened*, 40–3; Horace Russell, *Savings and Loan Associations*, 2nd edition (Albany, NY: Matthew Bender & Co., 1960), 98–101.

[19] John Fahey, "Federal Insurance is a Public Responsibility," *ABAN* 57 (September 1937), 491–3; Oscar R. Kreutz, "Insurance of Accounts to Build Larger and Stronger Associations," *Building and Loan Annals, 1938*, 300–3; Morton Bodfish, "Insurance of Share Accounts," *ABAN* 55 (July 1935), 295–7; Fred T. Greene, "Share Insurance – Federal and State," *ABAN* 55 (October 1935), 295–7; "New Act Broadens Savings Insurance," *The New York Times*, 9 June 1935, sec. 9, 2; "New Loan System Adding Members," *The New York Times*, 7 July 1935, sec 11&12, 1; *Confidential Bulletin* M85 (25 May 1938), quote 8.

to get as exercised over federal savings and loan associations as some of the folks."[20]

Like the other federal thrift programs, the federal S&L system received a boost when these industry concerns were met. In 1936 the Board introduced a new charter that broadened the powers of the "federals" and placed them on a par with state-chartered thrifts. The League interpreted this new Charter K as a "business-wide go ahead signal" for federalization, and as public opinion on federal charters appeared to be increasingly favorable, many thrift leaders saw the "federal" name as a way to restore confidence in the business. A final factor encouraging the growth of these associations was the inability of state regulators to prevent their spread. From the moment Congress created the federal thrift charter, the states tried to limit their use, primarily because they saw this as another intrusion by Washington into their business. In 1937 Wisconsin regulators sued the FHLBB alleging that federal charters did not conform to state law. The United States Circuit Court of Appeals, however, ruled the charter constitutional since it met the "public welfare" clause. These changes led to a slow but steady increase in the number of federal associations to 24 percent of all S&Ls by 1945.[21]

THRIFTS AND OTHER NEW DEAL PROGRAMS

Aside from government programs that directly affected the industry, other New Deal agencies required the League's attention. The three most important of these were the National Recovery Administration (NRA), the Home Owners' Loan Corporation (HOLC), and the Federal Housing

[20] Horace Russell, "Federal Savings and Loan Associations," *Building and Loan Annals, 1933,* 21–8; "Features of Federal Savings and Loan Associations," *American Builder* 56 (February 1934), 55–6; T. D. Webb, "Development of Federal Savings and Loan Associations," *ABAN* 54 (April 1934), 165–6; "Federal Savings and Loan System," *FHLB Review* 2 (February 1936), 178; *Savings and Loan Fact Book, 1956* (Chicago: United States Savings and Loan League, 1956), 85–6; A. D. Theobald, "The Pros and Cons of Federalization," *Building and Loan Annals, 1933,* 325; Kreutz, *The Way It Happened,* 25; *Confidential Bulletin* M24 (15 May 1933), 3; *Confidential Bulletin* M32 (21 August 1933), 8; *Confidential Bulletin* M39 (2 February 1934), quote 6; *Confidential Bulletin* M45 (12 July 1934), quote 12; M. E. Bristow, "Federalization of Building and Loan Associations," *Building and Loan Annals, 1934,* 325–35; Russell, *Savings and Loan Associations,* 65–7.

[21] Harold Wessels, "Federalization from the Standpoint of a Small Association," *ABAN* 54 (August 1934), 361, 373; L. A. Hickman, "What Federalization Has Done for Our Association," *ABAN* 55 (August 1935), 353–4, 378; John Ballard, "My First 60 Days Managing a Federal," *ASLN* 60 (January 1940), 42–5; "Board Announces Federal Charter Revisions," *ABAN* 57 (January 1937), 17; "New Charter Says 'Go Ahead,'" *FHLB Review* 3 (January 1937), quote 114; Fred Catlett, "Significance of the New Federal Charter," *ABAN* 57 (October 1937), 556–60; "New Charter is Favorably Received," *FHLB Review* 3 (February 1937), 145; Ewalt, *A Business Reborn,* 79–87; *Confidential Bulletin* M85 (25 May 1938), 8; "Constitutionality of Federal Savings and Loan Associations Upheld," *FHLB Review* 4 (July 1938), 348–50; "Savings Bodies Use New Charter," *The New York Times,* 9 May 1938, 9.

Administration (FHA). The NRA, created in 1933 and hailed by the League as "a historic change," proved to have the least impact on thrifts because of its short duration and diffuse objectives. Thrifts were part of the NRA's Group 1700, "Miscellaneous Commercial and Professional," subheading "Financial," which included commercial banks, savings banks, trust companies, brokerage and finance companies, insurance companies, real estate agents, and pawn shops. The NRA required all industries, including thrifts, to draft codes of fair competition, and since the law made trade associations a major unit in business and industrial government, the League assumed this task. The NRA adopted the thrift code in December 1933, and the agency gave the League great latitude in its administration and enforcement. While the NRA ended in 1935, the overall experience was positive for the League because it gave the trade association valuable national exposure and recognition. The League also saw the code as contributing to its work to make the industry more unified.[22]

The most significant nonregulatory New Deal agency in the short term was the HOLC, whose main objective was to provide immediate relief to homeowners in danger of losing their houses. The HOLC accomplished this goal by refinancing a homeowner's existing mortgages with government funds. Petitioners applied directly to the Corporation for a loan through a nationwide network of agency offices. If it approved the request, the HOLC issued government bonds of up to 80 percent of the appraised value to the existing lien holder in payment of the old debt. Homeowners continued to make their monthly payments and if a default did occur, the government would compensate the lender. The main benefit of refinancing with the HOLC for the homeowners was that the new loans were fifteen years long and had below-market interest rates, which resulted in a lower monthly payment. Also, HOLC mortgages were direct-reduction loans, which meant that the interest portion of each payment fell as the principal balance declined. This repayment method, which most thrifts had used for decades, was more beneficial to borrowers than the traditional sinking fund calculation method and far superior to straight interest-only loans used by most banks.[23]

---

[22] *Confidential Bulletin* M37 (26 December 1933), 1; *Confidential Bulletin* M45 (12 July 1934), 13; Harold T. Donaldson, "The Code of Fair Competition Thanks to the US League," *ABAN* 54 (June 1934), 259–60; Edward J. Frye, "Beneficent Results of NRA Code Beginning to be Felt," *ABAN* 54 (August 1934), 369–70; Morton Bodfish, "Appraising the NRA," *ABAN* 53 (December 1933), 559–60, 585; *Confidential Bulletin* M32 (21 August 1933), 1–3, quote 1; *Confidential Bulletin* M36 (21 December 1933), 3; Harold T. Donaldson, "A Code of Fair Competition for Building and Loan Associations," *ABAN* 53 (September 1933), 417, 439; "B-L Bodies Go Under NRA Code," *The New York Times*, 2 January 1934, 49.

[23] *Confidential Bulletin* M41 (24 April 1934), 1; William Stevenson, "How to Procure Loans from the Home Owners' Loan Corporation," *ABAN* 53 (July 1933), 309, 322–3; William Stevenson, "Home Owners' Loan Corporation and the Home Loan Bank System," and W. E. Wood, "The Home Owners' Loan Corporation," *Building and Loan Annals 1933*, 225–38, 299–305; Russell, *Savings and Loan Associations*, 57–8.

Within days of its creation, the HOLC was inundated with thousands of loan requests from both individuals and institutions that wanted to trade delinquent mortgages for government bonds. The agency responded so quickly and effectively to these requests that the HOLC became one of the most successful of all New Deal programs. At its peak in 1934, the HOLC operated 458 local, state, and regional offices, employing nearly 21,000 people. When lending operations ended in 1938, it had processed more than 1.88 million applications worth nearly $6.2 billion. The agency approved more than one million of these requests totaling $3.1 billion, and thrifts eventually acquired $770 million in HOLC bonds, an amount that represented 13 percent of total thrift industry assets. While the majority of these loans were repaid in full, the HOLC did foreclose on almost 20 percent of its borrowers. Remarkably, when it wound up its business in 1946, HOLC operations did not cost taxpayers any money, and it even returned a profit to the United States Treasury.[24]

Because the scope of HOLC operations was so broad, its practices and procedures had a tremendous impact on home lenders. One of the most significant outcomes was the widespread adoption of the direct-reduction mortgage, which was easy for consumers to understand, accrued lower interest costs, and had fixed monthly payments. HOLC administrators later claimed that this ability to "blaze the trail" in the use of long-term amortizing mortgages was their greatest contribution to residential home finance. The HOLC also encouraged home lenders to make higher-leverage and longer-term mortgages. A third important benefit of the HOLC experience was that it revealed the tremendous potential of making home improvement loans. The HOLC initiated the first large-scale home modernization program in the nation, which resulted in the reconditioning of more than 500,000 houses. For thrifts, making rehabilitation loans not only helped in the disposal of foreclosed housing, but also was a profitable way to generate business from existing customers.[25]

[24] John H. Fahey, "To Liquidate Home Loans Use New Federal Institutions," *Bankers Monthly* 51 (March 1934), 131–3; John H. Fahey, "The Resumption of Home Building," *The Architectural Record* 76 (October 1934), 221–3; "Federal Financial Participation in Home Financing, Home Building and Housing," *FHLB Review* 1 (December 1934), 72–4; Ewalt, *A Business Reborn*, 38–43; George Dock, "Federal Home Loan Program Affects 10 Million Families," *The New York Times*, 18 March 1934, 3; "HOLC Loans Approach Four Hundred Million Mark," *ABAN* 54 (April 1934), 166; "Progress in Strengthening of the Nation's Thrift and Home Financing Structure," *FHLB Review* 2 (March 1936), 193; "HOLC Closing Out with Profit to U.S." *Boston Globe*, 7 April 1946, 23; *Home Owners' Loan Corporation Historical Facts and Figures* (Washington, DC: USGPO, 1947 June 30), n.p.

[25] Russell, *Savings and Loan Associations*, 59–61; Ben R. Mayer, "Direct Reduction Loan Plan Gaining Headway," *ABAN* 54 (May 1934), 221–2; C. A. Schroetter, "Direct Reduction Loans," *ABAN* 58 (September 1938), 408–11; Memorandum from J. Francis Moore to John H. Fahey, 27 December 1945, quote 6, and memorandum from W. D. Baker to John H. Fahey, 11 December 1945, quote 4; Regional Managers Conference; Correspondence of Chairman

Another HOLC innovation was the use of property security maps to evaluate loan risks. These maps compiled the characteristics of different neighborhoods and classified them into one of four categories. Category "A" included the best areas, which were stable with consistent development, followed by "B" neighborhoods, which had older properties, or lower pride of ownership, but were still desirable to live in. The "C" neighborhoods were "definitely declining," with "influences that cause[d] original owners to move to another community." "D" neighborhoods were considered hazardous living environments with a distinct "undesirable element"; the majority of urban slums fell into this category. By 1936, the FHLBB began to encourage thrifts to create their own security maps using a "scientific analysis of the entire community." It cautioned thrifts however, against relying too much on neighborhood traits in making loan decisions, maintaining that properties located in even the worst areas could be good risks provided the lender used proper precautions.[26]

A final effect of the HOLC experience was on residential appraisal practices. In order to accurately evaluate property conditions and produce values that were high enough to pay off existing mortgages, the agency created an appraisal system that consisted of three different valuation methods. Commonly known as the sales comparable approach, cost approach, and income approach, these three methods provided a comprehensive range of values from which to arrive at a final valuation. Also, because these appraisals relied primarily on factual data, not opinion, the property values had a higher degree of reliability. As part of this valuation process, the HOLC required appraisers to describe the neighborhood and determine its stability by examining factors like zoning, access to schools, and types of development. Appraisers also had to provide the race and ethnicity of the residents, which the appraisal form initially limited to four classifications – "American, Foreign, Negro, Oriental." Appraisers then used all this information to justify any value adjustments for properties that did not conform to existing developments, or if they were in areas that were improving or declining. Since the HOLC made more than one million valuations, equal to about

John Fahey, 1940–47 (Fahey Papers); RG 195; NACP; "A Summary of New Lending Features to Attract the Home-Owner," *FHLB Review* 2 (July 1936), 354–6; E. Harrison Merrill, "This Building and Loan Business of Ours," *ABAN* 56 (August 1936), 367; William Husband, "Loan Terms and the Rate of Interest for Home Finance," *The Journal of Land & Public Utility Economics* 27 (February 1934), 39–40; David L. Wickens, "Developments in Home Finance," *The Annals of the Academy of Political and Social Science* 189 (March 1937), 77–9; "Another Argument in Favor of Modernization," *ABAN* 54 (February 1934), 72; "Modernize," *ABAN* 57 (July 1937), 371.

[26] "Show Loan Rating of Neighborhoods," *The New York Times*, 23 August 1936, sec. 9, 1; "Security Maps for Analysis of Mortgage Lending Areas," *FHLB Review* 2 (August 1936), quotes 389–91; "The Effect of Home-Financing Practices on Neighborhood Stability," *FHLB Review* 4 (March 1938), 199–203; "Appraisal Methods and Policies," *FHLB Review* 3 (August 1937), 372–3.

10 percent of all nonfarm homes in the nation, its appraisal practices and forms quickly became the standard for all residential appraisers and were adopted for use by the FHA and virtually all institutional mortgage lenders.[27]

While the use of HOLC appraisals yielded an unprecedented amount of detailed information on housing and home ownership, the inclusion of racial and ethnic data also created the opportunity for some lenders to discriminate against certain classes of borrowers. This process, known as "redlining," involved making arbitrary decisions not to lend in certain areas on the basis of the general characteristics of the neighborhood rather than the property being mortgaged. Significantly, redlining was found to some degree in all financial industries, and its most common form was the use of a borrower's race as a lending criteria. Although defended by some as helping to preserve neighborhood stability and enhancing property values, the racist undertone of this process caused it to become a target for reform by civil rights leaders; eventually the use of race, gender, or ethnicity as the basis of a consumer finance decision was made illegal.[28]

When Congress created the HOLC in 1933, the League agreed in principle with its goals, but also regarded its operations with trepidation. Because it feared that the HOLC would become a permanent agency, the League insisted that Congress make it self-liquidating. Also, thrift leaders did not like the fact that borrowers with the ability to repay their mortgages sometimes sought HOLC refinancing just to lower their interest rates. As the HOLC's operations grew, League concerns mounted, and in 1934 it called the agency "the most serious problem we face today." In response to industry protests, Congress passed legislation that restricted HOLC loans only to applicants who could prove they were in default or faced the loss of their homes due to tax sale. It also extended the government guarantee on HOLC bonds from just interest payments to include bond principal, which increased the willingness of thrifts to accept government debt for existing mortgages. Despite such changes, Bodfish still wondered if the HOLC would "be the end or the beginning of government financing in the home ownership field."[29]

[27] Russell, *Savings and Loan Associations*, 57–9; "Effect on Home Values of Appraisals by the Home Owners' Loan Corporation," *FHLB Review* 1 (December 1934), 119–22; "Appraisal Methods and Policies," *FHLB Review* 3 (November 1936), 36–8, "Appraisal Methods and Policies," *FHLB Review* 3 (January 1937), 110–13, "Appraisal Methods and Policies," *FHLB Review* 3 (December 1936), 76–9, "Appraisal Methods and Policies," *FHLB Review* 3 (February 1937), 146–8, "Appraisal Methods and Policies," *FHLB Review* 3 (April 1937), 219–21, "Appraisal Methods and Policies," *FHLB Review* 3 (July 1937), 331–41; "Building a Modern Appraisal Plant," *FHLB Review* 4 (December 1937), 85–6; "Appraisal Conferences and Techniques," *FHLB Review* 6 (January 1940), 106–9.

[28] Kenneth T. Jackson, *Crabgrass Frontier: The Suburbanization of the United States* (New York: Oxford University Press, 1985), 195–203.

[29] "Important Resolutions Passed at Executive Meeting," *ABAN* 53 (May 1933), 199, 232; *Confidential Bulletin* M23 (15 April 1933), 2; *Confidential Bulletin* M39 (22 February 1934), quote 2; *Confidential Bulletin* M41 (24 April 1934), 2; Morton Bodfish, "The Home Owners'

The New Deal agency that had the greatest long-term impact on thrifts was the FHA. Created in 1934 by the National Housing Act, the FHA was responsible for administering several programs intended to improve the availability and affordability of residential finance. One of these involved the chartering of national mortgage associations, originally conceived as a way to bring home loans to areas poorly served by existing lenders. This program, however, failed to meet expectations because thrift leaders were able to significantly alter the mission of these government-operated entities. Following intense League lobbying, the final version of the National Housing Act prohibited these associations from making direct home loans to consumers, and instead limited their activities to the buying and selling of FHA-insured mortgages made by other lenders. Given such a narrow focus, only one association was formed over the next three years. As a result, Congress ended this program and in 1938 authorized the creation of the Federal National Mortgage Association to assume responsibility for building and maintaining a secondary market for home loans made by private lenders and insured by the FHA.[30]

A second more successful program that increased the availability of home loans focused on providing federal mortgage insurance as a way to reduce the risk of lenders losing money in the event of foreclosure. Under this plan, if a borrower defaulted, the government would step in and continue making the regular payments until the loan matured. Although the League objected to this further intrusion of government into home finance and lobbied hard to kill this program, White House support was so strong that Congress approved it with few changes. An important aspect of ensuring the success of the FHA was making it relatively easy for borrowers to qualify for coverage. The FHA insured loans up to a maximum loan to value ratio of 80 percent, and a maximum term and an interest rate of 20 years and 5 percent, respectively. The borrower, in turn, paid an insurance premium equal to 1 percent of the loan amount at closing. This program, however, got off to a slow start and after three years of operation only 18 percent of all mortgages had FHA insurance. To make mortgage insurance more attractive, in 1938 Congress modified the FHA loan guidelines, and raised the maximum loan to value ratio to 90 percent, increased the term to 25 years, and cut the insurance premium in half. The changes had the desired effect, and by the end of World War II 34 percent of all mortgages had FHA insurance.[31]

Loan Corporation," *ABAN* 56 (August 1936), 338–9; David A. Bridewell, *The Federal Home Loan Bank and Its Agencies* (Washington, DC, 14 May 1938), 350–5; McDonough, "The Federal Home Loan Bank System," 680.

30 "Will Title II of the Housing Act Affect Building and Loan?" *ABAN* (June 934) 249–50; *Confidential Bulletin* M45 (12 July 1934), 7; *Confidential Bulletin* M47 (9 September 1934), 9; *Confidential Bulletin* M53 (18 March 1935), 7–8; Ansel Beckwith, "New FHA Loan Laws," *ABAN* 58 (February 1938), 74–5; "National Housing Act Amendments of 1938," *FHLB Review* 4 (March 1938), 196–8, 215.

31 Joseph D. Coppock, *Government Agencies of Consumer Instalment Credit*, Studies in Consumer Installment Financing, no. 5 (New York: National Bureau of Economic Research, 1940),

Significantly, thrifts were not large providers of FHA-insured loans. Most associations avoided FHA lending because of the federal "red tape" involved, as well as the fact that Congress set strict limits on interest rates for these loans. Thrifts did, however, use federal mortgage insurance for riskier types of lending such as home improvement loans, which were typically secured by second liens on the property. The result was that thrifts accounted for just 10 percent of all FHA loan volume between 1935 and 1945, with the majority of these loans taken out by commercial banks and mortgage bankers. The ability to get these institutions involved in making smaller, long-term amortizing loans was what FHA Commissioner Stewart McDonald later described as a key achievement for the agency. Eventually, as these lenders became a greater competitive threat, the thrift industry made sure its traditional loan terms kept pace with changes in the FHA program.[32]

SURVIVING THE GREAT DEPRESSION

While a more active League and improvements in the federal programs yielded strong benefits for the thrift industry, the most pressing concern for thrift managers was simply surviving the Great Depression. The most daunting challenges they faced were maintaining their liquidity and avoiding operating losses. The problem of not having enough available cash, which occurred when deposit withdrawals increased and loan payments fell, could be alleviated by borrowing from the home loan bank. Some associations, however, lacked the necessary amount of current mortgages needed to pledge as collateral for these loans. The more critical problem was managing the level of operating losses, since steady losses would quickly erode a thrift's net worth and force it to close. One way to control losses was by not foreclosing on borrowers, but instead carrying the loans as past due. Such a strategy had two advantages. First, the S&L did not acquire an asset that had not only declined in value but would be hard to resell without incurring a loss. Second, giving the borrower more time to repay a loan meant that the property

4–7; John R. B. Myers, "Building and Loan and the Federal Housing Administration," *ABAN* 55 (January 1935), 9–10; *Confidential Bulletin* M45 (12 July 1934), 1–5; John H. Cover, "The House that Franklin Built," *The Journal of Land & Public Utility Economics* 24 (August 1938), 237–9; "The House Not-So-Beautiful," *Fortune* 17 (May 1938), 94; *Federal Housing Administration Annual Report* (Washington, DC: USGPO, 1946), 44.

[32] Morton Bodfish, "Commercial Banks and Real Estate Loans," *ABAN* 55 (March 1935), 105–6; *Confidential Bulletin* M77 (30 August 1937), quote 2; John C. Hall, "Making Title II of the Housing Act a Building and Loan Aid," *ABAN* 55 (May 1935), 199–200, 236; *Confidential Bulletin* M55 (29 May 1935), 10; *Confidential Bulletin* M78 (15 November 1937), 5; L. D. Ross, "Lending Policies Today," *ABAN* 58 (August 1938), 261–4; "Loans Being Made at Varying Terms," *The New York Times*, 16 January 1938, 10; "Buyers Profiting by New Mortgages," *The New York Times*, 7 April 1939, sec. 9, 1; *Twenty-Seventh Annual Report of the Federal Housing Administration* (Washington, DC: USGPO, 1960), 37; *Federal Housing Administration Annual Report* (Washington, DC: USGPO, 1939), 41; Coppock, *Government Agencies*, 7.

remained occupied and maintained (which helped preserve its value) and offered the opportunity to renegotiate loan terms. The major disadvantage was that the past due status of some loans became so long, up to two years, that managers violated certain accounting rules by not writing off the loan. Still, foreclosures did occur, and by 1935 the amount of real estate owned by thrifts peaked at $1.6 billion or nearly 20 percent of industry assets.[33]

In some cases, thrifts that experienced a significant number of foreclosures and large deposit withdrawal requests became "frozen" and unable to conduct normal business. Despite such dire circumstances, a frozen thrift was not necessarily doomed to failure. Instead, managers took advantage of a legal concept called "segregation of assets" to stay in business. When a thrift segregated its assets, it was essentially divided in two. The first part of the association consisted of all remaining good mortgages, and the second part held the frozen assets. The ratio of good assets to total assets was calculated, and each member's account was written down to reflect the smaller "good" thrift, which then returned to business. Members also received a certificate of participation for the balance of their original accounts in the "bad" thrift, and as management "thawed" the frozen assets by selling them, members received any proceeds in the form of liquidating dividends.[34]

In practice, segregating assets proved to be an effective way to fix impaired thrifts, and in many cases shareholders actually lost nothing on the liquidation of the frozen assets, although liquidation often took years to accomplish. A second, quicker solution to repair a frozen thrift was to undergo reorganization, a process that many troubled associations did as a prerequisite to obtaining state or federal deposit insurance. A typical reorganization involved the cancellation of all outstanding thrift shares, with the original shares replaced by new shares written to reflect current asset values. The main difference between these two ways of dealing with frozen thrifts was that a reorganization produced an entirely new association, while the segregation of assets was more accounting-based. In either case, however, shareholders voted on the decision, which was never made at the sole discretion of managers or directors.[35]

---

[33] L. K. Meek, "Modern Operation of a Building and Loan Association," *ABAN* 51 (October 1931), 450–1; L. K. Meek, "Modern Operation of a Building and Loan Association," *ABAN* 51 (November 1931), 502–3; "To Pay or Not to Pay," *ABAN* 52 (April 1932), 148; "Bay State Starts Reserve System for Savings Institutions," *Business Week*, 4 May 1932, 27–8; "Some Suggestions on Management – How to Avoid Foreclosures," *ABAN* 52 (May 1932), 198; "What to Do with Repossessed Property," *ABAN* 52 (February 1932), 56–7; "The Problem of Real Estate Owned by Institutions," *FHLB Review* 4 (June 1938), 308–10; "How Long Shall We Carry a Delinquent Borrower?" *ABAN* 53 (January 1933), 53.

[34] "What Can Be Done With Frozen Assets?" *FHLB Review* 1 (October 1934), 7–8; Bodfish, *Depression Experience*, 13–14.

[35] "Experience of a Building and Loan Association in Segregating its Assets," *FHLB Review* 1 (January 1935), 124–5; "Effect of Segregation of Assets on Public Confidence," *FHLB Review* 2 (September 1936), 437–8; Ewalt, *A Business Reborn*, 115–8.

While the problem of frozen thrifts essentially ended by the mid-1930s, the problem of liquidating foreclosed properties was a much more drawn out process. One solution was modernizing these properties to improve their appeal for resale, but many lenders balked at this out of the fear of throwing good money after bad. These attitudes changed when managers saw how the HOLC used rehabilitation lending to successfully dispose of properties. Thrifts also encouraged borrowers still in possession of their homes to keep them up to date as a way to help retain value. To do this, thrifts offered maintenance mortgages that gave borrowers a credit line for property repair and upkeep. While such efforts did partially reduce the level of foreclosed real estate, what ultimately allowed the industry to whittle away at this backlog was the demand for housing caused by World War II. During the late 1930s, the level of real estate owned by thrifts fell steadily, and by 1942 this backlog was just $206 million or 3 percent of total assets.[36]

By the late 1930s, the financial condition of many associations had improved to such an extent that managers could begin to focus on improving the physical appearance of their offices. This issue was important to the League because most S&L offices looked like commercial banks and were not in keeping with the more modern image the trade group was trying to project for the industry. Unlike the marble fixtures and "tellers's cages" found in most banks, the new thrift offices were less austere and tried to create comfortable consumer-oriented environments. Many managers tried to make their offices look like family living rooms, with carpeted lobbies, customer lounges, photomurals on the walls, and color-coordinated drapes and furniture. To emphasize the ties between the thrift and the community, more offices also had meeting rooms and recreational facilities available for group gatherings. Between 1938 and 1941, more than 1,000 associations moved to new quarters, and the trend of keeping thrift offices modern and inviting became a trademark of the industry.[37]

[36] "McCullough is Optimistic on Building and Loan Outlook," *Ohio League Section of ABAN* 51 (August 1931), iv; "A Summary of New Lending Features to Attract the Home-Owner," *FHLB Review* 2 (July, 1936), 354; "Remodeling Foreclosed Properties," *ABAN* 52 (April 1932), 166, 187; *Confidential Bulletin* M55 (29 May 1935), 12–13; Thomas Pemberton, "Management and Handling of Real Estate Owned," *ABAN* 57 (October 1937), 550–5; Morton Bodfish, "Time Marches On in Thrift and Home Financing," *Building and Loan Annals, 1936* (Chicago: United States Building and Loan League, 1936), 72–4; "Maintenance Mortgages," *ASLN* 60 (October 1940), 434–5; A. Walling Levin, "Management Problems," *ASLN* 60 (May 1940), 211; "Loan Groups Cut Realty Holdings," *The New York Times*, 29 January 1939, sec. 9, 1; *Savings and Loan Fact Book, 1957* (Chicago: United States Savings and Loan League, 1957), 45.

[37] A. E. Goss, "What to Do with Repossessed Property," *ABAN* 53 (January 1933), 56; E. Clinton Wolcott, "Proper Quarters for a Federal Associations," *Building and Loan Annals 1937*; 188–94; "The Value of Modernization," *FHLB Review* 6 (September 1940), 404–7; Ewalt, *A Business Reborn*, 189–90; Bodfish and Theobald, *Savings and Loan Principles*, 423–6.

THRIFTS IN WARTIME

As had been true during World War I, when America entered World War II the thrift business saw its deposit base soar while lending opportunities dwindled. For the country, the most important economic consequence of the war was that it ended the Great Depression. As industries converted into an "arsenal for democracy," unemployment fell sharply and personal income rose steadily. The war also reduced the opportunities for people to spend their money on consumer goods, which naturally led to strong growth in personal savings. Like all financial institutions, thrifts were major beneficiaries of this windfall, and during the war deposits skyrocketed by 60 percent. S&Ls, however, had few ways to invest these funds, since the war also forced a virtual cessation of residential construction, as rationing of building materials caused new housing starts to plummet by nearly 66 percent from 1939 to 1945.[38]

Although wartime restrictions on residential construction meant that thrifts had few opportunities to make new mortgages, they could still generate business by encouraging customers to refinance existing loans. The lack of new building also allowed S&Ls to liquidate most of their foreclosed properties. The most important role of the thrift industry during the war, however, was as a buyer and seller of government war bonds. The League even organized a bond purchase program for its members, allotting quotas for each state. Between 1941 and 1945, thrifts sold more than $1.6 billion in war bonds to outside investors and acquired an additional $1.7 billion for their own portfolios. By the end of the war, nearly 28 percent of all thrift assets were in government securities.[39]

EVALUATING THE INDUSTRY

Even though the number of S&Ls had fallen by nearly half, at the end of World War II the thrift industry had fully recovered from the economic crisis of the 1930s, as seen in Table 4.1.

---

[38] Paul Endicott, "A New Responsibility," *ASLN* 61 (August 1941), 340–1; Oscar Kreutz, "Holding and Building Savings Volume During the War Period," *ASLN* 62 (April 1942), 147–8; "Too Much Money," *Business Week*, 28 November 1942, 101–2; Everett Smith, "A Bond Portfolio of Savings and Loan Associations," *ASLN* (November 1942), 515–9; Ewalt, *A Business Reborn*, 176–7; *Confidential Bulletin* M120 (19 December 1941), 3; *Historical Statistics of the United States*, 393.

[39] "A Loan Problem," *Business Week*, 24 October 1942, 36–7; "About the Home Loan Banks," *Business Week*, 12 December 1942, 119; "WPB Answers Questions on Conservation Order L-41," *ASLN* 62 (May 1942), 234–5; Fred T. Greene, "Attaining Loan Business in War Times," *ASLN* 63 (September 1943), 424–6; John Blandford, "Our Present Job – War Housing," *ASLN* 62 (November 1942), 488–91; *Confidential Bulletin* M120 (19 December 1941), 6–7; Ewalt, *A Business Reborn*, 177, 205–9.

TABLE 4.1. *Number of Thrifts and Assets – 1930 to 1945*

Year	No. B&L	Change/Year	Assets (000,000)	Change/Year
1930	11,777	–	$8,829	–
1937	9,225	(3.4%)	$5,682	(6.3%)
1941	7,211	(5.9%)	$6,049	1.5%
1945	6,149	(4.0%)	$8,747	9.6%

Source: *Savings and Loan Fact Book, 1955* (Chicago: United States Savings and Loan League, 1955), 39.

One significant trend during this period was the consolidation of the industry, as the total number of thrifts in business fell by half in fifteen years. While failures accounted for part of this decline, another factor was the rise in urban-area thrift mergers toward the end of the 1930s. A second trend was the strong rebound in total industry assets in the 1940s. Assets fell every year in the 1930s, but in 1941 the improving economy produced the first annual increase. The rise in consumer savings during the war helped the industry recover to such an extent that by 1945 total assets were essentially at the same level as in 1930. The third industry trend was that most thrifts significantly increased their reserves. In 1930, the average S&L paid out 91 percent of earnings as dividends, but by 1937 this figure had fallen to 77 percent, reflecting the general decline in dividend rates as well as the need to build capital in order to absorb losses on real estate owned. A final milestone achieved during this period was that thrifts became the single largest source for residential mortgages in the country, accounting for 35 percent of all long-term home loans in 1945, up from 20 percent in 1929.[40]

As they revived and expanded, thrifts faced an increased need for better-trained personnel, which indirectly benefitted female employees. By the late 1930s, more and more S&Ls created specific departments that performed well-defined functions, like accounting, appraisals, and government lending. Because of this change, managers could no longer be jacks-of-all-trades, but instead had to hire professionals to fill these specialized positions. By the outbreak of World War II, a growing number of these new people were women, which resulted in greater opportunities to advance within the firm. The increase in female thrift employees was so large that by the end of the war, 42 percent of all personnel, including 44 percent of all junior executives, were women. As in other businesses, however, most high-level women lost their jobs when the men came home, which

---

[40] "Home Building's No. 1 Financier," *Architectural Forum* 71 (November 1939), 399–402; Bodfish and Theobald, *Savings and Loan Principles,* 23; Ewalt, *A Business Reborn,* 107–10; "Trends in the Savings and Loan Industry," *FHLB Review* 7 (January 1941), 107–10; "Analysis Reveals Interesting Savings and Loan Trends," *ASLN* (January 1940), 16; Fred T. Greene, "Significant Post-Depression Changes," 34–6; *Savings and Loan Fact Book, 1960,* 47.

meant that future jobs for women were lower-skilled clerical and teller positions. However, because most thrifts continued to follow their traditional policy of promoting from within, over time women reemerged as executive managers.[41]

The war years also produced a major change for the League. By the 1940s, Bodfish's quest for power over the previous ten years had produced a growing resentment toward the League leader. This was especially true among government officials, many of whom loathed him. The White House disliked Bodfish's criticisms of the New Deal, which Bodfish described as "brilliantly conceived in theory but its execution has been unsatisfactory." Regulators were angered by his interference in the affairs of the home loan banks, which included seeking special treatment for friends as well as unsolicited recommendations for new rules. One reason for this animosity was that Bodfish resented not being reappointed to serve on the FHLBB in 1933. Stories circulated that he had to be physically removed from the Board office when his successor tried to move in. Although he consistently pointed out how any new Board appointees lacked thrift industry experience, Bodfish did not necessarily want to return to Washington, since he had already "saved the country once."[42]

Other thrift leaders also resented Bodfish's often arrogant and dictatorial control of the League. When people refused to do his bidding, Bodfish was known to try to "get" them, and sometimes these disagreements devolved into public shouting matches. Other officials saw his 1935 acquisition of a controlling interest in the $11 million First Federal Savings and Loan of Chicago as another major problem, since it not only took away from the time Bodfish devoted to League activities, but also raised conflict of interest concerns. Eventually, Bodfish made a number of enemies within the Illinois thrift community, because he expected its members to defer to his judgment in Chicago banking matters. Despite such criticism, the executive manager still had a close-knit group of loyal supporters that included former and current League presidents, and this power base made it virtually impossible to remove Bodfish from power. In fact, the League made Bodfish executive vice president in 1940, a move which infuriated his enemies.[43]

Because of the seemingly irreconcilable differences between the pro- and anti-Bodfish factions, a handful of his staunchest critics broke away from

---

[41] Naomi Ranson, "Women Wanted," *ASLN* 62 (April 1942), 151–3; Ewalt, *A Business Reborn*, 210–11; Marion Carlton, "Woman's Future in Our Business," *ASLN* 64 (May 1944), 181; Judge Lillian M. Westrop, "New Horizons for the Postwar Woman," *ASLN* 65 (February 1945), 52–5.

[42] *Confidential Bulletin* M35 (15 November 1933), quotes 1, 4; *Confidential Bulletin* M22 (29 March 1933), 3–4; *Confidential Bulletin* M32 (21 August 1933), 1.

[43] *Confidential Bulletin* M30 (10 May 1933), quote 4; Kreutz, *The Way It Happened*, 88–96; Ewalt, *A Business Reborn*, 305; Theobald, *Forty-Five Years*, 138–41.

the League in 1943, to establish the National League of Savings and Loan Associations (NLS&LA). In a letter to League members, NLS&LA officials said they did this not over policy differences with the League, but because they considered Bodfish's very bad relations with federal regulators and other government officials the key reason why no League-sponsored legislation of consequence was being considered or passed. Initially, all NLS&LA members were headed by people who hated Bodfish, but over time others joined because they liked being in a smaller, more personable trade group. Most of the new members, however, also retained their original League memberships. While the NLS&LA never had more than 600 members and did not achieve the same political power as the League, it did help the industry by giving legislators an alternative point of view on thrift issues. In 1953, merger talks between the two groups failed because, according to an NLS&LA official, "whether we have been right or wrong, it was one personality who caused the rift, and it has been that same personality that has made it impossible for anyone to consider even for a moment a regrouping."[44]

FAHEY VS. THE INDUSTRY

A final effect of World War II on thrifts was the change in the structure of federal regulation. The mobilization for war led to the creation of dozens of new government agencies, including the National Housing Agency. Created by Executive Order 9070 on February 24, 1942, the Agency consolidated the FHLBB, the FHA, and the U.S. Housing Authority, which administered public housing, into one super-agency as a way to coordinate wartime housing and home finance. This change not only ended the Board's existence as an independent body, but its five members were replaced by a single commissioner. While wartime conditions warranted this move, the League still saw it as a significant blow to the prestige of the industry, since the Board now played a very minor role in Washington. An even greater concern was that putting a single person in control of thrift regulation created the potential for arbitrary decision making.[45]

The commissioner of the home loan bank during the war was John H. Fahey, a longtime government official who was very familiar with the thrift industry and the League. A patrician figure with a distinctive Van Dyke beard, Fahey had served as FHLBB chairman since 1934 and had headed the HOLC between 1933 and 1938. Fahey was an authoritarian administrator

44 "Report of the First Convention of the National Savings and Loan League," *ASLN* 64 (June 1944), 225, 240; "Generes Reports on League Start," *National Savings and Loan Journal* 11 (June 1956), 36–7; Letter from Philip Lieber to Walter McAllister, 3 August 1953, quote; National Savings and Loan League Consolidation, 1953; Correspondence of Chairman Walter W. McAllister 1952–56; RG 195; NACP.

45 Kreutz, *The Way It Happened*, 110; *Confidential Bulletin* M124 (27 February 1942), 1–5.

whose main objective as chief S&L regulator was to make certain the thrift reserve banking system served the public interest. One way to accomplish this involved reducing the influence of the League in the operation of the individual home loan banks. Because these banks were owned by the thrift members, the League felt strongly that they were primarily for the benefit of the industry and that it in turn would use them to serve the public. Fahey, however, felt that industry dominance over bank management and operations was potentially dangerous, and as early as 1937 he wanted to set limits on how many thrift executives could serve as bank directors.[46]

The issue of whether the regulator or the regulated should control the home loan banks finally came to a head in 1944. That year, the Los Angeles home loan bank elected as their new leader a thrift executive supported by a small group of members headed by Thomas Gregory, the flamboyant president of Long Beach Federal Savings and Loan Association. Gregory was in many ways the epitome of new-style bankers that the more traditional S&L executives called "the fast-buck boys." These younger executives took advantage of rapidly growing markets in states like Florida and California to aggressively expand their associations. Many of these people also owned businesses outside their S&Ls, which often led to conflicts of interest. Gregory acquired Long Beach Federal in the late 1930s and quickly expanded it into a large $26 million institution. Allegations circulated that this growth occurred because Long Beach Federal made large loans to a real estate developer who bought construction materials from a company that Gregory had a half interest in.[47]

In the face of these allegations, Fahey quickly developed a strong distrust of Gregory and his "willful and ambitious" followers. He suspected that they were trying to use the Los Angeles home loan bank election to increase their control of the bank for their own gain. To prevent this, Fahey exercised his right as commissioner to approve the choice of all home loan bank officers, and refused to approve the election results. For the next year and a half, Gregory and his supporters worked feverishly to pressure Fahey to change his decision. Using his connections in Congress, Gregory tried to initiate an investigation of the FHLBB, and he also increased his public attacks on the commissioner. With tensions rising, Fahey announced in March 1946 that the Los Angeles FHLB would be abolished and consolidated with the smaller Portland FHLB. The new bank would then be moved to San Francisco. Two months later he authorized the seizure of Long Beach Federal and the removal

---

[46] "House Not-So-Beautiful," 95; Kreutz, *The Way It Happened*, 91; *Confidential Bulletin* M77 (30 May 1937), 7–8.

[47] Kreutz, *The Way It Happened*, 85–7, 96; Thomas Marvell, *The Federal Home Loan Bank Board* (New York: Frederick A. Praeger, Publishers, 1969), 27, 58–61, 177–9; E. L. Barnett, "The FHLB Controversy," *Savings and Loan Annals*, 1946 (Chicago: United States Savings and Loan League, 1946), 89–95.

of Gregory as president. Although Fahey said he did this because the S&L was engaged in certain "unsafe and unsound practices," the seizure was the first time regulators ever took over a healthy thrift. This event led to considerable local publicity and sparked a run on deposits, which drained $6 million from the thrift in just one week.[48]

In June 1946, the months of congressional lobbying by Gregory finally led to the formation of the Special Subcommittee to Investigate the FHLBB, which held hearings on the recent events. Angry committee members lambasted Fahey for abusing his power, and in its final report they demanded the reinstatement of the Los Angeles FHLB and urged that Long Beach Federal be returned to Gregory. Fahey, who did not like anyone questioning his authority, flatly refused, and Gregory took the matter to court. With the case still pending, in July 1947 Congress tried to dilute Fahey's power by expanding the Board to three members. However, because Fahey was still chairman, he successfully prevented any consideration of these issues. The Long Beach controversy finally ended when President Harry S. Truman refused to reappoint Fahey when his term expired in December 1947. A month later the FHLBB gave Long Beach Federal back to Gregory. The Board, however, did not reinstate the Los Angeles FHLB, in part because the new bank in San Francisco was successful and was following more conservative lending policies, and also because it also wanted to prove it could not be swayed by thrift industry leaders.[49]

[48] "...And Then There Were Eleven," *Savings and Loan News* 66 (May 1946), 11–12; Kreutz, *The Way It Happened*, 97–8; Memorandum from John Fahey to Harry S. Truman, 3 January 1947, 1–5; Los Angeles Federal Home Loan Bank Election of President, Letter to U.S. President; Records Relating to the Seizure of the Los Angeles Federal Home Loan Bank and Long Beach Federal Savings and Loan Association (Long Beach Records); RG 195; NACP; Memorandum from A. V. Ammann to Harold Lee, 7 June 1946, 1–3; Los Angeles Federal Home Loan Bank # 12, Associations, Long Beach Federal Savings and Loan Association; Long Beach Records; RG 195; NACP; Arthur O. Whitney, "One Banker Defies Federal Usurpation," Enclosed in Letter from Harold S. Taylor to John H. Fahey, October 23, 1946; E. L. Bennett, "The Story of the F.H.L.B Controversy," *The Savings and Loan Journal* 20 (January 1947), 6; "The California Controversy," *Savings and Loan News,* 66 (September 1946), 29–31; "Fahey Testimony Gives FHLBA Side in the Seizure of Long Beach, Cal., S&L," *American Banker,* 26 June 1946, 11; Ray Richards, "HLA Accused of Causing Bank Run," *Los Angeles Examiner,* 15 June 1946, 14; Ray Richards, "Abolition of US Loan Bank Regime Hinted," *Los Angeles Examiner,* 14 June 1946, 17.

[49] Kreutz, *The Way It Happened*, 100–1; Marvell, *The Federal Home Loan Bank Board,* 185–7; "More on the California Controversy," *Savings and Loan News* 66 (November 1946), 23; Memorandum from Kenneth Heisler to John Fahey, 7 July 1947, 1–2; Los Angeles Federal Home Loan Bank #12, Long Beach Federal Savings and Loan Association – Civil Action, Supreme Court Decision, General 1947; Long Beach Records; RG 195; NACP; "Status of the F.H.L.B. Settlement," *The Savings and Loan Journal* 22 (March 1949), 13–14; Letter from J. Howard Edgerton to William K. Divers, 30 December 1948, and letter from William K. Divers to E. L. Barnett, 29 October 1948, 1; Los Angeles Federal Home Loan Bank, Consolidation – Recision; Long Beach Records; RG 195; NACP.

CONCLUSIONS

The Great Depression was one of the most significant periods in the development of thrifts as modern financial institutions. Between 1930 and 1945, fundamental changes occurred that produced greater internal organization, improved business procedures, and greater interaction between thrifts and the federal government. A key force behind the creation of these new business practices was the League and its executive manager Morton Bodfish, who helped modernize the operations of the trade association and improve member services. One of the more underrated League accomplishments, however, was its ability to change the public image of the thrift business away from that of a semi-philanthropic movement and toward a true financial industry. Since the earliest days of the thrift business, its leaders referred to their work in almost evangelic tones, noting the moral and spiritual benefits of saving and home ownership. While this approach helped attract members and aided growth, as thrifts became more professional, the League realized that the business also needed a more modern identity. Related to this was the nearly universal adoption of the term "savings and loan" to describe an association. Not only did it emphasize the dual roles thrifts provided to consumers, but it also achieved greater industry uniformity.

A second major development during the 1930s was the rise of federal thrift regulation. While commercial banks also experienced increased regulation during the depression, they paled in comparison to the scale and scope of federal government involvement in the thrift business. Between 1932 and 1934, the government created a mortgage reserve bank, designed federal charters for associations and implemented a deposit insurance system. Despite the potential benefits these agencies offered to promote growth and public confidence, many thrifts were wary of them, which resulted in managers adopting a "wait and see" attitude toward participation. As these new agencies established their rules and practices, this hesitancy declined and industry participation rose.

The final major challenge that faced the industry lay in dealing with the economic turmoil caused by the Great Depression. To survive the waves of deposit withdrawals, thrift managers relied on the positive agency relationships they had with members to maintain investor confidence. When foreclosures rose, managers adopted a number of innovative solutions to manage these assets and avoid large losses. By the end of the 1930s, the major crises facing thrifts had passed, and managers were again actively seeking lending opportunities for home renovation and new construction. While World War II offered few opportunities for home lenders, given the restrictions on construction, thrifts still found ways to increase their role as financiers. Defense housing loans rose during these years, but the more significant change was in the growth of personal savings. These funds would be a crucial source to finance the homes demanded by returning serviceman. Despite the turmoil of the 1930s and 1940s, thrifts were in an excellent position to help millions of Americans realize the dream of home owner-ship in the postwar period, which would help propel the industry to greater heights.

5

THE GLORY YEARS, 1946–1955

In the decade following World War II, the savings and loan industry grew at the fastest rate in its history, and the key to this expansion was the tremendous postwar demand for new homes. Because residential construction nearly dried up during the Great Depression and the war, when peace came the need for new houses exceeded all expectations. The result was an unprecedented demand for mortgages, and S&Ls responded by offering innovative mortgage products that met customer needs, while also designing better ways to attract deposits to fund these loans. The result was that by the mid-1950s the thrift industry was not only the preeminent source for home finance, but also became the second largest repository for consumer savings. Another reason for the expansion of S&Ls was their effort to adopt a more progressive business image that combined their traditional role of community institutions with modern convenience and efficiency. The League assisted in this work by expanding management education programs and promoting more effective advertising methods. It also worked with the Federal Home Loan Bank Board to design industry-friendly regulations. These relations grew so close that Congress eventually investigated the role of the League in government activities.

While the expansion of the thrift industry in the early 1950s was indeed remarkable, some changes during the period seemed threatening for the future. Chief among these was the greater role of the government in home finance, as the Federal Housing Administration, Federal National Mortgage Association, and the Veteran's Administration all expanded their mortgage lending activities. Another major change came in 1955 when the continued demand for home loans produced the first significant postwar credit crunch that signaled an end to this period of easy growth. While the thrift industry would continue to expand for years to come, these experiences had a major impact on internal relations as well as the regulatory environment.

.

PLANNING FOR SUBURBIA

When government and housing industry leaders began to consider the post-war housing needs for the nation in 1942, their primary concern lay in trying to prevent the severe shortages that had plagued the country after World War I. These fears stemmed from the fact that for the past fifteen years the construction of new homes had not kept pace with demand. From a peak of 900,000 new homes built in 1925, housing starts fell steadily during the last half of the 1920s, before plummeting to an all-time low of 90,000 in 1933. While construction did increase steadily over the remainder of the 1930s, the number of houses built in any one year never matched the annual increase in new families. Complicating matters was the virtual ban on nondefense-related building and the restrictions on home renovations during World War II. When the war ended, not only was there a shortage of new homes, but millions of dwellings also required repairs and reconditioning. Housing officials predicted that more than 7 million new non-farm homes would have to be built by 1950, and up to 16.1 million by 1955.[1]

In deciding how best to meet this shortfall, some former New Deal officials wanted to create large-scale planned communities reminiscent of the Greenbelt town projects of the late 1930s. Their plans stressed federal control over new building to ensure that development was well-balanced among inner cities, suburbs and rural areas, with a particular emphasis on low-cost homes. Congressional leaders weary of centralized planning opposed these ideas, and in 1944 the task of deciding how to meet postwar housing needs moved to the Senate, which was still discussing the issue when the war ended the following year. Drafting plans for new housing were delayed further as legislators responded to the pressure from consumers and businesses for an immediate end to all wartime economic controls. Although Congress did end most rationing and wage restrictions quickly, it kept the controls on building materials and home prices in place because of fears that their removal would lead to high inflation. Because builders lacked the resources to resume full-scale construction, this inaction resulted in a housing crisis of unprecedented magnitude. Conditions were so severe that by the end of 1945 more than 30 percent of all married veterans lived in trailers or "doubled-up households." In 1946, Congress finally eliminated the remaining wartime

[1] Leon Keyserling, "Planning for Postwar Housing," *American Savings and Loan News* [hereafter *ASLN*] 62 (March 1942), 121; Joseph Shister, "The Postwar Housing Boom," *ASLN* 63 (May 1943), 194–6; Abner Ferguson, "Private Enterprise in War and Post-War Housing," *ASLN* 63 (June 1943), 257–61; "After the War, What Will We Need in Housing?" *Federal Home Loan Bank Review* [hereafter *FHLB Review*] 11 (October 1944), 41–3; "Post World War I – A Straw in the Wind?" *FHLB Review* 11 (October 1944), 3–5, 14; "Planning for Postwar Housing," *ASLN* 64 (January 1944), 10–11; "Why the Housing Shortage?" *FHLB Review* 12 (April 1946), 201–2; Edward Gavin, "Housing Needs for the Next 15 Years," *Savings and Loan News* [hereafter *SLN*] 66 (May 1946), 23–5.

building restrictions; and, while this action did cause home prices to soar more than 50 percent above their prewar levels, it also gave developers freedom to build new homes. Much of this construction occurred in the suburbs, marking the latest phase in the long-term evolution of American cities.[2]

Although the growth of suburban communities was one of the defining characteristics of postwar America, it was not a development unique to the 1950s, since suburbs had been a part of cities for centuries. Traditionally, most urban areas had been compact and densely built with the wealthiest living closest to the center, and the poor relegated to the periphery. As late as the 1830s, a suburb was regarded as a substandard place in which to live. One reason for this living pattern was that in the eighteenth century work and home life were intertwined with little real distinction between the two. A more important reason, however, was that most cities lacked efficient transportation systems, which meant that pre-industrial urban centers were "walking cities." This situation began to change in the 1850s with the perfection of the short-distance railroad. Because the railroad was an efficient and reliable form of transportation, city residents could now commute to work; but, since it was also expensive to take the train regularly, the wealthy were the only people who could afford the service. Consequently, the upper classes were the first to relocate away from the crowded city center and into communities characterized by large custom-built homes on richly landscaped multi-acre lots.[3]

A second major wave of suburban development came in the 1890s following another critical innovation in transportation, the electric streetcar. The streetcar was a convenient and cheap way to travel around the city, and it allowed urban planners to design integrated mass transit systems everyone could use. This flexible form of transit also made it possible for middle-class professionals to live farther away from work, resulting in the growth of "streetcar suburbs." These communities were often located five to ten miles from downtown, and consisted of moderately priced homes on smaller

---

[2] Josephine Hedges Ewalt, *A Business Reborn: The Savings and Loan Business, 1930–1960* (Chicago: American Savings and Loan Institute Press, 1962), 240–3; "Postwar Housing Problems in Perspective," *FHLB Review* 12 (December 1945), 63–5, 73; Dorothy Rosenman, "Housing Our Postwar Economy," *ASLN* 64 (March 1944), 84–5, 90–1; "The Outlook for Home Financing," *FHLB Review* 12 (October 1945), 3, 15; Morton Bodfish, "Report of the Executive President," *Savings and Loan Annals, 1945* (Chicago: United States Building and Loan League, 1945), 54–5; "Postwar Increase in Prices Seen," *The New York Times*, 26 January 1945, 25; John Hancock, "The New Deal and American Planning: The 1930s," in Daniel Schaffer, editor, *Two Centuries of American Planning* (London: Mansel, 1987), 213–18; "G. I. Joe's Housing Plans," *FHLB Review* 13 (October 1946), 9–11.

[3] J. John Phelan, *The Suburbs* (New York: McGraw-Hill, 1995), 28; Robert Fishman, *Bourgeois Utopias: The Rise and Fall of Suburbia* (New York: Basic Books, 1987), 21–6, 125–7, 142–5; John F. Kasson, *Amusing the Million: Coney Island at the Turn of the Century* (New York: Hill and Wang, 1978), 46–8; Peter O. Muller, *Contemporary Suburban America* (Englewood Cliffs, NJ: Prentice-Hall, 1981), 23.

lots that were within walking distance of the streetcar lines. In established cities such as Boston, streetcar suburbs eventually overwhelmed the original suburbs of the wealthy, who would sell their large lots to developers and move to newer communities farther out from the city. In the newer cities of the West, the building of streetcar lines and middle-class suburbs occurred in tandem, and it was common to find the same people controlling both projects. For example, Los Angeles transit system owner Henry Huntington used his development of suburbs to support his rail service. This combination of affordable housing and dependable transportation caused that city's population to grow from 11,200 in 1880 to more than 319,000 by 1910.[4]

A third wave of suburban development came in the 1920s, and again was tied to a revolution in transportation. The automobile, which became widely available and affordable after World War I, led to massive road construction programs, and eventually the creation of a new type of community, the "automobile suburb." Like the streetcar suburb, the automobile suburb was intended for the middle class, since the flexibility of roads offered greater access to cheap land. The availability of land also allowed planners more freedom to design communities that were similar to those of the wealthy, with the result that the homes in automobile suburbs tended to be on larger lots and located along winding roads. Developers also used zoning laws more frequently, as a way to increase the exclusivity of neighborhoods. While intended to separate and control residential and commercial development, zoning laws also had discriminatory side effects as developers used them to exclude "undesirable" housing and residents. Ultimately, zoning laws and deed covenants would be a way to separate suburbanites based on race, ethnicity, religion, and economic status.[5]

The fourth significant wave of suburban growth came after World War II, but unlike the earlier patterns of residential development this new exodus from the city was not in response to a new mode of transportation. Rather, the 1950s suburbs were more a response to the explosion of new families that appeared after the war. Almost as soon as World War II ended and for several years thereafter, the rate of new marriages across the country soared, and with this marriage frenzy came a corresponding increase in the birth rate. Consequently, the number of households rose at the fastest rate in

---

4 Sam Bass Warner, *Streetcar Suburbs* (Cambridge: Harvard University Press, 1962), 52–8. Kenneth T. Jackson, *Crabgrass Frontiers: the Suburbanization of America* (New York: Oxford University Press, 1985), 118–19; Phelan, *The Suburbs*, 50–55 William B. Friedricks, *Henry E. Huntington and the Creation of Southern California* (Columbus, OH: Ohio State University Press, 1992), 44–67; Fishman, *Bourgeois Utopias*, 158.

5 New York City created the first zoning ordinances in 1916. Jackson, *Crabgrass Frontiers*, 17; Phelan, *The Suburbs*, 89; Mark S. Foster, *From Streetcar to Superhighway: American City Planners and Transportation, 1900–1940* (Philadelphia: Temple University Press, 1981), 56–73, 154; Mansel G. Blackford, *The Lost Dream: Businessmen and City Planning on the Pacific Coast, 1890–1920* (Columbus, OH: Ohio State University Press, 1993), 93–4.

American history, from 37.5 million in 1945 to 47.8 million by 1955. This so-called "baby boom" also sparked a sharp increase in consumer purchases, and one of the major beneficiaries of this spending was the automobile industry. Between 1945 and 1955, car registrations jumped from 31 million to 62.7 million; and, because this change demanded new roads, highway construction by state and federal governments rose from 18,000 miles per year to 76,000 miles per year over the same period.[6]

This network of roads and highways was critical to meeting the postwar housing demand because it opened up large tracts of land to residential development. This made it possible for home builders to design communities that allowed residents to commute to their urban jobs but also have access to local shopping and recreation facilities. Builders, however, still faced the problem of finding more efficient construction methods that would allow them to build high-quality homes in a quick and cost-effective manner. Meeting this requirement was difficult since most traditional home building methods relied on skilled trade workers. While using prefabricated materials was a potential solution, the high cost of using this method meant that the prices of these homes often were outside the price range for most aspiring buyers. The best solution involved applying mass-production technologies to home construction, processes that were pioneered by Bill and Alfred Levitt in the construction of Levittown on Long Island.[7]

The Levitts used elements of big business organization and mass-production techniques to produce simple yet adequate homes which almost anyone could afford. The construction methods used by the Levitts relied on scientific management principles in which work crews performed discrete functions and moved from house to house in assembly-line fashion. This division of labor proved so efficient that during peak production a new house was completed every fifteen minutes. These efforts to minimize costs allowed the Levitts to sell their homes 20 percent below the price of the

---

[6] "The Current Boom in Marriages," *FHLB Review* 12 (June 1946), 264–5; "Post-V-J Day Migration," *FHLB Review* 12 (October 1945), 4–5; "Slow Down in Savings," *FHLB Review* 13 (November 1946), 49–50; "The Pattern of New Savings," *FHLB Review* 13 (February 1947), 145–6; John B. Rae, *The American Automobile Industry* (Boston: Twayne Publishers, 1984), 178–9; Bureau of the Census, *Historical Statistics of the United States, Colonial Times to 1957* (Washington, DC: USGPO, 1960), 15, 30, 176–177; Muller, *Contemporary Suburban America*, 53; Phelan, *The Suburbs*, 51–7.

[7] *The Prefabrication Industry and Housing Costs* prepared for the Housing and Home Finance Agency for the Subcommittee on Housing Costs, 9 January 1948; Prefabrication; Correspondence of Chairman William K. Divers (Divers Papers); Records of the Federal Home Loan Bank Board, Record Group 195 (RG 195); National Archives, College Park (NACP); Letter from Harry J. Durbin to William K. Divers, 12 May 1948; Du; Divers Papers; RG 195; NACP; "Kreutz Talks on Mass Production in Postwar Housing," *ASLN* 64 (July 1944), 268–9; Jackson, *Crabgrass Frontiers*, 233–4; Joseph M. Guilfoyle and J. Howard Rutledge, "Levitt Licks the Housing Shortage," *Coronet* 25 (September 1948), 112–16; "High Housing Costs are Laid to Profits for Distributors," *The New York Times*, 15 November 1947, 1.

competition, while still realizing a 15 percent profit per house. The Levitts further improved the efficiency of their operations by integrating vertically through the ownership of lumber yards, nail works, and a sales and finance company – a change that produced scale economies and improved long-range planning. Although criticized as "cookie-cutter" developments, the New York Levittown was so popular that the Levitts completed a similar community near Philadelphia. Other builders also followed the Levittown model, and by 1950 the growth rate of suburbs was ten times that of the central city. Such changes were so pronounced that in 1958 the Census Bureau created a new population measurement, the Standard Metropolitan Statistical Area, to define the phenomenon.[8]

FINANCING THE AMERICAN DREAM IN THE 1950S

The postwar years redefined the role of S&Ls in American finance, as the tremendous demand for mortgages caused by the housing boom produced unprecedented industry growth. The prosperity for S&Ls was so seemingly effortless that it was alleged that all a thrift executive had to do to succeed was to follow the "3-6-3 Rule" – pay 3 percent on savings, charge 6 percent on loans, and be on the golf course by 3 p.m. In reality, the success following World War II resulted not so much from a windfall to lending opportunities, but from concerted efforts of thrifts managers to provide consumers with innovative products and services. These included affordable mortgage plans, flexible high-yield savings accounts, and a business environment in keeping with the image of thrifts modern and progressive financial institutions. These changes produced an industry that bore but scant resemblance to the one that had existed before the war.[9]

Like government officials, lenders also anticipated a sharp rise in the demand for housing and home finance after the war, and to meet these needs S&L managers and the League created a number of new lending options to assist home buyers. Significantly, many of these products incorporated unique and innovative features that made them superior to competing loan structures. The most creative loan package offered was the Uniform Savings Loan Plan, or the US Loan Plan, which combined features of several types of

[8] Jackson, *Crabgrass Frontiers,* 235–8; Eric Larrabee, "The Six Thousand Houses that Levitt Built," *Harper's Magazine* 197 (September 1948), 79–88; John T. Liell, "4000 Houses a Year," *Architectural Forum* 90 (April 1949), 84–93; William M. Dobriner, *Class in Suburbia* (Englewood Cliffs, NJ: Prentice Hall, 1963), 22; Phelan, *The Suburbs,* 63–66; "Census Shows a Better Housed Nation," *SLN* 72 (June 1952), 9–10; Richard U. Ratcliff, Daniel Rathbun, and Junia Honnold, *Residential Finance, 1950,* prepared for the Social Science Research Council in cooperation with the U.S. Dept. of Commerce, Bureau of the Census (New York: J. Wiley & Sons, 1957), 157–9.

[9] Charles R. Morris, *Money, Greed, and Risk: Why Financial Crises and Crashes Happen* (New York: Random House, 1999), 83.

loans into one flexible financing package. This plan was beneficial to builders because it simplified closing and funding procedures, while borrowers liked the long twenty-year repayment term and the option to defer temporarily payments after the first three years. The US Loan Plan also allowed borrowers to obtain additional advances after the loan closed for home improvement projects, an option that eliminated the need for refinancing or seeking a second mortgage. This "open-end" provision became so popular that by 1953 mortgages with this feature accounted for nearly $330 million of total industry assets.[10]

As the thrift industry saw its loan volume grow, it turned its attention to finding ways to increase its share of consumer savings. Although thrift deposits rose by almost 60 percent during World War II, in the seven years after the war total industry deposits soared by 117 percent, a gain that dwarfed the 22 percent increase for commercial banks during the same period. The main reason for this phenomenal growth was that S&Ls, unlike banks, faced few restrictions on the interest rates they could pay on savings. Under the Banking Act of 1933, bank regulators could limit commercial bank savings account rates. This rule, known as Regulation Q, did not apply to thrifts, and since the rule had not been changed for nearly twenty years, the average annual yield on bank deposits in the early 1950s was less than half the rate for S&Ls. Because bankers strongly objected to this disparity, federal officials began to raise rates by the middle of the decade, and as deposit competition increased some thrifts responded with their own rate increases. The League, however, discouraged rate competition and instead urged S&Ls to attract funds by enlisting as members the estimated 40 percent of all American families that did not have savings accounts. Associations did tap into this resource, and by 1955 over one-third of all S&L deposits were coming from new members.[11]

[10] "New US Loan Plan Proposed," *ASLN* 64 (July 1944), 290–2 "What's New in Loan Plans," *SLN* 66 (November 1946), 15–17; Frederick T. Backston, "The Packaged Mortgage," *SLN* 67 (March 1947), 9–12; Morton Bodfish, "Shylock has Gone Out of Style," *House Beautiful* 86 (October 1944), 84–5; Franklin Hardinge, "Open-End Mortgage Offers Strong Support to Booming Home Improvement Market," *SLN* 70 (May 1950), 9–12; Fred Church, "Open-End Provision Builds Business While Minimizing Mortgage Loan Risk," *SLN* 72 (July 1952), 17–19; "Lending Operations," *SLN* 73 (July 1953), 47; "'Built-In Flexibility' Can Make Your Loans Attractive, Competitive," *SLN* 75 (March 1955), 57–60.

[11] "What Has the War Done to Savings?" *FHLB Review* 11 (January 1945), 107–10; "Dividend Rates," *SLN* 73 (June 1953), 47; Walter W. McAllister, "Developing Future Loans by an Own-A-Home Savings Club," *SLN* 55 (October 1945), 5–8; "Good American Home Program Sells Middle-Income Home Ownership," *SLN* 70 (April 1950), 9–12; "The Case for Give-Aways," *SLN* 69 (August 1949), 25–6; "Shop Talk Sessions," *Savings and Loan Annals, 1952* (Chicago: United State Savings and Loan League, 1952), 85–9; "Savings Institutions or Loan Companies," *SLN* 69 (June 1949), 6; Henry Kingman, "Real Competition for Savings," *SLN* 70 (January 1950), 27–8; *Savings and Loan Fact Book, 1959* (Chicago: United States Savings and Loan League, 1959), 22–3; "Sleeping Giant Stirs," *SLN* 72 (March 1952), 11–13; Norman Strunk, "Savers," *SLN* 74 (April 1954), 18–22; George Mooney, "Survey Shows

Beyond working to build loans and deposits, a third area of attention for thrift managers lay in improving business efficiency by using new office automation technologies thermofax photocopying and microfilming. Larger thrifts also adopted more formal organizational structures with functions such as loan processing and appraisals assigned to specific departments and managers. These and other changes produced significant savings, as the ratio of total operating expenses to gross income for the thrift industry fell steadily between 1945 and 1954. Furthermore, S&L workforces became more efficient as the number of employees per $1 million in assets declined from 1.7 to just 1.0 over the same period. Finally, the trend towards modernizing thrift offices continued, as more than 85 percent of all S&Ls either moved into new quarters or modernized existing spaces. These new offices usually offered more customer services such as night deposit boxes and drive-in windows. More thrifts were also opening suburban branches or satellite offices in shopping centers and supermarkets. By 1955, S&Ls began using what was to become the symbol of the postwar thrift, the time and temperature sign.[12]

THE LEAGUE IN THE GLORY YEARS

The 1950s also was a time of significant change for the United States Savings and Loan League, as evidenced by an expansion of member services. One of its goals in the postwar period was to help S&Ls advertise in more innovative ways, since the public still did not fully understand the nature of the thrift business. One sign of this appeared in a 1948 survey in which only 15 percent of respondents felt that S&Ls were the best places to get a mortgage, while just 7 percent said they would save money there. Although newspaper advertising was the dominant form of publicity used by associations, the League did not feel that it was "of the quality or size that is befitting a $13 billion business." To change this, it recommended that S&Ls emphasize service, not rates, in their advertising and, above all, to make sure the advertisements were well designed and run frequently. The League also

41% of Families in U.S. Lack Savings Accounts," *The New York Times*, 18 April 1954, sec. 3, 1; *Savings and Loan Fact Book, 1958* (Chicago: United States Savings and Loan League, 1958), 9–13, 54–6.

12 "Personnel Trends," *SLN* 72 (February 1952), 9–10; "Microfilm for the Savings Association," *SLN* 70 (August 1950), 26–8; "The Electron and Our Business," *SLN* 75 (June 1955), 14; "Management and Staff: Both Have Rights and Responsibilities," *SLN* 76 (October 1955), 45–7; "New Office Stresses Employee Facilities," *SLN* 69 (January 1949), 34; "Shedding Light on Office Modernization," *SLN* 65 (August 1945), 8–11; Robert L. Schutt, "Planning for New Office Quarters," *SLN* (January 1948), 7–8; J. B. Gander, "The 'New Look,'" *SLN* 68 (March 1948), 20–24; "Extra Services Win Customer Approval," *SLN* 69 (April 1949), 22–5; "Drive-Ins Cater to the Carriage Trade," *SLN* 72 (December 1952), 40–3; "Drive-Ins, Community Room Mark Suburban Style," *SLN* 73 (March 1953), 55–6; "Managers Cite Many Benefits of New Offices," *SLN* 69 (November 1949), 22–6; "Super Savings Market," *SLN* 73 (April 1953), 36–7; "Office Quarters," *SLN* 74 (February 1954), 67.

encouraged thrifts to use new office openings to show their commitment to the community, and their financial statements to promote their strength. As television became more common, S&Ls also sponsored shows such as *Hop-a-long Cassidy* as a way to attract young savers.[13]

Another way the League wanted S&Ls to reach the public was through the use of specialized publications or house organs. While these publications usually focused on the issuing S&L, many, like *The Second Federalist* of the Second Federal Savings and Loan Association of Cleveland, pledged to readers that the newsletter "will not be overloaded with advertising of this association, but it will be an assembling of brief news items that should interest men and women who love their homes and are ambitious to get ahead." To assist S&Ls unable to produce their own house organs, the League printed *Home Life*, a glossy color magazine that could be tailored to the exact needs of each individual association. Through these more personal and direct forms of advertising, the League hoped to build an industry image focused on meeting the needs of the family and the community, ideals that harkened back to the older spirit of the thrift movement.[14]

A second objective of the League during this period was to see that thrift employees were well-educated professionals. Between 1948 and 1955, the total industry workforce more than doubled; and while many of the new thrift executives hired after the war were college educated, the League wanted to ensure that these managers were properly trained in S&L business methods. To accomplish this, in 1946 the American Savings and Loan Institute (ASLI) resumed its Graduate School for thrift executives which was suspended during the war. At its new home at Indiana University, the Graduate School met during the summer and offered classes in thrift law, financial systems, home construction, advertising, personnel management and training, regulation and supervision, and business economics. The program took three years to complete, and students had to submit a thesis and pass an oral defense to graduate. By the mid-1950s, the annual enrollment in the Graduate School exceeded 300, of which nearly 100 were women. While most managers went

---

[13] "Dr. Gallup Started Something," *SLN* 68 (August 1948), 19–23; Ed Hiles, "What the Public Thinks of Our Business," *SLN* 68 (September 1948), 23–4; Morton Bodfish, "The Need for Merchandising," *Savings and Loan Annals, 1948* (Chicago: United States Savings and Loan League, 1948), 69–77; Robert Perrin, "Reflections on 4,500 Newspaper Ads," *SLN* 69 (November 1949), 53–5, quote 55; Nathaniel Griffin, "Making the Most of Moving to New Quarters," *SLN* 69 (May 1949), 32–5; "A 'New Look' for Financial Statements," *SLN* 69 (May 1949), 10–14; J. L. Fifer, "Merchandising a Modern Loan Plan," *SLN* 66 (November 1946), 15–17; Robert Perrin, "The Advertising Side," *SLN* 68 (June 1948), 31–3; Phyllis Edmunds, "A Program for Business Development," *SLN* 74 (January 1954), 38–9; "S&L Men Teach Bankers a Lesson," *Time*, 29 November 1954, 92.

[14] Josephine Hedges Ewalt,. "The Publicity Department," *SLN* 68 (August 1948), 31–2; "House Organs – Their Content, Make-Up and Use," *SLN* 67 (January 1947), 19–24; "House Organs – Their Content, Make-Up and Use," *SLN* 67 (February 1947), 30–3; Helen Heggie, "League Publications," *SLN* 68 (January 1948), 33–4.

to the Graduate School to obtain a solid financial education, the school also offered a unique opportunity to network with other thrift leaders.[15]

The third major objective of the League involved increasing its role in the design of thrift legislation and regulation. Although the League had always monitored political affairs as they related to S&Ls, the growing complexity of housing laws and federal regulations necessitated a more permanent presence on Capitol Hill. In 1942, the League hired Stephen Slipher to coordinate the industry's government affairs work, and eight years later it formally opened a Washington office. As the League's chief lobbyist, Slipher worked closely with legislators and provided them with information on housing and home ownership. He was so effective and well respected that during his thirty-year tenure in Washington, D.C. Slipher was known as the "dean of financial lobbyists." Also, to keep members informed about legislative issues, the League created the *Flash News*, which could be sent to all members within twenty-four hours. This rapid dissemination of information allowed it to mobilize the industry for grassroots lobbying.[16]

The increased League presence in Washington eventually led the Justice Department in 1948 to use the trade association as the test case for the recently-passed Lobbying Registration Act. Although a judge dismissed the case in 1949 as "too vague and indefinite," the House Select Committee on Lobbying Activities still launched an investigation of the League the following year. The House probe focused on what role the League had played in the formation of housing legislation over the previous three years; and, while the committee found that people like League leader Morton Bodfish had unusually close relations with key legislators, its final 749-page-long report did not directly criticize the trade group. In fact, chairman Rep. Frank Buchanan (D-PA) concluded that the League presented a "good over-all picture of positive lobbying in operation.... [T]hey desired to help their business, and they set about obtaining legislation carefully and methodically." Such a positive assessment both vindicated the League and was an acknowledgment of its increased political clout.[17]

---

[15] Ben H. Hazen, "Training the Crew for the Job Ahead," *SLN* 66 (January 1946), 18–19; Arthur M. Weimer, "Training and Leadership in Housing and Home Finance," *SLN* 66 (March–April, 1946), 35–6; "The Institute in the New Era," *SLN* 66 (May 1946), 18–20; "Graduate School of Savings and Loan Continues at Indiana University," *SLN* 67 (June 1947), 30–1; Parker Hazen, "Graduate School Integral for Learning," *SLN* 69 (April 1949), 40–1; "The 1950 Graduate School," *SLN* 70 (April 1950), 18–20; "Graduate School Helps Train Top-Flight Savings Association Executives," *SLN* 70 (October 1950), 26–7; Letter from William K. Divers to Edward E. Edwards, 2 September 1952; American Savings and Loan Institute, 1948; Divers Papers; RG 195; NACP.

[16] Horace Russell, "The Legal Side," *SLN* 68 (March 1948), 31–3; Ewalt, *A Business Reborn*, 303.

[17] "Loan League Cited on Lobbying Charges," *The New York Times*, 31 March 1948, 22; "What is a Lobbyist?" *Washington Times-Herald*, 21 April 1949, quote 21; U.S. Congress, House, 81st Cong., 2nd sess., "The United States Savings and Loan League," Report of the

As the League expanded its scope of operations, it also underwent internal changes. By 1950, more than 50 percent of all thrifts were League members, and the trade association employed more than 150 people in its Chicago headquarters. It also had six major affiliated organizations and published ten different periodicals on a wide range of subjects related to housing and the thrift industry. While Bodfish was instrumental in helping the League expand operations, by the late 1940s he had become such a lighting rod for controversy that some within the League saw him as a liability. Although opponents of Bodfish tried to reduce his power in 1947 by moving him into the largely ceremonial post of Chairman of the Executive Committee, he still insisted on running the trade group personally. His ability to do so, however, was affected by a series of personal setbacks including a divorce, and by the early 1950s the chairman was drinking heavily and taking frequent unannounced trips to his Arizona ranch.[18]

Eventually, even Bodfish's staunchest supporters decided something had to be done, and in 1952 the League named Norman Strunk as executive vice president. Strunk joined the trade association in 1938 after having earned an MBA from Northwestern University, and was in many ways the mirror opposite of Bodfish. Strunk was a mild-mannered leader who worked to achieve consensus decisions, and his more relaxed style was a welcome relief from the confrontational tactics of his predecessor. Although Strunk's unassuming personality caused some to question his ability to lead the League, his superior knowledge of the thrift business helped him flourish on the new job. In 1953, Bodfish formally left the League to focus on running First Federal Savings and Loan of Chicago, the thrift he had organized in 1935 and which had become one of the largest in the nation. While the departure was cordial on the surface, Bodfish was bitter about leaving the spotlight, and until his death in 1963 he continued to provide solicited and unsolicited advice to industry and government leaders.[19]

House Select Committee on Lobbying Activities Created Pursuant to HR 298 (Washington, DC: USGPO, 1950), 153–77; "Dirkson is Linked to Lobbying Group," *The New York Times*, 4 November 1950, 10; Morton Bodfish, "Report of the Chairman of the Executive Committee on Legislative Matters," *Savings and Loan Annals, 1950* (Chicago: United States Savings and Loan League, 1950), 146–7.

[18] Ralph M. Smith, "How the U.S. League Serves You," *SLN* 67 (December 1947), 12–13; Carl Distlehorst, "The American Savings and Loan Institute," *SLN* 68 (January 1948), 22–4; Leonard Dodson, "The Accounting Division," *SLN* 68 (March 1948), 33–4; *Savings and Loan Fact Book, 1954* (Chicago: United States Savings and Loan League, 1954), 1; Heggie, "League Publications," 33; Norman Strunk, "The U.S. League in Action," *SLN* 71 (November 1951), 32–5; Ewalt, *A Business Reborn*, 335–7; A. D. Theobald, *Forty-Five Years on the Up Escalator* (Chicago: privately published, 1979), 58–9, 148, 171–2.

[19] Letter from Walter McAllister to Don Geyer, 14 November 1953; United States Savings and Loan League 1953–, General; Correspondence of Chairman Walter W. McAllister 1953–1956 (McAllister Papers); RG 195, NACP; Norman Strunk "A Look Behind and a Look Ahead," *Savings Association Annals 1979* (Chicago: United States League of Savings Associations,

TABLE 5.1. *Number of Thrifts and Assets – 1945 to 1955*

Year	No. S&L	Change/Year	Assets (000,000)	Change/Year
1945	6,149	–	$8,747	–
1949	5,983	(0.7%)	$14,622	13.7%
1952	6,004	0.1%	$22,585	15.6%
1955	6,048	0.2%	$37,800	18.8%

Source: *Savings and Loan Fact Book, 1955*, 43; *Savings and Loan Fact Book, 1956*, 45.

EVALUATING THE GLORY YEARS

Given the tremendous demand for housing following World War II, the thrift industry recorded unprecedented expansion as shown in Table 5.1.

The most remarkable trend of this period was the spectacular asset growth rate for the thrift business – not only an industry record, but also the highest in any home financing industry. In states such as California, thrifts recorded a spectacular 380 percent jump in assets in the first postwar decade, while in the Northeast the growth was a more modest 240 percent. Also, the industry experienced a decline of the number of thrifts, resulting from both the closing of associations that still suffered from Depression era problems, as well as thrift mergers. This continued trend toward consolidation caused the average size of a thrift to rise to more than $6 million, up from $770,000 before the war. Similarly, in 1955 the industry remained the single largest source of residential mortgages, providing 36 percent of all home loans, which was nearly twice the amount provided by commercial banks. Furthermore, S&Ls were the primary mortgage providers for middle-class and lower-middle-class borrowers, as well as for nonwhite borrowers. Finally, by 1954 thrifts had assumed the position as the second largest repository for personal savings, and had in fact narrowed the gap that separated them from the largest depository, commercial banks. Between 1945 and 1954, thrift savings grew by almost 16 percent each year, which was twice the rate of increase for banks. By 1955, S&L deposits were 70 percent of bank savings, up from just 25 percent a decade earlier.[20]

1979), 171–2; Letter from Morton Bodfish to Walter W. McAllister, 9 November 1954; Bodfish, Morton, 1953– ; McAllister Papers; RG 195, NACP; Theobald, *Forty-Five Years*, 174.

[20] *Savings and Loan Fact Book, 1954*, 12–14; *Savings and Loan Fact Book, 1955* (Chicago: United States Savings and Loan League, 1955), 28, 38–40; Norman Strunk, "Business Will Continue to Grow Because We Build Service," *SLN* 75 (September 1955), 18–21; "Savings and Loan Associations Boom," *Business Week*, 17 May 1952, 148–50; "S&Ls are the Fastest Gainers," *Business Week*, 21 July 1956, 117–20; "The Rocketing S&Ls," *Business Week*, 16 February 1957, 134–5; Gaylord Freeman, *Mutual Competition* (Chicago: n.p., 1959), 27–9; Ratcliff, Rathbun and Honnold, *Residential Finance, 1950*, 40–46.

The federal home loan bank, the federal savings and loan system, and the Federal Savings and Loan Insurance Corporation (FSLIC) also expanded. Between 1940 and 1955, membership in the home loan bank grew from 77 percent to 96 percent of all thrifts, and this increase in subscriptions allowed the Federal Home Loan Bank Board (FHLBB) finally to liquidate the government's original $125 million investment in the reserve bank by 1950. At the same time, more than 90 percent of all industry assets were covered by deposit insurance by 1955, up from 70 percent fifteen years earlier. At the same time, because only one insured thrift failed during this period the FSLIC's insurance reserve also grew steadily. Unfortunately, large thrifts continued to dominate FSLIC membership and as late as 1955 an astounding 41 percent of all thrifts had not joined this organization. Finally, the federal savings and loan system saw modest growth with just over a quarter of all thrifts having federal charters. These same S&Ls, however, were quite large, accounting for more than half of total industry assets.[21]

FINE TUNING FEDERAL THRIFT PROGRAMS

The main reason for the growth of federal S&Ls was that regulators created a new charter for these associations, which unleashed the potential of these thrifts. Issued in 1949, Charter N simplified thrift operations by reducing the number of different types of savings accounts from five to one, allowed full withdrawal requests in a timely manner, and increased the maximum loan amount and loan-to-value ratio for mortgages. A technical, but important, improvement allowed federal thrifts to take advantage of regulatory changes without having to obtain permission from the shareholders to amend the thrift charter. Another technical change under Charter N involved the rules regarding the terms they could use to describe their business activities. The charter dropped all phraseology associated with shares, such as share accounts and share repurchases, and replaced them with the common terms of savings accounts and withdrawals. At the same time that it issued this charter, the Board announced it would also have a "free hand" to approve branches for federal thrifts, without regard to state laws.[22]

---

[21] "Ten Years of Federal Savings and Loan Associations," *FHLB Review* 9 (June 1943), 255–65; "Ten Years of Savings and Loan Insurance," *FHLB Review* 10 (July 1944), 261–6; *Savings and Loan Fact Book, 1955,* 40, 66–8; *Savings and Loan Fact Book, 1959,* 70–1, 102–4, "Residential Financing in the U.S.," *SLN* 74 (February 1954), 17–19.

[22] Theobald, *Forty-Five Years,* 170; Letter from William K. Divers to John Bricker, 25 April 1949; Federal Savings and Loan Rules and Regulations 1949; Divers Papers; RG 195; NACP; Memorandum from John M. Wyman to Home Loan Bank Board with attachments, 9 April 1952; Federal Savings and Loan Charters; Divers Papers; RG 195, NACP; Letter from William K. Divers to William J. Hallahan, 6 June 1952; Home Loan Bank Board 1948; Divers Papers; RG 195, NACP; Memorandum from Harold Lee to Mr. Fahey with attachments, 5 December 1947, National Savings and Loan League General 1948–1949; Divers Papers;

Federal thrifts quickly adopted Charter N, and by 1952 almost half of all federal thrifts operated under the new charter. That same year, the Board issued a revised Charter K so that associations which liked the more detailed document could also benefit from the new rules. The new charters also led state regulators to enact similar provisions for state-chartered thrifts so as to avoid their conversion to federal S&Ls. While the League gave these changes only a tepid endorsement, the American Bankers Association (ABA) was outraged because it saw the new terms as an attempt to mislead people into thinking that thrift and bank accounts were identical. They were not, since thrift deposits were actually investments towards the purchase of shares. The Board denied these accusations and countered that the banking industry did not have a "God-given right" to the use of terms such as withdrawal, deposit, or savings account. Still, the changes in terminology did make S&Ls appear more like banks in the mind of the public.[23]

Like the increase in the federal savings and loan system, the rise in FSLIC membership resulted from efforts by the FHLBB to make it easier for S&Ls to join. One reason that thrift managers did not have deposit insurance was that the premium for coverage was higher than that charged for banks under the Federal Deposit Insurance Corporation (FDIC). There were other differences between the FDIC and the FSLIC that discouraged thrifts from becoming members, and eventually banks began to use this to their advantage. In a 1938 pamphlet called "The Bank Customer Inquires," the ABA contended that because of the differences between the two deposit insurance programs, the FDIC was superior to the FSLIC, and by extension banks were safer than thrifts. The League responded with its own negative publicity, and the conflict became so heated that by 1948 regulators of both industries urged an immediate cessation to these smear tactics. The best way to end this type of competition was to eliminate the differences between the two programs, a goal for which the League began to lobby.[24]

RG 195, NACP; Memorandum from John M Wyman, 6 May 1949; Federal Savings and Loan Associations Rules and Regulations 1949, Divers Papers; RG 195, NACP.

[23] "Banker's Holiday," *The New Republic* 130 (5 July 1954), 4; "FHLB Seen Opening Saving-Loan Field," *The New York Times*, 31 March 1949, 39; George Mooney, "Bankers Surprised by Code Revisions," *The New York Times*, 24 July 1949, sec. 3, 1; Memorandum from O. E. L. to Mr. Divers, 1 April 1949; Federal Savings and Loan Association Rules and Regulations American Bankers Association 1949, Divers Papers; RG 195; NACP; Notes for FDIC Conference 1 June 1948; FDIC Controversy on Publicity 1948; Divers Papers; RG 195, NACP, quote 3.

[24] When the draft thrift deposit insurance bill circulated for comment in 1935, Assistant Treasury Secretary and former Utah banker Marriner Eccles insisted the FSLIC charge a higher premium than the FDIC in order to gain White House support. Horace Russell, *Savings and Loan Associations*, 2nd edition (Albany, NY: Mathew Bender & Company, 1960), 99–100; Memorandum for the files from W. H. Husband, 8 July 1948; FDIC Controversy on Publicity; Divers Papers; RG 195; NACP; Memorandum from O. E. L. to Mr. Divers, 6 January 1948; FDIC Comparison with FSLIC 1948; Divers Papers; RG 195; NACP; Memorandum

Although the FHLBB also disliked anything that made the FSLIC appear inferior to the FDIC, regulators did not recommend that Congress follow the League's requests to make both programs equal. They, in fact, thought that their insurance premium should stay high to allow FSLIC reserves to grow at the same pace as industry assets. The Board also thought this was needed to counter the general decline in the reserve ratio of the industry, which had fallen from 8.2 percent in 1942 to 7.6 percent in 1949. Even though it did not have the support of regulators, the League rallied its members to push for change, and in 1950 when it held its annual convention in Washington, D.C., hundreds of S&L executives descended on Congress. As a result, the industry got a bill introduced that would make the FSLIC equal to the FDIC in terms of premiums, insurance coverage, and payout of insured accounts. Curiously, approval of this law received the assistance of southern legislators who used it to block an important civil rights bill; Congress quickly passed the FSLIC bill in order to get to the civil rights measure before the session ended.[25]

Another issue involving the FSLIC was the 1956 effort by the Eisenhower Administration to remove it from the control of the FHLBB as part of a larger government restructuring effort. Under the White House plan, the FSLIC was to be run by a three-man Board of trustees as a separate government agency, much like the FDIC. The reason for creating two separate bodies was that the Board was perceived as having too much influence over the FSLIC, and the White House felt that there was a strong conflict of interest. Specifically, the Administration argued that providing home loan bank loans and insuring deposits involved contradictory objectives. On the one hand, the Board had to make sure thrifts operations were as sound as possible to protect the insurance fund reserves. This goal may be compromised, however, by the ready availability of bank advances which S&Ls might use to make speculative loans.[26]

W. H. Husband to William K. Divers, 11 October 1948, quote 1 and Notes for FDIC Conference June 1, 1948, 5–7; FS&LIC Consolidation with FDIC 1948; Divers Papers; RG 195; NACP; "Bankers Planning Retaliation in Savings Association Dispute," *The New York Times*, 30 May 1940, sec. 3, 1; "Banks Push Fight on Loan Methods," *The New York Times*, 2 May 1948, sec. 3, 1; William Reinhardt, "Insured Savings and Loan Associations – State and Federal," *ASLN* 63 (May 1943), 201–3.

[25] Fred L. Morse, "Liquidity Must Be Maintained," *SLN* 67 (August 1947), 13–15; "Reserves," *SLN* 73 (August 1953), 55; Memorandum from W. H. H. to Mr. Divers and Mr. Adams, Premium Reduction Pros and Cons, 28 January 1948; Divers Papers; RG 195; NACP; Draft Article of "Your Money and the Savings and Loan Association," for *Good Housekeeping* magazine, n.d., 1–7; Good Housekeeping 1955; McAllister Papers; RG 195; NACP; "How Savings are Insured," *U.S. News and World Report*, 25 March 1955, 97; "Savings-Loan Gain is Based on New Law Cutting Insurance Premium," *The New York Times*, 2 July 1950, sec. 3, 2; Walter Biggs, "A Manager Views Account Insurance," *SLN* 69 (November 1949), 36–8; *Savings and Loan Fact Book, 1955*, 45; Ewalt, *A Business Reborn*, 294–6.

[26] Separating the FSLIC from the FHLBB was one of the recommendations in the report from the Hoover Commission on Organization of the Executive Branch of Government, and

The Board strongly opposed this move in part because there were no operational problems to justify the change, with one member noting that "if the machine is running well, don't try to make it run better." It also argued that a separate FSLIC would create a supervisory problem for federal savings and loan associations, since all federal thrifts also had to have deposit insurance. The League also opposed the change, citing increased inefficiency and regulatory costs, as well as the potential adverse effects the change would have on the prestige of the FHLBB and the industry. After intense lobbying, the House defeated the proposal, which was the only time that a government reorganization effort failed to become law during the 1950s.[27]

INCREASED COMPETITION FROM GOVERNMENT

Although the 1950s was a period of tremendous prosperity for S&Ls, it was also a decade in which the federal government dramatically expanded its role in home finance. A key event in this process came in 1944 when Congress passed the Servicemen's Readjustment Act, a law intended to say "thank you" to an estimated 16 million veterans for their years of service to the nation. Dubbed the "G. I. Bill of Rights," the law offered veterans numerous benefits ranging from long-term medical care to education tuition, as well as generous financial assistance to prospective home buyers. Veterans could obtain mortgage payment guarantees from the Veterans Administration (VA) that were so complete that veterans were able to buy homes without any down payment and with the lender providing 100 percent financing. In addition, to ensure that monthly payments were affordable, the law capped interest rates on these loans.[28]

was similar to earlier reorganization proposals made by the General Accounting Office ten years earlier. U.S. Senate, Committee on Banking and Currency, *Federal Home Loan Bank Board and Federal Savings and Loan Insurance Corporation: A Study of Relationships.* Hearings by a Subcommittee of the Committee on Banking and Currency, 84th Cong., 2nd sess. (Washington, DC: USGPO, 1956), 32, 78–97; United States Savings and Loan League, "Why Reorganization Plan No. 2 Should Be Rejected"; Reorganization Plan No. 2 of 1956; McAllister Papers; NACP; RG 195; Thomas B. Marvell, *The Federal Home Loan Bank Board* (New York: Frederick A. Praeger, 1969), 259–61.

27 Letter from Walter W. McAllister to John F. Kennedy, 25 June 1956; Reorganization Plan No. 2 of 1956; McAllister Papers; RG 195; NACP; Handwritten comments by McAllister on the White House Transmittal Letter for Reorganization Plan No. 2; Reorganization Plan No. 2 of 1956; McAllister Papers; RG 195; NACP; *Federal Home Loan Bank Board and Federal Savings and Loan Insurance Corporation: A Study of Relationships,* 18–22. quote 20; Walter H. Dreier, "The Year In Retrospect," and Brent Spence, "A Staunch congressional Friend Promises Fair Treatment," *Savings and Loan Annals, 1956* (Chicago: United States Savings and Loan League), 8–9, 14–15; Ewalt, *A Business Reborn,* 74.

28 Allen Knowles, "GI Joe Returns," *ASLN* 64 (October 1944), 388–9; "While You Were Away," *SLN* 66 (March–April 1946), 27–8; Miles L. Colean and Alan F. Thornton, "Characteristics of GI Home Loans," *SLN* 69 (August 1949), 9–10; "The 'GI Bill of Rights' A Summary of Regulations," *FHLB Review* 13 (November 1944), 35–6, 43–4; Harry W. Colmery,

The League enthusiastically supported the G. I. Bill of Rights and helped draft the mortgage-guarantee provisions. Viewing their participation in the program as a patriotic duty, thrifts provided 80 percent of all VA-guaranteed mortgages in the first year of operation. Over the next four years, however, thrifts made only between 35 and 40 percent of VA loans, and by 1955 this share had fallen to just 20 percent. While this decline reflected the frustration S&L managers had with complying with the "red tape" and paperwork associated with VA loans, it also was a sign that congressional caps on interest rates were below market rates. Consequently, even though thrifts wanted to make VA mortgages, their desire to maximize loan yields meant that participation in this program waxed and waned in step with congressional changes to the maximum VA rates.[29]

The Federal Housing Administration (FHA) also expanded its operations in the 1950s when Congress passed laws that extended mortgage insurance coverage to loans for apartment buildings and inner-city projects, and made it easier for borrowers to qualify for insurance coverage. These changes caused the volume of loans with FHA insurance to grow by more than 450 percent between 1945 and 1954, at which time VA and FHA loans accounted for almost half of all new home mortgages. Significantly, because S&Ls did not make many of these loans, the main beneficiaries of these changes were competing lenders. While some managers wanted to make thrift mortgage terms equal to those of government-backed loans as a way to give their business a "shot in the arm," there was even greater opposition to any change from conservative managers. In fact, when the Board did try to move in this direction it "raised such a storm of protest throughout the business" that regulators quickly backed off, and it would be years before S&Ls offered the same consumer-friendly terms offered by the FHA.[30]

"Background and Broad Objectives of the 'GI' Bill," *Savings and Loan Annals, 1944* (Chicago: United States Savings and Loan League, 1944), 21–36; Oscar Kreutz, "GI Bill of Rights Opens Up $16 Billion Housing Market," *ASLN* 64 (October 1944), 316–17, 333–4; National Housing Administration, *Home Loans Under the G.I. Bill of Rights* (Washington, DC: USGPO, 1946), 2–5.

[29] "83% of GI Home Loans Made by Savings and Loan Business in 1945," *SLN* 66 (March–April 1946), 15; Harold Robb, "GI Loans – Insured or Guaranteed?" *SLN* 66 (May 1946), 15–6; Franklin Hardinge, "Secondary Market for GI Loans," *SLN* 67 (July 1947), 25–7; "Trends in GI Loans," *SLN* 69 (May 1949), 43; T. B. King, "Revival of the GI Loan," *SLN* 70 (November 1950), 27–31; Norman Strunk, "A Re-Examination of the GI Loan," *SLN* 72 (April 1952), 16–18; Lawrence V. Conway, *Principles of Savings and Loans* (Chicago: American Savings and Loan Institute Press, 1960), 351–91; Ratcliff, Rathbun, and Honnold, *Residential Finance, 1950*, 27; Ewalt, *A Business Reborn*, 246.

[30] Raymond Foley, "How the FHA Plans to Serve," *SLN* (January 1946), 7–9; Ray Westerfeld, "The Interest Factor," *ASLN* (February 1946), 17; "Government Activity in Home Mortgage Lending," *SLN* 71 (April 1951), 32; "The New Look in FHA: More Liberal Terms Ahead," *SLN* 74 (April 1954), 12; "Installment Principle Seen Making 100% VA-FHA Mortgages Sound," *The American Banker*, 22 July 1954, 12; Federal Housing Administration, *The FHA*

Finally, the Federal National Mortgage Association (FNMA or "Fannie Mae"), also underwent major changes to increase its role in home finance. Since its creation in 1938, the primary function of Fannie Mae was to buy FHA-insured mortgages from the lenders who made them. These transactions gave lenders the funds needed to make more insured loans. In 1954, Congress allowed the FNMA to both buy and sell all types of government-insured mortgages, which created a formal secondary market for FHA and VA loans. Fannie Mae could also sell mortgage-backed securities on the open market to buy these loans, which made the agency a self-funding entity. While expanding the FNMA provided thrifts with a resource to help manage their government-loan exposure, the changes also resulted in greater competition since they gave new life to mortgage companies, which had been essentially moribund since the 1930s. Because these firms specialized in making and selling loans to outside investors, the changes to the FNMA allowed them to become the largest originators of FHA and VA mortgages.[31]

The improvements in the VA, FHA, and FNMA mortgage programs after World War II had an effect on home ownership and finance that was nothing short of revolutionary. One accomplishment of these programs was that it now became possible for millions of Americans, who otherwise did not have adequate financial resources, to buy homes. Between 1940 and 1955, the level of home ownership rose from 41 percent to 57 percent, the fastest increase in American history. Another consequence of this "democratization" of home ownership was its impact on shaping the values of the postwar middle class, causing most people to view owning a home as an inalienable right. Finally, government involvement in home finance forced other mortgage lenders to adopt uniform practices in areas ranging from appraising to underwriting, as well as making loan terms more consumer oriented. Lenders also began

---

Story In Summary (Washington, DC: USGPO, 1959), 18–21; James Coppock, *Government Agencies of Consumer Instalment Credit,* Studies in Consumer Installment Financing, no. 5 (New York: National Bureau of Economic Research, 1940), 15–17; Ewalt, *A Business Reborn,* 262–67, 320–1; *Savings and Loan Fact Book, 1956* (Chicago: United States Savings and Loan League, 1956) 27, 35–7; Letter from David Ford to Walter W. McAllister, 7 December 1954, letter from Norman Strunk to Walter W. McAllister, 10 December 1954, quote, letter from Walter W. McAllister to Morton Bodfish, 7 January 1955, and memorandum from E. E. Reardon to Walter McAllister, 14 February 1955; Federal Savings and Loan Associations, Lending Liberalization, 1954– ; McAllister Papers; RG 195; NACP.

31 Memorandum from William K. Divers to Paul Heisler, 14 August 1953; Federal Home Loan Bank System, General; McAllister Papers; RG 195; NACP; "Housing Act of 1954," *SLN* 74 (August 1954), 10; Stephen Slipher, "Report on Legislative Matters," *Savings and Loan Annals, 1954* (Chicago: United States Savings and Loan League, 1954), 75–6; Ewalt, *A Business Reborn,* 142, 323; "Mortgage Insurance," *SLN* 74 (March 1954), 17–21;. "Mortgage Insurance (continued)," *SLN* 74 (June 1954), 44–50; E. P. Juel, "Selling Mortgages to FNMA," *SLN* 69 (September 1949), 9–12; Miles Colean, "Federal Lending and Insuring Practices," *SLN* 73 (February 1953), 9–11.

using the term "conventional" to describe any mortgage not under the FHA or VA programs.[32]

THE REGULATED COZIES UP TO THE REGULATOR

At the same time that the federal government was increasing its roles in housing, the FHLBB was beginning to form closer relations with the industry it oversaw. Before this could be done, however, the Board first had to be restored as an independent government agency. The Board first lost this status in 1934 when Congress placed it under the FHA; and, while it retained significant autonomy within the FHA, the League interpreted the move as a blow to the prestige of the industry. The status of the FHLBB diminished further during World War II when Roosevelt issued Executive Order 9070, which created the National Housing Agency (NHA) to coordinate all defense-related housing. This order not only reduced the size of the Board from five members to one, but it also dropped the word "federal" from the agency name, changes that the League again strongly disliked.[33]

In 1947, Congress expanded the Board from one to three members after the Los Angeles home loan bank controversy revealed the problems of having a single powerful commissioner oversee the industry. Legislators, however, ignored the League's pleas to make the Board a separate agency and instead made it part of the new Housing and Home Finance Agency (HHFA). While the Board regained more operational autonomy under the HHFA, the League still felt the thrift industry deserved a separate regulatory agency. This finally occurred in 1955 when the League launched a massive lobbying effort to defeat legislation that would give the HHFA administrator complete control over Board policies. Industry pressure was so effective that rather than diminish Board powers, the final version of the Housing Amendments Act of 1955 gave the FHLBB its independence. Even though the White House strenuously opposed this change, the broad scope of the overall bill forced President Dwight D. Eisenhower to reluctantly sign it into law.[34]

---

[32] "'Crisis' Confirms Conventional Loan," *SLN* 71 (August 1951), 6; Miles Colean, "The Euthanasia of Private Mortgage Lending," *SLN* 70 (July 1950), 33; Miles Colean, "Federal Mortgage Lending and Insurance Practices," *SLN* 73 (February 1953), 9–11; "Panel on Interest Rates, Terms, Percentages and Project Loans," *Savings and Loan Annals, 1949* (Chicago: United States Savings and Loan League, 1949), 96–100; "A Significant Change in Thinking," *SLN* 75 (April 1955), 10.

[33] Henry Stam, "Necessity of Independent Status for Savings and Loan Associations, *ASLN* 65 (April 1945), 124–5; "President Merges Housing Agencies," *The New York Times*, 25 May 1942, 24; Morton Bodfish, "Home Ownership - The Primary Defense Against Socialism," *Savings and Loan Annals, 1947* (Chicago: United States Savings and Loan League, 1947), 72–6; "Does the FHLB System Need to Live?" *SLN* 67 (April 1947), 15–17.

[34] Memorandum from O. E. Loomis to Mr. Fahey, 22 October 1947, memorandum from O. E. L. to Mr. Divers, 29 April 1949, and memorandum from O. E. L. to Mr. Divers,

The fight to gain FHLBB independence showed how important it was to the industry that thrifts, like commercial banks, have an autonomous regulatory agency. It also reflected the League's desire to have a regulatory body they could consult with and craft policies to promote growth and enhance the public image of the industry. This desire for a cooperative relationship between the regulator and the regulated was in large measure fulfilled after World War II, as evidenced by the actions of the three Board chairmen who served between 1947 and 1961. Although the chairmen varied widely in background, they shared the opinion that to build a safe and healthy industry required working closely with thrift leaders to design appropriate regulations. The first of these, William K. Divers was an experienced federal housing administrator who established this pattern of cooperative relations.[35]

Divers wanted to create a regulatory environment that gave both the industry and supervisors sufficient latitude to make decisions. Because he strongly believed that savings and loan associations can "be among the least regulated and best supervised financial institutions in the United States," Divers reduced the number of rules thrifts faced and often sought the advise of League leaders before issuing new regulations. Such actions did not necessarily mean, however, that thrifts always got what they desired, since Divers' main concern was ensuring safe and sound operations. For example, when executives of several large associations petitioned the Board for permission to pay "bonus" dividends in order to attract funds, Divers refused, contending the change was not in the public interest. The decision was unpopular, but adhered to Divers' philosophy of "strong but quiet supervision" of an

27 September 1949; Commission on the Organization of the Executive Branch of Government 1947; Divers Papers; RG 195; NACP; Memorandum from Walter W. McAllister to J. Aldrich Hall, 21 March 1955, Memorandum from J. Aldrich Hall to Walter W. McAllister, 21 March 1955, Letter from Walter W. McAllister to Herbert Hoover, 18 December 1953, and Reorganization Plan No. 1 of 1954 Clearance Draft; Reorganization of Home Loan Bank Board, 1953; McAllister Papers; RG 195; NACP; Memorandum from J. F. M. to Walter W. McAllister with attachments, 13 January 1955, Reorganization of Home Loan Bank Board 1955; McAllister Papers; RG 195; NACP; Letter from Walter W. McAllister to Harold A. Fitzgerald with attachments, 8 September 1955, Federal Home Loan Bank Board Independence Effective August 11, 1955, Correspondence of Chairman Albert J. Robertson 1956–1961 (Roberston Papers); RG 195; NACP, 2; Letter from Walter W. McAllister to Norman Strunk, 8 August 1955, McAllister Papers; RG 195, NACP; "HLB Board Independence Voted in Congress" *SLN* 75 (July 1955), 8; "Congress Grants Independence to HLB Board" *SLN* 75 (August 1955), 10; "A Message From Your President," *SLN* 75 (September 1955), 14; Ewalt, *A Business Reborn*, 306.

35 Marvell, *The Federal Home Loan Bank Board*, 219; Oscar Kreutz, *The Way It Happened* (St. Petersburg, FL: St. Petersburg Printing Co., 1972), 100–1; Letter from William K. Divers to E. L. Barnett, 29 October 1948, 1; Records Relating to the Seizure of the Los Angeles Federal Home Loan Bank and Long Beach Federal Savings and Loan Association; RG 195; NACP; "League Discusses Policy with Bank Board," *SLN* 71 (March 1951), 17–18.

industry that "is in too good a shape to permit a few reckless or poorly managed associations to damage its reputation."[36]

Another way Divers showed his support for the industry was his work in establishing the Savings and Loan Foundation in 1951 to educate the public about the thrift business. The idea of creating the Foundation – an independent nonprofit organization funded by member S&Ls – resulted from the work of the Federal Savings and Loan Advisory Committee, a body formed by the FHLBB in 1935 to develop ways to promote the thrift industry. Divers strongly supported the Foundation and instructed each regional home loan bank to encourage member thrifts to help fund it. Unfortunately, even though industry leaders were consulted on the goals of the Foundation, the League did not like the fact it had no control over its operation, and thus gave it only lukewarm support. Consequently, the Foundation had difficulty in attracting funds, and it was three years before it could launch its first national publicity campaign. This campaign, which consisted of full-color advertisements in popular magazines such as the *Saturday Evening Post*, proved so successful that in 1955 alone membership tripled; by 1960 over one-third of all S&Ls belonged to the Foundation. Divers' commitment to the Foundation's mission to "teach millions of new savers to save modest amounts regularly" was such that he left the Board in 1953 to become its president.[37]

Replacing Divers as chairman was thrift executive and former League president Walter McAllister. Although McAllister was the first industry leader to hold this position, senators did not seriously question his ability

---

[36] Speech Notes, Indiana Savings and Loan League Meeting, 16–17 September 1948, quote; Divers Papers; RG 195, NACP; Speech Notes, Kansas Savings and Loan League, 15 May 1953, quote; Divers Papers; RG 195; NACP; Speech Notes, Illinois Savings and Loan League Meeting, 12 October 1948; Divers Papers; RG 195; NACP; Letter from William K. Divers to John A Davis, 9 June 1952; Advertising and Broker Solicitations Insured Associations Dividend Bureau; Divers Papers; RG 195; NACP; Letter from Everett C. Sherborn to William K. Divers, 25 April 1952; Federal Savings and Loan Associations, 1950 Shares, Bonus On; Divers Papers; RG 195; NACP; Memorandum from John M. Wyman to Board, 15 September 1950; Federal Savings and Loan Associations, 1950 Shares, Bonus On; Divers Papers; RG 195; NACP; William K. Divers, "Current Savings and Loan Association Picture," *Savings and Loan Annals, 1950*, 18–20.

[37] Memorandum from William K. Divers to All Bank Presidents, Public Relations Program, 19 May 1950; Savings and Loan Foundation 1950; Divers Papers; RG 195; NACP; Letter from George W. West to Joseph W. Hart, 11 March 1952, Quote; Savings and Loan Foundation 1950; Divers Papers; RG 195; NACP; Ernest T. Trigg to the Chairman of the Board of Directors and to the Presidents of Each FHLB, 8 June 1951, Savings and Loan Foundation 1950, Correspondence of Chairman William K. Divers, RG 195; NACP; Theobald, *Forty-Five Years*, 177; Ewalt, *A Business Reborn*, 334; Address by Louis W. Grant to the Presidents of the Federal Home Loan Banks, 15 February 1954; McAllister Papers; RG 195; NACP; Letter from William K. Divers to Albert J. Robertson, 30 November 1956, and Letter from W. R. Youngquist to William K. Divers, 12 February 1957, Savings and Loan Foundation 1956, Robertson Papers; RG 195; NACP.

to run the Board in an impartial manner, and based on the support of Divers and the two major industry trade groups he was easily confirmed. Curiously, the main reason McAllister agreed to become chairman was to help secure the Board's independence from the HHFA, not to be a regulator. Consequently, throughout his tenure McAllister was uncomfortable as an administrator and warned friends not to "start thinking of me as a bureaucrat." League leaders, however, considered him to be "part of the family," and as a result FHLBB members were such frequent guests at trade group functions that some thrift executives complained that it was "easier to 'talk shop' without the 'policemen' around."[38]

Unlike Divers, whose term in office was relatively uneventful, McAllister faced a number of issues that required regulatory action. As the chairman confessed to his friend Bodfish, "I find the pressure to issue regulations right and left for this and that." The most persistent and troublesome problem McAllister had to deal with was finding a way to regulate the use of "give-away" promotions used by S&Ls to attract deposits, a practice first used in the 1920s. While most thrifts wooed savers with low-cost items such as pen and pencil sets, others that aggressively sought deposits offered customers expensive gifts such as kitchen appliances. Initially, McAllister relied on moral suasion and pleas by League leaders to limit these practices, but much to his dismay these "jaw-boning" efforts rarely worked. Finally, in 1956 the Board reluctantly issued a rule limiting the value of gifts any one customer could receive to $2.50 per account. Although McAllister knew this regulation was not perfect, it did end the most grievous abuses and set a precedent that subsequent Boards would build upon.[39]

[38] Transcript of meeting between Board members Divers and Adams, League executive vice president Gehrke and Savings and Loan Foundation executive Trigg, n.d., McAllister, Walter W., 1952; Divers Papers; RG 195, NACP; Letter from Walter W. McAllister to Morton Bodfish, 31 July 1953; United States Savings and Loan League 1953 – General; McAllister Papers; RG 195, NACP; Letter from Ben H. Wooten to Walter W. McAllister, 15 August 1953; Wooten, Ben; McAllister Papers; RG 195, NACP; Letter from Walter W. McAllister to Ben H. Wooten, 20 August 1953; Wooten, Ben; McAllister Papers; RG 195; NACP; Letter from Walter McAllister to Norman Strunk, 4 August 1953; United States Savings and Loan League, General; McAllister Papers; RG 195; NACP; Letter from Walter McAllister to Allan Shivers, n.d.; Sh; McAllister Papers; RG 195, NACP; Letter from Walter McAllister to W. W. Townsend, 5 January 1954, quote; Townsend, W. W. 1953– ; McAllister Papers; RG 195, NACP; Letter from Norman Strunk to Walter McAllister, 20 April 1954, quote; United States Savings and Loan League Manager Conference, 1953; McAllister Papers; RG 195; NACP; Letter from Norman Strunk to Walter McAllister, 13 August 1954, quote; United States Savings and Loan League Meetings; McAllister Papers; RG 195; NACP.

[39] Letter from Walter W. McAllister to Morton Bodfish, 2 October 1953; United States Savings and Loan League 1953 – General; McAllister Papers; RG 195; NACP; Letter from Walter McAllister to Henry Bubb, 25 July 1956, letter from Walter McAllister to Roy Larson, 1 June 1955, letter from Norman Strunk to Walter McAllister 10 May 1954, letter from Ira Dixon to Fred Greene, 29 April 1955, letter from Walter W. McAllister to Neill Davis, 30 March 1954, and letter from Norman Strunk to Walter W. McAllister with attachment, 1 October 1953;

The use of brokered deposits as a way to build savings was another issue the McAllister Board tackled. Like the use of "give-aways," some managers were abusing this source of funds to achieve rapid growth. Deposit brokers were firms that solicited money from investors throughout the country and placed them in associations that paid the highest rates; these institutions paid the brokers a fee for this service. Because brokers moved funds whenever rates changed, these deposits were known as "hot money," and thrifts sometimes engaged in rate wars to attract and retain these funds. Given this volatility, both the League and Board condemned as unsound the excessive use of brokered deposits to fund mortgages but to little avail. The San Francisco home loan bank, pressured by its members, even insisted there should be no attempt to prohibit these practices by regulation. By 1953, the continued abuse of these funds led the Board to limit the territory from which thrifts could solicit brokered deposits. The Justice Department, however, nullified this rule since it restricted competition. A thoroughly frustrated McAllister dropped efforts to regulate these funds, and opted to let later Boards wrestle with this issue.[40]

In 1956, President Eisenhower named as the new Board chairman Albert J. Robertson, who was a career bureaucrat with little knowledge of the thrift industry. Robertson had been Assistant Postmaster General prior to coming to the Board, and his early policies conformed to the same pro-industry positions of Divers and McAllister. During his five-year tenure, Robertson did not significantly expand thrift powers, and most changes simply codified new authorities granted by Congress. One such rule allowed thrifts to make loans of up to 5 percent of total assets for the acquisition and development of unimproved residential sites, while the most beneficial rule gave S&Ls permission to buy and sell loan participations to other thrifts. By allowing S&Ls to buy and sell up to half of a loan, as long as the originating institution retained at least the other half of the loan, the Board hoped to improve the distribution of surplus funds across the country and allow thrifts to finance

Advertising "Give-Away" Programs, 1953– ; McAllister Papers; RG 195; NACP and Letter from Walter W. McAllister to Perry Marsh, 22 November 1953; Advertising and Broker Solicitation, 1955; McAllister Papers, RG 195; NACP.

[40] Memorandum from R. R. Burklin to Mr. Divers and Mr. McAllister, 2 September 1953, Letter from Leo W. Tosh to Walter W. McAllister, 2 December 1953, and Memorandum from T. Wade Harrison to members of the Board, 11 November 1953; Advertising and Broker Solicitations, 1953; McAllister Papers; RG 195; NACP; Memorandum from T. Wade Harrison to members of the Board, Department of Justice Views on Proposed Regulations, 9 August 1954; Advertising and Broker Solicitations, 1954; McAllister Papers; RG 195; NACP; Letter from Walter W. McAllister to Perry Marsh, 22 November 1955; Advertising and Broker Solicitations, 1955; McAllister Papers; RG 195; Letter from Walter W. McAllister to Norman Strunk, 19 July 1956; United States Savings and Loan League 1953 – General; McAllister Papers; RG 195; NACP.

larger housing projects. In 1960, the Board amended this rule to allow loan sales to pension funds.[41]

While the League maintained generally cordial relations with the Robertson Board, sometimes the chairman grew annoyed with persistent industry requests for broader business powers. When the FHLBB raised the limits on apartment loans to 75 percent of appraised value for a maximum term of fifteen years, Strunk applauded the decision as "a step in the right direction." An incredulous Robertson noted to the other Board members "if this is only a step in the right direction, what is the ultimate goal, 100% in perpetuity?" Despite such instances of apparent frustration with industry desires, Robertson, like previous chairmen, was content to give the industry considerable latitude to police itself. This was especially evident in how Robertson dealt with the continued abuse of "give-aways," in which he conceded, "we can't do much better on the subject. Our best guess is to give the industry a free hand with the hope that sooner or later it will recognize the futility of overdoing these programs."[42]

The Robertson Board also relied on traditional "jaw-boning" to persuade thrifts to change their ways, especially if self-policing failed to achieve the desired outcome. This approach was used when thrifts began to raise dividend rates in 1958 and 1959. Robertson tried to convince managers that by raising rates thrifts would not gain a competitive advantage, but would rather create a floor that all other S&Ls would have to meet to avoid losing funds. When these appeals failed, the chairman told thrift leaders in 1960 that, while he opposed regulation, he hated unnecessary competition even more, and warned that rate controls such as those for commercial banks would be inevitable if the destructive rate wars persisted. Although he had no intention of following through on this threat, his willingness to raise the issue of extending Regulation Q over S&Ls was a sign that regulatory goodwill did have limitations.[43]

---

[41] Memorandum from Charles M. Torrance to Albert J. Robertson, 25 August 1958; Federal Savings and Loan Insurance Corporation, Loans, Participation, 1957– ; Robertson Papers, RG 195; NACP; Letter from Daniel Flood to Albert J. Robertson, 8 May 1958, and Letter from Albert J. Robertson to David Ford, 23 October 1958; Federal Savings and Loan Associations, Loans – General, 1956–1959; Robertson Papers, RG 195; NACP; Henry C. Newman, "Participation Loan Program of Savings and Loan Associations," *Construction Review* 4 (December 1958), 8–12; Ewalt, *A Business Reborn*, 322–3.

[42] Letter from Norman Strunk to Albert J. Robertson, 22 August 1958, and Attachment from Albert J. Robertson to Dixon and Hallahan, 25 August 1958, quote; Federal Savings and Loan Associations, Loans, General; Robertson Papers; RG 195; NACP; Letter Albert J. Robertson to Hamilton Patton, 4 February 1960; P; Robertson Papers; RG 195; NACP; Letter from Albert J. Robertson to G. E. Karlan, 11 February 1960, quote; Advertising – Give Aways; Robertson Papers; RG 195; NACP.

[43] Ed W. Hiles "Do We Want a Regulatory Dividend Ceiling?" *SLN* 78 (February 1957), 32–6; Speech by Albert J. Robertson to the Little Rock Federal Home Loan Bank Shareholders

The Board was, however, successful in finally controlling the use of bro-kered deposits by fast-growing thrifts. Robertson, like McAllister, was con-cerned that managers were relying too heavily on this unstable funding source, especially in states such as California where some S&Ls depended on brokers for more than 50 percent of their deposits. Not only did Robertson see this concentration of funds as a hazard, but he feared that the high rates paid to retain these funds would force managers to make riskier loans. Furthermore, the increase in rates was draining funds from S&Ls in other parts of the country. By 1959, Robertson had received enough complaints from other thrifts in the East and Midwest to draft a rule that limited bro-kered deposits to 5 percent of assets and restricted the fees brokers could receive. While the League did not take a strong stand on this issue, the brokered deposit community immediately tried to prevent passage of the new rules. Despite their public relations efforts to sway Board opinion, the rule was not modified and, according to Robertson, appeared to solve the problem.[44]

On the surface, the policies of these three ideologically pro-industry chair-men gave the impression the industry had "captured" the FHLBB and had essentially made it a third S&L trade association. In reality, however, the Board was not entirely sympathetic to industry needs, but generally sup-ported the conservative mainstream of the industry as evidenced by rules that promoted the activities of smaller associations and discouraged rapid expansion. Divers, for example, noted that "size alone is no criterion; it is O.K. if it means service to common encouragement of thrift and economical finance, but no good if done for size alone." Similarly, the Boards of the 1950s did not let the industry dictate the rule-making agenda and in several instances specifically rejected any attempt by the League to influence opin-ion. Even McAllister, who was the closest to the industry, felt that on some issues the Board had to act independently and not look to the "so-called trade associations for advice." The conclusion to be drawn about this period of

---

Meeting, 4 April 1960; Federal Savings and Loan Associations, Dividends – Ceiling; Robertson Papers, RG 195; NACP.

[44] Letter from Albert J. Robertson to F. Marion Donahoe, 8 July 1958; Advertising and Brokers, Regulations, September 1956–1958; Robertson Papers; RG 195; NACP; Letter from Clarence Smith to John E. Barriere, 11 February 1959; Advertising and Brokers, Regulations, 1959; Robertson Papers; RG 195; NACP; Letter from Albert J. Robertson to F. Marion Donahoe, 8 July 1958; Advertising and Brokers, Regulations, September 1956–1958; Robertson Papers; RG 195; Letter from Norman Strunk to Member Managers, 2 December 1959; Advertising and Broker Regulations, 1959; Robertson Papers; RG 195; NACP; Letter from Albert J. Robertson to Philip A. Hart, 5 August 1960; Advertising and Brokers, Regulations, 1960; Robertson Papers; RG 195; NACP; H. R. Amott, "Savings and Loan Broker Restrictions Not in Public Interest," *Investment Dealers Digest* 26 (8 February 1960), 5; Marvell, *The Federal Home Loan Bank Board*, 133–6.

regulation was that the Board wanted industry growth as long as it did not compromise industry safety.[45]

THRIFTS HIT SOME BUMPS IN THE ROAD

Although the S&L industry generally viewed the postwar years as the best of times, it also suffered some legislative and business setbacks. The first of these was the Housing Act of 1949, which formally made it the responsibility of the federal government to "guarantee a decent home and suitable living environment for every American family." Although the first federal housing assistance program had appeared in 1937, the role of the government in housing the needy received greater attention in the postwar period. One of the champions of increasing federal support was Sen. Robert Taft (R-OH), who was an ardent supporter of free enterprise, but who also believed that the government did have an obligation to house the least advantaged. As chairman of a wartime subcommittee examining postwar housing needs, Taft renewed the debate on federally financed public housing, and from 1945 to 1948 he co-sponsored legislation each year to establish a federal housing program for the poor.[46]

While the League agreed that there was a need for low-income housing, it strongly opposed any effort to provide this through public housing. Industry leaders argued that a broad government housing program would hurt the building industry by driving up labor and material prices, and that the tremendous cost of any public housing plan would increase taxes for all Americans, including the poor. Aside from these economic arguments the League had strong ideological objections to this potential intrusion of government into housing. It contended that subsidized housing was pure socialism, an extension of the welfare state, and a direct threat to private enterprise. League officials also pointed to the problems of subsidized housing

---

[45] "Setting the Record Straight," Address of William K. Divers before the Annual Convention of the National Savings and Loan League Meeting, 17 June 1949, quote; National Savings and Loan League Meeting, June 15–18, 1949; Divers Papers; RG 195; NACP; Letter from Walter W. McAllister to R. V. Walker, 5 December 1955, quote; Federal Savings and Loan Associations, Conversions, 1955 October–December; McAllister Papers; RG 195; NACP; Marvell, *The Federal Home Loan Bank Board*, 267–8.

[46] Wm. Brock, "President's Address," and Morton Bodfish, "Report of the Executive Vice President," *Savings and Loan Annals, 1945* (Chicago: United States Savings and Loan League, 1945), 5–6, 38–43; F. G. Addison, "Bankers Testify on Wagner-Ellender-Taft Bill," *SLN* (January 1946), 25–8; Henry Irr, "President's Address," *Savings and Loan Annals, 1946* (Chicago: United States Savings and Loan League, 1946), 4–5, 9; Charles Fletcher, "Constructive Program Needed to Combat Public Housing," *Savings and Loan Annals, 1947*, 48–56; Morton Bodfish, "Report of the Chairman of the Executive Committee on Legislative Matters," *Savings and Loan Annals, 1948* (Chicago: United States Savings and Loan League, 1948), 292.

in Great Britain as proof that such an experiment should not be tried in America. Such arguments helped defeat every attempt to create government-subsidized housing through 1948, and many government officials at the time believed as Governor John Bricker (R-OH) did, that housing can "only be met by the savings and loan, real estate, and home building industries. Government cannot and should not do it."[47]

The prospect of creating a broad public housing program gained strength when several key House and Senate housing committee members lost in the 1948 election. Public housing advocates interpreted their defeat as a mandate to improve the deteriorating condition of inner cities. They also contended government had to be the source of urban housing since other lenders were focused almost exclusively on suburban development. Such repeated attacks caused the League to become very defensive, and allowed supporters to introduce desired reform bills. The Housing Act of 1949 called for the construction of 810,000 public housing units over six years, and a five-year campaign to clear urban slums. The League was aghast by the scope of the bill and saw it as the first step toward government control of housing. Recently elected Senator John Bricker concurred with this assessment and asked "Where do we stop?... With the Government threatening to encompass between one-third to one-half of the home-financial field, [the thrift industry's] very existence is at stake." Still support for the measure as strong, and some representatives who personally opposed it voted in favor because "it was what my people want." Although subsequent funding for these programs was reduced and only a fraction of the proposed units was built, the Housing Act of 1949 had nonetheless created the opening that became the basis for future federal programs to build public housing.[48]

---

[47] "Bankers Testify on W-E-T Bill," *SLN* 66 (January 1946), 25–9; "Why We Are Against Government-Subsidized Housing," *SLN* 69 (June 1949), 23; M. K. McMurray, "Socialism on the Doorstep," *Savings and Loan Annals, 1949*, 11–12; Viola Billings, "The Dangers of Disinterest," *SLN* 66 (August 1946), 30–32; "Financing and Building Problems, *SLN* 69 (January 1949), 30–3; "It *Can* Happen in the Savings and Loan Business," *SLN* 68 (July 1948), 17–19; "So Sorry – Too Late," *SLN* 70 (July 1950), 6; Leon T. Kendall, editor, *Thrift and Home Ownership: The Writings of Fred T. Greene*, Occasional Paper No. 1 (Chicago: United States Savings and Loan League, 1961), 21–3; Henry Rosenthal, "Pooled Planning," *ASLN* 64 (February 1944), quote 43.

[48] The total cost of these programs was estimated to be $15–20 billion. U.S. House of Representatives, *Housing Amendments of 1949*, Hearings Before the Committee on Banking and Currency, 81st Cong., 1st sess., HR 5637 (Washington, DC: USGPO, 1949), 275–8; U. S. Senate, *Housing Amendments of 1949*, Hearings Before the Committee on Banking and Currency, 81st Cong., 1st sess., S 2246 (Washington, DC: USGPO, 1949), 1–10; J. D. McLamb,"Eight Inning to the Government Housers," *SLN* 69 (August 1949), 6; Stephen Slipher, "A Glance Behind the Housing Act," *SLN* 69 (August 1949), 13–14; John W. Bricker, "Government Encroachment on Individual Freedom," and Morton Bodfish, "Report of the Chairman of the Executive Committee on Legislative Matters," *Savings and Loan Annals, 1949*, 13–19, quote

A second legislative defeat came when Congress finally made S&Ls subject to federal income tax laws. The League had long been able to secure an exemption from federal taxes for the thrift industry by arguing that thrifts were not-for-profit associations similar to other self-help charities. The growth of thrifts after World War II, however, made it more difficult for League leaders to maintain this position, and even the industry trade journal joked that thrift executives "feel like a million – tax-free of course!" In 1950, this situation changed for the first time when the House, responding to pressure from commercial bankers, passed the first revenue bill that would tax S&Ls at the same rate as other corporations. While the League successfully lobbied to defeat the measure, the industry was not fully unified in opposing it. The National Savings and Loan League even told Congress it was willing to support a tax bill provided it exempted thrifts with reserves below some reasonable percentage of total assets. Such a concession not only angered many in the League, but became the basis for including S&Ls under federal tax laws.[49]

The next year, the House passed its annual revenue bill, and to the delight of the League it contained no S&L tax language. The Senate, however, shocked the industry by amending the bill so that any association with loan-loss reserves in excess of 10 percent of total assets would be taxed. The change was a sign that some legislators finally felt that industry profits were just too high to escape taxation. The League again lobbied for changes in the bill, but unlike the cases in earlier fights, thrift leaders no longer hoped to prevent passage of a tax. They were just trying to minimize its impact. By arguing that the proposed tax would penalize associations with large surpluses and discourage managers from making prudent allocations for potential loan losses, the League was able to change the bill so that S&Ls would be taxed, but only after they built up a reserve equal to 12 percent of assets. While the League disliked losing its cherished tax-exempt status, and regulators feared managers would use dubious accounting procedures to avoid paying taxes, overall the new law had very little effect on the industry since only a handful of thrifts maintained a 12 percent reserve. Still, the perverse logic of taxing thrifts with large reserves provided little incentive for increasing an association's safety cushion.[50]

A third challenge for the industry came during the Korean War when Congress passed the Defense Production Act of 1950. Like previous efforts

---

18–19, 142–8; "The Battleground of the Housing Fight," *SLN* 68 (May 1949), 18–20, quote 19; Theobald, *Forty-Five Years*, 168–9.

[49] Cartoon, *SLN* (May 1952), 19; George Mooney, "Savings Units Join to Fight Taxation," *The New York Times*, 21 May 1950, sec. 3, 3; Memorandum from O. E. Loomis to Mr. Divers, 28 February 1950, 6–7; Taxes Mutual 1950; Divers Papers; RG 195; NACP.

[50] Morton Bodfish, "A Look at the Year Ahead," *Savings and Loan Annals, 1950*, 26–7; Memorandum from John M. Wyman to Files, 10 September 1952; Taxes Mutual 1952; Divers Papers; RG 195; NACP; Marvel. *The Federal Home Loan Bank Board*, 136–8; Ewalt, *A Business Reborn*, 300–1; Theobald, *Forty-Five Years*, 187.

to convert the economy from domestic to wartime production, this law restricted residential construction. It did so, however, through indirectly controlling home finance, as opposed to the direct control of building materials imposed during World War II. The law led to the creation of Regulation X, which gave the Federal Reserve authority to reduce the loan-to-value ratios for home loans and require shorter loan maturities, all in an effort to reduce the demand for non–defense-related housing. At the same time, the Federal Reserve reduced the money supply, which increased mortgage interest rates. Although such controls seemed harsh, the provisions of Regulation X proved to be more palatable than strict rationing; and, since the Federal Reserve administered the rules flexibly, the impact of these changes on thrifts and consumers was gradual, which helped in its general success.[51]

The final crisis the industry faced came in 1954 when the nation experienced its first major credit crunch since the end of World War II. That year, the booming economy finally began to show signs of weakness, and slid into a mild and brief recession. The dip in the economy did not, however, dampen consumer spending; and, as personal income fell, people began using their savings to pay for expensive goods such as automobiles and televisions. Unfortunately, the market for home loans also remained red-hot; and, as thrifts saw savings withdrawals increase in early 1955, they reacted by raising dividend rates to hold onto this money. This tactic, however, was not successful, and in an effort to make more loans, thrifts borrowed heavily from the home loan banks. Between August 1954 and May 1955, home loan bank advances rose 25 percent to $821 million, and in just three months advances exceeded $1.2 billion. This rapid increase forced the Board to authorize an unusually large bond issue to fund these advances in June 1955. The sale of these notes, however, almost failed because it occurred when debt markets were already saturated and the Federal Reserve Board was curbing the flow of credit to banks.[52]

The Board realized that because banks were the primary buyers of their debt, it would have to offer the bonds at higher interest rates to ensure future sales, a move that would likely fuel inflation. In September 1955, the Board announced a moratorium on new borrowing from the bank, which McAllister justified by telling thrift executives "you had a lender's paradise.... but if the trend [of increased bank loans] had been continued

---

[51] Morton Bodfish, "A Look at the Year Ahead," *SLN* 70 (December 1950), 16; Morton Bodfish, "Report of the Chairman of the Executive Committee on Legislative Matters," *Savings and Loan Annals, 1950*, 137–42; "Vigorous Policies Urged in Inflation," *The New York Times*, 25 January 1951, 35; Charles Fisher, "Regulation X," *SLN* 70 (December 1950), 26–7; "Regulation and Frustration," *SLN* 71 (September 1951), 6; Ewalt, *A Business Reborn*, 235.

[52] Theobald, *Forty-Five Years*, 191; "U.S. Acts to Slow Mortgage Boom," *The New York Times*, 18 September 1955, sec. 3, 1; "Another Big Year for Mortgage Lenders," *Business Week*, 6 February 1954, 64–6; 'Easy Mortgage' Warning Given as Rates on Savings are Raised," *The New York Times*, 3 April 1955, sec. 3, 10.

we would have been responsible for contributing an unnecessary inflation" to the national economy. This sudden cut off of liquidity had an immediate effect on the availability of S&L home loans. During the first nine months of 1955, the volume of thrift mortgages had increased by 28 percent over the same period in 1954, but in the fourth quarter lending fell below the levels a year earlier. In November, the Board lifted its restrictions, but tight money conditions eased only slightly as the country again moved toward a recession. For industry leaders, the events of 1955 indicated the seemingly limitless growth of the "glory years" were near an end and that future expansion would require greater management skills and business innovation.[53]

CONCLUSIONS

By all accounts, the late 1940s and early 1950s was the most successful period in the history of the thrift industry, and a large part of this success resulted from the major social changes that the nation experienced during these years. The return of millions of servicemen who were eager to take up their prewar lives led to a dramatic increase in marriages and new families, and related to this "baby boom" was the need for new homes. Although postwar housing shortages were not new in America, the way in which this problem was solved in the 1940s was different. Improvements in automobile transportation and construction techniques allowed builders to develop large suburbs of single-family houses in order to meet the unprecedented demands of prospective homeowners. Because these communities combined the benefits of being close to the city with the space and freedom of country living, millions of Americans became suburbanites establishing a trend that would dominate residential development for the rest of the twentieth century. The demand for homes and the large-scale development of suburbs proved to be a financial windfall for the savings and loan industry as S&Ls aggressively pursued lending opportunities with mortgage plans designed to meet the needs of the postwar consumer.

The thrift industry trade association was an important force in helping thrifts attain a major role in America's financial structure during the 1950s. The League advised S&Ls on how to advertise their services effectively, offered more education programs, and expanded its own internal organization all in an effort to push the industry forward. Business growth was

---

[53] "Take It Easy" *Business Week*, 31 January 1953, 87; "Home Loan Banks to Tighten Credit," *The New York Times*, 15 September 1955, 47; "Money Hunt Is On for Mortgages," *the New York Times*, 16 October 1955, sec. 3, 1; "Home Loan Bank Board Relaxes Credit Curbs It Imposed Sept. 8," *The New York Times*, 19 November 1955, 25; "Savings Squeeze is Felt by Banks," *The New York Times*, 16 December 1955, 1; "FHLBB Chairman Climaxes Conference Program," *California Savings and Loan League Journal*, n.d., quote; California Savings and Loan League 1953; McAllister Papers; RG 195; NACP; Theobald, *Forty-Five Years*, 191.

also aided by changes in federal regulations. Redesigned charters for federal associations and more favorable requirements for deposit insurance led to strong increases in thrift participation in these major programs. At the same time, federal regulators became more industry-friendly by issuing rules that supported S&L growth and expansion. Eventually, the increasingly close relationship between the regulator and the regulated combined with the political clout of the League became a concern of other Washington officials, but few efforts to change it proved successful.

By the middle of the 1950s, the thrift industry bore little resemblance to the business that had existed in the 1930s. S&Ls controlled over $37 billion (U.S. billion) in assets, provided nearly half of all home mortgages, and were the second largest private industry repository for consumer savings. Despite these impressive gains, signs were appearing that the industry was beginning to fragment. These included differences over issues like thrift taxation, the use of brokered deposits, and dividend rate policies. Over the next ten years divisions between large and small thrifts as well as between S&Ls in the East and the West would grow and eventually lead to greater internal dissent and legislative scrutiny.

6

EXTERNAL CHALLENGES AND INTERNAL DIVISIONS, 1956–1966

The second decade after World War II presented far more challenges and uncertainties for the thrift industry than the earlier "glory years." One major challenge thrifts faced was finding lending opportunities and ways to attract funds, problems tied to slower economic growth and the significant increase in competition from other financial industries and the federal government. A second critical concern was the need to give greater attention to the home ownership needs of minority groups, resulting from the growth of a national civil rights movement. Finally, thrifts had to contend with more vigorous federal oversight, a situation that reflected the work of several dynamic regulators. Despite such challenges, the thrift industry maintained a very strong growth rate in the late 1950s and early 1960s, during which time it surpassed the $100 billion (U.S. billion) asset milestone and achieved control of nearly half the residential home finance market. This expansion, however, also led to greater divisions within the thrift industry. Differences between large and small thrifts, those in the eastern half of the country and those in the faster growing West, as well as between mutually owned and publicly traded S&Ls were all signs that the industry was becoming fragmented. For its part, the League tried to bridge these rifts, but by the mid-1960s it was apparent that these gaps had instead widened. The most significant challenge for the League and the industry, however, lay in trying to prevent the imposition of legal controls on savings rates. Despite their best efforts, thrift officers were unable to keep this from happening, and in 1966 S&Ls became subject to the same rate controls banks faced under Regulation Q. This development not only formally ended the years of easy S&L growth, but ushered in a new period of uncertainty that would culminate in industry deregulation.

THE ECONOMY COOLS OFF AND COMPETITION HEATS UP

During the late 1950s and early 1960s, S&Ls found it more difficult to attract business than in the previous glory years for a variety of reasons.

A general slowdown in the economy made it impossible to maintain the growth rates recorded in the first ten years after World War II. Between 1945 and 1954, the Gross National Product (GNP) and level of personal spending rose at an annual rate of 6.6 percent and 8.1 percent, respectively, but over the next ten years, these figures declined slightly, to 5.5 percent and 5.9 percent, respectively. Furthermore, unlike the case in the immediate postwar decade, which was a time of almost uninterrupted expansion, the country went through brief recessions in 1954, 1958, and 1961, and as a result unemployment, which averaged just 3.7 percent through 1954, was at 5.4 percent by 1965. The main reason the economy was not as prosperous in the late 1950s as it had been in the early part of the decade was that manufacturing had caught up with the tremendous postwar demand for consumer goods, and had entered a more normal production cycle.[1]

Like the economy as a whole, the level of home construction in the second decade after World War II was erratic. Between 1945 and 1954, housing starts rose in every year except 1951, and on average increased at an annual rate of 6.6 percent. Over the next ten years, however, housing starts rose and fell nearly every other year, and the result was an average annual increase between 1955 and 1965 of just 0.2 percent. This anemic performance reflected not only the fact that the large postwar housing shortage had finally been met, but also the lower rate of new household formation, which caused the demand for homes to fall slightly. Because of these conditions, the increase in home ownership, which had risen at an average annual rate of 2.6 percent between 1940 and 1950, slowed to just 1.2 percent during the 1950s, and was virtually unchanged between 1961 and 1965. The one positive trend of this period was that during the 1950s the average annual rate of personal savings more than doubled to 5.7 percent of household income.[2]

While an uneven economy and slow-growth housing industry presented one set of problems to S&Ls, another equally important challenge came from other financial institutions, notably commercial banks. Although banks had not traditionally been major home mortgage lenders, during the early 1960s they expanded their activity so that by the middle of the decade, banks accounted for more than 14 percent of the total residential mortgage market. The main reason for this development lay in the work of Comptroller of the Currency James J. Saxon, a former banker who took office in 1961. He helped transform the formerly staid banking industry into a modern financial force.

---

[1] Bureau of the Census, *Historical Statistics of the United States, Colonial Times to 1970* (Washington, DC: USGPO, 1976), 37.

[2] *Savings and Loan Fact Book, 1960* (Chicago: United States Savings and Loan League, 1960) 47; *Savings and Loan Fact Book, 1961* (Chicago: United States Savings and Loan League, 1961) 44; *Savings and Loan Fact Book 1969* (Chicago: United States Savings and Loan League, 1969) 8, 19, 21; A. D. Theobald, *Forty–Five Years on the Up Escalator*, (Chicago: privately published, 1979) 195–6; U.S. Bureau of the Census, *Historical Statistics of the United States*, 5, ˙6, 24, 27, 487.

During his controversial five-year tenure, Saxon issued more than 6,000 new regulations, many of which liberalized bank lending powers. Among these were rules that allowed banks to make residential mortgages on essentially the same terms as S&Ls, thereby making both types of institutions equal competitors for the first time in their histories.[3]

Commercial banks also provided a new competitive threat in the contest to acquire consumer savings. Historically, banks had several advantages that allowed them to dominate the market for long-term savings. Banks did not require customers to become members, allowed more convenient withdrawals, offered broader services, and to a lesser extent were perceived as safer and more professional than thrifts. The main reason why banks attracted more deposits, however, was their ability to offer savings rates comparable to thrifts. This situation changed with the creation of interest rate controls under Regulation Q in 1933. Because only Federal Reserve members had to comply with Regulation Q, thrifts were able to offer higher rates on deposits, and by the late 1940s they held a 2 to 3 percent interest rate advantage over banks. As a result, even though banks still controlled the majority of all consumer savings, from 1945 to 1954 thrifts attracted nearly 60 percent of all new deposits as compared to around 20 percent for banks.[4]

Following years of banker complaints, in 1954 the Federal Reserve changed Regulation Q for the first time, and over the next ten years regulators worked to keep bank rates competitive with thrifts. As a result, by 1965 banks had reversed the trend of the 1950s and were attracting 60 percent of all new savings, while thrifts received just 19 percent. Bank savings received another boost following the creation of a secondary market for long-term certificates of deposit (CDs) in 1962. Although term CDs were not covered by Regulation Q, their traditional lack of liquidity meant that

---

[3] "Capitalists with a Common Touch," *Coronet* (December 1960), 126–30; Eugene Mattock "Advising Bankers to Go Slow in Mortgage Lending," *Savings and Loan News* [hereafter *SLN*] 85 (August 1964), 28–32; "Banks are Fighting Back" *Business Week*, 23 February 1958, 39–40; Highlights of the "National Banks and the Future" Report of the Saxon Advisory Committee 1-6; Federal Home Loan Bank Board [hereafter FHLBB] Task Force Members, Lists of Materials Sent, 1961–; Correspondence of Chairman Joseph P. McMurray, 1961–1965 (McMurray Papers); Record Group 195 (RG 195); National Archives College Park (NACP); "The New Frontiersman of Banking," *Business Week*, 22 September 1963, 96–9; "Rift on Control of Banking" *US News and World Report*, 23 March 1963, 47–51. "Banks Boardinghouse Reach," *SLN* 87 (June 1966), 32–7; "New Blueprints for the Banks," *Business Week*, 22 September 1962, 148–9; "The Fed Hits Back in the Saxon Feud," *Business Week*, 14 September 1963, 171–2; Robert Sheehan, "What's Rocking Those Rocks the Banks?" *Fortune* (October 1963), 108–15; "Off Their Duffs," *Newsweek*, 9 November 1964, 83; H. Erich Heinemann, "Saxon Leaving a Vastly Changed Comptrollers Office," *The New York Times*, 6 November 1966, 1, 11; "No Saxon Conquest, *Barron's*, 30 September 1963, 1.

[4] American Bankers Association *Response to Change: A Century of Commercial Bank Activity on the Savings Field* (New York: n.p., 1965), 64–81,134; *Savings and Loan Fact Book, 1967* (Chicago: United States Savings and Loan League, 1967), 14–6; "Does Higher Interest Lure More Money Into Savings?" *Business Week*, 16 March 1957, 190–5.

few banks could use them as a funding source for short-term loans. The ability to buy and sell these market-rate certificates made them liquid financial instruments, and the result was that between 1961 and 1965 more than half of the increase in bank deposits came from the issuance of term CDs.[5]

While banks and thrifts tended to dominate the fight for funds, they were not the only financial institutions in this battle. Mutual funds emerged as an important competitor for investor money after the passage in 1940 of the Maloney Act, which placed companies that offered mutual funds under regulations similar to issuers of stocks and bonds. This law helped remove the taint of scandal that mutual funds had acquired in the early 1930s, when federal investigations showed that several prominent fund managers had engaged in fraud and pyramid schemes that had cost investors millions. Many of the new firms of the 1950s, like Merrill Lynch, also followed more diversified investment strategies that helped reduce market risks and boost investor confidence. The result was that during the 1950s investments in mutual funds increased at an annual rate of 45 percent, and by 1965 accounted for more than $17 billion in consumer savings, up from just $1 billion twenty-five years earlier. While still a minor part of the overall allocation of national savings, by the 1970s mutual funds would have a dramatic effect on how well thrifts retained funds.[6]

A third source of competitive pressure came from the federal government, which continued to expand federal housing programs under the Federal Housing Administration (FHA) and the Veterans Administration (VA). During the 1950s, Congress significantly liberalized the requirements for federal mortgage insurance by raising the maximum loan-to-value ratio for mortgages from 75 percent to 95 percent and increasing the maximum term from twenty to thirty years. Aside from making FHA and VA loans more consumer-friendly, Congress also improved their marketability, and in 1954 it redesigned the Federal National Mortgage Insurance Administration (FNMA) so it would focus solely on buying and selling FHA-insured and VA-guaranteed loans. This creation of a secondary market allowed mortgage

---

[5] "Up Bank Ceiling Move" *SLN* 78 (January 1957), 17. James Hollensteiner "Time Deposits: The Story Behind the Growth," *SLN* 79 (December, 1958), 33–7; "Banks are Fighting Back," *Business Week*, 23 August 1958, 39–40; *Savings and Loan Fact Book, 1969*, 71; *Savings and Loan Fact Book, 1967*, 14–6; "The Narrowing Rate Advantage," *SLN* 78 (February 1957), 14; Norman Strunk, "Commercial Banks Come Alive," *SLN* 86 (September 1965), 18–26; "How Commercial Banks Reach for CD Funds" *SLN* 87 (July 1966), 7; American Bankers Association, *The Commercial Banking Industry* (Englewood Cliffs, NJ: Prentice Hall, 1962), 75–84; "Testimony on Bills to Limit Use of CD's Presented by Chairman John E. Horne Before Banking Committee," *Digest / Federal Home Loan Bank Board* [hereafter *FHLB Digest*] 8 (May 1966), 2.

[6] Norman Strunk "Who is Our Real Competition?" *SLN* 78 (April 1956), 30–5; "A Scramble for Your Savings," *US News and World Report*, 22 January 1962, 5–7; *Savings and Loan Fact Book, 1969*, 7; Edwin J. Perkins, *From Wall Street to Main Street: Charles Merrill and the Rise of Middle-Class Investors* (New York: Cambridge University Press, 1999), 127–43, 237–57.

bankers, who relied on a uniform clearinghouse to finance operations, to become major providers of these loans. As a result, mortgage companies originated two thirds of these loans by 1965, up from 43 percent twelve years earlier. With these changes, the volume of outstanding government-insured loans rose from $38.9 billion to $72.2 billion between 1955 and 1965. While mortgages backed by the FHA and VA never exceeded 3 percent of the total market, their more consumer-friendly terms forced thrifts to make similar changes for their home loans.[7]

AN INCREASED FOCUS ON MINORITY HOUSING

Yet another major issue facing S&Ls in the late 1950s was the growing attention given to the housing needs of African Americans. Following the 1954 Supreme Court ruling in *Brown vs. Board of Education*, civil rights leaders began pushing for greater equality, including greater access to housing and home ownership. While achieving this goal required changing social attitudes on race relations and integration, it also required expanding the availability of home financing for minority applicants. For decades, blacks had had trouble obtaining mortgages because white-owned institutions frequently discriminated against minority applicants with financial tests, such as large down payments, that whites did not have to meet. This treatment, combined with the harsh reality of segregation in the South, was one reason why African Americans had to form their own banks and insurance companies after the Civil War as a way to get loans. By the turn of the century, dozens of minority-owned financial institutions operated throughout the South, and some, such as the North Carolina Mutual Insurance Company, were substantial operations with hundreds of members.[8]

[7] Josephine Hedges Ewalt, "The FHA is known for Efficient Operations and Technical Excellence," *SLN* 78 (July 1957), 28–33; *Savings and Loan Fact Book, 1956* (Chicago: United States Savings and Loan League, 1956) 107–9; *Savings and Loan Fact Book, 1969*, 126, 128; Josephine Hedges Ewalt, "Fanny May and its $3.6 Billion Portfolio," *SLN* (October 1957), 43–6; Leon Kendall, *The Savings and Loan Business Its Purposes, Functions, and Economic Justification; A Monograph Prepared for the Commission on Money and Credit* (Englewood Cliffs, NJ: Prentice-Hall, 1962), 48–52; "Housing Act Has Broad Mortgage Lending Impact," *SLN* 86 (September 1965), 7; Memorandum from Robert C. Weaver to Joseph A. Califano with two attachments, 6 August 1965; EX FG 245, Housing and Home Finance Agency, June 11, 1965 to July 23, 1965; White House Central Files (WHCF) Subject File Financial Groups (FG); Lyndon B. Johnson Presidential Library, Austin, Texas (LBJPL); Miles Colean, *Mortgage Companies: Their Place in the Financial Structure; A Monograph Prepared for the Commission on Money and Credit* (Englewood Cliffs, NJ: Prentice-Hall, 1962), 20–4, 34–9.

[8] Juliet K. Walker, *The History of Black Business in America: Capitalism, Race and Entrepreneurship*, (Prentice-Hall International: London, 1989), 83–91, 187–193; Walter B. Weare, *Black Business in the New South: A Social History of the North Carolina Mutual Life Insurance Company* (Urbana, IL: University of Illinois Press, 1973), 3–29, 133–54; *The Freedmen's Savings Bank and Trust Company: Charter and By-Laws* (New York: W. C. Bryant, 1865).

African Americans also organized their own S&Ls to help urban blacks acquire homes. The earliest minority-owned building society was formed in Kinston, North Carolina, in 1865, and the first association based on the traditional building and loan plan appeared in Baltimore in 1881. By the end of the nineteenth century, seventeen African American thrifts were in operation, and in cities such as Philadelphia and Charlotte North Carolina, the leaders of these associations formed their own local trade associations to promote their business interests. One reason why African Americans could easily form a thrift was that most states did not impose strict financial requirements for charters. Also, attracting new members was not very hard because many early African American S&Ls held meetings at local churches, which were primary social institutions in the black community. In the early 1900s' Booker T. Washington claimed that, "perhaps the most numerous and popular form of cooperative business in which our people have engaged is that of the building and loan associations." He also noted that half of the homes owned by blacks in Virginia were built using loans from minority-owned thrifts.[9]

Aside from forming minority-owned thrifts, African Americans often found it possible to become members of white-owned associations. Throughout the South, many S&Ls allowed blacks to join on an equal status with whites. In 1896, the League reported that nearly 7 percent of all Louisiana thrift members were African American men and women, and that the majority of the thrifts in that state drew "no line of distinction on color" when making loans. By the 1910s, many associations accepted members of "any age, sex, color, vocation, or habitation." One reason for doing so was that industry leaders saw their business as a way to encourage self-help and moral uplift. As one white Southern thrift leader noted, "it is the providence of the building associations in the South to educate the colored man along the lines of economy and savings and home building, and from this work more good will come than from all the vaporings of all the politicians in the land." This sentiment was shared by many blacks, and one minority-owned thrift advertised, "think of the habits of saving as how it makes for independence of the individual and of the race."[10]

---

[9] The first thrift to admit black members was in 1841. See: H. Morton Bodfish, "The Spread of the Building and Loan Movement in the United States," in Bodfish, editor, *History of Building and Loan,* 78–9; "Colored Building and Loan Associations," *American Building Association News* [hereafter *ABAN*] 19 (May 1900), 129; "Negro State League of North Carolina," *ABAN* 25 (December 1906), 227; Walker, *The History of Black Business in America,* 171–2; J. H. Harmon Jr., Arnett G. Lindsay, and Carter G. Woodson, *The Negro as a Business Man* (Washington, DC: The Association for the Study of Negro Life and History, Inc., 1929), 10; Howard N. Rabinowitz, *Race Relations in the Urban South, 1865–1890* (New York: Oxford University Press, 1978), 81; Booker T. Washington, *Negro in Business* (Chicago: Afro-Am Press, 1969), quote 161.

[10] Samuel A. Rosenberg, *Negro Managed Building and Loan Associations in the United States* (Hampton, VA: Hampton Institute, 1940), 2–5, 39, 68; Don A. Davis, "Using a Building and Loan Association," *Southern Workman* 36 (November 1927), 493; John E. Huffman,

The early phase of the development of African American thrifts, which lasted from the 1880s into the early 1900s, was followed by solid expansion after the First Great Migration of World War I. The lure of jobs in the urban North led millions of blacks to leave the South, and between 1915 and 1930 minority populations in Chicago and Philadelphia rose by 63 percent and 114 percent, respectively. While blacks in the North did not face the problem of legal segregation that existed in the South, there was still a *de facto* policy to separate the races, and this policy led to rising racial tensions, especially in cities such as Detroit and St. Louis. Housing was one area where the races were separated by practice, and black leaders alleged that landlords and banks often conspired to restrict blacks to certain neighborhoods. In these circumstances, northern blacks also began forming their own S&Ls. Unlike what had been the case in the 1880s, the League appeared to be quite interested in their work. Industry leaders noted that increasing home ownership among blacks not only helped reduce mortality, but also strengthened their commitment to the community, which helped ease racial tensions. Philadelphia, which was the home of the American thrift movement, also had the most active collection of minority-owned thrifts in the country.[11]

Because Philadelphia historically had a large African American population, it also had a well-organized network of minority-owned businesses whose leaders took an active role in forming black S&Ls. The first African American thrift in the city appeared in 1886, and by 1926 there were thirty-six associations serving black members. These thrifts also had their own

"The Building Association Movement in the South," *Financial Review and American Building Association News* [hereafter *FRABAN*] 14 (November 1895), 19–22; "The Louisiana Homestead League," *FRABAN* 19 (February 1893), 24; "United States League Meeting," *ABAN* 21 (August 1902), quote 228; *The Weldon Building and Loan Association, Organized in July, 1914* (n.p.), quote 1; J. H. Westover, "Building Associations in the South," *FRABAN* 16 (January 1897), quote 25; John E. Huffman, "A Review of the Building and Loan Association Movement in the Southern States," *Proceedings of the Second Annual Meeting of The United States League of Local Building and Loan Associations* (Chicago: The Press of the Financial Review and American Building Association News Press, 1894), 134; "Black Owned Association in New York," *ABAN* 18 (March 1899), quote 69; "How to Solve the Race Problem," *ABAN* 18 (April 1899), 115.

11 "The American Negro," *ABAN* 17 (July 1918), 296; "Ohio's Negro Population," *ABAN* 36 (October 1927), 455; Davis, "Using a Building and Loan Association," 495–7; "Negroes Becoming Homeowners," *ABAN* 25 (December 1906), 227; F. D. Wheelock, "A Community Asset: People's Building and Loan Association of Hampton, VA," *Southern Workman* 30 (December 1921), 345–50; H. S. Rosenthal, "Possibilities of the Building and Loan Movement," *Proceedings of the Thirty-Sixth Annual Meeting of the Building Association League of Illinois* (Chicago: American Building Association News Publishing, 1916), 106; D. A. Tompkins, "Building and Loan Associations, The Means for Co-operative Savings by Southern Working People," *Manufacturers' Record* 78 (25 August 1904), 110–2; D. A. Tompkins, "Building and Loan Associations, Philanthropy and Working People," *Manufacturers' Record* 78 (1 September 1904), 150–2; D. A. Tompkins, "Building and Loan Associations, Opportunities and Benefits," *Manufacturers' Record* 78 (8 September 1904), 226–8.

trade group and monthly magazine. Philadelphia was not unique; almost every major city in the North with a sizable African American population had at least one black-owned S&L, including Baltimore, with ten, and Chicago, with three. In addition, Newark, New York, Milwaukee, Cincinnati, Dayton, and Los Angeles each had at least one African American S&L. By 1930, seventy-three minority-owned thrifts controlled more than $6.5 million in assets, and operated in fourteen states from coast to coast. Because these S&Ls focused on meeting the home finance needs of members drawn from the local neighborhoods, the average thrift was small, with about $75,000 in assets. Just two had more than $400,000 in assets; by comparison, the industry average was more than $700,000.[12]

Although relatively few in number, the activities of African American S&Ls in the 1920s did help increase the level of black home ownership. Between 1910 and 1930, the number of black homeowners nationwide rose from 20 percent to an estimated 28 percent, and in cities where thrifts were active the change was even larger. In Philadelphia, 12 percent of all black families owned their own homes in 1920, up from just 5 percent in 1910, while Dayton saw an increase from 23 percent to 29 percent over the same period. Minority home ownership also rose significantly in the South, and in Norfolk, Virginia, and Charlotte, the value of black-owned property rose 46 percent and 53 percent, respectively. A federal study of minority housing credited the roles of white- and black-owned thrifts for these changes, noting, "Negro buyers fare better in communities where building and loan associations are prominent. Many communities have thriving Negro associations, and white associations often welcome Negro clients."[13]

Following growth in the 1920s, minority-owned thrifts suffered during the Great Depression, recording a failure rate well above that of the thrift industry in general. Between 1930 and 1938, the number of African American thrifts fell 37 percent to 47 percent, while the assets managed by these associations dropped by 46 percent to $3.5 million over the same period. In contrast, the entire thrift industry experienced only a 26 percent decline in associations and a 36 percent drop in assets. While unusually high black unemployment and the sharp drop in real estate values provide a partial explanation for the decline of minority-owned thrifts, other problems, including poor management, were also factors. Moreover, black shareholders

---

[12] I. Maximilian Martin, *Negro Managed Building and Loan Associations in Philadelphia: Their History and Present Status* (Philadelphia: Associated Real Estate Brokers of Philadelphia, 1936), 1–5; Rosenberg, *Negro Managed Building and Loan Associations*, 43–8; "A New Movement in the South," *ABAN* 36 (August 1927), 405.

[13] Blanch Halbert, "Home Improvement Among Negro Families," *Southern Workman* 60 (May 1932), 209–16; Blanch Halbert, "Leadership for Better Homes," *Southern Workman* 56 (April 1927), 169–74; Charles S. Johnson, *Negro Housing: Report of the Committee on Negro Housing* (Washington, DC: The President's Conference on Home Building and Home Ownership, 1932), 79–86, 92–6, quote 96.

appeared to have less confidence in their institutions, since minority-owned S&Ls had more incidents of deposit runs than other thrifts. Despite these problems, the Great Depression provided valuable lessons for those African American thrifts that survived, and in turn helped them take advantage of growth opportunities in the 1940s.[14]

As had been true during World War I, the Second Great Migration of World War II brought millions of blacks out of the South to the North and West, and this movement produced a third wave of expansion for African American thrifts. Between 1938 and 1949, the total assets controlled by black-owned associations soared to more than $16.4 million, but because their number had fallen to twenty-nine, these thrifts were much larger. Furthermore, their credit quality was fairly strong, with one black manager reporting in 1949 that his thrift had had no foreclosures in its entire fifteen-year history of lending to mostly black homeowners. One important reason for this growth was that blacks had more access to housing after the common practice of maintaining "colored neighborhoods" was found unconstitutional in 1948. In the landmark ruling of *Shelley v. Kraemer*, the Supreme Court outlawed the use of restrictive deed of trust covenants that barred the sale of property to blacks. This decision created a technical opening for blacks to move into traditionally-all-white neighborhoods.[15]

The mass movement of African Americans from the South also led the thrift industry as a whole to again realize the business potential of lending to minorities. This was especially true after Congress passed the GI Bill of Rights in 1944, an act that required lenders making mortgages under this law to do so without regard to race, creed, or color. By 1950, the League had brought to the attention of its membership the need to lend to minorities, stressing that African American borrowers were generally excellent credit risks. Surveys in 1946, 1948, and 1954 by the FHLBB on lending to minorities confirmed that the rate of loan delinquencies for black and white borrowers was similar, and noted that most thrifts tended to approve or reject a loan on the basis of financial eligibility and not race. Interestingly, the Board could not compile accurate statistics on the actual number of minority loans made by S&Ls since none of the associations surveyed separated their accounts on the basis of the race of the applicant.[16]

[14] Johnson, *Negro Housing*, 99–102; Martin, *Negro Managed Building and Loan Associations*, 5–9; Rosenberg, *Negro Managed Building and Loan Associations*, 35; *Savings and loan Fact Book, 1955* (Chicago: United States Savings and Loan League, 1955), 39, 43.

[15] Other major cases on ending racially segregated neighborhoods include *Buchanan v. Warley* 245 US 60 (1917), *Harmon v. Tyler* 273 US 668 (1927), *City of Richmond v. Deans* 281 US 704 (1930). Rosenberg, *Negro Managed Building and Loan Associations in the United States*, 49–54; Robert R. Taylor, "Financing Minority Group Homes," *SLN* 69 (January 1949), 33; Memorandum from John Fahey to Office of the Chairman, 21 February 1941, with attachments; "He"; Correspondence of Chairman Lohn Fahey, 1940–1947; RG 195; NACP.

[16] Robert R. Taylor, "Financing Opportunities Among Minority Groups," *Savings and Loan Annals, 1949* (Chicago: United States Savings and Loan League, 1949), 144–6; George Streator,

Despite the surface positive attitude of white thrift managers toward African American mortgage applicants, there were still signs that discrimination existed within the industry. While one lender maintained that associations in his state "with no exception that I know of" discriminated against minorities, he added that "it is only when the Negro applicant expects special or preferential treatment that we run into difficulty." In particular, he commented on how some builders of minority housing demanded "much looser and more generous" terms than the S&L normally granted. At the same time, this executive noted "if there is any factor which is limiting the spread of home ownership among the colored folks, it is because they have not yet acquired the habit of thrift to the same extent as the white." Such attitudes indicated that black applicants still experienced a perception problem in the home lending process.[17]

Given this persistent and subtle discrimination, some African American thrift leaders felt they needed an organization that would address the problems facing minority home buyers. Although the League did not discriminate in its membership, and allowed African American thrift employees equal access to education and other trade association services, several state Leagues did prohibit black S&Ls from joining. These conditions contributed to the formation of the American Savings and Loan League (AS&LL) in November 1948 to represent the interests of African American S&Ls. Like the larger League, the AS&LL worked to promote thrift and home ownership, but it also sought ways to increase lending to minorities and discourage the use of race-based criteria in evaluating African American loan applications. Thus, AS&LL leaders pushed regulators to make it easier for blacks to form their own associations and to create a new position within the FHLBB to focus on minority housing issues.[18]

"FHA Aide Outlines Negro Housing Bar," *The New York Times*, 23 April 1949, 26; "'Non-Racial' Colony of Houses at $7,000 Will Open Tomorrow at North Amityville," *The New York Times*, 27 January 1950, 41; Edwin W. Zwergel, "Our Experience with Negro Loans Adds Up to Profitable Mortgage Lending," *SLN* 75 (May 1955), 53–57; Johnson, *Negro Housing*, 103–5; Memorandum from Douglas Rosenbaum to William K. Divers, 3 September 1948; "R"; Correspondence of Chairman William K. Divers, 1948–1952 (Divers Papers); RG 195; NACP; Memorandum from William K. Divers to J. S. Baughman with attachment, 14 September 1948; "R"; RG 195; NACP; Memorandum from William K. Divers to Walter McAllister, 6 December 1954, quotes; Housing, Minority 1954– ; Correspondence of Chairman Walter W. McAllister, 1953–1956 (McAllister Papers); RG 195; NACP.

[17] Rosenberg, *Negro Managed Building and Loan Associations in the United States*, 22–3; Divers to McAllister, 6 December 1954, and Letter from Everett C. Sherbourne to William K. Divers, 8 November, 1954, quotes 1–3; Housing, Minority 1954– ; McAllister Papers; RG 195; NACP.

[18] The Board eventually refused to establish a special assistant to the Chairman for minority housing issues citing its "tight" budget. "Fourth Report of Savings and Loan Associations Operated by Negroes," January 1951, 2–3; Savings and Loan Associations, 1952–1953; Divers Papers; RG 195; NACP; H. A. Howard, "The American Savings and Loan League: Its Founding, Its Future," Address before the Fourth Annual Conference on "The Negro in

While the FHLBB agreed with the AS&LL that there should be more minority thrifts, there were limits to this support. Board chairman Divers expressed a "desire to see Negroes help themselves" in becoming homeowners, but also emphasized that only "strong groups [with] resources, strong community support [and] a reasonable likelihood of success" should form new thrifts. Because he wanted to make sure that no new S&L would become a problem for the FSLIC, Divers felt it was inappropriate to lower the minimum capital requirements and to make it easier for minorities to organize thrifts. Such a position did not help the AS&LL since blacks traditionally had only very limited access to capital. The Board ultimately recognized this gap between rhetoric and action in 1961. In a report submitted to the Commission on Civil Rights, regulators conceded that "we are not aware that the 1940s was a period of unusual encouragement" for African American thrifts. They instead attributed the growth in new minority S&Ls during this period to the national Civil Rights Movement. Still, the FHLBB maintained it was more supportive of minority thrifts, as evidenced by an approval rate for black applications that exceeded the rate for white applicants.[19]

Although the AS&LL did not make substantive headway with federal regulators in increasing the number of minority-owned thrifts, the work of the existing associations continued to expand into the 1960s. While the majority of these S&Ls remained small, with less than $7 million in assets, some were large and prosperous concerns. In New York City, Carver Federal Savings and Loan, which began in 1949 with $225,000 in subscribed capital and only $15,000 in actual cash had grown to more than $24.4 million in assets by 1963. This thrift was so well-known that Vice President Richard M. Nixon visited it in 1957 to highlight the Eisenhower Administration's commitment to civil rights. The largest African American thrifts, however, were in California. Los Angeles had four black-owned thrifts, which controlled nearly $154 million in assets, while San Francisco was home to the biggest, Trans-Bay Federal, with more than $74 million in assets. Overall, thirty-four African American thrifts held more than $400 million in total assets, and from this modest beginning, minority-owned thrifts continue to

Business," Washington, DC, 22 April 1949, 4–6; American Savings and Loan League, 1949; Divers Papers; RG 195; NACP; Memorandum from American Savings & Loan League to Walter W. McAllister, 24 September 1954, and memorandum from American Savings & Loan League to Albert M. Cole, 24 September 1954; American Savings and Loan League, 1954; McAllister Papers; RG 195; NACP.

19 Letter from William K. Divers to H. N. Faulkner, 25 April 1949, and handwritten notes "Chairman's Story" (?) (n.d.), quotes; American Savings and Loan League, 1949; Divers Papers; RG 195; NACP; Letter from Maurice E. Collette to William K. Divers, 8 October 1949; "Co"; Divers Papers, RG 195; NACP; Letter from William R. Hudgins to Walter W. McAllister with attachment, 14 October 1954 and letter from H. Caulsen to William B.[sic] Hudgins, 29 October 1954; American Savings and Loan League, 1954; McAllister Papers; RG 195; NACP; Memorandum from Dan I. McKeithen to Ira Dixon, 28 April 1961, 2–4; Civil Rights Commission, 1961– ; McMurray Papers, RG 195; NACP.

meet the mortgages to both black and white applicants into the twenty-first century.[20]

S&LS AND THE LEAGUE CONTINUE TO GROW

Despite the various challenges facing all S&Ls, the industry continued to grow in the late 1950s and early 1960s. Federal regulators broadened thrift lending powers to include apartment and condominium mortgages, which were growing and lucrative fields. The League, however, urged caution when making these loans since they involved additional risks; multifamily apartments were often nonowner-occupied and condominiums involved unique legal considerations. Another regulatory change was the right to make short-term "trade-in" financing to help borrowers gain access to their equity in existing homes that could be used to purchase new houses. S&Ls also got permission to sell up to 75 percent of loans to other associations, a change that allowed thrifts to come together to meet loan requests that exceeded the legal lending limits of a single association. This increased ability to sell loan participations also improved the flow of mortgage funds across the country. Finally, the Board allowed thrifts to lend for home-related items such as appliances and furniture, which opened the door to consumer lending, albeit in a limited way.[21]

[20] "Saving Agency Gains in Harlem," *The New York Times*, 25 November 1962, sec. 3, 9; Letter from Joseph P. McMurray to Cornelius A. Page with attachment, 30 December 1963, "N"; McMurray Papers; RG 195; NACP; Memorandum from CSS to Mr. McMurray with attachments, 16 August, 1962; Housing, Nondiscrimination; McMurray Papers; RG 195; NACP; Memorandum from Albert Hampton to Chairman Martin, 23 December 1969, 1–4 and "EDA 'Seed Money' Grant Aids Black-Owned S&Ls," *The Washington Post*, n.d., n.p.; American Savings & Loan League; Correspondence of Chairman Preson Martin, 1969–1972; RG 195; NACP; William Bradford, *The Viability and Performance of Minority Controlled Savings and Loan Associations*, Research Working Paper No. 62 (Washington, DC: Office of Economic Research, Federal Home Loan Bank Board, 1975), 40–2; "Minority Associations Mix Success and Struggle with Moves to Adapt," *SLN* 103 (May 1982), 40–6; Theresa Watson, "Minority Savings and Loan Industry," *Journal* [Federal Home Loan Bank Board], 17 (April 1984), 122–38.

[21] Arthur Neeley "Apartment House Financing – Some Yardsticks," *SLN* 81 (September 1960), 20–2; Horace Russell "Be Modern But Be Safe," *SLN* 83 (November 1962), 38–40; "Round Up Report on Condominiums: Its Problems and Potential," *SLN* 85 (January 1964), 44–8; Memorandum from Charles M. Torrance to the Board, 25 August 1958; Federal Savings and Loan Associations [hereafter FS&LA], Loans, General; Robertson Papers; RG 195; NACP; "Increase of Loans on Home 'Trade-Ins' Approved by FHLBB," *The American Banker*, 10 October 1961, 15; "Ins and Outs of Trade-In Financing," *SLN* 84 (January 1963), 30–3; Wyn Warman "Loan Participations – A New Savings and Loan Mortgage Tool," *SLN* 79 (April 1958), 30–3; Wyn Warman, "Buying, Selling Loan Participations," *SLN* 80 (July 1959), 25–8; "National Loan Market Expands" *SLN* 87 (January 1966), 22–7; Thomas Marvel, *The Federal Home Loan Bank Board* (New York: Praeger, 1967), 240–3; Press Release, 28 May 1964; FS&LA, Loans, Nationwide, 1962; McMurray Papers; RG 195; NACP; Memorandum from John J. Brady to Joseph P. McMurray, 19 October 1964; Advisory Council, General, 1964;

Congress also helped the thrift industry with new legislation, the most significant of which was the Housing Act of 1964. This law expanded the lending authority of thrifts to finance the acquisition and development of raw land for residential purposes, a critical change that made it possible for a single association to finance all aspects of home construction; it also gave the industry a new competitive tool over national banks, which could not make loans on undeveloped land. Other changes included allowing S&Ls to make education loans, a doubling of the lending territory in which a federal S&L could make direct loans up to 100 miles from the home office, and the authority to invest up to 5 percent of S&L assets in any standard metropolitan statistical area, which effectively established nationwide lending. Finally, the law allowed S&Ls to invest up to 1 percent of their assets in unregulated service corporations, which thrifts used initially to manage "backroom" activities like data processing. Over time, however, service corporations would be an important way for thrifts to enter business fields prohibited by regulators.[22]

The League also tried to help the industry stay competitive during this period by creating more innovative lending and saving options. To promote a more efficient flow of mortgage funds, the League received regulatory permission in 1955 to form the Voluntary Home Mortgage Credit Program (VHMCP). Under this program, associations with excess funds joined with other thrifts to make FHA and VA loans in rural areas. The League promoted the VHMCP to show how thrifts were committed to meeting mortgage demand in all parts of the country, and also to blunt any efforts to increase government involvement in financing homes. In terms of finding ways to

McMurray Papers; RG 195; NACP; Letter from Norman Strunk to Joseph P. McMurray, 12 December 1962; FS&LA Loans Consumer 1961– ; McMurray Papers; RG 195; NACP; "Consumer Loan Field Eyed for S&L Groups," *The Dallas Times Herald*, 28 October 1964, 1; Memorandum from Clarence S. Smith to Joseph P. McMurray, 18 April 1963; Committee on Applications for Branches and Charters, November 23, 1962– ; McMurray Papers, RG 195; NACP.

22 "A Savings Account for That College Education," *Good Housekeeping* (September 1958), 148; Letter from Philip Lieber to Harold Bauman, 27 February 1956, FS&LA, Lending, 1953– ; McAllister Papers; RG 195; NACP; Press Release, 5 October 1964; FS&LA Loans, Educational; McMurray Papers; RG 195; NACP; "Education Loans: Will Associations Rise to the Challenge?" *SLN* 86 (April 1965), 36–42; "Education Loans: Associations Rise to the Challenge," *SLN* 87 (February 1966), 30–6; Press Release, 25 May 1964; Federal Savings and Loan Insurance Corporation [hereafter FSLIC], Reserves, Regulations and Press Releases, 1963–1967; McMurray Papers; RG 195; NACP; Press Release, 25 January 1965; FS&LA, Loans, Extending Lending Area, 1961– ; McMurray Papers; RG 195; NACP; "Property Improvement Lending," *SLN* 83 (April 1962), 59–69; "Survey Reveals Swing to Greater Use of Own Plan Property Improvement Loans" *SLN* 76 (November 1955), 78–92, 104; Press Release, 21 December 1963; FS&LA, Loans, Acquisition and Development of Land 1961– ; McMurray Papers; RG 195; NACP; Stephen G. Slipher, "Report of the Legislative Director on Legislative Matters," *Savings and Loan Annals, 1964* (Chicago: United States Savings and Loan League, 1964), 234–7.

attract more stable savings, although the League failed to win approval to pay variable rates on savings, it convinced regulators to allow S&Ls to pay quarterly dividends as well as bonus dividends on large deposits held for at least one year. Thrift leaders argued that this incentive was justified since it promoted systematic saving and encouraged customers to plan for the long term.[23]

While the industry gained many new powers, it did not get everything it wanted. One such failure was a federal mortgage insurance program for conventional loans that the League wanted as a way to compete against the improvements to the FHA and VA mortgage programs. Although years of lobbying did not work, an acceptable alternative was private mortgage insurance through firms like the Mortgage Guaranty Insurance Corporation, which insured the portion of a mortgage that exceeded 80 percent of appraised value. A second failure was the inability to create a secondary market for conventional loans through the FNMA. Although the League argued that the ability to buy and sell traditional mortgages would improve liquidity and the overall flow of funds, Congress was generally opposed to providing thrifts with what some saw as a direct federal subsidy. Finally, the League failed to win approval for its idea to create a consumer bill paying service, since regulators considered it to be too much like regular bank checking accounts. Thrift leaders did not give up, however, and by the mid-1970s the industry had a secondary market for conventional mortgages as well as the ability to offer quasi-checking accounts.[24]

[23] Eugene Mortlock, "The Voluntary Home Mortgage Credit Program and the Savings and Loan Business," *SLN* 78 (January 1957), 48–50; Memorandums from Paul Pfeiffer to Mr. Dixon, 25 October 1955, and 27 March 1956, and letter from Albert Cole to Walter W. McAllister with handwritten comments from William K. Divers, 10 June 1954; Mortgage Credit Program – Voluntary 1954; McAllister Papers; RG 195; NACP; Letter from Paul Pfeiffer Jr. to Ira Dixon, 27 May 1958; Mortgage Credit Program, Voluntary; Correspondence of Chairman Albert J. Robertson, 1956–1961 (Robertson Papers); RG 195; NACP; "Greater Flexibility in Dividend Payments by Federals Authorized," *FHLBB Digest* 4 (December 1961), 2; Letter from G. W. Davis to Walter W. McAllister, with attachment, 7 October 1955; FS&LA, Dividends, 1953– ; McAllister Papers; RG 195; NACP; Memorandum from Harry Schwartz to Joseph P. McMurray, 19 November 1964; FS&LA Dividends, Variable; McMurray Papers; RG 195; NACP; "U.S. Approves Bonus Dividends of Savings and Loan Institutions," *The New York Times*, 6 June 1961, 48.

[24] "Guaranteeing the Top Portion of Conventional Loans," *SLN* 78 (May 1957), 12; "Private Mortgage Insurance Firm Expands," *SLN* (March 1958), 11; "Opposition to Loan Guaranty Plan Mounts as House Hearings End," *SLN* 79 (July 1958), 9; Letter from Albert J. Robertson to Ira Dixon to 10 May 1960; Federal Home Loan Banks, Lending – Secondary Market, 1956– ; Robertson Papers; RG 195; NACP; Arlen J. Large, "New Resale Market Sought for Mortgages of Conventional Type, *The Wall Street Journal*, 16 May 1962, 2; Speech by Joseph P. McMurray, 6 February 1963, letter from Norman Strunk to Joseph P. McMurray, 25 February 1963, 1–4, and memorandum from A. D. Theobald to Hobart C. Carr, 28 December 1961, 1–3; Secondary Mortgage Market Facility, 1961– ; McMurray Papers; RG 195; NACP; Memorandum from Alan J. Moscow to Joseph P. McMurray, 2 September 1962,

TABLE 6.1. *Number of Thrifts and Assets – 1959 to 1965*

Year	No. S&L	Change/Year	Assets (000,000)	Change/Year
1955	6,048	–	$37,800	–
1959	6,223	0.8%	$63,401	13.7%
1963	5,992	(0.9%)	$107,559	14.1%
1965	6,071	0.7%	$129,442	9.7%

Source: Savings and Loan Fact Book, 1966, 92–4.

EVALUATING THE INDUSTRY

Despite increased competition for loans and deposits, the growth of the thrift industry continued to amaze outside observers and League officials. Between 1955 and 1965, the industry passed a number of major milestones and posted one of the fastest growth rates of any financial industry, as shown in Table 6.1.

By 1965, S&Ls controlled 26 percent of consumer savings and provided 46 percent of all single-family home loans – tremendous gains over the comparable figures of 7 percent and 23 percent, respectively, for 1945. The financial condition of the industry also was strong, as operating income and net income in 1965 of $7.1 billion and $5.3 billion, respectively, were both records. By comparison, these same figures in 1955 were $1.7 billion and $1.2 billion, while in 1950 they were only one tenth of the 1965 level. Although the net margin for the industry declined, it was not because of a drop in operating efficiency, but rather from increased spending for advertising and office expansion. Operating efficiency, in fact, improved significantly, as the increased use of office automation caused the average number of thrift employees per $1 million in assets to fall from 1.7 people in 1945 to .62 people by 1965.[25]

The rapid industry expansion, combined with the slower formation of new thrifts, meant that the average S&L in 1965 was significantly larger than it had been just ten years earlier. From having less than $6 million in assets in 1955, the average thrift in 1965 had nearly $21 million in assets, and

1–4; Mortgage Guaranty Insurance Corporation; Correspondence of Chairman John E. Horne, 1965–1968 (Horne Papers); RG 195; NACP; Letter from Norman Strunk to Joseph P. McMurray, 26 September 1963; USS&LL and National League, 1961–; McMurray Papers; RG 195; NACP; Letter from John E. Horne to Charles Borson, 15 June 1967, and letter from Norman Strunk to John E. Horne, 28 August 1967; USS&LL Bill Payer Withdrawal System; Horne Papers; RG 195 NACP.

[25] *Savings and Loan Fact Book 1969*, 22–4, 65–7; *Savings and Loan Fact Book, 1960*, 25–7, 70–2; "Savings Come Back in Style," *US News and World Report*, 12 September 1960, 120; "Banks Lag in Luring Savings," *US News and World Report*, 7 August 1961, 89; "Scramble for Savers," *Time*, 2 February 1962, 62; Roy Marr, "To Meet Our Competition, Let's Roll Up Our Sleeves and Sell, Sell, Sell," *SLN* 78 (April 1957), 38–43; Ira U. Cobleigh, *$100 Billion Can't Be Wrong* (New York: Cobleigh & Gordon, 1964), 23–7.

the League attributed this growth in part to the industry's continued effort to provide better customer service than competitors. Thrifts were among the first financial institutions to incorporate drive-up teller windows and locate branches in suburbs closer to their customers. By 1965, 22 percent of all associations had at least one branch, and the total for the industry exceeded 2,500. Branching, however, had a number of potential problems, and League groups like the Savings Institutions Marketing Society provided advice on how best to locate branch offices and market their services. Finally, the trade association continued to grow, and by 1965 more than 80 percent of all thrifts were League members.[26]

A less positive trend, however, was the slow but steady decline in the industry reserve ratio, which averaged just 6.7 percent by 1965, a level far below the 11.5 percent average for commercial banks. The main reason for the disparity was the continued emphasis by thrifts on paying high dividends, which was reflected in the decline in the average share of net income allocated to reserves from 30 percent in 1955 to 16 percent by 1965. While the majority of all thrifts maintained reserves well above regulatory minimums, regulators were still very concerned with the slow pace of reserve growth, especially since the level of real estate owned by the industry soared from $60 million to more than $1 billion over the same ten-year period. Because reserves were the only financial cushion thrifts had to absorb these losses, serious problems would result if these trends continued.[27]

A second adverse development during this period involved the tax status of the industry. Although S&Ls had become subject to federal taxes in 1952, few actually paid any taxes because the law allowed generous exemptions for associations with low levels of reserves, provisions that were staunchly defended by League lobbyists. By the early 1960s, however, the surge in industry earnings made it even harder to defend the traditional idea that thrifts

[26] "Microfilming Ensures Full Service at Branch," *SLN* 83 (June 1962), 51; "Have You Heard About Data Processing?" *SLN* 79 (October 1958), 60–3; "New Policies, Management, Building Effect Major Organization Change," *SLN* (June 1959), 34–7; "Management's Aim: A Flexible Organization," *SLN* (January 1961), 18–21; *Savings and Loan Fact Book, 1969*, 59–61, 108; Norman Strunk, "Our Business Will Continue to Grow Because We Build on Service," *SLN* 76 (September 1955), 19–21; James Hollensteiner, "Drive-Ins are Here to Stay, But . . ." *SLN* 79 (May 1958), 22–5; Josephine Hedges Ewalt, *A Business Reborn: The Savings and Loan Story, 1930–1960* (Chicago: American Savings and Loan Institute Press, 1962), 330–3; "What US League Survey Reveals About Branch Operations," *SLN* 79 (April 1958), 36–41; Oliver M. Chatburn, "Introducing SIMSA," *Savings and Loan Annals, 1965* (Chicago: United States Savings and Loan League, 1965), 57–60; Theobald, *Forty-Five Years*, 228.

[27] *Trends in the Savings and Loan Field, 1966* (Washington, DC: Federal Home Loan Bank Board, 1968); *Savings and Loan Fact Book, 1966*, 102–5; United States Savings and Loan League, *Report of the Special Committee to Study the Federal Home Loan Bank System* (Chicago: United States Savings and Loan League, 1956), 5–6; M. L. Dye, "The Problems You Face," *SLN* 83 (October 1962), 34; Letter from Albert J. Robertson to Ira Dixon, 10 May 1960; Federal Home Loan Banks, Lending, Secondary Market, 1956– ; Robertson Papers; RG 195; NACP.

should not be taxed because they were not-for-profit associations. As a result, when the League attempted to use this argument to defeat the provisions of the Revenue Act of 1962 that would make thrifts subject to "full taxation," President John F. Kennedy threatened to "blast against savings and loans 'such as he gave steel'" if they were successful. Although the League acquiesced, and accepted changes that required most S&Ls to pay taxes on 50 percent of their earnings, they did prevent enactment of the full taxation language originally considered by legislators.[28]

THE INDUSTRY SHOWS SIGNS OF DIVISION

Another dominant trend of the late 1950s and early 1960s was increased tension and fragmentation within the thrift industry based on region, size, and form of ownership. One source of division was between thrift leaders in the East and Midwest, and those in the Southwest and West. While nearly every S&L prospered in the 1950s and 1960s, those in the West and Southwest were especially successful, because of the tremendous postwar population growth in these areas. During World War II, millions moved to California in pursuit of defense industry jobs, and in the postwar period this migration continued. By 1960, the state's population was 125 percent higher than in 1940. In contrast, states like New York, Ohio, and Pennsylvania experienced more modest population gains ranging between 20 and 40 percent. Such changes had a broad effect on shifting the balance of economic power from the industrial North to the West and Southwest.[29]

Related to this change was the widening gap between large and small thrifts. In 1965, nearly 600 S&Ls had more than $50 million in assets, while at the other end of the spectrum 2,700 associations had fewer than $5 million in assets, of which 1,032 had less than $1 million. By contrast, the one hundred largest S&Ls controlled 26 percent of total industry assets, and many of these thrifts, including three that held $4.7 billion in assets each, were in California. Because the large thrifts often fueled their growth by

[28] League lobbying was exceptionally well organized, and during the 1962 tax debate two Congressmen reported receiving 120,000 letters from constituents opposing the S&L tax provisions. USS&LL Memorandum to Members with attachments, 2 February 1962, and 13 February 1962; Taxes, Mutual, January–June 1962; McMurray Papers; RG 195; NACP; "Savings and Loan Taxation," *SLN* 79 (March 1958), 27–32; Norman Strunk, "Our Present Tax Status: Why it is Right for Us," *SLN* 80 (June 1959), 25–30; W. O. DuVall, "Taxation," *SLN* 83 (October, 1962), 22–7; Wright Patman "A Banker's Bonus Bill," *SLN* 82 (November 1961), 35–40; "ABA Set for New Attack on Association Tax Law," *SLN* 82 (November 1961), 10; "S-L Men Rip JFK Tax Bill," *Los Angeles Herald-Examiner*, 10 May 1962, 9; *Confidential Memorandum*, undated, quote 1; *Membership Bulletin*, M303 (23 February 1962), 1; "Tax Post-Mortem," *Savings and Loan Annals 1962* (Chicago: United States Savings and Loan League, 1962), 66–8; "A Tax Crackdown on S&L Companies," *US News and World Report*, 28 January 1963, 44.

[29] *Historical Statistics of the United States*, 56–60.

offering above market dividends, leaders of the smaller S&Ls referred to these managers derisively as "the high-rate boys," and pleaded with League officials to rein in their practices. Adding to this dissent was the fact that it was common for groups like the large-S&L-dominated California Savings and Loan League to take policy positions that were opposite to those of the League. Furthermore, since these same thrifts wielded tremendous political influence in Congress it was impossible for the Board to ignore their demands. Their power was such that when the Los Angeles-based Council of Savings and Loan Financial Corporations wanted to meet with President Lyndon B. Johnson to discuss thrift legislation, a White House staffer admitted "I'm afraid of this group."[30]

A third source of internal industry tensions lay in splits between mutually owned thrifts and those that issued stock to the public. Although most S&Ls in the mid-1960s were owned by their members, a handful of associations were controlled by stockholders. This type of ownership first appeared in 1909, when the California legislature required all thrift organizers and managers to own guaranteed stock in their associations as part of a permanent guarantee fund. This law was designed to assure depositors that these thrifts would meet their required dividend payments, since the permanent capital fund would be used to make the payments if regular income was insufficient to meet the needs. If this occurred, the stockholders had to replenish this fund with their own money. Conversely, if income exceeded dividends, the stockholders were allowed to reap the benefits. This arrangement gave management an incentive to stay with their association and operate it efficiently. Despite the advantages of the guaranteed stock plan, only a handful of other states followed the example of California.[31]

Thrift managers began to seek the right to issue stock to the public like any corporation by the late 1940s. This was especially true in states where

---

[30] "100 Largest U.S. League Member Institutions," *SLN* 74 (March 1954), 22–3; "Vital Statistics of 100 Largest Associations," *SLN* 81 (February 1960), 50–1; "Vital Statistics of 100 Largest Associations," *SLN* 86 (February 1965), 55–5; Herbert Kay, "California's S.& L.'s: The Boom the Bankers Knock," *Fortune* 70 (August 1964), 119–23; *Savings and Loan Fact Book, 1966*, 34–7; Letter from Henry Bubb to John E. Horne, 22 December 1965, quote; Advertising, Out of State; Horne Papers; RG 195; NACP; Marvel, *The Federal Home Loan Bank Board*, 127–9; Memorandum from White House Conferees to Bill Moyers and Jack Valenti, 15 December 1965, 1–7, letter from Tom Bane to Harry McPherson, 12 March 1966, and memorandum from Irv Sprague to Harry McPherson with handwritten comments by McPherson, with attachment, 27 July 1967, quote; Savings and Loan; Office Files of Harry McPherson; LBJPL.

[31] Wilfred George Donley, "An Analysis of Building and Loan Associations in California, 1920–1935," (Ph.D. dissertation, University of California, 1937), 20–27, 70–83; "California Associations," *FRABAN* 13 (December 1894), 292; Floyd F. Burtchett, "What's Behind the Growth of California Associations?" *ABAN* 49 (May 1929), 282–3; "The Savings and Loan Business in Los Angeles and California," *SLN* 74 (November 1954), 32–7; Ewalt, *A Business Reborn*, 326–8.

the demand for loans exceeded the local availability of funds, and by 1967 twenty-three states allowed state-chartered S&Ls to sell stock on the open market. While only 12 percent of all thrifts were stock associations by this time, they were also very large and controlled more than 20 percent of total industry resources; in California publicly held S&Ls accounted for more than 60 percent of thrift assets. The ability to sell stock also created the opportunity to use more complex ownership structures such as holding companies. These were umbrella organizations that issued stock to the public but had little or no hard assets. The real financial resources were with subsidiaries that were holding company–owned. For thrifts, the holding company structure had not only legal advantages, but was a way for investors to own and operate multiple S&Ls, as well as unregulated nonfinancial businesses. The New York investment banking firm Lehman Brothers organized the first thrift holding company, Great Western Financial Corporation, in 1955. Within five years it controlled more than twenty different S&Ls, as well as land development companies and an insurance agency. By 1966, ninety-eight holding companies controlled 134 thrifts with more than $16 billion in assets, or one eighth of the industry total.[32]

The wisdom of thrifts issuing stock and forming holding companies was hotly debated within the industry. Supporters claimed that selling stock allowed thrifts to better fund loan demand, and provided a permanent source of capital that limited the liability of the FSLIC since it represented an additional reserve. Similarly, since the managers of these S&Ls were often also the owners, they had a vested interest in making sure the thrift was sound financially. Opponents charged that stock associations limited ownership opportunities and raised conflict of interest problems, especially if a holding company owned nonregulated businesses. Similarly, the idea of stock associations ran counter to the original concept of thrifts as local institutions controlled by the membership. Regulators also suspected, but could not prove, that closely held stock associations ignored local lending needs to pursue risky business in order to maximize profits for investors. As federally insured institutions, such operations posed a potential problem for the well-being of the FSLIC.[33]

---

[32] "S&L Holding Company on Coast Makes Public Offering of Shares," *The New York Times*, 25 August 1955, 1, 11; Donald D. Hester, *Stock and Mutual Associations in the Savings and Loan Industry* (Washington, DC: Federal Home Loan Bank Board, 1968), 8–14, 24; Eugene F. Brigham, *Savings and Loan Holding Companies, Their Development and Operation* (Los Angeles: University of California Graduate School of Business Administration, 1966), 5–10; Marvel, *The Federal Home Loan Bank Board*, 202–4, 241–245; "Those S&L Stocks," *Business Week*, 27 June 1959, 112–4; Stephen G. Slipher, "Report of the Legislative Director on Legislative Matters" *Savings and Loan Annals, 1960* (Chicago: United States Savings and Loan League, 1960), 243–5; Ewalt, *A Business Reborn*, 329.

[33] Draft memorandum to members of the Federal Savings and Loan Advisory Committee with attachment, 9 March 1955, 1–2; FS&LA, Conversions, 1954; McAllister Papers; RG 195;

Because of these concerns, federal regulators, supported by the League, began in 1956 to seek legislation restricting the activities of savings and loan holding companies. When Congress finally took up the issue in 1959, testimony from thrift leaders reflected the high level of division within the industry. The League wanted the law to help protect the reputation of mutual S&Ls, while holding company leaders, all of whom were from California, opposed it because there was "no evidence that anyone has been hurt." The Savings and Loan Holding Company Act, whose most important provision limited holding companies from owning no more than one thrift, did pass in 1960, but legislators considered it a stop-gap measure to allow for further study of the issue. Unfortunately, the law was not strengthened for years, with the result that holding companies accounted for more than half of all regulatory problems faced by the Board in 1965.[34]

A REVITALIZED REGULATORY ENVIRONMENT

A related major challenge for the thrift industry was the end to the passive regulatory policies of the 1950s. When Albert Robertson resigned as Board chairman in 1961, President Kennedy named former New York City housing commissioner and past consultant to the Senate Banking Committee, James P. McMurray, to replace him. A stocky and energetic individual, McMurray immediately set out to revitalize the Board and reassert its authority over the industry. During his first year in office, he established a division to collect and analyze housing and thrift industry data, hired more home loan bank personnel and, following the first in-depth organizational study of the

NACP; Letter from Wm. Mosely to Walter W. McAllister, 1 February 1956, 1–4; FS&LA, Conversions, 1955, October–December; McAllister Papers; RG 195; NACP; Memorandum from A. D. Theobald to Joseph P. McMurray, December 1961; FS&LA Conversions, 1961–; McMurray Papers; RG 195; NACP; Letter from J. Ralph Stone to John E. Horne, 28 December 1967; United States Savings and Loan League (hereafter USS&LL), General; Horne Papers; RG 195; NACP.

34 Letter from Neill Davis to Walter W. McAllister, 3 February 1955; FS&LA Conversions, 1954; McAllister Papers; RG 195; NACP; Letter from Morton Bodfish to Walter W. McAllister, 27 June 1955; FS&LA Conversions, 1955 April–September; McAllister Papers; RG 195; NACP; Letter from A. J. Robertson to A. Willis Robertson, 12 August 1959; Holding Companies; Robertson Papers; RG 195; NACP; "Fight Brewing on Savings and Loan Holding Companies" *Business Week*, 2 March 1963, 54; Memorandum from Len Creighton for July 15, 1963 Meeting, letter from Norman Strunk to Joseph P. McMurray, 2 March 1963 and memorandum from Harry Schwartz to Joseph P. McMurray, 23 May 1963; Holding Companies, 1961–1963; McMurray Papers; RG 195; U.S. Senate, *Hearings Before the Committee on Banking and Currency on HR 7244 and S 2517*, 86th Cong., 1st sess. (Washington, DC: USGPO, 1959), 45–9, 64–6, quote 46; "Testimony Given by Chairman on Holding Company Bill," *FHLBB Digest* 9 (June 1967), 1; "S&L Merger Set; Horne Answered by Californian," *The New York Times*, 15 November 1967, 61, 65; Memorandum from MJC to Mr. Watson, June 21, 1967; EX FG October 1, 1966–August 28, 1967; WHCF Subject File FG; LBJPL.

agency, created a centralized Division of Examination and Supervision. As one League official later noted, McMurray "was a mover, a doer [and] by all odds the most interesting chairman since John Fahey."[35]

McMurray also formed a twelve-man task force composed of thrift leaders and outside advisors to consult on issues facing the Board. The new chairman thought that the Board should be supportive of the industry it oversaw, but also wanted to make sure that it did not engage in practices that would tarnish its image. He described his role as "that of a good old-fashioned Irish policeman who smiles and jokes with the people on his beat, but can be tough with them when he has to." To make certain the industry was aware of this more active government-business relationship, the new chairman issued dozens of new policies that he called "the rules of the game." He was also more than willing to use not-so-subtle threats that went beyond simple moral suasion to make the industry "toe the line." While McMurray received very favorable public reviews, several within the industry grumbled over the changes.[36]

Although McMurray wrestled with issues long familiar to the Board, such as "giveaways" and brokered deposits, his greatest concern was the trend of rising dividend rates, something that he wanted to end for several reasons. First, if the Board could reduce rate competition it would also solve many of the other problems it faced. Second, when local rate wars did occur, S&Ls across the country typically had to match the higher rates to retain deposits. Finally, higher dividends usually required riskier loans to generate income, which in turn resulted in more defaults. This was especially true in the early 1960s' as the level of delinquent loans for the entire industry rose an average

---

[35] Gurney Breckenfield, "Joe McMurray of the Home Loan Bank Board," *House and Home* (May 1962), 47–8; Letter from Joseph P. McMurray to Edward E. Edwards, 17 July 1962; Edwards, Edward E., 1961– ; Murray Papers; RG 195; NACP; McMurray Papers; RG 195; NACP; Letter from Stephen Slipher to Joseph P. McMurray, 17 April 1961; FHLBB Task Force, McMurray Desk File, 1961– ; McMurray Papers; RG 195; NACP; Notes on First Meeting of Task Force, 27–29 May 1961; FHLBB Task Force Meetings, Notes 1961– ; McMurray Papers; RG 195; NACP; Letter from Joseph P. McMurray to Dante Fascell, 11 March 1962; FHLBB Survey (Booz-Allen Hamilton), 1961– ; McMurray Papers; RG 195; NACP

[36] "Wider Role Urged for Savings Units," *The New York Times*, 26 September 1963, 47; "The Man Who Makes the Savings and Loans Toe the Mark" *Business Week*, 8 January 1964, 72–4 quote 72; "The Irish Policeman," *The Wall Street Journal*, 24 June 1963, quote 22; James Cameron, "S&L Regulation by McMurray: Larger Industry, More Powers," *The American Banker*, 27 August 1962, 8; "McMurray Speaks Out," *SLN* 84 (March 1963), 32–7; "S&L Watchdogs Growl Louder," *Business Week*, 26 October 1963, 45; "New Rules for Savings and Loan: What 1964 Will Bring," *US News and World Report*, 6 November 1963, 94–5; James Gavin, "Joe McMurray ... A Man with a Mission," *American Savings and Loan Weekly*, 13 July 1964, 2, 10; Memorandum from Gardner Ackley to Lyndon B. Johnson, 1 December 1964, 2; FI 2, April 25, 1964 to December 31, 1964; WHCF General Financial Institutions (FI); LBJPL. Memorandum from Walter Heller to Lyndon B. Johnson, 5 February 1964; FI 5-4 Housing, November 23, 1963 to May 11, 1965; WHCF General FI; LBJPL.

of 35 percent per year, and in California, where rate competition was fierce, the same annual increase approached 60 percent.[37]

While McMurray warned California thrifts they would "find a heavy supervisory hand on their shoulders" if they did not end their "avid" dividend practices, his pleas produced few changes. As a result, in March 1962 the chairman announced new rules that would make it harder to pay more on savings by requiring thrifts to set aside reserves for both scheduled items and their annual increase in savings. In addition, all thrifts had to contribute to the formation of a new secondary reserve for the FSLIC that would equal 2 percent of total insured savings. Saying he could "no longer wait for moral suasion to take its course," the announcements shocked the industry, and League leaders told McMurray that "the business was never more 'up in arms' over a regulation." When these new rules failed to end rate competition, the chairman tightened them by linking annual reserve contributions to total asset growth, which forced the fastest growing thrifts to set aside the most in reserve.[38]

The second major issue McMurray faced during his tenure was checking the activities of stock associations and holding companies. The Board believed that state regulators were allowing too many state-chartered, but

[37] Regulations, Legislation, and Policy Statements, 1–16; Regulations, Legislation, and Policy Statements; McMurray Papers; RG 195; NACP, 3–5, 14; "Luring the Investors," *Newsweek*, 11 April 1960, 104; "Crackdown on Lures for Investors," *US News and World Report*, 25 April 1961, 89; W. O. DuVall, "Intra-Business Competition," *SLN* 81 (June 1960), 27–30; Memorandum from John Wyman to Joseph P. McMurray, 6 July 1961; Advertising, Give Aways, 1961–1962; McMurray Papers; RG 195; NACP; Ed W. Hiles "Do We Want a Regulatory Dividend Ceiling?" *SLN* (February 1957), 32–6; Memorandum from George W. Murphey to Joseph P McMurray, 12 June 1963; Advertising, Give Aways, 1963; McMurray Papers; RG 195; NACP; Letter with handwritten comments from Carol Fish to Joseph P. McMurray 12 December 1963; Brokers, General; McMurray Papers; RG 195; NACP; *Savings and Loan Fact Book, 1966*, 108; Gladwin Hill, "Loan Warriors to Call Truce and Bury Premiums, *The New York Times*, 28 May 1961, sec. 3, 1; "Board Members Discuss Three Major Problems Before U.S. League," *FHLBB Digest* 4 (September 1961), 3–5, 11.

[38] "'Adventurous' S&Ls Warned by McMurray," *Los Angeles Times*, 10 October 1963, quote 15; Edward Cowan, "Move on Savings Draws Criticism," *The New York Times*, 16 December 1963, 55; "No Help for Home Buyers," *The Wall Street Journal*, 22 July 1963, 15; "Letter to Editor," *The Wall Street Journal*, 12 August 1963, 17; Joseph P. McMurray, "The Savings and Loan Industry in Transition," *Savings and Loan Annals, 1963* (Chicago: United States Savings and Loan League, 1963), 18–22; "Scrambling Towards a Worthy Goal," *The American Banker*, 3 January 1964 4; Letter from Joseph P. McMurray to Herman Talmadge, 20 July 1962, and speech by Joseph P. McMurray, 21 October 1963, 11–3; FS&LA, Dividends, Ceiling on, 1961– ; McMurray Papers; RG 195; Letter from Leonard Rautenberg to Joseph P. McMurray, 6 February 1964, and letter from Joseph P. McMurray to Nath Turner, 19 February 1964; FSLIC, Reserves, January–February, 1964; McMurray Papers; RG 195; "California 5 Percenters Face New Federal Pressure," *The Miami Herald,* 3 October 1963, 9C; Albert Jedlicka, "S&L Reserve Rise Proposed to Curb Rate," *Chicago Daily News*, 4 November 1963, 6; Letter from Norman Strunk to Joseph P. McMurray, 13 December 1963, quote; FSLIC Reserves December 1963 Letters; McMurray Papers; RG 195; NACP.

federally insured, thrifts to convert from mutual to stock ownership, and it suspected that many of these conversions were done simply to enrich management. The Board used this reasoning to place a moratorium on the conversion of federal S&Ls from mutual to stock ownership in 1955. This position, however, was strongly opposed within the industry, and in 1961 the Board lifted the ban. The number of conversions immediately soared, but unfortunately so did the reports of abuse, especially by insiders who opened large accounts just before a thrift was to issue stock. Because it was clear that not all existing members were receiving equitable treatment in such cases, McMurray reimposed the prohibition on conversions in 1963, and this order would stay in place for the next ten years.[39]

In 1965, McMurray retired from the Board, and President Johnson named John E. Horne as the new chairman. Horne was a soft-spoken Alabaman who had been a staffer for Senate Banking Committee chairman John Sparkman (D-AL) from 1947 to 1961 and FHLBB member since 1963. Like McMurray, Horne believed in vigorous oversight to end practices he termed "inimical to the best interests of the industry." His interest in closer supervision was driven in part by a surge in the number of problem thrifts. These included the failure of three S&Ls in 1965 and 1966 that cost the FSLIC more than $118 million. Investigations later revealed that lender misconduct played a major role in each insolvency. In addition, the number of current supervisory cases was such that the FSLIC estimated it may have to pay out make an additional $425 million to insured account holders over the next two years. Such unprecedented statistics led regulators to wonder for the first time in the history of the FSLIC if the insurance fund would be able to meet these needs.[40]

---

[39] "Saving and Loan: A Troubled Year," *The New York Times*, 6 January 1964, 110; "Ceiling on Dividends," *Barron's*, 6 May 1963, 1; Marvel, *The Federal Home Loan Bank Board*, 199–208, 243–8; Letter from Walter W. McAllister to Daniel Robinson, 16 June 1955; First Federal Savings & Loan Associations, M-Z; McAllister Papers; RG 195; NACP; Letter from Walter W. McAllister to R. V. Walker, 5 December 1955; FS&LA, Conversions, 1955, October–December; McAllister Papers; RG 195; NACP; Memorandum from W. H. Husband to Len Creighton, 30 March 1962; FS&LA, Conversions, 1961– ; McMurray Papers; RG 195; NACP; Memorandum from Rex Baker to Joseph P. McMurray, 31 July 1962; Stock Associations, 1961– ; McMurray Papers; RG 195; NACP.

[40] Actual FSLIC liabilities for this two-year period were considerably less at just over $150 million. Marvell, *The Federal Home Loan Bank Board*, 270–1; Edward Cowan, "Election by Bank Watched Closely," *The New York Times*, 7 March 1964, 27; "Savings-Loan Men Relieved as McMurray Prepares to Resign HLB Post," *The Wall Street Journal*, 14 September 1964, 16; Letter from Thomas T. Timons to Walter Purmort with attachment, 9 January 1968, quote; Advertising, Out of State; Horne Papers; RG 195; NACP; Memorandum from Robert P. Perrin to John E. Horne, 4 April 1968; Coordinating Committee Meeting, 7 May 1968; Horne Papers; RG 195; NACP; "Hounding the S&Ls' Own Watchdog," *Business Week*, 20 August 1966, 51–3; Memorandum from Jery D. Worthy to Board Members, 25 August 1965; FSLIC, Debentures, General; Horne Papers; RG 195; NACP; Memorandum

To remedy this, Horne pressed Congress to give the Board stronger supervisory powers. Traditionally, if regulators wanted to end improper business practices, they had three options – send management a written reprimand, revoke FSLIC coverage, or seize the association. Regulators complained that restricting their options forced them to "use a bludgeon when all we want to apply is a restraining hand." In 1966, Congress passed the Financial Institutions Supervision Act, which gave the Board the authority to issue cease-and-desist orders that would force a thrift to change its practices without putting it out of business. These orders could be used against any "unsafe and unsound practices," whose definition was kept purposely vague so regulators had some latitude to apply this new tool. They could also issue a permanent injunction, which often required a court hearing to become effective, or a temporary order, which took effect immediately but also required greater evidence of wrongdoing.[41]

CREATING RATE CONTROLS

The most significant development in the period 1955 to 1966 was the imposition on the thrift industry of the same type of interest rate controls that the banking industry had operated under for more than thirty years. When Congress passed the Banking Act of 1933, federal regulators got the authority to regulate the interest rates that commercial banks could pay on most types of deposits, including a complete prohibition on the payment of interest on demand deposits like checking accounts. While these rules, which were codified under Regulation Q, had helped restore stability to the banking system during the Great Depression, they also gave thrifts a major competitive advantage, since S&L managers had much greater freedom to determine their own rates. Despite warnings from the Board and the League not to use this

form Kenneth Scott to Board Members, 8 May 1967, 1–34; Federal Home Loan Bank Board, Plans and Objectives; Horne Papers; RG 195; NACP.

[41] Letter from Morris D. Crawford to Joseph P. McMurray, 12 June 1961; FS&LA, Conservators and Receivers, 1961–1963; McMurray Papers; RG 195; NACP; Memorandum from John Wyman to Kenneth Scott, 14 February 1964, Memorandum from Joseph P. McMurray to Kenneth Scott, 14 February 1964, and Memorandum from Thomas H. Creighton to Board members, 30 April 1964; FS&LA, Conservators and Receivers, January–August 1964; McMurray Papers; RG 195; NACP; Edward Cowan, "U.S. Seeks to Aid Saving Concerns," *The New York Times*, 21 January 1963, 13; H. Erich Heinemann, "Dispute Boiling in Thrift Field," *The New York Times*, 14 November 1965, sec. 3, 1, 9, quote 9; John E. Horne, "Chairman's Address," *Savings and Loan Annals, 1965*, 30–1; John E. Horne, "Federal Savings Bank Bill," *Vital Speeches of the Day* 32 (1965–66), 364–5; Memorandum from John E. Horne to Marvin Watson with attachment, 17 September 1966, memorandum from John E. Horne to Mr. Jacobson with attachment, 5 October 1966, and letter from John E. Horne to Marvin Watson with attachment, 3 November 1967; LE/FI 2, February 22, 1966–; WHCF LE/FI 2; LBJPL. Letter from John Horne et al. to the Speaker of the House, 29 March 1966; Federal Home Loan Bank Board; Wright Patman Papers; LBJPL; Marvel, *The Federal Home Loan Bank Board*, 32–4.

advantage to lure deposits, several short but fierce rate wars erupted in 1954, 1957, 1959, and 1962.[42]

By the early 1960s, banker complaints over the unfair restrictions they faced under Regulation Q reached the sympathetic ear of Comptroller of the Currency Saxon. He wanted banks to be more competitive in the marketplace, and encouraged the Federal Reserve to raise Regulation Q ceilings. In 1961, the Federal Reserve initiated the first of a series of rate increases that helped narrow the average gap between banks and thrift interest rates to less than 0.5 percent by 1965. Because thrifts, especially in California, responded with increases of their own, the result was a spiraling pattern of higher rates. Adding fuel to this competition for money was the federal government, which began issuing more debt to finance the growing American involvement in the Vietnam War.[43]

The rate competition between banks and thrifts escalated sharply in August 1965, when S&Ls in California and Florida raised dividend rates. Although bankers demanded a change in Regulation Q to match the increase, Saxon was reluctant to add fuel to this latest rate war. In December, however, the Federal Reserve unexpectedly set Regulation Q at the same level as thrift rates, and for the first time in recent history savings rates for banks and thrifts were at parity. Thrifts responded with another round of increases, and by February 1966 the back-and-forth rate escalation had become so fierce that the leaders of both industries called for a truce. By April, market conditions had stabilized, and in August the Federal Reserve finally lowered rates under Regulation Q to further defuse the conflict. Because the rate war of 1965–1966 was the most serious to date, Congress held hearings in May 1966 to consider extending Regulation Q controls

---

[42] "Thrifts Get U.S. Plea on Rates," *The New York Times*, 21 December 1961, 39; "U.S. Curbs Urged on Thrift Rates," *The New York Times*, 28 September 1963, 23; Murray Teigh Bloom, "In Quest of the Higher Percentage," *The New York Times Magazine*, 22 July 1962, 21, 34; Reserve Regulations: A Way to Limit Rate Wars, 11 March 1965,; Federal Home Loan Bank Board, Questions and Answers; Horne Papers; RG 195; NACP; Transcript of "The Frank McGee Report," 17 July 1966; California, State of; Horne Papers; RG 195; NACP; Ewalt, *A Business Reborn*, 314–6; Theobald, *Forty-Five Years*, 225.

[43] "Savings and Loan Associations Time of Troubles," *Forbes* 89 (15 February 1962), 23–5; Edward Cowan, "Boom in Savings Poses Dilemma," *The New York Times*, 13 April 1963, 75; "Savings Agencies Raise Rate to 5%," *The New York Times*, 28 September 1963, 23; Edward Cowan, "Savings agencies in West Discover Headaches Come with Bigness, but Business is Considered Sound," *The New York Times*, 4 November 1963, 55; Eileen Shanahan, "Bankers and Agencies Question US Savings-Bond Advertising," *The New York Times*, 7 February 1966, 43, 46; "How Scramble for Savings is Hurting S&Ls," *US News and World Report*, 30 May 1966, 75–7; Memorandum from Jake Jacobson to Lyndon B. Johnson with attachment, 6 January 1966, and memorandum from Lyndon B. Johnson, to Henry Fowler, 18 January 1966; EX FI 8 Interest Rates, December 4, 1965 to March 22, 1966; WHCF Subject File FI; LBJPL; Letter with attachment from Jim Freeman to Wright Patman, 8 December 1967; United States Savings and Loan League Correspondence; Wright Patman Papers; LBJPL.

to include S&Ls. The session ended, however, before any legislation was passed.[44]

Although McMurray indicated a desire to make thrifts subject to Regulation Q in 1962, the Board never seriously considered using rate controls to solve the problem of funds competition. The events of early 1966, however, changed Board attitudes, and in August Horne announced his support for an extension of Regulation Q to the thrift industry, a move he felt was needed to prevent the continued rate wars from having an adverse effect on the economy. Privately, Horne did not think that rate controls would accomplish much, since most thrifts would invariably set their rates to equal the ceiling, thereby making "the maximum rate the minimum." Despite such misgivings, Horne thought he had no alternative, and as he told one League official, "I see headaches with dividend controls, but presently there are more headaches without it."[45]

The White House also supported rate controls, and in March 1966, President Johnson recommended Congress enact appropriate legislation. When the session ended without action, Rep. Wright Patman (D-TX) announced he would introduce a bill to permanently roll back rates on all CDs, a move that would essentially overrule the authority of the Federal Reserve. The Johnson Administration, however, feared this would "cause chaos in the financial

---

[44] "Bankers Bait the Hook for Deposits," *Business Week*, 22 October 1966, 88–92; "Regulation Q Revisited," *SLN* (January 1965), 51; "Problem is Seen for Thrift Units," *The New York Times*, 30 January 1966, sec. 3, 9; H. Erich Heinemann, "Now a Question: 'Where to Save?'" *The New York Times*, 23 January 1966, sec. 3, 1, 12; "Action to Help Savings and Loans," *US News and World Report*, 7 June 1966, 88; "U.S. Eliminates All Curbs on Rates of Savings Units," *The New York Times*, 2 July 1966, 1; H. Erich Heinemann, "Not Enough Savings, Not Enough Loans," *The New York Times*, 28 August 1966, sec. 4, 4; Marvel, *The Federal Home Loan Bank Board*, 195–7; "Business Asks Curbs on Regulation Q Authority," *SLN* 87 (January 1966), 5–7; "Did the Fed Make a Mistake?" *Journal of Commerce*, 12 May 1966, 4; Letter from Henry Bubb to John E. Horne, 22 December 1965; Advertising, Out-of-State; Horne Papers; RG 195; NACP; Memorandum from Michael Greenebaum to John E. Horne, 30 August 1966; Dividends, Controls, General Meetings 1967; Horne Papers; RG 195; NACP; Memorandum from Arthur Okun to Lyndon B. Johnson, 28 June 1966; FI 2, August 7, 1965, to April 12, 1966; WHCF General FI; LBJPL; Memorandum from Henry Fowler to Lyndon B. Johnson, 1 July 1966; FI 2, April 13, 1966 to July 31, 1966; WHCF General FI; LBJPL.

[45] "Rate War Joined by U.S. Agencies," *The New York Times*, 29 June 1966, 61; Eileen Shanahan, "U.S. Seeks Powers on Savings Rates," *The New York Times*, 27 May 1963, 41; H. Erich Heinemann, "Lawmakers Map Savings-Unit Aid," *The New York Times*, 5 June 1966, 1; Letter from Thomas T. Timmons to William Purmort with attachment, 9 January 1968; Advertising, Out-of-State; Horne Papers; RG 195; NACP; Speech by John E. Horne to the Alabama Savings and Loan League, 19 August 1966; Alabama Savings and Loan League; Horne Papers; RG 195; NACP; Letter from William J. Kerwin to John E. Horne with attachment, 20 February 1967, quote; Dividends and Certificate of Deposit Controls; Horne Papers; RG 195; NACP; Memorandum from Arthur Okun to Lyndon B. Johnson, 13 July 1966; EX FG 2 March 1966 to 6 July 1967; WHCF Subject File FG 229 EX; LBJPL; Letter from John E. Horne to Stephen Slipher, 6 September 1966, quote; USS&LL General; Horne Papers; RG 195; NACP.

markets" and scrambled to dissuade him, while at the same time working behind the scenes to convince others not to support the bill. Although there was little support for his measure, if Congress refused to consider the bill, Patman threatened to use parliamentary tactics to prevent anything from being approved during the short summer session. To avoid a public and embarrassing clash with this loyal friend of the President, the White House reached a compromise with Patman that limited the term of the rate control bill to one year, which would give regulators more time to lower CD rates to levels acceptable to the congressman.[46]

Although the League strenuously opposed rate controls, when it became apparent that some form of rate restriction would be passed, thrift lobbyists focused on finding ways to minimize the financial impact it would have on the industry. While they liked the one-year limit on the bill because it placed the onus on Congress to renew it each year, their main focus was ensuring that thrifts be allowed to pay higher rates than banks. Using the justification that S&Ls deserved a rate advantage given their important role as home financiers, the League succeeded in having Congress insert in the Interest Rate Control Act of 1966 a guarantee that the S&L industry be allowed to pay more on savings than banks. On the basis of this provision, the Board and the Federal Reserve eventually agreed to set rates that would allow thrifts to pay 0.25 percent more than banks on savings. This rate differential became part of regulatory policy until the 1980s, when rate controls were eventually phased out under deregulation.[47]

---

[46] "Escalating Interest Rates," *The New York Times*, 4 July 1966, 14; Memorandum from Gardner Ackley to Lyndon B. Johnson, 28 June 1966, 1–3 and memorandum from Joseph Barr to Lyndon B. Johnson, 12 May 1966, 1–4; FI 2, 13 April 1966 to 31 July 1966; WHCF FI; LBJPL; Memorandum from Larry Levinson to Lyndon B. Johnson, 25 March 1966 and memorandum from Arthur Okun to Lyndon B. Johnson, 26 May 1966; LE/FI 2 February 22, 1966– ; WHCF LE/FI 2; LBJPL; Memorandum from Joseph Barr to Lyndon B. Johnson, 22 July 1966; EX FG 2 March 1966 to 6 July 1967; WHCF Subject File FG 229 EX; LBJPL; Memorandum from Joseph Barr to Marvin Watson, 15 August 1966; EX FG August 5, 1966–September 30, 1966; WHCF Subject File FG; LBJPL; Memorandum from Joseph Barr to Marvin Watson, 15 August 1966, memorandum from Henry H. Wilson Jr. to Lyndon B. Johnson with attachment, 23 August 1966, memorandum and memorandum from Joseph Barr to Marvin Watson with attachment, 1 September 1966; Letter from William J. Kerwin to Wright Patman, 22 July 1966; National League of Insured Savings and Loan Associations; Wright Patman Papers; LBJPL.

[47] "Thrift Units Fight Rate-Curb Measure," *The New York Times*, 5 August 1966, 40; Letter from Norman Strunk to John E. Horne, 28 August 1965; USS&LL Recommendations; Horne Papers; RG 195; NACP; Kerwin Letter, 20 February 1967; Dividend and Certificate of Deposit Controls; Horne Papers; RG 195; NACP; Greenebaum Memorandum, 30 August 1966; Dividends, Controls, General Meetings 1967; Horne Papers; RG 195; NACP; "House Passes Bill on Interest Rates," *The New York Times*, 9 September 1966, 1; "New Interest Rate Ceilings Go into Effect Quickly," *The New York Times*, 22 September 1966, 67, 71; Theobald, *Forty-Five Years*, 225–7; Stephen G. Slipher, "Report of the Legislative Director on Legislative Matters," *Savings and Loan Annals*, 1966 (Chicago: United States Savings and Loan League, 1966) 192–3.

Because the rate differential gave S&Ls the right to always offer higher rates than banks on savings accounts, the League quickly became the staunchest supporter of keeping rate controls in place. By the late 1960s, thrift officials predicted dire consequences to the availability of home financing if Congress refused to renew the law, and their testimony was critical each year in securing an extension. Unfortunately, such blind support for rate controls proved to be misplaced. In the 1970s, when Congress took up the issue of deregulating financial industries, the League's refusal to make any concession on reducing their historical rate advantage killed virtually every piece of reform legislation. As a result, thrift deregulation was consistently postponed until it virtually became a necessity in the early 1980s.[48]

CONCLUSIONS

Unlike the glory years thrifts enjoyed immediately after World War II, the period from 1956 to 1966 presented a number of potential barriers to the continued expansion of the thrift industry. One was the slower-growth economy, which depressed new home construction at times, while a second factor was increased competition from banks, mortgage companies, and federal housing programs. A more general challenge for the industry during this period was an active federal regulatory environment that was unwilling to give the industry the same degree of *carte blanche* it enjoyed in the past. Despite these challenges, the thrift industry managed to record phenomenal growth: by 1965 S&Ls commanded more than $125 billion in assets and made nearly half of all residential mortgages in the country. A key reason for the sustained growth was that thrift managers and industry leaders continued to be proactive in the development of innovative lending and savings option.

While this expansion pleased League leaders, it also caused increased tension within the industry, as managers of the more traditional, smaller mutually owned thrifts clashed with those of the billion-dollar publically held behemoths in the West. These divisions were seen in greater infighting within the League and periods of intense rate competition for deposits. Following a particularly intense interest rate war that affected the whole country, Congress finally intervened to restore some sense of order. The result was the Interest Rate Control Act of 1966, which extended rate controls under Regulation Q over both commercial banks and S&Ls. Although thrifts retained their traditional ability to pay higher savings rates than banks, the passage of this act marked an end to the days of easy growth for the thrift industry.

[48] Letter from Franklin Hardinge Jr. to Robert L Rand, 25 November 1968 and Letter from Norman Strunk to Robert L. Rand, 18 December 1968, and memorandum from RLR to Horne and Greenbaum with attachment, 2 October 1968; Coordinating Committee Meetings; Horne Papers; RG 195; NACP.

7

LOST OPPORTUNITIES, 1967–1978

From the inclusion of thrifts under Regulation Q to the onset of deregulation, the business environment for S&Ls grew increasingly more complex. A major reason for this situation was that the economy of the 1970s was very unstable, characterized by slow growth, rising inflation, and high interest rates. This condition, called "stagflation," forced thrifts to redesign traditional mortgages to make them affordable to borrowers, and create new savings instruments to attract funds from investors. A second factor was that technological innovations revolutionized finance and dramatically altered the way in which consumers could use their money. While many of these changes benefited the thrift industry, they also led to greater competition with other financial intermediaries. Finally, the rise of a consumer movement forced lenders to pay more attention to the problem of lending discrimination and be more responsive to the needs of individuals and communities. This not only led to the passage of several pro-consumer laws, but also gave consumers more agency in how S&Ls conducted business. While S&Ls continued to expand and maintain their dominant role as mortgage providers during these difficult years, such broad changes in the marketplace led the League and government officials to reassess the basic structure of thrift regulation. Nonetheless, conflicts over different issues, both within the industry and from other interest groups, delayed any substantive action for years. As a result, the industry was ill prepared to deal with the economic decline that began late in 1979, and as Congress rushed toward deregulation it was clear that the failure to pass reform laws earlier was a critical lost opportunity.

CONTENDING WITH STAGFLATION

The central challenge facing the thrift industry in the 1970s was responding to a slow-growth economy marked by persistent inflation and rising interest rates. While the economy, as measured by the gross national product (GNP), grew at an annual rate of 3.1 percent between 1969 and 1979, the expansion was very uneven and punctuated by recessions in 1969, 1974–5, and late 1979. The period was also marked by high inflation, as the consumer price index (CPI) rose at an average annual rate of 6.7 percent between 1970 and 1975, and 8.9 percent between 1975 and 1980. In contrast, from 1960 to 1968 GNP had grown at an average annual rate of 4.5 percent, while the CPI had risen by less than 2 percent per year. One important effect of these conditions was why it was difficult for government and business leaders to make long-term financial plans.[1]

A central reason why the 1970s economy was so unsettled was that for the first time since the end of World War II, energy costs in America rose significantly. Between 1951 and 1970, the country had enjoyed low and stable energy costs, as the average price of imported crude oil stayed between $2.66 and $3.00 per barrel. Prices, however, surged dramatically in October 1973 when the Oil Producing Exporting Countries (OPEC) declared an embargo on America for supporting Israel in the Yom Kippur War. Because America relied on OPEC for more than 60 percent of its oil, the subsequent tripling of oil prices caused inflation and helped create a sharp two-year recession. Oil prices remained high through the 1970s, which limited overall economic growth and caused inflation to remain a major problem. Such unusual conditions led economists to coin the term "stagflation" to describe them.[2]

The problem of inflation was exacerbated by rising interest rates, caused in part by increased federal deficits. Between 1963 and 1969, federal spending soared, and since revenues did not keep pace, the government had to sell more debt. The result was that in the last three years of the decade, short-term interest rates more than doubled, which also led to higher rates for consumer loans. Long-term mortgage rates, which had averaged 5 percent in the mid-1960s, rose to 8.5 percent by 1970 and then to 11 percent by 1978. This adverse change, combined with a near tripling of the average price of a home during the decade, meant that it was very difficult for borrowers to qualify for a conventional fixed-rate mortgage. In response to these problems, home lenders devised products collectively referred to as alternative mortgage instruments (AMIs) to improve the ability of home buyers to get a mortgage. These innovative financial products, while designed out of necessity given the economic environment, were additional examples of how the thrift industry tried to operate in a proactive manner to help consumers and meet increased competition.[3]

---

[1] Bureau of the Census, *Statistical Abstracts of the United States, 1988*, 109th edition (Washington, DC: USGPO, 1982), 445, 450.

[2] Bureau of the Census, *Statistical Abstracts of the United States, 1980*, 101st edition (Washington, DC: USGPO, 1980), 477–82; *Statistical Abstracts, 1988*, 754, 766; *The World Almanac and Review of Facts, 1980* (New York, Newspaper Enterprise Association, 1980), 922, 925, 933.

[3] *Savings and Loan Fact Book 1963* (Chicago: United States Savings and Loan League, 1963), 51; Scott Derks, editor, *The Value of a Dollar, 1860–1999* (Lakeville, CT: Grey House

One way that AMIs tried to lower the barrier to home ownership was by reducing the initial monthly mortgage payments, and the two main products that used this approach were the flexible mortgage and the graduated-payment mortgage. Under the flexible mortgage, borrowers made interest-only payments for up to five years, with full principal and interest payments made for the remaining term. The graduated-payment mortgage used a tiered payment structure that required only partial principal and interest payments during the early years of the loan, with the payment amount increasing on set dates to allow for full amortization. While both these plans helped lower the initial monthly payments, each had certain drawbacks. Using a flexible mortgage prevented the early accumulation of borrower equity in the property, while the graduated-payment mortgage resulted in negative amortization in which the loan balance initially increased in size. Lenders, however, justified these risks, claiming that borrowers would "grow" into the loan as their income increased.[4]

A second way AMIs tried to help consumers lay in provisions to protect the borrower and/or the lender from changes in interest rates. One such AMI, the rollover mortgage, did not have a fixed interest rate, but rather allowed the rate to be renegotiated at set intervals of three, five, or seven years. A similar plan was the step-rate mortgage, which had an initial below-market interest rate that increased during the life of the loan by preset amounts; the loan payment was also recalculated at each change date to ensure full amortization. Finally, variable-rate mortgages mitigated interest rate risk by tying the loan rate to a broader rate index, like that of the six-month Treasury bill; and, as the index changed, the loan rate and monthly payment changed accordingly. The main problem with all these plans was that it was difficult to protect both the borrower and lender, since consumers faced "payment shock" if rates increased suddenly, and negative amortization resulted if payments were kept too low. Because of such risks, only California allowed its state-chartered thrifts to make variable-rate mortgages during the 1970s. Federal S&Ls were not allowed to make variable-rate mortgages until April 1981.[5]

Publishing, 1999), 196; *Savings and Loan Fact Book '80* (Chicago: United States League of Savings Institutions, 1980), 36.

4 "Getting Money for Homes: Why Its Tough . . . and the Outlook," *US News and World Report*, 8 August 1966, 82–5; "Flexible Mortgages," *The New York Times*, 18 March 1974, 40; "Say Good Bye to the Great American Dream," *Savings and Loan News* [hereafter *SLN*] 96 (July 1975), 40–2; "New Moves to Revive the American Dream," *SLN* 97 (April 1976), 47–50; "Alternative Mortgage Instruments are Building," *SLN* 98 (August 1977), 50–3; "GPMs Help Relieve the Financial Burdens of Home Ownership," *SLN* 100 (February 1979), 36–7; "Graduated Payments Keep Buyers and Lenders in the Housing Market," *SLN* 100 (September 1979), 56.

5 "A New Plan for Variable Rate Mortgages," *SLN* 88 (January 1967), 26–8; "Variable Rate Mortgages Prove a Sticky Wicket," *SLN* 88 (December 1967), 51; "Will Variable Rates Cure S&Ls' Woes?" *Business Week*, 4 July 1974, 32–4; "The Unvariable Rate Mortgage," *SLN*

While finding ways to help borrowers qualify for loans during these years of rising rates was one challenge for S&Ls, an equally important problem was attracting deposits. Because thrifts faced rate restrictions under Regulation Q, whenever market rates rose above the rate ceiling depositors would move their money into accounts that earned the higher rates, a process known as disintermediation. While the first instance of disintermediation in 1969 was short-lived, it still caused the thrift industry to post its lowest gain in new savings in three years. The second case of disintermediation, in 1973, was more severe: lasting for nearly a year, savers moved money constantly in response to the precipitous ups and downs of rates, and S&Ls lost and gained billions in funds nearly every month. Another major period of disintermediation in 1979 saw interest rates soar so high that thrifts experienced a 50 percent increase in the rate of withdrawals. Overall, this "yo-yo-ing" of deposits placed a serious strain on cash management, and made difficult any type of long-term planning.[6]

To counteract disintermediation, thrifts pushed regulators to let them offer innovative savings accounts capable of competing with investments earning market rates. The first of these was the $1,000 four-year certificate of deposit (CD), which was free of any Regulation Q controls. Appearing in April 1973, these "wild card" CDs caused fierce rate wars between thrifts and banks, and ultimately cost S&Ls more than $1.2 trillion in savings; by October, Congress essentially banned their use. In June 1974, regulators approved another market-rate CD that could mature in as little as thirty days, but the required minimum $100,000 investment limited their use to high net worth investors. The most effective savings innovation, however, was the money market certificate, or MMC, introduced in 1977. Because the interest rate on the MMC was indexed to the six-month Treasury bill, there was little risk of rate wars, and the smaller $10,000 minimum investment made these products accessible to broader groups of savers.[7]

95 (July 1974), 41; "Variable Rate Loan Plan Sparks Lively Debate in Congress," *SLN* 96 (May 1975), 12; "Variable Rates Defeated," *The New York Times*, 5 November 1975, 63, 70; "It's A Bird! It's a Plane! It's a . . . Variable Rate Mortgage?" *SLN* 97 (January 1976), 66–8; "California Federals are Slow to Offer Variable Rate Loans," *SLN* 100 (February 1979), 14; "Nationwide VRMs May Help Ease Lender's Profit Problems," *SLN* 100 (July 1979), 6; Jeff Gerth, "Savings Regulators End Mortgage Curbs," *The New York Times*, 24 April 1981, A1, B6.

6 "Savings & Loans Break Out of the Boom-Bust Mold," *Business Week*, 9 October 1971, 38; A. F. Ehrbar, "The Basic Problems of the S&Ls," *Fortune* 91 (June 1975) 67–8, 73; John H. Allan, "Rate Rivalry Wounds Savings Industry," *The New York Times*, 10 August 1974, 37, 39; "Rate Rise Scored by Thrift Groups," *The New York Times*, 23 July, 1973, 41, 42; *Savings and Loan Fact Book '75* (Chicago: United States League of Savings Institutions, 1975), 19–20; *Savings and Loan Fact Book '80*, 56–8.

7 "Associations Up Savings Rates, Adopt New CD Plans," *SLN* 94 (August 1973), 14; "How the Rate War Began," *SLN* 94 (August 1973), 27–9; "The Money War," *SLN* 94 (September 1973), 54–9; "Fed Limits 'Wild Card' Interest to 7 1/4 %," *The New York Times*, 18 October

Although MMCs were extremely popular and reduced the risk of rate wars, many in the thrift industry did not see these and other market-rate accounts as a long-term solution for retaining funds. Because these accounts paid rates higher than the limits set by Regulation Q, the resulting rise in interest expenses placed pressure on thrift earnings. Similarly, holders of MMCs and other market-rate accounts were prone to move their funds if they could find higher yields. This became a serious concern by 1978, when market-rate accounts made up 75 percent of industry savings, while more stable passbook accounts accounted for 25 percent. This was a major change from just twelve years earlier when passbook savings accounts provided 80 percent industry funds.[8]

Another way thrifts could obtain funds was through the sale of mortgage assets on the secondary market. In addition to the Federal National Mortgage Association (Fannie Mae), thrifts could use the Government National Mortgage Administration (Ginnie Mae), created in 1968, to buy and sell government-insured mortgages. This new market was different because it focused on small investors by trading small-denomination mortgage-backed securities called pass-through certificates. Guaranteed by Ginnie Mae, these negotiable instruments were very popular, and by 1979 their market exceeded $24.5 billion (U.S. billion). A third way to buy and sell home loans was through the Federal Home Loan Mortgage Corporation (Freddie Mac), formed in 1970. Controlled by the FHLBB, Freddie Mac was the fulfilment of a long-standing League goal because it traded securities backed by conventional mortgages, which improved the liquidity of these by staple S&L assets.[9]

1973, 73; "Regulatory Agencies Tame 'Wild Card' Certificate Plans," *SLN* 94 (November 1973), 16; "Regulators Hope New CDs Will Help Boost Funds for Housing," *SLN* 99 (June 1978), 16; "Initial Response to New CDs Proves Mixed," *SLN* 99 (July 1978), 14; Jerry Pohlman, "A 'Yes' Vote for MMC," *SLN* 100 (April 1979), 84–7; "Proxmire Wants MMC, Other CD Minimums Reduced to $1,000," *SLN* 100 (February 1979), 13.

[8] Memorandums from Orin Kramer to Stu Eisenstat, 7 November 1978, and memorandum from Orin Kramer to Stu Eisenstat, 13 October 1978; Banking Reform – Banking (General); Domestic Policy Staff (DPS) Subject Files, 1976–1981; Jimmy Carter Presidential Library, Atlanta, GA (JCPL); "MMCs Only Postpone the Day of Reckoning," *SLN* 100 (January 1979), 74–6; *Savings and Loan Fact Book '80*, 57; William E. Donoghue, "Banking's Time Bomb: Six Month Money," *The New York Times*, 11 May 1980, sec. 3, 16.

[9] Congress created another secondary market, the Student Loan Marketing Administration (SLMA or Sallie Mae) in 1973 to buy and sell education loans. Arlen J. Large, "New Resale Market Sought for Mortgages of Conventional Type," *The Wall Street Journal*, 16 May 1962, 2; "Mortgage Securities Make It Big on Wall Street," *SLN* 98 (December 1977), 33; "Quest for New Funds Leads to Spate of Loan Backed Bonds," *SLN* 98 (July 1977), 14; "A New Way to Turn Mortgages into Money," *SLN* 99 (April 1978), 50; "Debenture Pools: Testing the Waters," *SLN* 94 (May 1973), 46–8; "More Firms Handle Pass-Through Issues, Improve Market Access," *SLN* 100 (June 1979), 7; "They Can Get It to You Wholesale," *SLN* 95 (August 1974), 30; "The 'In-Between' Commercial Loan Market," *SLN* 95 (March 1974), 52–7; "Sallie Mae 'Ready to Buy' Student Loans," *SLN* 95 (August 1974), 22; "New Legislation:

A REVOLUTION IN FINANCIAL TECHNOLOGY

A second factor making the 1970s a more complex environment for thrift managers was the sweeping technological advances occurring in finance. Although S&Ls first began using computers in the 1950s, their large size and high cost limited them to only the most labor-intensive operations like data processing. While improved technology reduced the cost of computers, what made these machines a virtual necessity for all financial institutions was the perfection of electronic funds transfer (EFT) services in the early 1970s. EFT allowed firms to move money quickly and accurately between different accounts or institutions, and this ability to track money electronically led to the introduction of a host of new consumer products, including automated teller machines (ATM), automatic bill payments, direct deposit, and point-of-sale (POS) terminals. While these innovations created the possibility of a "paperless" society, their broad acceptance by financial institutions still faced a number of hurdles.[10]

The main reason many banks and S&Ls were leery of adopting new technologies was that they were still more expensive than traditional manual methods. As late as 1977, the cost of processing ATM transactions was eight times the cost for paper checks, which posed a significant barrier to achieving scale economies. Managers were also concerned about the potential for technological obsolescence, security risks, and any adverse public reactions resulting from working with machines instead of human tellers. These fears diminished, however, when terminals became more standardized and reliable, and consumers, especially younger people, realized that using an ATM was more efficient and saved time. The result was that the number of ATM machines used by all institutions skyrocketed from just 1,858 in 1973 to 14,190 by 1979, an average annual increase of more than 110 percent. This growth did not mean that ATMs radically altered financial transactions, as more than 90 percent of all terminals were still located on-premise.[11]

Pulling It All Together," *SLN* 100 (February 1979), 38–9; Thomas Halclarke, "Can a New Mortgage Market Narrow the Housing Gap?" *The Evening Star* (Washington, DC), 20 February 1970, F4; *Savings Institutions Sourcebook, '89* (Chicago: United States League of Savings Institutions, 1989), 25–9, 65–6.

[10] "The U.S. Has a Date with Electronic Banking," *Forbes* 108 (1 July 1976), 69–70; "EFTS Technology Spawns New Payment Systems," *SLN* 94 (October 1973), 90–1; Paul Samuelson, "Regulating Banks," *The New Republic*, 3 April 1976, 13–14; "Checkless Banking is Bound to Come," *Fortune*, June 1977, 118–20; "Banking by Computer," *US News and World Report*, 7 March 1977, 81–2.

[11] "What Ever It is, Electronic Money Is Not a Customer Service," *SLN* 94 (April 1973), 66; "If It's a Good Product, Why Aren't More People Using It?" *SLN* 94 (June 1973), 62; "No Passbook Savings: Not a Question of Whether, Only How Soon," *SLN* 94 (November 1973), 57; "Pick a Teller," *SLN* 97 (July 1976), 50; "TMS: Will It Swing in the Marketplace?" *SLN* 95 (May 1974), 50–1; Rose, "Checkless Banking," 121–2; "The U.S. Has a Date," 70; Letter

The first major S&L EFT system was the Transmatic System (TMS) developed by First Federal Lincoln of Omaha, Nebraska, in 1971. Initially, customers accessed TMS by telephone, and they could only use it to authorize direct deposits and mortgage payments. By 1974, however, remote TMS terminals inside local supermarkets could be used for check authorization, deposits, withdrawals, and bill payments. Also, by using a plastic debit card issued by the thrift, customers could buy goods from select merchants. This service made TMS a direct point-of-sale system and turned the traditional savings account into a quasi-checking account. In the first six weeks of operation, TMS generated more than $600,000 in new deposits, and this favorable acceptance caused other thrifts in Ohio, Delaware, and Washington to develop their own EFT systems. Since many of these operations were unique, the League tried to get S&Ls to adopt one uniform electronic banking card and standard system. Uncharacteristically, the League failed in this effort as most institutions became allied with Visa or MasterCard, whose credit card systems were accepted by merchants nationwide.[12]

A negative consequence of EFT technology for S&Ls was that it produced new sources of competition. State-chartered banks began using automated transfers to allow customers to move money between their savings and checking accounts, which essentially allowed them to earn interest on demand deposits. Securities firms like Merrill Lynch also used EFT systems to create the money market account in 1974. These accounts invested savings in low-risk but high-yield instruments like Treasury securities or commercial paper, and customers could access these funds by writing checks called negotiable orders. Money market accounts were so popular that within five years they controlled more than $34 billion, or 13.5 percent, of total household savings. In response to the increased competition created by these investments,

from Robert W. Minor to Jack Carter, 13 September 1972; In-House Files, September 1972; In-House Files, October 1972; Congressional Correspondence of Acting Chairman Carl O. Kamp (Kamp Papers); Records of the Federal Home Loan Bank Board, Record Group 195 (RG 195); National Archives, College Park (NACP); Allen H. Lipis, Thomas R. Marschall, and Jan Tinker, *Electronic Banking* (New York: John Wiley & Sons, 1985), 8–12; "More Associations Install More ATMs," *SLN* 103 (February 1982), 104–5; "ATM Networks Span the Nation," *SLN* 104 (April 1983), 48–52.

[12] "Now a Bill-Paying Service by S&Ls," *US News and World Report*, 4 January 1971, 38; "An S&L Puts the Teller in the Supermarket," *Busiuness Week*, 20 April 1974, 88–91; "TMS: What Hath John Dean Wrought?" *SLN* 94 (May 1974), 44–9; "TMS Plan Gains," *SLN* 95 (March 1974), 18; "WSFS Lesson: Don't Invade a Market Without a Better Product," *SLN* 97 (January 1976), 58–60; "Bill Payments: Is the Answer in the Telephone?" *SLN* 98 (March 1977), 55–6; "Pick a Card, Any Card. Or Should You?" *SLN* 95 (May 1974), 51; "Bank Credit Cards Setting the Scene for Future EFTS," *SLN* 100 (August 1979), 74; "Biggest Association First to Issue Nationwide Card," *SLN* 94 (June 1973), 15; "Major Credit Cards Get and S&L Imprint," *Business Week*, 14 June 1979, 26–7; Letter from Norman Strunk to Paul Nelson, 23 February 1973; United States Savings and Loan League Correspondence; Wright Patman Papers; Lyndon B. Johnson Presidential Library, Austin, TX (LBJPL).

in 1972 a Massachusetts savings bank used a loophole in state regulations to create the negotiable order of withdrawal (NOW) account, a product similar to the money market account. Because customers wrote checks for money taken directly from their insured interest-bearing savings accounts, the NOW account was the first to combine the flexibility of demand deposits with the earning potential of savings. They were such a success that within a year NOW accounts were available at savings banks throughout New England.[13]

Despite the broad public acceptance of NOW accounts and ATMs, regulators were skeptical about the legality of these new products, many of which they saw as blatant attempts to circumvent regulations. They questioned whether remote terminals constituted illegal branching, since they provided the same services as traditional brick-and-mortar facilities. There was also the problem of how the higher cost of maintaining POS services or paying interest on NOW accounts would affect S&L earnings. Still, not allowing federally chartered thrifts in New England to offer similar accounts was costing these institutions millions in savings. As a result, in 1973 Congress made it legal for thrifts in states that permitted NOW accounts to have the same option. A year later, Congress formed a commission to make recommendations on how best to direct future EFT growth. Despite such moves, products like NOW accounts remained controversial and would ultimately influence the debate over how to modify thrift regulations.[14]

[13] "Passbook Disintermediation," *SLN* 99 (October 1978), 46; "The Thundering Herd Leads the Pack of Competitors," *SLN* 98 (November 1977), 54–6; *Savings and Loan Fact Book, '80,* 9–11; "Money Funds Drain Housing's Primary Source of Credit," *SLN* 100 (November 1979), 33; Dimitris N. Chorafes, *Electronic Funds Transfers* (London: Butterworths, 1988), 144–6; Robert J. Cole, "The Fight Over Savings-Bank 'Checking' Accounts," *The New York Times,* 2 July 1974, 49, 54; "Senate Vote Limits NOW Accounts," *The New York Times,* 23 May 1973, 62; "'NOW' Accounts: A New Payments Mechanism, or a Short Lived Experiment?" *SLN* 94 (May 1973), 58–62; Edwin J. Perkins, *Wall Street to Main Street: Charles Merrill and Middle-Class Investors* (New York: Cambridge University Press, 1999), 257–59.

[14] Edward G. Nelson, "NOW – There's No Free Checking," *The New York Times,* 31 July 1977, 12; "Congress Mulls NOW Plans, Rate Control Extension," *SLN* 94 (April 1973), 33; Rose, "Checkless Banking," 118, 120; "What's a Nice Card Like You Doing in a Place Like This?" *SLN* 95 (May 1974), 42–3; "EFTS Commission Report: A Savings and Loan View," *SLN* 98 (April 1977), 52–8; Memorandum from Preston Martin to the Board, 2 November 1972; In-House Files, October 1972; Kamp Papers; RG 195; NACP; "H. Erich Heinemann, "Martin Resigns as Chief of Home Loan Bank Board," *The New York* Times, 15 November 1972, 77; B. G. Hartzog, *The Impact of NOW Accounts on Savings and Loan Behavior and Performance,* Research Working Paper No. 78, 1978 (Washington, DC: Federal Home Loan Bank Board, Office of Economic Research, 1978), 17; "New Rules for Electronic Banking," *Consumer Reports* (November 1978), 12; Memorandum with attachment from Rick Newstadt to Si Lazarus, Bob Marson, Steve Simmons, Orin Kraemer, 27 April 1977; Electronic Funds Transfers (EFTs), Privacy Issue; Richard M. Meustadt, Jr., Files on Government Reform, 1976- ; JCPL.

THE RISE OF CONSUMER ACTIVISM

A third major challenge facing S&Ls by the late 1960s was consumer activism. Beginning in the early 1960s, a consumer rights movement embodied a variety of efforts to make business more responsive to the needs of society. In the area of consumer finance, activists attacked the use of racist or sexist criteria like job stability, debt history, or marital status as the basis for a lending decision. (Some lenders even asked female borrowers the type of birth control they used, or required them to a sign an agreement not to have babies as a precondition for a loan!) Another form of financial discrimination consumer activists wanted to end was "redlining," the practice of denying a loan request based on the location of the property. The term referred to the use of red ink by lenders to outline neighborhoods, mostly in the inner city, in which they would not lend.[15]

One of the obstacles to ending these forms of discrimination, however, was proving that such biased methods were the primary tools used to evaluate borrowers. Since most lending decisions required a wide range of information about the applicant or property, trying to show that one issue like race or sex was used to deny a loan was often impossible. Consequently, consumer rights groups wanted financial institutions to prove they did not discriminate through greater disclosure of lending policies and patterns. Organizations like National People's Action, a coalition of more than seventy-five civil rights and consumer groups, also demanded that financial institutions open more inner-city offices and create liaison groups with community leaders to monitor lending activity. While traditional forms of protest like picketing bank offices was the most common way to gain attention to this cause, another very effective tactic was the threat of savings withdrawals, called "greenlining," to achieve change.[16]

---

[15] "Associations Learn How to Finance Mortgages for Minorities," *SLN* 89 (October 1968), 37; "Loans to Women: A Case for Questioning Loan Criteria, " *SLN* 95 (January 1974), 36–7; "Loans to Women: A Case for Questioning Loan Criteria," *SLN* 95 (January 1974), 38; "Mortgage Redlining: The Urban Disinvestment Dilemma," *SLN* 95 (June 1974), 39; "Lenders Can't Ignore Economic Facts of Life," *SLN* 95 (May 1974), 105; "Are Facts Discriminatory?" *SLN* 95 (February 1974), 120; "Check Lending, Forms for Discrimination," *SLN* 89 (October 1968), 10; Thomas Doehrman, *Background Analysis on Redlining* (Indianapolis: Indiana Center on Law and Poverty, Inc., 1977); Federal Home Loan Bank Board, 1/3/77–3/17/77; Landon Butler Files, 1977–1981; JCPL; A. Thomas King, *Redlining: A Critical Review of the Literature with Suggested Research*, Research Working Paper No. 82 (Washington DC: Federal Home Loan Bank Board, Office of Economic Research, 1979), 11–42; Confidential Memorandum for the January 31, 1969, Coordinating Group Committee Meeting on Bank Regulation; Interagency, Federal Reserve Board, Federal Deposit Insurance Corporation and Federal Home Loan Bank Board; Correspondence of Chairman Preston Martin, 1969–1972 (Martin Papers); RG 195; NACP.

[16] Donald L. Thomas, "The Banks and Redlining," *Vital Speeches* 44 (15 April 1978), 407–10; Michael Massing, "Breaking the Bank," *Saturday Review*, 15 September 1979, 21–8; *Redlining: A Critical Review*, 2–10; "What to Expect from a CRA Protest," *SLN* 100 (April

In addition to approaching lenders directly, consumer activists also worked with the FHLBB to secure antidiscrimination regulations. The Board responded with rules making it illegal to deny a loan request based on the age of the property, or borrower criteria like education or criminal record. Regulators, however, refused to meet some demands like having thrifts meet annual quotas for loans to minorities and women, since doing so would interfere with legitimate business issues. Congress also provided thrifts with an incentive to increase minority lending by passing in 1974 Housing and Community Development Act; lenders received tax breaks for making inner-city neighborhood loans, and regulators could take into account this record of activity when considering new facility or merger requests. Other important congressional actions to end lending bias included the Fair Housing Act of 1968, which banned discrimination based on race, religion, or national origin, and the Equal Credit Opportunity Act of 1974, which extended the ban to include sex.[17]

Finally, consumer groups lobbied for laws to increase financial disclosure requirements, and in 1968 Congress passed the Truth-in-Lending Act, which the Board codified as Regulation Z. This law revolutionized consumer credit by requiring lenders to disclose an itemization of the amount financed, details on total finance charges, the annual percentage rate, the payment schedule, as well as prepayment and late payment policies. This law was followed by the Real Estate Settlement Procedures Act in 1974, which forced lenders to make available more information about a property, as well as give borrowers a chance to cancel a loan through the right of recision. While lenders questioned whether or not these new rules actually helped or confused borrowers, their main concern was that the regulations significantly increased the amount of compliance forms and paperwork lenders had to file.[18]

1979), 62–4;"Confrontation in Communities," *SLN* 95 (June 1974), 40; "What to Expect from Community Groups," *SLN* 100 (May 1979), 64–6.

[17] Massing, "Breaking the Bank," 22; "FHLBB Proposed Anti-Redlining Regulations Praised, Criticized," *SLN* 98 (December 1977), 14; "No Retreat at the FHLBB," *Fortune*, 21 May 1979, 45–6; A. D. Theobald, *Forty Five Years on the Up Escalator* (Chicago: privately published, 1977), 261–2; Letter from Ralph Nader to Preston Martin, 15 September 1970, 1–3; Ralph Nader; Martin Papers; RG 195; NACP; Judith Miller, "Redlining a Topic as Senate Airs Choice for S. & L. Job," *The New York Times*, 26 January 1977, 27; House Committee on Banking, Finance and Urban Affairs, Subcommittee on Housing and Community Development, *Housing and Community Development Act of 1977*, hearings, 95th Cong., 1st sess., pt. 3, 7 March 1977, 1874–7, 2572–9; Robert Dowling, "Nader Joins FHLBB in Fight for Reform of S&L Industry," *American Banker*, 16 September 1970, 8; "Spurring S&L Loans for the Inner City," *Business Week*, 25 April 1977, 86–7; Memorandum from Orin Kramer to Stu Eisenstat, 22 June 1977; Banking Reform – Banking (General); DPS Subject Files, 1976–1981; JCPL.

[18] Memorandum from Arthur Okun to Joseph Califano, 25 October 1967; EX FI 5, 24 October 1967 to 31 January 1968; WHCF Subject Files FI; LBJPL; Barefoot Sanders to Lyndon B. Johnson, 6 March 1968; EX FI 5, 1 February 1968 to 30 June 1968; WHCF Subject Files

The League was sympathetic to most of the issues raised by consumer groups, but it also defended some allegedly biased practices as being appropriate ways to measure risk. One of these was the use of real estate appraisal data on neighborhoods, which activists claimed lenders used to redline. The League countered that this information was needed to determine if neighborhood values were stable or changing, a key consideration for any secured lender. They also used government statistics to show that minority home ownership was rising, and that thrifts were the leading source of mortgages to these borrowers. Furthermore, they contended that they could serve minority applicants better if the Federal Housing Administration and the Veterans Administration would accept more inner-city loans for mortgage insurance. Despite such arguments, the negative publicity associated with consumer group protests led most S&Ls to work with these activists, primarily by forming mortgage review boards, opening more neighborhood offices, and hiring minority loan officers.[19]

Such efforts to satisfy consumer concerns did not, however, mean that lending discrimination had ended. One area that was extremely difficult to change was the perception held by lenders that minorities and the poor were unsuitable credit risks. One thrift officer maintained that a reason why these people did not use bank credit was because "financial institutions are imposing. They frighten lower income people." Demands to become more supportive and encouraging of low-income borrowers caused another officer to lament, "should our communication tell them how they can get a loan, or should it go further – encourage the initiative to rehabilitate? . . . Maybe

FI; LBJPL; Memorandum from Joseph Barr to Lyndon B. Johnson, 7 January 1968, and memorandum from Don Furtado to Matt Nimetz with attachment, 24 May 1968; LE/FI 5, 1 January 1968 to 24 May 1968; WHCF LE/FI 5; LBJPL; Letter from Ralph Nader to Jimmy Carter, 4 March 1977; Federal Home Loan Bank Board, 1/3/77–3/17/77; Landon Butler Files, 1977–1981; JCPL; "The Sticky Lessons of Settlement Standards," *SLN,* 96 (November 1975), 40; "CRA Exams: A Regulatory Can of Worms" *SLN* 100 (June 1979), 38; "Redlining 'Red Herring': Community Groups Snipe at Initial Loan Disclosure," *SLN* 97 (November 1976), 14; Letter from Steve Slipher to William A. Barrett, 14 March 1972; United States Savings and Loan League Legislative Program and Correspondence; Wright Patman Papers; LBJPL.

19 "How Do You Rate Loans? And Why?" *SLN* 95 (May 1974), 61; "The People v. Regressive Federal," *SLN* 99 (February 1978), 48–54; Andrew Brimmer, "Inner City Lending Would Increase Risk," *SLN* 98 (May 1977), 61–4; "Is It Prudent Loan Underwriting or is It Redlining?" *SLN* 98 (April 1977), 122; "Something's Wrong About Civil Rights," *SLN* 96 (October 1975), 114; "Savings Associations Lead in Negro Home Financing," *SLN* 88 (September 1967), 64–5; "Confrontation in Communities," *SLN* 95 (June 1974), 40; "Mortgage Redlining: The Urban Disinvestment Dilemma," *SLN* 95 (June 1974), 39; "The Minority Applicant Knows He's Different; Do You?" *SLN* 95 (February 1974), 58–64; "Redlining 'Red Herring': Community Groups Snipe at Initial Loan Disclosure," *SLN* 97 (November 1976), 14; "Mortgage Review Boards: The Second Chance," *SLN* 98 (September 1977), 43–5; "Subject: Neighborhood Deterioration," 1977 (?); Federal Home Loan Bank Board, 1/3/77–3/17/77; Landon Butler Files, 1977–1981; JCPL; Theobald, *Forty Five Years,* 256–7.

they've never thought to take down the rusted gutter and put up a new one for the $300 they might blow on a wild Saturday night? Should a lending institution go that far?" Such comments, which were in stark contrast to the spirit of uplift that permeated the thrift movement in the early 1900s, meant that the issues separating financial industries and consumer groups would remain problems for years.[20]

THE LEAGUE STRUGGLES TO ADAPT

Just as individual thrifts wrestled with the business challenges of the 1970s, the League faced its own problems in charting a future course. Because the increased complexity of consumer finance had blurred the traditional distinctions between financial industries, the League thought that it was necessary to redefine the S&L image. It, however, faced a dilemma since emphasizing the traditional role of thrifts as specialized home lenders could potentially limit industry expansion, while portraying S&Ls as being just like banks would likely lead to greater confusion. The solution was to position thrifts as "family financial service centers," institutions committed to serving the financial and investment needs of consumers. By broadening the focus of the industry to include residential and consumer finance, the League hoped that regulators would authorize broader lending and savings powers, while at the same time retaining benefits like the Regulation Q rate differential. To help instill this more comprehensive consumer identity within its membership, in early 1974 the League changed its name to The United States League of Savings Associations, the third name change in its history.[21]

The League worked with legislators to gain new powers needed to implement this "family financial service center" concept, and Congress responded favorably, passing several bills that benefited the thrift industry. The Housing and Urban Development Act of 1968 let thrifts finance mobile homes and

[20] Massing, "Breaking the Bank," 22, 24; "What to Expect from Community Groups," *SLN* 100 (May 1979), quote 65; "Coping with Confrontation: A Case History," *SLN* 95 (June 1974), 51; "Urban Revitalization Programs Provide Lending Opportunities," *SLN* 100 (December 1979), 62–8.

[21] "Savings and Loans Hunt for Funds – and a Future," *US News and World Report*, 11 May 1970, 95–7; "Can Thrifts be Competitive Lenders?" *SLN* 95 (December 1974), 58–64; Lloyd Bowles, "Alternatives for Future Development of Savings and Loan Associations," *Savings and Loan Annals, 1974* (Chicago: United States Savings and Loan League, 1974), 6–12; Lloyd Bowles, "President's Address" *Savings and Loan Annals, 1975* (Chicago: United States Savings and Loan League, 1975), 3–6; "How Does the Business Grow? Mostly Its Blooming," *SLN* 98 (November 1977), 63–7; Ned Eichler, *The Thrift Debacle*, Berkeley: University of California Press, 1989) 62; "Lenders Appeal for Asset Change at FHLBB Saver Hearings," *SLN* 100 (June 1979), 6; *The Impact of Regulation on the Provision of Consumer Financial Services by Depository Institutions: Research, Backgrounds and Needs* (West Lafayette, IN: Credit Research Center, Krannert Graduate School of Management, Purdue University, 1978), 79, 88–95; "It's Now the United States League of Savings Institutions," *SLN* 94 (December 1974), 13.

improvements for any type of real estate, issue debentures, and offer services like preauthorized bill payments. The Housing and Community Development Act also gave S&Ls the right to make lines of credit to builders, and the authority to invest 5 percent of assets in loans "a thrift might otherwise not make," like unsecured lending. Finally, federal S&Ls received permission to make consumer loans in states where state-chartered thrifts had that right.[22]

Another gain for the League was the expanded use of unregulated service corporations. The industry first obtained the right to invest up to 1 percent of assets in service corporations in 1964, and most S&Ls used these businesses to manage nonfinancial operations like data processing. In the early 1970s, the industry had broadened the use of service corporations, so that by the end of the decade they were used to issue long-term debt, make direct consumer loans, broker mortgages, sell insurance, and operate land development companies. The use of these firms by smaller S&Ls received a boost after 1970 when the Board allowed thrifts to pool their resources and invest in one service corporation used by all the owners. While service corporations were often a valuable source of profits for some S&Ls, their continued expansion into areas further afield from home finance would become an important issue in the era of deregulation.[23]

While the League achieved some success in expanding thrift lending powers, in other areas, like the use of NOW accounts, it was far less effective.

[22] State-chartered thrifts in Texas had been making all forms of consumer loans since 1967. Shelby J. Smith, *Texas S&L's: Implications for Consumer Lending*. Research Working Paper No. 13 (Washington, DC: Office of Economic Research, Federal Home Loan Bank Board, Office of Economic Research, 1976), 1–5; "Housing Measure Aids Thrift Units," *The New York Times*, 23 August 1968, 47; "Savings League Ends Bid for Law," *The New York Times*, 12 November 1968, 63; H. Erich Heinemann, "Thrift Units Gain Payment Service," *The New York Times*, 17 August 1970, 41, 43; "Savings and Loans Get More Power – But Will It Be Enough?" *Business Week*, 31 August 1968, 31–2; "What to Expect in Consumer Lending," *SLN* 89 (November 1968), 31; "The Nader Report," *SLN* 94 (December 1973), 66–72; "The Case for Consumer Lending," *SLN* 94 (November 1973), 60–2; "Consumer Credit: Do Savings Associations Really Want In," *SLN* 94 (May 1973), 36–8; "Bomar Presses Need for Consumer Lending," *SLN* 94 (October 1974), 24; Norman Strunk, "Know Your Competition," *SLN* 98 (May 1977), 46; "Consumer Credit: What You Should Know Before You Take the Plunge," *SLN* 98 (August 1977), 60; Letter from Kenneth G. Heisler to Wright Patman, 3 July 1968; National League of Insured Savings Associations; Wright Patman Papers; LBJPL; Letter from Norman Strunk to Wright Patman, 4 June 1968, and letter from Raleigh W. Creed to Richard E. Ehlis, 25 September 1968; United States Savings and Loan League Correspondence; Wright Patman Papers; LBJPL.

[23] "Family Finance Center? It Could be a Service Corporation," *SLN* 95 (September 1974), 68–71; Letter from Joseph E. Linville to Preston Martin, 22 April 1970, Ohio Savings & Loan League, General; Martin Papers; RG 195; NACP; "Service Corporations: A Little Bundle of Joy," *SLN* 96 (September 1975), 44; "Service Corporations Mature with Success," *SLN* 100 (October 1979), 110–12; William Wallis, "Why You Should Own a Service Corporation" *Savings and Loan Annals*, 1971 (Chicago: United States Savings and Loan League, 1971), 133–5.

Even though these products were very popular with consumers, the trade group proved unable to take a definitive position on their use. Finally, in 1976, after three years of being neutral on the use of NOW accounts, the League came out in favor of nationwide use of NOW accounts. The following year, however, it reversed itself after Congress indicated it would end the Regulation Q rate differential as a condition of approval, and for the next two years it went back and forth on the issue. A key reason for this indecision was that thrifts were also very divided on NOW accounts: large S&Ls wanted them, but smaller associations did not. When the League first favored NOW accounts in 1976, the presidency was held by the leader of a $1 billion thrift, while the year it opposed their use the president was from a $100 million association. Such changes reflected the deepening of the divisions between large and small S&Ls that first appeared in the 1950s.[24]

REGULATORS IN LIMBO

The Board, like the League, had some trouble setting its agenda for the 1970s, in part because there were six different chairmen between 1968 and 1979. The first chairmen of this period was Robert L. Rand, who assumed the position in 1968 following the departure of John E. Horne. Rand's tenure ended the following year when newly elected president Richard M. Nixon named Preston Martin as Board chairman, a choice supported by many of the executives who headed the large California S&Ls that had contributed heavily to Nixon's campaign. Martin came to the Board after serving two years as the chief thrift regulator in California, and it quickly became apparent that he was intent on following the same proindustry policy making that characterized his work at the state level.[25]

Only 48 years old, Martin was determined to ease the pattern of close scrutiny established by Joseph McMurray and Horne, and his actions helped make him one of the most important regulators of the decade. His working motto of "another week, another rule" meant that regulations were constantly revised, with many of these changes favoring the industry. Shortly after coming to office, Martin made it easier for S&Ls to merge, a move that

[24] Letter from Wright Patman to Gilbert Roessner, 6 January 1972; United States Savings and Loan League Correspondence; Wright Patman Papers; LBJPL; "1975 Legislative Program: Not NOWs but Checking Accounts Instead," *SLN* 96 (March 1975), 76–9; "US League Sets Legislation Objectives," *SLN* 97 (March 1976), 72–4; Norman Strunk, "The Case for NOW Accounts," *SLN* 97 (March 1976), 44–8; "Bankers 'Cry Wolf' over NOW Account Legislation," *SLN* 98 (September 1977), 64; "US League Returns to a Neutral Stance on NOW Accounts," *SLN* 99 (April 1978), 74; "US League Sets Legislative Goals," *SLN* 100 (April 1979), 74; "With POW and ATS, What Happens Now?" *SLN* 100 (January 1979), 50–4; "Past Presidents of the League," *Savings Associations Annals*, 1979 (Chicago: United States League of Savings Associations, 1979), xiii.

[25] "Home Loan Bank Loses Chairman after Infighting," *The New York Times*, 12 March 1969, 59; Sanford Rose, "The S&Ls Break Out of Their Shell," *Fortune* (September 1972), 152–3.

sparked a wave of thrift combinations that lasted through the mid-1970s. The Martin Board also increased the authority for thrifts to lend statewide, and allowed virtually any S&L to open an unregulated service corporation without prior regulatory approval. Although he disliked NOW accounts, advising thrifts to "move slowly" in this area, he also felt that if states continued to let savings banks offer the product, then thrifts should be given a similar right.[26]

While many thrift leaders liked "Pres" Martin, other financial leaders were less enthusiastic about the chairman's work. One former Federal Reserve Board member grumbled that "Martin was less a regulator than an industry cheerleader." There were also concerns within the FHLBB that some of his plans could hurt the financial health of the industry and potentially increase the risk to the federal deposit insurance fund. As one Board official remarked with prescient words to his associates, "maybe we should eliminate all regulations and let them compete openly – and realize that the FSLIC may get a heavier future load." Although there was a wide range of opinions on the work of Martin, one important legacy was that his actions helped lay the foundation for many of the regulatory changes contemplated by legislators toward the end of the decade.[27]

Martin left the Board in 1972, and over the next seven years, four different people held the post of chairman. The first, Carl O. Kamp, a Board member since 1969, was acting chairman from 1972 to 1973, but was never confirmed by the Senate. Thomas Bomar replaced Kamp as chairman and served to 1975, when he was succeeded by Board member Garth Marston as acting chairman. Between 1975 and 1977, the Board only had two members, until

---

[26] "S&Ls Look for Sympathy at the Top," *Business Week*, 29 March 1969, 72–6; "Administration Spurring S&Ls Lending Style to Boost Lending, Martin Says," *Los Angeles Times*, 7 May 1970, 13; H. Erich Heinemann, "New Policy Asked for on Housing Funds," *The New York Times*, 30 April 1969, 61, 67; Press Release, 20 August 1969; Exchequer Club; Martin Papers; RG 195; NACP; Memorandum to all Member Institutions from Preston Martin, 1 July 1970,; Service Corporations; Martin Papers; RG 195; NACP; Memorandum from Preston Martin to Art Leibold, 27 August 1970; Statewide Lending; Martin Papers; RG 195; NACP; Letter from Alexander Mintz to Preston Martin, 17 September 1970, with handwritten comments, and letter from Alexander Mintz to Preston Martin, 7 September 1971, with handwritten comments; Mintz, Alexander; Martin Papers; RG 195; NACP; Memorandum from Preston Martin to the Board, 2 November 1972; In-House Files, October 1972; Kamp Papers; RG 195; NACP; Letter from Preston Martin to Spiro Agnew, 7 March 1970; Legislation; Martin Papers; RG 195; NACP; Memorandum from Mr. Stattin to Supervisory Agents, 24 August 1970, quote; Information Disclosure "R" Series (file); Martin Papers; RG 195; NACP; Rose, "The S&Ls Break Out of Their Shell," 152–6, 158, 163–4, 196–70, quote 154.

[27] Heinemann, "Martin Resigns as Chief of Home Loan Bank Board," 65, 77; Rose, "The S&Ls Break Out of Their Shell," quote 153; Memorandum from Harris C. Friedman and Dan Gordon to R. Bruce Ricks, 12 May 1970, quote; Information Disclosure "R" Series (file); Martin Papers; RG 195; NACP; Joseph D. Hutuyan, "Preston Martin is S&L's Hero Despite Dubious Rate Outcome," *American Banker*, 23 January 1970, 7.

TABLE 7.1. *Number of Thrifts and Assets – 1965 to 1979*

Year	No. S&L	Change/Year	Assets (000,000)	Change/Year
1965	6,071	–	$129,442	–
1970	5,669	(1.4%)	$176,183	6.4%
1974	5,023	(2.9%)	$295,545	13.8%
1979	4,709	(1.3%)	$579,307	11.8%

Source: *Savings and Loan Fact Book*, 1980, 48–51

President Jimmy Carter named Indiana S&L executive William McKinney as chairman in 1977. McKinney held the job through the end of 1979, when Jay Janis, a prominent home builder who also served in the Department of Housing and Urban Development, ended the decade as chairman. While much of this turnover resulted from changes in the executive branch, the fact that no one individual was Board chairman for more than three years affected the consistency of regulatory oversight. Furthermore, because these chairmen spent most of their time responding to crises like disintermediation, there was little opportunity for them to set long-term strategic plans for the agency. The result was that in 1979, when plans to deregulate thrifts were gaining speed, the Board did not play a leading role in the process.[28]

EVALUATING THE THRIFT INDUSTRY

Although the problems of stagflation and increased competition produced a number of concerns for thrift leaders, the industry still managed to post solid asset growth between 1967 and 1979, as shown in Table 7.1.

The strong growth of the thrift industry during the 1970s is noteworthy first, because it occurred during difficult economic conditions, and second, fewer S&Ls were in operation in 1979 than at the start of the decade. This later trend was important, since it represented the first time since the end of World War II that the number of thrifts had fallen by an appreciable amount. The main reason for the change was the wave of acquisitions of smaller thrifts by large S&Ls that were seeking to expand their markets and achieve economies of scale. Between 1969 and 1975, there were at least 95 thrift mergers annually, peaking at 132 in both 1971 and 1974. A related development was the stunning growth of S&L branches, which increased at an average annual rate of 27 percent. The result was that from 1965 to 1979, the ratio of branches to main offices rose from 1:2 to 3:1; by comparison,

[28] Memorandum from Robert McKinney (?), 14 May 1977, and Consumers Federation of America, Press Release, 11 May 1977; Federal Home Loan Bank Board President, 2/1/77–11/1/77; Landon Butler Files, 1977–1979; JCPL; William B. O'Connell, *America's Trauma: How Washington Blunders Crippled the U.S. Financial System* (Winnetka, IL: Conversation Press, 1992), 65–6.

in 1955 there had been one branch for every ten offices. These two trends, the growth of new branches and the overall institutional consolidation, produced a nearly sixfold increase in the average size of a thrift to more than $120 million in assets in just fifteen years.[29]

The growth in the average thrift size was not representative of the entire industry, but instead highlighted the continued widening gap between large and small institutions. By the end of the decade, nearly 75 percent of all thrifts remained fairly small, with less than $100 million in assets; fully 56 percent had less than $50 million. At the other end of the spectrum, the largest two hundred associations controlled 41.5 percent of industry assets. Furthermore, twelve of the fifteen largest thrifts were headquartered in California, including the top five associations, which held a total of $50 billion in assets. One significant consequence of this gap between big and small thrifts was that dissent within the industry grew during the 1970s, and it ultimately led to the formation of smaller niche trade groups focused on issues relevant only to their members. Some large S&Ls, like the $9.2 billion Home Savings of Los Angeles, even maintained their own separate lobbying presence in Washington, DC. Such developments led William O'Connell, who was the top League official from 1979 to 1989, to say that his biggest task in leading the trade association was finding ways to "keep the business together."[30]

Another troubling trend for the thrift industry was the decline in profitability. Because rising short-term interest rates produced sharp increases in the cost of funds for most thrifts, the industry net profit margin during the decade was between 7 percent and 10 percent, well below the average net margin of near 25 percent experienced during the 1950s. One consequence was that more thrifts relied on low-rate advances from the home loan bank to fund operations, and by 1979 these loans accounted for nearly 10 percent of total industry liabilities, a threefold increase from twenty years earlier. An even more disturbing consequence of the lack of strong income growth was that total capital for the industry continued to fall. Between 1970 and 1977, the ratio of regulatory capital to total assets dropped 1.3 percentage points to 5.6 percent; by comparison, this ratio for banks fell just 0.9 percentage points to 7.5 percent over the same period.[31]

---

[29] *Savings and Loan Fact Book, '80*, 50–54; *Savings Institutions Sourcebook, '89*, 56; Walt Woerheide, *The Evolution of SLA Susceptibility to Interest Rate Risk During the Seventies*, Research Working Paper No. 96 (Washington, DC: Federal Home Loan Bank Board, Office of Policy and Economic Research, 1980), 18–19.

[30] *Savings and Loan Fact Book, '89*, 53; "Top 200 Savings Associations," *SLN* 99 (February 1978), 31–3; Donald D. Hester, "Special Interests: The *FINE Study*," *Journal of Money, Credit and Banking* 9 (November 1977), 652; Robert J. Samuelson, "Role of S&Ls Annual Meeting Sparks Feud," *The Washington Post*, 8 September 1970, D10; "Past League President O'Connell Retires," *Savings Institutions* 111 (January 1990), quote 7.

[31] "Capital Adequacy: How Much is Enough?" *SLN* 97 (November 1976), 84–8; Edward J. Kane, *The S&L Insurance Mess: How Did It Happen?* (Washington, DC: The Urban Institute

As the industry's capital "cushion" fell closer to the FHLBB required minimum of 5 percent, a debate developed over just what was considered adequate capital. The League wanted a general reduction in these requirements, arguing that the current rules, which dated back to the 1930s, did not reflect current financial conditions. The League thought that the definition of reserves should be expanded to include items like subordinated debt and deferred income, and believed that thrifts should also be allowed to achieve the minimum reserve level in thirty, not twenty-five, years. The League maintained that, if no changes were made, thrifts would not be able to grow, which could hurt the public interest by limiting the availability of mortgages.[32]

One solution to the problem of capital adequacy was to find ways to raise new equity, and during the 1970s the thrift industry pressed for permission to issue securities like preferred stock. Because preferred stock possessed characteristics of both debt and equity, the holders of this stock, like general debt holders, did not have voting rights. Furthermore, this type of stock required fixed dividend payments and could be retired over time by setting up a sinking fund for repayment. These dividend payments could also be deferred if there were a shortfall in profits. Moreover, in the event of a bankruptcy, these investors held a second lien on thrift assets. The main problem with issuing preferred stock was regulatory, since the FHLBB did not consider it to be true equity, and as such thrifts were unable to use this potential source of funds to help meet legal capital requirements.[33]

Another proposed solution to the problem of declining capital was to end the ban on conversions from mutual to stock ownership. Regulators, however, did not want to take this step because management insiders might reap large financial gains, and also embark on risky lending strategies to

Press, 1989), 29–33; Norman Strunk and Fred Case, *Where Deregulation Went Wrong: A Look at the Causes Behind the Savings and Loan Failures in the 1980s* (Chicago: United States League of Savings Institutions, 1988), 35–9.

[32] H. Erich Heinemann, "Debenture Sales by Thrift Units Urged," *The New York Times*, 6 October 1972, 59; "New Strategies Take On the Tests of Capital Adequacy," *SLN* 98 (April 1977), 98–104; Joseph Benedict, "The Future Will Bring New Strength," *Savings Association Annals*, 1979, 2–3.

[33] H. Erich Heinemann, "Revolution Ahead for US Savings," *The New York Times*, 12 November 1972, 1, 9; H. Erich Heinemann, "Stock Proposed in Savings Units," *The New York Times*, 9 January 1973, 49, 53; "A Capital Idea: How About Preferred Stick for Mutuals?" *SLN* 100 (February 1979), 66–9; James A. Verbrugge and Robert R. Dince Jr., "Alternative Sources of Equity Capital for Savings and Loan Associations," in *New Sources of Capital for the Savings and Loan Industry*, Proceedings of the Fifth Annual Conference (San Francisco: Federal Home Loan Bank of San Francisco, n.d.?), 59–90; "S&Ls Have New Way to Raise Money," *Business Week*, 8 September 1975, 58; Carter H. Golembe and Lewis N. Dembitz, "Capital Needs of S&L Association," *Changes in the Savings and Loan Industry*, Proceedings of the Second Annual Conference (San Francisco: Federal Home Loan Bank of San Francisco, 1977), 126–9.

boost earnings. Both these concerns lay behind their decision to impose the initial moratorium on conversions in 1961. In the early 1970s, however, observers were questioning the assumed superiority of mutual ownership, and contended that such firms were not efficiently managed and suffered from poor utilization of resources. Such critiques, combined with increased lobbying by leaders of large S&Ls, convinced Board chairman Martin to reexamine the issue. In 1970, he allowed Citizens Federal of San Francisco, which was managed by one of his longtime friends, to convert to stock ownership as a test case for lifting the ban. The success of this conversion led to more easing of the rules in 1973, followed by a full repeal in 1975.[34]

Almost immediately, S&L managers took advantage of this change, and over the next four years the number of stock S&Ls rose by more than 25 percent to 805, and combined, these thrifts held $148 billion in assets. The surge in stock conversions did not, however, mean that this form of ownership was necessarily sound or beneficial to thrift members. Reports prepared by the General Accounting Office found not only that insider abuse occurred in several stock conversions, but that after converting many of the new stock S&Ls also made riskier loans. Such findings, combined with factors like high interest rates and poor lending conditions, help explain why the aggregate reserve ratio for these S&Ls declined from 7.9 percent in 1973 to 4.8 percent by 1979. Despite such warnings, stock conversions continued into the 1980s and proved to be a major source of regulatory headaches.[35]

34 "As I See It," *Forbes* 101 (15 January 1968), 43–4; "Mergers Eased for Thrift Units," *The New York Times*, 21 August 1969, 57; "Savings Gripped by Merger Mania," *The New York Times*, 24 August 1969, 49; "The Big Switch," *Forbes* 110 (1 July 1972), 18; Heinemann, "Revolution Ahead for US Savings," 9; Alfred Nicols, *Management and Control in the Mutual Savings and Loan Association* (Lexington, MA: Lexington Books, 1972), 1–8, 11–22; Rose, "The S&Ls Break Out of Their Shell," 153–5; Memorandum from Start Halpert to Paul Nelson, 27 September 1972, and letter from Preston Martin to Wright Patman, 12 October 1972; United States Savings and Loan League Legislative Program and Correspondence; Wright Patman Papers; LBJPL; Letter from Wright Patman to Preston Martin, 11 August 1972, and letter from Preston Martin to Wright Patman, 15 September 1972; Federal Home Loan Bank Board Correspondence; Wright Patman Papers; LBJPL.

35 "Windfall for Depositors if Savings and Loans 'Go Public,'" *US News and World Report*, 22 January 1973, 63–4; "Conversions – A Search for Gold," *SLN* 98 (August 1977), 40–4; "Suppose Your Savings and Loan Becomes a Stock Company," *Changing Times* (February 1973), 45–8; "Savings and Loan Stock Plan Opposed," *US News and World Report*, 26 March 1973, 95; Robert D. Hershey Jr., "Savings & Loans Accused of Abuses in Ownership Shifts," *The New York Times*, 1 June 1977, D1, D11; "Why S&Ls are Pushing for Conversion Rights," *Business Week*, 24 May 1976, 34; "Conversions: Clamor Rises for Congress to Step In," *SLN* 100 (December 1979), 36–8; Letter from R. W. Crenshaw to Robert J. Lipshutz, 15 December 1977; Savings and Loan Associations, 12/78–2/79; Robert J. Lipshutz Files, 1977–79; JCPL; Anthony M. Santomero, "Risk and Capital in Financial Institutions," in *New Sources of Capital for the Savings and Loan Industry*, 39–40.

LURCHING TOWARD DEREGULATION

Although S&Ls continued to experience strong growth in the 1970s, changes in the marketplace convinced both industry and government officials that the basic regulatory structure of the thrift industry needed to be reassessed. This was not the first time that thrift regulation was examined. In 1961 the Commission on Money and Credit, formed by President Kennedy, had made comprehensive examinations of all major financial industries. Although the Commission produced a number of recommendations on how to improve the thrift industry, there was little effort to codify these findings into new laws, although some modest changes were made to FHLBB regulations.[36]

In 1966, the Board commissioned Dr. Irwin Friend of the University of Pennsylvania Wharton School of Business to prepare the first extensive examination into all aspects of the thrift industry. Completed three years later, the Friend Commission report was a massive four-volume academic work that made sweeping recommendations to improve the efficiency and scale economies of the industry. According to the report, thrifts needed more diversified asset bases, and should be allowed to make variable rate mortgages, and hold up to 10 percent of total assets in nonmortgage products, like consumer loans or select equity investments. To improve their liability mix thrifts should offer savings instruments with different maturities and account terms, and have limited authority to hold demand deposits like checking accounts. Finally, the Friend Commission called for an end to Regulation Q, and recommended that rate controls be used only on a standby basis to alleviate tight money conditions. Despite its broad scope, the report produced little action, in part because several of its recommendations mirrored what the League wanted.[37]

---

[36] The key reports include: Commission on Money and Credit, *Money and Credit: Their Influence on Jobs, Prices, and Growth; Report* (Englewood Cliffs, NJ: Prentice-Hall, 1961); Leon T. Kendall, *The Savings and Loan Business: Its Purposes, Functions, and Economic Justification; A Monograph Prepared for the Commission on Money and Credit* (Englewood Cliffs, NJ: Prentice-Hall, 1962); American Bankers Association, *The Commercial Banking Industry; A Monograph Prepared for the Commission on Money and Credit* (Englewood Cliffs, NJ: Prentice-Hall, 1962); George F. Break et. al, *Federal Credit Agencies; A Series of Research Studies Prepared for the Commission on Money and Credit* (Englewood Cliffs, NJ: Prentice-Hall, 1963); Miles Colean, *Mortgage Companies: Their Place in the Financial Structure; A Monograph Prepared for the Commission on Money and Credit* (Englewood Cliffs, NJ: Prentice-Hall, 1962).

[37] The Friend Commission received the full support of the League, which commissioned its own thrift industry study by Dr. Leo Grebler of the UCLA Graduate School of Business in June 1969. The Grebler Report made virtually the same recommendations as the Friend Commission. "New Rights Urged for Thrift Units," *The New York Times*, 10 April 1968, 70; "Diversify or Atrophy," *SLN* 90 (August 1969), 38; Leo Grebler, *The Future of Thrift Institutions: A Study of Diversification Versus Specialization* (Danville, IL: Interstate Printers and Publishers, 1971), 94–104; Irwin Friend, "Summary and Recommendations," Volume I, *Study of the Savings and Loan Industry* (Washington, DC: USGPO, 1969), 1–3, 29–4; "Savings Associations Called Sound in Study Urging Reforms," *The New York Times*,

The most influential study was prepared in 1972 by the President's Commission on Financial Structure and Regulation, more commonly known as the Hunt Commission after its chairman, the industrialist Reed Hunt. This concise 175-page report reaffirmed the findings of the Friend Commission on how to diversify thrift assets and liabilities, and also expanded upon them by recommending S&Ls be allowed to issue credit cards, hold subordinated debt, and sell mutual funds. The report also proposed that Congress create a new system of federally chartered mutual savings banks to complement the system of state-chartered institutions. Finally, the Hunt Commission called for an end to Regulation Q, with the rate controls phased out over a period of two to five years.[38]

The Hunt Commission Report was controversial on all fronts. The League claimed the changes represented "revolution not evolution" and would essentially destroy the separate identity of the thrift industry, while consumer groups charged that the commission did not go far enough in restructuring the financial systems. The most influential critic, however, was Rep. Wright Patman (D-TX), the powerful chairman of the House Banking Committee. Patman claimed that because the commission worked behind closed doors, its report was not in the public interest; he was also miffed that he was not consulted about the study. As a result, Patman prepared his own separate study, and the subsequent "Patman Paper" proposed far more radical changes for financial industries. These included letting federal thrifts convert to national banks, and creating a National Development Bank to make loans to small business owners during periods of tight money. Such differences of opinion indicated that writing the Hunt Commission Report into law would be a difficult task.[39]

---

8 September 1969, 1, 57; "Savings-and-Loan Curbs – A Rising Controversy," *US News and World Report*, 31 August 1970, 67–8; "Friend or Foe?" *Barron's*, 22 September 1969, 1; "Friend Report: Big Problems Demand Big Solutions," *SLN* 90 (November 1969), 53; Richard T. Pratt, *Savings and Loan Viability and Deposit Rate Ceilings*, Research Working Paper No. 14 (Washington, DC: Federal Home Loan Bank Board, Office of Economic Research, 1970), 1–5; Letter from John Horne to Wright Patman, 17 February 1970; Savings and Loan Associations; Wright Patman Papers; LBJPL; Memorandum from Marshall A. Kaplan to Joseph Sims with attachment, 10 August 1970; Federal Home Loan Bank Board Actions and Developments; Martin Papers; RG 195; NACP.

38 Other recommendations included a need for equal tax treatment for all financial institutions, as well as the same reserve requirements; it did not, however, want to end the system of separate bank and thrift regulators. H. Erich Heinemann, "Thrift: What Future?" *The New York Times*, 21 November 1971, 1, 16; President's Commission on Financial Structure and Regulation, *Report on the President's Commission on Financial Structure and Regulation* (Washington, DC: USGPO, 1972), 7–9, 23–6, 31–4; H. Erich Heinemann, "Revamping Is Urged for Nations' Financial Structure by Hunt Commission," *The New York Times*, 17 December 1971, 1, 65; Daniel Clay Draper, *The Thrift Industry, 1973* (New York: Practicing Law Institute, 1973), 26–32.

39 Edwin L. Dale Jr., "Nixon Proposes Major Changes in Banking System," *The New York Times*, 4 August 1973, 1, 33; "Banking Change Bill Sent to Congress," *The New York Times*,

Despite this controversy, the Hunt Commission Report became the basis of the Financial Institutions Act of 1973. The bill called for a five-and-a-half-year phase-out of Regulation Q, allowed thrifts to offer NOW accounts and invest up to 10 percent of assets in consumer loans. It also offered tax credits on real estate loans as a way to encourage thrifts to remain primarily mortgage lenders. Although this bill gave thrifts important new powers, the League refused to support it because it would end Regulation Q, and this opposition prevented the bill from moving out of committee. The second attempt at financial reform was the Financial Institutions Act of 1975, which virtually mirrored the earlier bill; the only substantive change allowed S&Ls to hold up to 30 percent of assets in commercial mortgages and consumer loans. Because it also mandated a five-year-phase-out of Regulation Q, the League refused to endorse it and although approved by the Senate, the bill quietly died in the House.[40]

Following the failure of these two bills, Rep. Ferdinand J. St. Germain (D-RI) launched a new study on financial reform. The report, known as the Financial Institutions and the National Economy Study, or FINE Study, sought to create a "homogenized" financial system that would be more competitive, efficient, and better serve consumer interests. While the FINE Study made many of the same recommendations as the earlier studies, its most radical proposals were to require thrifts to meet the same reserve requirements as banks, and create a "super agency," combining all federal bank and thrift regulators into one body to oversee all financial institutions. The League was aghast at the FINE Study recommendations, and when Congress began

13 October 1973, 51; "Hunt Reform Plans Panned and Praised," *SLN* 94 (December 1973), 26–7; "The Nader Report," *SLN* 94 (December 1973), 66–72; Edwin L. Dale Jr., "S&L Industry Fights Ceiling-Free Rates," *The New York Times*, 25 July 1973, 59, 65; Hester, "Special Interests: The *FINE Study*," 654; Letter from Ronald Albritton to Preston Martin with attachment, 18 September 1972, quote; In-House Files, September, 1972; Kamp Papers; RG 195; NACP; Letter from Steve Slipher to Wright Patman, 27 September 1972; United States Savings and Loan League Legislative Program and Correspondence; Wright Patman Papers; LBJPL; Warren, Gorham, & Lamont, "New Prospects for Banking Reform," 30 December 1972, and letter from Grover W. Ensley to Wright Patman, 16 December 1971; Hunt Commission, 1971; Wright Patman Papers; LBJPL; "Patman Paper 'Answers' Hunt Report," *SLN* 94 (September 1973), 41; "Restructuring of Reserve and Banking Groups Sought," *The New York Times*, 4 August 1973, 33; "Patman Says Loan Board Makes 'Ambitious Grabs,'" *The New York Times*, 14 November 1973, 65, 69.

40 "Big Changes for Thrift Institutions?" *US News and World Report*, 15 August 1973, 60–1; Senate. Committee on Banking, Housing and Urban Affairs. Subcommittee on Financial Institutions, *Financial Institutions Act, 1973*, hearings on S. 2591, 93rd Cong., 2nd sess., 13 May 1973, 6–9; "1974 Legislative Program," *SLN* 95 (March 1974), 86; "Hunt Reform Debate Resumes," *SLN* 95 (June 1974), 31; Senate. Committee on Banking, Housing and Urban Affairs. Subcommittee on Financial Institutions, *Financial Institutions Act of 1975*, hearings on S. 1267, S. 1475, and S. 1540, 94th Cong., 1st sess., 5–7, 14 May 1975; "Senate Votes Banking Bill; Widest Reform Since '30's," *The New York Times*, 12 December 1975, 1, 67.

to draft its latest version of financial reform legislation, intense industry pressure made sure that virtually none of the FINE Study recommendations were included. Instead, the Financial Reform Act of 1976 followed the same basic approach as the two earlier measures, with one major concession to the League's insistence of maintaining rate controls: this bill sought to phase out the rate differential between banks and thrifts over five years, but not for any S&Ls that held 80 percent or more of their assets in mortgage loans. Unfortunately, this bill also died in the committee.[41]

The only significant financial reform measure to win approval during this decade was the Financial Institutions Interest Rate Control Act of 1978, a relatively minor measure. This law allowed thrifts to invest up to 5 percent of assets in land development, construction, and/or education loans. It also raised the insurance coverage for IRA and Keogh retirement savings accounts from $40,000 to $100,000. One reason for the passage of this bill was that President Jimmy Carter had made financial reform a goal of its administration, and although the bill was far less comprehensive than what he wanted, he supported it in order to get some form of legislation on the books. A second reason was that it did not tamper with Regulation Q, which brought thrift industry support.[42]

WHY DID 1970S, FINANCIAL REFORM FAIL?

In many respects, the decade of the 1970s was an ideal time for League leaders and Congress to come together and create a plan to modernize federal

[41] House Committee on Banking, Finance, and Urban Affairs. Subcommittee on Financial Institutions Supervision, Regulation, and Insurance, *Financial Institutions and the Nation's Economy (FINE): "Discussion Principles,"* hearings, 94th Cong., 1st and 2nd sess., part III, 1620–3; James L. Pierce, "The *FINE Study*," *Journal of Money, Credit and Banking* 9 (November 1977), 606–14; "How Lobbyists Tripped Up Banking Reform," *Forbes* 118 (1 July 1976), 57–8; "The Rifts Over Financial Institution Restructuring," *SLN* 97 (February 1976), 60–6; "Business Stirred by 'Principle' for Restructuring Study," *SLN* 96 (December 1975), 12; Hester, "Special Interests: The *FINE Study*," 656–9; Letter from Carl O. Kamp to Ferdinand J. St. Germain with attachment, 1 March 1974, 1–4; St. Germain, Ferdinand J.; Kamp Papers; RG 195; NACP; House Committee on Banking, Currency and Housing Subcommittee on Financial Institutions Supervision, Regulation and Insurance Currency and Housing, *The Financial Reform Act of 1976*, hearings, 94th Cong., 2nd sess., 4, 9, 11, 16 March 1976, part I, 3–15, 216–26; Robert D. Hershey Jr., "Associations, Banks Clash Over House Draft Plan," *SLN* 97 (April 1976), 16; "House Subcommittee Gets Banking Bill for Redrafting," *The New York Times*, 4 May 1976, 55; "Why Financial Reform Died," *SLN* 97 (June 1976), 27.

[42] Memorandum from Orin Kramer and Stu Eisenstat to Jimmy Carter, 9 November 1978; Banking Reform – Banking (General); DPS Subject Files; JCPL; "New Legislation: Pulling It All Together," *SLN* 100 (February 1979), 38–42; "Congress Beats the Clock to Enact Giant Financial Bill," *SLN* 99 (November 1978), 33; House Committee on Banking, Finance, and Urban Affairs, *Financial Institutions Regulatory Act of 1978*, H-Rept., 95–1383, 95th Cong., 2nd sess., 1978, 1–5.

regulations governing thrifts. The economy of the period proved conclusively that these associations suffered problems when interest rates became volatile, and several independent studies showed that the system of rules put in place during the Great Depression was in dire need of updating. Despite such positive factors, there were at least three major roadblocks to getting financial reform legislation through Congress. One was the fact that although all the major reports on the S&L industry agreed on the need to diversify assets and liabilities, they had major differences about which remedies in particular should be pursued. The Patman Paper and the FINE Study added to this confusion by making recommendations that both industry officials and regulators considered too radical.[43]

A second factor that contributed to the failure of these reform measures was that, despite the difficult economic conditions, S&Ls recorded gains in assets and profits during this period, indicating that perhaps the industry was not in dire trouble. The lack of a true "S&L crisis" in the 1970s is significant because throughout the history of this industry the only major legislation affecting thrifts resulted from specific crises. During the collapse of the "national" B&Ls in the 1890s, nearly every state enacted some form of thrift regulation to protect these institutions and to protect small savers. Federal thrift regulations, although first considered in 1919, did not become law until the 1930s, when the Great Depression caused thousands of families to lose their homes. Furthermore, nearly every other piece of thrift legislation passed Congress at the end of the current session, indicating the difficulty of finding consensus on key issues.[44]

Related to this situation was the fact that Congress went through major changes in its membership during the 1970s. Following the Watergate incident, dozens of long-serving legislators either retired or were voted out of office, and this development created problems in the leadership of Congress. Patman, who opposed any efforts to give thrifts any new powers he thought were anticonsumer, was succeeded in 1974 by Rep. Henry Reuss (D-WI) as chairman of the House Banking Committee. In contrast, long-time Senate

---

[43] Eli Shapiro and Kent Colton, "The Process of Change in the Savings and Loan Industry," *Change in the Savings and Loan Industry*, 24–5; Strunk and Case, *Where Deregulation Went Wrong*, 2–5; Frederick E. Balberston, *Thrifts in Crisis: Structural Transformation of the Savings and Loan Industry* (Cambridge, MA: Ballinger Publishing Co., 1985), 19–24; Thomas F. Cargill and Gillian G. Garcia, *Financial Reform in the 1980s* (Stanford: Hoover Institution Press, 1985), 53; Thomas F. Cargill and Gillian G. Garcia, *Financial Deregulation and Monetary Control: Historical Perspective and Impact of the 1980 Act* (Stanford, CA: Hoover Institution Press, 1982), 25.

[44] Andrew S. Carron, "The Political Economy of Financial Regulation," in Roger S. Noll and Bruce M. Owens, editors, *The Political Economy of Deregulation: Interest Groups in the Regulatory Process* (Washington, DC: American Enterprise Institute, 1983), 69–96; "How Lobbyists Tripped Up Banking Reform," 58; Thomas K. McCraw, *Prophets of Regulation: Charles Francis Adams, Louis D. Brandeis, James M. Landis, Alfred E. Kahn* (Cambridge, MA: Belknap Press of Harvard University Press, 1984), 303–4.

Banking Committee chairman Sen. John Sparkman (D-AL) was less active because of his advanced age, and in 1978 was replaced by the proconsumer senator William Proxmire (D-WI). While the new chairmen were both experienced legislators, they did not have the same close relationships with the League that both Sparkman and Patman had possessed. This lack of confidential lines of communications with these critical committees affected the ability to push reform legislation forward.[45]

A third critical reason for the dearth of reform in the 1970s was the unwillingness of the League to compromise on the issue of Regulation Q. Although thrift leaders consistently supported the idea of passing new thrift regulations, they were inflexible about any proposal to change the rate protection they enjoyed under Regulation Q. Even though the League had vehemently opposed rate controls in 1966, by the 1970s the industry had become convinced that without the rate differential, thrifts would have trouble retaining funds to make home loans. According to one thrift executive, the only thing needed in order for thrifts to meet their financial role was "long-term extension of Regulation Q with a rate differential. There is no number two because the space between Q and everything else is so great." Such devotion to this single issue and intransigence ultimately cost the League its one golden opportunity to help create a new system of thrift rules that might have reformed the industry without forcing a loss of its unique identity.[46]

Finally, even though the League's formidable lobbying effort was "aggressive without being obnoxious and had one hell of a network," by the late 1970s it was becoming more disorganized. One reason for this was the death of League Vice President Stephen Slipher in 1973, who was known as the "dean of financial lobbyists," and the retirement of Norman Strunk in 1979, who had led the League for more than twenty-five years. A more critical problem, however, was the lack of consensus within the League on the need for reform, with large S&Ls in favor and smaller associations strongly opposed. As one senator later commented, "the S&L industry was conspicuous by its inability to say what it wanted and to stand up and fight for it. In many ways it seems like the AFL-CIO and the home builders had more to say about what was best for the S&L industry than what the S&Ls themselves did." This inability for the League to speak with one voice not only reflected

---

45 Letter from Preston Martin to Wright Patman, 17 March 1972, and letter from Wright Patman to Preston Martin, 25 August 1972; Federal Home Loan Bank Board Correspondence; Wright Patman Papers; LBJPL; "How Reuss Fumbled Financial Reform," *Business Week*, 14 June 1979, 26–7; "Congress Messes Up Financial Reform Again," *Business Week*, 19 November 1979, 50; Shapiro and Colton, "The Process of Change in the Savings and Loan Industry," 25; O'Connell, *America's Money Trauma*, 16–22.

46 "The Case for Savings Rate Differentials," *SLN* 98 (January 1977), 38–40; Eichler, *The Thrift Debacle*, 62–3; Anthony M. Frank, "Institutional Implications of the Changing Regulatory and Technological Framework of S&L Competition," *Change in the Savings and Loan Industry*, quote 247.

the divisions within the industry, but would be a major reason why this trade group would have troubles in the 1980s.[47]

CONCLUSIONS

The thirteen years following the passage of the Interest Rate Control Act of 1966 were among the most turbulent in the postwar history of the thrift industry. S&Ls faced many problems, the chief of which was contending with a slow-growth economy characterized by high interest rates and consumer prices. In response to these complex circumstances, thrift managers designed a number of innovative financial products, including alternative mortgage instruments and NOW accounts. Despite such challenges, S&Ls continued to grow and remain profitable during the 1970s, even as the actual number of thrifts steadily declined. However, the steady decline in the loan loss reserve ratio for the industry was a sign of potential financial weaknesses. These and other changes in financial markets led Congress to consider modernizing the basic thrift laws. Following the preparation of a host of independent studies, Congress considered several major pieces of reform legislation designed to help S&Ls diversify both their assets and liabilities. None of these measures won enough support from legislators and the League to become law. As a result, only one reform bill, the Financial Institutions Interest Rate Control Act, was enacted. As later events would soon prove, these failures to achieve reform in the 1970s were lost opportunities for the thrift industry.

[47] Thomas B. Marvell, *The Federal Home Loan Bank Board* (New York: Praeger, 1969), 147–8, Day, *S&L Hell*, 57; William K. Black, *The S&L Lobby: An Exercise in Customer Service* (Washington, DC: National Commission on Financial Institution Reform, Recovery and Enforcement, 1992), 2–4, quote 4; "Political Action: The Need to be Involved," *SLN* 99 (September 1978), 48–58; "Legislative Report," *Saving and Loan Annals, 1973* (Chicago: United States Savings and Loan League, 1973), 239; "O'Connell Vows to Strengthen Lobbying Efforts," *SLN* 100 (November 1979), 64–7; A. D. Theobald, *Forty Five Years on the Up Escalator* (Chicago: privately published, 1979), 247–8; Strunk and Case, *Where Deregulation Went Wrong*, 53–5; "US League Sets Legislative Objectives," *Savings and Loan News* 97 (March 1979), 73; US League Sets Legislative Goals," *Savings and Loan News* 100 (April 1979), 75; *FINE Discussion Principles*, part III, 1623, 1664–8; Colton, *Financial Reform*, quote 23.

8

DEREGULATION AND DISASTER,
1979–1988

The 1980s was the most difficult and trying decade for savings and loans since the 1930s. It began poorly when interest rates soared and the American economy slid into the deepest recession since the end of World War II. Such unprecedented economic conditions hurt all financial institutions, with the thrift industry experiencing record losses and even failures. The severity of these problems led Congress to pass the first significant financial reform legislation in nearly fifty years. In 1980, the Depository Institutions Deregulation and Monetary Control Act initiated deregulation by relaxing controls on interest rates and depository services, while the Garn-St. Germain Depository Institutions Act of 1982 completed the process by expanding thrift lending powers. The return of economic growth in 1983 helped the industry rebound as hundreds of S&Ls took advantage of the new business opportunities afforded by deregulation. Unfortunately, not all thrifts made the transition smoothly. The number of insolvent associations rose in the mid-1980s, and in 1985 there were even deposit runs reminiscent of the Great Depression. When federal regulators tried to impose greater discipline on the industry, efforts by the League, key legislators, and White House officials to downplay the severity of the crisis prevented any substantive changes. The bankruptcy of the Federal Savings and Loan Insurance Corp. (FSLIC) in 1987 finally forced Congress to act, but its responses proved inadequate and the number of insolvent thrifts (some of which involved fraud) grew larger. By the end of the decade, the financial condition of hundreds of S&Ls had deteriorated to such an extent that officials had little choice but to re-regulate the thrift industry.[1]

---

[1] The S&L crisis of the 1980s is the most thoroughly researched period of the thrift industry's history. For descriptions of more than 360 books, academic studies, and federal reports written between 1980 and 1992 on the subject, see Pat L. Talley, *The Savings and Loan Crisis: An Annotated Bibliography* (Westport, CT: Greenwood Press, 1993).

THRIFT DEREGULATION: ROUND ONE

Despite numerous failed efforts to modify S&L regulations in the 1970s, the push for deregulation intensified when seesawing interest rates forced hundreds of thrifts to the brink of insolvency. The rate volatility began in August 1979 when Federal Reserve Board chairman Paul Volker announced that, in an effort to curb inflation associated with the near doubling of oil prices, monetary policy would no longer seek to control interest rates but instead focus on managing the money supply. While inflation eventually subsided, the decision to let interest rates float freely caused turmoil in the money markets. Between July 1979 and April 1980, the benchmark Federal Funds rate rose from 10.47 percent to 17.61 percent; it fell to 9.03 percent three months later, but then soared to 19.08 percent by January 1981.[2]

The fluctuations in interest rates affected thrifts in two ways. First, because of Regulation Q rate controls, S&Ls (and banks) had limited ability to offer market rates on savings accounts. Consequently, these institutions lost billions in deposits to unregulated investments like money-market mutual funds, which grew from $9.5 billion (U.S. billion) in assets in 1978 to more than $236 billion (US billion) by the end of 1982. Second, since the bulk of thrift assets were fixed-rate mortgages, the income they produced was usually insufficient to offset the rise in the cost of attracting deposits. Furthermore, rising rates caused the market value of these long-term assets to decline; if they were sold, the S&L would have to record a loss. The result was that industry profits fell from $3.6 billion (US billion) in 1979 to just $781 million in 1980. More importantly, nearly half of all thrifts were technically insolvent, since their total capital had fallen below the required minimum of 5 percent of insured deposits.[3]

While disintermediation and declining profits were important factors in reviving the push for thrift deregulation, the main factor that led Congress to finally act on this issue was an adverse legal decision involving the use of financial technology. In 1978, consumer groups filed a suit against bank regulators alleging that accounts with investment restrictions, like high minimum deposit requirements, discriminated against small savers. In April 1979, a U.S. Circuit Court agreed, ruling in part, that allowing bank customers to

---

[2] Between 1978 and 1980, the consumer price index soared from 7.59 to 13.48 percent, but by 1983 inflation had fallen to just 3.21 and remained low for the remainder of the decade. Federal Reserve Bank, St. Louis, *FRED II*, *http://research.stlouisfed.org/fred2/*, accessed 31 August 2003; "Inflation: The Great Saver Rip-Off" *Savings and Loan News* [hereafter *SLN*] 100 (August 1979), 47.

[3] Money market accounts often invested in low-risk treasury notes and commercial paper. Norman Strunk and Fred Case, *Where Deregulation Went Wrong: A Look at the Causes Behind Savings and Loan Failures in the 1980s* (Chicago: United States League of Savings Institutions, 1988), 54; James Barth, *The Great Savings and Loan Debacle* (Washington DC: AEI Press, 1991), 26–7; Andrew S. Carron, *The Plight of Thrift Institutions* (Washington, DC: Brookings Institution, 1982), 9–11.

use electronic funds transfer (EFT) services to move money between checking and savings accounts violated the Banking Act of 1933 prohibition on
paying interest on demand deposits. As a result, all EFT services, including
popular consumer products like automated teller machines, were declared
illegal. The decision did not go into effect immediately, however, as the court
gave Congress until January 1, 1980, to draft new laws. Since Congress was
sure to enact some form of legislation to protect these important banking
services, the White House and consumer groups used this opportunity to
lobby for broader financial reforms.[4]

Responding to President Jimmy Carter's message to Congress urging the
"reform [of] a system which has become increasingly unfair to the small
saver," Senate Banking Committee chairman William Proxmire (D-WI) introduced a sweeping measure designed to overhaul existing banking laws.
In addition to legalizing the affected EFT services, the Proxmire bill called
for a phase-out Regulation Q, authorized all thrifts to offer interest-bearing
negotiable order of withdrawal (NOW) accounts, and allowed them to make
consumer loans of up to 10 percent of assets. Proxmire's zeal to end "blatant
discrimination against savers" was not, however, shared by House Banking
Committee chairman Henry D. Reuss (D-WI), who drafted a more narrow
piece of legislation that focused exclusively on the issues raised in the court
decision. Such differences prevented a bill from being passed in the first session of Congress, and with the court deadline looming legislators worked
feverishly to craft a measure acceptable to both houses. Agreement was finally reached in early 1980, and on April 1 the first substantive financial
reform in nearly fifty years became law.[5]

---

[4] "Banks' Automatic Shift of Savings to Checking Accounts Held Illegal," *The New York Times*,
21 April 1979, 1; "Spurred by Appeals Court, Congress May Once Again Try Its Hand at
Financial Reform," *SLN* 100 (June 1979), 27; "A Rewrite for the Banking Laws," *Business
Week*, 7 May 1979, 120–1; "Anti-Inflation Move Spurs Credit Crunch for Home Lenders,"
SLN 100 (November 1979), 6; Hobart Rowen, "Crusade of the Gray Panthers," *The
Washington Post*, 15 September 1979, A19; Memorandum from Stuart Eisenstat to "Senator,"
23 October 1979; Depository Institutions Deregulation Act of 1979; Domestic Policy Staff
(DPS) Subject Files, 1976–1981; Jimmy Carter Presidential Library, Atlanta, GA (JCPL).

[5] "Banking Changes Proposed," *The New York Times*, 21 February 1979, D1, 9; Judith Miller,
"Rate Ceilings Under Fire," *The New York Times*, 25 March 1979, C5; "Bank Law: Con-
sumers' Gains Cited," *The New York Times*, 2 April 1980, D1, D9; "Let the Banks Compete,"
The New York Times, 2 April 1980, A26; Memorandum from Orin Kramer to Stu Eisenstat,
28 February 1979, quote; memorandum from Stu Eisenstat, Jim McIntyre, and Orin Kramer
to Jimmy Carter, 17 May 1979, and memorandum to Members of the Regulation Q Task
Force from Robert Carswell, n.d.; Regulation Q – Banking; DPS Subject Files, 1976–1981;
JCPL; *Message from the President of the United States Transmitting His Recommendations for
Comprehensive Financial Reform Legislation* (Washington, DC: USGPO, 22 May 1979), 1–3,
quote 1; Senate Committee on Banking, Housing, and Urban Affairs. Subcommittee on Financial Institutions, *Depository Institutions Deregulation Act of 1979*, hearings, 96th Cong.,
1st sess., part 2, 1–6, quote 1; Richard H. Timberlake, "Legislative Construction of the Monetary Control Act of 1980," Papers and Proceedings of the Ninety-Seventh Annual Meeting

The Depository Institutions Deregulation and Monetary Control Act (DIDMCA) was a broad financial reform measure affecting both commercial banks and thrifts. The centerpiece of the legislation was the phaseout of interest rate ceilings over a six-year period, a process to be administered by the Depository Institutions Deregulation Committee (DIDC). It expanded thrift business powers by allowing S&Ls to offer charge cards and NOW accounts, engage in trust services, and operate statewide branches. In terms of lending authority, DIDMCA exempted thrift mortgages from state usury laws and expanded their ability to make acquisition development and construction loans. It also allowed thrifts to diversify their loan portfolios by holding up to 20 percent of assets in a combination of consumer loans, commercial paper, and corporate bonds.[6]

Another provision of the DIDMCA increased the coverage for deposit insurance from $40,000 to $100,000 per account. Critics would later contend that this change, which involved little congressional debate, was a key factor in the S&L crisis since it allowed households and deposit brokers to funnel millions into troubled S&Ls with little risk of loss if the thrift failed. Such arguments, however, ignore the fact that even before the increase customers had the ability to place very large sums in a single institution and still receive full coverage. Opening multiple accounts in the names of different household members, or maintaining joint or trust accounts, was a legal way to sidestep the deposit insurance restrictions. Interestingly, when regulators did try to limit insurance coverage to $100,000 for total funds from a single source, like a deposit broker, the courts ruled that such restrictions were illegal. While there was the risk that unscrupulous lenders would use insured funds improperly, the greater concern for both the White House and regulators was that consumers would lose confidence in S&Ls if coverage remained unchanged.

---

of the American Economic Association, *The American Economic Review* 75 (May 1985), 97–102; Kent Colton, *Financial Reform: A Review of the Past and Prospects for the Future.* Invited Research Working Paper No. 37 (Washington DC: Office of Policy and Economic Research, Federal Home Loan Bank Board, 1980), 17.

[6] "Thrift Units Win Wider Credit Powers," *The New York Times*, 4 July 1980, D1, D5; "S&Ls Get Ready to Kick Up Their Heels," *US News and World Report*, 29 September 1980, 17–18; "The Thrifts Tip-Toe into Credit Cards," *Business Week*, 29 September 1980, 72; Thomas F. Cargill and Gillian G. Garcia, *Financial Deregulation and Monetary Control: Historical Perspective and Impact of the 1980 Act* (Stanford, CA: Hoover Institution Press, 1982), 33–5; Ned Eichler, *The Thrift Debacle* (Berkeley: University of California Press, 1989), 59–62; Mark Carl Rom, *Public Spirit in the Thrift Tragedy* (Pittsburgh: University of Pittsburgh Press, 1996), 7–15; "Strong Currents are Changing the Shape of Financial Markets," *SLN* 100 (August 1979), 40–6; Kenneth Thygerson, "Financial Change: Have Reformers Overlooked the Real Issue?" *SLN* 100 (October 1979), 98–109; Littlewood, Shane, & Co., *The Depository Institutions Deregulation and Monetary Control Act of 1980: An Analysis and Interpretation* (Park Ridge, IL: Bank Administration Institute, 1981), 3, 7–8; *Leveling the Playing Field: A Review of the DIDMCA of 1980, and the Garn-St Germain Act of 1982* (Chicago: Federal Reserve Bank of Chicago, 1983), 7–26.

Such a crisis would likely produce new rounds of disintermediation, which, in the extreme, could lead to deposit runs and thrift failures.[7]

One major problem with the DIDMCA was that it did not give thrifts the ability to make variable-rate mortgages. Even though the White House and many legislators felt it was "intellectually indefensible" not to give S&Ls this power, they feared a political backlash from consumer groups who portrayed variable-rate mortgages as "the engine of inflation [in which] lenders can exercise a 'heads I win tails you lose' policy against borrowers." Also, making financial reform too broad could have weakened support for the measure and jeopardized passage of any legislation. Consequently, officials hoped that the Board would authorize S&Ls to make variable-rate mortgages through subsequent regulations. Unfortunately, until then the only way for thrifts to make loans that would keep pace with the changing rate environment was by using the new lending powers and diversifying into areas outside traditional home finance.[8]

THRIFT DEREGULATION: ROUND TWO

Although the DIDMCA reforms offered the promise for financial growth, they did not offer immediate help to an industry going through the worst

---

[7] Changing the insurance coverage for the FDIC and FSLIC from $40,000 to $100,000 was not unique; Congress had made the exact same increase in the insurance of IRA and Keogh retirement accounts in 1978. Letter from Anthony M. Frank to Stu Eisenstat, 28 February 1980; FI 5, 10/1/78-1/20/81; WHCF: Subject File – Finance; JCPL; Memorandum from Stu Eisenstat to Jimmy Carter, 29 March 1980, memorandum from Orin Kramer to Stu Eisenstat, 2 April 1980, and memorandum from Orin Kramer to Stu Eisenstat, 14 April 1980; FI 2, 2/1/80-1/4/81; WHCF: Subject File – Finance; JCPL; Federal Deposit Insurance Corporation (FDIC) Division of Research and Statistics, *History of the Eighties – Lessons for the Future*, vol. 1 (Washington, DC : FDIC, 1997), 93–4.

[8] Another omission in the DIDMCA was the right of thrifts to enforce due-on-sale clauses in real estate sales contracts, which consumer groups opposed because they prevented buyers from assuming lower-cost mortgages. While these changes were goals of future reform, interest in further thrift deregulation within the Carter administration waned after 1980. Memorandum form Rick Neustadt to Stu Eisenstat, n.d.; Stu Eisenstat, Correspondence and Memorandums to, 7/14/80-11/20/80; Richard M. Neustadt Jr., Files on Government Reform, 1976– ; JCPL; Senate Committee on Banking, Housing and Urban Affairs, *Depository Institutions Deregulation Act of 1979*, hearings on S. 1347, 96th Cong., 1st sess., part 3, quote 131, 21 June 1979; Memorandum from Michael Blumenthal to Jimmy Carter, 7 June 1977, 3; FI 2, 5/1/77-6/30/77; WHCF: Subject File – Finance; JCPL; Memorandum from Orin Kramer to Stu Eisenstat, 14 April 1980; FI 2, 2/1/80-1/4/81; WHCF: Subject File – Finance; JCPL; Memorandum from Orin Kramer to Stu Eisenstat, 28 February 1979, memorandum from Orin Kramer to Stu Eisenstat, 17 May 1979, quote, memorandum from Orin Kramer to Stu Eisenstat, 10 September 1979, and memorandum from Stu Eisenstat and Orin Kramer to Dan Tate, 19 October 1979; Regulation Q – Banking; DPS Subject Files, 1976–1981; JCPL; "The Differential is Worth $230 Billion to Home Buyers," *SLN* 100 (October 1979), 44; Rom, *Public Spirit in the Thrift Tragedy*, 137–48; Strunk and Case, *Where Deregulation Went Wrong*, 43–7.

national recession in nearly forty years. Because of high interest rates and weak demand for new homes, total thrift mortgage originations declined by 25 percent between 1979 and 1980. By 1981 the level of new mortgages was less than half the amount made three years earlier. While thrifts could lend in areas outside home finance most managers were "not eager to jump into new fields when old-timers were already having trouble earning a profit." Adding to the industry's woes was the decision by the DIDC to remove all restrictions on money market certificates within weeks of the passage of DIDMCA. Because these accounts represented more than 40 percent of all S&L deposits, interest expense for thrifts soared. The increased cost of funds combined with the lack of lending opportunities led to net losses for the industry in 1981 of a staggering $4.6 billion (US billion). Although the League pleaded for the reimposition of rate controls, officials chose not to intervene contending that "thrifts hadn't come to grips with the [competitive] implications of deregulation."[9]

As industry losses mounted, the net worth for hundreds of S&Ls fell sharply. By the end of 1981 the number of thrift failures approached levels last seen during the Great Depression. Responding to industry appeals for aid, Congress again considered financial reform legislation, but this time the new Republican-controlled Senate approached the problem intent on also fulfilling President Ronald Reagan's campaign promise of creating truly open financial markets. In October 1981, Senate Banking Committee chairman Jake Garn (R-UT), introduced a bill that provided assistance to S&Ls with insufficient new worth, and also called for a broad array of reforms ranging from the expansion of thrift lending powers to the consolidation of the FSLIC and the FDIC into one agency. The House, however, was still

[9] Alan S. Oser, "America's 'Dream Adrift'" *The New York Times*, 20 June 1982, R7, R14; "Bank Law: Consumers' Gains Cited," *The New York Times*, 2 April 1980, D9; "The Cost of Inflation Strikes Home," *The New York Times*, 14 May 1981, 26; "The Thrift Crisis the Result of High Rates and Bungled Deregulation," *SLN* 103 (April 1982), 44–8; George G. Kaufman, "The U.S. Banking Debacle of the 1980s: An Overview and Lessons," *The Financier: ACMT* 2 (May 1995), 11; National Commission on Financial Institution Reform, Recovery and Enforcement (NCFIRRE), *Origins and Causes of the S&L Debacle: A Blueprint for Reform* (Washington, DC: NCFIRRE, July 1993), 29–30; "Thrift Units Cautious on Expansion Plans," *The New York Times*, 12 January 1981, D1, D5, quote D1; Senate Committee on Banking, Housing and Urban Affairs, *Depository Institutions Deregulation Committee*, hearings to consider the actions of the Depository Institutions Deregulation Committee and S. 2927, 96th Cong., 2nd sess., 5 August 5, 1980, 96–9, 103–5; Memorandum from Orin Kramer to Stu Eisenstat, 27 June 1980, quote and memorandum from Stu Eisenstat to Jimmy Carter, 25 July 1980; FI 2, 2/1/80-1/4/81; WHCF: Subject File – Finance; JCPL; Rom, *Public Spirit in the Thrift Tragedy*, 142–8; William O'Connell, *America's Money Trauma: How Washington Blunders Crippled the U.S. Financial System* (Winnetka, IL: Conversation Press, 1992), 27–30; "As Savings & Loans Fight for Survival," *US News and World Report*, 30 March 1981, 76–7; "Casualties of the Revolution," *Time*, 11 January 1982, 67; "Too Many, Too Much," *Forbes* 128 (26 October 1981), 187–8; William J. Quark, "The Feckless Thrifts," *Harper's* 265 (February 1982), 8–13; Leonard Silk, "Savings Units Pressures Grows," *The New York Times*, 10 June 1981, D2.

under Democratic leadership, and Banking Committee chairman Ferdinand J. St. Germain (D-RI) introduced a much narrower bill in May 1982 that simply provided aid to the most troubled thrifts. As was true with passage of the DIDMCA, ironing out the differences between the House and Senate versions was a contentious process, but on October 15 (less than one hour before adjourning for the session) Congress approved the Garn-St. Germain Depository Institutions Act of 1982 (Garn-St. Germain).[10]

Garn-St. Germain completed the process of thrift deregulation begun with the DIDMCA by providing immediate relief to the beleaguered industry as well as new powers designed to promote long-term recovery. To assist thrifts with low net worth, Garn-St. Germain authorized the FSLIC to issue "net worth certificates" to any S&L with positive net worth of less than 3 percent of total assets. Because these certificates were actually government promissory notes that thrifts could use to increase their regulatory equity, the FSLIC was essentially making a direct capital investment in individual thrifts. Other ways Garn-St. Germain tried to help thrifts raise capital included relaxing the restrictions on mergers, and making it easier for associations to convert from mutual to stock ownership. S&Ls could even use the word "bank" in their corporate titles.[11]

The most significant reforms enacted by Garn-St. Germain, however, involved the expansion of S&L lending powers into a host of new areas, many of which bore little relation to the industry's core home finance mission. To help diversify their loan portfolios, the law allowed S&Ls to hold up to 40 percent of assets in commercial mortgages, up to 11 percent of assets in secured or unsecured commercial loans, and up to 3 percent of assets as direct equity investments in businesses. While these new lending areas offered higher earnings potential for struggling thrifts, they also involved greater risks, which increased the likelihood of loan losses if lenders made poor

---

[10] Robert Dince and James Verbrugge, "The Right Way to Save the S&Ls," *Fortune*, 10 August 1981, 133–8; Clyde H. Farnsworth, "Senate Bill Asks Bank Decontrol," *The New York Times*, 8 October 1981, D11; "How a Crisis is Speeding Deregulation," *Business Week*, 31 May 1982, 68; Kenneth B. Noble, "Aid Bill Emerging for Thrifts," *The New York Times*, 1 June 1982, D5; Kenneth B. Noble, "Thrift Unit Aid Falters in Senate," *The New York Times*, 5 August 1982, D3; Kenneth B. Noble, "Thrift Unit Aid Backed by Senate," *The New York Times*, 25 September 1982, 39, 42; "Garn Continued to Push for Thrift Bill," *SLN* 103 (August 1982), 7; Kenneth B. Noble, "Conferees Clear Bill to Shore Up Savings Industry," *The New York Times*, 30 September 1982, A1, D16; Jonathan Fuerbringer, "Behind the Scenes, Perhaps a Coup," *The New York Times*, 15 November 1983, A20; L. Richard Fischer, Elizabeth G. Gentry and Petrina M. E. Verderamo, *The Garn-St. Germain Depository Institutions Act of 1982: What's in It for You?* (Arlington, VA: The Consumer Bankers Associations, 1982), 5–8.

[11] "New Options Offer Hope to Ailing Thrifts Capital Problems," *SLN* 103 (June 1982), 64–9; Kerry Cooper and Donald R. Fraser, *Banking Deregulation and the New Competition in Financial Service*, (Cambridge, MA: Ballinger Publishing Co., 1984), 1–10; *Garn-St. Germain Depository Institutions Act of 1982 Conference Report*, 30–41; "New Names Designate Better, Broader Role," *Savings Institutions* [hereafter *SI*] 108 (January 1987), 60–4.

decisions. In more traditional lending areas, Garn-St. Germain broadened the types of consumer loans thrifts could make, and removed the loan-to-value ratio limits on mortgages. This made it possible for thrifts to offer 100 percent home financing to virtually any borrower. Finally, to help S&Ls attract funds, Garn-St. Germain required the Board to create a new money-market deposit account to compete with money-market mutual funds, and end any remaining Regulation Q controls by January 1984.[12]

One reason for the broad scope of Garn-St. Germain was that the League played a much more active role in the legislative process. Unlike the passage of the DIDMCA, which was influenced primarily by consumer interests, the League was able to mobilize strong grassroots support for deregulation. By arguing that the only way for the industry to recover financially was through growth and diversification, thrift leaders secured most of the new powers they desired and at the same time proved that the trade group still had political clout on Capitol Hill. Passage of the law also benefited from the support of the FHLBB, whose new chairman Richard T. Pratt was so involved in drafting Garn-St. Germain that some legislators called it the "Pratt Bill." Such cooperation between the industry and the White House led League executive William O'Connell to claim that Garn-St. Germain "wouldn't have happened without trade group support and wouldn't have passed without the support of the Reagan administration."[13]

REGULATORS EASE THE RULES

Pratt's role in the passage of Garn-St. Germain was not the first time he had displayed his passion for deregulation. Appointed by Reagan at the recommendation of Sen. Jake Garn, Pratt was a physically imposing academic/economist and former League employee who firmly believed that markets, not governments, should determine the success or failure of S&Ls. As a member of the DIDC, Pratt supported the quick removal of rate controls,

---

[12] House Committee on Banking, Finance, and Urban Affairs. Subcommittee on Financial Institutions Supervision, Regulation, and Insurance. *Garn-St. Germain Depository Institutions Act of 1982*, Report No. 97-899, 97th Cong., 2nd sess., 1982, 2–30; "Major Provisions of the Legislation," *The New York Times*, 1 October 1982, D4; "Saving the Thrifts, and Then Some," *The New York Times*, 1 October 1982, A30; "What New Bank Law Does for Consumers," *US News and World Report*, 10 October 1982, 66–7; *Leveling the Playing Field*, 28–51; Rom, *Public Spirit in the Thrift Tragedy*, 148–9; Lawrence J. White, *The S&L Debacle: Public Policy Lessons for Bank and Thrift Regulation* (New York: Oxford University Press, 1991), 67–74.

[13] Clyde H. Farnsworth, "Thrift Units Join Forces in Aid Plea," *The New York Times*, 21 January 1982, D13; Kenneth B. Noble, "Amid Debate, U.S. Panel Asks Wider Powers for Thrift Units, " *The New York Times*, 26 February 1982, D3; "Implementation of New Powers Awaits FHLBB, DIDC Rules," *SLN* 103 (November 1982), 6–8, quote 7; "Thrifts Enter a New Era," *SLN* 103 (November 1982), 36–42; Fischer, Gentry, and Verderamo, *The Garn-St. Germain Depository Institutions Act*, 5; "A Bail-out the S&Ls No Longer Needed," *Forbes* 128 (29 November 1982), 90.

and as Board chairman from 1981 to 1982 he liberalized regulations, making it easier for thrifts to obtain and invest funds. During his tenure, the Board authorized variable-rate mortgage lending and allowed thrifts to participate in the high-risk financial futures and options markets. It also removed restrictions on brokered deposits, essentially allowing thrifts to obtain as much money as they wanted from this volatile funding source. Pratt also believed that for the industry to survive, larger and more efficient thrifts be allowed to "swallow up" weaker institutions as a way to generate higher earnings and become more diversified. As a result, between 1980 and 1982, the Board approved, encouraged, or arranged the merger of 516 S&Ls and closed an additional 434 failing thrifts.[14]

One of the more controversial rule changes made by the Pratt Board was the decision to reduce the minimum number of thrift shareholders needed for a federal charter. Instead of requiring 400 individuals (of which at least 125 had to be from the "local community"), the new rules allowed even one person to own a federal S&L. Also, potential buyers could obtain 100 percent financing from the home loan bank to buy thrift stock, provided the buyers offered real estate assets to secure these loans. Making it easier for people to form S&Ls led to a sharp increase in the number of new associations. From 1980 to 1982, only twelve new federal thrifts were formed, but over the next three years 114 new thrifts received federal charters. Significantly, many of these new charters were issued to institutions in Texas and California. Critics would later identify this ownership rule change as a major factor in thrift failures since it allowed an association to become dominated by a handful of people who could use it as their "personal piggy bank."[15]

However, the one Pratt Board decision that had the greatest long-term effect on the thrift industry was the creation of new thrift accounting rules. In January 1982, the Board allowed S&Ls to use Regulatory Accounting Principles (RAP) to prepare their financial statements for regulators. Unlike

[14] In its entire history up to 1980, the Board had resolved only 165 failures. Clyde H. Farnsworth, "The Patron-Regulator of the Beleaguered Thrifts," *The New York Times*, 22 November 1981, 6–7; Jeff Gerth, "Savings Regulators End Mortgage Curbs," *The New York Times*, 24 April 1981, B6; John Merwin, "Enough is Enough," *Forbes* 127 (25 May 1981), 32–3; "A Step Closer to Rescuing the Thrifts," *Business Week*, 27 July 1981, 74; O'Connell, *America's Money Trauma*, 67–71; "Merger Trend in the Thrift Industry," *The New York Times*, 5 July 1980, 27, 37; "Beyond Crisis, Pratt Foresees Promising future," *SLN* 103 (April 1982), 74–5; Rom, *Public Spirit in the Thrift Tragedy*, 64.

[15] Brokered deposits were funds accessed from investors across the country and deposited in banks by brokers in the form of large-denomination federally insured certificates of deposit. Because the main criteria used to select a depository institution was high interest rates, brokers moved funds often as rates changed, which made this a highly volatile source of funds. "Why New S&Ls are Doing So Well," *Business Week*, 7 June 1982, 68; "New Associations Baby Members of a Better Business," *SLN* 103 (July 1982), 12–15; Alice P. White, *Evolution of the Thrift Crisis* (Washington, DC: Division of Research and Statistics, Division of Monetary Affairs, Federal Reserve Board, 1989), 20.

Generally Accepted Accounting Principles (GAAP), which most businesses used, RAP was more liberal and allowed thrifts greater latitude in how they reported their assets, equity, income, and expenses. For example, if a thrift sold an asset at a loss, under GAAP it would have to recognize the loss immediately. RAP allowed the thrift to spread the loss out over ten years and carry the unamortized portion of the loss as an "asset." RAP also permitted S&Ls to revalue any properties they owned, including their office buildings and branches, to market value and include this "appraised equity capital" in their net worth.[16]

Another critical change under RAP was how thrifts could treat "goodwill," an intangible asset created when businesses merged. Goodwill represents the difference between what a buyer pays for an asset and its market value. Under GAAP, thrifts reported goodwill as an asset and included it in their regulatory net worth calculations. However, GAAP also required that this asset be amortized as an expense within ten years, effectively offsetting the initial gains in equity. RAP extended this amortization period to forty years. The longer amortization led to a rise in thrift mergers, especially between healthy thrifts and those whose loans had lost value when interest rates rose. This was because when such a merger occurred the acquiring S&L would write down the assets to market value. As the loans matured, this write down amount would be amortized by increasing interest income. Significantly, the amortization period for the asset write down was only ten years. Since it was shorter than the goodwill amortization period, the income created by amortizing the asset write down exceeded the goodwill expense. The result was that S&Ls could "literally 'manufacture' earnings and capital by acquiring other thrift[s]." More importantly, regulators encouraged mergers that generated goodwill as a way to reduce the number of problem S&Ls. As a result, by 1983, 67 percent of total RAP regulatory equity was in the form of this intangible asset.[17]

In addition to changing how thrifts calculated their net worth, regulators also modified the industry's regulatory capital guidelines. Prior to 1980, the

---

[16] "Implementation of New Powers Awaits FHLBB, DIDC Rules," *SLN* 103 (November 1982), 8; "How S&Ls Can Hide Their Losses," *Forbes* 128 (14 September 1981), 159; Ahmad Salam, "Congress, RAP, and the Savings and Loan Debacle," *The CPA Journal* 64 (January 1994), 46–7; Bert Ely, *The Role of Accounting in the S&L Crisis*, Consultant Study No. 2 (Washington, DC: NCFIRRE, 1993), 37.

[17] GAAP has since prohibited the amortization of goodwill, and now goodwill is only adjusted for impairment. "Biting the Old Loan Bullet Today Could Mean Less Pain Tomorrow," *SLN* 103 (February 1982), 43–6; "Success in the New World May Depend on How Accountants Keep Score," *SLN* 104 (January 1983), 50–5; Salam, "Congress, RAP, and the Savings and Loan Debacle," 47–50; Ely, *The Role of Accounting in the S&L Crisis*, 37–8; NCFIRRE, *Origins and Causes of the S&L Debacle*, 38–39; Strunk and Case, *Where Deregulation Went Wrong*, 30–4; Rom, *Public Spirit in the Thrift Tragedy*, 63–4, 110–12; Barth, *The Great Savings and Loan Debacle*, 50; FDIC, *History of the Eighties*, quote 174.

FHLBB required the equity of a thrift be no less than 5 percent of total insured accounts. When hundreds of S&Ls could not meet this requirement, the Board was faced with the choice of tightening regulatory scrutiny and control of these technically insolvent thrifts, or lowering the net worth requirement. It chose the latter option. In November 1980 the Board lowered the capital requirement to 4 percent, and in 1982 reduced it further to 3 percent. These actions were significant for a number of reasons. First, lowering the net worth requirement reduced the ability of the Board to restrain thrifts that were most likely to pursue high-yield and high-risk lending strategies intended to improve earnings. Also, the lower equity increased the overall risks to the firms because there was less financial cushion to absorb loan losses. Finally, because the FSLIC was willing to subsidize capital with net worth certificates and generous allowances for intangible assets such as goodwill, the owners of poorly capitalized S&Ls had little incentive to contribute their own funds to the business.[18]

While critics charged that lowering capital requirements and using RAP papered over the problems within the industry, the changes were in many ways unavoidable given the dire condition of the industry in the early 1980s. On the basis of tangible net worth (which excludes goodwill), a total of 415 thrifts with $220 billion (US billion) in assets were insolvent in 1982. This represented 12.6 percent of all S&Ls and 32 percent of total industry assets. Using RAP, however, the Board reported that only 71 thrifts with $12.8 billion (US billion) in assets were insolvent. While RAP understated the true condition of the thrift industry, the more liberal accounting rules allowed regulators to delay closing troubled S&Ls, which helped conserve FSLIC resources. This was an important consideration because the cost of assisting failed thrifts had risen from just $160 million in 1980 to nearly $1.9 billion (US billion) in 1981; in 1982 the FSLIC spent more than $1.5 billion (US billion). Since the new standards reduced the number of regulatory insolvent thrifts, resolution costs fell to just $420 million in 1983. Although the Board contended that its net worth and accounting changes were made to give weaker S&Ls more time to recover, they also limited the ability of regulators to impose greater discipline on thrift managers, allowing some associations to grow into even larger problems.[19]

[18] Barth, *The Great Savings and Loan Debacle*, 133–8; Ely, *The Role of Accounting in the S&L Crisis*, 29–43; FDIC, *History of the Eighties*, 168; White, *The S&L Debacle*, 82–7, 112–15, 150.
[19] Edward J. Kane, *The S&L Insurance Mess: How Did It Happen?* (Washington, DC: The Urban Institute Press, 1989), 24–30; White, *Evolution of the Thrift Crisis*, 13; Allan Sloan, "A Contrarian View of the S&Ls," *Forbes* 128 (26 October 1981), 39–40; "S&Ls in the Candy Store," *Forbes* 131 (6 June 1983), 44–5; "The Saving of the Thrifts," *Newsweek*, 18 April 1983, 59; FDIC, *Managing the Crisis: The FDIC and RTC Experience, 1980–1994*, v. 1 (Washington, DC: FDIC, 1998), 795, 798, 803; White, *The S&L Debacle*, 80; Strunk and Case, *Where Deregulation Went Wrong*, 6–9, 23.

THE CRISIS BEGINS: 1983–1985

The prospects for the thrift industry brightened considerably when the recession ended and robust economic growth returned. Between 1983 and 1985, the gross national product rose an average of 8 percent per year, while short-term interest rates fell from near 11 percent to less than 7 percent; inflation also remained in check during the recovery. For thrifts, these economic conditions led to strong growth in assets and, more importantly, profits. After recording a $4.1 billion (US billion) loss in 1982, the industry posted a $1.9 billion (US billion) profit in 1983, and two years later reported record earnings of $4 billion (US billion). Total industry assets also surged, rising at an average annual rate of 17 percent between 1983 and 1985 to a record $1.1 trillion (US trillion). The result was that individual S&Ls were much larger, with the average association in 1985 holding $339 million in assets, up from the $171 million four years earlier. Furthermore, deregulation had caused these assets to become more diversified. By 1985, less than 44 percent of total industry assets were in traditional 1–4 family mortgages, down from 69 percent in 1979.[20]

While most institutions prospered during the mid-1980s, the gains were particularly impressive in states like Texas, Florida, and California, where some S&Ls actually quadrupled in size during the recovery. A key reason why thrifts in these three states grew so rapidly was because state regulators there had taken thrift deregulation to a new level. When dozens of S&Ls converted from state to federal charters to take advantage of the new lending powers under Garn-St. Germain, California legislators passed the Nolan Bill in December 1982. This law, which was essentially copied in Florida and Texas, removed nearly all lending restrictions on state-chartered thrifts and allowed them to invest up to 100 percent of their deposits in virtually any kind of venture. The expanded lending powers, combined with looser state supervision, caused thrifts in California, Florida, and Texas to mushroom in size. From 1982 to 1985, the combined thrift assets in these three states tripled to $214 billion, which represented 19 percent of total industry assets.[21]

---

[20] Economic growth continued through most of the decade, with an average GNP increase of at least 6 percent per year through 1988. Short-term interest rates also remained stable, never rising above 8.5 percent. Federal Reserve Bank, St. Louis, *FRED II*, *http://research.stlouisfed.org/fred2/*, accessed 31 August 2003; *Savings Institutions Sourcebook*, '86 (Chicago: United States League of Savings Institutions, 1986), 46–49; Robert A. Bennett, "Savings Institutions Are Healthier but Now Face Further Challenges," *The New York Times*, 30 December 1982, A1, D4; Nathaniel C. Nash, "Wall St. Rediscovers the Thrift Stocks," *The New York Times*, 1 December 1985, F10; White, *The S&L Debacle*, 100–1; Office of Thrift Supervision, *1999 Fact Book: A Statistical Profile on the United States Thrift Industry* (Washington, DC: Office of Thrift Supervision, June 2000), 10.

[21] The Nolan Bill required that these investments be held by the thrift's wholly owned, but loosely regulated, service corporation subsidiary. Ramon P. DeGennaro, Larry H. Lang, and

Another important factor in the industry's growth was the boom in construction that occurred following the passage of the Economic Recovery Tax Act of 1981. This law shortened the depreciation period for real estate investments from up to 60 years to 15 years, and made depreciation available to passive investors, not just owners and developers. The effect of these changes was twofold. First, the shorter depreciation period meant that after-tax returns rose significantly, so that initial investments would be earned back in only a few years. Second, extending the benefits to passive investors made real estate investing an ideal tax shelter for individuals, and soon hundreds of real estate investment trusts were funneling millions into new commercial projects.[22]

As the financial condition of most thrifts improved, the League began to encourage managers to take advantage of deregulation and diversify their mortgage loan portfolios. The trade association agreed with regulators that the future of the S&L industry lay in new deregulated business areas, and during the recession League officials singled out the success of several associations that had diversified as proof that this was a profitable strategy. The League, however, also advised thrifts to move cautiously when entering a new business field. It warned managers against making loans in areas they lacked expertise, and offered suggestions for how they could develop new lending skills. One way to acquire expertise was to work with more experienced lenders through the purchase of loan participations, which the League felt offered "big potential" in areas like commercial lending. While this was sound advice, some thrifts became so reliant on commercial and investment banks for new deals and advice that the lenders sometimes failed to conduct their own risk evaluations.[23]

Not all S&Ls followed this "go slow" approach with deregulation. Many of the fastest growing and most profitable thrifts of the mid-1980s were those

---

James B. Thomson, *Troubled Savings and Loan Institutions: Voluntary Restructuring Under Insolvency*, Research Working Paper 9112 (Cleveland, OH: Federal Reserve Bank of Cleveland, 1991), 9; "More Bungled Deregulation," *SLN* 104 (March 1983), 6; Barth, *The Great Savings and Loan Debacle*, 55–6.

[22] NCFIRRE, *Origins and Causes of the S&L Debacle*, 40–1; White, *The S&L Debacle*, 109; FDIC, *History of the Eighties*, 140–1.

[23] In 1982, *Savings and Loan News* profiled four thrifts that successfully took advantage of deregulation, and the League (which had changed its name to the United States League of Savings Institutions in 1983) praised these managers for their "aggressive" business style; by 1992, all four thrifts had failed. "What is the Future for Savings Associations?" *SLN* 103 (August 1982), 82–4; "Thrifts Enter a New Era," *SLN* 103 (November 1982), 37–8, quote 37; "Mutual to Stock Exchange Puts Management in a Fishbowl," *SLN* 104 (January 1983), 50–5; "New Commercial Lenders Swing in the Jungle," *SLN* 104 (May 1983), 50–5; "Hard-Charging Managers Strive for Triumph in New Environment," *SLN* 103 (August 1982), 38–42; "A Market Driven Association Leaps into Consumer and Mortgage Banking," *SLN* 103 (November 1982), 46–50; "Savings Institutions Becoming a Super Business," *SI* 104 (July 1983), quote 46; "Look for a New Name," *SLN* 104 (June 1983), 8.

that quickly embraced new business opportunities outside traditional home finance. In 1984, S&Ls that grew at an annual rate of less than 15 percent held 68 percent of their assets in residential loans, while institutions that grew by more than 50 percent annually held just 53 percent of their assets in mortgages. Furthermore, the slower-growing thrifts relied on traditional retail deposits for nearly 81 percent of their funds, while the "highflying" S&Ls obtained only 59 percent from local markets. Despite the apparent success of the highfliers, and the overall improvement in industry finances, some in Congress feared that the growth associated with deregulation was causing thrifts to stray from their primary mission of meeting the home finance needs of local communities.[24]

These concerns were not, however, shared by the Board and its new chairman Edwin Gray. A San Diego thrift executive and longtime friend of President Reagan, Gray became chairman "because he was supposed to be a dope and patsy who would go along with whatever the U.S. League and the Reagan administration wanted." After taking office in March 1983, Gray's actions appeared to fulfil this assessment as he dutifully supported the spirit of deregulation and continued to give the industry greater business latitude. One such change was the May 1983 decision to let thrifts invest up to 10 percent of assets in high-risk "junk" bonds. Gray also followed Pratt's desire to reduce the level of direct oversight, as evidenced by the 26 percent decline in the number of thrift examinations between 1981 and 1984. While there were fewer thrifts to examine, the reduction also reflected the fact that there were fewer examiners. More importantly, the majority of these examiners had less than two years' experience, in part because low salaries had caused high turnover. This was a potential problem given the increasingly complex lending activities many S&Ls were pursuing.[25]

Gray's "laissez faire" attitude toward the industry ended abruptly in 1984 when regulators closed Empire Savings and Loan of Mesquite, Texas. The liquidation of this one-office, suburban Dallas thrift was notable not just because it required the largest insurance payout in the history of the FSLIC

---

[24] "An Innovator Out Races Problems Via Growth and Astute Investing," *SLN* 103 (August 1982), 48–53; "Freed Institutions Set Sail on Varied Courses," *SI* 104 (July 1983), 72–6; Patrick I. Mahoney and Alice P. White, "The Thrift Industry in Transition," *Federal Reserve Bulletin* 71 (March 1985), 137–56; White, *The S&L Debacle*, 102–6; Rom, *Public Spirit in the Thrift Tragedy*, 158–62; Barth, *The Savings and Loan Debacle*, 25.

[25] Martin Mayer, *The Greatest-Ever Bank Robbery: The Collapse of the Savings and Loan Industry* (New York: Charles Scribner's Sons, 1990), quote 117; Kenneth B. Noble, "Reagan's Friend at the Bank Board," *The New York Times*, 29 May 1983, F17; "New FHLBB Chairman Gray Outlines Goals," *SLN* 104 (June 1983), 9; "Savings Institutions Must Restructure for Survival, New FHLBB Chairman Urges," *SI* 104 (September 1983), 85–91. "Gray Defends Bolstering of Fragile Savings Institutions," *SI* 104 (October 1983), 35; "Changing Institutions Seek New Identity," *SI* 104 (July 1983), 51–6; White, *Evolution of the Thrift Crisis*, 13; White, *The S&L Debacle*, 88–90; Rom, *Public Spirit in the Thrift Debacle*, 87–100; Barth, *The Great Savings and Loan Debacle*, 129; Strunk and Case, *Where Deregulation Went Wrong*, 138–46.

up to that time, but also because it resulted from massive insider fraud. The presence of fraud convinced Gray to reverse the process of deregulation, and for the remainder of his tenure the Board imposed stricter regulatory and supervisory measures to refocus the industry on home finance. Over the next two years, the Board reinstated limits on deposit brokers (seen as a cause of the Empire failure), restricted the ability of thrifts to make direct invests in equity securities, required all new thrifts to have at least 7 percent in owner equity, and began raising the minimum net worth requirement for the entire industry toward a goal of 6 percent of assets.[26]

Gray also tried to increase the level of supervision by transferring control of the federal examiners who conducted S&L audits from the Board to the individual home loan banks. Because the thrift industry owned the home loan banks, critics charged that the move was tantamount to "the fox watching the hen house." The move, however, meant that thrift examiners were no longer federal employees, which allowed officials to hire more staff and raise their salaries. As a result, by 1986 examiner salaries had increased by a third while the size of the examination force had nearly doubled. Although League officials publically applauded Gray's initiatives, calling them effective ways to "prevent more damage [caused by] a host of problems brought on by deregulation," in private they were much less supportive. Thrift lobbyists pressured Gray not to pursue his get-tough policies, and on Capitol Hill they portrayed the Board chairman as overly pessimistic about industry problems. Even the Reagan administration failed to support Gray, as both Pratt and chief of staff Donald Regan openly criticized his work.[27]

THE CRISIS INTENSIFIES: 1985–1987

The League's insistence that the industry was financially sound was seriously questioned in 1985 when thrift failures in Ohio and Maryland sparked statewide consumer panics. In March, Home State Savings Bank in Cincinnati, a $1.4 billion (U.S. billion) thrift, experienced deposit runs after it lost more than $540 million in an elaborate securities scam perpetrated by Florida-based ESM Government Securities Inc. What made the problems at Home State particularly serious was that, like most Ohio thrifts, it was insured by a private state insurance program, not by the FSLIC. As the panic spread, it became apparent that the state fund could not meet depositor

[26] Nathaniel C. Nash, "Bank Board's Embattled Chief," *The New York Times*, 4 November 1985, D1, D6; "Making S&Ls Pay for Living Dangerously," *Business Week*, 9 September 1985, 30–1; Gary Hector, "The Thrift Industry is Under Siege Again," *Fortune*, 15 October, 1984, 175–7, 180, 184–5; Eichler, *The Thrift Debacle*, 104–6; NICFIRRE, *Origins and Causes of the S&L Debacle*, 56; Rom, *Public Spirit in the Thrift Debacle*, 97–8.
[27] Nash, "Bank Board's Embattled Chief," quote D6; Kathleen Day, *S&L Hell: The People and the Politics Behind the $1 Trillion Savings & Loan Scandal* (New York: W.W. Norton & Co., 1993), 148–52, 178–9, 181–95; NICFIRRE, *Origins and Causes of the S&L Debacle*, 57.

claims and within days Gov. Richard F. Celeste ordered all 71 state-insured institutions closed for three days to stem the runs. This closing, which allowed officials to examine the thrifts and move the healthy institutions to federal insurance, was the first bank holiday since the Great Depression.[28]

Two months later, the Maryland state insurance fund experienced similar runs when reports surfaced of a criminal investigation involving fraudulent lending practices at Old Court Savings and Loan in Baltimore. Depositors besieged the $850 million thrift demanding their funds, and within days it had to be closed by the state. By mid-May, all 102 Maryland thrifts covered by the state deposit insurance program were experiencing deposit runs, and, in order to prevent the complete collapse of the program, Gov. Harry R. Hughes ordered that monthly withdrawals be limited to $1,000 per account. The crisis began to subside in June after the Maryland legislature passed a law requiring all state-insured S&Ls to become members of the FSLIC within six months or face liquidation. By the end of the year, the panics in Ohio and Maryland were over, but both insurance funds had been bankrupted at a cost of more than $250 million to state taxpayers.[29]

Significantly, the problems in Ohio and Maryland were not isolated, and by 1986 hundreds of thrifts were again losing millions. That year, the losses reported by the 27 percent of the industry that was unprofitable nearly equaled the combined profits of all the remaining thrifts. In 1987 the share of the industry losing money rose to 35 percent, and the $14.4 billion (US billion) in losses they incurred far exceeded the $6.6 billion (US billion) in income posted by the profitable S&Ls. One reason so many thrifts were losing money was that the Southwest, especially Texas, had entered a sharp regional recession brought on by a decline in domestic crude oil prices. Oil prices began to fall in 1984, and by August 1986 the price of oil had dropped more than 60 percent to just $10 per barrel. Since the Texas economy lost an estimated 25,000 jobs and $100 million in revenues with each $1 drop in the price of oil, the collapse in energy costs also led to a decline in real estate values and a rise in office vacancy rates. In Houston, nearly a third of all its

[28] Gary Klott, "71 Savings Institutions Shut for 3 Days in Effort to Stem Run," *The New York Times*, 16 March 1985, 1; Donald L. Maggin, *Bankers, Builders, Knaves, and Thieves: The $300 Million Scam at ESM* (Chicago: Contemporary Books, 1989), 140–5, 173–7; J. Huston McCulloch, "The Ohio S&L Crisis in Retrospect: Implications for the Current Federal Deposit Insurance Crisis," and Edward J. Kane, "Who Should Learn What From the Failure and Delayed Bail-out of the ODGB?" in *Merging Commercial and Investment Banking*, Proceedings of a Conference on Bank Structure and Competition (Chicago: Federal Reserve Bank of Chicago, 1987), 230–51, 306–26; Day, *S&L Hell*, 17–20.

[29] Eric N. Berg, "Maryland Assess Thrift Unit Woes," *The New York Times*, 1 July 1985, D1; Eric N. Berb, "Maryland Thrift Unit Moratorium," *The New York Times*, 20 August 1985, D1; Walker F. Todd, *Similarities and Dissimilarities in the Collapses of Three State-Chartered Private Deposit Insurance Funds*, Federal Reserve Bank of Cleveland, Working Paper No. 9411, October 1994, 7–8; Day, *S&L Hell*, 21–7; Kane, *The S&L Insurance Mess*, 129–40; Day, *S&L Hell*, 21–7.

office space was unoccupied, and 17 percent of all homes and apartments were vacant. For local thrifts, the economic decline was devastating. Once held up as examples of how deregulation had succeeded, by 1986 dozens of Texas S&Ls were losing millions.[30]

A second factor that contributed to the drop in industry profits was an overall reduction in real estate construction. While the decline was caused in part by an oversupply of commercial space, changes in federal tax laws were also a factor. The Tax Reform Act of 1986 lengthened the depreciation periods for real estate and limited the ability of passive investors to use these investments as tax shelters. These tax incentives were important in fueling the building boom of the early 1980s, and their elimination led to a sharp reduction in new real estate investment. After growing fivefold between 1981 and 1985 to $16 billion (US billion), total sales of real estate partnerships plummeted, and by 1989 were attracting just $1.5 billion (US billion) in new capital. The decline in investment funds led to a corresponding drop in non-residential construction, with states such as Texas, Arizona, and California being hit the hardest.[31]

Ironically, the true financial condition of the industry was much worse than regulators thought, since dozens of S&Ls in serious financial difficulty found ways to escape regulatory scrutiny. One way managers of troubled thrifts hid their problems was by trading their bad loans for the bad loans of another association, a process known as "swapping dead cows for dead horses." Even though the loans were still nonperforming after these transactions, regulatory accounting rules allowed them to be treated as new assets that gave managers up to six more months before they had to write them down. These and other bizarre deals led one journalist to quip that if Frank Capra made his move *It's a Wonderful Life* about an S&L owner in the 1980s, Jimmy Stewart's speech to the angry depositors would be "Your money's not here. Why your money's in racehorses, a bordello in Nevada, a share in the Dallas Cowboys, a nitrogen-cooled tank filled with vials of buffalo semen, vacant shopping malls, and unneeded condominiums. . . ."[32]

DEALING WITH THE DEBACLE: 1985–1987

Even though the vast majority of all S&Ls were profitable during the mid-1980s, the steady rise of unprofitable associations was a major concern for the Board and the FSLIC. In 1985, regulators reported that 130 thrifts

---

[30] FDIC, *History of the Eighties*, 169, 294–6; FDIC, *Managing the Crisis*, 795, 798, 808; White, *The S&L Debacle*, 114, 136–8, 149–50; Rom, *Public Spirit in the Thrift Tragedy*, 178; NCFIRRE, *Origins and Causes of the S&L Debacle*, 60–1.

[31] FDIC, *History of the Eighties*, 303–5; White, *The S&L Debacle*, 109–11; Barth, *The Great Savings and Loan Debacle*, 45.

[32] James Ring Adams, *The Big Fix: Inside the S&L Scandal* (New York: John Wiley and Sons, 1989), 220; Day, *S&L Hell*, 191–2, quote 192.

were insolvent on the basis of RAP, up from 71 the year before. By 1986, 255 thrifts with $68 billion in assets were RAP-insolvent. As the number of insolvent thrifts rose, the cost of assisting them also skyrocketed. After spending $800 million in 1984 to resolve failed thrifts, the FSLIC spent $7.4 billion in 1985 and $9.1 billion in 1986. As a result, the reserves of the thrift insurer, which were $6.2 billion in 1980, fell to less than $2 billion by the end of 1986. This was especially troublesome since the total insured deposits covered by the FSLIC had risen from $459 billion to almost $810 billion over the same period.[33]

As FSLIC resources declined, regulators tired to employ more cost-effective means of managing failed thrifts. One approach was the management consignment plan (MCP), in which existing thrift management was replaced by new officers "on consignment" from other S&Ls. Applied to thrifts that were unlikely to follow supervisory orders, the goal of the MCP, which began in 1985, was not to bring the S&L back to health but to give the FSLIC more time to dispose its assets. The new managers were to "clean up" the thrift by bringing losses under control and making accurate assessments of its problems. This would hopefully increase the value of the thrift and make it easier to sell. While most people agreed that the MCP was a good idea, it did not work out as planned. MCP managers were given little incentive to put in the effort needed to turn around these institutions, and in some cases the executives simply acted as caretakers. Furthermore, the decline in FSLIC resources meant that the MCP became a "dumping ground" for some of the sickest institutions. As a result, some thrifts remained in this frozen state of limbo for up to three years as regulators tried to sell them.[34]

The increase in failed thrifts also meant that the FSLIC had to dispose of millions in thrift assets, and to assist in this process regulators formed the Federal Asset Disposition Association (FADA), an organization dedicated to managing and selling these loans. Also created in 1985, FADA was essentially an S&L whose stock was owned entirely by the FSLIC. Intended to operate like the HOLC in the 1930s, FADA bought bad loans from the FSLIC and sold them to outside buyers. Since FADA was not a government entity, it was exempt from federal disclosure rules and federal hiring guidelines. This allowed FADA to pay the high salaries needed to attract the skilled professionals required for the evaluation and sale of these loans. While FADA, like the MCP, was conceptually sound, it too failed to meet expectations. Legislators resented the independence of FADA, and often clashed with its officials on matters of fiscal accountability. This was especially true after

---

[33] White, *The S&L Debacle*, 114; FDIC, *Managing the Crisis*, 795, 798, 808; Office of Thrift Supervision, 2002 *Fact Book: A Statistical Profile of the Thrift Industry*. (Washington, DC: Office of Thrift Supervision, April 2003), 11.

[34] White, *The S&L Debacle*, 144; FDIC, *Managing the Crisis*, 68; Richard W. Stevenson, "A Good Idea Gone Sour: Savings Talent on Loan," *The New York Times*, 8 June 1988, D1, D9.

accusations surfaced of political favoritism within the association. The persistence of these criticisms hindered the effectiveness of FADA, and in 1989 Congress legislated it out of existence.[35]

By early 1986, regulators realized that the magnitude of the problems they faced far exceeded the resources of the FSLIC. Consequently, to end the thrift crisis and maintain consumer confidence, a full recapitalization of the insurance fund was needed. In April 1986, the White House sent Congress a formal plan to recapitalize the insurance fund by $15 billion, but legislators did not act on the request with any sense of urgency. One source of delay was from legislators who wanted the Board to first crack down on thrift abuses before the FSLIC received more money. Another problem was finding the budget cuts needed to comply with the Gramm-Rudman-Hollings anti-deficit law. Even the Reagan administration did not push Congress to act, in part because it wanted to avoid unfavorable publicity. As a result, the Senate did not pass its version of FSLIC recapitalization until the last day of the session in October 1986. Unfortunately, House Banking Committee chairman St. Germain was indignant of being put in "a take-it-or-leave-it position" and refused to consider the Senate bill. As a result, it would be at least six more months before the FSLIC could begin to receive more money.[36]

When the 100th Congress met in January 1987, FSLIC recapitalization was at the top of its agenda, but as was true in the previous session quick passage of legislation to replenish the depleted insurance fund did not occur. This time, the stumbling block was the fact that both the Senate and House approved measures that combined FSLIC funding with other more complex financial reforms. The Senate version included provisions that limited the ability of commercial banks to underwrite securities and placed new restrictions on unregulated financial institutions. These reforms were prompted in part by the Ivan Boesky stock insider-trading scandal. The House bill, which was strongly supported by the new House Speaker, Jim Wright (D-TX), required regulators to follow new guidelines in their supervision of troubled

[35] Nathaniel C. Nash, "Plan to Sell F.S.L.I.C.'s Bad Assets," *The New York Times*, 6 November 1985, D1; Stewart B. McKinney, "Blame Management and Budget for Thrifts Mess," *The New York Times*, 22 October 1985, A27; "Who's Killing the Thrifts?" *Newsweek*, 10 November 1986, 51–2; John H. Crockett, *On the Good Bank/Bad Bank Restructuring of Failed Thrifts*, Research Working Paper No. 129 (Washington, DC: Federal Home Loan Bank Board, May 1987); Eichler, *The Thrift Debacle*, 101–2; Martin Lowy, *High Rollers: Inside the Savings and Loan Debacle* (New York: Praeger, 1991), 212–13.

[36] Nathaniel C. Nash, "400 Thrift Units Called Effectively Unsound," *The New York Times*, 3 June 1985, D1, D14; "High-Rollers Among the Thrifts," *The New York Times*, 16 October 1985, A26; "Its Touch-and-Go for Troubled Thrifts," *US News and World Report*, 4 March 1985, 92; "Washington Wrangles as Thrift Crisis Deepens," *Business Week*, 27 May 1985, 127–30; "Powerful Prescript for Ailing Thrifts," *Business Week*, 4 November 1985, 29; *Savings Institutions Sourcebook*, '89 (Chicago: United States League of Savings Institutions, 1989), 52, 64; Eichler, *The Thrift Debacle*, 102; Rom, *Public Spirit in the Thrift Tragedy*, 171–4; NICFIRRE, *Origins and Causes of the S&L Debacle*, 57–9.

thrifts. The bill required regulators to "forbear" and allow thrifts with very low net worth ratios (as little as 0.5 percent of liabilities) to continue to operate provided they met other "good faith" tests. In terms of new borrowing authority for the FSLIC, the Senate and House gave the insurer $7.5 billion and $5 billion, respectively. Significantly, both figures were a fraction of the amount originally requested by the Board and the White House.[37]

While some legislators resisted giving the FSLIC more money out of budget concerns, the main reason both the House and Senate insisted on lower aid amounts was that legislators had bowed to the intense pressure of League lobbying. Industry leaders maintained that the Board was exaggerating the level of industry problems, and League executive William O'Connell even stated that regulators had precipitated the crisis. While it generally opposed recapitalization, the League assured legislators that the lower aid amounts would be "absolutely more than enough" to meet the FSLIC needs given the fact that the majority of the industry was both healthy and profitable. Another sign of the League's power was its ability to secure regulatory forbearance in the House bill, even though the White House strongly opposed it. Siding with the League position that harsh and arbitrary regulatory actions were interfering with legitimate business operations and that the Board needed to be "put on a short leash," Speaker Wright made it clear that no bill would be passed without forbearance. Significantly, this was not the first time that Wright had displayed his willingness to support the thrift industry. In 1986, he met with Edwin Gray at the request of several Texas thrift executives to protest how the Board was supervising S&Ls in his state, actions that led to accusations that Wright was meddling in regulatory affairs.[38]

Although the final bill passed by both chambers in July 1987 increased the FSLIC funding to $8.5 billion (US billion), the White House still threatened a veto unless the amount was raised further. One reason for the Reagan administration's insistence on this position was that a recent General Accounting Office report found that the FSLIC spent more in 1986 than

---

[37] Nathaniel C. Nash, "Financial Legislation, Perhaps," *The New York Times*, 8 January 1987, D1, D7; Noel Fahey, "US League Self-Help Plan Calls for FSLIC Funding, 'Two-Tiered' Supervision," *SI* 108 (February 1987), 51, 60–2; "US League Renews Push for FSLIC Funds, Forbearance," *SI* 108 (April 1987), 54–7; Robert D. Hershey Jr., "F.S.L.I.C. Aid Gains in Senate," *The New York Times*, 11 March 1987, D1; White, *The S&L Debacle*, 135–42.

[38] The power of the thrift lobby was reflected by one executive who said, "My congressman, who is a Republican, called me up and asked me how he should vote, and I told him the $5 billion package. He said 'The White House is telling me to vote on the $15 billion, but if you say so, I'll go with the $5 billion.'" Richard L. Berke, "Officials Say House Speaker Intervened in Texan's Case," *The New York Times*, 22 June 1987, 17; "Wright Pushes Thrift Unit Aid," *The New York Times*, 9 February 1987, quote D2; Nathaniel C. Nash, "Savings-Loan Units Flex Their Lobbying Muscles," *The New York Times*, 26 June 1987, sec. IV, 4; Nathaniel C. Nash, "Experts Express Pessimism on Savings Industry's Future," *The New York Times*, 8 May 1987, A1, D2, quote D2; Nathaniel C. Nash, "Bank Board to Ease Net-Worth Rules for Ailing Thrifts," *The New York Times*, 27 February 1987, D6.

previously reported, and that it had in fact been bankrupt since the end of that year. Furthermore, the GAO estimated that the thrift insurer now had a *negative* net worth of $6.3 billion (US billion). Fearing that news of an FSLIC bankruptcy would cause a consumer confidence crisis and deposit runs, Treasury Secretary James Baker met with congressional leaders to craft a compromise and avoid a veto. In exchange for raising the FSLIC recapitalization amount, the White House agreed to accept forbearance provided it was phased-out in three years, and on August 11, 1987, President Reagan signed the Competitive Equality Banking Act (CEBA) into law.[39]

CEBA gave the FSLIC $10.8 billion in new funding, and essentially reaffirmed the full faith and credit of the government behind all federal deposit insurance programs. To avoid increasing the federal deficit, these funds would be raised "off budget" and come from the sale of government-backed bonds through a special-purpose entity known as the Financing Corporation (FICO). While the recapitalization of the FSLIC was the centerpiece of CEBA, there were other important provisions. To encourage thrifts to make more home loans, the law established the Qualified Thrift Lender (QTL) test that required all S&Ls to hold a minimum 60 percent of assets in areas related to residential finance. If a thrift did not meet the test, its ability to borrow from the home loan banks would be restricted. CEBA also required regulators to follow more lenient procedures when supervising thrifts in economically depressed areas. This applied to any "well-managed and viable" S&L that had equity capital of 0.5 percent or more and was experiencing financial problems that were "beyond its control."[40]

Although CEBA reassured the public that their deposits were "now good," critics attacked it as flawed legislation that limited the ability of regulators to end the S&L crisis. For example, even though the FSLIC received $10.8 billion in new funding, the amount that could be borrowed in any twelve-month period was limited to just $3.75 billion. This restriction meant that regulators still had to exercise restraint in how they allocated insurance funds. More importantly, regulatory forbearance was interpreted as a signal for regulators to "back off." Although it was intended to give shaky but well-managed thrifts more time to recover, forbearance had the perverse effect of allowing poorly run S&Ls engage in riskier lending and grow larger.

[39] Nathaniel C. Nash, "Anatomy of the Skirmishing for a Veto," *The New York Times*, 13 July 1987, 14; Nathaniel C. Nash, "Final Battles Shape Up On Major Banking Bill," *The New York Times*, 27 July 1987, D1, D6; Nathaniel C. Nash, "Deal Made on Major Bank Bill," *The New York Times*, 29 July 1987, D1; Nathaniel C. Nash, "Senate Accepts Compromise Bill on Banking System," *The New York Times*, 5 August 1987, A1, D5.

[40] House Committee on Banking, Housing, and Urban Affairs, *Competitive Equality Banking Act of 1987*, 100th Congress, 1st sess., Report 100-261 (Washington, DC: USGPO, 1987), 1–15; Nash, "Senate Accepts Compromise Bill on Banking System," D5; Robert D. Hershey Jr., "Unit to Aid F.S.L.I.C. is Set Up," *The New York Times*, 29 August 1987, 35, 37; FDIC, *Managing the Crisis*, 81; Barth, *The Great Savings and Loan Debacle*, 125–6.

The result was that when these institutions did finally fail, the cost to the FSLIC was significantly higher.[41]

Although regulators now had the means to attack the S&L crisis in earnest, the delays in recapitalizing the FSLIC had allowed it to deepen. By 1987, 351 thrifts, or about 11 percent of the industry, were RAP-insolvent, and these institutions controlled more than $99 billion in assets. The situation was especially bad in Texas, where 109 thrifts, equal to 40 percent of all S&Ls in the state, were RAP-insolvent, and the losses of these institution accounted for more than half of all S&L losses nationwide in 1987. Even healthy Texas thrifts were affected by the problems of sick S&Ls as depositors, already leery of the health of the FSLIC, began demanding higher rates. Eventually, most Texas thrifts had to pay 0.5 percent more than what other S&Ls paid just to retain their deposits. This "Texas premium" added millions to operating costs and threatened to push even more S&Ls into insolvency.[42]

These problems, however, did not appear to alarm the new Board chairman M. Danny Wall. A staff director for Sen. Jake Garn, Wall became chairman shortly before the passage of CEBA, and unlike Gray, he had no prior experience in finance and lacked an analytical knowledge of the thrift industry. He was a natural optimist who consistently assured legislators that the crisis was not very severe and that everything was under control. Even after the agency announced that the industry had lost nearly $4 billion in the first quarter of 1988, Wall maintained that he had "no reason to change my position that we can handle the problems with the resources we have." Although Wall, like all previous Board chairmen, underestimated the true magnitude of the S&L crisis, his persistently rosy forecasts for recovery (many of which ran counter to the more dire reports from independent agencies like the congressional Budget Office) hurt his credibility with Congress. Eventually, some legislators and staffers on Capitol Hill began to refer to the Board chairman as M. Danny Isuzu (after the chronic liar on a television commercial) or as M. Danny Off-the-Wall.[43]

[41] Nash, "Senate Accepts Compromise Bill on Banking System," quote A1; White, *Evolution of the Thrift Crisis,* 20; Adams, *The Big Fix,* 40–8, quote 40. Not all critics agree that passing a more stringent law would have ended the thrift crisis quicker. See White, *The S&L Debacle,* 140–2, and Rom, *Public Spirit in the Thrift Tragedy,* 171–8, 186–8.

[42] White, *The S&L Debacle,* 151; Thomas C. Hayes, "Even Strong Suffer in State Thrift Crisis," *The New York Times,* 18 May 1987, D1, D5; NCFIRRE, *Origins and Causes of the S&L Debacle,* 59.

[43] Nathaniel C. Nash, "Staying Calm – Maybe Too Calm – in the Midst of a Crisis," *The New York Times,* 26 June 1988, sec. 3, 7; DeGennaro, *Troubled Savings and Loan Institutions,* 2–3; White, *Evolution of the Thrift Crisis,* 20; Adams, *The Big Fix,* 53–5, 57–60; Rom, *Public Spirit in the Thrift Tragedy,* 66–7; Day, *S&L Hell,* 284, 292.

Skepticism of Wall's credibility increased during 1988 when the Board initiated the "Southwest Plan," an ambitious effort to sell dozens of insolvent thrifts and eliminate the Texas premium. The goal of the plan was to sell groups of adjacent or complementary thrifts to new investors, who would then consolidate operations, close overlapping branches, and hopefully return the institution to profitability. Regulators chose this approach because unlike liquidation, finding an acquirer for an S&L was generally the least costly method of disposition, since it minimized direct cash outlays and preserved the "going concern" value of the association. Unfortunately, since the liabilities of these S&Ls exceeded the value of assets, the FSLIC had to offer a number of incentives to attract buyers, including loans and promises of future payments to offset losses. The main reason buyers were expected to participate was that they could include the losses from the acquired thrift in their overall financial results, which could result in significant tax savings. Because this benefit would expire at the end of the year when new tax laws went into effect, all sales had to be completed before January 1, 1989.[44]

By marketing the thrifts to a wide array of prospective investors, including other S&Ls, commercial banks, corporations like Ford Motor Company, and even wealthy individuals, the Board had high hopes for the Southwest Plan. Initially, however, it had trouble arranging sales. While bureaucratic "red tape" was one source of problems, the main reason for the slow progress was that there were few prospective buyers. Because no one was certain that "things have hit bottom," investors were reluctant to buy S&Ls without broad financial support from the FSLIC. Consequently, only two deals were completed by June 1988. Furthermore, because investors contributed only $30 million while the FSLIC pledged to provide more than $2.3 billion (US billion) in aid, Rep. Ferdinand J. St. Germain derided them as "more bail-out than workout." Criticism intensified when Wall told Congress in July that the estimated cost of the Southwest Plan would be $15 billion and not the $7 billion he had stated just six weeks earlier. Such pessimistic forecasts, combined with industry statements vowing to contribute "no more than an additional few billion dollars" to help Congress deal with the S&L crisis, caused legislators for the first time to talk about the need for a taxpayer bail-out.[45]

Despite the early problems, in the second half of the year the number of sales under the Southwest Plan increased, and by the end of November

44 White, *The S&L Debacle*, 157–60; NCFIRRE, *Origins and Causes of the S&L Debacle*, 60; Adams, *The Big Fix*, 57–8; Rom, *Public Spirit in the Thrift Tragedy*, 83–5; Day, *S&L Hell*, 282–3; Lowy, *High Rollers*, 199–204.
45 Nathaniel C. Nash, "Bank Board Doubles Texas Cost Estimate," *The New York Times*, 8 July 1988, D1, D2; Thomas C. Hayes, "Doubts Emerge About Plan to Aid Texas Savings Units," *The New York Times*, 9 July 1988, 35, 37, quote 31; Nathaniel C. Nash, "Fight Seen on Savings Insurance," *The New York Times*, 1 November 1988, D1, D2, quote D1; Day, *S&L Hell*, 290–1.

the Board had resolved 104 thrifts. With the tax deadline approaching, the number of sales rose sharply, and in the first twenty-five days of December regulators disposed of 41 more S&Ls. Round-the-clock negotiations during the last five days of the year resulted in the sale of an additional 34 thrifts. In the largest transaction, Fort Worth financier Robert M. Bass bought a thrift with $30 billion in assets for $500 million and $1.7 billion of federal guarantees against future losses. A group led by Revlon chairman Ronald Perleman invested $315 million to buy five thrifts, and got tax deductions valued at $897.3 million. In the last week of the year alone, the Board agreed to spend $13.8 billion over the next ten years to cover the future losses of the acquired S&Ls. Still, the frenetic pace of activity allowed the FSLIC to resolve a record number of thrifts in 1988. For the entire year, regulators disposed of 205 thrifts with $102 billion (US billion) in assets at an estimated cost of $36 billion (US billion); the Southwest Plan accounted for $32.6 billion (US billion) of this amount.[46]

The cost and generous concessions made by regulators under the Southwest Plan, however, surprised many in Congress. Sen. Howard M. Metzenbaum (D-OH) charged that the sales were "short sighted, irresponsible, and ultimately unfair to the U.S. taxpayers." Although critics derided the 1988 deals as windfalls for the wealthy, the Board defended them as an efficient way to stretch thin resources. Furthermore, they argued that the transactions were not "giveaways" but designed to maximize the returns to the government. For example, while it was true that the FSLIC would incur future losses if a buyer sold thrift assets for less than book value, if the buyer sold the assets for more than book value the government was entitled to receive a share of the gain. The Southwest Plan deals also allowed regulators to repurchase assets if they felt the original buyer was not managing or selling them properly. Finally, when the FSLIC sold the insolvent thrifts it received warrants that it could convert into a percentage of the stock in the new thrift should it prosper under the new owner. Despite these mechanisms to minimize costs, adverse publicity created the impression that the Texas transactions were a government bail-out of the industry. Furthermore, because there were still 250 RAP-insolvent thrifts with nearly $81 billion in assets at the end of 1988, the S&L crisis appeared far from over.[47]

---

[46] The total resolution costs for 1988 would later be revised upward to $46.6 billion. Thomas C. Hayes, "13 More Savings Bail-outs Set," *The New York Times*, 30 December 1988, D1, D12; Nathaniel C. Nash, "Financiers Sense an Opportunity in the Savings Industry's Distress," *The New York Times*, 1 January 1989, sec. 1, 16; Nathaniel C. Nash, U.S. Bank Board Adds Seven More Ailing Savings and Loans to Its Pile of Bail-outs," *The New York Times*, 1 January 1989, sec. 1, 16; Nathaniel C. Nash, "Bank Board's Wild Week of Round-the-Clock Deals," *The New York Times*, 3 January 1989, A1, D8; Mayer, *The Greatest-Ever Bank Robbery*, 249–59; Paul Zane Pilzer, *Other People's Money: The Inside Story of the S&L Mess* (New York: Simon and Schuster, 1989), 203–32; Adams, *The Big Fix*, 58.

[47] Nash, "Bank Board's Wild Week of Round-the-Clock Deals," quote D8; "Regulators Bungled Texas S&L Bail-outs, Study Says," *The Washington Post*, 2 January 1991, D3; White,

PROFILES OF FAILURE

Toward the end of the 1980s, several best-selling books and magazine articles detailing the seamier aspects of the crisis further tarnished the already damaged reputation of the thrift industry. These accounts typically focused on the activities of "highflying" S&Ls, many of which were led by executives who were the antitheses of the traditional conservative thrift leaders. These flamboyant managers included Stanley Adams of Lamar Savings and Loan in Austin, Texas, who filed for an application with regulators to open a branch on the moon, and Don Dixon of Vernon Savings and Loan in Dallas, who used bank funds to buy a private plane used to conduct "market studies" of world-class restaurants in France. Dixon also had the bank pay for his $1.8 million in luxury cars and $2 million beach house, which cost an additional $200,000 to furnish; this figure included the $36,760 his wife spent for flowers. By the end of the decade both these S&Ls were insolvent. Lamar Savings and Loan, with $1.9 billion in assets, cost more than $2 billion (US billion) to clean up, while at the $1.7 billion Vernon Savings and Loan, 94 percent of its loans were nonperforming.[48]

Another highflying S&L was Columbia Savings and Loan of Beverly Hills California. Its failure highlighted the problems associated with diversifying into areas outside home mortgages. Columbia took advantage of deregulation by investing heavily in high-risk, high-yield securities known as junk bonds. Working with the leading architect of the junk bond market, investment banker Michael Milken of Drexel Burnham Lambert, Columbia grew from $373 million in assets in 1981 to more than $10 billion (US billion) in just five years. With nearly $3 billion (US billion) in junk bond assets, Columbia had become one of the most profitable thrifts in the nation, and its chief executive Thomas Spiegel was receiving media attention for the success of his nontraditional investment strategy as well as his $5.4 million annual salary. The praise for Columbia, however, was shortlived. Between 1989 and 1990, the collapse of junk bond prices, combined with stricter accounting rules, had produced $1.3 billion (US billion) in losses for Columbia, and placed it nearly $900 million short of its minimum capital requirements. In January 1991 regulators took control of the thrift, and in September

---

The *S&L Debacle*, 159–60; Rom, *Public Spirit in the Thrift Tragedy*, 86; Mayer, *The Greatest-Ever Bank Robbery*, 256; Lowy, *High Rollers*, 204–11; FDIC, *History of the Eighties*, 186.

[48] Examples of magazine articles that appeared between 1988 and 1990 include "High-Rolling Texas: The State That Ate FSLIC," *Business Week*, 31 October 1988, 138–40; James K. Glassman, "The Great Banks Robbery," *The New Republic* (8 October 1990), 16–17; "Bonfire of the S&Ls," *Newsweek*, 21 May 1990, 20–5; Steven Waldman and Rich Thomas, "How Did It Happen?" *Newsweek*, 21 May 1990, 27–32; "Villians of the S&L Crisis," *U.S. News and World Report*, 1 October 1990, 53–9; P. J. O'Rourke, "Piggy Banks," *Rolling Stone Magazine*, 24 August 1989, 43–4; James O'Shea, *The Daisy Chain: How Borrowed Billions Sank a Texas S&L* (New York: Pocket Books, 1991), 25–30; Adams, *The Big Fix*, 220–1; Strunk and Case, *Where Deregulation Went Wrong*, 89–95.

began the largest payout in banking history of $3.25 billion (US billion) to depositors.[49]

One of the most widely publicized insolvencies was that of Lincoln Savings and Loan and its owner Charles Keating. Keating, an influential figure in the Arizona and California Republican parties, acquired Lincoln in 1984 and in five years expanded it from a $1 billion S&L into a $4.9 billion (US billion) behemoth. Keating achieved this growth by transforming Lincoln from a thrift that made exclusively home loans into an S&L that financed multimillion-dollar hotels, invested in speculative stocks and junk bonds, but made almost no mortgage loans. In 1987, when the regional home loan bank recommended Lincoln be seized immediately after an audit uncovered evidence of fraud and other criminal acts, Keating turned to his political connections for help. In April, 1987 Senators Dennis DeConcini (D-AZ), John McCain (R-AZ), Alan Cranston (D-WY), John Glenn (D-OH), and Donald Riegle (D-MI) met with Board chairman Gray to question the appropriateness of the Lincoln investigation and urge that it be curtailed. When it was revealed that these five senators (known as the "Keating Five") received a combined $1.3 million in direct and indirect campaign contributions from Keating, they became the subject of a congressional ethics investigation. Interestingly, Gray was not dissuaded by the Keating Five, but when Wall became chairman, regulatory pressure on Lincoln eased; Wall would later resign in December 1989 in part because he did not push for more aggressive oversight of Lincoln. When the thrift finally failed in 1989 it cost taxpayers over $2.6 billion (US billion).[50]

Possibly the most egregious displays of excess involved Edwin T. McBirney of Sunbelt Savings in Dallas. McBirney bought Sunbelt in 1981 when he was 31 years old, and within four years he had expanded it from $90 million in assets to more than $3.2 billion (US billion). Nicknamed "Gunbelt" Savings, the thrift was notorious for its reckless lending. "Fast Eddy" McBirney negotiated so many multibillion-dollar deals on the tablecloth of his favorite Dallas eatery that the owner began covering the table in paper. Like Dixon, McBirney had his thrift pay for lavish parties at his palatial home, a chauffeured limousine, and a fleet of seven planes which he used to make frequent

---

[49] The actual cost to the government of closing Columbia was $274 million. Connie Bruck, *The Predators' Ball* (New York: Penguin Books, 1989), 91–3; Richard W. Stevenson, "Savings and Loans that Prosper," *The New York Times*, 28 February 1989, D1; "Warning on Savings Unit Reported," *The New York Times*, 4 December 1989, D9; "$3.5 Billion 'Junk Bond' Sale Sought," *The New York Times*, 15 March 1990, D1; Michael Lev, "U.S. Seizes Columbia Savings," *The New York Times*, 26 January 1991, 43; Michael Lev, "Columbia Savings Shut Down By U.S.," *The New York Times*, 15 March 1990, D6.

[50] Mayer, *The Greatest-Ever Bank Robbery*, 165–225; Glassman, "The Great Banks Robbery," 18–19; Michael Binstein and Charles Bowden, *Trust Me: Charles Keating and the Missing Billions* (New York: Random House, 1993), 209–88; Lowy, *High Rollers*, 146–52; Day, *S&L Hell*, 344–5.

trips to Las Vegas. The failure of Sunbelt in 1988 cost the government nearly $3.8 billion (US billion), an amount made all the more remarkable by the fact that the thrift's assets at the time were worth only $2.2 billion. Such stories of fraud and abuse incensed the public to such an extent that when Congress held hearings on S&L fraud in 1990, a banner hung over the Senate committee that read "When are the Savings and Loan Crooks Going to Jail?"[51]

CONCLUSIONS

The events of the 1980s severely damaged the image of all thrifts, and nearly devastated the industry. Between 1980 and 1989, a total of 890 S&Ls with $347.8 billion (US billion) in assets went out of business, and a review of the S&L failures reveals some common characteristics. First, many of the insolvencies in the early 1980s were smaller S&Ls with an average of $302 million in assets, and many failed because of losses associated with high interest rates and the recession. The thrifts that failed after 1985 were much larger, with an average of $467 million in assets, and these insolvencies had a higher-than-average percentage of assets in deregulated lending areas, including commercial mortgages, land loans, and direct equity investments. Other characteristics are that a disproportionate number of insolvencies had state charters, were stock organizations, and had grown significantly faster than the rest of the industry. Also, nearly a third of all thrift failures occurred in California, Texas, and Florida, states with liberal banking laws and generally lax oversight. Finally, early investigations of the most prominent insolvencies showed that some form of fraud or lender misconduct had occurred. Such characteristics indicate that these thrifts did not use deregulation for prudent diversification, but rather invested funds in ways that increased – not decreased – their risks.[52]

Despite the loss of nearly 35 percent of the nation's thrifts, those that survived grew to such an extent that total industry assets nearly doubled during the decade, as seen in Table 8.1.

The thrifts that survived the S&L crisis also share a number of characteristics. Some merged with other financial institutions or were acquired by

---

51 "Showdown at 'Gunbelt' Savings," *The New York Times*, 12 March 1989, sec. 3, 1; Adams, *The Big Fix*, 224; Day, *S&L Hell*, 223–4; House Committee on Banking, Finance and Urban Affairs Subcommittee on Financial Institutions Supervision Regulation and Insurance, *When Are The Savings and Loan Crooks Going to Jail?* hearings, 101st Cong., 2nd sess., 28 June 1990, 1–5; Senate Committee on Banking, Housing, and Urban Affairs, *Fraud in America's Insured Depository Institutions*, hearings, 101st Cong., 2nd sess., 1–2 August 1990, 65–8; FDIC, *Managing the Crisis*, 863.

52 James R. Barth, Philip F. Bartholomew, and Carol J. Labich, *Moral Hazard and the Thrift Crisis: An Analysis of the 1988 Resolutions*, Research Working Paper No. 160 (Washington, DC: FHLBB, 1989); White, *The S&L Debacle*, 113–15.

TABLE 8.1. *Number of Thrifts and Assets – 1980 to 1988*

Year	No. of S&Ls	Change/Year	Assets (000,000)	Change/Year
1980	3,993	–	$603,777	–
1983	3,146	(7.1%)	$813,770	11.6%
1985	3,274	4.4%	$1,109,789	18.2%
1988	2,969	(3.1%)	$1,368,843	7.8%

Source: Office of Thrift Supervision, 1999 *Fact Book: A Statistical Profile on the United States Thrift Industry* (Washington, DC: Office of Thrift Supervision, June 2000), 1, 4.

"white-knight" businesses, but the majority of thrifts that remained independent were mutual associations that held a high percentage of traditional residential mortgages in their portfolios. While many "survivors" did take advantage of deregulation, they often did so cautiously and chose areas that complemented existing lines of business. This determination to "stick to the knitting" and stay true to the core mission of meeting local financial needs was another defining trait of success. Finally, many of the S&Ls that prospered were among the oldest in the industry. Since these firms had experienced both good and bad business conditions, they more than likely understood the volatility of financial markets. The effects of these long-term institutional memories on business practices also indicates the importance of management continuity in surviving in the turbulent 1980s.[53]

---

[53] In Ohio nearly 90 percent of S&Ls still in business were founded in the nineteenth century. House Committee on Banking Finance and Urban Affairs, *The Other Side of the Savings and Loan Industry*, 100th Cong., 1st sess. (Washington, DC: USGPO, 1989), 5–46; Bird, *Can S&Ls Survive?* 48–50, 66–7; Maye Smith and Faye Hudson, *Maye and Faye's Building and Loan: The Story of a Remarkable Sisterhood* (New York: Harper Collins, 1997), 145–98; *Thomson Savings Directory* (Skokie, IL : Thomson Financial Publishing, 1998), R20–5; FDIC, *Managing the Crisis*, 9; White, *The S&L Debacle*, 72–4, 76–80, 112–6; James R. Barth and Michael Bradley, "Thrift Deregulation and Federal Deposit Insurance," *Journal of Financial Services Research* 2 (September 1989), 231–59; James R. Barth, Carl D. Hudson, and John S. Jahara Jr., "S&L Closures and Survivors: Are There Systematic Differences in Behavior?" in Cottrell et. al, editors, *The Causes and Costs of Depository Institution Failures*, 10–13; Anat Bird, *Can S&Ls Survive?: The Emerging Recovery, Restructuring & Repositioning of America's S&Ls* (Chicago: Bankers Publishing Co., 1993), 9, 19–23.

9

RESOLVING THE CRISIS,
RESTORING THE CONFIDENCE,
1989–1995

By the end of 1988, it was clear to most policy makers that the initial efforts to contain the S&L crisis were inadequate and that unprecedented measures were needed to bring the debacle to an end. With hundreds of insolvent thrifts losing millions each week and public indignation growing, Congress took the first step in the recovery process when it passed the Financial Institution Reform, Recovery and Enforcement Act of 1989. This landmark legislation created the Resolution Trust Corporation, which operated through 1995 and disposed of billions in failed thrift assets. More importantly, the law also overhauled the thrift regulatory structure and began the process of industry re-regulation. By the early 1990s, what remained of the sector was working to restore public confidence. One element of this process involved emphasizing how thrifts were community organizations committed to serving local financial needs by offering an array of consumer products and services. Significantly, this approach was strikingly similar to the messages used to promote the industry in the late nineteenth century. Another concern in the wake of the thrift debacle was identifying how and why it had happened. Given the scale and scope of the crisis, there was no one overarching explanation, but rather it resulted from a combination of factors, of which ill-advised lending decisions and lax oversight were the most important. Significantly, fraud was not a major cause of thrift failures despite its prominence in several high-profile insolvencies. By the mid-1990s, the S&L crisis was effectively over, and the industry, albeit fewer in numbers, was again growing and profitable.

TOWARD RE-REGULATION

When the FHLBB completed its sales of insolvent thrifts under the Southwest Plan, officials were shocked at not only the costs involved, but by the fact that hundreds of associations were still in trouble. Even though the FSLIC closed a total of 205 thrifts in 1988, at the end of the year 250 thrifts with nearly

$81 billion (U.S. billion) in assets were still RAP-insolvent. If only tangible net worth was used, the figures ballooned to 508 S&Ls, with $297 billion in assets. Regulators also estimated that the largest of these troubled thrifts were losing more than $1 billion (US billion) every month. Furthermore, the FSLIC, which was responsible for insuring all thrift deposits, ended 1988 with a *negative* net worth of $75 billion. While officials essentially conceded that a taxpayer bail-out was unavoidable, most politicians still wanted the industry to pay for its mistakes. Consequently, when newly elected president George Bush proposed to fund a bail-out by levying a fee on all insured accounts at banks, credit unions, and S&Ls, in January 1989 he was roundly criticized as being unfair to depositors of well-managed institutions. Bush responded to the opposition by candidly stating that "whatever we come up with will not be popular.... But we've got to get on and get the problem solved."[1]

On February 6, 1989, the Bush administration presented Congress with its plan to finally resolve the thrift debacle. The government would create a temporary agency and allocate it $50 billion (US billion) to liquidate the assets of insolvent thrifts. To avoid a significant increase in the deficit, $30 billion of this amount would be raised "off budget" through the sale of long-term bonds issued by the Resolution Funding Corporation (REFCORP), a private agency owned by the government. While taxpayers and the thrift industry would share the burden of paying the interest on these bonds, the industry was expected to repay the principal through higher insurance premiums and taxes on the net worth and future profits of the industry-owned home loan banks. In terms of thrift regulation, the Bush plan would abolish the FHLBB and the FSLIC, giving the task for insuring thrift deposits to the FDIC and oversight responsibility to a new agency within the Treasury Department. Regulations would also be tightened, with all thrifts required to double their regulatory capital to 6 percent of assets by June 1991. Furthermore, goodwill would no longer be counted as equity. Finally, the Justice Department would receive $50 million to prosecute S&L fraud.[2]

---

[1] Federal Deposit Insurance Corporation (FDIC) Division of Research and Statistics, *History of the Eighties – Lessons for the Future*, vol. 1 (Washington, DC: FDIC, 1997), 168. Nathaniel C. Nash, "Big Problem Awaiting Bush: Who Pays for the Savings Crisis," *The New York Times*, 1 December 1988, D1, D6; Thomas C. Hayes, "Shifts Studies for Financial Regulators," *The New York Times*, 16 January 1989, D1, D6; Peter T. Kilborn, "Bush is Criticized for Not Dropping Savings-Fee Plan," *The New York Times*, 30 January 1989, A1, D2; Nathaniel C. Nash, "Bush Aides' Plan on Savings Units Is Said to Place Cost on Industry," *The New York Times*, 4 February 1989, 1, quote 45; "The S&L Mess – And How to Fix It," *Business Week*, 31 October 1988, 130–6; "The Bust of '89," *Business Week*, 23 January 1989, 36–46.

[2] Like the bonds issued by FICO to recapitalize the FSLIC in 1987, the REFCORP bonds would be guaranteed by zero coupon Treasury bonds. Maureen Dowd, "Bush Savings Plan Calls for Sharing the Cost Broadly," *The New York Times*, 7 February 1989, A1, D9; Nathaniel C. Nash, "Bush Aide Who Put The Pieces Together," *The New York Times*, 8 February 1989, D9; FDIC, *Managing the Crisis: The FDIC and RTC Experience, 1980–1994*, (Washington,

The Bush plan was "the most significant attempt by any Administration" to deal with the S&L crisis, and the president was applauded for "dealing with the problem squarely." Legislators found it appealing since it did not call for new taxes, or raise the federal deficit. Also, because it placed most of the financial costs on the thrift industry, politicians could argue that it was not a bail-out. More importantly, the program reaffirmed the government's commitment to maintaining the integrity of financial institutions. Still, critics wondered if it was adequate to end the S&L crisis, especially if an economic downturn caused more failures. Another concern involved the method of financing. Because of the president's campaign promise not to raise taxes, issuing the bonds through REFCORP, and not the Treasury Department, would increase annual interest expense by $600 million to $1 billion (US billion). Taxpayer costs, which were estimated to be $39.9 billion (US billion) over ten years (about 40 percent of the total cost), could also increase significantly if the revenue from the sale of thrift assets failed to meet projections.[3]

The League, while generally supportive, also had serious problems with the Bush administration proposal. Given how much the trade group cherished the independence of the FHLBB, it naturally opposed placing oversight of the industry under the Treasury Department. The greater concern, however, was the steep increase in capital requirements, which it considered too extreme because it would have the undesired consequence of pushing marginal thrifts into insolvency. The League even contended that the exclusion of goodwill as capital represented a breach of contract since regulators had used it to encourage thrifts to acquire troubled S&Ls in the 1980s. Legislators, however, turned a deaf ear to these arguments. During Senate hearings on the bill, Sen. Richard C. Shelby (D-AL) told League chairman O'Connell, "you have no credibility here today. It seems to me you have already destroyed your own industry." Sen. Phil Gramm (R-TX) echoed this sentiment, saying "if anyone has been irresponsible here it has been the League. I know you have lots of friends, but less than you previously had." Such sharp criticisms reflected the broad feeling in Capitol Hill that the League had duped Congress in the 1980s by consistently downplaying and underestimating the severity of industry problems.[4]

DC: FDIC, 1998), 122; Lawrence J. White, *The S&L Debacle: Public Policy Lessons for Bank and Thrift Regulation* (New York: Oxford University Press, 1991), 176; James Barth, *The Great Savings and Loan Debacle* (Washington, D.C.: AEI Press, 1991), 79.

[3] Nathaniel C. Nash, "Deft Politics, Fiscal Doubt," *The New York Times*, 7 February 1989, A1, D9; Robert D. Hershey Jr., "Praise on Capital Hill for Rescue Proposal," *The New York Times*, 7 February 1989, D9; "Facing the S&Ls, Not So Squarely," *The New York Times*, 7 February 1989, A28; Brian D. Cooney, "Thrifts, A New Chapter," *Mortgage Banking* 50 (October 1989), 93; White, *The S&L Debacle*, 177.

[4] John Cranford, "Bush Faces Powerful Foes as Bail-out Battle Nears," *Congressional Quarterly Weekly Report* 47 (18 February 1989), 303–11; Nathaniel C. Nash, "Savings Industry Ready

Although the Senate attacks on the League were not surprising given the public mood, officials still expected the trade group to use its legendary lobbying power to remove the most onerous provisions from the final bill. This, however, did not happen. By April it was clear that deep divisions within the industry had caused the League's power to dissipate. For the first time in memory, senators were hearing two distinct pleas from S&Ls. One came from the weaker thrifts that urged leniency, while the other came from healthy S&Ls that were tired of opposing efforts to improve the industry and were now willing to "stick it to those other guys." In fact, the three largest S&Ls in California hired their own Washington lobbyists to push for "the tightest capital and accounting standards we can get." The result was that on April 19, 1989, the Senate approved the Bush proposal virtually unchanged by the lopsided vote of 91 to 8.[5]

Swift passage in the House, however, was not assured, especially after Banking Committee chairman Henry D. Gonzalez (D-TX) broadened the measure by attaching an amendment to provide $100 million a year in interest rate subsidies for low-income mortgages. Another problem was that because the League had more lobbying clout in the House, several influential members, including House Republicans, were willing to modify the bill further. Consequently, when Rep. Henry Hyde (D-IL) attached several proindustry amendments, it appeared as if the trade group had achieved its overall goal of diluting the worst aspects of the bill. The victory, however, was short-lived. On the day of the final vote, Rep. Jim Leach (R-IA) introduced an amendment to strip the bill of all special-interest provisions, and under the glare of CSPAN television cameras, support for the League-inspired changes evaporated. The House voted 412 to 7 for the Leach amendment, indicating how much legislators did not want to look beholden to the League. The full Congress then approved the bill on the last day of the session, and on August 9 President Bush signed the Financial Institution Reform, Recovery and Enforcement Act of 1989 (FIRREA) into law.[6]

---

to Fight the Bush Plan," *The New York Times*, 8 February 1989, D6; Nathaniel C. Nash, "Critics of Bush Savings Plan Face Senate," *The New York Times*, 8 March, 1989, D1, D13, quotes D13; "S&Ls Send Out an SOS," *Time*, 8 June 1989, 68–9; Cooney, "Thrifts, A New Chapter," *Mortgage Banking* 50 (October 1989) 94.

[5] Nathaniel C. Nash, "Rifts Run Deep in Savings Bill Debate," *The New York Times*, 17 April, 1989, D1, D5, quotes D1; Nathaniel C. Nash, "Savings Bill is Cleared by Senate," *The New York Times*, 20 April 1989, D1, D17; Nathaniel Nash, "As the Thrift Bail-out Plan Gets Backed Up, The Meter Keeps Running for Congress," *The New York Times*, 4 June 1989, sec. 4, 4.

[6] Nathaniel C. Nash, "House Banking Panel Backs Help for Poor Home Buyers," *The New York Times*, 27 April 1989, D1, D6; Nathaniel C. Nash, "Some in G.O.P. Deserting Bush on Savings Plan," *The New York Times*, 25 May 1989, A1, D7; Nathaniel C. Nash, "Near Upset on Savings Vote Shows Power of Lobbyists," *The New York Times*, 29 May 1989, 31, 34; Nathaniel C. Nash. "Bush Savings Plan is Passed by House," *The New York Times*, 16

FIRREA was a landmark legislation that altered the regulatory structure of the thrift industry, increased the restrictions on lending activities, and established a means to dispose of the billions in assets held by insolvent thrifts. The organizational restructuring focused on dividing the multiple powers once held by the FHLBB into separate agencies. Industry oversight was given to the new Office of Thrift Supervision (OTS), which was under the Treasury Department, and the independent FHLBB was abolished. The FSLIC was also eliminated, and responsibility for insuring deposits was transferred to the FDIC, which was to establish a new and separate reserve, the Savings Association Insurance Fund (SAIF), for this purpose. Finally, while the twelve individual home loan banks remained intact, their oversight was given to a new agency, the Federal Housing and Finance Board. Such changes reflected a feeling that the problems of the 1980s occurred in part because the Board was too powerful and too close to the industry.[7]

The main focus of industry re-regulation was on improving the level of thrift equity and establishing stricter net worth requirements. This was accomplished by creating a three-tiered system of capital ratios. The first tier required all S&Ls to have tangible capital of at least 1.5 percent of assets by the end of 1989. Second, thrifts had to have core capital (which consisted of tangible capital plus up to 1.5 percent of goodwill) equal to 3 percent of assets; the use of goodwill as capital was to end, however, by the end of 1994. Third, the OTS was to impose risk-based capital requirements on the industry that would force thrifts to set aside more capital if they engaged in risky lending. If a thrift failed to meet these requirements it had to submit a capital restoration plan to regulators, and its access to advances from the home loan banks would be restricted. These rules would force thrifts to hold "harder" forms of equity (like direct owner investments) and make managers more responsible for their business decisions.[8]

June 1989, A1, D6; Nathaniel C. Nash, "House and Senate Pass Plan to Rescue Savings and Loan," *The New York Times*, 5 August 1989, 1, 33; Nathaniel C. Nash, "After Savings and Loan Rescue, Lawmakers Go Home," *The New York Times*, 6 August 1989, 18; O'Connell, *America's Money Trauma*, 96–103; Michael Waldman, *Who Robbed America? A Citizen's Guide to the S&L Scandal* (New York: Random House, 1990), 104–9; Cooney, "Thrifts, a New Chapter," 94; White, *The S&L Debacle*, 175–6.

7 Bank deposits would be insured by a separate fund, the Bank Insurance Fund. Robert D. Hershey Jr., "Bush Signs Savings Legislation; Remaking of Industry Starts Fast," *The New York Times*, 10 August 1989, A1, D2; White, *The S&L Debacle*, 176–80, quote 180; Raymond Natter, *Financial Institutions Reform, Recovery Act of 1989* (New York: Matthew Bender, 1989), 40–3; Kenneth E. Scott, *Never Again: The Savings and Loan Bail-out Bill* (Stanford, CA: Hoover Institution Press, 1990), 18–19.

8 John T. Rose, "The Thrift Crisis: Evolution, Resolution and Reform," *Baylor Business Review* 8 (Winter 1990), 12–15; Maggie Mahar, "The $100 Billion Fiasco," *Barron's*, 11 September 1989, 24; Eric Luse, Samuel J. Maliza, and John J. Spidi, "The Capital Conundrum," *Bottomline* 6 (December 1989), 31–5; White, *The S&L Debacle*, 179; Barth, *The Great Savings and Loan Debacle*, 84–6.

The new thrift capital guidelines were similar to those for commercial banks, and the use of lending-risk measures reflected the broader international trend to improve the supervision of financial institutions. The key event in this process was the issuance of the Basle Accords in 1988. Created by the Basle Committee, an international body of banking supervisors and central bank governors from the ten major industrialized countries, the Basle Accords advocated the adoption of risk-based capital ratios as a way to reflect the real credit risks of institutions. Significantly, these measures would measure the risks of both on- and off-balance sheet items. Since the United States supported the Basle Accords, the inclusion of risk-based capital requirements in FIRREA was a sign of the Bush administration's commitment to adhere to the new standards.[9]

Other regulatory changes under FIRREA included reinstating restrictions on thrift lending powers to refocus the industry back on home finance. The law raised the Qualified Thrift Lender test so that all thrifts had to hold at least 70 percent of assets in areas related to residential real estate by 1991. If a thrift failed this test, it had to convert to a state or national bank charter. Thrifts also had five years to divest all their junk bond holdings and to reduce the amount of commercial real estate mortgages in their loan portfolios from 40 percent of assets to four times their net worth. Furthermore, the maximum loan size a thrift could make to a single borrower was lowered from 100 percent of net worth to 15 percent, and state-chartered S&Ls were required to limit their activities to those permitted federally chartered thrifts, regardless of state authorizations. Finally, commercial banks for the first time had the right to purchase healthy thrifts. While intended to correct the mistakes of the past, critics charged that the changes limited the ability of S&Ls to diversify, and that the new rules opened the door for further consolidation of the thrift and banking industries.[10]

To administer the liquidation of insolvent thrifts, the law created the Resolution Trust Corporation (RTC), and gave it two years and $50 billion to complete this process. The RTC was to structure the sale of assets so as to maximize the return to the government, while at the same time it was to avoid hurting local real estate and financial markets. The RTC also had a social

---

[9] Kern Alexander, *The Role of the Basle Standards in International Banking Supervision*, ESCR Centre for Business Research Working Paper No. 153 (Cambridge: University of Cambridge, March 2000), 1–16.

[10] The QTL test would later be reduced by the OTS to 65 percent of assets. Nicholas Ordway, "Key Provisions of the FSLIC Bail-out Bill," *Real Estate Finance* 6 (Fall 1989), 83–4; William A. Cooper, "The QTL Test Sends Savings & Loans Back to the Future," *Bottomline* 6 (December 1989), 25–8; James R. Barth and Philip R. Wiest, *Consolidation and Restructuring of the U.S. Thrift Industry Under the Financial Institution Reform, Recovery, and Enforcement Act* (Washington, DC: Office of Thrift Supervision, Department of the Treasury, 1989), 1–5; Rose, "The Thrift Crisis," *Baylor Business Review* 8 (Winter 1990) 11; Cooney, "Thrifts, A New Chapter," 91; White, *The S&L Debacle*, 179–82.

mission, since Congress required it to increase the availability of affordable housing and use women- and minority-owned firms to assist in the resolution process. In addition, legislators instructed the RTC to review all 1988 FSLIC transactions to see if costs could be saved through restructuring. Finally, in terms of oversight and rules enforcement, while the OTS had supervisory power over both federally and state-chartered institutions, the FDIC had the right to terminate insurance coverage even if the OTS objected. Penalties for rules violations increased, and some forms of misconduct would incur fines of up to $1 million per day. The Justice Department also received $75 million to prosecute criminal activities related to thrifts and banks.[11]

Called by some an "act of anger," FIRREA reflected how much attitudes towards the thrift industry had changed in only a few years. According to former Board member Lawrence White, as late as 1987 "the Congress had thought that all thrift operators were Jimmy Stewart in *It's a Wonderful Life*; in 1989 the Congress thought they were all Warren Beatty in *Bonnie and Clyde*." Rep. Charles Schumer (D-NY) noted that House members were "just ticked off at the thrifts, the industry that created the problems, [and that] the industry that wasn't contrite about it. . . . Laissez-faire is over. Leaving it up to the thrifts and regulators doesn't work anymore." While the harshest provisions of the law were directed at thrifts and their regulators, other financial institutions were also affected. Commercial banks saw insurance premiums rise by 50 percent, as well as a significant strengthening of their capital requirements. Overall, the distinctly populist elements in the law indicated to some that FIRREA was the beginning of "a new period of Federal management of corporate America."[12]

ENTER THE RTC

Within days of the passage of FIRREA, the RTC (whose motto was "Resolving The Crisis, Restoring The Confidence") began operations, and its first task was to develop procedures for closing and resolving hundreds of insolvent S&Ls. Not surprisingly, these procedures were similar to those used by the FDIC and the FSLIC. The first step in resolving an insolvent thrift was to legally transfer it to the RTC. This was done by establishing a conservatorship that placed the thrift under the direct supervision of the RTC. Significantly, a thrift in conservatorship was still open for business,

---

[11] Paulette Thomas, "New Agency to Handle Sick S&L Assets," *The Wall Street Journal*, 18 May 1989, A1; James Chesson, "Strong Medicine," *ABA Banking Journal* 81 (October 1989), 67–9; Rose, "The Thrift Crisis," 8–10; FDIC, *Managing the Crisis*, 297–8; Barth, *The Great Savings and Loan Debacle*, 86–8.

[12] Nathaniel C. Nash, "In Savings Bill, a Populist Message," *The New York Times*, 17 June 1989, 31, 34, quote 31; White, *The S&L Debacle*, quote 180; Cooney, "Thrifts, A New Chapter," *Mortgage Banking* 50 (October 1989) 93; Chesson, "Strong Medicine," 67; FDIC, *History of the Eighties*, 101–2.

with an RTC-appointed managing agent overseeing the thrift's original employees who conducted day-to-day operations. Next, the RTC sold the assets and placed the deposits of the thrift with other institutions. Any assets and liabilities that could not be sold were transferred to a receivership for final disposition, and once this was completed, the receivership was ended and the resolution over.[13]

When disposing of loan assets and deposit liabilities, the RTC, like the FDIC, had essentially two basic options. The first was simple liquidation, in which the thrift was closed, the insured depositors paid off, and the assets assumed by the government. This was the least-favored approach since it involved large direct cash outlays that could only be recovered when the assets were sold. The second method, known as purchase and assumption, involved finding a buyer for the thrift who was willing to assume both the assets and liabilities. Since the buyer was acquiring assets that were worth less than the liabilities, this method also required government funds to compensate for the difference. Rarely did this involve direct cash payments, however, as most buyers received notes, loan guarantees, or tax breaks. Significantly, the ultimate cost to the government under both resolution methods was essentially the same.[14]

Although the RTC followed many of the same procedures used by the FDIC, the uniqueness of the RTC mission forced it to adopt different disposal strategies. Unlike the FDIC, which tried to sell the maximum amount of assets to the acquirer at final resolution, the RTC focused on selling assets while a thrift was in conservatorship, and often sold a limited amount of assets to the acquirer at resolution. One reason for this was that the average S&L conservatorship lasted thirteen months, which gave the RTC ample time to evaluate and market the loans. Furthermore, given the sheer volume of assets controlled by the RTC and its limited financial resources, it made sense to sell assets piecemeal and avoid long negotiations. Also, breaking up a thrift and separating the assets and liabilities often attracted more buyers; for example, in 1990 when the RTC tried to sell a $1.5 billion thrift as a whole, it received no bidders, but had 87 parties interested in buying the thrift's branches.[15]

Another difference between the FDIC and the RTC disposition methods was, because it was common knowledge that RTC institutions were insolvent, the Corporation had the benefit of conducting a more public marketing process. This began by placing advertisements in publications like *The Wall*

[13] FDIC, *Managing the Crisis*, 117–18.

[14] RTC, *Statistical Abstract, August 1989/September 1995* (Washington, DC: Office of Planning, Research and Statistics, 1995), 10; Mark Carl Rom, *Public Spirit in the Thrift Tragedy*, (Pittsburgh: University of Pittsburgh Press, 1996), 84–6; White, *The S&L Debacle*, 154–7.

[15] FDIC, *Managing the Crisis*, 116–19; Steve Cocheo, "Brother Can You Spare a Few Billion?" *ABA Banking Journal* 82 (February 1990), 19; "Selling Branches Is a Booming Business, *United States Banker* 101 (January 1991), 20–2.

Street Journal to solicit tentative bids from interested parties. If the bids were acceptable, the RTC forwarded detailed information on the loans to the bidders so they could conduct their own due diligence investigations. Once this was completed, buyers submitted final sealed bids and the RTC awarded the assets to the least cost bidder. Because of its mandate, however, the RTC had the right to reject all offers if officials felt they could earn a higher return using different disposal methods. While the sealed bid process was the most common way to dispose of assets, the RTC also conducted open auctions where prospective buyers gathered at one location to bid competitively on assets like furniture, cars, and loans.[16]

A third major difference between the RTC and FDIC disposition strategies was that the RTC was required by law to rely on private contractors to assist in the process. The main contractor program used was the Standard Asset Management and Disposition Agreement (SAMDA), and through 1995 the RTC issued 199 contracts to 91 different SAMDA firms. A typical SAMDA contract lasted three years, and awarded loan assets to a contractor who was responsible for management, maintenance, and, if possible, final disposition. The contractor received set fees for this work, and could also receive bonuses if it sold assets for more than the estimated recovery value. The main advantage of using SAMDAs was that delegating asset management authority to these private-sector contractors gave the RTC more flexibility in managing its own workforce and expenses. Also, using SAMDAs allowed the RTC to focus its efforts on selling thrift assets. While the RTC considered this program a success, the large number of contractors (many of which were small start-up firms) initially made it difficult for officials to effectively monitor their operations.[17]

When the RTC was created it had just three employees, who were responsible for 292 failed S&Ls. The Corporation inherited these thrifts from the FDIC, which, because the FSLIC was insolvent, had assumed responsibility for closing failed S&Ls in January 1989. Unfortunately, the FDIC lacked the statutory authority and funding to actually resolve them. While the immediate challenge was to raise a staff to manage this huge case load, the RTC also had to start resolving the S&Ls quickly, since Congress stipulated that $18.8 billion of the total $50 billion allocated under FIRREA be used before the fiscal year ended on September 30. With just fifty-two days to spend this money, the RTC decided its best course of action was to close the sickest thrifts first and pay depositors directly, and within six weeks it completed

---

[16] "RTC between a Rock and a Hard Place," *United States Banker* 101 (March 1991), 29–30; "In the Trenches for the RTC," *ABA Banking Journal*, 82 (April 1990), 52; Jeffrey Marshall, "Learning From the RTC," *United States Bankers* 103 (September 1993), 17–18; FDIC, *Managing the Crisis*, 119–22.

[17] Donald F. Kettl, "The Savings-and-Loan Bail-out: The Mismatch between the Headlines and the Issues," *PS: Political Science and Politics* 24 (September 1991), 445–6; "RTC between a Rock and a Hard Place," 30–1; FDIC, *Managing the Crisis*, 354–64.

24 of these cash-intensive resolutions. It also used a portion of the funds to refinance high-rate deposits to lower the overall interest expense of the other S&Ls in conservatorship.[18]

By the end of 1989, RTC resolved a total of 37 thrifts at a cost that would ultimately approach $51 billion. While legislators knew all along that the initial funding under FIRREA was not sufficient to clean up the S&L mess, they were nonetheless shocked and outraged that so much money was spent closing so few S&Ls. The RTC came under a firestorm of criticism for wasting "precious time" selling off the worst thrifts first, and for focusing on selling individual assets and not entire associations. RTC chairman L. William Seidman countered that the high costs were unavoidable given the horrible financial condition of the S&Ls that were sold. He also argued that worsening economic conditions and fears of a glut in the real estate market were scaring off buyers. For example, of the 7,500 parties invited to bid on thrifts in the first quarter of 1990, only 263 actually performed due diligence, and just 194 bids were received. Congressional leaders, however, were not swayed and pressured Seidman to move faster.[19]

In March 1990, Seidman responded with Operation Clean Sweep, an ambitious plan to sell 141 thrifts by June 30 and prove to legislators, prospective buyers, and the public that the RTC was making progress. While most people doubted that the RTC could dispose of so many thrifts in just ninety days, when the deadline arrived Seidman reported that the agency had resolved 155 thrifts at a total cost of just $18 billion. The overall success of Operation Clean Sweep was tempered by the fact that the RTC gave the buyers the option to return unwanted assets to the government within ninety days for a full refund of the sales price. As a result, the agency eventually reacquired more than half of the loans sold. While these assets were eventually disposed of, the need to manage them in the interim added to the agency's logistical problems.[20]

For all of 1990, the RTC resolved 315 institutions at a total cost of just over $20 billion, but despite this improvement the agency was still a target for attack. One reason for this was that the RTC had become a bureaucratic behemoth seemingly overnight. By 1991, the RTC had over 8,000 employees,

---

[18] Nathaniel C. Nash, "Weighing Plan to Take Over 350 Insolvent Savings Institutions," *The New York Times*, 5 February 1989, 1, 23; Nathaniel C. Nash, "Bank Regulators Assuming Control of 4 Savings Units," *The New York Times*, 8 February 1989, A1, D6; Thomas, "New Agency to Handle Sick S&L Assets," A1; FDIC, *Managing the Crisis*, 122–5.

[19] Paulette Thomas, "Fire Sale: The Government's Job – Persuade Someone to Buy a Thundering Herd of White Elephants," *The Wall Street Journal*, 10 August 1990, R20-1; "Can't Anybody Here Sell Some Property?" *Business Week*, 10 December 1990, 56, 58; RTC, *Statistical Abstract*, 25, 29; Mahar, "The $100 Billion Fiasco," 28; FDIC, *Managing the Crisis*, 122–5.

[20] "The $1 Billion-a-Day Cleanup," *U.S. News and World Report*, 21 May 1990, 31–34; "Lighting a Fire Under the Thrift Fire Sale," *Business Week*, 21 May 1990, 142–3; FDIC, *Managing the Crisis*, 126–8.

with regional offices in Atlanta, Dallas, Denver, and Kansas City, and sales centers in 28 cities throughout the country. Potential buyers complained that the RTC's complex, and sometimes conflicting, organizational structure made it difficult to determine who had the authority to approve sales. Also, rules and procedures changed so often (for example it took eighteen 18 months for the RTC to issue a bidding manual) that one investor suggested that officials were "making it up as they go." The General Accounting Office (GAO) also criticized the RTC for not having the systems in place to monitor the hundreds of contracts being awarded, and for not using a nationwide computer system to track assets. The inability to catalogue assets in a central database not only made it hard to obtain accurate loan information, but was also a reason why the RTC admitted in 1991 that its Denver office had "lost" more than $7 billion in thrift property.[21]

Critics also challenged RTC claims of high recovery rates on the assets sold. Although officials reported that they had recovered 97 percent of the original book value of assets sold in 1989 and 1990, this was expected since most of the assets sold were cash, marketable securities, and highly desirable properties. Furthermore, because investors had the option to put back assets, many resolutions were incomplete. Through March 1991, only 31 percent of failed-thrift assets were in the hands of private investors, with the balance held by the RTC. This warehousing of loans incurred substantial carrying costs, which according to one official could "quickly eat up any profit... [and] wipe out value more quickly than you might imagine." Finally, reports that investors were buying loans for as little as 14 percent of book value, or earning up to 100 percent returns on investments made some RTC transactions appear like the infamous 1988 Southwest Plan deals.[22]

[21] Paulette Thomas, "Congress Watchdog is 'Disappointed' with S&L Cleanup," *The Wall Street Journal*, 20 February 1990, B4; John McCloud, "RTC, One Year Later: Going No Where Fast," *Journal of Property Management* 56 (January/February 1991), 22–7, quote 22; Greg Hitt, "Resolution Trust Corp. Initiates Review that Could Lead to Changes in Agency," *The Wall Street Journal*, 22 April 1991, B6; "GAO Says RTC Records Show 'Control Weaknesses,'" *The Wall Street Journal*, 18 October 1991, A4; Steven Wilmsen, "Soldiers of Fortune," *The Washington Monthly Magazine*, January/February 1993, 20–24; Edward J. Kane, "Principal-Agent Problems in the S&L Salvage," *Journal of Finance* 45 (July 1990), 755–64; FDIC, *Managing the Crisis*, 297.

[22] The book value of assets was based on the value of the assets when acquired by the RTC. "The 'Toxic Waste' of the Thrift Crisis," *Business Week*, 27 March 1989, 104–5; "Bail, Bail, Blub Blub, The S&L Plan is Sinking," *Business Week*, 9 April 1990, 20–1; Christopher J. Pike and James B. Thomson, "The RTC and the Escalating Cost of the Thrift Insurance Mess," *Federal Reserve Bank of Cleveland Economic Commentary*, 15 May 1991, quote 2; Paulette Thomas, "RTC Under Fire to Sell Real Estate of Insolvent S&Ls," *The Wall Street Journal*, 25 January 1991, C8; Paulette Thomas, "Hidden Treasures: Dead S&Ls' Bad Loans Prove to Be Bonanzas for Big, Rich Players," *The Wall Street Journal*, 9 November 1992, A1; Jonathan Silvers, "Motivated Seller," *The New Republic*, 25 January 1993, 12–14; "The $1 Billion-a-Day Cleanup," 32; "Can't Anybody Here Sell Some Property?" 56.

The RTC was also under close scrutiny because its officials were already asking Congress for more money at the end of 1990. Since a lack of working capital was hindering recovery efforts, legislators gave the agency $30 billion under the RTC Funding Act in March 1991. This allowed officials to resolve an additional 232 S&Ls for the year. The end of the cleanup, however, was still nowhere in sight since the RTC still held 91 thrifts with $130 billion in assets and was acquiring even more insolvent S&Ls. With its funds again nearly exhausted, Congress appropriated an additional $25 billion in November 1991 under the RTC Refinance, Restructuring and Improvement Act. However, because the RTC had to use these funds by April 1992, it was clear that support for the cleanup on Capitol Hill was waning, and that the thrift bail-out had become a political nightmare for both parties.[23]

In late 1991, former American Airlines CEO Albert Casey replaced Seidman as chairman, and one of his top priorities was to find ways to make the RTC more efficient when selling off assets. One solution was to increase the sale of loans in bulk as mortgage-backed securities to outside investors. This was possible in part because, contrary to the popular belief that the RTC held only worthless properties, more than 96 percent of its residential mortgages (which accounted for nearly 23 percent of total RTC assets) were performing and current. In fact less than 20 percent of *all* RTC loans were delinquent, and just 12 percent of RTC assets were classified as "real estate owned." Given these characteristics, the RTC could sell its mortgages in much the same way that Fannie Mae conducted its secondary market loan sales. Like Fannie Mae, the RTC bonds were guaranteed by a government-sponsored entity that gave them investment-grade ratings, and they were repaid by "passing through" to the investors the regular payments made by the borrowers of the underlying loans. The bonds were very popular, and by 1992 the RTC was selling between $1.5 and $2.1 billion each month of what Wall Street dubbed "Ritzy Maes." When the RTC ended operations, more than 21 percent of all mortgages it held were sold under this securitization program.[24]

In addition to selling mortgage-backed securities, the RTC began issuing bonds backed by commercial loans. This was a highly unusual form of debt offering since commercial loans were generally less standardized and involved greater risks than residential mortgages. To offset these risks, the RTC created a reserve fund equal to 30 percent of the face value of the

---

[23] RTC, *Statistical Abstract*, 10, 15, 18.
[24] Paulette Thomas and Greg Hitt, "Top RTC Post Expected to Go to Albert Casey," *The Wall Street Journal*, 18 September 1991, A3; Paulette Thomas, "Mortgage-Backed 'Ritzy Maes' Stroll Down the Street with RTC," *The Wall Street Journal*, 12 July 1991, C1; Martin Mayer, "Turnaround at the RTC," *The Wall Street Journal*, 22 December 1992, A10; Abby Schultz, "Will First Ritzy Mae Create Hot Market for Wall Street?" *The Investment Dealers' Digest* 13 January 1992, 16–20; RTC, *Statistical Abstract*, 60–1; Pike and Thomson, "The RTC and the Escalating Cost of the Thrift Insurance Mess," 3–4.

securities to protect investors against defaults. The fund allowed the bonds to hold investment-grade ratings, which lowered their interest costs, and if there were no defaults, the government kept the money. In addition, using a reserve fund let the RTC combine performing and nonperforming loans, which led to higher recovery rates on the weaker assets; reserve funds were also used to sell bonds backed by delinquent mortgages. Such innovative disposal methods caused the ratio of delinquent loans to total loans held by the RTC to fall from 21 percent in 1992 to 14 percent in 1993. More importantly, critics now generally agreed that these deals were giving the government fair prices. As one real estate investor noted, the agency was "moving the stuff at prices the taxpayers ought to be happy with. They're getting top dollar under the circumstances."[25]

The RTC also made greater progress in going after the people considered responsible for the S&L mess. Between 1992 and 1995, the gross recovery of fines from accounting firms, lawyers, and thrift executives totaled $2.4 billion, with $1 billion coming from the bankrupt investment bank Drexel Burnham Lambert and the head of its junk bond unit Michael Milken. Criminal prosecutions also increased, and between 1988 and 1995 the Justice Department obtained 5,500 convictions for various thrift and bank fraud crimes. Of this, about a third involved former thrift and bank executives, including such "highfliers" as Don Dixon, who was sentenced to five years in prison for his role in the failure of Vernon Savings and Loan, and Charles Keating who got a fifteen-year sentence for the Lincoln S&L fiasco. Unfortunately, the RTC was less successful in collecting the more than $1 billion in court-ordered restitution, netting only $100 million through 1995. A key reason was that convicted executives often used legal trusts and state homestead laws to shield their wealth from seizure.[26]

Unlike the rapid disposal of thrifts in 1990 and 1991, the RTC resolved only 69 thrifts in 1992. The main reason for the poor performance was a lack of funding. Because Congress refused to extend the April 1992 deadline for using the $25 billion allocated late in 1991, legislators spent most of the year debating whether to give the RTC the $18.3 billion that remained unspent. The stalemate continued into 1993 as new allegations of RTC mismanagement, overspending on contracts, and political infighting delayed action. In the interim, the lack of funding forced the corporation to virtually shut down. Not only did this cause morale problems and the loss of personnel (including

[25] Paulette Thomas, "RTC Securitizes Commercial Property Loans," *The Wall Street Journal*, 12 February 1992, C1; FDIC, *Managing the Crisis*, 408–20; Mark D. Fefer, "Time to Speed Up the S&L Cleanup," *Fortune*, 16 November 1992, 116–17, quote 117; "Resolved: Resolution Trust Corp. is Doing a Credible Job," *Business Week*, 20 April 1992, 100–4.

[26] "Resolution Trust Reports Wider Recoveries," *The Wall Street Journal*, 16 May 1994, B16; "Savings-and-Loan Scandals: The Texas Tally," *The Economist*, 5 May 1994, 26; Albert Karr, "In Cold Pursuit: RTC Chases Billions from Failed Thrifts but Nets Small Change," *The Wall Street Journal*, 2 September 1994, A1; FDIC, *Managing the Crisis*, 283–7.

Casey, who resigned shortly after Bill Clinton became president), but the de-layed sale of thrifts cost taxpayers an estimated $3 million a day. Finally, in November 1993, Congress passed the RTC Completion Act, which gave the corporation access to the remaining $18.3 billion. It also prohibited the RTC from seizing any more thrifts, and gave it until December 1996 to sell off its remaining assets.[27]

While the funding problems meant that only 26 thrifts were resolved in 1993, a greater concern was that the recovery rate on the assets sold (which was 94 percent in 1991 and 86 percent in 1992) fell to just 77 percent. Al-though resolution activity more than doubled in 1994, the recovery rate had dropped to 65 percent, and by 1995 was down to 62 percent. The steady declines in the ratio of sales and collections to asset book value was not a sign that the RTC was making bad deals, however, but reflected the fact that what remained in its inventory were mostly hard-to-sell properties such as unfinished buildings and raw land. Disposing of these assets, known within the RTC as the "toxic waste," often required creative financing. One such solution was the formation of equity partnerships between the RTC and private investors. In these partnerships, the RTC contributed the assets and financing while an outside firm provided equity capital and asset manage-ment services. Using partnerships to dispose of impaired assets instead of selling them directly tended to be more profitable for the RTC, since the agency was entitled to receive funds both at closing and throughout the life of the partnership. For investors, the main incentive to participate was the potential for high returns if they effectively managed their portfolios. By pur-suing these and other more traditional disposal methods, the RTC completed its last resolutions, and in July 1995 the agency effectively ended operations when it transferred its remaining $7.7 billion in unsold assets to the FDIC.[28]

In just over six years, the RTC resolved 747 S&Ls and disposed of $402.6 billion in assets. Described by one official as "the largest transfer of real estate assets since the Louisiana Purchase," the agency recovered just over 78 percent of the book value on *all* the assets it sold, and toward the

[27] Jeffrey Marshall, "Critics Throw Plenty of Darts," *United States Banker* 103 (September 1993), 34–5; Albert Karr, "Resolution Trust Corp. Nears Standstill as Personnel, Funding Problems Mount," *The Wall Street Journal*, 15 November 1993, A2; Kenneth Bacon, "Law-makers Craft Proposal to Renew Thrift Cleanup," *The Wall Street Journal*, 4 August 1993, A10; "House Votes $18.3 Billion to Fund Resolution Trust," *The Wall Street Journal*, 15 September 1993, A8; RTC, *Statistical Abstract*, 10, 15; Mike McNamee, "The Stalemate Over Sick Thrifts is Enough to Make You Sick," *Business Week*, 20 April 1992, 101; "S&L Mess: The End is Near. At Last. Maybe," *Time*, 29 March 1993.
[28] Albert Karr, "RTC Gets Ready For Toughest Sell, Sees Lower Returns on Remaining As-sets," *The Wall Street Journal*, 1 April 1993, A4; RTC *Statistical Abstract*, 10, 15; Adrienne Linsenmeyer-Hardman, "Move 'Em Out," *Financial World* 161 (23 June 1992), 84–6; FDIC, *Managing the Crisis*, 433–6, 452–4; Jack Mazzeo, "Thrift Agency Sells Last Group of S&Ls Under Its Control," *The Wall Street Journal*, 14 March 1995, B12; "Curtain Falls on the RTC," *United States Banker* (May 1995) 17.

end was receiving favorable reviews from former critics. The GAO, which lambasted the RTC in 1990, reported in 1994 that officials had significantly improved internal controls and that the agency's balance sheet was "reliable in all material aspects." Others noted how the RTC bond sales helped create a new market for the bulk sale of commercial loans. Another accomplishment was the RTC affordable housing program, which took more than 81,000 units of multifamily housing and nearly 28,000 units of single-family housing financed by failed thrifts and resold them to low- and moderate-income individuals. Possibly its greatest feat, however, was that the RTC directly spent just $87.5 billion to complete its mission, a fraction of the quarter-trillion dollar cost many had originally predicted.[29]

WHY DID 1980S FINANCIAL REFORM FAIL?

While the RTC was busy resolving hundreds of S&Ls, scholars and government officials were working to identify the overall causes of the 1980s thrift debacle. Although thrifts failed for a variety of reasons, the major causes can be grouped into two broad areas. The first involves the problems associated with the rigidity of institutional and regulatory environments that hindered the ability of thrift managers and regulators to respond to the rapid and unexpected economic turmoil in the late 1970s. Such conditions meant that many of the thrift failures of the early 1980s were unavoidable. The second area focuses on human-error causes, including flawed deregulation, lax oversight, fraud, and misguided lending decisions. These were among the chief causes of thrift failures after 1983, and given their nature could have been better controlled and possibly avoided. This, in turn, supports my assertion that while numerous thrifts were destined to fail in the 1980s, the ultimate scale and scope of the crisis need not have been so extensive.[30]

One key reason why the S&L crisis was inevitable is that the financial structure of thrifts made them ill-prepared to deal with the economic upheavals of the late 1970s and early 1980s. One aspect of this institutional rigidity was the inherent mismatch between thrift income and expenses. Since S&L earnings came from long-term, fixed-rate mortgages that were funded by relatively short-term deposits, when interest rates rose expenses increased rapidly while loan income did not. Rising rates also caused these fixed-rate

---

[29] "The 'Toxic Waste' of the Thrift Crisis," 104; "Bail, Bail, Blub Blub, The S&L Plan is Sinking," 20; Jeffrey Marshall, "Learning from the RTC," *United States Banker* 103 (September 1993), 28–9, quote 28; Birge Watkins, "Examining the Past and Present of the RTC," *National Real Estate Investor* 36 (June 1994), 138–9; FDIC, *Managing the Crisis*, 113, 137–8, 140, 373.

[30] FDIC, *Managing the Crisis*, 794–8; National Commission on Financial Institution Reform, Recovery and Enforcement (NCFIRRE), *Origins and Causes of the S&L Debacle: A Blueprint for Reform*. (Washington, DC: NCFIRRE, 1993), ix–x, 1–10; John Steele Gordon, "Understanding the S&L Mess," *American Heritage* 42 (February/ March 1991), 49–68.

assets to lose value, which produced further losses if sold. Unfortunately, most thrifts lacked the capital cushion to absorb sustained periods of net losses. This was because S&Ls traditionally held low loan loss reserves and low levels of owner equity and retained earnings. Such traits, however, were not unusual since home loans are generally lower-risk forms of lending with lower delinquency and foreclosure rates than commercial loans. Similarly, the low equity reflected the mutual ownership of most S&Ls and their historic tradition of distributing most of the profits to their members; even federal tax policies gave managers incentives to maintain low levels of equity.[31]

A second factor that contributed to thrift failures was the problem of regulatory lag, which involved regulators failing to respond to changing market conditions in a timely manner. Regulatory lag occurred at two levels: The first involved the rigidity of the FHLBB organizational structure. Like most bureaucracies, the FHLBB rule-making process was time-consuming and often required going through a hierarchy with multiple (and sometimes contradictory) lines of authority. Compounding this problem was the oversight role of Congress. Since Board powers were derived from the legislative branch, political infighting between the House and Senate often hindered the ability of regulators to implement change. The second form of regulatory lag involved retaining policies that were made obsolete by changes in the economy and/or technology. While following a "wait and see" approach is sometimes appropriate, regulators often failed to revise rules even after financial innovations were proven – examples include the delays in authorizing adjustable-rate mortgages and negotiable order of withdrawal accounts. Significantly, industry lobbying, consumer interests, and politics played critical roles in preventing regulatory change.[32]

While institutional and regulatory rigidity contributed to the failure of dozens of thrifts, the scale and scope of the overall crisis most likely could have been better managed had certain events occurred differently. One was the piecemeal nature of thrift deregulation. Because the DIDMCA dealt primarily with liabilities, not assets, S&Ls were in the awkward position of

---

[31] Barth, *The Great Savings and Loan Debacle*, 37–42; Frederick E. Balderston, *Thrifts in Crisis: Structural Transformation of the Savings and Loan Industry* (Cambridge, MA: Ballinger Publishing Co., 1985), 4–6; George J. Benston, *An Analysis of the Causes of Savings and Loan Association Failures*, Monograph Series in Finance and Economic, Monograph 1983 – 4/5 (New York: Salomon Brothers Center for the Study of Financial Institutions, Graduate School of Business Administration, New York University, 1985), 10–12; NCFIRRE, *Origins and Causes of the S&L Debacle*, 29–38; Norman Strunk and Fred Case, *Where Deregulation Went Wrong: A Look at the Causes Behind Savings and Loan Failures in the 1980s*, (Chicago: United States League of Savings Institutions, 1988), 43–7.

[32] Thomas K. McCraw, *Prophets of Regulation: Charles Francis Adams, Louis D. Brandeis, James M. Landis, Alfred E. Kahn* (Cambridge: Belknap Press of Harvard University Press, 1984), 305–7; Richard H. K. Vietor, *Contrived Competition: Regulation and Deregulation in America* (Cambridge, MA: Harvard University Press, 1994), 314–15; NCFIRRE, *Origins and Causes of the S&L Debacle*, 7–8.

being able to offer variable-rate savings instruments but not variable-rate mortgages. While Garn-St. Germain corrected this imbalance, the changes to thrift lending powers were too broad and generous. Significantly, the changes under both laws were not phased-in, but were implemented within weeks of passage. Another regulatory misstep was the easing of ownership rules, which had the effect of turning some S&Ls into personal wealth machines. In addition, the use of Regulatory Accounting Principles not only ran counter to the idea that market forces should determine success, but had the perverse effect of propping up failing thrifts and allowing their problems to worsen.[33]

The most critical human errors, however, were those that reduced the level of regulatory oversight and enforcement. This made it easier for lenders (both honest and dishonest) to make bad business decisions. More importantly, maintaining adequate oversight was critical given the role of federal deposit insurance. While deposit insurance instilled consumer confidence in the safety of a thrift, it also transferred the risk of losses resulting from the problem of "moral hazard" from depositors to the government. Consequently, account holders had little incentive to impose any discipline on how their funds were used, a situation that would have been different had their savings been more at risk. Since the government was the at-risk investor, regulators had the dual responsibility of not only preventing outright criminal acts, but also the moral hazard attitude "if a loan worked the thrift made money, if it goes bad insurance covered the losses." The adoption of policies like forbearance, however, indicates that legislators lost sight of the distinction between these two regulatory goals, and were not willing to hold lenders to the level of accountability needed to prevent a drain on insurance resources.[34]

[33] Strunk and Case, *Where Deregulation Went Wrong*, 54–75; NCFIRRE, *Origins and Causes of the S&L Debacle*, 41–3; William O'Connell, *America's Money Trauma: How Washington Blunders Crippled the U.S. Financial System* (Winnetka: IL: Conversation Press, 1992), 23–6; Edward J. Kane, *The S&L Insurance Mess: How Did It Happen?* (Washington, DC: The Urban Institute Press, 1989), 76–8; Rom, *Public Spirit in the Thrift Tragedy*, 104; Bert Ely, *The Role of Accounting in the S&L Crisis*, Consultant Study No. 2 (Washington DC: NCFIRRE, 1993), 43–51; White, *The S&L Debacle*, 114; L. J. Davis, "Chronicle of a Debacle Foretold: How Deregulation Begat the S&L Scandal," *Harper's Magazine* 281 (September 1990), 50–66.

[34] Kenneth B. Noble, "Examining the Bank Examiners," *The New York Times*, 25 November 1983, D1; Strunk and Case, *Where Deregulation Went Wrong*, 54–75; O'Connell, *America's Money Trauma*, 33–7; Kane, *The S&L Insurance Mess*, 57–60, 76–8, 121–9; Rom, *Public Spirit in the Thrift Tragedy*, 112–14; White, *The S&L Debacle*, 114; James Ring Adams, *The Big Fix: Inside the S&L Scandal* (New York: John Wiley and Sons, 1989), 32, 175; Benston, *An Analysis of the Causes of Savings and Loan Association Failures*, 13–16; NCFIRRE, *Origins and Causes of the S&L Debacle*, 76–7; Benton Gup, *Bank Fraud: Exposing the Hidden Threat to Financial Institutions* (Rolling Meadows, IL: Bankers Publishing Co., 1990), 3–6; Davita Silfen Glasberg and Dan L. Skidmore, "The Role of the State in the Criminogenesis of Corporate Crime: A Case Study of the Savings and Loan Crisis," *Social Science Quarterly* 79 (March 1998), 110–28; James F. Gilsinan, James E. Fisher, William B. Gillespie, Ellen

While the reduction in resources dedicated to supervisory activities hampered efforts by regulators to countervail against the latent potential for morally hazardous behavior, it also weakened their ability to prevent criminal fraud. This was especially problematic since fraud was a factor in several high-profile, multibillion-dollar failures. Unfortunately, because lender misconduct is, according to one government official, "the easiest thing to focus on and understand," many observers have incorrectly portrayed fraud as the leading cause of the S&L crisis. While illegal activities contributed to individual thrift failures, quantifying the industrywide extent of such abuses is extremely difficult. This is because few people can agree upon what separates true white-collar crime from bad business judgment. For some, only clear criminal misconduct constitutes fraud, while others define criminal activity as anything that violates a banker's fiduciary responsibility. Consequently, it is not surprising that the estimated cost of the thrift bail-out attributed to fraud ranges from as little as 3 percent of the total to as much as 33 percent. While most observers accept a figure of between 10 and 15 percent of the total direct costs of resolving S&Ls, and agree that fraud was not a major factor in the industry's collapse, the cost to taxpayers for thrift lender misconduct that occurred between 1980 and 1994 was still between $16 and $24 billion.[35]

The most important, and most controllable, reason S&Ls failed, however, was that lenders simply made bad loans in fields in which they lacked expertise. Significantly, many times these decisions were simply well-intentioned efforts to attract business. This problem occurred because most thrift managers were only experienced in the specialized, lower-risk fields of consumer and mortgage finance. As a result they often lacked the skills to successfully identify, evaluate, and mitigate lending risks in the more complex business areas opened by deregulation. This was especially true for unsecured commercial lending, merchant banking, and direct equity investments – all of

---

F. Harshman, and Fred C. Yeager, "From Regulation to Deregulation to Re-regulation: Rhetorical Quicksand and the Construction of Blame in the U.S. Savings and Loan Crisis," in Barry Rider, editor, *Corruption: The Enemy Within* (Boston: Kluwer Law International, 1997), 138–40.

[35] "Report on Bank Failures," *The New York Times*, 2 October 1984, D18; Gup, *Bank Fraud*, 1–3; Barth, *The Great Savings and Loan Debacle*, quote, 44; NCFIRRE, *Origins and Causes of the S&L Debacle*, 70. Popular and academic works that tend to focus exclusively on fraud include Paul Zane Pilzer, *Other People's Money: The Inside Story of the S&L Mess* (New York: Simon and Schuster, 1989); Gilsinan et al., "From Regulation to Deregulation to Re-regulation," 136–7; Davita Silfen Glasberg and Dan L. Skidmore, "The Dialectics of White-Collar Crime: The Anatomy of the Savings and Loan Crisis and the Case of Silverado Banking, Savings and Loan Association," *The American Journal of Economics and Sociology* 57 (October 1998), 423–49; Kitty Calavita, Henry N. Pontell, and Robert H. Tillman, *Big Money Crime: Fraud and Politics in the Savings and Loan Crisis* (Berkeley: University of California Press, 1997); Stephen Puzzo, Mary Fricker, and Paul Muolo, *Inside Job: The Looting of America's Savings and Loans* (New York: McGraw-Hill, 1989).

which require sophisticated financial analysis skills to make intelligent decisions. Lending outside of the normal market territory added an additional layer of risk, especially if officers relied on the judgment of others and not their own due diligence when making these loans.[36]

Another reason why bad loans were be made was because many lenders were under tremendous pressure to generate profit. Given the losses of the early 1980s, the ability to move into deregulated lending fields where interest rates and fees were significantly higher proved irresistible. Also, lenders (especially in Texas) had the firm conviction that oil prices would remain high, and made real estate loans on that assumption. When prices did the unthinkable and fell in the mid-1980s, these loans quickly became impaired. Moreover, even if lenders made good loans, the risk of growing too fast could imperil their institutions. Many thrifts got into trouble for not having adequate support staff to monitor their larger, more diversified loan portfolios. Finally, if lending needs outstripped the local availability of funds, lenders encountered additional risks by relying on money from alternative sources like brokered deposits.[37]

While I believe that lax oversight and well-intentioned but misguided business decisions are the two most important causes of the S&L crisis, it is critical to emphasize that for the thrift crisis to have occurred a combination of these and other factors was necessary.[38] For example, if thrifts held larger equity reserves and had a more diversified asset base, the slow economy of the 1970s and the sudden rise in interest rates might not have had as severe an effect on industry finances. Similarly, if thrift deregulation was more

---

[36] NCFIRRE, *Origins and Causes of the S&L Debacle*, 69–70; Gregory A. Lilly, "The Savings and Loan Debacle: Moral Hazard of Market Disaster?" in Allin F. Cottrell, Michael S. Lawlor, and John H. Wood, editors, *The Causes and Costs of Depository Institution Failures* (Boston: Kluwer Academic, 1995), 119–21; Robert A. Bennett, "A Daring New World for Thrifts In the Making," *The New York Times*, 24 July 1983, F1; Strunk and Case, *Where Deregulation Went Wrong*, 98–101.

[37] John L. West, "Set the Record Straight on the S&L Crisis," *ABA Banking Journal* 83 (November 1993), 133–5; Lilly, "The Savings and Loan Debacle: Moral Hazard of Market Disaster?" 155–9; Strunk and Case, *Where Deregulation Went Wrong*, 98–101; Bennett, "A Daring New World for Thrifts In the Making," F1; Interview, Kenneth Law, Law and Riddle, Belton, Texas, by the author, 5 July 1985; David L. Mason, "The Failure of Empire Savings and Loan Association of Mesquite, Texas" (unpublished M.A. thesis, The University of Texas at Austin, 1985), 45–7.

[38] Other frequently cited causes include the decision to raise deposit insurance coverage to $100,000, the rise of the brokered deposit markets, problems in real estate appraisals, lax state regulation, the Tax Reform Act of 1986 that repealed many of the commercial real estate investment tax credits contained in the Economic Recovery Tax Act of 1981, and the general increase in competition between thrifts, banks, and other financial institutions. See NCFIRRE, *Origins and Causes of the S&L Debacle*, 7–10; Timothy Curry and Lynn Shibut, "The Cost of the Savings and Loan Crisis: Truth and Consequences," *FDIC Banking Review* 13 (December 2000), 27; Robert Litan, "Deposit Insurance: Gas on the S&L Fire," *The Wall Street Journal*, 29 July 1993, A10; and White, *The S&L Debacle*, 211–22.

balanced and limited, many of the bad loans made in areas completely unrelated to home finance would have been avoided. Furthermore, had League executives and politicians like Richard Pratt, Donald Regan, and Rep. Jim Wright not encouraged lax oversight and policies like regulatory forbearance, insolvent thrifts could have been closed sooner and lender misconduct (while not preventable) detected earlier. These observations, however, are not intended to suggest that the S&L crisis could have been avoided but simply illustrate the point that the scale and scope of the crisis could have been better controlled and most definitely reduced.

THE "NEW" THRIFT INDUSTRY

By all measures, the S&L crisis of the 1980s and early 1990s was one of the most expensive financial collapses in American history. Between 1980 and 1994, a total of 1,295 S&Ls with $621.2 billion (U.S. billion) in assets ceased to exist; the ten largest S&L failures (all of which involved some degree of fraud) accounted for $112 billion (U.S. billion) of this figure. The direct cost of disposing of thrift assets was also staggering. During this same fourteen-year period, the federal government directly spent $161.4 billion (US billion) on resolving failed thrifts, of which $60 billion (US billion) was attributable to the policy of regulatory forbearance under CEBA. These figures do not, however, include the interest payments on the long-term bonds issued by FICO and REFCORP. If these costs are factored in, the S&L mess could eventually cost taxpayers nearly $500 billion (US billion). Some consider this unreasonable, however; as one economist dryly noted, "no debt ever gets paid off at the governmental level."[39]

Given the financial and political fall-out of the thrift debacle, many commentators predicted an end to the industry, arguing that these specialized institutions had outlived their usefulness. In fact, throughout the 1990s, the industry did shrink significantly, as seen in Table 9.1.

While the decline in the number of S&Ls and total industry assets was expected given the resolution activities of the RTC, the consolidation also resulted from other factors, including an increase in the number of mergers between healthy thrifts and commercial banks. When FIRREA legalized these transactions, large profitable thrifts became targets of banks seeking to expand their service territory and deposits. Between 1991 and 1995 commercial banks acquired 188 thrifts with $78 billion (US billion) in assets. Also,

---

[39] Barth, *The Great Savings and Loan Debacle*, 30–6; Curry and Shibut, "The Cost of the Savings and Loan Crisis, " 30–3; Congressional Budget Office, *The Economic Effects of the Savings and Loan Crisis* (Washington, DC: USGPO, January 1992), 1–2, 29–30; Kathleen Day, *S&L Hell: The People and the Politics Behind the $1 Trillion Savings & Loan Scandal* (New York: W. W. Norton & Co., 1993), 294–5, 375, 381. *Managing the Crisis*, 795, 796, 798; RTC, *Statistical Abstract*, 9; DeGennaro, *Troubled Savings and Loan Institutions*, 4–7; Marshall, "Learning from the RTC," quote 31.

TABLE 9.1. *Number of Thrifts and Assets – 1989 to 1995*

Year	No. of S&Ls	Change/Year	Assets (000,000)	Change/Year
1989	2,616	–	$1,186,906	–
1991	2,110	(9.7%)	$895,296	(12.3%)
1993	1,669	(10.4%)	$774,775	(6.7%)
1995	1,437	(6.9%)	$770,982	(0.2%)

Source: Office of Thrift Supervision, 2002 *Fact Book: A Statistical Profile on the Thrift Industry*, at http://www.ots.treas.gov/docs/48080.pdf, accessed 31 August 2003, 1, 4.

many thrifts converted to bank charters, both to expand their services and to exit the undercapitalized and expensive SAIF. By the mid-1990s, thrifts in the SAIF were paying significantly higher premiums than commercial banks because the fund not only had to build reserves but use a portion of its income to repay the bail-out bonds. While the RTC Completion Act made it easier for the SAIF to meet its reserve requirements, the prospect that premiums would remain high was one reason why 79 thrifts with $27 billion (US billion) in assets became banks in the first half of the 1990s.[40]

Despite this consolidation and calls to "kill the thrifts," the industry still managed a remarkable financial turnaround between 1989 and 1995. After reporting losses of $6.8 billion (US billion) and $3.8 billion in 1989 and 1990, respectively, industry profits rose steadily, from $1.2 billion in 1991 to a record $5.3 billion by 1995. More importantly, the industry's return on assets ratio rose from just 0.1 percent in 1991 to 0.7 percent over the same period, reflecting the fact that more thrifts were making adjustable-rate mortgages and selling their loans on the secondary market. Another important trend was the strengthening of industry capital. Although assets fell steadily in the early 1990s, equity capital of OTS-regulated thrifts rose by nearly 20 percent. As a result, the ratio of capital to assets nearly doubled from 4.1 percent to 7.9 percent. Furthermore, the increase in the tangible capital ratio from 3.1 percent to 7.4 percent indicates that more of this equity

---

[40] The Deposit Insurance Funds Act of 1996 imposed a one-time assessment on all SAIF members to bring the fund up to its reserve requirements, which led to lower premiums. FDIC, *History of the Eighties*, 110; Robert Bennett, "Get 'em While They Last," *United States Banker* 103 (October 1993), 19–20; Steven Taub, "Hey Buddy, Want to Buy an S&L?" *Financial World* 163 (1 September 1994), 8–10; William P. Osterberg and James B. Thomson, "Making the SAIF Safe for Taxpayers," *Federal Reserve Bank of Cleveland, Economic Commentary*, 1 November 1993, 1–7; William P. Osterberg and James B. Thomson, "SAIF Policy Options," *Federal Reserve Bank of Cleveland, Economic Commentary*, June 1995, 1–4; Mathew Schifrin, "The Merger-Conversion Game," *Forbes*, 15 June 1993, 43–5; Steve Cocheo, "Is It a Bank? Is It a Thrift? It's a Colossal Flanking Maneuver," *ABA Banking Journal* 87 (May 1995), 7–9; Jeffrey Marshall, "Is Time Running Out for Thrifts?" *United States Banker* 105 (August 1995), 42–4; William Cooper, "It's Time to Eliminate Thrifts," *United States Banker* 105 (July 1995), 72–5; OTS, 2002 *Fact Book*, 37.

was in the form of "hard" capital. Finally, because the share of industry assets in nonresidential and commercial loans plunged from 9.3 percent to 5.1 percent, the total capital to risk-based asset ratio surged from 7.2 percent to 15.2. Significantly, all these capital measures were well above regulatory minimums.[41]

While strong economic growth, low interest rates, and the closing of unprofitable institutions accounted for most of the industry's improvement in the early 1990s, another factor was that consumers began to have more confidence in thrifts. Between 1989 and 1995, the share of industry assets in areas tied to home and consumer finance and the level of core deposits from small savers rose steadily. While regulators forced thrifts to focus more on these activities, another key reason for the change was that thrifts were marketing themselves as community banks providing a broad spectrum of personal financial services. Interestingly, this focus on relationship banking was in many ways a return to the ideals that helped the industry first grow in the late nineteenth century. The early thrifts thrived by promoting the close ties that existed between customers and management, and emphasizing how they could provide financial security for their members. In the late twentieth century, these themes resonated with consumers dissatisfied with the impersonal nature of large multistate banks, and the increased use of low-cost automated systems.[42]

The community banking approach was especially well suited for small S&Ls, given their traditional reputation for personalized service, but it also was an effective growth strategy for larger S&Ls, including the so-called super thrifts. Found mostly in California, super thrifts were capable of competing directly with commercial banks, but instead used their superior customer service and extensive branch networks to attract local business opportunities and create diversified sources of deposits and loans. While the rise of super thrifts has contributed to the steady increase in the average size of thrifts from $454 million in 1989 to $537 million in 1995, the industry remains dominated by small S&Ls serving local markets. In 1995, nearly 48 percent of all S&Ls had less than $100 million in assets, and more than 73 percent of all thrifts held under $250 million. By contrast, 8 percent of S&Ls held more than $1 billion in assets. Significantly, smaller associations had higher

[41] OTS, 2002 *Fact Book*, 6, 19, 23; "S&L Finances Improve as Industry Shrinks," *Journal of Accountancy* 176 (December 1993), 6; "Back in the Saddle Again," *Mortgage Banking* 55 (October 1994), 138–42.

[42] Rodger Shay, "From Thrift to Community Bank," *America's Community Banker* 5 (January 1996), 38–44; Karen Shaw, "Backing Into the Future: Positioning Savings Associations for Profit in the 1990s," *Bottomline* 6 (November 1989), 17–21; Joe Garrett, "Like on the Edge: A Survivor's Story," *Mortgage Banking* 56 (November 1995), 36–46; Preston Martin, "Regulatory Chokehold: Turn Ailing Thrifts into Community Banks," *The Wall Street Journal*, 6 July 1993, A12; Jeffrey Marshall, "Adapting to a New Climate," *United States Banker* 103 (April 1993), 4–7; "Out of the S&L Ashes," *Business Week*, 24 March 1997, 112.

capital ratios than the super-thrifts (10.3 percent vs. 7.3 percent), as well as higher return on asset ratios (0.77 percent vs. 0.6 percent). The continued ability of small thrifts to coexist side by side with larger, more diversified associations and thrive indicates that there was no one clear path to success in the years following deregulation.[43]

One problem with the community banker strategy, however, is that it has further blurred the distinction between thrifts and banks. Because thrifts offer more of the same products and services as banks these firms have lost their marketing advantage as mortgage specialists, and as such have seen their share of the residential mortgage market fall sharply. Between 1980 and 1995, the share of total 1–4 family mortgages originated by thrifts fell from 47 percent to 15 percent; by comparison, thrifts originated 61 percent of all 1–4 family mortgages in 1970. While some legislators have used the decline in the industry's share of mortgage lending to justify eliminating the S&L charter and legally consolidate the thrift and banking industries, support for a separate thrift business remains strong, indicating that these firms will remain a part of America's financial system for years to come.[44]

Although the thrift industry has made significant progress in rebuilding its image and finances, insolvent thrifts were not the only casualties of the S&L crisis. One was the thrift industry trade association, the United States League of Savings Institutions. The League's involvement in the deregulation process, and its efforts to delay re-regulation had so severely tarnished its image and reputation that by the end of the 1980s the trade group was losing large influential key members. In 1991, one year shy of its 100th anniversary, the League announced its merger with the National Council of Savings Institutions, the same group that had split from the League in 1942 over differences in trade association management. The new organization, called America's Community Bankers, with headquarters in Washington, DC, became the chief trade association for the nation's thrifts, savings banks, and commercial community banks.[45]

---

43 John F. Lawrence, "How to Succeed in a Lousy Business," *Forbes*, 3 July 1989, 125–8; Shaw, "Backing into the Future," 18; *Savings Institutions Sourcebook '89*, 46–50; *The U.S. Savings Institutions Directory* (Chicago: Rand McNally & Co., 1989), R46–R48; OTS, *2002 Fact Book*, 7.

44 In 1995, mortgage companies made 56 percent of all 1–4 family home mortgages, up from just 22 percent in 1980. Bureau of Statistics, *Statistical Abstract of the United States 1997* (Washington, DC: Dept. of the Treasury, 1998), 518; Bureau of Statistics, *Statistical Abstract of the United States 1981* (Washington, DC: Dept. of the Treasury, 1982), 771; Nathaniel C. Nash, "Death Rattle for a Dated Industry," *The New York Times*, 19 February 1989, Sec. 3, 1, 26; "Out of the S&L Ashes," 112; John Wilke, "Bill to Shore Up S&L Fund by Requiring Thrifts to Convert to Banks Is Planned," *The Wall Street Journal*, 1 June 1995, B6; "Hear the Banks Howling? The S&Ls are Back," *Business Week*, 7 December 1998, 54; Gary Silverman, "It's a Wonderful Loophole," *Business Week*, 22 March 1999, 90.

45 Nathaniel C. Nash, "Power Fades for Savings Lobbying Group," *The New York Times*, 4 July 1989, A41; Sharon Reier, "Let's Make a Deal," *Financial World* 158 (27 July 1989), 50; Debra

Another casualty of the thrift crisis was, curiously, the term "savings and loan." At the urging of the League, the use of this uniform nomenclature became common after the Great Depression, and by the 1970s more than 90 percent of all thrifts used it in their corporate titles. The failure of hundreds of S&Ls, however, affected the image of all savings and loans. In 1989, public opinion polls revealed that just 14 percent of respondents felt that thrifts were safer than banks, and even 36 percent of those who said they were thrift customers considered banks safer. As part of the process of improving their public image, dozens of S&Ls renamed themselves. By the late 1990s, only 60 percent of all associations with a thrift charter used the term "savings and loan" in their corporate titles, while 20 percent used just the words "savings" or "savings bank"; the remaining 20 percent simply used the word "bank" to describe their businesses. While many institutions changed names to distance themselves from the thrift crisis, industry leaders said the changes were needed to tell consumers that thrifts offered a broader variety of services and products. Despite these efforts, more still needs to be done to rehabilitate the industry's image. Evidence of this was seen when a thrift executive told a friend that he was the president of a bank, and the person suspiciously responded, "is that really a bank, or are you just one of those savings and loans pretending to be a bank?"[46]

CONCLUSIONS

Following the problems of the 1980s, the thrift industry faced the seemingly impossible task of rebuilding its business and reputation. While the government disposed of billions in failed thrift assets through the RTC, thrift managers had to adjust to a new regulatory environment and find ways to compete more effectively in an increasingly competitive market. The overall trend of the 1990s was that thrifts have adopted more of the services traditionally provided by banks and grown larger. Significantly, thrifts have not been alone in dealing with these challenges, as commercial banks also experienced significant consolidation. Between 1980 and 1995, more than 1,600 banks with $302.6 billion in assets went out of business; Texas was hit particularly hard, as more than 300 institutions failed between 1988 and 1989.[47]

Cope and Robert Garsson, "National Council and U.S. League Agree to Merge," *American Banker*, 11 December 1991, 1; "A Marriage Made in Adversity," *Bottomline* 9 (May/June 1992), 25–9.

[46] In Louisiana and Massachusetts the more traditional terms "homestead association" and "cooperative bank" were used. Richard W. Stevenson, "Betting That 'Bank' Smells Sweeter," *The New York Times*, 5 July 1989, D1, D6; OTS institution directory *http://www.ots.treas.gov/instsql/default.cfm?catNumber=70*, accessed 31 August 2003; Garrett, "Life on the Edge," quote, 38.

[47] In addition to the problems in the local economy, the high rate of failures in Texas was also affected by the state's antibranching laws. Nathaniel C. Nash, "Adjusting to 100 Failed Banks," *The New York Times*, 16 November 1985, 35, 37; FDIC, *History of the Eighties*, 291–419; FDIC, *Managing the Crisis*, 794, 797, 807.

The 1990s also witnessed an increase in the number of banking mergers as managers sought to reduce costs and achieve scale economies. Furthermore, many of the regulatory barriers bankers faced have been modified or removed, the most significant of which involved the restrictions in the Banking Act of 1933. While the growth of large multiservice financial institutions has produced major changes in how consumers can access and manage their money, the fact that small thrifts, commercial banks, and savings banks continue to operate profitably suggests that there is still room for lenders with "the local touch."

IO

THE AMERICAN SAVINGS
AND LOAN INDUSTRY
IN PERSPECTIVE

The history of the American savings and loan industry from 1831 to 1994 is essentially a story of how local institutions helped millions of American families acquire homes and save for the future. From the start, S&Ls achieved these goals by requiring thrift members to adhere to the basic principles of mutual cooperation and systematic savings. Because these nascent institutions were easy to organize and used relatively simple operating procedures, S&Ls were especially popular with working-class men and women who joined them in order to improve their lives financially. This idea of self-improvement was echoed by industry leaders who portrayed S&Ls as being part of a broader social movement. By the end of the nineteenth century, S&Ls had become so numerous that they formed trade organizations, first at the state and local levels, later at the national level. The thrift business prospered in the early twentieth century, but like most financial sectors suffered serious losses during the Great Depression. Even in the 1930s, though, some progress occurred as Congress enacted the first federal thrift regulations. The high point for the S&L industry came after World War II, when the demand for housing resulted in strong expansion and enhanced profitability. In the 1960s and 1970s, however, increasing divisions within the thrift industry, combined with growing economic uncertainties and new sources of competition, fueled an effort toward deregulation in the 1980s. While the thrift industry experienced significant upheaval during this decade, it ended the twentieth century stronger in total assets (albeit fewer in numbers) than at any point in its history. My analysis of the S&L industry reveals these fundamental elements: essential continuity interrupted by competitive threats from other financial institutions; crises that threatened the image of the business; and a growing reliance on government support to help the industry support itself.

THRIFTS AS AN INDUSTRY

To illustrate this continuity, we can point out that the operating characteristics of a successful S&L shared many traits with the personalized businesses of preindustrial America. One characteristic was the close relationship between management and customers, something made possible in part by the fact that early S&Ls were financial cooperatives that served narrowly defined markets. Since thrift members shared in the profits of the association, it was in their interest to maintain sound administration. A second characteristic was that asset size was not critical to profitability and the industry was dominated by small S&Ls. Because finance is inherently labor-intensive, scale economies are difficult to achieve. Similarly, the specialized nature of home finance allows a thrift to operate without significant management hierarchies. Furthermore Congress and regulators encouraged fragmentation of the industry with restrictions on lending territories and chartering requirements.[1]

When thrifts diversified into fields beyond residential finance, however, the requirements for success changed. Management hierarchies were needed to coordinate information flows and evaluate different lending risks, tasks made easier by the use of specialized reporting systems. Similarly, the use of computer technologies (including data processing and electronic funds transfers) allowed larger thrifts to achieve some scale economies. Because not all thrifts sought diversification or significant growth, however, such changes in operating practices were sometimes not necessary. Since there were few significant barriers to entry, it was also possible for small thrifts to coexist with their larger peers.[2]

Historically, thrifts used a wide variety of ownership structures. When all thrifts were mutually owned, the array of ownership plans reflected a desire to tailor operations to suit the needs and requirements of the members. Although these plans became more uniform during the early twentieth century, nearly every thrift was still owned by its members. By the late 1950s, thrift leaders began to question the wisdom of such limited ownership, especially when a growing S&L needed more deposits than local resources could supply. To remedy this problem, some thrifts became publicly held corporations, and while selling stock allowed access to larger pools of funds, the diversity

---

[1] For histories on business in preindustrial America, see Edwin J. Perkins, *The Economy of Colonial America* (New York: Columbia University Press, 1988); and Edwin J. Perkins, *American Public Finance and Financial Services, 1700–1815* (Columbus: Ohio State University Press, 1994). For a review of the development of small business, see Mansel G. Blackford, *A History of Small Business in America* (New York: Twayne Publishers, 1991); and Philip Scranton, *Figured Tapestry: Production, Markets, and Power in Philadelphia Textiles, 1885–1941* (New York: Cambridge University Press, 1989).

[2] The changes in the requirements for financial success as firms grow in size was common in other industries. See Alfred D. Chandler Jr., *The Visible Hand: The Managerial Revolution in American Business* (Cambridge, MA: Belknap Press, 1977).

of ownership also brought the potential problem of eroding the ties between management and customers. Still, because size was not critical for success, it was possible for a small thrift to remain mutually owned and still operate successfully.

One factor that often influenced the decisions to diversify or grow was the level of competition, and throughout their history many S&Ls saw markets become increasingly complex. When the industry began, there were few competitive threats because national banks could not make residential loans, and state banks were unwilling to offer the same long-term, fully amortizing mortgages made by S&Ls. They also could not match the significantly lower down payment requirements of a thrift mortgage, a critical benefit for people with limited resources. The relative lack of competition that thrifts enjoyed for nearly a century ended when the federal government entered the field of home finance in the 1930s. Although the government was not an active direct lender (the Home Owners' Loan Corporation was a notable exception), federal housing programs did make it possible for other financial institutions to compete directly with thrifts. This change was especially true with the creation of mortgage insurance and secondary markets for the sale of home loans, both of which gave commercial banks and mortgage companies greater access to home lending markets. Competition further stiffened when advances in financial technology pitted thrifts against nontraditional lenders like investment banks and brokerage firms.

The S&L industry responded to these competitive changes in essentially two ways. In terms of lending, thrifts expanded their range of products to eventually encompass all elements of consumer finance; deregulation broadened the horizon to include commercial lending. In terms of depository services, S&Ls developed a variety of long- and short-term accounts to meet consumer needs and attract funds. The result was some S&Ls became large, diversified firms capable of competing successfully with the largest banks. Not all associations, however, reacted to competition through growth and diversification. Many chose to adopt only those new loan products and services that complemented their core role as community-oriented home lenders, a strategy that may have limited significant growth opportunities but was still capable of producing profitable business. At the end of the twentieth century, nearly 85 percent of all thrifts held less than $500 million in assets, and of this 44 percent held less than $100 million. These institutions were also financially strong, with an equity capital ratio of 10.8 percent, well above the industry average of 7.7 percent. This ability to choose between alternative paths of business success was another element of continuity in the thrift industry.[3]

---

[3] Office of Thrift Supervision, 2002 *Fact Book: A Statistical Profile of the Thrift Industry* (Washington, DC: Office of Thrift Supervision, April 2003), 6, 7.

THE ROLE OF THE TRADE ASSOCIATION

As historians have observed with respect to other industries, trade associations played an important role in the development of the thrift industry. Although state trade groups appeared in the late 1880s, it was the national trade association, the United States Savings and Loan League that had the greatest long-term effects on the industry. The League began as a forum for thrift leaders to discuss business concerns, and one of its first tasks was to repair the damage done to the industry's reputation by the problems associated with the fraudulent "national" building and loans. Because these associations used unsound lending practices and made false claims of high earnings for depositors, the failure of these popular institutions in the 1890s cost small savers millions and threatened to undermine the credibility of legitimate thrifts. One way the League tried to restore faith in the industry was by cultivating an image that portrayed thrifts as part of a broader social self-help movement focused on assisting working-class Americans to become homeowners. They also emphasized that members of locally owned thrifts had greater contact with management, which gave them greater confidence in the safety of operation. Such efforts rehabilitated the public perception of S&Ls and, in turn, became a useful marketing tool to attract business.

This quaint homespun image of thrifts eventually became a liability when the public began to feel that thrift managers were professionally inferior to bankers. The League responded by encouraging the adoption of uniform business standards and creating formal and professional education programs. These efforts received a significant boost in 1929 when the League hired Morton Bodfish as its executive manager. Bodfish was critical in transforming the League from a collegial "club" of S&L executives into an efficient organization capable of directing the internal and external development of the industry. This reorganization gave the League the capacity to play a more active role in not only shaping the popular image of S&Ls as innovative and modern financial professionals, but also in enhancing the business potential of the industry. The most significant way the League accomplished this latter goal was its work in securing federal regulations that both protected thrifts from competition and promoted growth.

While the work of the League was similar to trade associations' activities in other industries, there are several reasons why the thrift trade group was particularly effective. One was the fact that between 1929 and 1979 just three people served as the head of the League, and many key officials served for as long as thirty years. This stability in senior management resulted in strategic planning continuity and the creation of close relationships between the thrift industry and government. Another factor was that, unlike some trade associations that tried to erect entry barriers to limit internal competition and enhance the industry's prestige; the League actively encouraged the formation of new firms, especially federal S&Ls. Finally, because most S&Ls

were members of both the League and state trade groups (an attribute that reflected the local nature of their business), the national trade group had to work closely with regional associations to ensure the industry maintained a united front.[4]

The work of the League in the development of the thrift industry supports the paradigm known as the "organizational synthesis." This school of thought emphasizes the importance of organizations in mediating among individuals in the United States. A key assertion of the organizational synthesis is that in many aspects of American life, face-to-face contact among individuals has given way to less personal contacts between organizations in both the private and public sectors. While personal contact was a defining characteristic of how thrifts conducted business, in terms of broader institutional relations, the League was the primary point of contact with officials from other housing industries and the government. Without the presence of such a powerful trade group, thrifts most likely would not have been such an essential part of America's financial system.[5]

THRIFTS IN AMERICA'S POLITICAL ECONOMY

While the League was important in defining the mission and image of S&Ls, another critical force that shaped the industry was state and federal regulation. Initially, thrifts were not subject to many state laws, primarily because local governments considered them to be semi-philanthropic, not-for-profit businesses. The "nationals" crisis combined with the Depression of 1893 changed this environment and by the end of the nineteenth century, nearly every state had created some form of S&L regulation. Significantly, thrift leaders helped draft many of these laws since they saw regulation as a way to establish minimum operating standards and raise public confidence in all S&Ls. While there was little uniformity between the various state laws, the net effect of early regulation was both to protect consumer interests and to promote the thrift business.[6]

Like state regulation, federal oversight of thrifts came in response to industry problems and economic turmoil. When the Great Depression caused

---

[4] For the development of trade groups in the textile industry, see Louis Galambos, *Competition & Cooperation; the Emergence of a National Trade Association* (Baltimore: Johns Hopkins Press, 1966). For trade association activities in trucking see William R. Childs, *Trucking and the Public Interest: The Emergence of Federal Regulation, 1914–1940* (Knoxville: University of Tennessee Press, 1985).

[5] The organizational synthesis is elaborated in Louis Galambos, "The Emerging Organizational Synthesis in Modern American History," *Business History Review* 44 (Autumn 1970), 279–90; and Louis Galambos, "Technology, Political Economy, and Professionalization: Central Themes in the Organizational Synthesis," *Business History Review* 57 (Winter 1983), 472–93.

[6] The lack of uniformity in state regulation was also a problem for the railroad industry, and contributed to the formation of federal rules. See K. Austin Kerr, *American Railroad Politics, 1914–1920; Rates, Wages, and Efficiency* (Pittsburgh: University of Pittsburgh Press, 1968).

hundreds of S&Ls to fail, increased regulation was prescribed as the cure. With the active involvement of industry leaders, Congress created a credit reserve bank, a system of federal charters, and a deposit insurance program for thrifts, all of which mirrored similar programs for commercial banks. Although there was tremendous disagreement within the industry about the need of federal involvement in their business, it soon became apparent that these programs would produce many of the same positive effects associated with state regulation. Such benefits included access to low-cost funds, more uniform financial standards, and the formation of new S&Ls in areas poorly served by other lenders.

The nature of government oversight of the thrift industry resembled the pattern of regulation in other industries. Thrift regulations were designed to fit the specific characteristics of this industry. For example, because thrifts were not-for-profit mutuals, they received preferential tax treatment. Also, regulators worked to ensure the ready availability of mortgage finance by giving thrifts competitive advantages over banks in their ability to attract funds. These included allowing thrifts to pay higher rates on savings and hold lower reserves than banks. Finally, like officials in other regulated industries, S&L leaders often tried to influence the degree of oversight, a condition that critics charged resulted in the "capture" of the regulators by the regulated industry.[7]

Although S&Ls clearly came to rely on government support to protect and promote their work as home lenders, this pattern of relations does not conform to the classic "life cycle" theory of regulatory failure. First put forth in the 1950s, the life-cycle theory maintains that regulatory agencies go through distinct phases. They begin with strong attention given to serving the public interest but they culminate in regulatory capture. While there were periods when the industry did appear to have undue influence over regulators, there was no real consistency or true control. In fact, during the tenures of FHLBB chairmen James P. McMurray and John E. Horne in the 1960s, regulatory oversight was revitalized and sought to balance public and industry interests; similar attempts occurred in the 1980s under Edwin Gray. The ability of powerful personalities to shape the degree of regulation runs counter to a basic point of the life-cycle theory and confirms what other researchers have identified as weaknesses in the idea of regulatory capture.[8]

---

[7] For a discussion of the life-cycle theory of regulation and regulatory capture, see Thomas McCraw, "Regulation in American: A Review Article," *Business History Review* 49 (Summer 1975), 159–83; and Thomas McCraw, editor, *Regulation in Perspective: Historical Essays* (Cambridge, MA: Harvard University Press, 1981).

[8] Kenneth J. Meier and John P. Plumlee, "Regulatory Administration and Organizational Rigidity," *The Western Political Quarterly* 31 (March 1978), 80–95; and William D. Berry, "An Alternative to the Capture Theory of Regulation: The Case of State Public Utility Commissions," *American Journal of Political Science* 28 (August 1984), 524–58.

In the final analysis, federal regulation of the thrift industry must be considered an overall failure, but one that was marked by periods of notable success. Federal regulation did serve the public interest by expanding the availability of home finance through programs like deposit insurance and the system of federal charters for S&Ls. Regulation also produced a number of benefits for S&Ls, since federal rules often protected thrifts from competition. The failures of regulation, however, are more numerous. The rigidity of the regulatory process hindered the ability of thrifts to respond to economic changes and market competition. Similarly, rules such as interest-rate controls created artificial and inefficient business environments that sometimes stifled innovation. The greatest failure of regulation was the lack of consistency in oversight, a condition that undermined the overall effectiveness of regulation and was an important factor in the S&L crisis of the 1980s.[9]

THRIFT, HOME OWNERSHIP, AND AMERICAN SOCIETY

A final broad theme permeating this history was the role S&Ls had in raising the level of home ownership in America. This was especially true during the late nineteenth century when thrift leaders advocated home ownership among the working class as a way to alleviate the problems of social urbanization. While the League touted the financial benefits of not paying rent, it also emphasized how owning a home created the ideal environment to raise a family and instill both moral and spiritual values. These included greater personal pride and self-responsibility, as well as increased community participation and interest in good government. Most importantly, home ownership was a sign of national patriotism, a theme expressed best in the official motto of the League – "The American Home. The Safeguard of American Liberties."

Aside from helping to redefine the popular conception of the home, thrifts also played a crucial role in the rise of suburbia. Although suburbs were common to most American cities by the 1920s, they became the dominant form of middle-class residence in the 1950s when the post–World War II "baby boom" produced an unprecedented demand for housing. Since consumers associated S&Ls with home lending, these institutions became the leading source of institutional mortgage finance, helping thousands of families acquire this key element of the American Dream. Furthermore, the availability of affordable credit also helped transform America from a nation of renters to one where nearly two-thirds of all households now own their own home, and made equity in a home the single largest source of wealth for most households.

[9] For a broader discussion of the role regulatory oversight had in the S&L crisis, see National Commission on Financial Institution Reform, Recovery and Enforcement, *Origins and Causes of the S&L Debacle: A Blueprint for Reform*, 1993, 4–7.

The history of S&Ls also reveals a strong element of social inclusiveness. For example, women traditionally represented nearly a third of all thrift members, and S&Ls typically treated their female members equally with male members. This acceptance reflected how women used their traditional leadership role in home affairs to assume a greater role in the financing of homes. The degree of involvement was such that women served as S&L managers, organized their own associations, and held leadership posts within the trade associations long before similar gains were realized in commercial banking.[10] Ethnic Americans and recent immigrants also had an important role in the growth of S&Ls. One reason why ethnic-owned S&Ls were so popular with immigrants was that they were neighborhood institutions that typically conducted business in the members' native language. Also, because home ownership was associated with good citizenship, membership in a thrift helped these people to assimilate into their new cultures and prove their desire to become "true" Americans.

Finally, African Americans were active in the thrift industry, although their work was more akin to their experiences in other financial industries. During the years of segregation in the South, African Americans formed S&Ls to serve their communities, much as was also the case for minority-owned banks and insurance companies. When blacks migrated to cities in the North and West, African American S&Ls followed and became so active in residential finance for minorities that they formed a separate trade group to promote their interests. One significant aspect of African American involvement in S&Ls was that as early as the 1890s several associations were biracial, a trend that was extremely rare in other financial industries.

THE 1980S IN HISTORICAL PERSPECTIVE

Finally, my history of the thrift industry sheds new light on the S&L crisis of the 1980s. The thrift debacle began after an economic slowdown and volatile interest rates in the late 1970s caused legislators to pass legislation deregulating the thrift industry. These laws gave S&Ls greater powers to attract deposits and make loans in areas beyond home finance, and were intended to help these firms become more diversified and competitive. Unfortunately, deregulation, combined with other factors including lax oversight, fraud, and unwise (but well-intentioned) lending decisions, produced one of the greatest financial crises in American history. The events of the 1980s not only caused the industry to shrink in absolute numbers, but led to the demise of the national thrift trade group and the creation of new regulations intent on returning S&Ls to their original focus of providing consumer lending services.

[10] For background on women in banking, see Genevieve N. Gildersleeve, *Women in Banking* (Washington DC: Public Affairs Press, 1959).

Although the S&L debacle is the most thoroughly discussed and analyzed aspect of the thrift industry, only a few authors place the events in any historical context. As a result, many accounts portray the period as an aberrant time for the industry. As my history shows, however, the S&L crisis of the 1980s was not unique but was similar to the "nationals" crisis of the 1890s, and to a lesser extent the crisis of the 1930s. In these periods all produced thrift failures and a decline in public confidence in the industry. Similarly, the crisis of the 1980s was not limited to S&Ls, since commercial banks also experienced severe hardships. Between 1980 and 1994, nearly 12 percent of the nation's banks (controlling $303 billion in assets) required some form of government assistance. Furthermore, while American Savings and Loan of California with $33.8 billion in assets was the largest failure of any financial institution in the 1980s, the next four largest failures (with a total of $104.5 billion in assets) were all commercial banks.[11]

Despite the turmoil of the 1980s, the S&L industry continues to thrive. One reason for this success is that many thrifts remain committed to meeting the financial needs of consumers and small businesses. Significantly, the majority of these thrifts are relatively small, community-oriented institutions that continue to exhibit close relations between management and members. While a handful of large firms have come to dominate the modern thrift industry, the Hollywood image of the Bailey Bros. Building and Loan remains a vital part of this business, as dozens of "George Baileys" continue to follow the same guiding principles that thrift managers have adhered to for more than 150 years.

[11] Federal Deposit Insurance Corporation (FDIC), *Managing The Crisis: The FDIC and RTC Experience, 1980–1994*, (Washington, DC: FDIC, 1998), 10–15.

APPENDIX 1. FRAUD, FORBEARANCE, AND FAILURE: THE CASE OF EMPIRE SAVINGS & LOAN ASSOCIATION

One of the most oft-cited reasons for the failure of thrifts in the 1980s was management fraud. The focus on white-collar crime, however, produces a misleading picture about why thrifts failed, since most insolvencies resulted from a variety of factors. One of the most important of these factors was negligence on the part of regulators to intervene in a timely manner. This problem is well illustrated in the case of Empire Savings and Loan Association of Mesquite, Texas (Empire S&LA), which failed in 1984 directly as a result of massive insider fraud. This one-office thrift made millions in loans for the construction of condominiums in an area outside Dallas, and within a matter of months grew from an institution possessing $13 million in assets to one having more than $330 million in assets. This growth caused thrift managers and their associates to became fabulously rich and the envy of the entire industry. This success, however, was not based on prudent lending practices, but instead resulted from abuses, the most grievous of which was the way thrift insiders conspired to inflate the value of the land for which they made loans. Ironically, these activities attracted the attention of regulators, and almost from the start they had some knowledge that Empire S&LA's management was engaged in fraud.

Despite such early warnings, regulators failed to act quickly to end abuses, in part because of weaknesses in their enforcement powers and in part because of bureaucratic inertia. The result was a thrift failure that was at the time the largest in the history of the thrift industry – an important example of how complex economic, political, and business forces could combine to produce problems for thrifts in the 1980s. No single factor brought down Empire S&LA.[1]

[1] This chapter is based on my Masters of Business Administration thesis at the University of Texas at Austin titled "The Failure of Empire Savings and Loan Association of Mesquite Texas" completed in August 1985, and my paper "Fraud, Forbearance and Failure: The Failure

THE STORY OF FAILURE

Although the failure of Empire S&L in 1984 led to the largest payout of insured deposits in the then-fifty-year history of the Federal Savings and Loan Insurance Corporation (FSLIC), the S&L had humble beginnings. Organized in 1973 as Town East Savings and Loan, the thrift operated out of a nondescript office located in a strip shopping center in Mesquite, Texas, a suburb east of Dallas. Only $13 million in size, Town East served its 2,000 local depositors with traditional thrift products, including mortgages, car loans, and term certificates of deposits (CDs). As a state-chartered and federally insured institution, the thrift was under the oversight of both the Texas State Savings and Loan Department and the Federal Home Loan Bank Board (FHLBB), but like most small associations it attracted little regulatory attention. The one major difference between this and other traditional S&Ls was that Town East was a privately held stock corporation controlled by a handful of investors not mutually owned by its members.[2]

In March 1982, Spencer Blain, who was the president of First Federal Savings and Loan Association of Austin, came to Mesquite to become the majority owner of Town East S&L. Blain was a respected Texas thrift executive, and during his ten years in the industry had served as a director of the Federal Home Loan Bank in Little Rock, Arkansas, vice chairman of the executive committee of the Federal Home Loan Mortgage Corporation Advisory Board, and president of the politically powerful Texas Savings and Loan League. Blain was credited with making First Federal into a highly profitable S&L; and, although his departure was unexpected, many people assumed he left because he wanted to run his own association, something that was not possible at the mutually owned First Federal. By August 1982, Blain had acquired 67 percent of the stock of Town East and renamed it Empire S&LA.[3]

Because of his reputation, regulators viewed this move by Blain as positive; but even at this early date there were signs that his new S&L might become

of Empire Savings and Loan Association of Mesquite, Texas" delivered at the Southwest Social Science Association conference on 12 March 1996 at Houston TX.

[2] D. W. Nauss, "Inside View of Empire," *The Dallas Times Herald*, 3 February 1985, 10; Allen Pusey, "Fast Money and Fraud," *The New York Times Magazine*, 23 April 1988, 32; Rick Atkinson and David Maraniss, "In Texas, Thrifts went on a Binge of Growth," *The Washington Post*, 11 June 1989, 1.

[3] It was only later that it was revealed Blain and the directors of First Federal disagreed over how to best expand the Austin thrift. Allen Pusey and Christi Harlan, "S&L President Made $16 Million in Land Deals," *The Dallas Morning News*, 16 December 1983, 1; U.S. Congress. Committee on Government Operations. Subcommittee on Commerce, Consumer, and Monetary Affairs, *Hearings on the Adequacy of the Federal Home Loan Bank Board Supervision of the Failure Empire Savings and Loan Association of Mesquite Texas*, 98th Congress, 2nd sess. (Washington, DC: USGPO, 1984), 43; Interview with Charles Beil, President First Federal Savings and Loan, Big Spring, Texas, by the author, 18 November 1984; Allen Pusey, "Fast Money and Fraud," 34.

a problem institution. Federal regulations required the Board to give prior approval for any change in the ownership of a thrift, but Blain simply ignored this requirement. This step should have automatically prevented him from acquiring Empire's stock and becoming chairman, but rather than blocking the change, the Board simply notified Blain of the regulatory violation by mail and requested he submit the necessary application for retroactive approval. After seven months of repeated requests, in March 1983 Blain finally asked for Board approval for the change of ownership. By that time, however, he had already implemented the business plan that would make Empire S&LA one of the fastest growing financial institutions in the country, and ultimately one of its costliest thrift failures.[4]

Blain acquired Empire S&LA primarily because he wanted to transform the thrift from a marginally profitable association into an industry leader by using several of the new powers allowed by deregulation. Under his plan, Empire S&LA would make short-term loans to acquire raw land for the development, and construction of condominiums.[5] While finding borrowers who wanted to live in the condominiums would have been ideal, the majority of the loans actually went to investors who intended to profit from the resale of the units. To fund these acquisition, development, and construction (ADC) loans Blain intended to use brokered deposits, made possible by a market that had grown significantly after deregulation removed many of the rules restricting their use. This money would be held in the form of federally insured $100,000 short-term certificates of deposits known as jumbo CDs.[6] After selling the condominiums to the final homeowners, Empire S&LA intended to refinance the ADC loans with long-term mortgages, which would then be sold to the Federal National Mortgage Association, with the proceeds used to pay off the CDs as they matured. Blain thought it would take two to four years to complete this cycle, after which he would let his S&L shrink in size while retaining large profits for himself.[7]

---

4 David Hurlbut, D. W. Nauss, and Stuart Silverstein, "Loan Inquiries Glut Stifle Ray Hubbard Condo Boom," *The Dallas Times Herald*, 22 January 1984, 22; Andrew Albert and Richard Ringer, "Questions Raised by 'Penn Square of Thrifts' Gets Scrutiny in congressional Hearing Today," *The American Banker*, 25 April 1984, 1, 12; *Hearings on FHLBB Supervision of Empire S&LA*, 83, 355.

5 Although thrifts gained the right to make land development loans in 1959 and construction loans in 1978, ADC lending gained a major boost when the Garn-St. Germain Depository Institutions Act of 1982 removed virtually all restrictions on this type of business. Barth, *The Great Savings and Loan Debacle*, 119–132.

6 In the 1980s deposit brokers used sophisticated computer programs to track CD interest rates and terms at institutions across the country and electronically transfer funds in exchange for CDs that they then sell to individual investors. David Cates, "The Case for Brokered Deposits," *United States Banker* 95 (May 1984), 46–8; Sanford Rose, "In Praise of Brokered Deposits," *The American Banker*, 20 March 1984, 1.

7 Blain also formed a nonregulated subsidiary, Statewide Service Corporation, to assist in the lending process and also generate additional income for the thrift. *Hearings on FHLBB*

To make this plan work, Blain needed a suitable region to build condominiums, and he found it east of Dallas along Interstate-30, between Interstate-635 and Lake Ray Hubbard. Known locally as the "I-30 Corridor," this ten-square-mile stretch of land had a number of characteristics that made it ideal for residential development. It was an easy and direct commute to downtown Dallas, was close to recreation and shopping, and was large enough and sufficiently undeveloped to support the level of activity envisioned by Blain. While the I-30 Corridor was a good location for construction, ensuring the success of the projects Empire S&LA would finance required using real estate developers experienced in designing, building, and marketing this type of housing.[8]

The main developer of the Empire S&LA projects was Danny Faulkner, a Mississippi native who had dropped out of school after the sixth grade and who was unable to read or write. Faulkner came to Dallas in the early 1970s, where he began a house-painting company, through which he met insurance executive Ken Murchison. The millionaire Murchison was taken by the folksy manner of the illiterate house painter and helped him grow his business to such an extent that by the end of the decade Faulkner was looking for ways to invest his growing wealth. He was one of the first to build condominiums near Lake Ray Hubbard, and their quick sale convinced him to expand his holdings in the area. Faulkner also made an investment in Town East Savings and Loan; and in 1981, when its president decided to leave, he convinced Blain to become the new executive officer. Faulkner even provided Blain with a $850,000 loan to acquire a controlling interest in the thrift. In addition to Faulkner, the other key figures in the I-30 Corridor were Clifford Sinclair, a former National Home Builders Association "Salesman of the Year" with only a limited background in the development of condominiums, and Jim Toler, a former mayor of Rowlett, Texas, who had no real estate experience.[9]

Within months of Blain's acquisition of Empire S&LA, the once barren I-30 Corridor was teeming with construction crews throwing up condominiums. While most of these projects were fairly small in size; some, like The Park, a 3,100-unit development, were miniature cities. Empire S&LA

Supervision of Empire S&LA, 151–2; Day, *S&L Hell*, 148; Pusey, "Fast Money and Fraud," 35; Atkinson and Maraniss, "In Texas, Thrifts went on a Binge of Growth," 1.

[8] Rick Atkinson and David Maraniss, "Only Ambition Limited S&L Growth," *The Washington Post*, 12 June 1989, 1; Allen Pusey and Christi Harlan, "Condo Land Deals Price Spiral Probed," *The Dallas Morning News*, 27 November 1983, 1; Day, *S&L Hell*, 148–50; "In Empire's Wake, a Dynasty Shakes," *The American Banker*, 7 February 1984, 1, 11; *Hearings on FHLBB Supervision of Empire S&LA*, 45–6.

[9] Albert and Ringer, "Questions Raised by 'Penn Square of Thrifts' Gets Scrutiny in congressional Hearing Today," 12; Pusey, "Fast Money and Fraud," 35; Atkinson and Maraniss, "Only Ambition Limited S&L Growth," 1; Hurlbut, Nauss, and Silverstein, "Loan Inquiries Glut Stifle Ray Hubbard Condo Boom," 22; Allen Pusey and Christi Harlan, "Condo Developer Was Indicted in Two States," *The Dallas Morning News*, 4 December 1983, 1, 10.

TABLE A1.1. *Financial Statistics for Empire Savings and Loan Association – 1981 to 1983*

($000)	12/31/81	6/30/82	12/31/82	6/30/83	12/31/83
Mortgages	13,013	27,471	85,064	257,904	437,228
Less: LIP*	(2,738)	(11,584)	(29,990)	(81,343)	(105,745)
Total Assets	16,958	31,436	67,690	178,461	332,512
Broker Deposits	1,206	14,574	48,437	139,054	291,410
Net Worth	781	838	2,068	8,201	11,695
Interest Income	587	924	2,815	11,510	16,068
Fee Income	49	301	1,516	4,021	5,270
Net Income	16	56	1,230	6,133	3,495

* Loans in Process.

Source: *Financial Statements of Empire Savings and Loan Association of Mesquite, Texas* (Federal Home Loan Bank of Dallas, unpublished document), 1–2.

provided the majority of the millions in loans that financed this flurry of building, and the result was significant growth for the thrift, as seen in Table A1.1.

By December 1983, just eighteen months after taking control of Empire S&LA, Blain appeared to have engineered a financial miracle in Mesquite. Each *month*, the net loan portfolio and level of brokered deposits at the one-office thrift rose at average rates of 82 percent and 105 percent, respectively. While such stunning growth seemed highly unusual, the fact that both net income and net worth also soared made it appear as if the expansion was being managed properly. The growing equity appeared to mitigate the fact that Empire S&LA made more condominium loans than any bank in Texas and convinced some that deregulation was indeed working.[10]

As the size of the I-30 projects expanded, Empire S&LA began to bring other thrifts into these transactions, both to reduce its concentration of loans to individual developers and to generate additional fee income. While dozens of financial institutions nationwide took part in the I-30 Corridor loans, five Texas S&Ls – Bell Savings & Loan of Belton, First Savings & Loan Association of Burkburnett, Investex Savings in Tyler, State Savings & Loan in Lubbock, and Lancaster First Federal Savings & Loan – held the largest participations and accounted for nearly half of the more than $750 million invested in the region. This business resulted in the rapid growth of these five associations: in just six months the assets of Bell S&L rose 350 percent to $77 million, while Lancaster Federal grew an astounding 610 percent to $101 million. Finally, the success of Empire S&LA garnered national

---

[10] One reason why net worth did not rise as fast as net income was because Blain and others at the thrift rewarded themselves for their success with large bonuses and other financial perks. *Financial Statements of Empire Savings and Loan Association*, 1–4.

recognition when the trade publication *National Thrift News* named it the top-rated institution for 1983.[11]

While large fees and high interest rates were important reasons these lenders were eager to work with Empire S&LA, another was the fact that the Texas thrift industry was facing hard times following the collapse of the regional economy after several years of strong growth. In the late 1970s, the Texas economy boomed because of a surge in oil and gas prices tied to the OPEC oil embargo in 1979. Business leaders were convinced that energy prices would stay high, and this assumption had prompted banks to make millions in oil production and real estate loans. By 1981, however, oil prices had returned to their pre-embargo levels, and this drop caused many overextended firms to default on their loans. In such depressed lending conditions, the fact that Empire S&LA found a way to grow profitably convinced many that Blain had found the way to achieve long-term success.[12]

Some lenders also wanted to become involved in the I-30 Corridor because they were clearly awed by the increased wealth and conspicuous consumption of Blain and his associates. Among the gifts the chairman gave himself were a $1.1 million condominium at the posh Colorado ski resort of Steamboat Springs and a luxurious blue Rolls Royce. Faulkner indulged in an even gaudier display of wealth, owning luxury cars, jets, and helicopters. He also gained a reputation for giving away money to friends and strangers. Faulkner often left $100 tips at the small neighborhood diner where he arranged many of the condominium projects, and he gave away dozens of Rolex watches and stick-pins with a diamond encrusted letter "F" as tokens of his appreciation. For his son's wedding he hired the Tulsa Symphony Orchestra to perform the theme from "Rocky" at the reception. He even built a billboard along I-30 near his projects proclaiming "Danny Faulkner Welcomes you to Garland." Despite such ostentatious displays, Faulkner also contributed money to a variety of charities; and his down-home manner led one person to describe him as "a good-old boy from Mississippi whom everyone likes."[13]

---

[11] The addition of other lenders also helped Empire S&LA comply with federal regulations regarding how many loans one thrift could make to one borrower. Allen Pusey and Christi Harlan, "Savings Firms Face Problems from Land Loans," *The Dallas Morning News*, 5 December 1983, 1; Hurlbut, Nauss, and Silverstein, "Loan Inquiries Glut Stifle Ray Hubbard Condo Boom," 22; Interview, Kenneth Law, "Law and Riddle," Belton, Texas, by the author, 5 July 1985; Interview, L. Linton Bowman III, Texas Savings and Loan Commissioner, by the author, 3 July 1985; Atkinson and Maraniss, "In Texas, Thrifts Went on a Binge of Growth," 1.

[12] Pusey and Harlan, "Condo Land Deals Price Spiral Probed," 1; *Hearings on FHLBB Supervision of Empire S&LA*, 131; Albert and Ringer, "Questions Raised by 'Penn Square of Thrifts' Gets Scrutiny in congressional Hearing Today," 12; Bowman Interview; Law Interview; Day, *S&L Hell*, 146–7.

[13] Eric Miller, "Trouble in Dannyland," *D Magazine* (February 1984), 111–13; Beil Interview; Atkinson and Maraniss, "In Texas, Thrifts went on a Binge of Growth," 1; Pusey, "Fast Money and Fraud," 33; Day, *S&L Hell*, 147; Beil Interview.

While Empire S&LA was amazing industry observers, and Blain and Faulkner were living the high life, regulators were also finding out that all was not well at the thrift. In October 1982, federal regulators began a regular, periodic supervisory examination of the thrift, which they finished in December. While the final report noted the high income and net worth of the S&L, it also detailed several improper lending practices, such as the absence of borrower equity from most of the loans. In addition, Empire S&LA had committed dozens of rules violations involving loan documentation because its financial records were in disarray. Finally, the report provided information on a September 1982 sale of land by Blain, which he had bought just six months earlier for $1.6 million, to an associate of Faulkner for $16 million. Because Empire S&LA financed all these transactions, the examiners thought that this represented a conflict of interest violation.[14]

Given these findings, the examiners called for, and FHLBB rules required, that immediate supervisory action be taken against the thrift. However, because Empire appeared financially healthy, the Board choose not to meet with Blain, but rather followed its normal bureaucratic procedure of resolving problems by mail. In January 1983, the Board sent a letter asking Blain how he planned to correct the problems cited in the examination and after receiving no response sent additional letters in February and March. Blain finally replied to the original request in April with a noninformative letter that indicated he was working to correct the issues raised in the report. Regulators later characterized this response as a "kiss-off."[15]

As the FHLBB was trying to get Blain to address the problems raised in its examination, the accounting firm Coopers & Lybrand was completing its own audit of the thrift, an examination needed to prepare year-end financial statements for regulators. Beginning in September 1982, it took ten months for auditors to sift through loan documents that were now in a marked state of confusion. Their report not only confirmed many of the findings from the earlier audit, but also cautioned that the financial condition of Empire S&LA was in fact grossly overstated. Because few of the ADC loans made by the thrift had any borrower equity, the accountants contended that these transactions were actually investments, and asserted that any fee income received should be recorded only after the properties had been sold to the

---

[14] The report also uncovered a profit-sharing agreement between Blain and Statewide Service Corp. that entitled Blain to receive a $250,000 bonus. Although regulators later struck this down, the directors of Empire voted to give their chairman a Christmas gift in the same amount. *Hearings on FHLBB Supervision of Empire S&LA*, 191–251.

[15] Allen Pusey and Christi Harlan, "Dallas Appraisal Firms Probed in Condo Deals," *The Dallas Morning News*, 30 December 1983, 10, 12; Nauss, "Inside View of Empire," 18; U.S. Congress. House, Committee on Government Operations. Subcommittee on Commerce, Consumer, and Monetary Affairs. *Report on the Federal Home Loan Board Supervision and the Failure of Empire Savings and Loan Association of Mesquite Texas*, H. Rept. 98–953, 98th Congress, 2nd sess. (Washington, DC: USGPO, 1984), quote 19.

final owners. Since this up-front income represented the bulk of the earnings for Empire S&LA, the Coopers & Lybrand recommendation would result in a significantly weaker financial condition for the thrift. The Board, however, was reluctant to act on this recommendation, in part because it was based on definitions of loans and investments that the accounting profession itself did not completely agree upon. This lack of consensus, combined with the fact that Empire S&LA was complying with existing FHLBB accounting rules, led the Board not to press for any changes.[16]

In May 1983, regulators received additional evidence that Empire S&LA was engaging in unsafe business practices, when Texas regulators completed their own supervisory review of the thrift. This third audit in less than nine months revealed that Empire S&LA was mired in deep financial trouble, and this conclusion caused Texas State Savings and Loan Department commissioner L. Linton Bowman III to arrange a meeting between himself, Blain, and FHLBB chairman Edwin Gray at the annual Texas Savings and Loan League convention in June. Although this was the first time Gray learned about Empire S&LA, even before the meeting took place he realized that this institution was indeed a special thrift. Blain met Gray at the airport in his Rolls Royce, and on the drive to the convention the Board chairman asked the thrift executive how he could afford such a luxury car. Blain simply responded "We're just very profitable down here in Texas."[17]

The June 1983 meeting produced the first substantive regulatory action designed to reign in Blain and his thrift. Texas regulators entered into an agreement with the executive to allow them to supervise the thrift for the next three months, while federal regulators decided to order another audit of the thrift. This special limited examination was completed in October, and it showed that Empire S&LA was hopelessly entangled in a web of mismanagement, featuring loan records that had not been maintained or updated for months. Furthermore, the examiners found that many of the loans were grossly overstated because they were based on artificially inflated land values. Although the report gave the thrift its lowest possible rating and strongly recommended immediate supervisory action, the Board demurred and instead ordered new appraisals of the I-30 Corridor properties to determine the accuracy of these new findings.[18]

By the end of 1983, however, it was a virtual certainty that this thrift was going to fail. Because it relied on short-term jumbo CDs to fund its

---

[16] Andrew Albert, "Panel Blasts Bank Board over Empire Failure," *The American Banker*, 1 August 1984, 3; *Hearings on FHLBB Supervision of Empire S&LA*, quote 240, 334, 336; *Report on FHLBB Supervision of Empire S&LA*, 28.

[17] Atkinson and Maraniss, "In Texas, Thrifts went on a Binge of Growth," 1; Pusey, "Fast Money and Fraud," 33; Day, *S&L Hell*, quote 150.

[18] *Hearings on FHLBB Supervision of Empire S&LA*, 88, 307, 369; Allen Pusey and Christi Harlan, "State Assumes Control of Empire Savings," *The Dallas Morning News*, 12 January 1984, 1.

short-term ADC loans, Empire S&LA needed a steady stream of condominium sales to pay off these obligations as they matured. By one estimate, a minimum of 200 units had to be sold each month to meet these cash needs. An average of just four condominiums sold each month, and this low sales rate highlighted a basic flaw in Blain's original plan to expand his thrift. Because the I-30 Corridor was only ten square miles in size, experts estimated it could absorb only 75 new condominium units per month. A healthy level of units on the market at any one time was 675, or approximately a nine-month supply. Blain and the project developers apparently ignored these factors since in just over two years they built more than 2,000 units and had permits to construct an additional 4,000 units. To make matters worse, other developers entered the region to build condominiums, which according to one city official, "spread like brush fire." By the end of 1983, cities along the I-30 Corridor had issued more than 30,000 condominium permits, which one research firm estimated was enough to supply demand for the next twelve years.[19]

While this "condo glut" posed obvious problems for Empire S&LA, the situation worsened in November 1983 when *The Dallas Morning News* ran the first in a series of articles detailing overbuilding in the Lake Ray Hubbard area. This adverse publicity depressed sales even more, so that by January 1984 just 779 of the thousands of completed units built were occupied. Entire projects were totally vacant. The lack of sales meant that Blain did not have the funds needed to pay off the short-term CDs as they matured, and by early 1984 the thrift faced a liquidity crisis, which it narrowly averted after Faulkner agreed to pay off $32 million of these obligations. Also, the inability to refinance the ADC loans meant that Blain could not sell them to the Federal National Mortgage Association, which refused to buy them because of their high risks. Furthermore, since few of the investor/borrowers for these loans had the financial ability to repay them, Empire S&LA was forced to write them off as they matured. As a result, even though the thrift continued to lend money, the level of nonperforming loans soared. By year-end 1983 more than $8.4 million in loans were in default or foreclosure.[20]

As the situation at Empire S&LA grew bleaker, federal regulators at the regional home loan bank in Dallas finally intervened. In December 1983, the supervisory staff made criminal referrals to the U.S. District Attorney's Office concerning the September 1982 land transaction involving Blain, and

---

[19] Richard Ringer, "Dallas County Housing Glut Hurts Local Lenders," *The American Banker*, 16 March 1984, quote 16; Albert and Ringer, "Questions Raised by 'Penn Square of Thrifts' Gets Scrutiny in Congressional Hearing Today," 22; Hurlbut, Nauss, and Silverstein, "Loan Inquiries Glut Stifle Ray Hubbard Condo Boom," 23.

[20] Albert and Ringer, "Questions Raised by 'Penn Square of Thrifts' Gets Scrutiny in Congressional Hearing Today," 22; *Hearings on FHLBB Supervision of Empire S&LA*, 22, 72, 120, 153; Andrew Albert and Richard Ringer, "Regulators Evaluating Empire's Costs," *The American Banker*, 26 March 1984, 1; Bowman Interview.

ordered Empire S&LA to stop accepting brokered deposits. On January 5, 1984, the FHLBB issued a temporary cease and desist order that prohibited further lending, and directed the FSLIC to try to arrange for a merger between Empire S&LA and another institution. Three days later, Texas regulators moved in and assumed control of the thrift, although they still allowed Blain to remain as chairman. By the end of the month, after determining that a merger was impractical, the Board formally removed Blain from the management of Empire S&LA; but, incredibly, it did not close the thrift because it thought that it needed still more evidence that the thrift was in danger of becoming insolvent.[21]

On March 14, 1984, real estate appraisers the Board had assigned in January to revalue the I-30 Corridor projects presented their findings, and their report included a videotape filmed from an airplane of the condominium projects financed by Empire S&LA. The tape showed hundreds of acres of vacant condominiums, many of which were partially built, falling apart, or the victims of arson. The scene so shocked the Board that, Gray said later, "I couldn't believe what I was seeing. It was like a pornographic movie. I had to turn away." The Board immediately declared Empire S&LA insolvent, and the next day federal regulators descended on it in such numbers that one thrift executive commented, "it wasn't so much an examination as it was an invasion. We didn't have that many people in Normandy on D-Day." Shortly afterward, the FSLIC began paying off insured depositors – payments which eventually exceeded $273 million, making Empire S&LA the largest thrift failure in the history of the thrift deposit insurance program to that time.[22]

IDENTIFYING THE FACTORS OF FAILURE

A month after regulators closed Empire S&LA, a subcommittee of the House Committee on Government Operations began hearings seeking to determine why the thrift failed. While it was clear that management fraud caused the collapse, legislators wanted to know if any other factors played a role in the failure. Their investigation led the subcommittee to conclude that regulators also played a major role by not properly monitoring the thrift. Even though he was loathe to admit it, Board chairman Gray eventually agreed with this assessment, conceding that "the manner in which this case was handled by the regulatory apparatus, was deficient in a number of ways." He even speculated that had regulators acted quicker Empire S&LA "would not have failed and possibly it could have been saved." Despite this admission

[21] Kenneth Noble, "Empire Savings of Texas Is Shut Down," *New York Times*, 15 March 1984, Sec. D, 4; Pusey and Harlan, "State Assumes Control of Empire Savings," 1; *Hearings on FHLBB Supervision of Empire S&LA*, 93, 155, 158.

[22] Albert and Ringer, "Regulators Evaluating Empire's Costs," 1; David Hurlbut, "Mesquite S&L Closed over Condo Loans," *The Dallas Times Herald*, 15 March 1984, quote 1; Pusey, "Fast Money and Fraud," quote 37.

of guilt, regulators claimed that the real reasons for the collapse were fraud and the fact that Empire S&LA had access to an unlimited supply of money from deposit brokers who used federal deposit insurance to protect themselves against losses.[23]

Although deposit brokers had worked with thrifts since the 1950s, in the 1980s they came under increased scrutiny because of the perception that they were engaged in what some considered unethical practices. Because deposit brokers primarily looked for high rates when selecting a financial institution for investment, it was common for them to move their money whenever rates changed. This threat of sudden withdrawals, regulators charged, caused thrift managers to find ways to keep rates high, which resulted in making riskier loans that would generate sufficient income. Despite this increased risk, brokers protected themselves by only opening accounts that qualified for deposit insurance, a task made easier by the 1980 increase in the coverage amount from $40,000 to $100,000. Regulators alleged that this was exactly what happened in the case of Empire S&LA, since just 3.7 percent of its accounts were not covered by deposit insurance, even though 85 percent of total deposits came from brokers. According to Gray, the use of brokered deposits was a "spreading cancer on the federal deposit insurance system."[24]

Outside industry experts, however, strongly disagreed with these arguments, and contended that they obscured the real reason why thrifts failed. According to one banking analyst, "the emphasis on brokered deposits as some sort of major cause of bank failure is simply misleading. Mismanagement is the cause of bank failures." Several brokers who worked with Empire S&LA also told legislators that "on paper the thrift looked very well. But we weren't actually given enough information to make a proper evaluation, so we didn't know all their problems." On the basis of this testimony, the subcommittee concluded that deposit brokers were not to blame for the problems with Empire S&LA, and in its final report virtually exonerated their activities, saying that "brokered deposits were not the proximate cause of Empire's failure. Brokered deposits did indeed provide additional fuel, but the fire had been raging, and was not originally ignited by the brokered funds."[25]

[23] *Report on FHLBB Supervision of Empire S&LA*, 41, 43; *Hearings on FHLBB Supervision of Empire S&LA*, quote 121.
[24] William O'Connell, *America's Money Trauma: How Washington Blunders Crippled the U.S. Financial System* (Winnetka, IL: Conversation Press, 1992), 63; Christi Harlan, "Empire S&L Closed, Declared Insolvent," *The Dallas Morning News*, 15 March 1984, 1; *Financial Statements of Empire Savings and Loan Association*, 3–4; *Hearings on FHLBB Supervision of Empire S&LA*, 28, 83, 245, *Report on FHLBB Supervision of Empire S&LA*, 48; Lisa J. McCue, "Brokered Funds Issue," *The American Banker*, 22 June 1983, 10; Nancy L. Ross, "Bank Board Liquidates Texas S&L; 'Cancer' of Brokered Funds Cited," *The Washington Post*, 15 March 1984, quote 1.
[25] Federal Deposit Insurance Corporation (FDIC). *Managing the Crisis: The FDIC and RTC Experience*, (Washington, DC: FDIC, 1998), 210–11; National Commission on Financial

THE ROLE OF FRAUD

Although brokered deposits did "provide additional fuel" for Empire S&LA, the basic reason why the fire began lay in broad and systemic corruption inside and outside the thrift. One aspect of these unethical practices involved how the thrift abused what were otherwise acceptable lending practices. For example, while it was common for lenders to include up-front fees as part of the loan amount, in the case of Empire S&LA these fees were more than 400 percent higher than normal, which in turn greatly increased the size and risk of these loans. The thrift also followed slipshod loan-closing procedures involving the omission of required disclosure documents, and the outright alteration and falsification of other loan materials. While this was done to hide illegal activities, it was also necessary to allow Empire S&LA to close loans rapidly, often at all times of the day and night. According to one investor, "it was not unusual to drive by and see the lights on in the office past midnight, with people inside signing papers and eating pizza."[26]

The most serious instance of fraud, however, involved how developers deliberately inflated land prices as a way to reap significant profits for themselves. They did this by using a real estate technique known as a "land flip," which involves the multiple sale and resale of land within a short period of time, often between buyers and sellers who know each other. While land flipping is uncommon but legal if done over a period of months or years, along the I-30 Corridor developers often sold land among themselves several times in just a matter of hours. Furthermore, since the land price increased with each transaction, when these paper-shuffling exercises ended it was common for the final sales price to have risen by more than 800 percent over the original acquisition cost. In one such series of land flips, a sixty-acre tract of land was resold ten times among seven individuals in one afternoon; the price of this raw land rose from $1 per square foot to over $6 per square foot. Since Empire S&LA financed each flip, these transactions produced huge paper profits.[27]

Institution Recovery, Reform and Enforcement, *Origins and Causes of the S&L Debacle*, (Washington, DC: USGPO, 1993), 6, 35–7; Andrew Albert and Richard Ringer, "Some Brokers Shunned Empire But Others Fueled Its Growth," *American Banker*, 23 March 1984, 1; Jay Rosenstein, "Gray Says Linkage Exists Between Money Brokers and Failures," *American Banker*, 20 March 1984, 12; *Hearings on FHLBB Supervision of Empire S&LA*, quote 24; *Report on FHLBB Supervision of Empire S&LA*, quote 48.

26 The senior broker of the Dallas Title Company, which closed most of the Empire S&L, was also a director of the thrift. Albert and Ringer, "Questions Raised by 'Penn Square of Thrifts' Gets Scrutiny in Congressional Hearing Today," 12; Pusey and Harlan, "Condo Land Deals Price Spiral Probed," 1; Law Interview; Hurlbut, Nauss and Silverstein, "Loan Inquiries Glut Stifle Ray Hubbard Condo Boom," 27–8; Nauss, "Inside View of Empire," quote 10.

27 *Hearings on FHLBB Supervision of Empire S&LA*, 130; Pusey and Harlan, "Condo Land Deals Price Spiral Probed," 20.

After inflating the price of land, developers subdivided the parcels into small tracts, which were then sold to outside investors unaware of the land flips. This process of "slicing the pie" into smaller pieces both concealed the flips and allowed the developers to realize the actual profits of their flipping. Again, Empire S&LA financed these transactions, which produced millions more in fee income. Since dozens of borrowers were now involved in these deals, the thrift could finance an entire project while still complying with federal regulations that restricted the number of loans a thrift could make to one individual. Although the final borrowers generally did not question these transactions, some worried that they might not be able to repay their loans, especially because these debts often exceeded their actual net worth. Thrift lawyers typically told the borrowers that 'if worse came to worst, [they] could always declare bankruptcy." Finally, signing bonuses of between $21,000 and $43,000 per loan alleviated any lingering concerns. As one borrower later said, "they hit you in a place one would like to think is not vulnerable – they hit you right in your greed."[28]

As outrageous as the land flips were, regulators initially had trouble uncovering them, because the developers found a way to make the inflated land values appear to reflect actual market conditions. They did this by using independent appraisers who followed the standards established by the two leading appraisal societies, the Society of Real Estate Appraisers (SREA) and the American Institute of Real Estate Appraisers (AIREA). According to these groups, a properly prepared appraisal should use three different valuation methods: the cost approach, income approach, and sales comparison approach. The sales comparison approach, which is the most accepted way to determine values for condominium and land sales, uses the sales prices of at least three comparable properties to determine the value of the subject property. While the definition of a comparable property is open to personal judgement, the AIREA and SREA require an appraiser to take into account the location, sales date, and physical similarities when choosing a comparable property. The appraiser should then make adjustments based on any major differences and provide an explanation for each change.[29]

While using multiple approaches to arrive at a real estate's value is one aspect of the appraisal process, another equally important consideration involves evaluating whether or not the proposed use for the property represents its "highest and best use." For development properties like those in

---

[28] Similar payoffs were made to other thrifts that made loans in the I-30 Corridor, with participation bonuses sometimes exceeding $500,000. Bowman Interview; Pusey and Harlan, "Condo Land Deals, Price Spiral Probed," 1, 10, quote 10.

[29] American Institute of Real Estate Appraisers, *The Appraisal of Real Estate*, 8th ed. (Chicago: American Institute of Real Estate Appraisers, 1983), 11–12, 210, 435; R. A. Rhodes, *Valuation of Chandler's Landing Marina, Lake Ray Hubbard Texas* (unpublished manuscript), 1, 2, 4.

the I-30 corridor, the recommended way to determine the highest and best use is with a feasibility analysis in which the appraiser compares a proposed project to existing and competitive projects in the surrounding area. It takes into account demand and supply projections, the expected absorption rate for the development, as well as development constraints such as zoning and location. These various valuation techniques and methods of analysis make an appraisal not just a report on market values, but a way to answer questions on the economic feasibility of a project, and its compatibility with the surrounding community.[30]

While virtually anyone can prepare an appraisal, the most highly regarded reports are from appraisers certified by the AIREA with the designation of "Master Appraisal Institute," or MAI. These appraisers must meet the highest professional, educational, and ethical standards of the AIREA. The MAI designation "mean[s] as much in real estate appraising as CPA does in accounting and MD does in medicine." Despite all the efforts to make appraisals unbiased and reliable, their final values are still estimates, which can vary on the basis of different assumptions; as one appraiser wryly admitted, "the only 'true value' is a hardware store." This inherent flexibility makes appraisals open to influence, and critics charge that anyone can "buy" an appraisal, or that an MAI appraisal is in reality "Made As Instructed." Still, the overall integrity of appraisers is high, and many outside institutions place ultimate faith in these people to make unbiased valuations. As one thrift president noted, "If you can't trust an MAI appraiser, who can you trust?"[31]

Given the importance of this certification to lenders, Empire S&LA used MAI appraisers to make more than 90 percent of all the valuations in the I-30 Corridor. To ensure these reports supported the inflated values created by the land flips, the developers paid cash bonuses to the appraisers and let them invest in the properties they were evaluating. As a result, it was not surprising that the appraisers ignored many professional ethics guidelines, as well as several federal regulations. Most of the sales comparables bore little resemblance to the subject, and the appraisers rarely adjusted their valuations to reflect these differences. If any adjustments were made, they were seemingly done at random with no supporting documentation. Despite such sloppy procedures, the signature of an MAI appraiser on each report gave

---

[30] *Hearings on FHLBB Supervision of Empire S&LA*, 130–3, quote 131; Byrl Boyce and William Kinnard, *Appraising Real Property* (Lexington, MA: Lexington Books, 1983), 109; David C. Lennhoff, "What's All the Ruckus Over R-41b?" *The Appraisal Journal* 52 (July 1984), 444.

[31] American Institute of Real Estate Appraisers, *Standards of Professional Practice* (Chicago: American Institute of Real Estate Appraisers, 1982), quote Section 1; Interview with Dr. Terry Grissom, MAI SREA, Associate Professor of Real Estate, University of Texas at Austin, Austin, Texas, by the author, 15 November 1984, quote; Pusey and Harlan, "Dallas Appraisal Firms Probed in Condo Deals," quote 1.

them an air of legitimacy, which "any S&L would accept and rely on...as gospel." Unfortunately, over time honest appraisers used these fraudulent valuations as comparables to determine the value of properties unrelated to the thrift scandal, which resulted in "a vicious cycle in which the inflated appraisal supported an inflated loan for an inflated land sale. And soon those land sales were used as comparables for other sales."[32]

Despite such systematic fraud, Blain testified that he was not to blame for the failure of his thrift, but rather it was due, he claimed, to the overall decline of the Dallas real estate market. His only fault, he said, was succumbing to the "boom psychology" that pervaded the region. Blain also blamed the massive construction in the I-30 Corridor by developers not associated with Empire S&LA for depressing sales and asserted that without this additional activity he would have been able to meet his goals. Furthermore, if regulators had been willing to work with him instead of "inducing a destructive process, all the tragic consequences of Empire's liquidation might have been avoided." Blain's arguments were echoed by others who participated in the projects. The president of Bell S&L addressed the issue of high fees, noting that the deals were not out of line with market condition. Regulators instead ignored this since it "made more sense for [regulators] to say 'look at how greedy they were.' Yes they were good deals and good offers, but that's what the deals were making at the time. The point was if you take everything out of context it looked crazy."[33]

THE ROLE OF REGULATORS

Although the fraud that permeated the activities at Empire S&LA was sufficient to cause the insolvency, the House subcommittee also found that the magnitude of the crisis was heightened by the lack of timely regulatory intervention. In their defense, regulators claimed that it was hard to reign in the thrift because at the time it appeared to be the model of success. As Bowman stated, "the biggest problem we were faced with was that at least on paper – and as a matter of fact according to the *National Thrift News* – [Empire S&LA] was a leader in the industry.... This makes it that much more difficult for us to walk in the front door and say 'I'm sorry Number 1, but we're

---

[32] Allen Pusey and Christi Harlan, "I-30 Land Appraiser Reaped Gains," *Dallas Morning* News, 10 February 1984, 1; Christi Harlan, "Some I-30 Condo Properties Overvalued 70%, Board Finds," *Dallas Morning* News, 13 April 1984, 8; *Hearings on FHLBB Supervision of Empire S&LA*, 131; *Report on FHLBB Supervision of Empire S&LA*, 39; Christi Harlan, "I-30 Appraiser Admits Inflating," *National Mortgage News*, 29 April 1985, 1; Law Interview, quote; Pusey and Harlan, "Dallas Appraisal Firms Probed in Condo Deals," quote 10.

[33] Nancy L. Ross Empire Chairman Denies Wrongdoing in Collapse," *The Washington Post*, 26 April 1984, C13; *Hearings on FHLBB Supervision of Empire S&LA*, 155–61, quote 161; Law Interview, quote.

going to close you down.' So we felt we had to develop a fairly complex set of evidence to allow us to go into court and defend our position." Ironically, one reason why Empire S&LA could appear to be the model of sound health was that it complied with regulatory rules regarding the distinction between loans and investments.[34]

As the 1982 Coopers & Lybrand examination revealed, the main reason Empire S&LA appeared financially strong was that it classified its real estate transactions as loans, which allowed it to boost profits with fee income earned when the loan was made. In reality, nearly all of these loans were really investments since the borrowers made no equity contributions; nor did they intend to occupy the properties upon completion. Consequently, the thrift should have deferred its fee income until after the units were sold, a change that would have dramatically reduced earnings and net worth. The Board, however, faced a dilemma, since dozens of thrifts, including many in poor financial condition, used the exact same accounting procedures as those followed by Empire S&LA. As a result, if it forced this one thrift to make changes, every association would have to change, thereby increasing the number of problem institutions and the potential for more failures. To avoid putting pressure on the deposit insurance fund, regulators took refuge in the indecision within the accounting profession on this issue as a way to delay their own action.[35]

The House subcommittee found this position inexcusable, and lambasted regulators for what it characterized as a catch-22 situation. Its final report contended that regulators used circular logic in dealing with Empire S&LA, noting that "so long as the association showed steady earnings and high net worth, the regulators would not take supervisory or regulatory action. The association would continue to show high earnings and net worth if it took fees and points on real estate activities up-front, simply because it characterized these activities as loans rather than investments. It remained for the regulators to intercede and break the cycle.... It should not have taken the accounting profession's lead for the agencies to be able to distinguish between a loan and an investment." While this indictment of the Board for not setting clear rules that defined the difference between loans and investments was specifically cited as a cause of the failure of Empire S&LA, it could also have been applied elsewhere, since loose regulatory accounting principles helped hide the true financial conditions of other failed thrifts.[36]

---

[34] Richard Sizemore, "Bowman Ready to Go After Troubled Texas Thrifts," *National Mortgage News*, 9 September 1985, 33; Albert, "Panel Blasts Bank Board over Empire Failure," 3; *Hearings on FHLBB Supervision of Empire S&LA*, 132–4, quote 133.

[35] *Hearings on FHLBB Supervision of Empire S&LA*, 134–5; *Report on FHLBB Supervision of Empire S& LA*, 28; Pusey, "Fast Money and Fraud," 33; "Professional Notes," *Journal of Accountancy* 156 (November 1983), 51–4.

[36] Day, *S&L Hell*, 165–6; *Report on FHLBB Supervision of Empire S&LA*, 31–3, quote 32.

TABLE A1.2. *Peer Group Analysis for Empire Savings and Loan Association – 1981 to 1983*

(%)	June 1981–June 1982 Empire S&LA	June 1981–June 1982 Peer Group	June 1982–June 1983 Empire S&LA	June 1982–June 1983 Peer Group	June 1983–Dec 1983 Empire S&LA	June 1983–Dec 1983 Peer Group
Change in Mortgages	276.7	1.9	4,395.3	12.2	231.5	11.0
Change in Total Assets	170.7	9.6	327.3	34.6	172.6	31.8
Change in Net Worth	14.4	(19.3)	593.2	19.4	85.2	32.1
Net Income/Net Worth	28.7	(37.4)	1,186.4	22.4	170.4	53.8
Fee Income/ GOI*	22.4	3.3	26.3	8.1	25.4	9.0
Loan Yield	11.23	10.66	25.83	10.78	17.03	11.44

* Gross Operating Income.
Source: *Financial Statements of Empire S&LA*, 3–4.

The lack of attention to detail became even more apparent when subcommittee members asked why regulators did not identify any of the unusual trends based on the repeated audits of the thrift. As financial analysis experts later noted, if regulators had reviewed their own reports of Empire S&LA and compared them to the performance figures of similar thrifts in its peer group, several inexplicable contrasts between the failed thrift and other associations in terms of the growth rates, financial ratios, and loan yields would have been very apparent, as seen in Table A1.2.

One of the most revealing trends from this comparison between Empire S&LA and other thrifts that were both similar in size and location is the extremely large increase in total mortgages and assets, especially between June 1982 and June 1983. While these trends were unusually high, because net worth also rose, again at a rate well above that of the peer group, it is understandable that Empire S&LA might escape close regulatory scrutiny. The more revealing trend was the high percentage of total income that came from up-front fees and other one-time payments. This should have caused regulators to question if the high earnings growth was sustainable. Similarly, the loan yield, which was more than double the rate for other thrifts between 1982 and 1983, is an indication that the loans made by Empire S&LA were higher-risk than traditional mortgages. These statistics, which were just a portion of the dozens available on this thrift, were all signs that at the very least Empire S&LA was an unusual institution.

The most remarkable aspect of these comparisons was that they were all taken directly from reports generated by the FHLBB. Unfortunately, the computers used by regulators were not programmed to analyze data in a way that would provide early warnings of potential problems. Similarly, while manual analysis of these reports was possible, supervisors had little time for this, because of the lack of personnel and the large number of problem institutions they had to contend with in the early 1980s. Therefore, it was not surprising that as long as the thrift reported positive net worth and net income, regulators did not investigate any further. For the subcommittee, this set of circumstances provided further evidence that federal regulators were not being proactive in preventing problem situations.[37]

Legislators also bemoaned the bureaucratic inertia that gripped regulators. For example, it took seven months for the Board to resolve the change-of-control rule violation by Blain when he first acquired Empire S&LA, and it took nearly a month for the 1982 federal examination of the thrift to be mailed from Dallas to Washington, DC. Similarly, when Coopers & Lybrand conducted their audit, they filed more than seven deadline extensions with the Board, each of which was approved "in a stylized bureaucratic fashion." A related problem cited by the subcommittee was that the FHLBB was inefficiently organized, because the people who examined the thrifts were managed from Washington, DC, while their supervisors reported to the regional home loan banks. This arrangement, legislators charged, led to confused and incomplete lines of communication, which allowed problem thrifts to fall through the cracks.[38]

In addition to the lack of communication within the FHLBB system, there was a communication gap between federal officials and state regulators. For example, the Board did not learn about the supervisory agreement Texas regulators had with Blain until *after* it closed the thrift. The most embarrassing moment, however, occurred in January 1984. As regulators were ready to move against Blain and Faulkner, the Office of the Comptroller of the Currency inexplicably approved Faulkner's application to buy a controlling interest in the First National Bank of Garland. According to Bowman, "the day [Faulkner] bought the bank, it was announced in the paper and everybody went crazy. They called us and said are you telling me the Office of the Comptroller of the Currency did not trade information with the FSLIC. That's exactly what I told them. Then I got a call from the Comptroller's office in Dallas saying can't you start talking to us on a regular basis and I said sure. I'm still waiting to hear from them."[39]

Finally, regulators working on Empire S&LA were affected by bad timing. Just as the thrift began to grow, the regional home loan bank responsible for thrifts in Texas, Arkansas, Louisiana, and New Mexico began the process of relocating its offices from Little Rock to Dallas. Curiously, there were no operational reasons for making this move, and it occurred primarily because

[37] *Hearings on FHLBB Supervision of Empire S&LA*, 33–7; *Report on FHLBB Supervision of Empire S&LA*, 39; *Financial Statements Empire S&LA*, 1–2.

[38] "Ensuring That Empire Doesn't Strike Back," *The American Banker*, 19 June 1984, 4; Day, *S&L Hell*, 166–7; *Report on FHLBB Supervision of Empire S&LA*, 41–4.

[39] Bowman Interview, quotes; Sizemore, "Bowman Ready to Go After Troubled Texas Thrifts," 33.

the Texas Savings and Loan League used its political leverage in Congress to give its state the bank headquarters it thought it deserved. The move was a disaster, as only 20 percent of all bank employees went to Dallas. More importantly, of the nearly fifty supervisory agents who worked in Little Rock, only two were at the new headquarters. Unfortunately, these two agents were still responsible for overseeing the work of 116 examiners and activities of 510 thrifts that comprised this district. The result was a huge backlog of review and oversight cases that meant that only the most serious problems received attention. Consequently, because Empire S&LA seemed healthy, it was understandable that the supervisors gave it little attention.[40]

THE AFTERMATH

Following the closure of Empire S&LA in March 1984, federal regulators had to sort out the mess the thrift had created. Their main task involved finding ways to dispose of thousands of condominiums, many of which were only partially complete or vandalized. Because new appraisals of these projects showed that their actual values were as little as 2 percent of the original valuations, the FSLIC would lose millions if it tried to auction them off in their "as is" condition. As a result, the government invested thousands to improve these properties, and by 1986 had converted 1,900 of these units into a small leasable city, with an additional 1,000 units in the process of rehabilitation. The FSLIC, however, also razed hundreds of units considered beyond repair; and this activity was followed closely by journalists, including the television show *60 Minutes*, which aired a segment on the I-30 Corridor in late 1984.[41]

A second consequence of the Empire S&LA failure was its impact on the thrifts it worked with. While dozens of associations across the country had to write off all or portions of their investments in the I-30 Corridor, seven thrifts failed directly as a result of this lending. These included all five of the Texas thrifts that had the largest loan exposures, and the cost of bailing them out exceeded $360 million. A third result from this fiasco was an effort by regulators to crack down on deposit brokers. Despite the virtual absolution of brokers' activities by the House subcommittee, federal thrift

---

[40] *Hearings on FHLBB Supervision of Empire S&LA*, 110; Pusey, "Fast Money and Fraud," 34; Atkinson and Maraniss, "Only Ambition Limited S&L Growth," 1; Day, *S&L Hell*, 165–6.

[41] One sign of the overvalued appraisals appeared when a bidder at auction paid only $600,000 for a property originally valued at $20 million. Mark Edgar, "Depositors Make Final Withdrawals at Empire S&L," *The Dallas Morning News*, 18 March 1984, 37; Christi Harlan, "Garland Feels Effect of Boom Gone Bust," *The Dallas Morning News*, 16 March 1985, 11; Christi Harlan, "FSLIC Sells I-30 Condos," *The Dallas Morning News*, 6 May 1984, 10; Christ Harlan, "I-30 Units Still FSLIC Headache; Condos May Cost $25 Million," *National Mortgage News*, 24 February 1986, 1; Pusey, "Fast Money and Fraud," 33; Esther M. Bauer, "FSLIC Empire Units Will Go Up in Smoke," *National Mortgage News*, 16 March 1987, 5.

and bank regulators still wanted to tighten rules regarding their operations. In March 1984, they issued new rules that required all brokers to register with the FDIC and limited the amount of money any one broker could place in a financial institution to $100,000. The Securities Industries Association challenged these rules and three months later a federal judge ordered them repealed. The FHLBB sought legislative controls on brokers with the Financial Services Competitive Equity Act, but when this bill failed to pass Congress the Board finally decided to abandon the issue.[42]

The final chapter in the Empire S&LA saga involved prosecuting the people involved in the failure. By the end of 1985, federal officials had brought to trial more than ninety people and forty-eight corporations associated with the I-30 Corridor projects. They secured convictions in nearly every case. In October 1987, a federal grand jury handed down an 88-count indictment for racketeering and conspiracy against Blain, Faulkner, Toler, and Sinclair. After the first trial in 1989 resulted in a hung jury, Sinclair reached a plea bargain agreement with prosecutors, and on the basis of his testimony a second jury found Blain, Faulkner, and Toler guilty on nearly all counts in November 1991. Blain and Faulkner received twenty-year sentences each, and were fined $22 million and $40 million, respectively. Toler received a ten-year sentence and $38 million fine. A 1995 civil suit against Faulkner resulted in an additional judgment of more than $340 million in damages. All told, these legal actions were one of the most successful prosecutions against criminal financial activity in the history of thrift regulation.[43]

A more positive outcome of this saga was its effect on strengthening the basic tools regulators used to deal with wayward thrifts. The most important change involved expanding the definition of "unsafe and unsound practices" under which the FHLBB could issue temporary cease-and-desist orders. Although Congress created this power to help the Board swiftly end certain

---

[42] Richard Ringer and Andrew Albert, "Regulatory Closing Hinted for Second Texas Thrift," *American Banker*, 21 March 1984, 11; Christi Harlan, "Condo-Loan S&L Put in Conservatorship," *The Dallas Morning News*, 20 March 1985, 28; Christi Harlan, "Former Officers Charged in Suit," *National Mortgage News*, 30 September 1985, 1; Kathleen Day, "Texas Thrift Chairman, 6 Others Charged with Defrauding S&Ls," *The Washington Post*, 8 October 1987, C3; Rosenstein, "Gray Says Linkage Exists between Money Brokers and Failures," 10; U.S. Congress. Senate. Committee on Banking Housing and Urban Affairs, *The Financial Services Competitive Equity Act*, S. Report. S-2851. 98th Cong., 2nd sess. (Washington, DC: USGPO, 1984).

[43] Christi Harlan, "1st I-30 Investigation Conviction Obtained," *National Mortgage News*, 22 July 1985, 22; Christi Harlan, "FSLIC Sues 91 on Empire Loans," *National Mortgage News*, 9 December 1985, 1; Christi Harlan, "88-Count Indictment Stems from Texas Thrift Collapse," *National Mortgage News*, 12 October 1987, 56; Dennis Cauchon "A Texas-sized scandal; S&L trial: 'Folk heroes' or Crooks?" *USA Today*, 27 February 1989, 1B; "4 Convicted of Fraud in Condo Case," *The New York Times*, 7 November 1991, D5; "Dallas Appraiser Gets Six-Year Jail Sentence," *The Wall Street Journal*, 26 July 1993, B6; "Blain Gets Sentenced to Term of 20 Years," *National Mortgage News*, 27 January 1992; "FDIC Wins Suit in Texas S&L Case," *The New York Times*, 18 April 1995, D6.

practices without actually closing a thrift, it could only use an order to stop practices that would likely cause an insolvency. Since none of the rules violations exposed in the repeated audits would have directly threatened the financial condition of Empire S&LA, regulators needed more evidence to justify issuing a cease-and-desist order against Empire S&LA. Even after the August 1983 examination revealed unsafe and unsound practices, the Board thought it had to prove these practices would lead directly to a failure, which led to a two-month delay that allowed Empire S&LA to make an additional $50 million in loans. To prevent this in the future, Congress broadened the use of cease-and-desist orders to include instances of incomplete and inaccurate record keeping at a thrift or any of its unregulated subsidiaries.[44]

A second positive result from the Empire S&LA experience was that Board chairman Gray began to press for a more vigorous regulatory approach toward the thrift industry. After seeing the videotape showing the waste caused by this S&L, Gray became a convert of re-regulation and lobbied both the White House and the industry to accept tighter regulations. In both areas, however, his efforts fell on deaf ears; as Gray stated at the time, "we have a major crisis here, and I can't get anyone's attention." One reason for this lack of support was that within the White House several close associates of President Reagan, including Treasury Secretary Donald Regan, disliked Gray and criticized him for not supporting the free-market spirit of the administration. From the thrift industry, leaders of many large thrifts contended that Gray was an alarmist who exaggerated the magnitude of industry problems. One of the people who wanted Gray to tone down his proposals was Charles Keating, whose own thrift, Lincoln Savings & Loan, would become the one of the largest thrift failures in history.[45]

CONCLUSIONS

The case of Empire S&LA is a prime example of how criminal activities that enriched a handful of people both within and outside a thrift sometimes led to a failure costing taxpayers millions. Like other failures involving fraud, the rise and fall of this Texas thrift was remarkably short. Empire S&LA began as Town East Savings and Loan in 1973, and for eight years it remained a small association that served local customers. In early 1982, Town East became Empire S&LA after Spencer Blain became the majority shareholder.

[44] Although the Board could issue a permanent injunction to end virtually any type of thrift practice, the fact these orders often involved a trial meant they were slow to take effect. Noble, "Empire Savings of Texas Is Shut Down," Sec. D, 4; Albert, "Panel Blasts Bank Board over Empire Failure," 3; *Hearings on FHLBB Supervision of Empire S&LA*, 97; *Report on FHLBB Supervision of Empire S&LA*, 7–8, 36–7, 52.

[45] Rick Atkinson and David Maraniss, "Turning Anger into Action," *The Washington Post*, 13 June 1989, 1; Rick Atkinson and David Maraniss, "Hardening of S&L Battle Lines," *The Washington Post*, 14 June 1989, 1; Day, *S&L Hell*, 181–95.

His main objective was to make the thrift an industry leader. Blain wanted to increase lending for the acquisition, development and construction of condominium projects outside Dallas. Teaming up with developers, Blain quickly put his plan into operation and soon Empire S&LA was on its way to become one of the fastest-growing thrifts in the country. The prosperity of this thrift, however, was illusory as examiners and accountants found out during their periodic reviews of its financial statements.

Despite indications of malfeasance, regulators were slow to react to the problems. At both the state and federal levels, officials had several opportunities to limit the activities at Empire S&LA, but in each instance failed to act decisively. In March 1984, just eighteen months after Blain took control, regulators finally closed the thrift down, but by then it had become so large that the payout of insured deposits by the FSLIC was the largest in the history of the agency up to that time. Immediately following the collapse, Congress held hearings to determine exactly why this thrift had failed, and its investigation revealed how a variety of forces can often combine to cause financial ruin.

APPENDIX 2. SUCCESS THE OLD-FASHIONED WAY: THE CASE OF MEDFORD COOPERATIVE BANK

In contrast to the case study of Empire Savings and Loan Association of Mesquite, Texas, an analysis of Medford Co-operative Bank[1] (MCB) provides an instructive example of how many thrifts survived the era of deregulation. MCB, like hundreds of savings and loans, began business in the late nineteenth century with the mission of helping people of modest means save for the future and become homeowners. Located in a suburb of a large urban center, this small association grew steadily, and over time developed a conservative business style that made it appear stodgy and resistant to change. While such characteristics were positive attributes that benefited MCB through the 1960s, by the 1970s some within the thrift saw them as liabilities.

Nonetheless, MCB dealt remarkably well with the challenges of the 1980s. The main reason why it thrived when others failed is that management found ways to incorporate change while at the same time adhering to their traditional focus of serving the local community. This practice of "sticking to the knitting" meant that MCB's management was conservative but open to innovation, provided such changes complemented existing business lines and enhanced customer service. Furthermore, when it did enter into new business areas, the thrift did so cautiously, which gave it the opportunity to evaluate the results. In the 1990s, MCB made a number of significant changes, including conversion to a stock association and expansion into commercial lending, but the outlook of its leaders did not change. They remained focused on serving the financial needs of the community, a tradition MCB had been following for over a century. While MCB may seem unique, a closer examination of the thrift industry shows that dozens of S&Ls followed a similar path to success.[2]

---

[1] Massachusetts savings and loan associations are known as cooperative banks.

[2] Thomas J. Peters and Robert H. Waterman Jr., *In Search of Excellence: Lessons from America's Best-Run Companies* (New York: Warner Books, 1982), 15. This chapter is based on material

THE SETTING OF MEDFORD CO-OPERATIVE BANK

The town of Medford, Massachusetts, the home of the Medford Co-operative Bank, was founded in 1630 and has deep roots in American history. Organized as the seventh town in British North America, Medford is located on rolling and wooded countryside along the Mystic River about five miles from Boston. For more than two centuries, Medford thrived on its renowned shipbuilding and rum-distilling industries, and in 1852 it became the home of Tufts University. The town was also the site of several contributions to Americana, including the song "Jingle Bells" by James Pierpont and the poem "Over the River and Through the Wood" by abolitionist Lydia Child. Although Medford did attract many upper-class residents from Boston who lived in large riverside summer retreats, it was essentially a quiet rural community whose population through the mid-nineteenth century never exceeded 5,500.[3]

Medford began to change in the 1860s following construction of a streetcar line that connected it to Boston. Such affordable transportation allowed more middle-class Bostonians to move away from the urban center and into suburbs like Medford. The result was that between 1870 and 1890 Medford's population more than doubled to 11,200. Fifteen years later it exceeded 22,000. By 1930, the number of residents leveled out at just over 60,000, a figure that would not change much for the next sixty years. Significantly, many of the new Medfordites were working-class Irish and Italians who had jobs in Boston. Although this population growth helped make Medford a true bedroom community for the larger city, the town still maintained a strong separate identity. A number of small manufacturers and service companies had offices in Medford, and its economic base received a major boost with the opening of the regional Lawrence Memorial Hospital in 1965. At the same time, this new source of stable employment reflected the fact that the local population was aging rapidly.[4]

THE BEGINNINGS OF THE MEDFORD CO-OPERATIVE BANK

In May 1886, forty-five leading citizens from Medford and Boston founded the Medford Co-operative Bank as the thirty-ninth thrift in Massachusetts.

obtained from MCB and its employees. All bank prepared financial statements, and directors' meeting manuscripts are located at the main office of MCB at 60 High St., Medford, MA. Interviews with key personnel were conducted by the author at the bank offices, and all relevant material from these conversations is in the possession of the author.

[3] Carl Seaburg and Alan Seaburg, *Medford on the Mystic* (Medford, MA: privately published, 1980), 3–4, 100, 104, 114.

[4] Kenneth T. Jackson, *Crabgrass Frontiers: The Suburbanization of America* (New York: Oxford University Press, 1985), 118–19; Sam Bass Warner, *Streetcar Suburbs: The Process of Growth in Boston, 1870–1900* (Cambridge: Harvard University Press, 1978), 47–64; Seaburg and Seaburg, *Medford on the Mystic*, 16, 21, 30, 59, 74, 78–9, 83, 118.

TABLE A2.1. *Medford Cooperative Bank, Members and Assets – 1888 to 1910*

Year	Members	Change/Year	Assets	Change/Year
1888	320	–	$28,883	–
1895	576	11.4%	$264,421	116.5%
1900	645	5.9%	$362,038	7.4%
1905	915	8.3%	$593,548	10.2%
1910	1,401	10.5%	$842,717	8.4%

Source: *Medford Cooperative Bank Financial Statement, 1887* (Medford, MA: Medford Cooperative Bank, 1887); *Annual Report of the State Banking Commissioner, Part III*, Public Document no. 8 (Boston: Commonwealth of Massachusetts Bank Commissioner, 1895), 120–1. *Annual Report of the State Banking Commissioner, Part III*, Public Document no. 8 (Boston: Commonwealth of Massachusetts Bank Commissioner, 1900) 145–6; *Annual Report of the State Banking Commissioner, Part III*, Public Document no. 8 (Boston: Commonwealth of Massachusetts Bank Commissioner, 1905), 167–8; *Annual Report of the State Banking Commissioner, Part III*, Public Document no. 8 (Boston: Commonwealth of Massachusetts Bank Commissioner, 1910), 154–5.

MCB had many characteristics common to nineteenth-century thrifts. It was a mutual association that helped people acquire homes and save for the future by issuing series of shares, each worth $200, twice each year, which members paid for in monthly installments. A board of directors elected by the members approved all loans and set general business policies. The only paid employee of MCB was its secretary and treasurer, Medford retailer James Sturtevant, who along with his wife managed the day-to-day activities of the bank. Membership was open to both men and women, and the majority of these people came from Medford and the surrounding communities of Arlington, Malden, and Somerville.[5]

Members met the first Wednesday of each month at a rented room in the Legion of Honor Hall for the regular "sale" of money. Prospective borrowers submitted bids on the interest rates and premiums they were willing to pay for loans, and prior to disbursing funds a Security Committee of thrift directors evaluated the "character" of the borrowers, and inspected the property, a process that took up to three months to complete. Share and loan payments were due monthly; and, depending on the rate of dividends, shares and loans matured within five to eight years. Despite the tedious loan approval process and lack of formal office space, the new cooperative was a financial success and grew quickly, as seen in Table A2.1.

By the early 1910s, MCB had become a profitable and healthy mid-sized institution. After expanding rapidly during the economic boom that preceded the depression of the mid-1890s, growth became more uniform. Similarly,

---

[5] Quarterly sales of shares began in 1920. *Fifty Years of Security* (n.p.: 1936), 10–12; *Directors Meetings Minutes, May 28, 1886 to April 2, 1902* [hereafter *DMM 1886–1902*] (unpublished manuscript, Medford Cooperative Bank, Medford, MA), 1, 21.

management followed conservative lending practices, as evidenced by the absence of any loan defaults for the first ten years of operations. One reason for this superior performance might be that many of the borrowers were more well-to-do, since the average MCB mortgage was more than what the typical working-class home of the period cost. Another reason may be that loans were often made on the "character" of the borrowers, not just financial considerations. Personal relations between management and members were very strong, and the Board did not see the need to have any written lending policies, a practice that would continue into the 1980s. Interestingly, many MCB members used the bank as a way to save for the future, since the ratio of borrowers to total members did not exceed 5 percent until the mid-1910s. Such considerations may also explain why MCB's reserve ratio, which was just 0.93 percent of assets in 1895, actually fell to 0.43 percent of assets by 1910.[6]

Like other thrifts, MCB used very little outside advertising to solicit business, but instead relied on word-of-mouth advertising from existing shareholders to attract new members. In fact, its first publicity campaign did not occur until 1914, and consisted of a mass mailing and a display at the new moving picture theater. This low-key approach to business carried over into MCB's physical presence: aside from the monthly meeting, the only way for members to make payments was to visit Treasurer Sturtevant at his home on one of the two days each week that he accepted money. While Sturtevant was not a trained accountant, during his twenty-five years with the bank he kept meticulous records in a general ledger using a double-entry system that he balanced each business day. Sturtevant finally resigned as treasurer, at the suggestion of the Board, after the state mental hospital found him to be permanently incapacitated.[7]

GROWTH BRINGS CHANGE

As MCB matured as a financial institution, it began to adopt more formal business procedures. By the start of World War I, MCB had moved into a spacious office on the top floor of the new Medford Trust Building downtown and was open every business day. The bank began making loans at rates set by the Board, and had reduced the time between loan approval

[6] At the first money auction in July 1886, J. O. Goodwin bid for $1700 at 6 percent interest and a 5 percent premium; he received his money in September. The first loan to a woman was in 1888. Similarly, the first foreclosure occurred in 1891, when fire destroyed collateral property. *Fifty Years of Security*, 6–7; DMM 1886–1902, 1–2, 9–15, 43, 95; *Medford Cooperative Bank Financial Statement*, 1887; *Annual Report of the State Banking Commissioner, Part III* (1895), 120–1.

[7] DMM 1886–1902, 133, 227; *Directors Meetings Minutes April 9 1902 to April 3 1912* [hereafter DMM 1902–1912] (unpublished manuscript, Medford Cooperative Bank, Medford, MA), 126–32, 254; "Letter to the Editor," *Medford Mercury*, 17 October 1913, 7.

and disbursement to a few days. Although it did not have any branches, customers were allowed to make payments at one of several retail stores in South Medford, West Medford, and Boston that were owned by an MCB shareholder. MCB also adopted the use of matured shares, which allowed members to keep their money in the thrift after paying for their original shares in full.[8]

Like those of many thrifts in the late nineteenth century, as MCB grew in size, it became involved in state banking affairs. Although Massachusetts cooperatives were not seriously affected by the "nationals" crisis of the 1890s, their leaders, like thrift executives across the country, realized that they needed a state trade association to protect their business interests. In 1888, they formed the Massachusetts Co-operative Bank League as a way for members to exchange ideas, to improve their financial education, and to "assist in any needed legislation" that would support their businesses. MCB joined the state League in 1890 and was active in trade group functions and state lobbying efforts, like many small thrifts it did not join the national trade association believing that this group was too remote to have a critical role in its affairs.[9]

By the 1920s, the rising population of Medford had attracted several new financial institutions to the area. In addition to two banks, Medford Savings and Medford Trust, both of which had been in business since the mid-1800s, the town received two new thrifts, the Hillside-Cambridge Co-operative Bank and West Medford Co-operative Bank, as well as branches of several Boston banks. Although competition rose sharply, MCB management refused to match the more liberal practices of these newer thrifts, evidenced by the fact that MCB consistently paid lower dividend rates than the competition and charged loan rates that were just above the market. Such conservative policies, however, did not cost the cooperative much business, and from the mid-1910s to the end of the 1920s MCB recorded solid growth, as seen in Table A2.2.

This fifteen-year span was the first period of sustained and exceptional growth for MCB. The thrift surpassed $1 million in assets in 1913, and in less than fifteen years it had grown fivefold. This expansion came from meeting local loan demand, with more than 90 percent of all mortgages going to Medford residents. Furthermore, nearly a third of all borrowers were women. The co-op continued to improve customer service by opening

---

[8] Oreb M. Tucker, *Three Score and Ten Years: A History of Seventy Years of Co-operative Banking in Massachusetts* (Boston: Central Co-operative Bank, 1948), 88, 95; *DMM 1886–1902*, 241; *DMM 1902–1912*, 94; *Directors Meetings Minutes April 10, 1912 to October 8, 1924* [hereafter *DMM 1912–1924*] (unpublished manuscript, Medford Cooperative Bank, Medford, MA), 84, 93; *Fifty Years of Service*, 12.

[9] MCB first joined the League in 1927 shortly after it began admitting thrifts as members, but quit and rejoined several times over the next fifty years. *DMM 1886–1902*, 82; Tucker, *Three Score and Ten Years Ago*, 120–35, quote 124.

TABLE A2.2. *Medford Cooperative Bank, Members and Assets – 1915 to 1930*

Year	Members	Change/Year	Assets	Change/Year
1915	2,069	8.9%	$1,310,678	11.1%
1920	2,579	4.9%	$2,267,404	14.5%
1925	3,856	9.9%	$4,209,021	17.2%
1930	4,746	4.6%	$5,911,327	8.0%

Source: *Annual Report of the State Banking Commissioner, Part III*, Public Document no. 8 (Boston: Commonwealth of Massachusetts Bank Commissioner, 1915), 182–3; *Annual Report of the State Banking Commissioner, Part III*, Public Document no. 8 (Boston: Commonwealth of Massachusetts Bank Commissioner, 1920), 215–6; *Annual Report of the State Banking Commissioner, Part III*, Public Document no. 8 (Boston: Commonwealth of Massachusetts Bank Commissioner, 1925), 107–8; *Annual Report of the State Banking Commissioner, Part III*, Public Document no. 8 (Boston: Commonwealth of Massachusetts Bank Commissioner, 1930), 124–5.

three branches in the Medford area. Despite these changes, MCB continued to follow conservative policies designed to improve its financial condition. Because the Board had raised the amount of profits paid into reserves from 1 percent to 5 percent, the reserve ratio rose sharply from its prewar lows to 4.94 percent of assets by 1930, which was close to the state minimum of 5 percent. Similarly, the bank continued to attract long-term savers as members, as evidenced by the rise in value of matured shares from $33,200 in 1915 to $1.79 million in 1930.[10]

Another important achievement for MCB during this period came when the thrift acquired its own office building. In 1924, the Board decided to follow its own advice of "owning their own home" and began the search for a suitable location. In 1929, they purchased property on Medford Square in the heart of downtown and hired an architect to design a new building that would reflect not only the heritage of Medford but also the ideals of home ownership. The design chosen was a two-story red brick Georgian structure with fireplaces at either end. Not only was the new office functional and large enough for future growth, but it was inviting to customers, a trait not common to traditional bank buildings. Construction began the following year; and in 1931, when the thrift industry celebrated its centennial, MCB moved into its new home.[11]

---

[10] *DMM 1902–1912*, 44; *DMM 1912–1924*, 272–3, 276, 291–3, 322, 332–3. 322, 419, 494; *Directors Meetings Minutes Nov 12 1924 to Apr 13 1932* [hereafter *DMM 1924–1932*] (unpublished manuscript, Medford Cooperative Bank, Medford, MA), 4, 83–6, 130–1, 136, 350; *Annual Report of the State Banking Commissioner, Part III* (1915), 182; *Annual Report of the State Banking Commissioner, Part III* (1920), 215; *Annual Report of the State Banking Commissioner, Part III* (1925), 107–8; *Annual Report of the State Banking Commissioner, Part III* (1930), 124–5.

[11] *Historical Register, June 1931* (Medford, MA: n.p., 1931) 30–4; *DMM 1912–1924*, 459; *DMM 1924–1932*, 209–10, 363; *Fifty Years of Service*, 16; "Medford Cooperative Bank Celebrating Its 45th Birthday in Beautiful Quarters," *Medford Daily Evening Mercury*, 7 July 1931,

Amid this success, there were signs, however, of potential problems, especially in terms of increased loan delinquencies and foreclosures. While it was true that the quality of MCB's loan portfolio was high, with an average annual loan loss of just $30 during its first forty-five years, the thrift also saw more members becoming borrowers. Between 1920 and 1928, the ratio of borrowers to total members rose from 16 percent to 36 percent, and many of these new borrowers appeared to be higher risks, since the proportion of loans more than six months past due increased from less than 0.2 percent to almost 1 percent of total loans during this period. Furthermore, foreclosures represented by real estate owned, which historically were virtually nonexistent, rose to about 0.6 percent of total assets. While these changes likely resulted from an overextension of credit, especially to developers, their sudden increase at the end of the decade indicated market weakness that would worsen as delinquencies rose.[12]

DEALING WITH THE GREAT DEPRESSION

Although the 1930s began for MCB on a positive note, with a gala celebration marking the opening of its new offices, the decade would prove to be one of the most challenging in its history. By late 1930, the Great Depression was having an effect on the Medford area, and one reason MCB began construction of its new office that winter was to help reduce local unemployment. As more people felt the financial effects of these hard times, bank directors tried to help members by allowing them to sign "loan reduction" agreements that let borrowers to apply the value of unpledged shares they owned to reduce their mortgage balances. Approved for use by the Massachusetts legislature in 1930, these agreements were a way to reduce the level of chronic loan delinquencies; but, since borrowers also had to subscribe to new shares as part of these agreements, they were not true debt forgiveness.[13]

In October 1931, MCB faced a major crisis when one of its depository banks, Medford Trust, experienced a run on deposits that forced it into voluntary liquidation. This closure posed a number of problems for the thrift. Not only did MCB face the risk of losing more than $100,000 in deposits it held at Medford Trust, but the loss of consumer confidence spread to MCB itself as over the next six months members withdrew more than $600,000. While such runs usually ended in failure, MCB survived in part because it maintained depository relationships with several large Boston banks that gave it access to the funds needed to meet withdrawals. Still, the experience

3–4; Angel Kwoleck-Folland, *Engendering Business: Men and Women in the Corporate Office, 1870–1930* (Baltimore: Johns Hopkins University Press, 1994), 94–128.

[12] *Annual Report of the State Banking Commissioner, Part III* (1920), 216; *Medford Cooperative Bank Financial Statements, October 1928* (Medford, MA: Medford Cooperative Bank, 1928).

[13] *Fifty Years of Service*, 20–2.

was very trying for the Board, and several directors were bitter that some members had such little faith in the strength of their association. A second impact of the Medford Trust closure on MCB was that it led to the resignation of several directors who served on the boards of both institutions. These resignations occurred after several local stock brokers were indicted for securities fraud; and while none of these directors was implicated, they likely left to avoid tainting the reputation of MCB.[14]

While the closure of Medford Trust was traumatic, MCB faced other persistent problems associated with the Great Depression. Like all lenders, MCB wrestled with the problem of loan delinquencies, which peaked in early 1933 at 5 percent of total loans, as well as foreclosures, which hit their high at the end of that year. Significantly, the experiences of MCB in both these areas were superior to those of the thrift industry as a whole, indicating that management worked with borrowers to find ways to help them stay current on their mortgages. In general, the Board was reluctant to foreclose on a borrower, not simply out of compassion for the homeowner, but because doing so would cause the thrift to acquire a property it would likely be unable to resell at a profit. Foreclosure, however, did occur; and between 1932 and 1940 the book value of real estate owned by the bank grew from more than $240,000 to $750,000, which was equal to 25 percent of its total mortgage portfolio.[15]

This high level of real estate held by the thrift eventually led state regulators in 1940 to order MCB to reduce its backlog of properties. The Board formed a new department to dispose of these assets, and within two years the level of real estate owned fell by more than 90 percent. While it did recover 88 percent of the original book value of these assets, MCB still had to absorb a $108,000 write-off, which reduced its equity by half. Remarkably, the thrift was in such good financial condition that even after this loss its reserve ratio was still well above state requirements. One reason for the high level of net worth was that the Board adopted cost-cutting policies, such as slashing dividend rates, closing branch offices, and freezing employees' salaries, all of which allowed it to post profits each year during the 1930s. Such actions did not, however, reflect a lack of concern for member needs, since the Board also authorized payment of special dividends in November 1932

---

[14] Following lawsuits filed by Medford Trust shareholders, the bank president was convicted of fraud in 1932. "Medford Trust Company Closed by Request of Its Board of Directors," *Medford Mercury*, 7 October 1931, 1; "Declare No Loss Will be Sustained by Depositors of Medford Trust Company," *Medford Mercury*, 8 October 1931, 1; DMM *1924–1932*, 353, 439, 451–3, 462, 628; *Fifty Years of Service*, 17.

[15] DMM *1924–1932*, (8 October, 1930), 354; *Directors Meetings Minutes May 4 1932 to June 12 1935* [hereafter DMM *1932–1935*] (unpublished manuscript, Medford Cooperative Bank, Medford, MA), 453, 513, 555, 573, 597, 702, 894; *Annual Report of the State Banking Commissioner, Part III*, Public Document no. 8 (Boston: Commonwealth of Massachusetts Bank Commissioner, 1930), 125; *Annual Report of the State Banking Commissioner, Part III*, Public Document no. 8 (Boston: Commonwealth of Massachusetts Bank Commissioner, 1935), 118.

and February 1933 to help shareholders during the worst period of the depression.[16]

The success MCB had in dealing with the challenges of the Great Depression was not unique among Massachusetts cooperatives, and in fact only 18 percent of all of the state's thrifts failed between 1927 and 1933. One reason for this low rate of failure was that the state trade association found ways to aid its members. In 1931, it created the Bay State Trust, which pooled money from its members in a fund that was available to the contributors for liquidity needs. The next year, the trade group proposed that the state create a central bank that would provide loans for all cooperatives, much like the federal home loan bank. While state regulators supported this plan, most state thrifts opposed it for many of the same reasons they opposed the national reserve bank. The opposition ended, however, when the state bank commissioner threatened to double the minimum reserve requirements if the central bank were not formed.[17]

In March 1932, the state legislature created the Cooperative Central Bank (CCB), and within a year more than 80 percent of all cooperatives, including MCB, were members. Like the federal home loan bank, the CCB provided an invaluable source of liquidity to its members. This was especially true during the national bank holiday in March 1933, since Massachusetts was one of the few states in which every thrift was allowed to reopen when the holiday ended. A second program that benefited cooperatives was the creation of a state share insurance fund in 1934. Like the CCB this initiative was supported by the state trade association but generally opposed by individual thrifts. Despite these divisions, the state created the insurance program, which produced an almost immediate restoration of public confidence in thrifts, thereby limiting the potential for disastrous deposit runs.[18]

MAINTAINING CONSERVATIVE BUSINESS PRACTICES

The impact of the Great Depression on MCB's management was profound, and even after prosperity returned in the 1950s the bank still followed very conservative policies. One reason was that most bank directors of the late 1920s and 1930s were still with MCB some thirty years later. In fact,

---

[16] *Medford Co-operative Bank Financial Statements, October 1928* (Medford, MA: Medford Cooperative Bank, 1928); *Medford Co-operative Bank Financial Statements, October 1932* (Medford, MA: Medford Cooperative Bank, 1932); *Medford Co-operative Bank Financial Statements, October 1936* (Medford, MA: Medford Cooperative Bank, 1936); *Medford Co-operative Bank Financial Statements, October 1940* (Medford, MA: Medford Cooperative Bank, 1940); DMM 1924–1932 352, 597, 733, 814, 976–8; *Directors Meetings Minutes July 10 1935 to May 14 1941* [hereafter *DMM 1935–1941*] (unpublished manuscript, Medford Cooperative Bank, Medford, MA), 1365–7, 1449–50, 1498–90; *Directors Meetings Minutes June 11, 1941 to May 11 1949* [hereafter *DMM 1941–1949*] (unpublished manuscript, Medford Cooperative Bank, Medford, MA), 1617, 1677.

[17] DMM 1924–32, 378, 439, 462.

[18] Tucker, *Three Score and Ten Years*, 112, 122–38.

TABLE A2.3. *Medford Cooperative Bank, Members and Assets – 1935 to 1955*

Year	Members	Change/Year	Assets	Change/Year
1935	3,510	(5.1%)	$5,041,591	(2.9%)
1940	3,419	(0.5%)	$4,586,491	(1.8%)
1945	3,321	(0.5%)	$3,653,749	(4.0%)
1950	3,484	0.9%	$3,612,761	(0.2%)
1955	5,468	11.3%	$5,262,186	9.1%

Source: *Annual Report of the State Banking Commissioner, Part III* (1935), 118; *Medford Co-operative Bank Financial Statements, October 1940; Annual Report of the State Banking Commissioner, Section A* (1945), 109; *Medford Cooperative Bank Financial Statements, 1950* (Medford, MA: Medford Cooperative Bank, 1950).

during its first sixty years of existence MCB had just three presidents and four treasurers, and most of the directors served well into their seventies. The influence of these "survivors of hard times" in setting business policies is evident in the slow growth of MCB from 1935 to 1955, as seen in Table A2.3.

During World War II, MCB did not experience as great a surge in savings as the thrift industry as a whole, and in fact during the war years deposits declined by an average of 3.5 percent per year. The main reason for this drop was that MCB kept dividend rates low, not only because the state bank commissioner had requested in 1942 that all thrifts reduce their rates, but also because the lack of home building during the war had depressed profits. Even though the resumption of residential construction resulted in rapid expansion for most thrifts, MCB continued to show anemic loan growth. During the last half of the 1940s, the Board rejected dozens of loan requests as being too risky, and most business came by way of traditional word-of-mouth referrals as opposed to formal advertising. Instead of aggressive lending, MCB kept its dividend rates low and focused on rebuilding reserves depleted by the losses on asset sales in 1942. As a result, even though assets did not rise significantly, the reserve ratio for MCB did, jumping from 8.1 percent of assets in 1935 to more than 14.5 percent of assets by 1950, which was nearly three times the state-required minimum.[19]

[19] *Annual Report of the State Banking Commissioner, Part III* (1935), 118; *Annual Report of the State Banking Commissioner, Part III*, Public Document no. 8 (Boston: Commonwealth of Massachusetts Bank Commissioner, 1940), 114; *Annual Report of the State Banking Commissioner, Section A* (1945), 109; *Medford Co-operative Bank Financial Statements Medford Co-operative Bank Financial Statements, October 1944* (Medford, MA: Medford Cooperative Bank, 1944); *Medford Co-operative Bank Financial Statements, October 1946* (Medford, MA: Medford Cooperative Bank, 1946); *Medford Co-operative Bank Financial Statements, October 1947* (Medford, MA: Medford Cooperative Bank, 1947); *Medford Co-operative Bank Financial Statements, October 1948* (Medford, MA: Medford Cooperative Bank, 1948); *Medford Co-operative Bank Financial Statements, October 1949* (Medford, MA: Medford Cooperative

While these conservative business policies caused MCB to miss out on the initial postwar housing boom, they did not mean that the thrift was unwilling to change. The Board adopted several new lending products, including the direct-reduction mortgage, flexible mortgages, and home-improvement loans. MCB was also an active lender under the Veterans Administration loan program. Finally, to better correlate lending risks with loan returns, management began using a sliding scale for interest rates based on the quality of the borrower and/or property. By the mid-1950s, business had increased to such an extent that MCB hired its first new employees in nearly twenty years. The Board even considered microfilming bank records, not as a way to improve efficiency, but as a precaution against an attack on America by a foreign power.[20]

CHANGE BRINGS GROWTH

As MCB moved into the 1960s, some on the Board began to see the continued conservative attitudes of its directors and managers as a potential liability to the long-term growth of the thrift. Two significant changes, however, prevented MCB from becoming a staid institution. The first was the departure of most Board members who had served since the 1920s and 1930s, which created an opportunity to bring in a younger generation of bankers. Among the new directors were John Hand, a former Massachusetts state bank examiner, and Robert Surabian, a Medford retailer and real estate investor, both of whom came to MCB in 1967. By the early 1970s, Hand was the executive vice president of MCB in charge of daily operations, while Surabian was board chairman and responsible for long-term strategic planning. While these new officers brought a youthful exuberance to MCB, they were still committed to the bank's traditional goals of sound home finance, serving the local community, and focusing on customer service.[21]

The second major change came in 1970 when MCB acquired West Medford Cooperative Bank, a smaller association, but one with a more Progressive management team than the older thrift. West Medford Cooperative

Bank, 1949); *DMM 1935–1941*, 1050, 1150, 1410; *DMM 1941–1949* (5 December 1943), 1062, 1690–1.

[20] Like many savings and loan associations, MCB avoided making FHA loans because they typically earned lower interest rates than conventional mortgages. *Massachusetts Cooperative Bank News* n.v. (July 1967), 1–2; *DMM 1941–1949*, 1742, 1779, 1754, 1853, 1867–8, 1941; *Directors Meetings Minutes June 8 1949 to October 9 1957* [hereafter *DMM 1949–1957*] (unpublished manuscript, Medford Cooperative Bank, Medford, MA), 2085, 2382, 2422; *Fifty Years*, 17–21; Alan Seaburg, *Medford Cooperative Bank: 100 Years of Service to the Community* (Medford, MA: s.n., 1986), 27

[21] *Directors Meetings Minutes June 4, 1967 to Oct 23 1974* [hereafter *DMM 1967–1974*] (unpublished manuscript, Medford Cooperative Bank, Medford, MA), 3074; Seaburg, *Medford Cooperative Bank* 27; Interview, Robert Surabian, president and chief executive officer, Medford Cooperative Bank, Medford, MA, by the author, 12 August 1998.

had been organized in the 1920s, and by 1965 had grown to more than $4.59 million in assets with nearly 3,000 members. During the previous decade, it had experienced solid loan growth of nearly 8 percent annually, in part because it advertised more aggressively than MCB and paid higher dividends. Despite this, the smaller cooperative had a solid financial condition, with a strong reserve ratio of 6.9 percent. The acquisition came after months of overtures by MCB, and it was by all accounts a friendly combination in which members from both cooperatives served on the new Board. The acquisition also caused MCB to modernize its management structure in order to better delegate authority within the larger institution and improve business development. It created four new vice president and four new assistant treasurer positions, and significantly women occupied all the assistant treasurer posts.[22]

While men held the top management positions at MCB, as in the thrift industry in general, women were also an integral part of MCB's workforce. Most female employees were tellers, but because MCB promoted from within, women also could become managers. The first was assistant treasurer Olivia Crocker in 1948, followed by Cecilia Hussey as treasurer in 1962. Three years later, Hussey become a director and was the first woman in Medford to serve on any bank board. Despite these opportunities, MCB also, like other businesses, had a "glass ceiling" that kept women from ascending to high office. An example of this came in 1972 when the Board refused to promote assistant treasurer Lorraine Silva, who had first joined the bank in 1948, to bank treasurer because "they did not think a woman should be there." They instead hired a less qualified man, who ironically came under the supervision of Silva when the Board decided to make her vice president six years later, the first woman to hold such a position in Medford.[23]

MCB UNDER JOHN HAND

The changes in the Board, combined with the benefits of the acquisition of the West Medford Cooperative Bank, helped MCB record rapid growth, as seen in Table A2.4.

---

[22] West Medford spent an average of 54 cents per $1,000 in assets on advertising, while MCB spent only 27 cents per $1,000. *DMM 1967–1974*, 3005, 3127, 3145–7, 3333; Annual *Report of the Commissioner of Banking, Section A, 1960*, Public Document no. 8 (Boston: Commonwealth of Massachusetts Banking Commissioner, 1960), 96; *Report of the Commissioner of Banking, Section A, 1965*, Public Document no. 8 (Boston: Commonwealth of Massachusetts Banking Commissioner, 1965), 96.

[23] *DMM 1941–1948*, 1942; *Directors Meetings Minutes, Nov 13, 1957 to May 10 1967* [hereafter *DMM 1957–1967*] (unpublished manuscript, Medford Cooperative Bank, Medford, MA), 2731, 2883; *Directors Meetings Minutes, Nov 27, 1974 to June 25, 1980* [hereafter *DMM 1974–1980*] (unpublished manuscript, Medford Cooperative Bank, Medford, MA), 3807; Interview Lorraine Silva, director, Medford Cooperative Bank, Medford, MA, by the author, 11 August 1998; Seaburg, *Medford Cooperative Bank*, 27; "Co-op Bank Elects Woman," *Medford Mercury*, 24 May 1978, 6.

TABLE A2.4. *Medford Cooperative Bank, Members and Assets – 1960 to 1979*

Year	Members	Change/Year	Assets	Change/Year
1960	n/a	–	$6,867,116	6.1%
1965	4,866	–	$8,555,015	4.9%
1970	7,250	9.7%	$14,759,381	14.5%
1974	9,340	5.7%	$23,520,464	11.8%
1979	n/a	–	$51,169,264	23.5%

Source: *Annual Report of the State Banking Commissioner, Section A, 1960*, 62–3, 96–7; *Annual Report of the State Banking Commissioner, Section A, 1965*, 62–3, 96; *Annual Report of the State Banking Commissioner, Section A, 1970*, Public Document no. 8 (Boston: Commonwealth of Massachusetts Banking Commissioner, 1970), 51, 97; *Annual Report of the State Banking Commissioner, Section A, 1974*, Public Document no. 8 (Boston: Commonwealth of Massachusetts Banking Commissioner, 1974), 98; *Financial Statements of Medford Cooperative Bank April 1979* (Medford, MA: Medford Cooperative Bank, 1979).

During the late 1960s and 1970s, MCB experienced its most significant growth since the 1920s, a remarkable performance given the unevenness of the American economy during this period. The main reason for this expansion was that MCB modernized its lending policies and became a more aggressive financial institution. Like most New England thrifts in the 1970s, MCB began making personal loans for cars and education, and introduced new savings options like negotiable order of withdrawal (NOW) accounts. The bank significantly increased advertising, with expenditures on promotions rising from the 27 cents per $1,000 in assets in 1965 to 84 cents per $1,000 in assets by the mid-1970s. The more aggressive business posture did not, however, weaken the financial condition of the thrift. Although the reserve ratio for MCB fell from 8.9 percent of assets in 1965 to 6.3 percent of assets by 1977, it was still well above the legal minimum of 5 percent.[24]

Despite the efforts to make MCB a more "modern" thrift during the late 1960s and 1970s, it still retained an "old-fashioned" commitment to personal service and customer contact. Tellers typically knew the members by name, and it was common for people to line up in order to speak to their favorite teller. Executive Vice President John Hand worked closely with bank customers and had the authority to approve most nonmortgage loan requests. He also participated actively in community affairs, and in 1972 the Medford Chamber of Commerce named him "Man of the Year." His direct contact with the members was so strong that some people in Medford began to call MCB "John Hand's Bank." Vice President Lorraine Silva was also an important figure in Medford, earning accolades from community leaders.

[24] *Annual Report of the State Banking Commissioner, Section A, 1965*, 96; *Annual Report of the State Banking Commissioner, Section A, 1970*, 51, 97; *Annual Report of the State Banking Commissioner, Section A, 1974*, 98; *Financial Statements of Medford Cooperative Bank April 1979*.

Within the MCB, Silva and Hand encouraged an informal family-like work environment that caused bank employees to refer to them as "Ma and Pa."[25]

SURVIVING DEREGULATION

During the 1980s, America's volatile economy and the effects of deregulation took a large toll on all financial institutions in Massachusetts. Between 1980 and 1991, fifty-one commercial banks with more than $33 billion in assets failed, while eight federally chartered thrifts with $6.9 billion in assets went under. These failure rates were the ninth and eighteenth highest, respectively, in the country. At the same time, the number of state-chartered thrifts shrank from 134 in 1978 to just 95 twelve years later. Despite this upheaval, MCB managed to survive the decade in fairly good shape. One important reason for this survival was its continued focus on traditional home lending and conservative business policies. Throughout most of the decade, MCB invested between 15 and 20 percent of all funds in government securities, and it adopted new technologies like electronic funds transfer services after they had proven their worth in the marketplace. This conscious decision to "stick to the knitting" seemed unusual given the opportunities afforded by deregulation, but it also reflected the broader management philosophy of doing what the bank did best.[26]

One reason for this conservative business attitude was that even though many of the new managers like Hand and Surabian wanted MCB to be a modern institution, they were still strictly "old school" bankers. They believed that their cooperative should only add services that would complement existing mortgage business, and they specifically avoided high-risk fields like commercial lending and making out-of-state loans. Old-fashioned referrals continued to be a major source of business for most of the 1980s. Furthermore, even though Board membership had changed in the 1960s, a third of the directors still serving were old enough to remember the Great Depression, and this memory helped reinforce the idea that MCB was "Medford's Community Bank." As Surabian noted in 1983, although there was "a change in the philosophy of some thrift institutions . . . to serve

---

[25] Interview Deborah McNeill, senior vice president and treasurer, Medford Cooperative Bank, Medford, MA, by the author, 15 August 1998; Interview Henry Sampson, Vice President, Medford Cooperative Bank, Medford, MA, by the author, 15 August 1998; Silva Interview; "Bank Officer and Civic Activist is Retiring," *Medford Mercury*, 31 May 1991, 1, 8; Seaburg, *Medford Cooperative Bank*, 21.

[26] MCB bought its first automated teller machine in 1984, and joined an automated clearinghouse in 1989; prior to that the bank manually deposited its funds with other institutions. *DMM 1974–1980*, 3937; *Directors Meetings Minutes June 25, 1980 to February 26, 1986* [hereafter *DMM 1980–1986*] (unpublished manuscript, Medford Cooperative Bank, Medford, MA), 4075–6, 4152–3; Surabian Interview; McNeill Interview; Interview Ralph Dunham, chief financial officer and executive vice president, Medford Cooperative Bank, Medford, MA, by the author, 14 August 1998.

TABLE A2.5. *Medford Cooperative Bank, Assets and Reserves – 1980 to 1990*

Year	Assets (000)	Change/Year	Reserves (000)	Change/Year
1980	$51,989	–	$2,811	–
1985	$71,718	7.5%	$3,700	6.3%
1988	$87,396	7.2%	$6,292	23.2%
1990	$96,538	5.2%	$7,478	9.4%

Source: *Medford Cooperative Bank Financial Statements, 1980; Medford Cooperative Bank Financial Statements, 1985* (Medford, MA: Medford Cooperative Bank, 1985); *Medford Cooperative Bank Financial Statements, 1988; Medford Cooperative Bank Financial Statements, 1990* (Medford, MA: Medford Cooperative Bank, 1990).

businesses and commercial enterprises, our main business is still lending to home buyers."[27]

One sign of this enduring commitment to the ideals of individual thrift was the creation of the Educational Cooperative Bank at Medford High School in 1985. Formed with the assistance of the Medford school system, this first-of-a-kind Massachusetts bank was a branch of MCB that served both the student body and faculty. Run entirely by Medford high school students supervised by an MCB employee, the Educational Cooperative Bank allowed students to receive academic credit as well as hands-on work experience. The bank also helped teenagers develop the habits of thrift, budgeting skills, and the responsibility for paying back loans. Praised by community leaders, its number of student-members grew steadily, and the institution earned profits for the school while creating a potential pool of future MCB employees.[28]

With a deliberate focus on serving the community and conservative lending, MCB continued to grow and remain financially healthy in the 1980s, as seen in Table A2.5.

Despite the continued financial improvements for MCB during the decade, there were still times of near-panic within the cooperative. Like nearly every thrift, the unprecedented increase in interest rates in the early 1980s caused MCB to lose money. Although year-end losses in 1981 and 1982 were only $77,741 and $99,067, respectively, for the twelve months between June 1981 to June 1982 the thrift actually lost more than $300,000. According to Surabian this period was "one the most difficult... since the thirties," and management responded by cutting expenses, increasing fees on bank products, and making more loans that paid market rates, like personal loans and adjustable-rate mortgages. Significantly, the bank did not pursue the high earnings potential afforded by commercial lending, primarily because of one bad experience in this field. In 1984, MCB participated in a commercial loan

[27] *DMM 1980–1986*, 4153 quote 4413.
[28] "MHS, Medford Coop are Banking on Student's Ability," *Medford Mercury*, 10 October 1985, 1, 8; Sampson Interview; Silva Interview.

to renovate a downtown office building, but when the project encountered problems in finding tenants the loan had to be restructured. This created a "once burned, twice shy" mentality that led the Board to avoid all other commercial loan opportunities.[29]

Another major problem for MCB came in 1986, when a jump in Massachusetts thrift failures threatened the liquidity of the state deposit insurance fund. When this occurred the state bank commissioner ordered all cooperatives to apply for membership with the FDIC or the FSLIC. MCB joined the FDIC, but because its reserve ratio was below the 7.5 percent reserve level required by the federal agency, the bank had to take out a $1.4 million loan from the CCB, which it added to reserves to meet FDIC reserved requirements. Although embarrassed by this lack of financial cushion, especially because management had worked hard to build reserves over the years, MCB was able to repay the CCB loan and meet FDIC reserve regulations by the early 1990s.[30]

MCB also experienced a rise in loan delinquencies in the 1980s, and management dealt with this problem in much the same manner it did in the 1930s. The ability to follow this policy of "compassionate collections" was possible because the bank still made many loan decisions based more on the quality of the borrower than on the underlying collateral; in fact, up to the late 1980s MCB did not require appraisals or title insurance. The use of "character lending" also reflected the close ties between the bank officers and this community. Most directors still knew bank customers personally, and Lorraine Silva, who became a director in 1983, said she could not walk down the street without meeting at least a dozen people she knew, many of them borrowers from MCB. Given this close connection with the community, it was not surprising that many MCB borrowers felt like part of a family.[31]

RESTRUCTURING THE "FAMILY BUSINESS"

The big event of the 1980s was the celebration of MCB's 100th anniversary in 1986, and the similarities between this and its 50th anniversary are remarkable. Both involved lavish affairs attended by local dignitaries, both occurred during periods of modest recovery from crisis situations, and both preceded major changes in how MCB was run. By the late 1980s, the last of the bank directors to join in the 1950s had retired, and the Board was dominated by younger, more "business-minded" individuals. Furthermore,

---

[29] DMM 1974–1980, 3936–7; *Medford Cooperative Bank Financial Statements, 1980; Medford Cooperative Bank Financial Statements, 1970; Medford Cooperative Bank Financial Statements, 1988;* DMM 1980–1986, 4075, quote 4152.

[30] Surabian Interview; *Capital Assistance Agreement between Medford Cooperative Bank and the Cooperative Central Bank, February 28, 1986* (unpublished financial document); *Massachusetts Cooperative Bank League Bulletin,* 17 May 1985, n. p.

[31] Silva Interview, Surabian Interview, McNeill Interview, Sampson Interview.

Board service was no longer considered "a privilege" and rubber stamp for officer decisions, but rather a job that required an understanding of how banks worked. One result of having a more financially astute Board was the realization that MCB needed to maintain more sophisticated financial systems.[32]

In 1988, Ralph Dunham joined MCB as its first chief financial officer, and one of his first tasks was to formalize bank procedures. Under John Hand, MCB's management was highly centralized, with literally every piece of paper passing over his desk. Ledgers were still posted by hand, and no real financial monitoring existed. While this may have worked for a $25 million institution in the 1970s, by the end of the 1980s MCB was approaching $100 million in assets, and the inefficiencies of such informal procedures were beginning to show. Among the changes Dunham put in place were the following: a budget; the use of ratio analysis to measure productivity; asset and liability tracking reports; and increased use of computers. Surabian and the Board also began formal annual strategic planning reviews to chart a long-term course of the bank, and they encouraged employees to take more courses offered by the state thrift trade association.[33]

While mostly beneficial, these changes also had some costs, such as a decrease in responsibilities as jobs became more specialized. In the past, tellers "wore many hats" and had to know about all bank products and be able to give advice to members, but by the 1980s their duties were much more narrowly defined. Another casualty of change was the bank's informal business culture. Although management still treated employees like family, the atmosphere was different from when "Ma" Silva and "Pa" Hand had run things. In the "old days" work schedules were flexible, and it was common for the bank to celebrate any occasion with parties. By the end of the 1980s, with the bank having to monitor costs and raise reserves, these practices had to go. Finally, a more competitive environment contributed to the need for greater financial discipline. Begining in 1975, when just fifteen banks had a presence in Medford, the number of financial institutions making loans in the local market had doubled every ten years, and totaled sixty by 1995.[34]

EXPANDING MCB UNDER ROBERT SURABIAN

The final break with the past came in 1991 when Hand retired as executive vice president, and Surabian became president and chief executive officer.

---

[32] Surabian Interview.
[33] Dunham Interview; Surabian Interview; McNeill Interview; Sampson Interview; *DMM 1932–1936*, 1096–7; *Directors Meetings Minutes March 26, 1986 to January 23, 1991* [hereafter *DMM 1986–1991*] (unpublished manuscript, Medford Cooperative Bank, Medford, MA), 4548–9; *Medford Cooperative Bank Semi-Annual Report April 15, 1988* (Medford, MA: Medford Cooperative Bank, 1988).
[34] Surabian Interview.

Like Hand, the new CEO was active in the community and committed to keeping MCB a local institution. While he wanted to preserve the elements that had made MCB successful in the past, Surabian was also aware that the thrift needed to expand its business in order for it to survive as an independent entity into the next century. This idea of combining new and old ideas played itself out in the decision to expand the bank's offices. MCB had operated in the same building since the 1930s, and by the 1980s it needed more space to house a workforce that had grown from six in 1970 to sixteen by 1985, and that would later rise to forty-five by 1995. Although there was controversy as to how best to expand, in the end the Board found a design for a new addition that met the demands of the future while preserving the architectural integrity of the past.[35]

Another set of changes MCB had to contend with was increased scrutiny from officials seeking to "re-regulate" the thrift industry following the abuses of the 1980s. Among the dozens of new rules MCB had to comply with was a state requirement that it adopt and follow formal lending procedures. For MCB's managers, this meant an end to their traditional policy of "character loans," which they believed made perfect business sense because they knew most of the applicants personally. Although both customers and employees resented the change, it did improve the ability to collect statistical data on the loan portfolio. The 1990s also brought increased pressure on thrifts to demonstrate how they served low-income borrowers, and the bank responded with its "first-time home buyer plan," which met with broad acceptance from community leaders.[36]

The 1990s also represented a crossroads for MCB in that the thrift could no longer rely solely on Medford for future growth. One sign of this change was the decision to enter commercial lending in 1993. Although this move represented a major departure from MCB's traditional ways of doing business, the Board still followed a conservative approach to this type of lending, hiring skilled lenders and limiting business to borrowers from its existing service territory. By June 1998 MCB's commercial portfolio, which included a large number of loans to small family-owned firms, had risen to more than $29 million. Loan quality remained high, reflecting management's commitment to "keeping our risk low and our standards high." Finally, the Board decided to extend its territory to include communities to the north and west of Medford, and in 1998 MCB opened a branch in Lexington, and a branch in Arlington three years later.[37]

---

[35] "Interest of city at heart of Chamber honoree," *Medford Transcript*, 23 March 1992, 1, 5; McNeill Interview; Surabian Interview; Silva Interview.

[36] Surabian Interview; Sampson Interview; *Directors Meetings Minutes February 21, 1991 to January 4, 1995* [hereafter *DMM 1991–1995*] (unpublished manuscript, Medford Cooperative Bank, Medford, MA), 5673, 5898.

[37] Surabian Interview; *1998 Annual Report of Mystic Financial Inc.*, (Medford, MA: Mystic Financial Inc., 1998), quote 5.

TABLE A2.6. *Medford Cooperative Bank, Assets and Reserves – 1990 to 1999*

Year	Assets (000)	Change/Year	Reserves (000)	Change/Year
1990	$96,538	–	$7,748	–
1995	$124,966	5.8%	$10,366	6.7%
1998	$199,049	19.7%	$36,127	82.2%
1999	$215,214	8.1%	$34,052	(5.8)%

Source: *Medford Cooperative Bank Financial Statements, 1990; 1998 Annual Report of Mystic Financial Inc.*, 30–41; *1999 Annual Report of Mystic Financial Inc.* (Medford, MA: Mystic Financial Inc., 1999), 5–8.

The most significant change for MCB, however, was its conversion from mutual to stock ownership. Because the bank was entering new fields that required more funds than could be obtained from its members, the Board had to find new sources of finance. Although MCB began selling loans to the Federal National Mortgage Association in 1983, Surabian kept these transactions to a minimum because he knew MCB members wanted their loans to be serviced locally. While issuing stock to the public raised a number of potential problems, such as the loss of local control, the benefits of conversion, including more funds for technology-based services, was appealing. After wrestling with the issue of stock conversion for nearly a decade, the Board agreed to make the change in May 1997. In January 1998, MCB formed a holding company, Mystic Financial, and in its initial public offering raised more than $25.7 million.[38]

These various policy decisions and changes in business directions had a major impact on MCB operations, as seen in Table A2.6.

During the early part of the 1990s, the bank experienced many of the same problems it encountered a decade earlier. A slump in the high-tech sector of the economy caused the number of past due loans held by MCB to rise sharply, to $3.75 million by 1990. This was a troubling increase given the findings of an internal study that showed the bank could only absorb $500,000 in actual loan losses without violating reserve regulations. The Board created a "watch list" committee of directors to monitor specific troubled loans and adopted the first formal policies for managing foreclosed real estate. These actions, combined with an improving economy, helped MCB weather this crisis, and by 1998 nonperforming loans had shrunk to $154,000. The stock conversion also caused reserves to rise, and by 1999 MCB's reserve ratio was a healthy 12.8 percent of assets. At the end of the twentieth century and 114 years of operations, MCB was by most standards a modern financial institution offering a wide array of consumer and business banking services, as well as electronic banking products like ATM, debit cards, and on-line banking. Despite its expansion, the thrift remained

[38] Surabian Interview; Dunham Interview.

a conservative institution committed to meeting the needs of the local community, reflecting a desire to be "big enough to serve, and small enough to care."[39]

CONCLUSIONS

The dominant reason Medford Cooperative Bank operated successfully for more than a century lay in its conservative style of management and its commitment to serving the home financing requirements of the local community. Since its inception in the late nineteenth century, MCB maintained close ties to Medford and surrounding communities. MCB was able to gain the support of residents by focusing on their financial needs. As a result, MCB quickly became known as "Medford's Community Bank." The managers of the bank were critical in building this close relationship with the community, and it was common to find MCB management taking active roles in civic affairs. In fact, over the years three bank directors were mayors of Medford.

MCB management followed a conservative lending style that centered on promoting thrift and home ownership. From its founding, the leaders of MCB were unwilling to compromise these values simply to generate business, especially if risky business might impair the financial condition of the institution. This pattern of "sticking to the knitting" appeared repeatedly in the manner management set dividend policies, its wait-and-see attitude on non-mortgage-related lending, and its refusal to follow blindly practices set by competitors. Furthermore, when major business changes did come in the 1990s, the management followed a deliberate strategy of bringing in experienced lenders and "testing the waters" before making a large financial commitment to these new areas.

One reason that management was so conservative was that so many of these people had been with MCB for decades. Since its founding, MCB has had just eighty-eight directors, and their average tenure was twenty-two years. One director served for fifty-four years, while only two held office for less than one year. MCB also has had only ten presidents, each of whom was with the bank for an average of seven years. These long years of service resulted in management stability and produced a "long-term memory" that clearly affected business decisions. When management change did occur, the turnover was gradual since only about a third of the Board retired in any given decade. This situation allowed the new members to learn from the

---

[39] *DMM 1986–1991*, 4917–8, 4920; *DMM 1991–1995*, 5919; *1998 Annual Report of Mystic Financial Inc.*, quote 2, 30–41; *1999 Annual Report of Mystic Financial Inc.*, (Medford, MA: Mystic Financial Inc., 1999), 5–8.

older ones the traditional management style MCB had developed over the years.

The way in which MCB was managed was a key determinant in helping make it a profitable institution. Like hundreds of other thrifts, MCB followed a course of serving the local community with financial products tied to long-term saving and housing. This focus on helping people acquire the habit of thrift and become homeowners was why the savings and loan industry first began in the early nineteenth century, and supports the idea that there is still a place in an increasingly complex financial world for community bankers and specialized home lenders.

To evaluate whether the experience of MCB was unique among thrifts, an examination of when all thrifts currently in operation were founded is instructive. As of 1998, 62.4 percent of all thrifts across America were formed during or before the Great Depression, and more than 40 percent of all S&Ls began business prior to 1920. Furthermore, the vast majority of these thrifts had less than $100 million in assets, and were located in small towns. Even in states like California and Texas, which saw hundreds of S&Ls fail in the 1980s, these small community-focused associations continue to thrive. While it is inappropriate to draw too broad a conclusion from this summary review, the success of so many small S&Ls is not a fluke and likely reflects their insistence on adhering to many of the traditional business practices that made them prosperous in the first place.[40]

[40] For another history of a small thrift that adhered to conservative business practices see Maye Smith and Faye Hudson with Leslie Whitaker, *Maye and Faye's Building & Loan: The Story of a Remarkable Sisterhood* (Thorndike, ME: Thorndike Press, 1997). All industry statistics from *Thomson Savings Directory* (Skokie, IL : Thomson Financial Publishing, 1998) and *The U.S. Savings and Loan Directory* (Chicago: Rand McNally & Co., 1984).

BIBLIOGRAPHY

Primary Sources

Personal Papers

Calder, William [U.S. Senator]. Papers. The Herbert Hoover Presidential Library (West Branch, IA).

Carter, Jimmy. Papers. The Jimmy Carter Presidential Library (Atlanta, GA).

Fahey, John H. [Federal Home Loan Bank Board Chairman]. Papers. The Franklin D. Roosevelt Presidential Library (Hyde Park, New York).

Hoover, Herbert. Papers. The Herbert Hoover Presidential Library (West Branch, IA).

Johnson, Lyndon Baines. Papers. The Lyndon Baines Johnson Presidential Library (Austin, TX).

Patman, John William Wright [U.S. Representative]. Papers. The Lyndon Baines Johnson Presidential Library (Austin, TX).

Roosevelt, Franklin D. Papers. The Franklin D. Roosevelt Presidential Library (Hyde Park, New York).

Archival Sources – Government Agencies

Record Group 195: Federal Home Loan Bank Board (National Archives, College Park, MD).

Congressional Hearings and Reports

U.S. Congress. House of Representatives. Committee on Banking and Currency. *Housing Amendments of 1949*, hearings on H.R. 5631, 81st Cong., 1st sess., 25 July–9 August 1949.

U.S. Congress. House of Representatives. Committee on Banking, Currency and Housing. Subcommittee on Financial Institutions Supervision, Regulation and Insurance. *The Financial Reform Act of 1976*, hearings, 94th Cong., 2nd sess., 4–16 March 1976.

U.S. Congress. House of Representatives. Committee on Banking, Currency and Urban Affairs. Subcommittee on Financial Institutions Supervision, Regulation and Insurance. *Financial Institutions and the Nation's Economy (FINE): "Discussion Principles"* hearings, 94th Cong., 1st and 2nd sess., 2 December 1975–29 January 1976.

———. *Garn-St. Germain Depository Institutions Act of 1982*, H. Rept., 97–899, 97th Cong., 2nd sess., 1982.

———. *The Other Side of the Savings and Loan Industry*, hearings, 100th Cong., 1st sess., 9 February 1989.

———. *When Are the Savings and Loan Crooks Going to Jail?* hearings, 101st Cong., 2nd sess., 28 June 1990.

U.S. Congress. House of Representatives. Committee on Banking, Finance and Urban Affairs. *Financial Institutions Regulatory Act of 1978*. H. Rept., 95–1383, 95th Cong., 2nd sess., 1978.

———. Subcommittee on Housing and Community Development. *Housing and Community Development Act of 1977*, hearings, 95th Cong., 1st sess., 24 February – 9 March 1977.

U.S. Congress. House of Representatives. Committee on Government Operations. Subcommittee on Commerce, Consumer, and Monetary Affairs. *Adequacy of the Federal Home Loan Bank Board Supervision of the Failure of Empire Savings and Loan Association of Mesquite, Texas*, hearings, 98th Cong., 2nd sess., 25 April 1984.

———. *Proposed Restrictions on Money Brokers*, hearings, 98th Cong., 2nd sess., 14 March 1984.

———. *Report on the Federal Home Loan Bank Board Supervision and Failure of Empire Savings and Loan Association of Mesquite, Texas*, H. Rept. 98–953, 98th Cong., 2nd sess., 1984.

———. Select Committee on Lobbying Activities. *The United States Savings and Loan League*, H. Rept. 3139, 81st Cong., 2nd sess., 1950.

U.S. Congress. Senate. Committee on Banking and Currency. *Housing Amendments of 1949*, hearings on S. 2246, 81st Cong., 1st sess., 26–29 July 1949.

———. *Savings and Loan Holding Companies*, hearings on H.R. 7244 and S. 2517, 86th Cong., 1st sess., 18–19 August 1959.

U.S. Congress. Senate. Committee of the Committee on Banking and Currency. Subcommittee on Housing. *Federal Home Loan Bank Board and Federal Savings and Loan Insurance Corporation: A Study of Relationships*, Staff report pursuant to S. Res. 160, 84th Cong., 2nd sess., 1956.

U.S. Congress. Senate. Committee on Banking, Housing and Urban Affairs. *The Financial Services Competitive Equity Act*, S. Rept. 98–560, 98th Cong., 2nd sess., 1984.

———. *Competitive Equality Banking Act of 1987*, S. Rept. 100–19, 100th Cong., 1st sess., 1987.

———. *Depository Institutions Deregulation Committee*, hearings to consider the actions of the Depository Institutions Deregulation Committee and S. 2927, 96th Cong., 2nd sess., 5 August 1980.

———. *Fraud in America's Insured Depository Institutions*, hearings, 101st Cong., 2nd sess., 1–2 August 1990.

U.S. Congress. Senate. Committee on Banking, Housing and Urban Affairs. Subcommittee on Financial Institutions. *Depository Institutions Deregulation Act of 1979*, hearings on S. 1347, 96th Cong., 1st sess., 21–23 June 1979.

_____. *Financial Institutions Act, 1973,* hearings on S. 2591, 93rd Cong., 2nd sess., 13–17 May 1974.

_____. *Financial Institutions Act of 1975,* hearings on S. 1267, S. 1475, S. 1540, 94th Cong., 1st sess., 14–16 May and 11 June 1975.

Federal Home Loan Bank Board Journals

Federal Home Loan Bank Review (1934–47).
Digest / Federal Home Loan Bank Board (1961–68).
Journal / Federal Home Loan Bank Board (1971–80).
Federal Home Loan Bank Board Journal (1980–88).
Trends in the Savings and Loan Field (1961–68).

Federal Home Loan Bank Board Publications

Barth, James R. *Thrift-Institution Failures: Causes and Policy Issues.* Research Working Paper No. 117. 1985.

_____, Philip F. Bartholomew, and Carol J. Labich. *Moral Hazard and the Thrift Crisis: An Analysis of 1988 Resolutions.* Research Working Paper No. 160. 1989.

_____, R. Dan Brumbaugh Jr., and Daniel Sauerhaft. *Failure Costs of Government-Regulated Financial Firms: The Case of Thrift Institutions.* Research Working Paper No. 123. 1986.

_____, and Michael G. Bradley. *Thrift Deregulation and Federal Deposit Insurance.* Research Working Paper No. 150. 1988.

_____, and John J. Feid. *The Federal Deposit Insurance System: Origins and Omissions.* Research Working Paper No. 153. 1989.

_____, and Philip R. Wiest. *Consolidation and Restructuring of the U.S. Thrift Industry Under the Financial Institution Reform, Recovery, and Enforcement Act.* 1989.

Bradford, William. *The Viability and Performance of Minority Controlled Savings and Loan Associations.* Research Working Paper No. 62. 1975.

Bridewell, David A. *The Federal Home Loan Bank and Its Agencies.* 14 May, 1938.

Change in the Savings and Loan Industry. Proceedings of the Second Annual Conference. Federal Home Loan Bank of San Francisco. 1977.

Colton, Kent. *Financial Reform: A Review of the Past and Prospects for the Future.* Invited Research Working Paper No. 37. 1980.

_____, Donald R. Lessard, and Arthur P. Solomon. *Borrower Attitudes Toward Alternative Mortgage Instruments.* Working Paper No. 61. 1979.

Crockett, John H. *On the Good Bank/Bad Bank Restructuring of Failed Thrifts.* Research Working Paper No. 129. May 1987.

The Federal Home Loan Bank System, 1932–1952. 1952.

Federal Savings and Loan Associations: What They Are, Conditions Under Which They May Be Organized. 1934.

Fifty Years of Service: Federal Home Loan Bank Board. 1982.

Friend, Irwin, director. *Study of the Savings and Loan Industry Submitted to the Federal Home Loan Bank Board.* 1969.

Hartzog, B. G. *The Impact of NOW Accounts on Savings and Loan Behavior and Performance.* Research Working Paper No. 78. 1978.

Hester, Donald D. *Stock and Mutual Associations in the Savings and Loan Industry*. 1968.

King, A. Thomas. *Redlining: A Critical Review of the Literature with Suggested Research*. Research Working Paper No. 82. 1979.

New Sources of Capital for the Savings and Loan Industry. Proceedings of the Fifth Annual Conference. Federal Home Loan Bank of San Francisco. 1980.

Pratt, Richard T. *Savings and Loan Viability and Deposit Rate Ceilings*. Research Working Paper No. 14. 1970.

———, and Jamie Jay Jackson. *Agenda for Reform: A Report on Deposit Insurance to the Congress from the Federal Home Loan Bank Board*. 1983.

Russell, Horace. *Origins of the Federal Home Loan Bank*. 1935.

Savings and Loan Asset Management Under Deregulation. Proceedings of the Sixth Annual Conference. Federal Home Loan Bank of San Francisco. 1981.

Smith, Shelby J. *Texas S&L's: Implications for Consumer Lending*. Research Working Paper No. 13. 1976.

Tuccillo, John A., and Maurice Weinrobe. *Advertising and Competition: The Attraction of Deposits by Savings and Loan Associations*. Research Working Paper No. 15. 1970.

Woerheide, Walt. *The Evolution of SLA Susceptibility to Interest Rate Risk During the Seventies*. Research Working Paper No. 96. 1980.

National Commission on Financial Institution Reform, Recovery and Enforcement Publications

Black, William K. *Examination / Supervision / Enforcement of S&L's, 1979–1992*. Staff Report No. 4. 1993.

———. *Examples of S&L's Engaging in Substantial Interest Rate Gambles After 1983*. Staff Report No. 5. 1993.

———. *The Incidence and Cost of Fraud and Insider Abuse*. Staff Report No. 13. 1993.

———. *The Southwest Plan and the 1988 "Resolutions."* Staff Report No. 3. 1993.

———. *Substantive Positions of S&L Trade Associations, 1979–1989*. Staff Report No. 1. 1993.

———. *Thrift Accounting Principles and Practices*. Staff Report No. 20. 1993.

Ely, Bert. *The Role of Accounting in the S&L Crisis*. Consultant Study No. 2. 1993.

Hutnyan, Joseph D. *The S&L Lobby: An Exercise in Customer Service*. Consultant Study No. 3. 1992.

National Commission on Financial Institution Reform, Recovery and Enforcement. *Origins and Causes of the S&L Debacle: A Blueprint for Reform*. 1993.

Whiteford, Taylor, and Preston. *Issues Regarding the Role of Fraud and Other Criminal Misconduct in Causing Failures in the Thrift Industry*. Staff Report No. 14. 1993.

———. *The Role of Fraud and Other Criminal Misconduct in Causing Failures in the Thrift Industry*. Staff Report No. 12. 1993.

Other Federal Government Publications

Better Homes in America: Guidebook for Demonstration Week, May 11 to 18, 1924.

Bureau of the Census. *Historical Statistics of the United States, Colonial Times to 1957*. 1961.

Bureau of Statistics, Dept. of Treasury. *Statistical Abstract of the United States.* 1981, 1998.

Commission on Money and Credit. *Money and Credit: Their Influence on Jobs, Prices and Growth; Report.* Englewood Cliffs, NJ: Prentice-Hall, 1961.

Congressional Budget Office. *The Economic Effects of the Savings and Loan Crisis.* January 1992.

———. *Resolving the Thrift Crisis.* April 1993.

———. *Thrift Failures: Federal Enforcement Actions Against Fraud and Wrongdoing in RTC Thrifts.* August 1993.

Federal Deposit Insurance Corporation. *History of the Eighties – Lessons for the Future,* vol. 1. 1997.

———. *Managing the Crisis: The FDIC and RTC Experience, 1980–1994.* 1998.

Federal Housing Administration. *Annual Report.* 1939, 1940, 1960.

———. *The FHA Story in Summary, 1934–1959.* 1959.

Federal Reserve Bank of Chicago. *Leveling the Playing Field: A Review of the DIDMCA of 1980 and the Garn-St Germain Act of 1982.* 1983.

———. *Merging Commercial and Investment Banking.* Proceedings of a Conference on Bank Structure and Competition. 1987.

Federal Reserve Bank of Cleveland. *Economic Commentary.*

Gries, John M., and Thomas M. Curran. *Present Home Financing Methods.* 1928.

Home Owners' Loan Corporation Historical Facts and Figures. 30 June, 1947.

National Housing Administration. *Home Loans Under the G.I. Bill of Rights.* 1946.

———. *Housing After World War I: Will History Repeat Itself?* National Housing Bulletin No. 4. December 1945.

Office of Thrift Supervision. *2002 Fact Book: A Statistical Profile on the United States Thrift Industry.* April 2003.

President's Advisory Committee on Government Housing Policies and Programs. *Recommendations on Government Housing Policies and Programs.* 1953.

President's Commission on Financial Structure and Regulation. *Report of the President's Commission on Financial Structure and Regulation.* 1972.

President's Conference on Home Building and Home Ownership. *Housing Objectives and Programs.* 1933.

———. Johnson, Charles S. *Negro Housing: Report of the Committee on Negro Housing.* 1932.

Resolution Trust Corporation. *Statistical Abstract: August 1989/September 1995.* 1995.

Todd, Walker F. *Similarities and Dissimilarities in the Collapses of Three State-Chartered Private Deposit Insurance Funds.* Federal Reserve Bank of Cleveland. 1994.

White, Alice P. *Evolution of the Thrift Crisis.* Federal Reserve Board. 1989.

Wright, Carroll D. *Ninth Annual Report of the Commissioner of Labor, Building and Loan Associations.* 1894.

Massachusetts State Government Documents

Annual Report of the State Banking Commissioner, Part III, Public Document no. 8. Boston: Commonwealth of Massachusetts Bank Commissioner, 1895, 1900, 1905, 1910, 1915, 1920, 1925, 1930, 1935, 1940, 1945, 1950, 1955.

Annual Report of the State Banking Commissioner, Section A, 1960, Public Document no. 8. Boston: Commonwealth of Massachusetts Banking Commissioner, 1960.

Annual Report of the State Banking Commissioner, Section A, 1965, Public Document no. 8. Boston: Commonwealth of Massachusetts Banking Commissioner, 1965.
Annual Report of the State Banking Commissioner, Section A, 1970, Public Document no. 8. Boston: Commonwealth of Massachusetts Banking Commissioner, 1970.
Annual Report of the State Banking Commissioner, Section A, 1974, Public Document no. 8. Boston: Commonwealth of Massachusetts Banking Commissioner, 1974.
Annual Report of the State Banking Commissioner, Section A, 1980, Public Document no. 8. Boston: Commonwealth of Massachusetts Banking Commissioner, 1980.

Records of Private Organizations

Medford Cooperative Bank. *Directors' Meeting Minutes*. Medford, MA. 1886–1995.
Empire Savings and Loan Association. *Financial Statements*. Federal Home Loan Bank of Dallas. Dallas, TX. 1982–1984.

Interviews by the Author

Beil, Charles. President First Federal Savings and Loan Association of Big Spring, Austin, TX, 18 November 1984.
Bowman, L. Linton, III. Commissioner, Texas Savings and Loan Commission, Austin, TX, 3 July 1985.
Dunham, Ralph. Chief Financial Officer and Executive Vice President, Medford Cooperative Bank, Medford, MA, 14 August 1998.
Grissom, Terry V. MAI SPREA. Associate Professor of Real Estate, The University of Texas at Austin, Austin, TX, 15 November 1984.
Harlan, Christi. Staff Writer, *The Dallas Morning News*, Dallas, TX, 3 November 1984.
Law, W. Kenneth. Attorney, Law and Ridley, Belton, TX, 5 July 1985.
McNeill, Deborah. Senior Vice President and Treasurer, Medford Cooperative Bank, Medford, MA, 15 August 1998.
Sampson, Henry. Vice President, Medford Cooperative Bank, Medford, MA, 15 August 1998.
Silva, Lorraine. Director, Medford Cooperative Bank, Medford, MA, 15 August 1998.
Surabian, Robert. Chief Executive Officer, Medford Cooperative Bank, Medford, MA, 15 August 1998.

Dissertations and Theses

Bodfish, H. Morton. "Money Lending Practices of Building and Loan Associations in Ohio," M.A. thesis, The Ohio State University, 1927.
Braddock, Walter David, III. "Operation of a Regulatory Agency: The Case of the Federal Home Loan Bank Board," Ph.D. diss., Northern Illinois University, 1984.
Byers, C. Floyd. "Building and Loan Associations," M.A. thesis, The Ohio State University, 1927.
Carr, James W. "A History of Savings and Loan Associations in the State of Ohio," B.S. thesis, University of Cincinnati, 1949.

Cope, Donald. "The Advertising Policies and Practices of Savings and Loan Associations," M.A. thesis, The Ohio State University, 1952.

Donley, Wilfred George. "An Analysis of Building and Loan Associations in California, 1920–1935," Ph.D. diss., University of California, Berkeley, 1937.

Dunn-Haley, Karen. "The House That Uncle Sam Built: The Political Culture of Federal Housing Policy, 1919–1932," Ph.D. diss., Stanford University, 1995.

Ehrlich, Michael Alan. "An Investigation of United States Savings Institutions," Ph.D. diss., Princeton University, 1983.

Fox, Harry Daniel. "An Historical Study of the Federal Home Loan Bank System," M.B.A. thesis, The University of Texas at Austin, 1956.

Goldstein, Reuben M. "Building and Loan Associations of Ohio," B.A. thesis, University of Cincinnati, 1923.

King, Jules Edward. "Black Savings and Loan Associations as Distinct Entities of the Savings and Loan Industry," Ph.D. diss., Stanford University, 1985.

McMurray, Gerald Richard. "Congressional oversight of the Federal Home Loan Bank Board," A.B. thesis (honors), Harvard University, 1964.

Mason, David Lawrence. "The Failure of Empire Savings and Loan Association of Mesquite, Texas," M.A. thesis, The University of Texas at Austin, 1985.

Mechanic, Morris. "The Development of the Building and Loan Associations," M.A. thesis, Johns Hopkins University, 1921.

Olech, Francis W. "The Federal Housing Administration and the People It Serves," M.A. thesis, Kent State University, 1955.

Rowlands, David Thomas. "Two Decades of Building and Loan Associations in Pennsylvania," Ph.D. diss., University of Pennsylvania, 1940.

Scott, Raltson D. "The Federal Home Loan Bank System," Ph.D. diss., New York University, 1952.

Uhl, Joseph A. "Financing the Purchase of Real Estate," B.A. thesis, University of Cincinnati, June, 1928.

Wallace, Elbert S. "The Federal Home Loan Bank System," Ph.D. diss., Duke University, 1937.

Thrift Industry Publications

U.S. League Monthly Trade Journals

Financial Review and American Building Association News (1893–8).
American Building Association News (1899–1939).
American Savings and Loan News (1939–45).
Savings and Loan News (1945–83).
Savings Institutions (1983–91).
Savings & Community Banker (1992–5).
America's Community Banker (1995–6).

National League Trade Journals

National League Journal (1967–73).
National Savings and Loan League Journal (1974–83).
Bottomline (1983–).

Annual Publications

Proceedings of the United States Local League of Building and Loan Associations (1893–1926).
Proceedings of the United States League of Building and Loan Associations (1927–9).
Building and Loan Annals (1930–8).
Savings and Loan Annals (1939–73).
Savings Association Annals (1974–81).
Savings and Loan Fact Book (1954–80).
Savings and Loan Sourcebook (1981–3).
Savings Institutions Sourcebook (1984–9).

Other Trade Publications

Conference on Savings and Residential Finance (1958–61).
Confidential Bulletin of the United States Building and Loan League (1932–9).
Handbook of Savings and Loan (1965, 1970).
Massachusetts Cooperative Bank League Bulletin (1985).
Proceedings of the Annual Meeting of the Ohio Building Association League (1900–25).
Proceedings of the Annual Meeting of the Building Association League of Illinois (1905–20).

Books Used as Primary Sources

American Bankers Association. *The Commercial Banking Industry*. Englewood Cliffs, NJ: Prentice Hall, 1962.
———. *Response to Change: A Century of Commercial Bank Activity in the Savings Field*. New York: n.p., 1965.
American Institute of Real Estate Appraisers. *The Appraisal of Real Estate*, 8th edition. Chicago: American Institute of Real Estate Appraisers, 1983.
———. *Standards of Professional Practice*. Chicago: American Institute of Real Estate Appraisers, 1982.
Bell, F. W. *Building Associations, How Operated, Advantages, etc. Read before the Office Men's Club, June 10, 1886*. Pamphlets in American History, Cooperative Societies, s.l.: s.n., 1886.
Bingham, Robert F., and Elmore L. Andrews. *Financing Real Estate*. Cleveland: Stanley McMichael Publishing, 1924.
Bodfish, Morton. *Depression Experience of Savings and Loan Associations in the United States*. n.p., September, 1935.
———. editor. *History of Buildings & Loan in the United States*. Chicago: United States Building and Loan League, 1932.
———. *Lending Practices of Building and Loan Associations in Ohio*. Bureau of Business Research, Monograph No. 8. Columbus: The Ohio State University Press, 1927.
———. *Historical Balance Sheet Analysis of Ohio Building and Loan Associations*. Columbus, Ohio : Bureau of Business Research, College of Commerce and Administration, Ohio State University, 1928.
———, and A. D. Theobald. *Savings and Loan Principles*. Chicago: United States Building and Loan League, 1936.

Brigham, Eugene F. *Savings and Loan Holding Companies, Their Development and Operation*. Los Angeles: University of California School of Business, 1966.

Clarency, James. *The Value of Building Associations and How to Purchase a Home*. s.l.: s.n.

Clark, Horace F., and Frank A. Chase. *Elements of the Modern Building and Loan Associations*. New York, The Macmillan Company, 1925.

Cobleigh, Ira U. *$100 Billion Can't Be Wrong!* New York: Cobleigh & Gordon, 1964.

Colean, Miles. *Mortgage Companies: Their Place in the Financial Structure; A Monograph Prepared for the Commission on Money and Credit*. Englewood Cliffs, NJ: Prentice-Hall, 1962.

Conway, Lawrence V. *Principles of Savings and Loans*. Chicago: American Savings and Loan Institute Press, 1960.

Coppock, Joseph D. *Government Agencies of Consumer Instalment Credit*. Studies in Consumer Installment Financing. No. 5. New York: National Bureau of Economic Research, 1940.

Dexter, Seymour. *A Treatise on Cooperative Savings and Loan Associations*. New York: D. Appleton, 1889.

Eldridge, D. *Massachusetts Cooperative Banks or Building Associations*. Boston: G. H. Ellis, 1893.

Ewalt, Josephine Hedges. *A Business Reborn: The Savings and Loan Story, 1930–1960*. Chicago: American Savings and Loan Institute Press, 1964.

Fifty Years of Security. Medford, MA: n.p., 1936.

The Freedmen's Savings Bank and Trust Company: Charter and By-Laws. New York: W. C. Bryant, 1865.

Freeman, Gaylord. *Mutual Competition*. Chicago: n.p., 1959.

Fritze, James P. *Investment Building and Loan: Reasons Why*. Peoria, IL: n.p., 1892.

Grinspan, Mel G., editor. *Focus on the 90's: Economics at Home, Turmoil Abroad*. The M. L. Seidman Memorial Town Hall Lecture Series. Memphis, TN: Rhodes College, 1992.

Gunby, Jordan G. *The ABC Primer of a Building and Loan Association*. New York: Uncle Ben Publishing, 1889.

Hamilton, James Henry. *Savings and Savings Institutions*. New York: Macmillian Company, 1902.

Harmon, J. H., Jr., Arnett G. Lindsay, and Carter G. Woodson. *The Negro as a Business Man*. Washington, DC: The Association for the Study of Negro Life and History, Inc., 1929.

Kendall, Leon T. *The Savings and Loan Business: Its Purposes, Functions, and Economic Justification. A Monograph Prepared for the Commission on Money and Credit*. Englewood Cliffs, NJ: Prentice-Hall, 1962.

———. editor. *Thrift and Home Ownership; The Writings of Fred T. Greene*. Chicago: United States Savings and Loan League, 1961.

King, Clyde L., editor. *Modern Crime: Its Prevention and Punishment*. Philadelphia: The American Academy of Political and Social Science, 1926.

Kreutz, Oscar. *The Way It Happened*. St. Petersburg, FL: St. Petersburg Printing Co., 1972.

LaFollette, Robert Marion, editor. *The Making of America*, v. 10, *Public Welfare*. Chicago: The Making of America Company, 1908.

Loucks, William. *The Philadelphia Plan of Home Financing: A Study of the Second Mortgage Lending of Philadelphia Building and Loan Associations.* Chicago: Institute for Research in Land Utility and Public Economics, 1929.

Martin, I. Maximilian. *Negro Managed Building and Loan Associations in Philadelphia: Their History and Present Status.* Philadelphia: Associated Real Estate Brokers of Philadelphia, 1936.

Meyers, R. Holtby. *Building and Loans Explained.* Cincinnati: American Building Association News, 1924.

Mitchell, B. R. *European Historical Statistics 1750–1970.* New York: Columbia University Press, 1978.

Mutual Benefit Building and Loan Associations: Their History, Principles and Plans of Operation. Charleston: Walker and James, 1852.

National Building, Loan and Provident Association. *By-Laws of the National Building, Loan and Provident Association.* Wilmington, DE: National Building, Loan and Provident Association, n.d.

The National Building and Loan Association, Milwaukee, WI. *Plain Answers to Sensible Questions.* Milwaukee: n.p., 1894.

Natter, Raymond. *Financial Institutions Reform, Recovery Act of 1989.* New York: Matthew Bender & Co., 1989.

North, Nelson L., and DeWitt Van Buren. *Real Estate Finance.* New York: Prentice-Hall, 1928.

Ohio Savings and Loan League: A Century of Service. n.p., 1988.

Paine, Robert Treat, Jr. *Cooperative Savings Banks or Building Associations.* Boston: Tolman and White, 1880.

Paine, Willis. *The Laws of the State of New York Relating to Building Associations.* New York: L. K. Strousse, 1889.

The People's Building and Loan Association of Bloomington, IL. *The People's Building and Loan Association of Bloomington, IL.* Bloomington, IL: J. E. Burke, 1893.

Pieplow, William. *Century Lessons of Building and Loan Associations.* Appleton, WI: C.C. Nelson Publishing, 1931.

Piquet, Howard S. *Building and Loan Associations in New Jersey.* Princeton: Princeton University Press, 1931.

Quincy, Josiah. *A Plea for the Incorporation of the Co-operative Loan and Building Associations.* Boston: Wright & Potter, State Publishers, 1875.

Rankin, L. L. *Financial Panic of 1907 and Its Lessons to Building and Loan Associations.* Columbus: Champlain Printing Company, 1908.

Ratcliff, Richard U., Daniel Rathbun, and Junia Honnold. *Residential Finance, 1950.* New York: J. Wiley & Sons, 1957.

Rhodes, R. A. *Valuation of Chandler's Landing Marina, Lake Ray Hubbard Texas,* unpublished manuscript, 1984.

Riegel, Robert, and J. Russell Doubman. *The Building-and-Loan Association.* New York: J. Wiley & Sons, 1927.

Robinson, Bird. *A Paper on Building and Loan Associations.* s.l.: s.n.

Rosenberg, Samuel A. *Negro Managed Building and Loan Associations in the United States.* Hampton, VA: Hampton Institute, 1940.

Rosenthal, Henry. *Building, Loan and Savings Associations.* Cincinnati: The Press of the American Building Association News, 1911.

_____. *Cyclopedia of Building, Loan and Savings Associations*, 5th edition. Cincinnati: American Building Association News Publishing, 1928.

_____. *Manual for Building and Loan Associations*. Cincinnati: S. Rosenthal & Co, 1891.

Russell, Horace. *Savings and Loan Associations*. New York: Matthew Bender, 1962.

Sandberg, Richard T. *Introduction to the Savings Association Business*. Chicago: American Savings and Loan Institute Press, 1970.

Seaburg, Alan. *Medford Cooperative Bank: 100 Years of Service to the Community*. Medford, MA: n.p., 1986.

Shaw, Albert. *History of Cooperation in the United States*. Baltimore: Johns Hopkins University, 1888.

Siedman, William. *Full Faith and Credit: The Great S&L Debacle and Other Washington Sagas*. New York: Times Books, 1993.

Sinclair, Upton. *The Jungle*. New York: The Jungle Publishing, 1906.

Smith, Maye, and Faye Hudson with Leslie Whitaker. *Maye and Faye's Building & Loan: The Story of a Remarkable Sisterhood*. Thorndike, ME: Thorndike Press, 1997.

Sundheim, Joseph H. *Law of Building and Loan Associations*, 3rd edition. Chicago: Callaghan and Co., 1933.

Theobald, A. D. *Forty-Five Years on the Up Escalator*. Chicago: privately published, 1979.

Thomson Savings Directory. Skokie, IL: Thomson Financial Publishing, 1998.

Tucker, Oreb M. *Three Score and Ten Years: A History of Seventy Years of Co-operative Banking in Massachusetts*. Boston: Central Co-operative Bank, 1948.

The U.S. Savings and Institutions Directory, vols. I–II. Chicago: Rand McNally & Co., 1989.

The U.S. Savings and Loan Directory, vols. I–II. Chicago: Rand McNally & Co., 1983.

United States Savings and Loan League. *Report of the Special Committee to Study the Federal Home Loan Bank System*. Chicago: United States Savings and Loan League, 1956.

Washington, Booker T. *Negro in Business*. Chicago: Afro-Am Press, 1969.

Williams, H. *The Plain Guide to a Knowledge of the Practical Workings of the Mutual Loan and Fund Association*. Boston: Shoe and Leather Dealers Loan and Fund Association, 1854.

The World Almanac and Review of Facts, 1980. New York: Newspaper Enterprise Association, 1980.

Wood, Edith Elmer. *Recent Trends in American Housing*. New York: Macmillian, 1931.

Wrigley, Edmund. *How to Manage Building Associations*. Philadelphia: J.P. Lippencott, 1894.

_____. *The Workingman's Way to Wealth: A Practical Treatise on Building Associations; What They Are and How to Use Them*, 5th edition. Philadelphia: J. K. Simon, 1872.

Newspapers and Periodicals

The Annals of The American Academy of Political and Social Science.
American Banker.
American Bankers Association Journal.
American Banking Association Journal.

American Builder.
American Heritage.
American Lumberman.
The American Magazine.
The American Review of Reviews.
Architectural Forum.
Architectural Review.
The Atlantic Monthly.
The Bankers Magazine.
Barron's.
Boston Globe.
Building Age.
Building Age and National Builder.
Business Week.
Cassier's Magazine.
Changing Times.
The Charities Review.
Chicago Daily News.
The Chicago Daily Tribune.
Child Welfare Magazine.
Christian Science Monitor.
Collier's.
Congressional Quarterly Weekly Report.
Construction Review.
Coronet.
D Magazine.
The Dallas Morning News.
The Dallas Times Herald.
Engineering and Contracting.
Financial World.
Forbes.
Fortune.
Harper's Magazine.
House and Home.
House Beautiful.
Investment Dealers Digest.
Journal of Commerce.
Ladies Home Journal.
The Los Angeles Examiner.
The Los Angeles Herald-Examiner.
The Los Angeles Times.
The Magazine of Wall Street.
Manufacturers' Record.
Medford Daily Evening Mercury.
Medford Mercury.
Medford Transcript.
The Miami Herald.
Mortgage Banking.

National Real Estate Journal.
National Mortgage News.
National Real Estate Journal.
The New Republic.
The New York Herald-Tribune.
The New York Times.
The New York Times Magazine.
Newsweek.
The North American Review.
The Philadelphia Inquirer.
The Philadelphia Record.
Printer's Ink.
Proceedings of the Annual Convention of the American Bankers Association.
Proceedings of the National Conference on Housing.
Proceedings of the Academy of Political Science.
Review of Reviews and World's Work.
Rolling Stone Magazine
Saturday Review.
Scribner's Magazine.
Southern Workman.
St. Paul Pioneer Press.
St. Nicholas: An Illustrated Magazine for Young Folks.
The Survey.
Time.
The Washington Monthly Magazine.
The Washington Times-Herald.
The Washington Post.
The Wall Street Journal.
The Washington Star.
United States Banker.
US News and World Report.
USA Today.
Vital Speeches of the Day.
World's Work.

Select Articles Used as Primary Sources

Ashley, E. Everett. "Government Housing Activities," *Harvard Business Review* 19 (January 1941), 230–41.

Bodfish, Morton. "Toward an Understanding of the Federal Home Loan Bank System," *The Journal of Land & Public Utility Economics* 15 (November 1939), 416–19.

Burke, Addison. "The City of Homes and Its Building Societies," *Journal of Social Science* 15 (February 1882), 120–3.

Clark, Horace F. "The Extension of State Regulation to the Building and Loan Association," *The Journal of Political Economy* 32 (December 1924), 622–35.

Cover, John H. "The House that Franklin Built," *The Journal of Land & Public Utility Economics* 24 (August 1938), 237–9.

Dexter, Seymour. "Building and Loan Associations as Related to the Future Political and Social Welfare of the United States," *The American Journal of Politics* 1 (December 1892), 624.

————. "Cooperative Building and Loan Associations in New York," *Journal of Social Science* 25 (December 1888), 146–8.

————. "Cooperative Building and Loan Associations," *Quarterly Journal of Economics* 3 (April 1889), 335.

Greene, Fred T. "Significant Post-Depression Changes in Savings and Loan Practices," *Journal of Land and Public Utility Economics* 16 (February 1940), 31–4.

Hallowell, Anna. "The Care and Saving of Neglected Children," *Journal of Social Science* 12 (December 1880), 117–24.

Husband, William. "Loan Terms and the Rate of Interest for Home Finance," *The Journal of Land & Public Utility Economics* 27 (February 1934), 39–40.

Hestor, Donald D. "Special Interests: The *FINE Study*," *Journal of Money, Credit and Banking* 9 (November 1977), 652.

Lennhoff, David C. "What's All the Ruckus Over R-41b?" *The Appraisal Journal* 52 (July 1984), 444.

Mahoney, Patrick I., and Alice P. White. "The Thrift Industry in Transition," *Federal Reserve Bulletin* 71 (March 1985), 137–56.

Paine, Robert Treat, Jr. "Homes for the People," *Journal of Social Science* 25 (February 1882), 117–18.

Pierce, James L. "The *FINE Study*," *Journal of Money, Credit and Banking* 9 (November 1977), 606–14.

"Professional Notes," *Journal of Accountancy* 156 (November 1983), 51–4.

Sanborn, F. B. "Co-operative Building Associations," *Journal of Social Science* 25 (December 1888), 112–3.

Timberlake, Richard H. "Legislative Construction of the Monetary Control Act of 1980," Papers and Proceedings of the Ninety-Seventh Annual Meeting of the American Economic Association. *The American Economic Review* 75 (May 1985), 97–102.

Wickens, David L. "Developments in Home Finance," *The Annals of the Academy of Political and Social Science* 189 (March 1937), 77–9.

Secondary Sources

Books

Adams, James Ring. *The Big Fix: Inside the S & L Scandal: How an Unholy Alliance of Politics and Money Destroyed America's Banking System*. New York: Wiley, 1990.

Agee, James. *Agee on Film*. New York: Grosset & Dunlap, 1969.

Albritton, Harold D. *Controversies in Real Estate Valuation: A Commentary*. Chicago: American Institute of Real Estate Appraisers, 1982.

Alchon, Guy. *The Invisible Hand of Planning*. Princeton: Princeton University Press, 1985.

Alexander, Kern. *The Role of the Basle Standards in International Banking Supervision*, ESCR Centre for Business Research Working Paper No. 153. Cambridge: University of Cambridge, 2000.

Babcock, Henry A. *Appraisal Principles and Practice*. Washington, DC: American Society of Appraisers, 1980.

Balberston, Frederick E. *Thrifts in Crisis: Structural Transformation of the Savings and Loan Industry*. Cambridge, MA: Ballinger Publishing Co., 1985.

Barber, William J. *From New Era to New Deal*. New York: Cambridge University Press, 1985.

Barth, James. *The Great Savings and Loan Debacle*. Washington, DC: AEI Press, 1991.

Baskin, Jonathan Barron, and Paul J. Miranti Jr. *A History of Corporate Finance*. New York: Cambridge University Press, 1999.

Bean, Jonathan J. *Beyond the Broker State: Federal Policies Toward Small Business, 1936–1961*. Chapel Hill: University of North Carolina Press, 1996.

Bellman, Harold. *The Thrift Three Millions*. London: Abbey Road Building Society, 1935

Benston, George J. *An Analysis of the Causes of Savings and Loan Association Failures*, Monograph Series in Finance and Economic, Monograph 1983 – 4/5. New York: Salomon Brothers Center for the Study of Financial Institutions, Graduate School of Business Administration, New York University, 1985.

Binstein, Michael, and Charles Bowden. *Trust Me: Charles Keating and the Missing Billions*. New York: Random House, 1993.

Bird, Anat. *Can S&Ls Survive?: The Emerging Recovery, Restructuring & Repositioning of America's S&Ls*. Chicago: Bankers Publishing Co., 1993.

Blackford, Mansel G. *A History of Small Business in America*. New York: Twayne Publishers, 1991.

_____. *The Lost Dream: Businessmen and City Planning on the Pacific Coast, 1890–1920*. Columbus: Ohio State University Press, 1993.

Boyce, Byrl N., and Kinnard, William. *Appraising Real Property*. Lexington, MA: Lexington Books, 1984.

Bruck, Connie. *The Predators' Ball*. New York: Penguin Books, 1989.

Brumbaugh, R. Dan. *Thrifts Under Siege: Restoring Order to American Banking*. Cambridge, MA: Ballinger Publishing Co., 1988.

_____. *The Collapse of Federally Insured Depositories: The Savings and Loans as Precursor*. New York: Garland Publishing, 1993.

Burns, Helen M. *The American Banking Community and the New Deal Banking Reforms, 1933–1935*. Westport, CT: Greenwood Press, 1974.

Calavita, Kitty, Henry N. Pontell, and Robert H. Tillman. *Big Money Crime: Fraud and Politics in the Savings and Loan Crisis*. Berkeley: University of California Press, 1997.

Calder, Lendol. *Financing the American Dream: A Cultural History of Consumer Credit*. Princeton: Princeton University Press, 1999.

Cargill, Thomas F., and Gillian G. Garcia. *Financial Deregulation and Monetary Control: Historical Perspective and Impact of the 1980 Act*. Stanford, CA: Hoover Institution Press, 1982.

_____. *Financial Reform in the 1980s*. Stanford: Hoover Institution Press, 1985.

Carney, Raymond. *American Vision: The Films of Frank Capra*. New York: Cambridge University Press, 1986.

Carosso, Vincent. *Investment Banking in America: A History*. Cambridge, MA: Harvard University Press, 1970.

Carron, Andrew S. *The Plight of Thrift Institutions*. Washington DC: Brookings Institution, 1982.

Chandler, Alfred D., Jr. *The Visible Hand: The Managerial Revolution in American Business*. Cambridge, MA: Belknap Press, 1977.

Chernow, Ron. *The House of Morgan: An American Banking Dynasty and the Rise of Modern Finance*. New York: Atlantic Monthly Press, 1990.

Childs, William R. *Trucking and the Public Interest: The Emergence of Federal Regulation, 1914–1940*. Knoxville: University of Tennessee Press, 1985.

Chorafas, Dimitris N. *Electronic Funds Transfers*. London: Butterworths, 1988.

Cleary, E. J. *The Building Society Movement*. London: Elek Books, 1965.

Clarke, Sally H. *Regulation and the Revolution in United States Farm Productivity*. New York: Cambridge University Press, 1994.

Cooper, Kerry, and Donald R. Fraser. *Banking Deregulation and the New Competition in Financial Service*. Cambridge, MA: Ballinger Publishing Co., 1984.

Cottrell, Allin F., Michael S. Lawlor, and John H. Wood, editors. *The Causes and Costs of Depository Institution Failures*. Boston: Kluwer Academic, 1995.

Day, Kathleen. *S & L Hell : The People and the Politics Behind the $1 Trillion Savings & Loan Scandal*. New York: W. W. Norton & Co., 1993.

DeGennaro, Ramon P., Larry H. Lang, and James B. Thomson, *Troubled Savings and Loan Institutions: Voluntary Restructuring Under Insolvency*, Research Working Paper 9112. Cleveland: Federal Reserve Bank of Cleveland, 1991.

Derks, Scott, editor. *The Value of a Dollar, 1860–1999*. Lakeville, CT: Grey House Publishing, 1999.

Dobriner, William M. *Class in Suburbia*. Englewood Cliffs, NJ: Prentice Hall, 1963.

Draper, Daniel Clay Draper. *The Thrift Industry, 1973*. New York: Practicing Law Institute, 1973.

Eichler, Ned. *The Thrift Debacle*. Berkeley: University of California Press, 1989.

Finegan, Patrick G., Jr. *Master Financial Statements: Who Murdered Savings and Loans?* Washington, DC: The Palindrome Press, 1991.

Fink, Leon. *Workingmen's Democracy: The Knights of Labor and American Politics*. Urbana: University of Illinois Press, 1983.

Fischer, L. Richard, Elizabeth G. Gentry, and Petrina M. E. Verderamo. *The Garn-St. Germain Depository Institutions Act of 1982: What's in it for you?* Arlington, VA: The Consumer Bankers Associations, 1982.

Fishman, Robert. *Bourgeois Utopias: The Rise and Fall of Suburbia*. New York: Basic Books, 1987.

Flink, James J. *The Car Culture*. Cambridge, MA: The MIT Press, 1975.

Foster, Mark S. *From Streetcar to Superhighway: American City Planners and Transportation, 1900–1940*. Philadelphia: Temple University Press, 1981.

Freidricks, William B. *Henry E. Huntington and the Creation of Southern California*. Columbus: Ohio State University Press, 1992.

Furlough, Ellen, and Carl Strikwerda, editors. *Consumers Against Capitalism? Consumer Cooperation in Europe, North America, and Japan, 1840–1990*. Lanham, MD: Rowman & Littlefield, 1999.

Galambos, Louis. *Competition & Cooperation: The Emergence of a National Trade Association*. Baltimore: Johns Hopkins Press, 1966.

Gehring, Wes D. *Populism and the Capra Legacy*. Westport, CT: Greenwood Press, 1995.

Gilbert, Charles. *American Financing of World War I*. Westport, CT: Greenwood Press, 1970.

Gildersleeve, Genevieve N. *Women in Banking*. Washington, DC: Public Affairs Press, 1959.

Glaab, Charles N., and A. Theodore Brown. *A History of Urban America*. New York: Macmillan, 1976.

Glatzer, Richard, and John Raeburn, editors. *Frank Capra: The Man and His Films*. Ann Arbor: University of Michigan Press, 1975.

Goodwyn, Lawrence. *Democratic Promise: The Populist Movement in America*. New York: Oxford University Press, 1976.

Grebler, Leo. *The Future of Thrift Institutions: A Study of Diversification Versus Specialization*. Danville, IL: Interstate Printers and Publishers, 1971.

Gup, Benton. *Bank Fraud: Exposing the Hidden Threat to Financial Institutions*. Rolling Meadows, IL: Bankers Publishing Co., 1990.

Haber, Samuel. *Efficiency and Uplift: Scientific Management in the Progressive Era, 1890–1920*. Chicago: University of Chicago Press, 1964.

Hammack, David C., editor. *Making the Nonprofit Sector in the United States: A Reader*. Bloomington: Indiana University Press, 1998.

Hartmann, Edward. *The Movement to Americanize the Immigrant*. New York: AMS Press, 1967.

Hawley, Ellis W. *The Great War and the Search for a Modern Order*, 2nd edition. New York: St. Martin's Press, 1992.

_____, editor. *Herbert Hoover as Secretary of Commerce: Studies in New Era Thought and Practice*. Ames, IA: University of Iowa Press, 1981.

Hayes, Samuel L., III. *Financial Services: Perspectives and Challenges*. Boston: Harvard Business School Press, 1993.

Hays, Samuel P. *The Response to Industrialism, 1885–1914*. Chicago: University of Chicago Press, 1995.

Himmelberg, Robert F. *The Origins of the National Recovery Administration: Business, Government, and the Trade Association Issue, 1921–1933*. New York: Fordham University Press, 1993.

_____, editor. *Antitrust and Regulation During World War I and the Republican Era, 1917–1932*. New York : Garland Publishing, 1994.

_____, editor. *Business-Government Cooperation, 1917–1932: The Rise of Corporatist Policies*. New York: Garland Publishing, 1994.

Hixson, William F. *Triumph of the Bankers: Money and Banking in the Eighteenth and Nineteenth Centuries*. Westport, CT: Praeger, 1993.

Hoover, Herbert C. *The Memoirs of Herbert Hoover: The Cabinet and the Presidency, 1920–1933*. New York: The Macmillan Co., 1952.

Horne, H. Oliver. *A History of Savings Banks*. London: Oxford University Press, 1947.

Impact of Regulation on the Provision of Consumer Financial Services by Depository Institutions: Research, Backgrounds and Needs. West Lafayette, IN: Krannert Graduate School of Management, Purdue University, 1978.

Jackson, Kenneth T. *Crabgrass Frontier: The Suburbanization of the United States*. New York: Oxford University Press, 1985.

Johnson, James. *Showing America a New Way Home*. San Francisco: Jossey-Bass Publishers, 1989.

Kane, Edward J. *The S&L Insurance Mess: How Did It Happen?* Washington, DC: The Urban Institute Press, 1989.

Kassan, John F. *Amusing the Million: Coney Island at the Turn of the Century.* New York: Hill and Wang, 1978.

Kazin, Michael. *The Populist Persuasion: An American History.* Ithaca, NY: Cornell University Press, 1998.

Kennedy, Susan Estabrook. *The Banking Crisis of 1933.* Lexington, KY: University of Kentucky Press, 1973.

Kerr, K. Austin. *American Railroad Politics, 1914–1920; Rates, Wages, and Efficiency.* Pittsburgh: University of Pittsburgh Press, 1968.

Klebaner, Benjamin J. *American Commercial Banking: A History.* Boston: Twayne Publishers, 1990.

Kolko, Gabriel. *The Triumph of Conservatism: A Re-interpretation of American History, 1900–1916.* Chicago: Quadrangle Books, 1967.

Korman, Gerd. *Industrialization, Immigrants, and Americanizers; the View from Milwaukee, 1866–1921.* Madison: State Historical Society of Wisconsin, 1967.

Kwolek-Folland, Angel. *Engendering Business: Men and Women in the Corporate Office, 1870–1930.* Baltimore: Johns Hopkins University Press, 1994.

Lamoreaux, Naomi R. *Insider Lending: Banks, Personal Connections, and Economic Development in Industrial New England.* Cambridge: Cambridge University Press, 1994.

———, and Daniel M. G. Raff, editors. *Coordination and Information: Historical Perspectives on the Organization of Enterprise.* Chicago: University of Chicago Press, 1995.

Lipis, Allen H., Thomas R. Marschall, and Jan Tinker. *Electronic Banking.* New York: John Wiley & Sons, 1985.

Littlewood, Shane, & Co. *The Depository Institutions Deregulation and Monetary Control Act of 1980: An Analysis and Interpretation.* Park Ridge, IL: Bank Administration Institute, 1981.

Leaver, J. B. *Building Societies, Past, Present and Future.* London: J. M. Dent and Sons Ltd., 1942.

Lowy, Martin. *High Rollers: Inside the Savings and Loan Debacle.* New York: Praeger, 1991.

Mack, Arien, editor. *Home: A Place in the World.* New York: New York University Press, 1993.

Maggin, Donald L. *Bankers, Builders, Knaves, and Thieves: The $300 Million Scam at ESM.* Chicago: Contemporary Books, 1989.

Marvell, Thomas. *The Federal Home Loan Bank Board.* New York: Frederick A. Praeger Publishers, 1969.

Mayer, Martin. *The Greatest-Ever Bank Robbery: The Collapse of the Savings and Loan Industry.* New York: Charles Scribner's Sons, 1990.

McCraw, Thomas K. *Prophets of Regulation: Charles Francis Adams, Louis D. Brandeis, James M. Landis, Alfred E. Kahn.* Cambridge: Belknap Press of Harvard University Press, 1984.

———, editor. *Regulation in Perspective: Historical Essays.* Cambridge, MA: Harvard University Press, 1981.

McCulley, Richard T. *Banks and Politics During the Progressive Era: the Origins of the Federal Reserve System, 1897–1913.* New York: Garland Publishing, 1992.

McKillop, Donal, and Charles Ferguson. *Building Societies: Structure, Performance and Change*. London: Graham & Trotman, 1993.

McMath, Robert C., Jr. *American Populism: A Social History, 1877–1898*. New York: Hill and Wang, 1993.

Milkis, Sidney M., and Jerome M., Mileur, editors. *Progressivism and the New Democracy*. Amherst: University of Massachusetts Press, 1999.

Monkkonen, Eric H. *America Becomes Urban: The Development of U.S. Cities & Towns, 1780–1980*. Berkeley: University of California Press, 1988.

Morris, Charles R. *Money, Greed, and Risk: Why Financial Crises and Crashes Happen*. New York: Random House, 1999.

Muller, Peter. *Contemporary Suburban America*. Englewood Cliffs, NJ: Prentice-Hall, 1981.

Munn, Glenn G. *Encyclopedia of Banking and Finance*. Boston: Bankers Publishing Co., 1983.

Nicols, Alfred. *Management and Control in the Mutual Savings and Loan Association*. Lexington, MA: Lexington Books, 1972.

Noll, Roger S., and Bruce M. Owens, editors. *The Political Economy of Deregulation: Interest Groups in the Regulatory Process*. Washington, DC: American Enterprise Institute, 1983.

North, Douglass C. *Institutions, Institutional Change and Economic Performance*. New York: Cambridge University Press, 1990.

O'Connell, William B. *America's Trauma: How Washington Blunders Crippled the U.S. Financial System*. Winnetka, IL: Conversation Press, 1992.

O'Shea, James. *The Daisy Chain: How Borrowed Billions Sank a Texas S&L*. New York: Pocket Books, 1991.

Olney, Martha N. *Buy Now Pay Later: Advertising, Credit, and Consumer Durables in the 1920s*. Chapel Hill: University of North Carolina Press, 1991.

Olson, James S. *Herbert Hoover and the Reconstruction Finance Corporation, 1931–1933*. Ames, IA: Iowa State University Press, 1977.

Palen, J. John. *The Suburbs*. New York: McGraw-Hill, 1995.

Patrick, Sue C. *Reform of the Federal Reserve System in the Early 1930s: The Politics of Money and Banking*. New York: Garland Publishing, 1993.

Peters, Thomas J., and Robert H. Waterman Jr. *In Search of Excellence: Lessons from America's Best-Run Companies*. New York: Warner Books, 1982.

Perkins, Edwin J. *American Public Finance and Financial Services, 1700–1815*. Columbus, OH: Ohio State University Press, 1994.

_____. *The Economy of Colonial America*. New York: Columbia University Press, 1988.

_____. *From Wall Street to Main Street: Charles Merrill and the Rise of Middle-Class Investors*. New York: Cambridge University Press, 1999.

Pilzer, Paul Zane. *Other People's Money: The Inside Story of the S&L Mess*. New York: Simon and Schuster, 1989.

Pollock, Norman. *The Populist Mind*. Indianapolis: Bobbs-Merrill, 1967.

Price, Seymour J. *Building Societies: Their Origin and History*. London: Franey, 1958.

Puzzo, Stephen, Mary Fricker, and Paul Muolo. *Inside Job: The Looting of America's Savings and Loans*. New York: McGraw-Hill, 1989.

Rabinowitz, Howard N. *Race Relations in the Urban South, 1865–1890*. New York: Oxford University Press, 1978.

Rae, John B. *The American Automobile Industry*. Boston: Twayne Publishers, 1984.

Rider, Barry, editor. *Corruption: The Enemy Within*. Boston: Kluwer Law International, 1997.

Rom, Mark Carl. *Public Spirit in the Thrift Tragedy*. Pittsburgh: University of Pittsburgh Press, 1996.

Rose, Peter S., editor. *Readings on Financial Institutions and Markets*, 5th edition. Homewood, IL: Irwin, 1993.

Ruiz, Vicki L., and Ellen Carol DuBois, editors. *Unequal Sisters*, 2nd edition. New York: Routledge, 1994.

Seaburg, Carl, and Alan Seaburg. *Medford on the Mystic*. Medford, MA: n.p., 1980.

Shapiro, Samuel B. *A Coming of Age: A History of the Profession of Association Management*. Washington, DC: American Society of Association Executives, 1987.

Schaffer, Daniel, editor. *Two Centuries of American Planning*. London: Mansel, 1987.

Scott, Kenneth E. *Never Again: The Savings and Loan Bailout Bill*. Stanford, CA: Hoover Institution Press, 1990.

Scranton, Philip. *Figured Tapestry: Production, Markets, and Power in Philadelphia Textiles, 1885–1941*. New York: Cambridge University Press, 1989.

Sklar, Robert, and Vito Zagarrio, editors. *Frank Capra: Authorship and the Studio System*. Philadelphia: Temple University Press, 1998.

Strunk, Norman, and Fred Case. *Where Deregulation Went Wrong: A Look at the Causes Behind Savings and Loan Failures in the 1980s*. Chicago: United States League of Savings Institutions, 1988.

Talley, Pat L. *The Savings and Loan Crisis: An Annotated Bibliography*. Westport, CT: Greenwood Press, 1993.

Teck, Alan. *Mutual Savings Banks and Savings and Loan Associations: Aspect of Growth*. New York: Columbia University Press, 1968.

Temin, Peter, editor. *Inside the Business Enterprise: Historical Perspectives on the Use of Information*. Chicago: University of Chicago Press, 1991.

Vietor, Richard H. K. *Contrived Competition: Regulation and Deregulation in America*. Cambridge, MA: Harvard University Press, 1994.

Waldman, Michael. *Who Robbed America? A Citizen's Guide to the S&L Scandal*. New York: Random House, 1990.

Walker, Juliet K. *The History of Black Business in America: Capitalism, Race and Entrepreneurship*. London: Prentice-Hall International, 1989.

Warner, Sam Bass. *Streetcar Suburbs: the Process of Growth in Boston, 1870–1900*. Cambridge, MA: Harvard University Press, 1978.

Weare, Walter B. *Black Business in the New South: A Social History of the North Carolina Mutual Life Insurance Company*. Urbana, IL: University of Illinois Press, 1973.

Weibe, Robert H. *Businessmen and Reform: A Study of the Progressive Movement*. Chicago: Quadrangle Books, 1968.

―――. *The Search for Order, 1877–1920*. New York: Hill and Wang, 1967.

Weiss, Marc A. *The Rise of the Community Builders: The American Real Estate Industry and Urban Land Planning*. New York: Columbia University Press, 1987.

White, Lawrence J. *The S&L Debacle: Public Policy Lessons for Bank and Thrift Regulation*. New York: Oxford University Press, 1991.

Wilson, Joan Hoff. *Herbert Hoover: Forgotten Progressive*. New York: Little Brown & Co., 1975.

Zelizer, Viviana A. Rotman. *Morals and Markets: The Development of Life Insurance in the United States*. New York: Columbia University Press, 1979.

Articles

Alter, George, Claudia Goldin, and Elyce Rotella. "The Savings of Ordinary Americans: The Philadelphia Saving Fund Society in the Mid-Nineteenth Century," *The Journal of Economic History* 54 (December 1994), 735–67.

Balogh, Brian. "Reorganizing the Organizational Synthesis: Federal Professional Relations in Modern America," *Studies in American Political Development* 5 (Spring 1991), 119–72.

Barth, James, and Michael Bradley. "Thrift Deregulation and Federal Deposit Insurance," *Journal of Financial Services Research* 2 (September 1989), 231–59.

Baskin, Jonathan Barron. "The Development of Corporate Financial Markets in Britain and the United States, 1600–1914: Overcoming Asymmetric Information," *Business History Review* 62 (Summer 1988), 199–237.

Benston, George J., and George G. Kaufman. "FDICIA After Five Years," *The Journal of Economic Perspectives*, 11 (Summer 1997), 139–158.

Berry, William D. "An Alternative to the Capture Theory of Regulation: The Case of State Public Utility Commissions," *American Journal of Political Science* 28 (August 1984), 524–58.

Brumbaugh, R. Dan, and Andrew S. Carron. "Thrift Industry Crisis: Causes and Solutions." *Brookings Papers on Economic Activity* 1987 Issue 2 (1987), 349–77.

Curry, Timothy, and Lynn Shibut. "The Cost of the Savings and Loan Crisis: Truth and Consequences," *FDIC Banking Review* 13 (December 2000), 26–33.

Galambos, Louis. "The Emerging Organizational Synthesis in Modern American History," *Business History Review* 44 (Autumn 1970), 279–90.

———. "Technology, Political Economy, and Professionalization: Central Themes in the Organizational Synthesis," *Business History Review* 57 (Winter 1983), 472–93.

Glasberg, Davita Silfen, and Dan L. Skidmore. "The Dialectics of White-Collar Crime: The Anatomy of the Savings and Loan Crisis and the Case of Silverado Banking, Savings and Loan Association," *The American Journal of Economics and Sociology* 57 (October 1998), 423–49.

———. "The Role of the State in the Criminogenesis of Corporate Crime: A Case Study of the Savings and Loan Crisis," *Social Science Quarterly* 79 (March 1998), 110–128.

Havemans, Heather A. "Organizational Size and Change: Diversification in the Savings and Loan Industry After Deregulation." *Administrative Science Quarterly* 38 (March 1993), 20–50.

Kane, Edward J. "Principal-Agent Problems in the S&L Salvage," *Journal of Finance* 45 (July 1990), 755–64.

Kaufman, George G. "The U.S. Banking Debacle of the 1980s: An Overview and Lessons," *The Financier: ACMT* 2 (May 1995), 9–26.

Kettl, Donald F. "The Savings-and-Loan Bailout: The Mismatch between the Headlines and the Issues," *PS: Political Science and Politics*, 24 (September 1991), 441–447.

McCraw, Thomas. "Regulation in American: A Review Article," *Business History Review* 49 (Summer 1975), 159–83.

Meier, Kenneth J, and John P. Plumlee. "Regulatory Administration and Organizational Rigidity, "*The Western Political Quarterly* 31 (March 1978), 80–95.

Snowden, Kenneth A. "Building and Loan Associationa in the U.S., 1880–1893: The Origins of Localization in the Residential Mortgage Market," *Research in Economics* 51 (1997), 227–50.

———. "Mortgage Lending and American Urbanization, 1880–1890", *The Journal of Economic History* 48 (June 1988), 273–85.

INDEX